ISLAY
THE LAND OF THE LORDSHIP

ISLAY

The Land of the Lordship

David H. Caldwell

BIRLINN

This book could not have been written without
significant support and contributions from
Ian Brown, Michael Cressey, Alan Macniven, Roger McWee
and Nigel A. Ruckley

The Publisher gratefully acknowledges the support of Ardbeg Distillery towards the
publication of this book

First published in 2008 by
Birlinn Limited
West Newington House
10 Newington Road
Edinburgh
EH9 1QS

www.birlinn.co.uk

ISBN13: 978 1 84158 358 7
ISBN10: 1 84158 358 8

British Library Cataloguing-in-Publication Data
A catalogue record for this book is available from the British Library

Typeset by Hewer Text UK Ltd, Edinburgh
Printed and bound by MPG Books Ltd, Bodmin

Contents

List of Illustrations

Plates

Family trees

Figures

Abbreviations

ALI. Acts of the Lords of the Isles. See Munro and Munro, 1986.
AC. Annals of Connacht. See Freeman, 1983.
ADCP. Acts of the Lords of Council in Public Affairs. See Hannay, 1932.
AFM. Annals of the Four Masters. See O'Donovan, 1848.
AI. Annals of Inisfallen. See Mac Airt, 1988.
APS. The Acts of the Parliaments of Scotland. See Thomson and Innes, 1814–75.
AT. Argyll Transcripts, made by 10th Duke of Argyll (Photostat copy in the Department of Scottish History, Glasgow University).
AU. Annals of Ulster. See Hennessy and McCarthy, 1887–1901.
Birrell's Diary. 'The Diarey of Robert Birrell, Burges of Edinburghe, 1532–1605', in Dalyell, 1798.
BGS. The British Geological Survey.
C. Carew MSS. Calendar of the Carew Manuscripts. See Brewer, 1867.
Cawdor Bk. See Innes, 1859.
CBP. Calendar of Border Papers. See Bain, 1894.
CDS. Calendar of Documents Relating to Scotland. See Bain, 1881–88.
CELT. Corpus of Electronic Texts – the online resource for Irish history, literature and politics; a project of the History Department, University College Cork. <http://www.ucc.ie/celt/>
Chron. Auchinleck. See Craigie, 1923, ii, 215–44.
Chron. Fordoun. See Skene, 1872.
Chron. Guisborough. See Rothwell, 1957.
Chron. Knighton. See Lumby, 1895.
Chron. Lanercost. See Maxwell, 1913.
Chron. Man. Chronicles of the kings of Man and the Isles. See Broderick, 1996.
Chron. Wyntoun. See Laing, 1879.
CM. Cawdor Muniments, Cawdor Castle, Nairnshire.
Coll de Rebus Alban. See Iona Club, 1847.
CPL. Calendar of Papal Letters. See Bliss, et al., 1893–.
CPLS (1378–94). Calendar of Papal Letters to Scotland of Clement VII of Avignon 1378–1394. See Burns, 1976.

CSP Ireland Calendar of the State Papers relating to Ireland. See
    Hamilton, et al., 1860–.
CSP Scotland Calendar of State Papers relating to Scotland. See Bain, et
    al., 1898–.
CSSR. Calendar of Scottish Supplications to Rome. See Dunlop, et al.,
    1934–.
ER. The Exchequer Rolls of Scotland. See Stuart, et al., 1878–.
ES. Early Sources of Scottish History. See Anderson, 1990.
FA. The Fragmentary Annals.
Fasti. Fasti Ecclesiae Scoticanae. See Scott, 1923.
Foedera (2nd edition). See Rymer, 1816–69.
G. Gaelic (language).
*Henry VIII L&P. Letters and Papers Foreign and Domestic of the Reign
    of Henry VIII.* See Brewer, et al., 1864–1932.
HP. Highland Papers. See Macphail, 1914–34.
ICD. The Islay Cultural Database – a digital resource compiled by
    Roger McWee and accessible via The Finlaggan Trust Website.
IR. Innes Review.
Islay Bk. See Smith, 1895.
MIL. Museum of Islay Life, Port Charlotte.
ML. Mitchell Library, Glasgow:
    B10/15. (Glasgow) Burgh Registration and Deposit. Deeds, 1661–1959.
    TD 1284. Kildalton Papers.
    TD 1338. Islay Estate Papers.
    T-MJ. Records of Messrs Mitchells, Johnston & Co, Solicitors,
        Glasgow.
NAS. National Archives of Scotland, Edinburgh:
    CC12. Commissariat of the Isles (Testaments).
    CE81/6/2. Records of the Board of Customs and Excise, Port Ellen
        Outport and District Records, Official Correspondence (Collector
        to Board of Excise), 20 Feb. 1849 to 22 May 1856.
    CS. Court of Session Papers.
    E727/60/1 Forfeited Estates Papers, Letters of Campbell of
        Shawfield.
    RD. Register of Deeds.
    RH. Register House (Charters).
    RHP. Register House Plans.
    RS. Register of Sasines.
NLS. National Library of Scotland:
    ACC 6223/12. Sunderland Memoranda, included within the Papers
        of the Campbells of Craignish.
    Adv. MS 29.1.1. Murray of Stanhope Manuscripts.
    Adv. MS 29.1.2. Anderson Papers.
    MS 14986. 'The Queen of the Hebrides', by 'Finlagan' (John
        Murdoch), *c.*1859.

MSS 3819. Records of the 1st, 2nd and 3rd Argyll Battalions Home Guard.

NMRS. National Monuments Records of Scotland, housed with RCAHMS.

NRA(S). National Register of Archives, Scotland (available via NAS): 1277. Mr N. M. MacLean.

ODNB. Oxford Dictionary of National Biography. See Matthew and Harrison, 2004.

ON. Old Norse (language).

OP. Origines Parochiales Scotiae. See Bannatyne Club, 1851–55.

PSAS. Proceedings of the Society of Antiquaries of Scotland.

RCAHMS. Royal Commission on the Ancient and Historical Monuments of Scotland.

Retours. See Thomson, 1811–16.

RMS. Registrum Magni Sigilli (Register of the Great Seal). See Thomson, et al., 1882–1914.

Rot. Scot. Rotuli Scotiae in Turri Londinensi et in Domo Capitulari Westmonasteriensi Asservati. See Macpherson, et al., 1814–19.

RPC. Register of the Privy Council. See Burton, et al., 1877–.

RPS. The Records of the Parliaments of Scotland: <http://www.rps.ac.uk>.

RRS. Regesta Regum Scottorum. See Barrow, et al., 1960–.

RSS. Registrum Secreti Sigilli (Register of the Privy Seal). See Livingstone, et al., 1908–.

SA (1794), xi. The Statistical Account of Scotland. See Sinclair, 1794.

SA (1845), vii. The Statistical Account of Scotland. See Statistical Account.

Scotichronicon. See Watt, et al., 1987–97.

Shawfield's Day Bk. See Ramsay, 1991.

SHR. Scottish Historical Review.

SHS. Scottish History Society

SS. Scottish Studies.

Stent Bk. See Ramsay, 1990.

TA. Accounts of the Lord High Treasurer of Scotland. See Dickson, Balfour Paul, et al., 1877–.

TNA. The National Archive, Kew:
AIR. Air Ministry.
WO. War Office.

The sources for this book include a series of rentals and other documents. To save repetitive reference to them in the end notes, their details are given here in date order:

1408. Charter by Donald, Lord of the Isles, to Brian Vicar MacKay, of lands in Islay. *ALI*, no. 16.

1494. Charter by King James IV to John MacIan of Ardnamurchan of lands in Islay and elsewhere, and the office of bailiary of Islay. *RMS*, ii, no. 2216; *Islay Bk*, 24–26.

1499. Charter by King James IV to John MacIan of Ardnamurchan of lands in Islay and elsewhere. *Islay Bk*, 28–30.

1506. Charter by King James IV to John MacIan of Ardnamurchan of lands in Islay and Jura. *RMS*, ii, no. 3001; *Islay Bk*, 32–33.

1507. The ferms of Islay. *ER*, xii, 587–90.

1509. The ferms of Islay. *ER*, xiii, 219–221; *Islay Bk*, 484–5.

1541. Rental of Islay. *ER*, xvii, 633–41.

1542. Accounts of the receivers of ferms of Islay. *ER*, xvii, 541–56.

1545. Charter by Mary Queen of Scots to James MacDonald of Dunyvaig and the Glynns of the Barony of Bar. *RMS*, iii, no. 3085.

1561. Rental of the Bishopric of the Isles and Abbey of Iona. *Coll de Rebus Alban*, 1–4.

1562. Tack by Mary Queen of Scots to James MacDonald of Dunyvaig and the Glynns of lands in Islay and Kintyre. *RSS*, v (i), no. 1112; *Islay Bk*, 67–69.

1563. Tack by Mary Queen of Scots to James MacDonald of Dunyvaig and the Glynns of lands in Islay and Kintyre. *RSS*, v (i), no. 1259; *Islay Bk*, 70.

1564. Tack by Mary Queen of Scots to James MacDonald of Dunyvaig and the Glynns of lands in Islay and Kintyre. *RSS*, v (i), no. 1879; *Islay Bk*, 73.

1588. Charter by James VI to Hector, son and heir of Lachlan MacLean of Duart, of lands formerly belonging to the Abbot of Iona and Monastery of Derry. *Coll de Rebus Alban*, 161–79; *Islay Bk*, 88–93.

1614. Charter by James VI & I to Sir John Campbell of Cawdor of the lands and island of Islay. *RMS* (1609–20), no. 1137; *Islay Bk*, 199–230.

1631. Rental of Islay. CM, 655.

1654. Rental of Islay. CM, 655.

1686. Rental of Islay. *Islay Bk*, 490–520.

1694. A List of the Hearths within the shires of Argyll and Bute. NAS, E69/3/1: Islay, pp 55–59.

1722. Rental of Islay. *Islay Bk*, 521–44.

1733. Rental of Islay. *Islay Bk*, 545–54; *Shawfield's Day Bk*, 9–20.

1741. Rental of Islay. *Islay Bk*, 554–59; *Shawfield's Day Bk*, 37–44.

1751. 'View of Contents of the Baroney and Estate of Islay', reproduced in *Shawfield's Day Bk*, 63–67; probably produced by Stephen MacDougall.

1780 Rental of Islay. *Shawfield's Day Bk*, 194–204.

1798–99. Rental of Islay. *Shawfield's Day Bk*, 206–13.

1828. Black Book of Islay. ML, TD 1284/3/2/4.

1836. Rental of Islay. ML, TD 1338/1/3.

1841. Census. Consulted via ICD.

1848. Rental of the Lands and Barony of Islay. ML, TD 1338/1/3/81.

1851. Census. Consulted via ICD.

1853–61. Rentals of Islay. ML, TD 1338/1/3/32.

1861. Census. Consulted via ICD.

1878. Ordnance Survey Book of Names for Islay. Copy in RCAHMS, consulted via ICD.

Acknowledgements

I first set foot on Islay in the spring of 1988, making a visit to Finlaggan to assess its potential for archaeological excavation. Some of the first people I met on that occasion, committee members of the newly formed Finlaggan Trust, have remained friends ever since. Donald Bell, the late Mairi Macintyre, Rhona MacKenzie, John Cameron, Donald MacFadyen, Gina McAuslan and Donald James MacPhee have all provided me with much information on the island and its past. They, and other Ilich I have met in my regular visits ever since, have shown me nothing but kindness and support. These others include the management committee, staff and volunteers who have looked after the splendid Museum of Islay Life in Port Charlotte, not least Malcolm Ogilvie, Margot Perrons and Irene Miller; Eleanor MacNab and other members of the Islay Family History Society, the factors, gamekeepers and other staff of the main estates, the proprietors, staff and regulars of the Ballygrant Inn and Harbour Inn, Bowmore, and all the many other locals and visitors who I have met in my travels. Some, including Jane Ferguson, Aonghus MacKechnie and Magnus Bell have endured with good humour what they may well have regarded as an inquisition on growing up on the island. One of my biggest regrets is that I may not have been clever enough to ask all the above the right questions. I have, nevertheless, learnt a great deal from them all.

I have relied heavily on the resources of the library of the National Museums Scotland, the National Library of Scotland, the Mitchell Library in Glasgow, and the National Archives of Scotland. I am very grateful to the staff of all these institutions for facilitating my research. Colleagues, including Hugh Cheape and John Burnett of the National Museums, Ewen Cameron of Edinburgh University and Keith Sanger have helped me with information, sources and references, as have the two historians of Clan Campbell and Clan MacLean respectively, Alastair Campbell of Airds and Major Nicholas MacLean-Bristol.

My co-authors have contributed much more to my understanding and knowledge of Islay than is indicated by the pieces of text attributed to them. Nigel Ruckley and Roger McWee have been constant companions in much of the fieldwork that underlies this book, and Roger, in particular, has been responsible for developing the *Islay Cultural Database* that has been such a useful tool for me and many others.

I had the good fortune to be involved in the supervision of the doctoral research undertaken by Mike Cressey and Alan Macniven. Both produced considerable works of scholarship, beyond anything I could have achieved, and it has been gratifying to incorporate some of their findings here. Last, but not least, my museum colleague, Ian Brown, has contributed a piece on how Islay was affected by the two world wars of the twentieth century.

To all the above go my thanks and best wishes. I, however, accept responsibility for the remaining shortcomings and imperfections of this book.

DHC
Burntisland
January 2008

Preface

This book has grown out of a major archaeological project, sponsored by National Museums Scotland, that saw the excavation of Eilean Mor and Eilean na Comhairle, and a survey of the archaeological remains around Loch Finlaggan. While there have been several excellent surveys of Islay's history in recent times, not least those by Lamont, Storrie and Jupp, cited in our bibliography, they do not fully cover the same ground as this book, or take into account the results of research from the Finlaggan Project.

The focus here is on the people of Islay in historic times, and their way of life. It is hoped that this will appeal to students and visitors alike, as well as the increasing numbers, especially those overseas, who now recognise that their own roots are in Islay. A previous book, *Islay, Jura and Colonsay: A Historical Guide*, published by Birlinn in 2000, contains a gazetteer of Islay sites and monuments, which should be seen as complementing this volume.

As the title recognises, Islay was the home of MacDonald lords who played a significant role in the wider affairs of Britain and Ireland. Our story, therefore, often extends beyond the physical bounds of Islay itself. In so doing, Islay's status as 'Queen of the Hebrides' is being truly demonstrated.

Historians of the island are fortunate in having a wider range of documentation to draw upon than for many other parts of Scotland. The series of rentals extending back to the sixteenth century, supplemented by testaments, provides the opportunity to learn about some of the lesser folk. Other estate papers have been mined for information on farming life and the development of industries. For the period prior to the nineteenth century, nevertheless, the subject matter of this book is severely restricted by the availability of sources. For more recent times, difficult choices have had to be made as to what to cover, and in how much detail.

Those readers who have dealt with pre-modern texts will know the difficulties of dealing with a multitude of spellings of people's names and place-names. Here, the attempt has been made to standardise these. For people's names, the lead versions in Black's *Surnames of Scotland* have generally been adopted, and for place-names, the versions that appear on up-to-date Ordnance Survey maps – except where it has seemed appropriate to quote from the original documents. The name Kilarrow has caused us some problems. Kilarrow is the spelling we have used, though it is very often given as Killarow. English versions of people's names have normally been given rather than Gaelic, for example, 'John MacDonald' rather than 'Eoin MacDhomnuill', since we believe this will cause less confusion for readers, the vast majority of whom will have English as a first language. We apologise for the inconsistencies that will no doubt be discovered.

The Queen of the Hebrides

'The Queen of the Hebrides' wrote William MacDonald in 1850 of Islay, using a title already known. It has stuck to this day since it is so clearly well deserved.[1] The island was already recognised as the most fertile of the Western Isles, abounding in corn and metal, by the time of King James V's visit in 1540, and that monarch expected that direct ownership of lands there should bring good returns in rents.[2] Islay is certainly greener and more fertile than any of its large neighbours in the Hebrides. It was the centre of the Lords of the Isles and its whisky distilleries have brought it worldwide renown.

The Hebrides are divided into the Inner and Outer Isles with Islay being the southernmost of the Inner Hebrides and part of the old shire of Argyll. Formerly these western isles were divided into four groups in administrative terms, each grouped around a large island: Islay, Mull, Skye and Lewis. The Islay group included the islands of Jura, Colonsay and Oronsay. Islay is now, in terms of local government, part of the district of Argyll and Bute, represented along with Kintyre and the neighbouring islands by a councillor at council meetings in Lochgilphead. With the rest of Argyll and Bute, it is served in the Westminster Parliament by one MP. It is also represented by a constituency and list MSPs in the Scottish Parliament at Holyrood.

Islay is 19 miles wide and 25½ miles from north to south with an overall area of 235 square miles. It is the furthest south of the Hebrides, lying at about the same latitude as Glasgow and Edinburgh, about 15 miles to the west of the peninsula of Kintyre, and only about 23 miles from the north-east coast of Ireland, which is often clearly visible. It is separated from the neighbouring island of Jura to the east by the narrow Sound of Islay. The first detailed map of the island was published in Amsterdam in 1654 in Joan Blaeu's *Atlas Novus*. Blaeu's map was based on the unpublished work of the Scotsman Timothy Pont who mapped much of Scotland in the years from 1583 to 1596.[3] Whereas most of the maps in Blaeu's *Atlas* are of great value, little of worth can be extracted from the Islay map. Clearly something has gone dreadfully wrong in its drafting. The overall shape of the island is inaccurate but recognisable,

and most of the place-names can be identified, but many are positioned
incorrectly, as are hills and rivers.

The first really useful and accurate map of Islay was produced by the
surveyor Stephen MacDougall in the years from 1749 to 1751 for the
laird, Daniel Campbell of Shawfield. MacDougall had been tasked with
producing separate plans of the individual farms, and these were brought
together to make up a map of the whole island showing farm boundaries
and the position of the main townships, but little else (see Fig. A2.1 on
p. 284). This map was first printed in the mid nineteenth century when
the island was on the market. George Langlands' 1801 map of Argyllshire
(Fig. 1.1) has a reasonably accurate representation of the island, depicting
farms, hills, lochs, rivers and roads, though some of his place-names are
suspect or clearly wrong.[4] The first Ordnance Survey maps were published
in 1878 and are an amazingly detailed and accurate overview of the island
at that time.

A wide inlet of the sea, Loch Indaal, dissects the island's broad south-
west flank (Fig. 1.2). To the north-west of this loch is the peninsula
known as the Rhinns, an island until the time of Christ, separated from
the rest of Islay by a narrow channel extending from Loch Gruinart in
the north down to Loch Indaal.[5] Loch Gruinart, over four miles long
and hardly more than one mile wide is a shallow, sheltered tidal inlet of
the sea. Loch Gorm is Islay's largest freshwater loch, about a mile and a
half across. At the tip of the Rhinns are two small islands, Orsay and
Eilean Mhic Coinnich. Another, Nave Island, is positioned off Ardnave
Point at the mouth of Loch Gruinart. The Rhinns forms the parish of
Kilchoman.

At the southern extremity of Islay is another peninsula, rounded and
smaller than the Rhinns, called the Oa, which, with the adjacent coastal
areas extending north-eastwards to the Sound of Islay and northwards
along Laggan Bay to the River Laggan, is the parish of Kildalton and Oa.
Between the Oa and the rest of the south coast is Kilnaughton Bay and the
smaller sheltered Loch Leòdamais, now surrounded by the village of Port
Ellen. There are several small rocky islands off Islay's southern coast, the
most notable of which is Texa.

The rest of the island comprises the conjoined parish of Kilarrow and
Kilmeny, including a broad central valley extending from the head of Loch
Indaal almost to the Sound of Islay. It is watered by the River Sorn, which
is fed via the Ballygrant Burn by Loch Ballygrant, and via the Abhuinn
Gleann Mhartuin by Loch Finlaggan. Neither the Sorn nor any other river
on Islay is navigable.

The climate is maritime and influenced by predominantly westerly
winds. The average rainfall tends to be high with between 1300 mm and
1600 mm per year, but there is little frost and only rarely snow that lies.
Temperatures are generally a good 1°C below those of lowland England
with less variation between summer and winter.[6]

Figure 1.1 Map of Islay,
detail from George Langlands' map of Argyllshire, 1801.

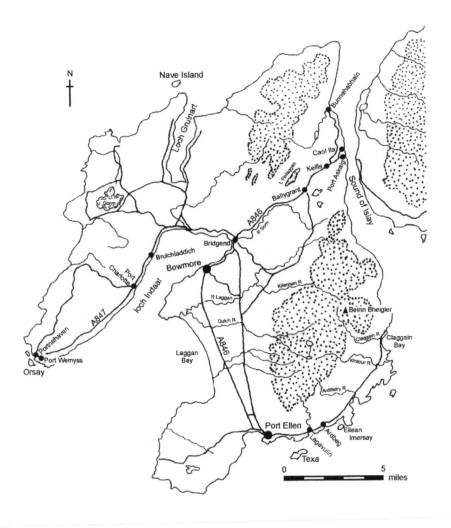

Figure 1.2 Map of Islay, the present day.

The underlying make-up

The geology of Islay is complex (Fig. 1.3).[7] The oldest rocks, particularly gneiss, are to be found in the Rhinns, the so-called Rhinns Complex, dating to about 1800 Ma (million years ago). Its rocks, which originated as sediments, have been metamorphosed and deformed over millions of years by enormous geological forces of heat and pressure. The northern portion of the Rhinns is overlain by sedimentary rocks of the Colonsay Group and the Bowmore Sandstone Group. Both are thought to be of late Precambrian Age, at least 620 Ma, and older than the Dalradian rocks that form the major land mass of the island.

The Dalradian Assemblage or Supergroup, extending right across Scotland in a great swathe, from Islay and Kintyre north-eastwards to the Moray Firth, and all the way round to Stonehaven, is divided by geologists into four groups. The oldest is the Grampian Group, dating to about 750 Ma, followed by the Appin Group (top c.655 Ma), the Argyll Group (top 595 Ma) and finally, the Southern Highland Group (top c.514 Ma). The Islay assemblage belongs to the Argyll, Appin and possibly the Grampian Groups, and represents a complex sequence of deposits that originally formed under the sea – sands, silts, muds and limestones. The tillites (derived from till laid down under ice sheets) included in this range of rocks are indicative of phases of glaciation, while intrusions of lavas provide evidence of volcanic activity.

During the Caledonian Period of mountain building, which peaked about 500 Ma, these rocks were metamorphosed. The sandstones, limestones and shales were turned into quartzites, crystalline limestones and slates respectively. The lavas and other igneous intrusions were metamorphosed into metabasites, amphibolites and metagabbros. Usually these rocks are of a greenish colour and form prominent NE/SW low ridges, the predominant topography of the south-east corner of Islay.

Tillites are generally found in the north and north-east parts of Islay. They belong to the Port Askaig Tillite Formation and make up the base of the Islay Subgroup, equivalent to the Argyll Group on the mainland. James Thompson was the first, in the 1870s, to claim an association with glaciation for the rocks of the Port Askaig Tillite Formation.[8] Although all geological researchers still recognise that they are glacial in origin, there are quite different interpretations concerning the mechanism of their deposition – either by grounded ice sheets, or by deposits dropped from floating ice sheets. More than forty-seven individual beds have been identified, cropping out along the coast from Fionn-phort in the Sound of Islay, past Port Askaig almost to Bunnahabhain, and extending inland for up to a mile.

Islay is criss-crossed by an intrusive suite of NW/SE quartz-dolerite dykes of Palaeogene (Lower Tertiary) age (60 to 52 Ma). Ranging from a metre or less to over 20 m thick, they often form prominent ridges. Similar

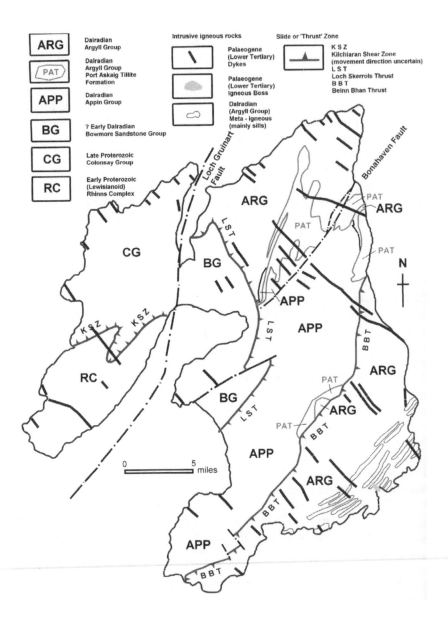

Dalradian
Argyll Group — ARG

Dalradian
Argyll Group
Port Askaig Tillite
Formation — PAT

Dalradian
Appin Group — APP

? Early Dalradian
Bowmore Sandstone Group — BG

Late Proterozoic
Colonsay Group — CG

Early Proterozoic
(Lewisianoid)
Rhinns Complex — RC

Intrusive igneous rocks

Palaeogene
(Lower Tertiary)
Dykes

Palaeogene
(Lower Tertiary)
Igneous Boss

Dalradian
(Argyll Group)
Meta - igneous
(mainly sills)

Slide or 'Thrust' Zone

K S Z
Kilchiaran Shear Zone
(movement direction uncertain)
L S T
Loch Skerrols Thrust
B B T
Beinn Bhan Thrust

Figure 1.3 Geological sketch map of Islay.

dykes also occur on Jura, Kintyre, Mull and Ardnamurchan. Their appearance was described, admirably, in the 1760s by the Revd Dr John Walker:

> The Champaign parts of the Island are Intersected with Dykes of a coarse whitestone [whinstone]. They are of various Degrees of thickness from 10 Inches to 20 or 30 Feet. In some places they are not above 100 Feet distant from one another and in others above a Mile. In many places they rise entire, several Feet above the Surface of the Grounds, and never intersect one another, running always parallel. In this way they look like the foundations of old Walls and Buildings and give the face of the Country a very odd Appearance.[9]

Good examples of Palaeogene dykes, of several metres' width, are located in the area bounded by Lochs Lossit, Ballygrant and Finlaggan. Within the limestone quarry at Ballygrant there is a dyke over 24 m wide with traces of mineralization (lead and associated minerals). Evidence for former mine workings was noted adjacent to the wall of the dyke when the quarry was visited in 2000. The conical hill of Cnoc Rhaonastil in the south-east of the island consists of a dolerite boss intruded in the same circumstances as the Palaeogene dykes.[10]

In the Quaternary Period, Islay was covered in ice sheets.[11] Striations on rock surfaces indicate fluctuations in the flow of ice, either WNW from the mainland, or WSW from Jura. The ice only finally disappeared about 10,000 years ago. Rising seas, caused by the melting of the ice, and a lifting of the land once the weight of ice was off it, caused fluctuations in the relative levels of the sea to land, producing a series of raised beaches around much of the island. Those around the north of Loch Indaal from Tràigh an Luig to Uiskentuie are notable, but those from Rubha Bholsa to Rhuvaal Lighthouse are on a par with the spectacular series of raised beaches of western Jura.[12] On its retreat the ice left deposits of till, sand, gravel and silt. The till is a tough clay containing many well-rounded boulders and is extensive on Islay, underlying later soils and peat. Some of the boulders have clearly been picked up by the ice elsewhere on the mainland or Jura before being deposited on Islay. Looking north from the road to Kilchoman, just east of Sunderland Farm, a prominent esker (a sinuous ridge of sand and gravel, formed by a sub-glacial stream) can be seen. The road from Sunderland Farm to Sanaigmore cuts it in two.

Much of the island is covered with peat or peaty soils unsuitable for cultivation. This mostly developed in the early first millennium BC when the climate was cooler and wetter than today. The useful soils, from the point of view of agricultural activity, fall broadly into three groups. Firstly, there are the soils, including brown calcareous soils, that have formed on windblown sands at Ardnave and Killinallan, on either side of Loch Gruinart, and at Machir Bay on the west coast of the Rhinns (machair).

Secondly, there are the podzols (leached, acidic soils) with some gleys (waterlogged or poorly drained soils), which have formed on the raised beaches around the coasts and extending up the valley of the River Laggan. Thirdly, there are the brown soils with some gleys. Those up the valley around Loch Finlaggan and extending over around Lossit, Airigh Ghuaidhre, etc., have formed on drift derived from Dalradian limestone. Others in the south of the island are on drifts derived from slates and phyllites.[13]

The Islay landscape

Islay has a variety of different landscape types, including sand dunes and machair (light sandy soils), lowland bog and moor, rocky moorland, coastal parallel ridges, and, predominantly, moorland plateau (Fig. 1.4).[14]

Moorland plateau covers the Oa and the hill country extending from behind Port Ellen over to the Sound of Islay and north to Rubh' a' Mhàil. It consists of undulating moorland with heather, rocky outcrops, upland lochs and blanket bog. Most of the Rhinns consists of rocky moorland, a rocky upland plateau dissected by deep gullies. It is exposed and wind-swept with extensive grassland broken by rocky outcrops and occasional patches of blanket bog and small lochs. The land between Laggan Bay and the moorland plateau, a fringe around Loch Gorm, and a strip running from Loch Gruinart to Loch Indaal are classified as Lowland bog and moor. It is characterised by extensive low-lying bog with a flat or hummocky landform. The landscape is open with tidal mud flats and marsh, and drainage channels.

The northern portion of the Rhinns and the opposite side of Loch Gruinart, a strip of land from Kilnaughton Bay to the bottom end of Laggan Bay, and the valley of the River Sorn up the middle of the island are described as marginal farmland mosaic. Typically there are geometric fields with patches of moorland, grassland, peaty marsh and woodland. Lastly, the fringe of land along Laggan Bay and Machir Bay, Ardnave, Killinallan and Sanaigmore are classified as sand dunes and machair. There are open windswept sand dunes, calcareous grasslands and patches of marram grass.

Agricultural activity, in the past or present, has taken place to some extent in all of these landscape areas. In a memorial prepared for the laird of Islay in 1780 it was reckoned that the island had 114,000 acres of which 27,720 (24.3 per cent) were in tillage and 8,507 (7.5 per cent) grass or green pasture.[15] The figure for tilled or arable land is likely to have risen even higher at the time of maximum population density in the early nineteenth century. The West Highland Survey of 1955 gives Islay's area as 150,585 acres and the extent of the 'inbye' (arable) land as 13.3 per cent of the total area. The actual area that was then cropped was reckoned as

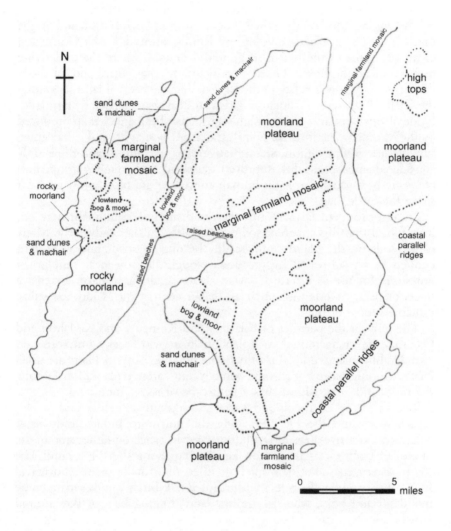

Figure 1.4 Map of Islay landscape types, after Environmental Resources Management, *Landscape assessment of Argyll and the Firth of Clyde.*

three-fifths of what it was in 1911 and only a little over 18 per cent of the
total inbye land.[16] It has continued to drop since then. This is a lower
proportion than in other areas of the West Highlands and Islands but
reflects the lack of crofting and prevalence of cattle raising.

There is farmland on the raised beaches around Loch Indaal, and on the
machair in the northern part of the Rhinns around Lochs Gorm and
Gruinart. Some of the best is to be found in areas where the underlying
rock is metamorphosed limestone, including the north end of Loch
Finlaggan. The lower valley of the Laggan and the neck of land separating
the Oa from the rest of Kildalton Parish are also characterised by farmland.
None of this farmland is rated highly in the land capability map produced
by the Macaulay Institute for Soil Research. At best, a little of it is deemed
suitable for producing a moderate range of crops, and most of it is only
considered appropriate for improved grassland and rough grazing. Few
crops are now grown on it for human consumption, mostly just grass for
silage for cattle feed.

Pre-improvement farmers, however, with limited equipment may not
have found that this apparent soil poverty affected them adversely. Many
of the soils on the island could readily be dug by spade and were light
enough to be cultivated by primitive ploughs. Ready local supplies of
limestone for use as a fertiliser were also a significant factor. Extensive
tracts of peat, covering as much as 25 per cent of the island, are still a
valuable source of fuel.

The bulk of the parishes of Kilarrow and Kilmeny, and Kildalton and
Oa, may be characterised as upland plateau with rocky outcrops and
rounded hills rising to heights of between 300 and 500 m. There are small
lochs, winding narrow glens and some recent forestry plantations among
the moorland. The Rhinns has a landscape of rocky moorland.

The coastline of the island varies from dramatic cliffs and stacks,
especially around the Oa and along the north, to broad sandy bays.
There are extensive areas of sand dunes, for instance on either side of the
mouth of Loch Gruinart and on Laggan Bay along the Big Strand. The
south-eastern coastal strip from Port Ellen to Ardtalla on the Sound of
Islay consists of parallel ridges with stunted oak-birch woods separated by
moorland and bogs, whereas the low land fringing Laggan Bay around
Duich is an expanse of boggy moor.

Mixed woods of deciduous trees were planted as windbreaks and for
ornamental purposes in the eighteenth and nineteenth centuries around the
great houses, especially Islay House, Dunlossit House and Kildalton House.
Since the 1960s conifer plantations have been planted for commercial
exploitation. There are large woods adjacent to Lochs Finlaggan and
Staiosha in the north-west, at Avenvogie and Kynagarry, at Cragabus in
the Oa, and extensive areas of the southern portion of the Rhinns.

Overall the flora and vegetation of the island is predominantly anthro-
pogenic – the result of human activity. Nevertheless there is a relatively

rich and varied flora, with some 800 taxa, for the most part species, recorded in a survey published in 1959.[17]

Animals, fish and birds

Cattle and sheep, and now pigs on the Dunlossit Estate, can be seen from the roadsides of the island. There are also significant populations of feral goats, largely confined to the Oa and the northern area around Bolsa. Large populations of wild red deer roam the moors, and there are also roe and fallow deer. There are otters and stoats, and Islay shrews and voles are considered to be distinct species. Rabbits abound, and surprising numbers of hares, but no foxes, weasels, moles or badgers. Common and grey seals are readily seen around the coasts. Potentially dangerous are the large population of adders, and, in some people's opinion, the midges that can appear in vast swarms in the summer months, though fortunately not when it is raining or there is a breeze.[18]

The freshwater lochs and streams of Islay are mostly well stocked with brown trout and eels, and salmon are caught in the River Laggan. Loch nam Breac on the Dunlossit Estate was well known for its stock of tail-deficient or 'dock-tailed' trout.[19] For many, however, the wealth of bird life is one of Islay's key points of interest. This is now one of the few places in the British Isles where choughs thrive. This member of the crow family is black, with a distinctive red beak and legs. They acquire many of the grubs, beetles, etc., that form a large part of their diet from breaking up cow pats. They can normally be seen around Kilchoman in the Rhinns. Birds of prey are well represented, especially buzzards and kestrels. Golden eagles can also be seen. The population of game birds, especially grouse and pheasant, is maintained by the estates.[20]

From October to April, Islay is home to vast flocks of geese, principally barnacle geese and white-fronted geese that come here from Greenland (Plate I). In 1983 it was reported that there were up to 20,000 barnacle geese overwintering on Islay out of a total Greenland population of 30,000 to 35,000. The total population of Greenland white-fronted geese was reckoned in 1983 as about 15,000, of which 4,000 turned up on Islay. All these geese are protected on Islay, with compensation payments being made to farmers for the depredations they make on their crops of grass. The main goose feeding grounds are in the Rhinns, including round Loch Gorm and Loch Gruinart, in the valley of the River Sorn, around the east coast of Loch Indaal and Laggan Bay.[21] The Royal Society for the Protection of Birds has a nature reserve at Loch Gruinart with a visitor centre at Aoradh from which birds on Loch Gruinart flats can be viewed by videocams.

The Ilich

The most obvious species on Islay, and the one which has had by far the most impact, is humankind. The Ilich – the people of Islay – as distinct from their leaders, are rarely delineated in early documents. Warlike they certainly were, 'that fair host of Islay' that in the thirteenth century tested their shooting as far as Loch Con in Ireland. They were among the 'Children of Conn of the Hundred Battles' in 1411 incited 'to remember hardihood in time of battle'. Their longships, galleys and birlings threatened the coasts of Ireland and the Firth of Clyde.[22]

In medieval times lavish entertaining was a key way for the Lords of the Isles and other chiefs to demonstrate their greatness, but hospitality and generosity were, and are, obvious characteristics of all the Ilich. Travellers in earlier times would expect to be offered food and lodging, even in quite humble dwellings.[23] The poor were looked after in their local communities with alms being provided through the Church.

Fosterage, the tradition which survived in Gaelic Scotland into the seventeenth century,[24] whereby links between families and clans were strengthened by the giving of babies to be brought up by others, is not specifically dealt with in surviving Islay documentation. The son and heir of John Mor of Dunyvaig and the Glynns, John 'Cathanach', may have acquired that name from having been fostered by the Ó Catháns in Ireland, while the fact that Sir James MacDonald was fostered by Lachlan MacLean of Duart played its part in the tragedy at Mulindry in 1586 (see Chapter 5). Foster parents might be of equivalent social rank to the foster child's, or might be their dependents. What is not known is how far down the social scale the practice went in Islay. Fosterage was clearly of particular importance in a society where marriage was not necessarily seen as so sacrosanct as elsewhere (Plate II). Cohabitation appears to have been prevalent among the upper ranks of society by the sixteenth century, and no doubt many took a lead from their social superiors.[25]

The Ilich mostly lived and worked on the land, growing crops and raising animals. They spoke the Gaelic language and preserved a rich heritage of folklore, some of which was recorded in the nineteenth century in the survey of West Highland tales compiled by John Francis Campbell, a great Gaelic scholar, who was also son of the last Campbell Laird of Islay (Plate XXIV). Heroes, fairies and dragons featured in these stories.[26]

Some of their beliefs and practices were inconsistent with the Christianity inculcated by their clergy. Thus in 1697 several had to be rebuked by their ministers in front of their congregations for the use of charms and divinations.[27] Martin Martin, writing about that time, disapproved of their custom of rowing about sunways (clockwise), three times, when they set out to sea, and seventy-five years later Thomas Pennant described other examples of spells and amulets.[28] Lingering unorthodox beliefs are demonstrated by the toothache stone near Port Charlotte, with quantities of nails hammered into it by sufferers in the hope that this would take away their pain (Plate III), and the hollows ground into the base of the cross at Kilchoman, one deep one invariably with coins hidden under the stone 'pestle' which has created it. The original idea was probably that the pestle should be turned sunways for a blessing, and withershins (antic-lockwise) for malediction, but in more recent times rotating the stone has been associated with expectant mothers anxious to conceive a boy.[29]

The Ilich delighted in playing games including shinty and trials of strength. Pennant was told in 1772 that sports and dramatic entertainments used to be performed at funerals. At the time of his visit wrestling and throwing the hammer were popular, and another, he assumed, more local trial of strength in which two men sat on the ground, foot to foot, jointly grasping a short stick, and attempted to pull each other over. Balancing skills and agility were encouraged by a game involving jumping and balancing on a pole. He also described a game that might be played by 200 or 300, formed in a circle, each with a stick in the ground in front of them. An 'odd man' in the middle of the ring had to retrieve his bonnet, which was being passed around the ring. He was succeeded as odd man by whoever he wrestled his bonnet from.[30]

The journalist, John Murdoch, describing his boyhood on Islay in the 1830s, said that stone throwing, shinty and running were leading pastimes. He describes how sticks with a natural crook could be cut near his home and turned into shinty clubs. He played the game at Traigh an Luig, on the shore of Loch Indaal, on Saturdays after school. He also describes a large shinty match at New Year in which the sides were captained by John Francis Campbell and Colin Campbell of Ballinaby.[31] Shinty has long since given way in favour among the youth of the island to football and rugby.

The minister of Kilchoman Parish in 1794 wrote how his parishioners 'had a natural ease and gracefulness of motion in the dance' and how many of them were good at playing the violin or bagpipes.[32] There may even be some genuine folk memory recorded in the mid nineteenth century of people doing the 'mazy dance' (May dance) on Eilean Mor at Finlaggan.[33] When their time on earth was done they were seen off with lavish hospitality for those left behind. The four gallons of whisky provided for the funeral of Robert Campbell of Sunderland in 1779, besides the two bottles for those who collected the coffin and the whisky, was probably not exceptional. Presumably this was Scots gallons at about twice the volume of English ones.[34]

The population of Islay is now only about 3,500, mostly settled in villages. The island capital, Bowmore, is the main centre for shops and businesses. Apart from Bowmore, the conjoined parish of Kilarrow and Kilmeny has small villages at Bunnahabhain, Caol Ila and Port Askaig on the Sound of Islay, inland at Ballygrant and at Bridgend at the head of Loch Indaal. The Rhinns has villages at Bruichladdich and Port Charlotte on the shore of Loch Indaal, and the contiguous hamlets of Port Wemyss and Portnahaven at the tip of the peninsula. In the parish of Kildalton there are small coastal settlements at Ardbeg, Lagavulin and Laphroaig with the main centre at Port Ellen on Loch Leòdamais Bay. Port Ellen rivals Bowmore in size and importance.

A network of roads connects these settlements, but there are none along the north coast or the full length of the Sound of Islay. Access to the island is provided by air services from Glasgow to Port Ellen airport and ferries from Kennacraig on West Loch Tarbert to Port Askaig and Port Ellen. There are also connections in the summer months to Colonsay and Oban, and a year-round service from Port Askaig to Jura. Some islanders and visitors sense a divide between Port Ellen and its hinterland, on the one hand, and the rest of the island. Port Ellen is sufficiently provided with shops and other facilities that there is little need for locals to traipse over to Bowmore. The two roads connecting Port Ellen to the rest of the island, one a single-track over the moors, the other straight through an interminable peat bog, add to the sense of separateness.

The majority of the population is still Islay bred – not, however, born, as most expectant mothers are shipped off to Glasgow to deliver their babies. Ilich of all ages have a pride in their island home and are very aware of their heritage and local traditions. A recent compilation of interviews undertaken with older Gaelic speakers, primarily with the aim of recording and preserving the island's Gaelic heritage, demonstrates that there is still a great wealth of knowledge of old traditions.[35]

Visitors to the island, however, may never hear Gaelic spoken. The locals are too polite to speak it in company where some may not understand it. There has also been a regrettable decline in the use of the language. At the end of the nineteenth century almost all the population was Gaelic-speaking with a significant number, over 40 per cent in the enumeration district of Grulinbeg and Sanaigmore according to the 1891 census, not speaking English (Plate IV). At that time English-only speakers were an insignificant minority, including incoming farmers, distillery workers, etc. Despite compulsory education in English, Gaelic remained strong until the 1930s. By the 1970s only the Rhinns had over 50 per cent of its population claiming to be Gaelic speakers and there were practically no islanders who could claim Gaelic as their mother tongue. Less than a third of Gaelic speakers could read the language, and even less could write it. Some steps are now in place, largely through schooling, to improve this situation, but there is a long way to go to turn around a situation which has looked dangerously like terminal decline.[36]

Prehistory and Early History[1]

With few written accounts surviving from the years before the twelfth century, the prehistory and early history of Islay is a canvas which can be painted only in very broad strokes. Archaeology is our sole source of information for the vast sweep of human occupation of the island prior to AD 100. The major themes of 'Dál Riatan warlords', 'Viking raiders' and 'MacSorley kings of the Isles' are relatively easy to pick out. Where these themes blend together, however, the image becomes blurred and difficult to decipher. To stand any chance of filling in the missing detail, the historical narrative must be extended to take in a wider range of evidence, including archaeology, place-names and the fuller documentary sources of neighbouring areas. By so doing, it is possible to trace a number of important developments in language, culture and politics prior to the arrival of the Gaelic sea-king Somerled mac Gilla-brigte and his sons in the middle of the twelfth century AD.

Prehistory[2]

Humans were attracted to Islay, at least seasonally, as the ice sheets were receding at the end of the last Ice Age. The recent discovery of a 'tanged point' flint tool at Bridgend, points to seasonal exploitation by hunter-gatherers in the late glacial or early post-glacial period (c.11000–8000 BC).[3] For several thousands of years hunting aurochs (wild cattle) and deer, fishing, and gathering seashells, nuts and berries, were the activities that sustained the people that visited or settled on the island. Several of their campsites, recognisable by scatters of flint waste from the manufacture of tools, have been explored in recent years in the Rhinns, for instance at Gleann Mor, Bolsay and around Loch Gorm. Practically all their equipment and possessions have perished with the passage of time, including the boats they must have used to get to and from Islay. Only the flints they fashioned to create composite blades, and scrapers and points, survive. This so-called Mesolithic ('Middle Stone Age') technology has given its prosaic name to the people.

The earliest evidence for farming, the growing of crops and raising of animals, only appears in the fourth millennium BC. Some of the impetus for this must have come as a result of the arrival of new people who already practised this new lifestyle. They may have co-existed with the local hunter-gatherer communities, and the latter may eventually have adopted the new ways. Archaeology has still not been able to provide a detailed overview of the processes of change.

By 4000 BC the island was largely covered with forest, but agricultural activity and better tools, including polished stone axes, led to a cutting back of the trees. Neolithic ('New Stone Age') farmers had sheep, goats and cattle, and grew barley. They also had hand-made pottery, an important new technology for cooking and storing foodstuffs. Metal tools, at first of bronze – thus heralding a Bronze Age – were only introduced about 2000 BC, perhaps as a result of trade, perhaps through the arrival of the bronze workers themselves. From the earliest to most recent times these twin processes of trade and migration have been two of the most potent factors in changing Islay and the Ilich.

The earliest known houses discovered on Islay are circular, represented in the landscape by hut-circles, low banks of turf and stones with diameters from about 9 m to 15 m. There are often groups of them with traces of early field systems, for example at An Sithean in the Rhinns.[4] A radio-carbon date from a round house at Ardnave indicates it was occupied in the late third millennium BC. The tradition of constructing circular houses continued for a remarkably long period of time. If we include in that shieling huts – up to the eighteenth century.

The burial and ritual monuments of the early farmers are more obvious in the landscape than their houses. Human remains, with food and equipment, seem to have been deposited in stone chambers formed of large stone slabs and lintels, incorporated in large stone cairns, many of which had an elongated shape, and a forecourt or façade that gave access to the chambers. The cairns have now mostly disappeared, leaving, in some cases, the chambers exposed, as at Balynaughtonmore (Plate V), Cragabus and Port Charlotte.[5] There was a major shift in burial practices in the third millennium BC, which saw many being buried individually, often in cists, or stone-lined graves, and archaeological excavations will probably demonstrate such burials under many of the round cairns on the island, like the large one at Carnduncan, overlooking Loch Gorm. Later still, there was a fashion for cremation burials, demonstrated by excavation of a small cairn, surrounded by kerb stones, at Cnoc Seannda, Finlaggan.[6]

Many of the standing stones of Islay, mostly positioned singly, may date back to Neolithic or Bronze Age times. Their function is not well understood. Some possibly mark boundaries, events or routes. Others may have had a ritual function. This seems reasonably clear with the stone circle at Coultoon in the Rhinns. It was actually elliptical in form, about

41 m by 35 m, with at least fifteen large stones defining its shape. Archaeological excavations have demonstrated that most of them were never actually erected and the monument was abandoned in its unfinished state sometime in the first half of the first millennium BC.[7]

Iron technology is believed to have arrived in Islay some time in the first millennium BC, but as with previous innovations, archaeology has still not provided a clear answer on whether this resulted primarily from major shifts in population or the dissemination of new ideas. The Iron Age is characterised by numerous defended settlements. Some are forts, normally crowning hilltops and encircled by one or more lines of ramparts. Impressive examples include Borraichill Mor, behind Port Ellen, and Dùn Bheolain, on the massive ridged headland near Smaull. Others are duns, small, often circular, stone-walled structures, perhaps occupied by a single family group. A particularly large and elaborate structure of this type, Dùn Bhoraraic, known as a broch, overlooks the Sound of Islay from the summit of a hill. It is about 23 m in diameter with walls 5 m thick, including mural chambers. It may originally have had a tower-like appearance.[8] Many of the smaller, simpler, duns may date to the first millennium AD. Although most Islay crannogs, artificial island settlements, appear to have medieval or later structures on them, they may also date back to the Iron Age.

Roman military intervention in what is now Scotland in the first and second centuries AD did not extend as far as Islay. The population that was here by that time was long established, utilised the resources of the whole island, and had continued to maintain contacts with the wider world right from earliest times. Throughout these millennia many people would have come and gone, peacefully and not so peacefully, changing and enriching the genetic stock of the islanders.

The Early Historic Period (AD *c.*100–*c.*800)

While Islay and its neighbours remained outside the immediate sphere of Roman interest, the region was not completely unknown to classical authors. In the early second century AD, for example, the Alexandrian geographer Claudius Ptolemy noted a group of five islands to the north of *Ivernia* (Northern Ireland) to which he referred collectively as *Eboudai*.[9] It is from Hector Boece's sixteenth-century misreading of this name that we get the modern (Inner) 'Hebrides'. According to Ptolemy, these islands were known from north-west to south-east as: *Eboudi*, *Eboudi* (sic), *Rhicina* or *Eggarikenna*, *Malaois* and *Epidion*. While only one of them, *Malaois* or Mull, can be identified with any certainty, the relative position of *Epidion* at the extreme south-east of the group puts it in the same general location we would expect to find Islay. Although the two names are quite different, it may be significant that Ptolemy also lists an *Epidion akron* (Kintyre peninsula) in this area. Linguistically speaking, both *Epidion akron* and *Epidion* share the same root – the ethnonym *Epidii* meaning 'horse people'. As Islay is adjacent to Kintyre, and traditionally famed for its horse-raising, there are at least tentative grounds for equating the two islands.

The language spoken by the inhabitants of second-century Islay is not known. With the place-name *Epidion* and the ethnonym *Epidii* appearing to be P-Celtic or Brythonic in origin – the branch of Celtic languages now represented by Welsh, Breton and Cornish – it is possible that the native tongue was not Gaelic, as it has been in more recent times. The likelihood that the locals shared a Brythonic language with the nearby Britons of Strathclyde, or the Picts of Skye or the Outer Hebrides[10] finds some support in traditional accounts of the settlement of Argyll by Gaels from Ireland in the late fifth century AD. Perhaps the best known of these appears at the beginning of the originally seventh-century text known properly as the *Miniugud Senchasa Fher nAlban* ('The Explanation of the Genealogy of the (Gaelic) men of Britain') but often referred to as the *Senchus fer nAlban* or simply the *Senchus*.[11]

According to the *Senchus*, the Gaelic or Scots colonisation of Alba (North Britain) was led by three sons of Erc, the ruler of Dál Riata in Ireland – an area roughly corresponding to County Antrim. This explains why the kingdom of the Scots in Alba was also known as Dál Riata. The newly conquered area appears to have had much the same boundaries as modern-day Argyll. While the bulk of it was shared between the *cenéla* or 'kindreds' of Fergus Mor and his brother Loairnd, Islay appears to have been held by that of the third brother, Angus. Interestingly, however, it is not Angus but his great-grandsons Lugaid, Conall and Canan, whose mother was Pictish, who are said to have divided the lands of Islay. This aspect of the Dál Riatan origin myth was previously thought to reflect the long-term acculturation of an erstwhile Brythonic island by incoming Gaels. However, modern scholars are not so sure. For one thing, the account must be balanced against classical sources, which hint at a Scots presence in North Britain since at least the fourth century AD, when alliances of Scots, Picts and other peoples are said to have harried the Roman Empire.[12] In fact, as recent excavations at Dunadd – the possible *caput regiones* or 'capital' of Early Historic Dál Riata – have produced no evidence for large-scale settlement or societal realignment at this time,[13] it seems more likely that the origin myth in the *Senchus* was penned to explain and legitimise seventh-century Scots' land claims in Ireland. Could it be that the Brythonic names recorded in classical texts were sourced from the Romans' Brythonic guides rather than the inhabitants of Islay itself?

Dál Riata

While the early Brythonic character of Islay remains a matter for speculation, the historical reality of the Scots kingdom of Dál Riata is well
attested in a range of contemporary literature from the seventh century
onwards. In terms of ethno-linguistic heritage, the most valuable of these is
Adomnán of Iona's late seventh-century *Vita Columbae* ('Life of St
Columba').[14] Although Adomnán himself wrote in Latin, the image he
paints of Argyll is that of an entirely Gaelic world where all of the place and
personal names are Irish. He refers to its people as the *Scotti* or 'Irish in
Britain' and presents Columba himself as such an unambiguous symbol
for the region's Gaelic ethnicity that he needs an interpreter when
travelling to non-Gaelic-speaking areas such as Skye.

It is in this context that we find the earliest reliable reference to the
island-name 'Islay' – albeit in the Latinised form *Ilea insula*.[15] As with
many ancient names, the meaning is obscure. Parallels have been sought in
Latin *ilium* (pl.), meaning 'guts, loins, flanks' and Welsh *ilio*, meaning
'ferment' – implying a sense of 'big-bottomed' and alluding to the shape of
the island. A more likely etymology, however, is provided by the Gaelic *I-
leithe* or Welsh *Y-ledd* – both meaning 'the divided isle' and pointing to the
virtual bisection of the island between Lochs Indaal and Gruinart. Unlike
the epithet 'big-bottomed', which would require a level of cartographic
knowledge unavailable to the pre-map-making cultures of Early Historic
Argyll, the fact that Islay has two relatively distinct parts would have been
obvious to anyone standing on the ridge of Cnoc Iolairean at the head of
Loch Indaal.

A more specific indication that the inhabitants of Dál Riatan Islay were
Gaelic-speaking is given by Adomnán in Book II, Chapter 23 of his *Vita
Columbae*.[16] Here, we learn of the demise of a rich man called Federach who
lived on the island. According to Adomnán, this Federach had been
entrusted with the care of a Pictish exile called Taran by no less than the
saintly Columba himself. Far from being the perfect host, however,
Federach soon tired of Taran and had him murdered. On hearing the
news, Columba 'predicted' that Federach would be seized by a sudden death
before he had tasted the first of that autumn's pork. Keen to beat this curse,
Federach had a pig specially fattened and slaughtered early. Just as he was
about to taste the pork, however, he dropped down dead – thus illustrating
Columba's divine authority and the terrible fate awaiting those who defied it!
In contrast to the Pictish Taran, we must assume that Federach was of Dál
Riatan – that is Gaelic – extraction. As he was also an acquaintance of
Columba, the kingmaker and eponymous founder of the monastic *familia*
based on Iona, it is clear that he too was of some social standing. By the time
Adomnán was writing, therefore, and almost certainly earlier, it seems that
Islay had a social hierarchy headed by Gaelic-speaking potentates with
important political connections in the outside world.

For more clues as to the nature of early Islay society, we must turn to the fuller documentary record of nearby Ireland. Early Irish society appears to have been strictly hierarchical.[17] If the general validity of law tracts such as *Crith Gablach* and *Uraicecht Becc* is accepted, every freeman was either a lord (*flaith*) or a client (*céle*) of a lord, and held one of a large number of ranks. While access to the higher ranks was determined to a certain extent by the status of one's ancestors, social standing generally was dependent on the amount of property owned.

By far the most important type of moveable property was cattle. The transfer of cattle from lord to client in return for goods and services played a central part in establishing and maintaining the status quo. Perhaps not surprisingly, however, the underlying basis of Irish society was the own-ership of land. So close, in fact, was the link between land and status that a freeman who sold or lost his lands also lost his free status. The likelihood that the Gaels of Argyll shared this system with their neighbours in Ireland has clear implications for the situation in Early Historic Islay. Despite popular allusion to the transient 'Celtic Cowboys' of the medieval *Gàidhealtachd*, we can be fairly sure that every part of the island was 'owned' by a settled community during its Dál Riatan heyday.

We can assume, on the basis of mainland parallels, that the economic mainstay of Dál Riatan Islay was mixed agriculture.[18] With rough estimates of the population ranging from 3,000 to 5,000,[19] it is likely that settlement was fairly widely dispersed across the island. There is currently very little evidence for the settlements or dwelling houses of the bulk of the population. It is possible that those of the upper ranks of society are represented by the duns, forts and crannogs which still dot the Islay landscape.[20] But we will not know for sure until there has been more archaeological excavation on these sites.

To date, there has been limited work on Eilean na Comhairle at Finlaggan. While the most conspicuous man-made features on this island are its medieval structures, these have been shown to overlie an artificial island or crannog made of brushwood, peat and stones, held in place by timber stakes. Radiocarbon dates have been extracted from two distinct deposits here, suggesting occupation in the last century before the Christian Era and in the early sixth century AD. The larger neighbouring island of Eilean Mor appears to have had a burial ground by the seventh century, and some remains of round houses may date to about the same time. All this suggests that Finlaggan was an important centre even at that time.

There are at least ten crannogs or island dwellings in Islay's freshwater lochs, many crowned with obvious medieval or later remains, but on the basis of the evidence from Finlaggan, it may be supposed that at least some of them were occupied in Early Historic times. They are mostly adjacent to land suitable for agricultural purposes.

Remarkably, the crannog of Eilean na Comhairle had a small, circular dun built on it, perhaps as early as the sixth century. This is the only evidence we have that Islay duns were built or occupied in the Early Historic Period. While it would be dangerous to extrapolate from this that all fifty or so of these structures were in use at this time, it is likely that many of them were. Many of Islay's duns are on rocky stacks or hillocks, on or near the sea. Like the crannogs, most of them are near land that could have been cropped. Whatever the day-to-day use of these structures may have been, it is not too fanciful to suggest that they also formed the focal point of local communities.

There are also thirty 'forts', larger stone/turf enclosures generally considered to be of Iron Age date, as well as a ruined 'broch' (a stone-walled tower), also dating to the Iron Age. Interestingly, the broch and five of the forts appear to have had Norse names, later Gaelicised: Dùn Bhoraraic, the broch overlooking the Sound of Islay, and Dùn Bhoraraig, near Lossit in the Rhinns: both incorporating Old Norse *Borga(r)vik,[21] 'the bay of the fort'; Borachill Mór, near Port Ellen, and Borachill Mór, near Bridgend: derived from Old Norse *Borga(r)ffall, 'the hill of the fort'; Am Burg, Coull: derived from Norse *Borg, 'fort'; Dùn Nosebridge (Plate VI), in the Glen: incorporates Norse *Hnausaborg, 'turf fortress'.

Norse names do not necessarily mean that these forts were occupied by Scandinavian settlers. They merely show that the structures were recognised as forts by these people, perhaps because they had been centres of resistance when they arrived on the island.

Dùn Nosebridge, overlooking fertile land in the valley of the River Laggan, is of particular interest because of the impressive tiered outline created by its three concentric ramparts, perhaps primarily intended to impart status to its owner rather than just add extra defences. In that respect, comparison with the royal Scottish fort of Dunsinane near Dunkeld is of significance. The fort of Dùn Ghùaidhre near Ballygrant, which overlooks fertile land in the valley of the River Sorn, is remarkably similar in size and appearance to Dùn Nosebridge, and there appears to have been another of these multivallate forts at Kilchoman, now flattened and partially under the houses beside the old parish church. It is only known from its defences showing up on aerial photographs.[22]

There are indications that land-holdings in Dál Riatan Islay, as elsewhere in Argyll, were formally organised for the purposes of taxation and military service. The origin myth in the *Senchus* is followed by a combined civil and military survey in which the landed interests of the *cenél nOengusa* are grouped into the assumed districts of Oidech, Freag, Cladrois, Ros Deorand, Loch Rois, Ardhes, Aitha Caissil and Caillnae.[23] Although their enumeration in terms of *tech* or 'houses' is reminiscent of a rental or taxation list, direct comparison of this survey with the better-understood fiscal material of the Later Medieval and Early Modern periods is perhaps unwise. While the *cenél nOengusa* are attributed 430 houses at the end of the document, only 350 of these are accounted for in the list. With a number of other inconsistencies in the body of the text, we cannot be sure, as is often taken for granted, that the list is complete, that all of the kindred's landed interests were actually in Islay, or whether further as yet undetected errors might not have crept into the text at the hands of later copyists.

While several attempts have been made to locate the presumed districts of the *Senchus* in Islay, few have been particularly convincing. The equation of Caillnae with the eastern part of Kildalton and Oa parish,[24] for example, like that of Loch Rois with the area around Loch Gorm,[25] and Ardhes with the high ground between the Sorn and Laggan valleys[26] is purely speculative. Indeed, if the popular identification of Ros Deorand with the southern tip of Jura is accepted,[27] there is no reason why these other places should not also be sought outwith Islay. It may be significant here that both Caillnae, meaning 'Wood of Nae', and Loch Rois, meaning 'loch of the promontory', find clear parallels in Galloway with its Loch Ryan and Forest of Nae.

Onomastic similarities have been noted in a number of studies between Freag and the now-lost farm district of *Ochdamh na Freighe* in the southern part of Kilarrow and Kilmeny parish.[28] Likewise, Aitha Cassil has been linked to the ruined fortification of Dùn Athad at the south-west extremity of the Oa;[29] Cladrois to the well-known farm district of Cladville in the southern part of the Rhinns;[30] and Oidech, through loss of the initial Oi, to the island-name Texa.[31] It should be noted, however, that none of these names have survived to more recent times in anything like their Dál Riatan forms. And while it can be conceded that Oidech and Cladrois seem to appear in other documents of the Early Historic period, it must also be noted that none of the other early forms are attested outside the *Senchus*.

If these designations were 'district-names', there is a strong possibility that they were transformed out of recognition by Norse activity during the Viking Age (see below) – which would explain the current difficulty in locating them on modern maps of Islay. Nevertheless, it must be wondered whether the elusive district-names of the *Senchus* are not, in fact, something of a red herring. Their lack of correlation with the administrative divisions and prestige centres of the Later Medieval Period suggests that they may never have signified physically contiguous districts. Considering that the landed interests of the *cenél Loairnd* in the *Senchus* are grouped clearly by sept and not district, it is possible that the Islay list might also represent a series of abstractions for dispersed tribal land-holdings – in other words, names that were only ever used in fiscal contexts and never actually existed in the landscape.

A further difficulty in reconstructing the socio-economic content in the *Senchus* is the interpretation of the word *tech* or 'houses'. There has been a temptation to assume that these houses represented individual, albeit prestigious, dwellings.[32] Rather than denoting physical 'houses', however, the term *tech* is perhaps better understood as a unit of relative productivity

– in a similar way to the region's Later Medieval and Early Modern 'extents'. It is not necessary that every extent of one house was centred on one particularly prestigious dwelling. On the contrary, several or perhaps even tens of 'houses' worth of land could have been held by one high status individual as a single 'estate' without the need for each individual unit to be demarcated or contain a symbolic structure. This postulated administrative nature of the *tech* finds support in the military details of the *Senchus*.

In Islay, as in Ireland, the local *rí túatha* ('king'), or his overlord, would have been entitled to raise a military force to defend his borders, suppress internal unrest or take pre-emptive action against potentially troublesome neighbours. According to the *Senchus*, each grouping of twenty 'houses' in Dál Riata was obliged to supply 'two seven benchers' towards the seagoing expedition of the authority for which the document was compiled[33] – most probably the *cenél Gabrain* king of Dál Riata.

Indirect study of these '20 house' groupings may hold the key to administrative delineation in Early Historic Islay. Although the grouping is not given a name, the probability that there were fewer than twenty of these on the island suggests that some of them would have defined substantial territorial divisions. Indeed, if, as seems likely, these units were largely defined by topographical features, it is possible that the boundaries themselves remained important long after their Dál Riatan function had been forgotten. Prior to the agricultural improvements of the mid eighteenth century, for example, there were around eighteen significant farm districts in Islay with names beginning with Gaelic *Cill-* ('church', 'graveyard'). With the number and island-wide distribution of these '*cill*-districts' providing a credible match for local '20 house' units, it would be reasonable to assume that the boundaries of the latter were still held to be important during the establishment of the parochial network in the late twelfth or early thirteenth century.[34]

The likely size of the '20 house' units and the levy that might be raised from them would also have had a bearing on the political clout of Islay's Dál Riatan headmen. While the exact meaning of the naval terminology 'two seven benchers' is open to interpretation, it is usually accepted that each bench would have seated two men. If helmsmen are figured into the equation, it is possible that the naval levy of the *cenél nOengusa*, based on the lower total of 350 houses, would have exceeded 500 men – a not inconsiderable force by the standards of the time. If this total were raised in Islay, we might expect the local chieftain(s) and their political exploits to have captured the attention of contemporary Irish annalists. On closer inspection, this is what we seem to find.

According to the *Annals of the Four Masters*, for example, Islay was harried in AD 565 by a fleet led by Conall, son of Comhgall, 'chief' of Dál Riata and an Irish king called Colmán Beg. Although the earliest extant version of this report can only be dated to the twelfth century, and is not corroborated by the generally more reliable *Annals of Ulster*, there is no reason to believe that the account is inaccurate. While it is clearly significant that the attack was led by Conall, it is perhaps even more noteworthy, given the blinkered political focus of the annalists, that this particular event was recorded at all.

When taken together, the origin myth and surveys of the *Senchus* give a strong sense that Dál Riatan Islay remained politically important into the seventh century. This impression also appears to be reflected in an account in the *Annals of Tigernach*, from some point between AD 620 and 643, of the defeat in battle of Domnall Brecc at a place called Calathros. While the location of this particular Calathros is by no means certain, one possibility is the Cladrois of the *Senchus*, which may have been in Islay. As Domnall Brecc was the head of the leading family group in Dál Riata – the *cenél nGabráin* – his presence on the island alone would have to be considered significant. As he was also the king of Dál Riata, the stakes in such a symbolic battle would have been high – amounting perhaps to the kingship itself. Although the victor is not known, the fact that Ferchar – head of the rival *cenél Comgaill* in Cowall – is recorded as reigning jointly with Domnall from the following year, suggests that he may have initiated the attack with this goal in mind.[35] Either way, the episode would appear to point to a regular aristocratic presence on the island, an acknowledged strategic or political advantage, or possibly all three.

Christianity

Another important conclusion that can be drawn from the early sources is that Dál Riatan society was Christian. Leaving issues of moral outlook to one side, this points to the existence of a sophisticated model of social control in Early Historic Islay.

Unlike the later medieval papal ideal, the 'Irish' or 'Celtic' Christianity in question had no single, centralised hierarchy. While the churchmen of this period were nominally subject to the pope,[36] there were, in reality, numerous monastic *familia* vying for local authority at any given time. We know of the operation of at least two of these in the Hebrides during the Early Middle Ages. One, which attributed its foundation to Máel Rhubha, had headquarters at Applecross on the mainland opposite Skye.[37] One of the parishes of Islay, Kilarrow, is named after him. It was the *familia* of Columba, however, with its *caput* on Iona, which appears to have had the greatest impact on Islay. The chapels at Keills and on Orsay were dedicated to him, and other churches on the island were named after his followers. Kilmeny, for example, is dedicated to the saint's mother, Eithne, and Finlaggan, named for Findlugán, one of his monks. This does not mean that the veneration of Columba, Máel Rhubha and their followers continued unabated from Dál Riatan times until the chapels were built and their names recorded in the later Middle Ages. It does suggest, however, that the traditional associations of these *familia* with the island remained strong enough in the *Gàidhealtachd* to warrant resurrection by later local rulers, keen to legitimise their position. But then, this is hardly surprising.

By the later part of the Dál Riatan Period, Iona had come to control a wide network of monasteries in Ireland, Scotland and Northumbria, with links to even further flung parts of mainland Europe and the Mediterranean. Given the likely role of its abbots in the introduction of new forms of organisation and authority to Argyll – and the profound impact this would have had on regional prosperity – it is difficult to imagine that the rulers of nearby Islay were not among the earliest beneficiaries of this process. Indeed, many scholars believe that the monastery of Hinba, founded by Columba when he first set foot in Scotland in 563, and before he moved on to Iona, was located at Cill Chaluim Chille, Tarbert, on the neighbouring island of Jura. Traces of large enclosures and early sculpture at Kilchoman (Plate VII) and on Nave Island suggest the location of similarly early monasteries on Islay.[38]

The size and intricacy of the two major, complete early Christian carved crosses on Islay suggest that the Columban *familia* was well rewarded by local aristocrats for its spiritual support. The free-standing ringless cross at Kilnave stands almost 3 m tall. Although the carving is restricted to one face, its five exquisite, albeit badly eroded, panels of spiral-work have clear similarities with the ring-crosses of Ahenny, County Tipperary – suggesting origins in the mid eighth century before the traditions of Central Scotland and Northumbria had come to bear on those of Ireland and the Isles.[39] The spirals and trumpet patterns of the slightly taller ring-cross at Kildalton (Plate VIII) are even more intensely Celtic in their execution, and characteristic of the so-called Iona school of cross-carving found in only two other examples on Iona itself. But as these are supplemented by scenes of typically Northumbrian religious imagery, they are unlikely to pre-date the flowering of ecclesiastical relations between Northumbria and Dál Riata in the late eighth century.[40]

As many of the numerous dry-stone chapels in Islay are traditionally associated with early saints, such as Slébhine, Ciaran, Cainnech, Lasair and Coman,[41] it is often assumed that they too must date to the Dál Riatan Period. While some of the smaller structures, such as Duisker 2,[42] may represent proprietary chapels, the larger and more elaborate examples, such as Duisker1, Cill Tobar Lasrach (Plate IX) and Cill a' Chubein at Trudernish, may well have been built as early parochial centres. It should be stressed, however, that the style and construction of these buildings find their closest parallels in the early ecclesiastical architecture of the Isle of Man rather than Ireland or Iona. On balance, therefore, it must be assumed that the majority date to a period of Manx influence following the Scandinavian *adventus*.[43]

The Scandinavian *adventus*

Towards the end of the eighth century, the Irish annals record the appearance of a new faction in Hebridean power politics – the heathen, Scandinavian seafarers now known as 'Vikings'. While there are no written accounts of any Viking activity in Islay, it is clear from the attested raids on nearby Rathlin Island and Iona that Scandinavian warlords were operating in the area as early as AD 795.[44] Whether these particular raids were target-specific, or part of a more ambitious campaign, is impossible to say. But considering the dramatic escalation in Norse violence recorded in main-land Ireland in the early ninth century, it is hard to imagine that Islay, with its pivotal maritime location, would have remained unaffected for long.

As the main recorded targets of the early Norse raids were Christian monasteries, it is commonly assumed that their primary motivation was a blasphemous lust for poorly defended ecclesiastical treasures.[45] Disap-pointingly for some, however, this morally loaded imagery of the barbar-ous Viking and his pious 'victim' owes more to the world view and philosophical agendas of Victorian Romanticists than the realities of the late eighth century.[46]

Far from being a specialist outpost of spiritual contemplation, the 'monastery' was the only type of religious institution in the Early Historic *Gàidhealtachd*. Moreover, of those said to have been attacked by Vikings, the majority appear to have been important centres of production, trade, political activity – or all three. It is also misleading to gloss their attackers as random accretions of barbarous freemen, when it is clear, from the lavish boat burials at Gokstad and Oseberg on the Oslofjord, that Norse society was highly stratified at this time.[47] The Norse chieftains who organised the recorded raids must have been very wealthy and powerful men even before robbing any monasteries. Considering the significant investment in resources and manpower needed to mount even a small expedition across the North Sea, it must be wondered whether the main impetus behind these endeavours was not political. The plundering of monasteries was, after all, neither the innovation nor the exclusive preserve of heathen Scandinavians. In Ireland, it had been a tried and tested part of the inter-dynastic struggle for centuries before the Viking Age.[48] That Iona was attacked four times by Norse gentiles between AD 795 and 825 may therefore serve to emphasise not how soft a target it was but the importance of its role as the spiritual anchor of the *cenél nGabráin* kings of Dál Riata.

Although the causes of the Viking expansion are complex and not yet properly understood, it may have been the determination of some Norse magnates to carve out kingdoms at home which forced others to con-centrate their efforts on the Scottish islands. Following the Icelandic saga tradition of the Later Middle Ages, the members of this last group are often cast as relatively insignificant local chieftains, subservient to the nascent kings of Norway. We are told in *Eyrbyggja Saga*, for example, that a certain Ketil Flatnose conquered the Hebrides in the late ninth century as a captain of the Vestfold king Harald Finehair[49] – fuelling the assumption that previous Norse activity in the Isles was limited to small-scale raiding and trading. More recently, however, this Ketil has been associated with the Caitil Find of the Irish Annals, a military leader who was active in Ireland while Harald was still a babe in arms.[50] That the political ambitions of Caitil and his compatriots stretched, moreover, to empire-building, appears to be confirmed by annalistic references to the Norse kingdom of *Laithlind, Laithlinn, Lochlainn, Lothlend,* etc., which emerged in the vicinity of the Irish Sea at some point prior to the mid ninth century.[51] While it is not possible to say whether this *Laithlind* was a direct precursor to the attested Kingdom of Man and the Isles, we can be reasonably certain that it was based, at least partly, in the Hebrides, and that it operated independently of any Vestfold overlords. As early as 853, and its first appearance in the *Annals of Ulster*, the son of the king of Laithlind had become powerful enough to assert himself over all the other Norsemen in Ireland.[52]

This last figure is generally associated with Olaf the White of saga fame, who, along with his son Thorstein the Red, is said to have gained control of 'half of Scotland'. Given the general problems of historicity and chronology associated with the Icelandic sagas,[53] it is possible that these accounts reflect a Norse partition, not of Scotland as later medieval Icelanders would have known it, but of Dál Riata.[54] This would explain the entry in the Frankish *Annals of St-Bertin* for the year 847, which records the Northmen '[getting] control of the islands all around Ireland, and [staying] there without encountering any kind of resistance from anyone'.[55]

To be worthy of mention, the islands in question must have included the Hebridean archipelago some 40 km to the north. Whether the complicity here was on the part of the population at large, or their leaders, is not clear. It is surely significant, however, that by this point, Dál Riata had come to be ruled by a Pictish dynasty based in north-east Scotland.[56] In the face of incursions by the increasingly powerful Anglo-Saxon kingdom of Wessex to the south, it is quite plausible that these absentee rulers would have sacrificed the insular part of Dál Riata to concentrate on the defence of the Pictish heartland. In so doing, they would also have been protecting their western flank from expansionist Irish factions such as the *cenél nEogain*. What happened to the native population of Islay and the isles as a result is not recorded. But it is interesting to note that none of the islanders who appear in the sagas are said to speak Gaelic or have any trouble communicating with Norse speakers from Iceland or Norway. While this could be seen as a literary convention, it might also preserve a folk memory of ethnic displacement.

In most overviews of Hebridean history, it is assumed that the majority of Norse incomers were very quickly absorbed into the native population to form a mixed *Gall-Gaidheal* or 'stranger-Gael' society where the dominant linguistic and cultural elements were Gaelic. Thus far, however, the little evidence that has been presented in support of this assumption must be dismissed as anachronistic, spurious or otherwise misleading.

While it is fair to assert that the established population of Islay was Gaelic-speaking in the centuries before and after the Viking Age, there is little evidence to suggest that this was also true in the intervening period. There may be no contemporary references to the island or its peoples between the earthquake of AD 740[57] and the death of Godred Crovan on the island *c.*1095.[58] It should be noted, however, that the term *Gall-Gaidheal* was rarely used before the later Middle Ages, when it was applied primarily to the contemporary inhabitants of Galloway.[59] There are a handful of obscure annalistic references to *Gall-Gaidheal* warriors in mid ninth-century Ireland.[60] But if these do point to Norse–native mingling in the Hebrides, there is no reason to believe that it was of anything other than the most sinister type. Rather than suggesting a peaceful or productive union of two ethnic groups, use of the term *Gall-Gaidheal* might just as easily reflect the flower of Gaelic manhood being subdued, press-ganged and sent overseas to die by incoming Norse warlords.

Attention can be drawn here to the large numbers of Norse place-names, which can still be found throughout the islands and adjacent stretches of mainland. In Islay the most conspicuous of these end in -bus (from ON *bolstaðr* 'farm') – e.g. Nerabus, Cornabus, Kinnabus; and -dale (from ON *dalr* 'valley') – e.g. (Glen) Egedale, (Glen) Astle, (Cnoc Mór) Ghrasdail – but there are many others. While it has been suggested that a significant portion of these names reflect seasonal exploitation as opposed to permanent settlement,[61] it is difficult to see how any such seasonal names would be preserved in a culturally hostile environment. Given the pre-map-making mentality of Viking Age Argyll, it seems highly unlikely that the local Gaels would preserve foreign Norse names in preference to their own, especially if left to their own devices for most of the year. It must be assumed, therefore, that the survival of Norse names *in situ* in Islay points to the one-time presence of a settled, Norse-speaking population.

Given that Norse farm- and nature-names can still be found in every part of the island at intervals rarely exceeding a mile or so, it seems likely that the Norse language and culture penetrated every level of society. While the introduction and survival of these names could, in theory, have resulted from a process of elite emulation, closer examination of the available name material suggests that the change from Gaelic to Norse was rather more abrupt.

In Islay, as elsewhere in the Hebrides, the form of many later Gaelic names such as Glenegedale (from G *gleann* + ON **Eik(ar)dalr*) or Beinn

Tart a'Mhill (from G *beinn* + ON **Hartafjall*), demonstrates how pre-existing Norse names came to be adopted by speakers of Gaelic towards the end of the Viking Age. Indeed, there are indications, such as the relatively high number of Norse loans in Gaelic beginning sg- and sk-, that these changes resulted, in part at least, from the adoption of Gaelic by an established Norse-speaking population.[62] On the other hand, however, there is no convincing evidence that pre-Viking Age Gaelic names were adopted in this way by speakers of Norse. We find no examples of **Gleannmordalr* or **Bailemartinstaðir* etc. Unpleasant as it may seem, the most likely explanation for this development is one of ethnic cleansing.

According to the Irish annals, Norse fleets of 100 ships and more were active in the Irish Sea region during the ninth century. Although doubts have been raised as to the accuracy of these figures, the existence of such large fleets is corroborated by contemporary European sources.[63] Considering the logistics of warfare and occupation in the Hebridean archipelago, it is entirely possible that a substantially smaller force could have subdued the whole area over a relatively short period of time. None of the islands are so big that they might not have been surrounded and captured by a handful of ships in a matter of days – no part of Islay is more than five miles from the sea. Once subdued, the natives would, moreover, have to be killed or at the very least enslaved and sent abroad in large numbers – lest their local knowledge and contacts allowed them to escape or unite and overwhelm their new masters. One potential sink for this excess population would have been the battlefields of Ireland. For less durable specimens, however, there were also the slave-markets of Dublin and Bristol.[64]

As the ratio of Norse to Gaelic place-names on modern maps of Islay is discernibly lower than in Lewis, it is nevertheless assumed that there must have been substantial Gaelic survival in the Inner Hebrides. In the late nineteenth century the ratios of Norse to Gaelic farm-names in the two islands stood at 1:2 and 4:1 respectively.[65] It must be stressed, however, that all such ratios published to date have ignored the effects of the radical demographic changes that are known to have followed the Viking Age. As a result, they provide only a highly degraded image of the earlier nomenclature. Although both Norse and Gaelic names have been lost as a result of immigration, emigration and changes in agricultural emphases, the vast majority of new names have been coined in either Gaelic or English, thus changing the relative proportion of Norse to Gaelic material. It seems likely that the unusually high proportion of Islay farm-names in Gaelic *cill-* (church or graveyard) and *baile-* (farm), for example, reflect ecclesiastical and administrative reorganisation at the hands of Gaelic-speaking potentates in the twelfth century or later.

If data were available from the height of the island's Norse Period – that is, the time during which the Norse language was spoken by the established population – it would no doubt show a much higher ratio of Norse to Gaelic names. But even complete ethnic cleansing would not necessarily preclude the retention of some pre-existing place-names or administrative divisions. During the early stages of Norse occupation, a knowledge of the more important settlements and territorial boundaries would have greatly facilitated the gathering of tribute and division of lands among Norse settlers. The preservation of the boundaries of '20 house' units in this way might explain their apparent reuse in the parochial system of the Later Middle Ages. It is possible that other names were translated rather than adopted outright. Given the example of the *Senchus*, however, and its now-lost nomenclature, it seems that any cultural exchange on this level was limited to the practicalities of take-over rather than the pre-servation of local culture and naming traditions.

The complete 'Norsification' implied by the place-name material finds a certain amount of corroboration in the archaeological record. While the soils and sand dunes of Islay have yet to yield a classic Viking ship burial, they have already released components of at least seven Viking graves and one coin hoard. The range and volume of diagnostically Scandinavian artefacts discovered near Ballinaby,[66] for example, is indicative of a Viking cemetery. Further mid- to high-status burials have been discovered at Newton Cottage near Bridgend,[67] and Cruach Mhor[68] on Laggan Bay, and a late-tenth-century hoard unearthed on nearby Machrie farm. It contained over ninety coins, including examples minted by the English king Aethelstan and the Viking kings of York, as well as some silver ingots.[69] It is clear that an element of Islay society had been participating in the Scandinavian prestige economy long after the initial Viking raids in the West. As all of these artefacts were recovered on, or near, relatively high-quality arable land, mostly light sandy soils, and included several typically female assemblages, it can also be assumed that this element was settled and socially significant.

To date, no convincing Viking Age houses or settlements have been positively identified on Islay. One of the forts mentioned above is perhaps worthy of further consideration as a Viking stronghold. That is Am Borg at Coull on the west coast of the Rhinns, a large, almost inaccessible rock stack surrounded on three sides by the sea. It is reminiscent in terms of its situation of other Norse forts like Peel in the Isle of Man and Birsay in Orkney. Nearby Am Burg is prized light sandy soil, and a mile to the north is the relatively sheltered sandy Saligo Bay, while Machir Bay is even closer to the south-east. Both of these bays would have been suitable for beaching Viking longships.

The Kingdom of the Isles

While the Norse language was clearly dead or dying in Islay by the introduction of the parish network in the twelfth or thirteenth century, the exact point of its demise will have been determined to a large extent by the direction and strength of the island's external connections. During the later part of the Viking Age, these were no doubt dominated by the Norse kingdoms of Man and Dublin and the concerns of Úi Ímar dynasts who ruled them.[70]

Although Dublin had become increasingly open to Irish influence by the middle of the tenth century,[71] the subsequent appearance of the sons of Harald in the Isles appears to have spurred a renaissance in the region's Norse identity.[72] All of the datable Viking artefacts in Islay, and many of those from elsewhere in the Hebrides, have been traced to this period. It is also during the second half of this century that the *Annals of the Four Masters* introduce a military faction led by the *Lagmannaibh* of the Isles.[73] Although previously thought to be a family of Gaelic islanders with Norse ancestry,[74] the appearance of these *Lagmannaibh* in the campaigns of Amlaíb Cuarán of Dublin and Magnus son of Harald (of Man) hints at an alternative explanation. With both Magnus and Amlaíb having striven for dominance in the Isles, it is not impossible that they were able to garner the support of the area's titular *lögmenn* (pl.) (ON 'lawmen, (legal) representatives', compare *lögmar/laghmann* (sg)) and their local levies. Further, albeit retrospective, evidence for the existence of such office-bearers is provided by certain sixteenth- and seventeenth-century accounts of the Lordship of the Isles. According to Dean Monro in his 1549 *Description of the Western Isles*, the Lordship of the Isles had a council of the region's leading lords, thanes and churchmen, which met on Eilean na Comhairle in Loch Finlaggan.[75] In Martin Martin's late-seventeenth-century *Description of the Western Isles* this council is further described as 'The High Court of Judicature', consisting of fourteen judges and hearing appeals from all the courts of the isles.[76]

By the end of the tenth century, however, the adoption of 'Irish' Christianity by the region's leading Norse magnates would have seen a steady rise in the status of Gaelic language and culture. Amlaíb Cuarán's retirement to, and subsequent demise on Iona in 981[77] could well reflect a Norse appropriation of the cult of Columba. Such a move may have been designed to legitimise the position of ailing Norse dynasties in the face of increasingly powerful Gaelic rivals. Saga tales of the violent proselytising of Norwegian king Olaf Tryggvason some two decades later can probably be equated with a more wide-ranging transition in local belief systems. Whether Olaf was personally responsible for the conversion of the Norse islanders or not, there is evidence that just such a change – that is the acceptance of Christianity by a culturally Norse society – did take place at this time. In Islay, the carved cross-slab found at Dòid Mhàiri near Tighcargaman in Kildalton parish is decorated with interlace patterns reminiscent of the Ringerike style of Scandinavian art – dating it to around the second half of the eleventh century.[78]

Around 1079, the Kingdom of Man and the Isles was seized by Godred Crovan. As Godred had fought alongside Harald Hard-Ruler at the Battle of Stamford Bridge, it would be surprising if his ascension had not strengthened political ties between the Isles and Norway. It has been suggested that Gaelic was already being used at the Manx court during Godred's reign.[79] As his father, Harald the Black, seems to have been a Norse dynast in Ireland, Godred may well have been equally at home in a Gaelic milieu. Ties with Norway were strengthened further, albeit temporarily, following his death. King Magnus Barefoot's invasions of 1098 – during which Islay is said to have been harried – and 1103 – during which Magnus himself was killed – saw the region fall subject to the Norwegian Crown.[80] It appears from the *Chronicles of Man* that close diplomatic relations were maintained between Norway and the Isles for at least another fifty years. While this is likely to have preserved some kind of Norse language use in Islay – if only at a diplomatic level – the foundation of the Diocese of Sodor and the Isles during, or shortly before, the reign of Godred's son Olaf,[81] cemented once and for all the Gaelic trajectory of Man and its political satellites.

As Islay is known to have been part of the Kingdom of Man and the Isles we can assume that these developments had a more local resonance. It is clearly significant in this respect that Godred Crovan should have died on the island in 1095. While local folklore associates him with the Ballygrant area,[82] where he is said to have slain a dragon, and the prestigious farm of Consiby (derived from ON *Konungsbýr* 'King's farm'), of which he may or may not have been the eponymous king, tradition dictates that he is buried under the standing stone known as Carragh Bhan ('White Rock') near Cornabus in Kildalton Parish (Plate X).[83] If, as seems likely, he died on royal procession, it is probable that the Gaelic language had also been promoted locally by his administration. Indeed, it is possible that Gaelicising reforms were more systematically enforced in Islay than the Manx homeland. The similarities between Islay's early dry-stone chapels and those of Man have already been noted. But whatever the extent of this process under Godred and his progeny, it seems likely that the final demise of Islay's Norse period followed shortly after the arrival of Somerled mac Gilla-brigte from mainland Argyll in 1153.

Somerled, the MacSorleys and Islay

Islay passed from the control of the Norse kings based in the Isle of Man in 1156 and became part of a new Kingdom of the Isles ruled by a rival dynasty. This change was effected by Somerled, described in early sources as ruler of Argyll. King Godfrey of Man was unpopular with many of his subjects, and one faction invited Somerled to supply his son Dugald to be their new king. Dugald was probably Somerled's eldest son, and may still have been a boy. He would have been preferred to his father as being of the royal blood since his mother was a daughter of King Olaf of Man. Dugald apparently received much support but this challenge to Godfrey's authority inevitably led to war. The same year, there was a sea battle between Somerled and Godfrey, which the former won. It is not clear that Somerled was campaigning with the support of any factions in the Isles to maintain his son's position rather than opportunistically seizing the chance to expand his own lordship. Certainly, the outcome of his victory was a partition of the Isles, Somerled taking the Southern Hebrides – those to the south of Ardnamurchan, including Islay and Mull, and probably also Arran and Bute.[1]

Two years later Somerled again defeated Godfrey, this time on the Isle of Man, and Godfrey was forced to flee to Norway. He only managed to re-establish himself in Man and the Northern Hebrides, Skye and Lewis, after Somerled's death.[2] Godfrey's descendants continued to rule Man and other territories including Lewis and Skye until they passed to the King of the Scots, Alexander III, by the Treaty of Perth in 1266. A rival dynasty of kings descended from Somerled ruled in the other islands and mainland parts of Argyll in the same period.

Traditionally Somerled has been seen as the leader of the Gaels in a struggle against Scandinavian interlopers in the West Highlands and Islands. His ancestry was believed to be Irish, traceable back to a ninth-century ruler of Airgialla in Northern Ireland, Godfrey the son of Fergus, who in 836 gave his assistance to the Scottish king, Kenneth MacAlpin.[3] The name Somerled, however, is likely to have its origins in the Old Norse *Somarlid(-)i*, which means 'summer warrior', a term used in early sources as an alternative for Viking, and Somerled was married to Ragnhild, (step-)sister of Godfrey of Man.

A recent re-examination of the genealogies recounting Somerled's ancestry concludes that Godfrey the son of Fergus is a fiction invented in the fourteenth century by Somerled's MacDonald descendants to give some depth to their support for the royal Scottish dynasty. Underlying this fable of an Irish adherent of Kenneth MacAlpin was, perhaps, the very real eleventh-century Scandinavian King of Man, Godred Crovan.[4] What is more, other recent research by a distinguished professor of genetics, Bryan Sykes, on the DNA of the present-day chiefs of Clan Donald and others surnamed MacDonald, MacDougall and MacAlister, has led him to identify the particular Y-chromosome that must have been inherited from Somerled himself, passed through the generations from father to son. This Y-chromosome is a classic Scandinavian type, distinctly different from early Irish ones.[5] All this demonstrates the extent of ongoing Scandinavian influence in the west of Scotland, even if later genealogists and clan historians preferred to play it down.

It is possible that Somerled, as a descendant of Godred Crovan, had a real sense of entitlement to rule his island kingdom. He emerges from obscurity in mainland Argyll, and sometime in the years from about 1120 to 1140 established himself as ruler there. Argyll was clearly part of the Kingdom of Scotland, but whether Somerled's accession to power was sanctioned, or indeed encouraged, by David I is not clear. His sister was married to one Malcolm, probably the bastard son of David's predecessor as king, Alexander I. Somerled was almost certainly one of the main backers of Malcolm in his rebellion in the 1120s, only quashed when Malcolm was captured and imprisoned in 1134. Somerled certainly rose, with others of the old Gaelic aristocracy, including the Lord of Galloway, in support of Malcolm's son Donald after the succession of David's grandson, Malcolm IV, to the kingship of the Scots. Somerled only made peace with King Malcolm in 1160.[6]

Somerled, again in rebellion against Malcolm IV, met his death in battle at Renfrew in 1164. He may have felt under considerable threat from the new Anglo-French lords in Scotland, especially the Steward, intent on expanding westwards. Bute had possibly just fallen into the Steward's hands. He would also have been aware, if not concerned, about the spread of Anglo-Norman lordship to the south, in Ireland.[7]

At his death he was styled King of the Isles (*Innse Gall*) and Kintyre, and his power was manifest in his ability to gather together an imposing fleet of ships, said to be 160 strong with contingents from Dublin as well as the Isles and Kintyre. Such a fleet of ships would have carried a fighting force of at least 6,000 men, and possibly considerably more than that.[8] The establishment of Somerled and his descendants in Kintyre and the Isles represented a considerable shift of power in the west away from the Isle of Man.

No residences or castles anywhere in the Isles or Argyll can be associated with Somerled. In the case of Islay, the castle of Dunyvaig is a possible centre of his lordship (Plate XI). Most of the ruins are of later date, but the core of this fortress, a small enclosure castle on a rock stack jutting into the sea, could well be of Somerled's time. It is possible that Islay provided an important base of operations for Somerled. There is, perhaps, a clue to this in an interesting Islay tradition that was picked up in the 1770s by the Welsh travel writer, Thomas Pennant:

> . . . while the Isle of Man was part of the kingdom of the Isles . . . the rents were for a time paid in this country: those in silver were paid on a rock, still called Creig-a-Nione, or, 'the rock of the silver rent': the other, Creg-a-Nairgid, or, 'the rock of rents in kind'. These lie opposite to each other, at the mouth of a harbour on the south side of this island.[9]

It is not clear from this whether the tradition meant that the rents of Islay alone were paid at these two rocks, or whether it was the rents of the wider kingdom, including Man. Given that the rocks are adjacent to a good sandy beach in the large bay that now shelters Port Ellen it is not unreasonable to suppose that ship-borne rents were envisaged. Could it be that the tradition did record a faint memory of rents coming from Man? If so, it would have been in the time of Somerled when Man was briefly in his power. The money rock, Creag nan Nithean, can still be seen near the junction of the road from Port Ellen to Bowmore and the road from Port Ellen to Kilnaughton. The rock of the articles, Creag an Airgid, was nearer Port Ellen, opposite the Ramsay Memorial Hall (Plate XII).[10]

On the death of Somerled in 1164 his lands were split between three of his surviving sons, Dugald, Ranald and Angus, who, along with their descendants, are known collectively as the MacSorleys. Precise evidence is lacking as to who got what, and there is no reason to think that the initial division remained static as the brothers fought among themselves and some of Somerled's gains were reclaimed by the rival dynasty descended from Godred Crovan. It is probable that they regained the territories they had retained in the partition of the Isles in 1156, including Man, Lewis, Harris and Skye.

The tripartite division among Somerled's sons seems to have involved Dugald taking a large piece of territory in the centre, including Lorn and Mull. Angus's share probably included Garmoran (the mainland districts of Moidart, Arisaig, Morar and Knoydart), and the islands of Rum, Eigg, the Uists, Benbecula, Barra, Bute and Arran. Of particular interest to us is Ranald since Islay is believed to have been part of his holding, and also Kintyre, Morvern and Ardnamurchan.[11]

More is known about Ranald than the other two, though much of it derives from a late source, the MacDonald history in The Black Book of Clanranald, compiled in the seventeenth century. It tells us:

> Ranald and his race went to the Hebrides and Kintyre, where his posterity succeeded him.

> Ranald, king of the Isles and Argyll, was the most distinguished of the Foreigners or Gael for prosperity, sway of generosity, and feats of arms. Three monasteries were erected by him, viz., a monastery of Black Monks (Benedictines) in Iona, in honour of God and Columba; a monastery of Black Nuns in the same place, and a monastery of Gray Friars at Saddel in Kintyre, and it is he also who founded the monastic order of Molaise.
>
> Be it known to you that Ranald with his force was the greatest power which King Alexander had against the King of Norway at the time he took the Islands from the Norse, and after having received a cross from Jerusalem, partaken of the Body of Christ, and received unction, he died, and was buried at Reilic Oran in Iona in the year of our Lord 1207.[12]

Although some of the information given here is clearly garbled, it can be demonstrated that much of it may essentially be true. Ranald certainly assumed the title of King of the Isles and Lord of Argyll and Kintyre. It was thus that he described himself in a charter to Saddell Abbey (not friary), unfortunately undated. His impressive title surely indicates that he gained dominance over his brothers.

His charter to Saddell Abbey is only known because it was produced for inspection in 1508. It was apparently the foundation charter of that Cistercian house. At the very least Ranald's gifts to it of lands in Kintyre and Arran indicates that he was in control of those territories.

The Benedictine Abbey of Iona was founded by 1203, plausibly by Ranald, and he may have founded the priory there, for Augustinian canonesses, about the same time. It was not a Benedictine nunnery as stated by the Book of Clanranald, and its first prioress was Ranald's own sister, Bethoc.[13] He surely must have been master of that island, perhaps wresting it from his brother Dugald. Another seventeenth-century Mac-Donald history attributed to a Skye *seneachie*, Hugh MacDonald, retains some memory of conflict between Ranald and his brother Dugald over the 'Isles of Mull'.[14]

A papal letter of 9 December 1203 records that Iona Abbey was then taken directly under the protection of the Pope, Innocent III, perhaps as a result of a quarrel with the Columban Church which may still have maintained a separate presence on the island. This dispute led to a raid on Iona by Irish clergy, including the head of the Columban Church, the Abbot of Derry, in the following year.[15]

The papal letter also gives a list of the abbey's possessions, some of which can be identified as being on Islay. These are the lands of Magenburg, Mangecheles, Herilnean and Abberade. Magenburg is an earlier form of Moyburg, the name for Loch Lossit in the Parish of Kilmeny in the sixteenth century. Mangecheles appears in Dean Monro's mid-sixteenth-century description of Islay as Moychaolis, also identifiable as an area in the parish of Kilmeny. It was still known as Mincholish in the eighteenth century. The name Herilnean suggests the district name 'The Herreis' by which the Mid Ward of Islay, the parishes of Kilarrow and Kilmeny, were known. Herilnean may be an earlier name for Lainty-manniche, identifiable from Dean Monro's account as land at the head of Loch Indaal.[16] Abberade is otherwise unknown, but might be an error for Ardnave, the five merklands of which, including Nave Island, did belong to the abbey by 1507. Some of these lands may have been earlier gifts to the Columban abbey on Iona, but some were presumably fresh grants through the generosity of Ranald.

There is evidence for what may be an early Christian enclosure on Nave Island, and the fragment of a cross from the island, along with the very fine eighth-century cross at Kilnave, demonstrate that Ardnave had a long history as a church centre prior to Ranald's time. The ruined church at Kilnave, however, could well date to his time.[17]

The reference to Ranald's foundation of the rule of Molaise must relate to the cult of that saint – Laisren, Abbot of Leighlin – centred on Holy Island off the west coast of the Island of Arran. In the sixteenth century Dean Monro believed that a house of friars had been founded there by John I Lord of the Isles in the fourteenth century, but perhaps an otherwise unattested religious house was of even earlier date. It may not have been long-lasting.[18]

One of the difficulties in reviewing Ranald's career is the likely confusion in documentary sources between him and his cousin Ranald, King of Man. The *Orkneyinga Saga* has it that Ranald of Man ('Rognvald Godrodarson, King of the Hebrides') was invited by King William I of Scotland to help him regain Caithness from the hands of Earl Harold Maddadson of Orkney. He gathered an army from the Hebrides, Kintyre and Ireland and occupied Caithness for a while, apparently in the summer of 1201. On the other hand, the English chronicler, Roger of Howden, says that Ronald, son of Somerled, King of Man, bought Caithness from King William. Recently David Sellar has made a convincing case that the Ranald in question really was Ranald son of Somerled. He could not have been, as the history in the Book of Clanranald has it, 'the greatest power which King Alexander had against the King of Lochlann', but perhaps therein is a distorted memory of his support for King William. The 'King of the Hebrides' in the saga version of events is described as the greatest fighting man in all the western lands. For three whole years he had lived on board longships and not spent a single night under a sooty roof.[19]

The only other military exploit that is known about Ranald is recorded in the *Chronicles of the Kings of Man*. There he is said to have been defeated by his brother Angus in 1192 in a battle in which many fell wounded. Perhaps this marked the eclipse of his leadership of the MacSorleys.[20]

The account that Ranald 'received a cross from Jerusalem' has been interpreted as meaning that he went on Crusade, presumably the Fourth Crusade that led to the sack of Constantinople in 1207. This, like the alleged date of his death in 1207, cannot be corroborated from other sources. There is the possibility that his piety and that of his wife, Fonie (Findguala?), led them to seek the shelter of a monastic life in their last years. They both offered generous gifts to Paisley Abbey and were granted the privileges of lay membership of that community.[21]

This grant to Paisley Abbey implies other interesting information about Ranald and his kingship. By it the abbey was to receive an initial gift of eight cows, and also two pennies from every house in Ranald's land from which smoke issued. In future years it was to receive one penny from each house. This hearth tax was presumably a percentage of the dues or rents that Ranald gathered in each year, and the fact that it was framed in terms of money suggests that there was a developing money economy in his kingdom. No coins are known to have been minted by Ranald, but issues from England and Scotland would have circulated here. Fonie offered a tenth of her inherited property as well as of all articles she sent by land and sea for sale, an oblique reference to the development of trade.

It is interesting to speculate on why Ranald was so generous to Paisley. There is no mention in the grant that he was recompensing the monks in any way for any action they had taken in respect of the nearby death of his father Somerled in 1164, and the grant instructs the monks to pray for himself, his wife, his heirs and subjects, not for his father. Paisley Abbey had been founded a year or so prior to Somerled's death by his arch-enemy, Walter the Steward. Ranald's interest in the abbey must, at the very least, demonstrate a rapprochement between the two families.

Ranald appears from all this as not just a great war leader in a Viking tradition but as a man who would be a new-style king as contemporary monarchs in England and Scotland. Like them, he used a double-sided seal, only known to us from a description in a notarial instrument of 1426 where it is said to have an image of an armed man sitting on a horse with a drawn sword, that is, the archetypal image of a knight. On the other side, rather than an image of himself seated on a throne, dispensing justice, it had a ship full of men-at-arms.[22] This showed the basis of his power, but did not overrate his status. After all, he had to recognise the King of Scots as his overlord for his mainland possessions, including Kintyre, and the King of Norway for his islands. Nevertheless his eminence as a lawgiver was long remembered. According to Dean Monro, writing in 1549, it was the laws of this 'King of the Occident Iles' that were used by the later Council of the Isles when it met at Finlaggan.[23] Archaeological excavations at Finlaggan on Islay also support this image of a leader who was embracing the culture and institutions of a wider European world. Here there is evidence for a castle with a large stone keep and earth and timberwork defences, defensive architecture of a type introduced to Britain and Ireland and developed there by the Normans. Unfortunately the building of the castle at Finlaggan cannot be dated very precisely, but Ranald seems a more likely candidate for its erection than his son Donald.

Only the foundations of the keep survive (Plate XIII), but it would have been some 20 m by 20 m square, perhaps not unlike the keep thought to have been built by Godrey II (1153–87) of the rival dynasty of the Isles at Rushen on the Isle of Man. The Finlaggan keep is sited on a small island, Eilean na Comhairle, in a freshwater loch, and was reached by a causeway, some 50 m long, from a larger neighbouring island, Eilean Mor, that in turn was connected to the shore of the loch by another causeway of about twice the length of the other. Eilean Mor was surrounded by a timber palisade with a circular earth-and-timber gatehouse securing the end of the causeway leading from the loch edge. Eilean Mor served as a bailey, no doubt with stores, workshops, sleeping quarters for retainers, and other buildings. There may also have been a chapel. None of his residences or centres of lordship, whether on Islay or elsewhere, are recorded in documentary sources.

It was possibly also in Ranald's time that a new parochial structure was devised for Islay leading to the creation of larger parishes centred on churches at Kildalton, Kilchoman and Kilarrow, and possibly also Kil-naughton, Kilchiaran and Kilmeny (see Chapter 8 for further discussion on this). The old parish church at Kildalton appears to date to Ranald's time (Plate XIV). The impetus for this reorganisation may have lain in the appointment prior to 1189 of a new bishop to the See of the Isles who was the protégé of Ranald or favourable to him rather than Ranald King of Man. This was Harold, later recognised as the first bishop of the See of Argyll with its cathedral on the island of Lismore. The partition of the Kingdom of the Isles had inevitably led to the creation of separate bishoprics bringing the Church into line with political spheres of influence, even if only for a brief period of time. The diocese of Argyll came to be limited to mainland Argyll (and Lismore) while the bishops of the Isles continued to administer to the religious needs of the Hebrides.[24]

Ranald's sons, known from other sources as Donald and Ruairi, are said to have defeated the men of Skye in 1209. They seem to have benefited from the death of their uncle Angus and his sons in unknown circumstances in the following year. In 1212 the brothers took part with the Earl of Atholl (Thomas, brother of the Lord of Galloway) in a devastating raid on Derry and Inishowen in Ireland in conjunction with the west Ulster kingdom of the *cenél Conaill*, and Ruairi alone is said to have joined Thomas on a further raid on Derry in 1214 when the treasures were removed from the abbey there. Was this revenge for the raid on Iona in 1204? Ruairi also supported rebellions against King Alexander II, who in 1221, and possibly 1222 as well, mounted expeditions into Argyll. Ruairi may have been the main target of Alexander's animosity, and was possibly forced out of his lands in Kintyre. He is also thought to have held Garmoran.[25]

Donald was the eponym of Clan Donald, the MacDonalds, probably with his main centre of power on Islay. Despite being immortalised through the MacDonald surname, little is known about him. The Book of Clanranald says that messages came from Tara (the traditional centre of royal power in Ireland) inviting him to take the headship of the Isles and of the greater part of the Gaels. Perhaps there is a faint echo here of events in Ireland in 1247 when a MacSorley King of Argyll fell in battle at Ballyshannon while assisting Mael Sechlainn O'Donnell, King of the *cenél Conaill* against the Norman lord of Sligo, Maurice Fitzgerald. This King of Argyll may have been Donald, who is also said by the Book of Clanranald to have been the progenitor of several Irish families.[26]

Hugh MacDonald's history has much more detail on Donald than the Book of Clanranald, some evidently wrong, like ascribing the erection of Saddell Abbey to him and giving his date of death as 1289. Of the rest, including his visit to Denmark (presumably Norway is meant) with his uncle Dugald and his subsequent murder of Dugald, there is nothing in early accounts to offer support.[27]

Donald had to contend with the increasing interest in Argyll and the west of King Alexander II of Scotland. We have already mentioned Alexander's expedition(s) into Argyll in 1221–22. This may have led to the erection of the royal castle at Tarbert, close to Donald's lands in Kintyre and controlling the isthmus that ships were taken over to avoid the long trip round the Mull of Kintyre. Dunoon Castle in Cowal is probably another royal castle of about the same time.[28] Hugh MacDonald may have been on the right lines in recording that Donald had to resist pressure from Alexander to be recognised as overlord for Donald's island as well as his mainland possessions.

Donald would also have been under pressure from the Kings of Norway. From at least the middle of the twelfth century the descendants of Godred Crovan had held their kingdom as a fief of the Norwegian Crown in return for a payment of ten gold marks payable to each King of Norway on his accession. Somerled and his descendants had resisted acknowledging Norwegian overlordship and paying this tribute.[29] The expedition sent to the Hebrides by King Hakon IV in 1230 was intended to bring the MacSorleys to heel under a king of Hakon's choosing, Uspak, possibly a son of Dugald, son of Somerled. Uspak sailed to the Sound of Islay where he rendezvoused with his supposed brothers, Duncan and Donald Screech. There is no mention in any of the sources as to their intentions in regard to Donald, whose sphere of interest they were in. Instead, it is recorded that there was a falling out. The expedition moved on to besiege and capture the Steward's castle of Rothesay on Bute, but Uspak died from a blow by a stone. Kintyre, presumably including Donald's lands, was plundered by the Norwegians on their way home after wintering in Man.[30]

It is difficult with the facts available to fully interpret these events. What is clear, however, is that King Hakon IV had demonstrated that he had the will, resources and determination to bring the MacSorleys to recognise his overlordship. In 1248, by which time, we assume, Donald had died in Ireland, Ewen (MacDougall), son of Duncan son of Dugald of Argyll, along with Dugald (MacRuairi) son of Donald's brother Ruairi went to Norway to compete for the title king, which Hakon gave to Ewen, presumably thereby recognising his dominance over the other descendants of Somerled. In the following year, however, Ewen, was superseded as king by Dugald.[31]

There is surprisingly little about Donald's son and successor, Angus Mor, in the seventeenth-century MacDonald histories. He was probably fairly young when he succeeded and he is known still to have been alive in the 1290s. Although he was technically the first of the MacDonalds, the surname MacDonald was not adopted by any of the main branches of the family until the sixteenth century. The title 'The MacDonald' was used by the Lord of the Isles alone as an indication of his status and headship of all the Clan Donald. As a surname, these lords and their immediate family adopted the designation *de Ile* (of Islay) while other members and branches of the family took the name *de Insulis* (of the Isles). The *de Ile* form first appears on the seal of Angus Mor, appended to a document of 1292. The seal, most appropriately, has an image of a longship or galley with its crew of warriors. His direct successors, the Lords of the Isles, were often known as 'of Islay'.[32]

A praise poem written for Angus Mor about 1250 by an Irish poet paints a picture of a warrior leading the host of Islay to raid and fight in Ireland:

> Thou hast come round Ireland; rare is the strand whence
> thou hast not taken cattle: graceful long ships are sailed
> by thee, thou art like an otter, O scion of Tara.

And:

> The host of Islay has been with thee beside Aran, to
> test their shooting as far as Loch Con; that fair host of
> Islay takes cattle from smooth Innse Modh.[33]

The poem is backed up by other contemporary sources, which suggest Angus was involved with the uprising of Brian O'Neill, King of the *cenel nEogain*, against the English from 1256 until his death in 1260. O'Neill aimed to have himself created High King of Ireland and it is pertinent to note that Angus's praise poem also calls him 'prince of Ireland'.[34]

Whether Angus recognised his cousin Dugald as king over his island domains is not known. In the crisis year of 1263 he was forced to serve alongside him, and also Magnus King of Man, in the fleet of King Hakon

IV. King Alexander II's son, Alexander III, had come of age and was clearly intent on acquiring the Western Isles. The immediate provocation for the Scandinavian invasion was a Scottish raid on Skye in 1262. Dugald and Magnus joined Hakon willingly. Ewen refused to do so on the basis of an oath he had sworn to the King of Scots and that most of his lands (Lorn) were held of him. Angus Mor and his brother Murchaid only joined Hakon after he had sent a force of fifty ships, including Dugald and Magnus, to ravage their lands in Kintyre.

Hakon sailed with his fleet into the Firth of Clyde, hoping to bring King Alexander to agree a peace deal. As the Scots refused to negotiate a force of forty ships, presumably the contingents from Man and the Isles, with King Magnus, King Dugald and his brother Alan, Angus and Murchaid, was detached to harry the Lennox, and possible lands further east. They sailed up Loch Long and dragged their ships overland into Loch Lomond. Meanwhile Hakon was forced to leave the Clyde after a battle on the coast of Ayrshire at Largs. He withdrew to Orkney for the winter and there sickened and died.[35]

On its way homewards from Largs, Hakon's fleet lay for two nights in the Sound of Islay and a tax of 300 head of cattle was laid on the island. Islay seems to have been the only island that was subjected to this burden, a not inconsiderable imposition, perhaps a fine on Angus Mor for previous refusal to recognise Norwegian overlordship. A small burial ground with one stone grave-marker, between Smaull and Ballinaby (NGR NR 216 677), may commemorate this visit. It is called Cladh Haco – Hakon's burial ground. Nearby is Tobar Haco – Hakon's well.

Hakon's expedition failed in its main objectives of establishing Norwegian authority in the Western Isles and protecting them from Alexander III of Scotland. In 1264 the Scots were on the offensive in the islands, forcing the submission of Angus of Islay and Magnus of Man. By the Treaty of Perth, which ceded the Western Isles to Scotland in 1266, Angus Mor and the other island leaders became subjects of the King of Scots for all their lands. The treaty specifically exempted any of the islanders from any retribution from the Scots for their support of King Hakon, but it is nevertheless possible that Angus suffered loss of his mainland possessions in Kintyre. When King John (Balliol) established sheriffdoms of Skye, Lorn and Kintyre in 1293 Angus was not trusted to be one of the sheriffs. The Steward was made sheriff of Kintyre thus establishing him in a position of power in that region. Angus's lands, perhaps including Ardnamurchan and Morvern as well as Islay, Colonsay and half of Jura, were included in the sheriffdom of Lorn, with Alexander (MacDougall) of Lorn as sheriff. The saga account that King Ewen's men had made a great shore-slaughter in Mull in 1263 may indicate the transfer of that island (back) to MacDougall lordship. The MacDougalls were more successful than the MacDonalds post-1263 at integrating with the political

establishment in Scotland. Angus Mor is known to have been in trouble, threatened with military action by the rest of the barons of Argyll if he did not enter Alexander III's goodwill.[36]

Later MacDonald tradition does not remember much about Angus Mor, not his career in Ireland nor his exploits as a leader of the Norwegian invasion fleet. Hugh MacDonald's history seems to confuse him with his son Angus Og and misses what appears to have been a collapse of MacDonald power and influence resulting from 1263 and the political changes that ensued. With the leaders of the other main MacSorley kindreds, Alexander (MacDougall) of Argyll and Alan MacRuairi, he made an appearance at the Council at Scone in February 1284 which recognised 'the Maid of Norway' as Alexander III's heir. These three tail an impressive list of Scottish earls and nobles in the official record, hardly a sign of integration, but perhaps a recognition of their status as lower than the rest of the barons of the Kingdom of Scotland, at least in the eyes of the existing mainland establishment.[37]

Two years later Angus and his son Alexander joined a group of Scottish nobles, including the Earls of Dunbar, Menteith and Carrick, the Steward and the Lord of Annandale at Turnberry Castle on the coast of Ayrshire. Their business was to subscribe a bond pledging their support to the Irish nobles Richard de Burgo, Earl of Ulster, and Thomas de Clare. Turnberry was the chief seat of the Earl of Carrick, the father of the future King Robert I, and this is interesting evidence for an alliance between the Bruces and MacDonalds prior to Robert's bid for the kingship. That this alliance was not new in 1286 and had some substance is suggested by the fact that Alexander confirmed a grant of his father Angus at this time of the church of Kilkerran in Kintyre to the Abbey of Crosraguel, a foundation of a previous Earl of Carrick. The meeting also indicates a continuing Mac-Donald interest in Ireland. At a practical level, the other signatories of the bond probably saw Angus's and Alexander's support as essential because of their resources in longships. In 1292 Angus and Alexander were granted English letters of safe-conduct for their men and merchants who frequented Ireland.[38]

Angus passes from the records in the 1290s. Hugh MacDonald records the tradition that he died at Kilchoman on Islay. The date he gives of 1300 is, however, almost certainly too late.[39] Until the emergence of his grandson John as 'first' Lord of the Isles in the 1330s there is much confusion and uncertainty in the records of Clan Donald, with the leaders of the main family not necessarily always being on the same side in the wars of independence that commenced in 1296 with the invasion of Scotland by Edward I of England and the deposition of King John Balliol.

A recent study of MacDonald genealogy by Noel Murray has suggested that Islay passed from Angus Mor to his son Alexander Og, and then to a son of Alexander Og, identified as Alexander 'Younger', Lord of Islay, Mull, Coll and Tiree, as well as *Ri Airir Gaedheal* (King of Argyll), through his mother Juliana of Lorn. On his death in 1318, Islay was inherited by Roderick (Ruairi) of Islay, probably a brother. His forfeiture in 1325, for unspecified crimes, laid the way open for Islay to be acquired or usurped by the bailie administering it on behalf of the Crown, none other than John, who later adopted the title of Lord of the Isles. He was the son of Angus Og, son of Angus Mor. In this model, Angus Og never held Islay, but was Lord of Lochaber, Morvern, Glencoe and Duror. Other descendants of Alexander Og – 'Clann Alexandair' – who founded Galloglas dynasties in Ireland, were denied their Scottish heritage.[40]

Murray's thesis is attractive in many ways, but it does depend on several leaps of faith in identifying, for instance, an Alexander and a Ruari as otherwise unknown sons of Alexander Og. It also runs contrary to MacDonald clan histories and Barbour's *Bruce* in the position it gives to Angus Og. Although these sources can hardly be regarded as reliable, it has seemed better to give, in what follows, what may be regarded as a more traditional explanation of MacDonald family history in the late thirteenth and early fourteenth centuries.

Angus Mor's son Alexander was probably already the effective leader of the MacDonalds before Angus Mor's death. The grant of the church of Kilkerran to Crosraguel Abbey demonstrates that the MacDonalds had retained or reacquired possessions in this area, and Alexander describes himself as a landowner in a letter written in 1296 to his overlord, Edward I. Earlier that year King Edward had appointed him bailiff for Kintyre and in the following year he appears as bailiff for Lorn, Ross and the Isles. In 1297 he complained to King Edward that Alexander (MacDougall) of Argyll had devastated and burnt his lands and killed his people. It is probable that MacDougall timed his raid to coincide with Alexander's on the MacRuairis. A long memorandum of 1297 gives an account of his activities in English service that year, including the capture of Lachlan and Ruairi MacRuairi. The enmity between the MacDonalds and MacDougalls that saw them take different sides in the Wars or Independence may have been exacerbated by an ongoing dispute over lands in Lismore.[41]

The Alexander MacDonald killed, according to Irish sources, in 1299 was probably not him, but a brother of Angus Mor. He is said to have been slaughtered together with many of his own people by Alexander MacDougall.[42]

Alexander the son of Angus Mor disappears from contemporary records after 1297 but a late source, Hugh MacDonald's history, describes how an Alexander of the Isles was besieged in Castle Sween in Knapdale by King Robert I, and when he was taken, imprisoned in Dundonald Castle in Ayrshire where he died.[43] It would be foolish to place too much trust in such a late and confused source but a possible context for these events would be to assume that Alexander remained loyal to the English king. The MacDougalls switched their allegiance to King Edward after Robert Bruce had himself crowned king in 1306, largely because Bruce had murdered John Comyn, a MacDougall ally and kinsman. This would have placed the MacDougalls in the same camp as Alexander who, in any case, had a MacDougall wife by 1295.[44] Some rapprochement between the MacDougalls and Alexander may have been a political necessity.

Any friendship with the Bruces engendered by his signing the Turnberry Bond in 1286 may have cooled by 1306. In 1296, in his role as bailiff, Alexander had taken over Kintyre from the Stewart, all except the castle, identifiable as the ancient stronghold of Dunaverty. King Edward then ordered him in the same year to give Kintyre to one Malcolm le fiz Lengleys (Malcolm MacQuillan) for reasons that are now obscure to us. The latter had exchanged Dunaverty in 1306 with Robert Bruce for another castle. As a Kintyre landholder and bailiff Alexander possibly resented that Dunaverty had slipped from his grasp into the hands of Bruce. It is perhaps not without significance that the church of Kilkerran, the gift of which Alexander had confirmed to Crosraguel Abbey in Carrick, was gifted by him, presumably at a later date, to Paisley Abbey. John Barbour's epic poem about Bruce, perhaps mistakenly, has Alexander's brother, Angus Og, rather than Alexander himself, welcome the fugitive king to Kintyre in 1306 and hand over Dunaverty Castle. At the same time Barbour indicates that Bruce did not totally trust his MacDonald host.[45]

Alexander had also been instructed by King Edward in 1296 to take over the lands of the Earl of Menteith in Argyll. This would have given him control of Castle Sween and explain why he was holding it against Bruce, possibly in 1309.[46]

Angus Og was also in English service. He is to be found in 1301 along with Hugh Bisset and John MacSween as a leader of a fleet in the waters around Bute and Kintyre. Much of their effort was apparently being directed against the MacDougalls.[47]

In 1306 Robert Bruce had himself crowned King of Scotland. His reign, however, got off to a shaky start and before the summer of 1306 was out he was a fugitive in his own kingdom. This was the point at which he sought shelter in Kintyre. Whether or not Angus Og welcomed the new king there, he did change his allegiance from Edward I to Bruce. It was the support offered by Angus Og to Bruce that was to be the foundation of the rise to power of the MacDonalds as the dominant lineage descended from Somerled and that was to lead to their effective re-creation of a unified Lordship or Kingdom of the Isles. King Robert also won the support of Donald of Islay who was probably the son of Angus Mor's brother Alexander.[48]

In September 1306 King Robert's enemies were hot on his trail and, after spending only a few days in Dunaverty Castle, he was off again for the island of Rathlin off the coast of Antrim.[49] Bruce's whereabouts over the next few months are unknown but it is possible that some of this time was spent with Angus Og in the comparative safety of his island possessions. When he returned to his own earldom of Carrick in February 1307, he appears to have been relying on the support of the Islesmen, and Irish contingents as well. Scottish sources specifically mention the help provided by Christina MacRuairi, Lady of Garmoran.[50] Changing allegiances in the west resulting from Robert Bruce's bid to rule Scotland had brought the MacRuaris and the MacDonalds under Angus Og together as allies.

Meanwhile, Robert's two brothers, Thomas and Alexander, along with Sir Reginald de Crawford, made a disastrous incursion into Galloway that was to result in defeat and the execution of all the leaders. They are said to have come in eighteen ships and galleys, clearly a substantial force, including the Lord of Kintyre and a certain kinglet of Ireland. This Lord of Kintyre was presumably the Malcolm MacQuillan that had given Dunaverty Castle to Bruce.[51] A year or so later King Robert's brother, Edward Bruce, and Donald of Islay commanded a force of Islesmen that killed many of the gentry of Galloway and subdued much of the region. Both commanders presumably felt they had a score to settle for the events of 1307. Donald then attended King Robert's first parliament at St Andrews in 1309.[52]

Angus Og brought his forces to fight at Bannockburn in 1314 and Bruce drafted them into the division under his personal leadership. Angus was duly rewarded by the king for his support. No charter survives, but later indexes of missing charters indicate that Angus received the lands of Morvern, Ardnamurchan, Lochaber, Duror and Glencoe. Of these Lochaber, formerly a possession of the Comyns, and Duror and Glencoe, MacDougall lands, were additions to his possessions, a reward for his services. On the other hand, Bruce retained Kintyre in his possession before granting it to his son-in-law Robert Stewart.[53]

Angus Og married Aine Ni Cathan, a daughter of the chief of the O' Cathans of Keenaght near Derry. Her wedding retinue is said to have had the ancestors of several Scottish families, including the medical family, the MacBeths (Beatons). It would be nice to believe that a description by Hugh MacDonald retains some genuine memory of Angus Og as 'a little black man, of a very amiable and cheerful disposition, and more witty than any could take him to be by his countenance'.[54]

There is no trace of Angus Og in the documentary sources after 1314 and it is probable that he died soon afterwards. He may have been succeeded by a son called Alexander.[55] A lost charter by Robert I granted the former MacDougall lands of Mull and Tiree to Alexander of Islay, and he, along with (Ruairi) the chief of the MacRuairis, joined Bruce's brother, King Edward, in Ireland. Both were among the Scots slain with him at Dundalk (Faughold) in 1318. Irish sources recognised Alexander as King of Argyll and Ruairi as King of the Isles. According to a credible English chronicle, the so-called '"Continuation" of Nicholas Trevet', Donald of Islay was also killed in this battle.[56]

The deaths of the leaders of the MacDonalds and MacRuairis at Dundalk, and the ongoing eclipse of the MacDougalls with their leader still in English service, created a power vacuum in the west. 'The "Continuation" of Nicholas Trevet' claims that Edward Bruce intended not only to conquer Ireland but the Isles as well. King Robert now took actions to bring the Isles more directly under his own control. He created a new Sheriffdom of Argyll, and founded a new castle and burgh at Tarbert on the isthmus where ships were dragged from West Loch Tarbert to Loch Fyne. In the Parliament held at Scone on 28 March 1325, Roderick (Ruairi) of Islay was forfeited. This Ruairi is otherwise unknown, but was surely a leading member of Clan Donald.[57] The MacDonalds must have felt under pressure from royal interest in Argyll. They had achieved much since the death of Donald son of Ranald, from whom they took their name. Their future as a major family was by no means assured in a Scotland led by Robert Bruce. He clearly expected absolute loyalty and the integration of the Gaelic West with the rest of his kingdom, but the MacDonalds and other West Highland families had no long or deep rooted tradition of playing their part in the Kingdom of the Scots, obeying its laws and taking their share of the responsibilities of administration and leadership. Bruce was not likely to tolerate Gaelic lords who did not play a full part in his kingdom and show absolute loyalty.

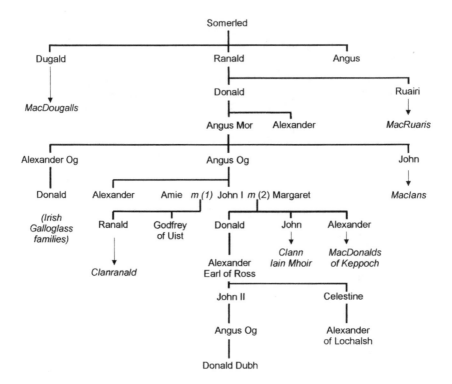

The MacDonalds, Lords of the Isles

The Lords of the Isles

King Robert I died in 1329 leaving his policy to take tighter royal control of the West Highlands and Islands unfinished. The power vacuum created by the death of West Highland leaders at the Battle of Dundalk in 1318 was now about to be filled by John of Islay, son of Angus Og. Clan Donald support for the Bruce regime must have been faltering towards the end of Robert I's reign and now there would be opportunities for the MacDonalds to consider a destiny well beyond the confines of Islay and their other lands. The story of these lords of Islay in the fourteenth and fifteenth centuries has to encompass a much larger world.

In the summer of 1335 John Randolph, Earl of Moray, one of the joint guardians on behalf of the young David II, was at Tarbert Castle to negotiate with John and win him back to the Bruce cause, but he failed. The following year the rival king, Edward Balliol, bought John's support through an indenture promising him the islands of Islay, Gigha, half of Jura, Colonsay, Mull, Skye and Lewis, and the lands of Kintyre, Knapdale, Morvern and Ardnamurchan. Missing from this list is Lochaber, one of the lands granted to the MacDonalds by Robert I. Balliol had to restore it to the Strathbogie family, although John was to retain it in ward until the Strathbogie heir came of age. Otherwise, Balliol's offer represented a vast increase in territorial power, spanning much of the west coast and islands of Scotland.[1]

Correspondence between the English king and John in the period 1336–38, and the issue to John of English letters of safe conduct, suggest that he was a valued ally. Edward III ratified the indenture his under-king, Edward Balliol, made with John.[2]

John must have been aware of his own royal heritage and would have seen the opportunity he had to assume the leadership of the MacSorleys, taking the title *Ri Innse Gall* (King of the Hebrides), as he is called in Irish sources, for himself. He had already taken this step by September 1336 when he described himself in a letter to Edward III, as *Dominus Insularum*. This title in Latin is translated into English as 'Lord of the Isles', and that is how John and his successors are now known. It is also now conventional to regard John as the first Lord of the Isles, but *Dominus Insularum* was also

an appropriate translation of the Gaelic *Ri Innse Gall*, and John and his
successors were seen as of kingly or princely status in the Irish and Gaelic
world. It may be of significance that he omitted this title in a letter written
the same day, on the same subject, to King Edward (Balliol) of Scotland.
Whereas he and his successors came to use the title regularly, the earliest
surviving evidence that it was recognised by central government is in 1431
when some charters issued by John's son and successor, Donald, were
confirmed under the Great Seal.[3]

One of the key characteristics of MacDonald lordship that demonstrates
its kingly nature is the way that it encompassed other clans at the highest
level. Other great Scottish magnates like the earls of Douglas, Hamilton
and Argyll rose to positions of prominence with extensive landholdings,
but their power was largely dependent on being head of their own kindreds
and sharing the fruits of their success with their own relatives. Professionals
in their service and other supporters were never treated as equals. In the
Lordship of the Isles, however, other clan leaders like MacLean of Duart
and MacLeod of Harris were accorded top status. This was one of the
strengths of the Lordship at the height of its power in the fifteenth century.
It was also one of the main reasons for its downfall under a weak lord.

Another sign of the kingly quality of the Lords of the Isles was their
inauguration ceremonies. Hugh MacDonald's *History* is the earliest source
for these. He inserts his account between the death of Angus Og and the
succession of John, perhaps because his sources indicated that John had
undergone such a ceremony. These took place at Finlaggan. There was a
stone with a footprint in it – now no longer to be seen – on which the new
lord stood. He was clad in a white robe and handed the symbols of his
authority, a white rod and a sword. Another late-seventeenth-century
description by the Skye scholar, Martin Martin, specifies that an orator
(poet) rehearsed a catalogue of his ancestors. All this took place in front of a
large assembly including churchmen and the nobles and the clan chiefs of
the Isles, and was followed by feasting. Although these descriptions are
considerably later than the events they describe they are believable, bearing
comparison to the known inauguration rites of Irish kings and, of course,
the kings of the Scots.[4]

The assemblies which witnessed the inaugurations were probably
convened annually, perhaps at midsummer. They would have been an
occasion for people from all over the Lordship to come together and show
their allegiance. They were an opportunity for the transaction of business,
trade, and indulging in games and sports. They were also the context for
meetings of a Council of the Isles. The Dean of the Isles, Donald Monro,
writing in 1549, tells us that the Council of the Isles met in the Council
House on Eilean na Comhairle (the Council Island), Finlaggan, and
consisted of four nobles: MacLean of Duart, MacLean of Lochbuy,
MacLeod of Harris and MacLeod of Lewis; four 'thanes': MacKinnon,
MacQuarrie of Ulva (?), MacNeill of Gigha and MacNeill of Barra; four

leaders of Clan Donald: MacDonald of Kintyre (Dunyvaig and the Glynns), MacIan of Ardnamurchan, Clanranald and MacDonald of Keppoch; and the Bishop of the Isles and the Abbot of Iona. This Council could be convened to offer advice to the lord wherever he was, but the meetings at Finlaggan were probably more formal, in effect a parliament constituted to give judgements and make laws. The model was the Manx Parliament, and the members of the Council of the Isles were the successors of those Hebridean delegates who had gone to the Tynwald in the Isle of Man prior to the mid twelfth century.[5]

Excavations on Eilean na Comhairle at Finlaggan have led to the identification of the Council House, a rectangular stone building, about 4.8 m by 7.5 m, built over the ruins of the earlier keep. Alongside it was a hall, perhaps the residence of a keeper or steward who looked after the place when the lord was not in residence.

The mention of thanes is of interest. Hugh MacDonald claims that John made many thanes, for the Lords of the Isles created thanes and sub-thanes at pleasure. Thane in this context is normally seen as an English translation of the Gaelic *toiseach*, the head of a kindred, but Hugh MacDonald may be indicating that these thanes were officers or coroners, local officials of the Lords of the Isles. It is known that such offices were held hereditarily by some families like the MacKays of the Rhinns of Islay. Hugh MacDonald also tells us that there was a judge in every island for settling of all controversies, and they were paid for their troubles with lands and the eleventh part of every action decided. On Islay this position was held hereditarily by a family that adopted the surname MacBrayne. The chief of the MacKinnons, based on Mull, was obliged to see weights and measures adjusted and the chief of the MacDuffies of Colonsay was the keeper of the records of the Lordship. All of this suggests that the MacDonalds had a fairly sophisticated system of administration, one appropriate for their kingly status.[6]

There were other professional families that provided clerics, poets, smiths, etc. (see Chapter 7), but the largest group of professionals by far were the warriors. The maintenance of a standing force was a characteristic of Gaelic lordship. These warriors, known in Lowland sources as caterans (Gaelic, *ceatharn*), were quartered on the local population and could extract blackmail from the surrounding areas. These were no doubt the enemies and rebels that David II had required John to expel in 1369. The MacLeans emerge in the fourteenth century from relative obscurity as a clan with a crucial military role in the Lordship. The two brothers, Hector and Lachlan, had been vassals or supporters of the MacDougalls but were given large grants of land in Mull by John, Hector receiving Lochbuie and Lachlan the lands of Duart. Lachlan seems also to have been appointed steward of John's household. A well-informed eighteenth-century geneal-ogist of the MacLeans has it that Lachlan was made the Lord of the Isles' Lieutenant General in time of war, a position passed on to his heirs. Hugh

MacDonald's *History* records that John kept a standing force of men under the command of Hector MacLean for the defence of Lochaber and the frontiers of his lands. Lachlan was given control not just of Duart Castle but also the fortresses in the Treshnish and Garvellach Islands. From these, with a force of galleys, he could command the waters around the Mull group of islands, Loch Linnhe and the coast of Lorn. Lachlan's son and successor Hector was given the command of the right wing of the army of the Lordship at the Battle of Harlaw in 1411 and is described by John Major, writing in the early sixteenth century, as the *Campiductorem* (drill-master).[7]

The lordship that John established for himself in the Isles was consciously one of kingly status. In the troubled years from the death of Robert Bruce in 1329 to the return of his son, David II, from exile in France in 1341 he had a relatively free hand to consolidate his position. David II could hardly, however, have looked upon him with kindness. John had backed Edward Balliol and sided with King Edward II of England, and it initially appeared that he would suffer the consequences, with a royal charter of many of his lands, including Islay, being issued, soon after David's return, to Angus, son of John de Insulis. This John de Insulis was Iain Sprangach, a younger brother of Angus Og and founder of the MacIans of Ardnamurchan.[8]

An English chronicler tells us that a dispute arose in Scotland in 1342 between John [of Islay] and David, and the king had to back down in order not to imperil his hold on his kingdom.[9] A meeting was arranged between the two parties at Ayr in June 1343, resulting in the granting to John of a charter of the islands of Islay, Gigha, Jura, Colonsay, Mull, Tiree and Coll with their small islands; Lewis; the lands of Morvern, Lochaber, Duror, Glencoe; the keepership of the adjacent castles of Cairn na Burgh More and Cairn na Burgh Beg in the Treshnish Islands, and the keepership of the castle of Dun Chonnuill in the Garvellachs. Skye and Kintyre, however, were withheld. A charter with the same date and place as John's was granted to Ranald MacRuairi of the islands of Uist, Barra, Eigg, Rum and the lands of Garmoran.[10]

John probably never offered any more than lukewarm support for David II. There is no evidence that he turned out to fight with the rest of the Scottish host in the campaign against the English that led to disaster and the capture of the king at Neville's Cross in 1346. Later that year he renewed his allegiance to Edward III, not as a mere subject but as an ally that could enter into a treaty.[11]

John was intent on building up his own power base in the west and making alliances with other important families around his sphere of influence. He married Amie, the sister of Ruairi, the chief of the MacRuairis. There is a papal dispensation for this marriage dated 4 June 1337. Ruairi was murdered by the Earl of Ross in 1346 and John unexpectedly fell heir to the MacRuairi inheritance. He had already, in

1342, concluded a marriage alliance with the Earl of Ross who had been granted Skye by David II, thus taking it away from the MacDonalds.[12]

About 1350 John married, secondly, Margaret, daughter of Robert the Stewart. The Stewarts were powerful rivals of the MacDonalds in the Firth of Clyde but for much of the reign of David II neither family was in favour at court.

Meanwhile the chief of the MacDougalls returned from exile in England in the 1350s. This was John Gallda (the foreigner), and in 1354 he and the Lord of the Isles patched up their family differences. The Lord of Lorn had to recognise the Lord of the Isles' control over his family's former possessions of Mull, Tiree, the upper part of Jura and the island fortresses of Cairn na Burgh More, Cairn na Burgh Beg and Dun Chonnuill. In return for this he was rewarded with a grant of the island of Coll and the neighbouring part of Tiree, and the Lord of the Isles recognised his right to build eight ships of sixteen or twelve oars.[13]

With David II a prisoner in England from 1346 to 1357 and his father-in-law, the Steward, acting as Lieutenant, John was again relatively free from outside interference. When the English finally agreed terms for David II's release in 1357 John, as an ally and adherent of the English king, was included in the truce between the two countries. He was also specifically excluded from having to make any contributions to David's ransom.[14]

Other lords with lands in the west, including Robert Stewart, the Earl of Ross, John MacDougall and Gillespie Campbell of Lochawe, were reluctant to pay taxes for the ransom but the king worked away at their resistance by a combination of bullying and offering rewards. The Lord of the Isles was a different matter, finally brought to a face-to-face meeting with David at Inverness in November 1369. Unlike their meeting at Ayr twenty-six years earlier John this time had to back down. We can only guess at the threats and the diplomatic efforts behind the scenes that persuaded John to go to Inverness in the first place and caused him to submit.

John was forced to admit that he had committed acts of negligence and he now undertook to obey royal officials and pay all the contributions and taxes that he owed. He had to expel enemies and rebels from his lands and lordship and he promised to send three hostages for his good behaviour to be warded in Dumbarton Castle – Donald his son, a grandson called Angus, and a natural son also called Donald. It is likely that David never saw any of the Lord of the Isles' money, and the death of the king in February 1371 removed any need for John to pay up.[15]

With the accession of Robert Stewart as King Robert II in 1371, John reaped yet more rewards. Within weeks of becoming king, his father-in-law confirmed his hold on the MacRuari lands, and in 1376 he granted him Kintyre and part of Knapdale. The extent of John's lordship was now considerable, possibly even rivalling that of the Kingdom of the Isles under

Godred Crovan and his own ancestor Somerled. John did not have the Isle
of Man or the islands in the Firth of Clyde, and it is not clear if he retained
control of Lewis. It was listed with the Earldom of Ross when it was
confirmed to the Countess Euphemia and her husband Alexander Stewart,
the Earl of Buchan, in 1382. Perhaps it had been taken from John by
David II as a punishment. Skye also belonged with the Earldom of Ross
but both islands, along with areas of Wester Ross may have been firmly in
John's sphere of influence. Possession of Lorn was to elude him. It passed
to John Stewart of Innermeath when John Gallda (MacDougall) died
sometime between 1371 and 1377 leaving no male heirs, and was acquired
by the Earl of Argyll in 1469. He had, however, the substantial territory of
Lochaber in Inverness-shire, part of the old province of Moray.[16]

As befits his kingly status there is evidence of the patronage exercised by
John, his building works, and the flourishing of a distinctive West
Highland culture. The Book of Clanranald records his devotion to the
Church. He kept monks and priests in his company, made donations to
Iona and built or restored the chapels on Orsay, at Finlaggan, both Islay,
and on Eilean Mor in Loch Sween. Remarkably, a half-groat of David II or
Robert II was recovered in excavations at the chapel at Finlaggan,
embedded in its mortar, confirmation of this account. He also erected
'the monastery of the Holy Cross' – presumably meaning Oronsay Priory,
one of the last priories or abbeys to be founded in Scotland.[17]

John's territories contained many castles and other dwellings, many of
which were inherited from his predecessors and the MacRuairis and
MacDougalls. He must have spent much of his time progressing around
his estates, enjoying local renders of rent in kind, dispensing hospitality
and ordering the affairs of his lordship. On Islay his main residence was at
Finlaggan on the site of the earlier castle.

Although protected by the waters of Loch Finlaggan it is striking that
the residential complex that developed on Eilean Mor in the fourteenth
century was not defended by fortifications. It was not a castle. There was a
chapel, already mentioned, with an associated burial ground, and several
houses, including workshops, stores and kitchens. At the end of the island,
adjacent to Eilean na Comhairle, there was an area separated off by a wall
from the rest of the island, containing a hall and other buildings, probably
the private quarters of the lords. The main building on the island was a
great hall with a slate roof. It would have dominated the view of Finlaggan
seen by visitors as they approached (Plates XV, XVI). It, rather than castle
walls, was an appropriate symbol of John's status in a society that measured
the greatness of its leaders by their generosity in entertaining.[18]

The late-fourteenth-century Chronicle of John of Fordun records that
the Lord of the Isles had the castle of Dunyvaig and two mansions on Islay.
Finlaggan was one of these mansions. The other was at Kilchoman. There
is no trace of this mansion today. It is probable that it survived into the
seventeenth century to be the 'choice mansion house' of the Campbell

Lairds of Islay. A report published in 1800 describes near Kilchoman 'an old, ruinous, gloomy building, which was once the seat of the turbulent Macdonald, prince of the Isles'. It was then occupied by the minister of the parish.[19]

On Islay and elsewhere in the West Highlands the vitality of culture in the Lordship of the Isles is evident in the many fine grave-slabs and commemorative crosses that survive from the Medieval Period. This tradition of sculpture seems to have lifted off in the time of John I Lord of the Isles. Fine examples that probably date to his lifetime include the cross at the old parish church of Kilchoman that commemorates members of the local medical family, the Macbeths or Beatons, and a small grave-slab, possibly a child's, in the chapel at Finlaggan (Plate XVII).

By the time of his death, probably in 1387, John had achieved a remarkable transformation of his family's fortunes, passing on a legacy that was to endure for over a hundred years. He is said to have died at his castle of Ardtornish on the coast of Morvern, and to have been buried with his father in St Oran's Chapel on Iona.[20]

By his first wife, Amie MacRuairi, John had several sons, the most notable of whom were Ranald, the eponym of Clanranald, and Godfrey of Uist. By his second wife, Margaret Stewart, his sons included Donald, his successor as Lord of the Isles; John (Iain Mor), the ancestor of the MacDonalds of Dunyvaig and the Glynns, leaders of Clan Donald South; and Alexander of Lochaber, ancestor of the MacDonalds of Keppoch.

Sometime prior to 1373 John granted his son Ranald the lands he had inherited from Amie MacRuairi. According to the Book of Clanranald, Ranald was already ruling the lordship as Steward at the time of his elderly father's death. It is surely significant that he had a commemorative cross erected to himself at the chapel of Texa, opposite Dunyvaig Castle on Islay (Plate XVIII). Perhaps this stronghold was the main centre of his administration prior to it being given to his younger half-brother John.[21]

Nevertheless, it was Ranald himself who is said to have proclaimed Donald, his younger half-brother, Lord of the Isles in succession to John. The Book of Clanranald says that Ranald had invited the nobles of the Isles and his own 'brethren' to Kildonnan on the island of Eigg and there handed him the sceptre. This nomination of Donald, however, was contrary to the opinion of the men of the Isles.[22] Possibly there was concern that Donald would turn away from his father's policy of building up a Gaelic kingdom in the Isles and would allow himself to be dominated by his mother's kin and Lowland culture. This was not to be the case. The law of primogeniture did not hold sway in Irish or Gaelic culture at this time and Donald must have owed his election to the fact that he was young and strong. Ranald, himself, may have been ruled out because of his age or health. He is said to have died six years after his father.[23]

Links, which could reasonably have been viewed as treasonable by the Scottish government, were maintained with the English court. King

Richard II authorised the Bishop of Sodor (Man) to treat with Donald, his brother John and half-brother Godfrey in 1388, and from 1389 to 1396 John is listed as an ally of Richard II in negotiations for the truce with France and her allies, including Scotland. There was a curious sequel to the MacDonalds' relationship with Richard II a few years later. It is claimed that Richard, having been deposed and imprisoned by his successor Henry IV, managed to escape and make his way to the Isles. Here he was recognised and discovered in the kitchen of Donald Lord of the Isles by either a jester who had been trained at Richard's court, or John MacDonald's Irish wife. Donald had him sent to the Scottish court where he was treated with respect and given royal honours. He died at Stirling Castle in 1419.[24]

The discovery of the deposed English king in Donald's kitchen – at Finlaggan? – must have been about 1401. It cannot reasonably be doubted that this Richard was an impostor. This must have been known to the MacDonalds and also to the leading figures at the Scottish court – so who was kidding whom and for what purpose? Was it a ploy by Donald and John to distract attention from the fact that in 1401 they were issued with safe conducts to go and treat with the new English king, Henry IV? It certainly suited the Scottish Governor, the Duke of Albany, to entertain this Richard and try and use him as a means of getting support from the French for war with England.[25]

It is clear from the above that the traditional interests of the MacDonalds in Ireland were not forgotten after the succession of Donald. There were by this time several MacDonald families of Galloglass (hereditary warriors) established in that island, some of them descended from Alexander son of Angus Mor. The main player from our point of view was Donald's younger brother John, not least because he was the progenitor of a branch of the MacDonalds that were important land-owners on Islay until the early seventeenth century. John was given the epithet 'great' and hence the clan that looked to him as its founder was known as Clann Iain Mhoir. It could also be referred to as the MacDonalds of Islay or Clan Donald South.

John married Margery Bisset, heiress of the Glynns of Antrim, about 1390. The Glynns are a substantial track of land in north-east County Antrim consisting of seven *tuatha* (countries or lordships) that were to remain with John's descendants until the eighteenth century. They gave John great power and prestige in the Isles, as well as Ireland, and put him in direct contact with the English kings Richard II and Henry IV.[26]

John had received from his father 120 merks of land in Kintyre and 60 merks of land in Islay. These Islay lands can be identified as those extending to almost 60 merks that were included in the Barony of Bar created in 1545 for John's descendant, James MacDonald (Fig. 5.1). They included lands in Kildalton, the Oa, Kilarrow and Kilmeny. John's main residence, from which he took his territorial designation, was the castle of

Figure 4.1 Map of Lordship of the Isles and Earldom of Ross.

Dunyvaig. By the time he acquired it, the small enclosure castle of the twelfth or thirteenth century had been developed into a much larger complex with a hall-house on the rock stack jutting into the sea, fronted by a small inner, and large outer, courtyard. This outer courtyard had a sea-gate large enough for drawing in galleys.[27]

Alexander, the younger brother of both John and Donald Lord of the Isles, is said by Hugh MacDonald to have refused his father's offer of Trotternish in Skye in favour of the Lordship of Lochaber. He expanded MacDonald power from Lochaber up the Great Glen by extortion and blackmail. An indenture of 1394 between him and Thomas Dunbar, Earl of Moray, shows how the earl had to pay Alexander a yearly fee of 80 merks as protection money for the lands of the Earldom and Bishopric of Moray. The document specifically lays down that Alexander will not burden these lands with his own men or other caterans. The indenture was for seven years, and in July 1402, presumably because it was not renewed, Alexander demonstrated the price of non-compliance by sacking the Chanonry of Elgin and burning much of the town of Elgin itself. In October of that year Alexander, having been excommunicated by the Bishop of Moray, felt compelled to return to Elgin to seek forgiveness and absolution, but he only did so at the head of a large army.[28]

Sometime between 1395 and 1398 Alexander also took the royal castle of Urquhart. The castle overlooks Loch Ness and controlled the route from Loch Linnhe through the Great Glen to Inverness and the Moray Firth. With Urquhart Castle under their control the forces of the Lordship would have been able to sail their galleys through the lochs of the Great Glen. This acquisition, however, was seen as a step too far by the government. A general council at Perth in April 1398 agreed that a large army should be sent against Donald, Lord of the Isles, and his two brothers. The leaders of this army were to be King Robert III's brother, the Earl of Fife (also called Robert), and the heir to the throne, his son the Earl of Carrick. Fife was now made Duke of Albany and Carrick Duke of Rothesay, perhaps as a deliberate propaganda drive to stress the role of the royal family as leaders and not persecutors of the Gaels. Both titles would have been seen to locate their spheres of interest in Gaelic regions of Scotland and suggested the Gaelic roots of the dynasty. The army was gathered at Dumbarton that summer and an expedition launched against the Lordship, resulting in the submission of Donald and his imprisonment of his brother Alexander. Despite the council's wish that Urquhart Castle should revert to royal control there is no certain evidence that this happened, and Donald had released his brother without royal permission by November 1399.[29]

Clearly the power and influence of the MacDonald brothers were not significantly curtailed by the events of 1398, and an even greater extension of MacDonald power was to come through the marriage of Donald with Mariota Leslie, sister of Alexander Earl of Ross, sometime prior to 1402

(Fig. 4.1). In that year, the earl died, leaving a daughter, Euphemia, as his heiress, but the earldom, which was the largest territorial earldom in Scotland, was claimed by Donald in right of his wife. Euphemia was supported by her grandfather, the Duke of Albany, who then governed Scotland on behalf of his brother, King Robert III. Donald may have been in effective control of much of the earldom, including its main castle of Dingwall, by 1411, when the forces of the Isles famously clashed with a royal army at Harlaw, near Inverurie in Aberdeenshire. The incitement to battle said to have been composed by a MacMhuirich bard prior to the conflict is a stirring string of exhortations for the 'children of Conn of the Hundred Battles' to be stout-hearted, vigorous and dexterous, for now was the time to win recognition.[30]

Writing in the early sixteenth century, the historian John Major saw the battle as a struggle between the wild and the civilised Scots, and tells how as a schoolboy it was the theme of his games. It was certainly the case that Donald's army, perhaps as many as 10,000 strong, was drawn from the Highlands and Islands while the forces that opposed him were largely contingents from the north-eastern Lowlands, commanded by Alexander Stewart, Earl of Mar. Donald's precise aims are not altogether clear, though contemporaries feared that he would take control of Scotland as far south as the River Tay. His route probably took him through the Earldom of Ross, picking up support as he went, and thence he moved on to threaten Aberdeen.[31]

The battle was hard fought with many casualties, the main one on Donald's side being Hector MacLean of Duart, the chief of the MacLeans. Both armies parted at the end of the day, perhaps neither very sure which had come off better. In the immediate aftermath, Albany, at the head of another army, recaptured Dingwall Castle from the MacDonalds, and the following summer gathered three forces to attack Donald. The latter came to him at Lochgilp and offered oaths and hostages to keep the peace and provide protection for the king's subjects.[32] In 1415 Albany's grand-daughter Euphemia resigned the earldom and it was re-granted by Albany to his son John, Earl of Buchan. After Buchan died in 1424 it was retained by King James I.

The reality on the ground, however, was undoubtedly somewhat different, with all or most of the lands of the earldom under MacDonald sway through to John II Lord of the Isles' forfeiture in 1475. Donald's grip on earldom lands was strengthened through the support he received from the main kindreds in Wester Ross, including the MacKenzies, Mathesons and Gillanders. A rare surviving charter issued by him in 1415 records a grant to Angus MacKay of Strathnaver, the head of another important northern clan, of lands in Sutherland associated with the Earldom of Ross.[33]

We mentioned above that the Bishop of Sodor was authorised by King Richard II of England to treat with Donald, his brother John and half-brother Godfrey in 1388. The negotiations, assuming they took place, must largely have been about ecclesiastical affairs, most importantly the schism in the Church that resulted in two lines of popes from 1378. The Roman popes were supported by the kings of England, and inevitably, the rival line of Avignonese popes was supported by the Scots. The Bishop of Sodor was based in the Isle of Man, the only part of his diocese under English control, and he adhered to the Roman Pope. Another bishop, Michael, was now installed in the Scottish part of the diocese, probably choosing Snizort on Skye as his cathedral. This marked another split in the Church in the Isles conforming to political realities. The new Scottish Bishopric of the Isles also broke its links with Nidaros (Trondheim), and when the Archbishopric of St Andrews was established in 1472 it was clearly fully part of the Scottish Church.[34] The break away of the Church in the Isles from the control of a bishop based in Man presumably suited Donald. It would have strengthened his hold on his vast lordship.

The date of Donald's death is given in Irish sources of the seventeenth century as 1422. He may, as indicated by the Book of Clanranald, have resigned control of the lordship to his son Alexander prior to his death. This history also states that he became a monk in the monastery at Iona, but afterwards passed away on Islay. Hugh MacDonald believed he died at Ardtornish in Morvern. The Book of Clanranald also credits him with giving land in Mull and Islay to Iona Abbey.[35]

In a Gaelic charter of 1408 relating to lands on Islay (see Chapter 7) Donald signs himself as *MacDhomnuill* (The MacDonald). This style of using the surname as a title parallels, if not anticipates, the way that Irish kings designated themselves in the fifteenth and sixteenth centuries. Donald did not, as far as is known, adopt the title of Earl of Ross, which he may have regarded as of lesser status than *MacDhomnuill* or *Ri Innse Gall*, though other contemporary documents refer to him as lord of the earldom.[36] In any case, Donald may have been prepared to aim much higher than a mere earldom. His main protagonist was the Duke of Albany, by 1406 ruling Scotland on behalf of his nephew King James I, a prisoner in England. Hector MacLean of Duart had been given an English safe conduct in 1405 to go and visit James I, presumably at the behest of Donald, but whether this was because James was looking for support from Donald, or vice versa, in a potential struggle with Albany, is not apparent. Donald must, like many of his contemporaries, have doubted whether James would ever succeed to the throne. His 1411 campaign may really have been about making a bid for the Kingdom of Scotland rather than just Ross.[37]

The Gaelic charter of 1408 is a unique survival of a type of document that might have been issued by Donald to many of the leaders of Isles society to record grants of land and other arrangements. His title, *MacDhomnuill*, appears to have been written in his own hand, and his doctor, Fergus Macbeth, also signed his own name. This is, perhaps, the oldest known deed in Scotland with the signature of laymen. It is the earliest surviving original document issued by a Lord of the Isles. The second oldest is a charter of 1410 issued by Donald at Aros on Mull in December 1410, confirming a grant by Christina MacRuairi. It is written in competent Latin of the period.[38]

These documents provide a tantalising glimpse of what may have been a considerable output of documents in the two languages, Gaelic and Latin. Although it appears that it was Fergus Macbeth who drew up the 1408 charter, it was probably more normal for such tasks to fall to the clergy who are noted by the Book of Clanranald as the companions of Donald, and John I before him. The Lords' chaplains may often have doubled as secretaries for such duties. The chapel at Finlaggan on Islay would have had an important role as a place where documents would have been drawn up and witnessed. The earliest surviving evidence of this is a notarial instrument of 14 June 1456, recording a decision of John II Lord of the Isles. Adjacent to the chapel the foundations of a house and byre (buildings H and J) have been discovered in excavations. These may have been occupied by the chaplain.[39]

By the time James I was released from English captivity in 1424 Albany had been succeeded by his son Murdoch, not just to the extensive Albany estates but also to the governorship of the realm. Neither he nor his father stretched themselves to achieve the release of their royal kinsman, and it is not greatly surprising that James moved against Murdoch early in 1425, as soon as he was confident he had enough support to achieve his ends. He was able to call upon the new Lord of the Isles, Alexander, to sit on the assize that tried and condemned Murdoch and other members of his faction.[40]

A desire to eliminate Albany may have been the only thing that the Lord of the Isles and his king had in common, and any rapprochement between the two was to be very short-lived. Indeed, the year after Duke Murdoch's execution the MacDonalds were supporting his son, James 'the Fat'. He had managed to escape to Ireland where he must have made contact with John of Dunyvaig and the Glynns. It was believed that he intended to invade Scotland and make a bid for the Crown. King James at this time had no children of his own and James 'the Fat' would have been seen as his heir.[41]

An Act of Parliament of March 1426 forbade unauthorised contact between Ireland and those parts of Scotland adjacent to it because of the presence of the king's rebels among the Irish.[42] Other actions by the king suggest that he was sizing up his options, if not actively planning for the downfall of the MacDonalds. These deeds included the sending of an embassy to King Eric of Denmark and Norway in 1426 to rearrange payments of the annual sum owed since 1266 for the Western Isles, thus presumably putting his overlordship of the Isles beyond any doubt. Hugh MacDonald was later to claim that Alexander refused to recognise the sovereignty of the Kings of the Scots over his island possessions. James also showed renewed favour to the MacDonalds' opponent at Harlaw, the Earl of Mar, bolstering his position in the north and in 1427 strengthening the royal castle of Inverness which was in that earl's keeping. The rights of Robert, a brother of Murdoch, late Duke of Albany, to the Earldom of Ross were probably bought out.[43] Most significant of all, there was no recognition by James of Alexander of the Isles' right to be Earl of Ross.

Whether the king was reacting to the MacDonalds' unfriendly actions or the MacDonalds to a hostile king cannot be known, but the two sides, while moving apart, were closing in on trouble. Alexander and his clerk, 'sir Nigel', were paid expenses by the royal treasurer in 1426, perhaps for a visit to court to resolve differences, but by 1428 there was clearly no thought of negotiation in the king's head when he invited Alexander, his mother and other leaders of northern society to come to his castle of Inverness for a parliament. There, in what can only be viewed as a breach of trust, he had them arrested and imprisoned. Apart from Alexander and the Countess of Ross, the prisoners included MacDonald allies like the chiefs of the MacKays, the MacKenzies and the Mathiesons.[44] The MacKenzies and Mathiesons were the two most important kindreds in Wester Ross at that time.

The king clearly now sought to find a more acceptable leader among the MacDonalds, one who would be more pliant to royal will. It appeared that John MacDonald of Dunyvaig might be that man. He was tanist or heir to the Lord of the Isles, ambitious and experienced. What realistic hopes James had to engineer a replacement of Alexander by his uncle John is not known but his plans went disastrously wrong when the royal go-between, James Campbell, murdered John at a meeting set up to discuss such matters. The king clearly did not feel strong enough at this point to dispense with the leaders of Clan Donald altogether and was left with no effective choice but to deal with Alexander. Alexander was offered a vision of loyal service bringing rewards, and was set free in 1429. His mother remained in custody, perhaps as a guarantee of his good behaviour.[45]

Whether the king understood it or not, there was little chance that Alexander would now be a good subject, even if he would have been happy with a life as a royal courtier. His position depended on his ability to lead his clansmen and there would have been no shortage of cries of revenge for the death of John MacDonald and other royal insults. The MacDonald response was almost immediate. Inverness was burnt and a fleet was sent to Ireland for James 'the Fat', to bring him home and have him established as king. This nightmare scenario for King James failed to materialise since the Albany heir died before being able to embark.[46] Meanwhile the king raised a large army and set off to encounter Alexander.

The two sides met in Lochaber on 23 June 1429. The MacDonald army was apparently as strong in numbers as at Harlaw but not so resolute for the fight. The Clan Chattan (MacKintosh) and Clan Cameron supporters of Alexander were not prepared to fight against the king in person, withdrew, and surrendered to royal authority. In the ensuing fight the MacDonald forces were routed. The king followed up this success by taking the castles of Dingwall and Urquhart and led a new force into Argyll to root out Alexander. Castle Sween and the castle of Skipness were taken and with Kintyre and Knapdale given into the joint keeping of two Ayrshire knights, Alexander Montgomery of Ardrossan and Robert Cunningham of Kilmaurs.[47] Alexander was forced to sue for peace. He was required to make a humiliating submission at Holyrood Abbey, where, clad only in his shirt and drawers, and on his knees, he had to offer up his sword to the king. He was imprisoned in Tantallon Castle in East Lothian.[48]

Even now, King James did not feel able or willing to dispose of this troubler of his peace, and the power of Clan Donald was soon to be manifest on another battlefield in Lochaber, this time at Inverlochy in September 1431. A royal army led by the earls of Mar and Caithness was routed by a much smaller force of Islesmen, Caithness himself being killed. The hero of the day for the MacDonalds was the eighteen-year-old Donald 'Balloch' (freckled), son of the murdered John MacDonald of Dunyvaig. He thus, in the chronicler Bower's words, 'raised his head from his lair', giving notice that he would be a power to reckon with.[49]

Remarkably, King James released Alexander from captivity very shortly afterwards. Perhaps he realised that his best hope of neutralising the threat posed by Donald Balloch was to restore Alexander to his lordship and leadership of his clan. Perhaps this time Alexander also saw a threat to his own position from his cousin Donald, who would, on the strength of his victory at Inverlochy, most likely be elected by the clan leaders as Lord of the Isles should Alexander falter or die.

Alexander had by 1431 married a Lowland wife, Elizabeth Haliburton, perhaps at the instigation of the king. She was from Dirleton, near his prison in Tantallon Castle. Hugh MacDonald believed that he took a contingent of 3,000 of his men to join the king's army at the siege of Roxburgh Castle in 1436. In his mother's lifetime he had called himself Lord of the Isles and Master of the Earldom of Ross, but by the beginning of January 1437 he had adopted the title of Earl of Ross, probably with King James's approval. The death of the Earl of Mar in 1435 would have meant that Alexander had no effective competitors as the most powerful lord in the northern parts of the kingdom. It was possibly also James who had Alexander appointed as justiciar north of the Forth, prior to his murder the following February. Alexander appears in government records from the middle of 1437 as earl, and as justiciar from the beginning of the following year.[50]

The rest of his life may have been spent as a loyal servant of the Crown. He was the first head of his kindred to be so integrated with mainstream Scottish society, and the only one to play a major role in the government and administration of the country. In the latter part of his life he was not only one of the most senior post-holders of the Crown but also one of the very few earls of adult age or any experience.

There is not much to be gleaned from documentary sources about his role as head of his kindred and administrator of the vast estates of the Lordship of the Isles and Earldom of Ross. He is known to have granted charters at Finlaggan in 1427 and 1432, and it may have been in his reign that Finlaggan reached its fullest development with a remodelled great hall and copious kitchens. He held the lands of Greenan on the coast of Ayrshire, just south of the burgh of Ayr. It is not known how or when these lands came into the possession of the MacDonalds but a foothold here would have provided useful access to the trading and manufacturing resources of Ayr and the other Ayrshire burghs. Inverness and Dingwall would have provided commercial opportunities for the lands of the Earldom of Ross.[51] Such activities are not well documented, but a grave-slab of the fourteenth or fifteenth century at the church of Kilchiaran on Islay may provide a clue. Its decoration includes a barrel, and an inscription identifies its owner as John and Donald, surely two merchants.

Alexander would certainly have had some say in the proposal by his uncle, Angus Bishop of the Isles, to move the cathedral of the Isles from Snizort in Skye to 'some honest place' and to create twelve canonries and as many prebends for the clergy to serve in it. The Pope was petitioned for licence to carry this out in 1433 but there is no evidence of the plan being realised.[52]

Alexander is said to have died at Dingwall on 8 May 1449 and to have been buried at the Chanonry of Ross – that is in the cathedral of the Diocese of Ross at Fortrose. He was succeeded as Earl of Ross and Lord of the Isles by his son John, then about fifteen years of age. John was betrothed, probably through an arrangement made by his father, to Elizabeth, daughter of James Livingston, the chamberlain and one of the most powerful men in the government during King James II's minority. A poem by Giolla Coluim that appears to date to the 1470s or '80s describes John as

> . . . the sternest to win land that is not yet thine;
> to oppose thee, thou king of Islay, great the effort![53]

A more accurate picture, possibly, is given by a later clan historian who claimed that John was a meek, modest man, brought up at court – a scholar more fit to be a churchman than to lead Clan Donald.[54] It was also in 1449 that James II took over personal government of his kingdom and began to turn against those that had held the reins of power in the preceding years. James Livingston was an early casualty, arrested that year and forfeited the following. This left John II Lord of the Isles stripped of powerful allies at court and denied any dowry for his new wife.

The death of Alexander of the Isles may also have had the effect of unleashing Donald Balloch. He is said to have fled to Ireland in the aftermath of his victory at Inverlochy in order to escape royal vengeance. Nothing much is heard of him from 1431 until the succession of John as Lord of the Isles but it is likely that in the intervening years he not only consolidated his family's hold in Ireland but also built upon his status in the lands of the Lordship. In 1433 he combined with the O'Neills in Ireland to inflict a series of defeats against the O'Donnells and other enemies.[55] He may already have been expanding his Scottish lordship eastwards to the island of Arran where one Ranald mac Alexander, possibly a close kinsman, was occupying royal lands in the north of the island, including Lochranza, from the 1430s onwards.[56]

It was probably Donald Balloch who persuaded the young and inexperienced John II to take by force what he was denied by an unsympathetic king. In 1451 he captured the royal castles of Urquhart and Inverness and destroyed Ruthven Castle in Badenoch. According to the Auchinleck Chronicler, John claimed he had been promised the keeping of Urquhart Castle for three years by the king and he now installed his father-in-law, James Livingston, as its keeper. His motive for destroying Ruthven Castle would undoubtedly have included damaging the interests of a new regional rival, the Earl of Huntly. Ruthven was the caput of his Lordship of Lochaber. In the following year Donald Balloch led a devastating raid on royal lands in the Firth of Clyde including Inverkip on the coast of Renfrewshire and the islands of Bute, Cumbrae and Arran. The castle of Brodick was destroyed.[57]

This second MacDonald raid was undertaken, at least partially, in support of the Black Douglases, all-powerful during King James's minority but now being viewed by him in a hostile manner. The Earls of Ross, Douglas and Crawford signed a bond of friendship, probably soon after the king began his personal rule.[58] This need not have been seen by the king as a hostile act. Such bonds were an important and characteristic way of nurturing friendship and avoiding misunderstandings among the Scottish nobility. James did, however, see that this bond posed a threat to himself, and perhaps he was not wrong. The refusal of the Earl of Douglas to renounce it was to lead to his murder at the king's hand in 1452.

James II achieved the extirpation of the Black Douglases before his warlike reign was cut short in 1460 by the blowing up of one of his own guns. John II remained beyond his reach and relatively quiet, and the king preferred to acquiesce to his taking of royal castles rather than have him join forces with the Douglases. There is some evidence of friction in the north between John II and the Earl of Orkney after the latter was awarded the Earldom of Caithness in 1455. The earl was a loyal and trusted supporter of James II, and the MacDonalds may have felt threatened by this development.[59] The king was more concerned to tackle Donald

Balloch, and there is evidence for a royal expedition to the Firth of Clyde in 1457 or 1458, probably to reclaim Arran. About the same time Colin Campbell of Lochawe was created Earl of Argyll. There can be no doubt that this loyal supporter of the Crown was seen as a bulwark against the MacDonalds.[60]

The minority of James III appeared to provide new opportunities for the MacDonalds. John II led a delegation of senior Islesmen to the first parliament of the new reign in February 1461 but got nothing for his troubles. He was clearly unhappy with the arrangements made for the minority government and the fact that the young king was to be looked after by the Earl of Orkney. His response was a devastating raid on Orkney that summer. Meanwhile Donald Balloch appears to have taken Arran again, raided Bute and besieged the royal castle of Rothesay. An attempt was made by the government to bring John back into the fold through a meeting held on Bute with Bishop Kennedy of St Andrews, but John had another option to pursue.[61]

This was one of the most infamous events in the whole history of the MacDonalds, the signing of the so-called treaty of Westminster–Ardtornish. It was actually an indenture between King Edward IV of England, on the one hand, and John II, Donald Balloch and Donald's son John, on the other, by which the latter would become subjects of the English king and receive wages from him. Furthermore, they agreed that should Edward conquer Scotland with MacDonald support then John II, Donald Balloch and his son would divide Scotland north of the Clyde–Forth isthmus equally among them while the exiled Earl of Douglas would be reinstated in his lands in the southern part of the country.[62]

Donald Balloch and his son clearly had more to gain from this than John. It is likely that Donald was the driving force, perhaps using his position as a landowner in Ireland to make the initial contacts. It was his brother Ranald along with Duncan, the Archdeacon of the Isles, who was appointed to go to England to draw up the agreement. Was this mere irresponsible opportunism, with John II being coerced by his uncle Donald Balloch, or were there deeper reasons? Given that John II felt excluded from court and government and had powerful enemies there, perhaps this was a logical approach – strike before stricken. There was no move, however, by Edward IV to conquer Scotland, nor did John gather his forces for a challenge against royal authority. Indeed, in Inverness in August 1464 John reached an accommodation with the Scottish administration, which probably covered several issues, including the activities of Donald Balloch in the Firth of Clyde and his support for his nephew, Allan MacDougall, in his bid to be head of the Clan Dougall, against the interests of the Earl of Argyll. Donald Balloch must have lost his grip on Arran by 1467 when Lord Boyd, then in control of the young King James III, had his son Thomas made Earl of Arran.[63]

Donald Balloch's main interest after 1461 may have been in his Irish lands, but the source of much of his power – manpower and ships – remained in Scotland. As a proven war leader he must have been able to attract a following from areas beyond his personal lordship, but several of the ships he led in the great raids of 1431, 1433 and 1452 would have been from Islay. A charter of the Tenandry of Lossit in 1617 indicates that this quarter land was to provide a boat with fourteen oars (or else £10) instead of the more normal mix of produce and money. This may be a unique survival of a type of service that was placed on several lands in Islay and elsewhere in the Lordship. From a 1615 report to the Privy Council on West Highland shipping it can be deduced that the Lossit boat was a birlinn, each of its fourteen oars pulled by three men. Many West Highland ships of the period would have been bigger vessels known as galleys, with eighteen to twenty-four oars each. The Auchinleck Chronicle gives Donald Balloch's forces in the raid of 1452 as 100 galleys containing a total of 5,000 to 6,000 men; that is somewhere in the region of fifty to sixty men and sixteen to twenty oars per boat. The overall size of this force may indeed be reported realistically at 5,000 or 6,000 men.[64]

Donald's main Scottish stronghold, Dunyvaig Castle on Islay, overlooks a sheltered bay, albeit difficult of access to those without local knowledge of the rocks that partially block its entrance. There is a boat landing, a cleared area among the rocks below the castle walls, and a sea-gate opposite it that a birlinn could be taken through.

It was probably no coincidence that James III became aware of the MacDonalds' agreement of 1461 with Edward IV in the aftermath of the Scottish–English Treaty of 1474. John II was summoned to answer charges of treason before Parliament in December 1475 but did not appear. Sentence of forfeiture was passed against him.[65] A determined king raised armies to hound him in the following year, empowering the MacDonalds' main rivals, including the earls of Argyll and Huntly, to join the chase. Donald Balloch, now in his sixties and perhaps within weeks of his own death, was not there to support his chief, and the latter submitted to royal authority.[66] That July he was stripped of his Earldom of Ross, Knapdale and Kintyre, the sheriffship of Inverness and the castles of Inverness and Nairn. He was allowed to keep Islay and all the other island territories he held before forfeiture, Morvern, Garmoran, the Lordship of Lochaber, lands of Duror and Glencoe, the lands of Greenan in Ayrshire and the lands of Kingedward in Aberdeenshire. To add insult to injury, he was created a lord of parliament as Lord of the Isles, a status that equated in no way to that he and his forebears had enjoyed as Lord of the Isles. Although the title was the same, his peers would have been in no doubt of the change.[67]

This humiliation of their clan chief evidently precipitated schisms among the MacDonald chiefs and other leaders of West Highland society. John continued to command the support of clan chiefs like MacLean of

Duart, MacLeod of Harris and MacNeill of Barra, perhaps because he rewarded them generously. Some of the MacDonald chiefs, however, looked to John's son, Angus Og, for leadership. Angus Og, born of a concubine rather than John's estranged wife, Elizabeth Livingston, had effectively been recognised as John's heir in the royal charter rescinding his forfeiture.[68] He was clearly made of sterner material than his father. Indeed one of the charges against his father in Parliament in 1475 was that he had usurped royal authority by appointing his bastard son as his lieutenant. Hugh MacDonald's history suggests that Alexander Og chased his father out of Islay. This may partially explain the liferent of lands in Kintyre given to John by King James III in 1481, perhaps in compensation, and as an attempt to bolster the authority of the pliant father against the unreasonable – from the king's viewpoint – son. Another reason was the effort John made in 1481 to capture the envoy sent by King Edward IV of England to encourage Donald Balloch's son and heir, John, to rebel against the King of Scots.[69]

A note in the Exchequer Rolls indicates that Arran had been devastated by the Islesmen about 1476, probably in a raid by Angus Og, also mentioned by Hugh MacDonald. Angus Og was not for giving up the Earldom of Ross without a fight. The king's uncle, John, Earl of Atholl, was rewarded in 1481 for his part in suppressing the rebellion of the Lord of the Isles, and Hugh MacDonald describes how Angus Og defeated an army led by Atholl at Logiebraid in Ross. It is not clear if Angus Og was campaigning in Ross in 1480–81 or whether Logiebraid took place in 1476 when King James III had mobilised considerable forces to bring down Angus's father. Atholl may have been taken prisoner by Angus and imprisoned for a spell on Islay. Whatever the case, as James III's authority disintegrated from 1482, leading to civil war and his murder in 1488, it is probable that Angus Og retained some control of the earldom.[70]

Continuing enmity between John II and Angus Og resulted in a naval engagement between father and son – 'the Battle of Bloody Bay' – fought near Tobermory, Mull, perhaps in 1484. John II and his supporters came off worse. Wider hostilities are suggested by a claim in 1542 that MacLean of Duart deeds to their lands in Islay had been destroyed at a time of deadly feud by Angus Og.[71]

A charter of November 1485 by Angus, described as Master of the Isles and Lord of Trotternish (in Skye) specifically states that it was granted with consent of his father and council. This is perhaps not so much an indication of rapprochement between father and son but the subservience of the former to the latter.[72]

Angus Og met his death in Inverness in 1490. This 'Islay's king of festive goblets' is said to have been murdered in his sleep by his Irish harper, Diarmid O'Cairbre. The Book of Clanranald says that Angus was entertaining the men of the North in Inverness. Possibly the murder, as inferred by Hugh MacDonald, was the result of hostility between Angus and the MacKenzies.[73] That Angus should have been with the men of the North in Inverness at this time suggests that he retained considerable authority in Ross and the Great Glen, presumably a large part of the reason he was killed. The Exchequer Rolls indicate that large areas of Ross were waste in 1485 and 1486, perhaps as a result of Angus Og's activities in expanding his power in the region.[74]

Angus had been married to a daughter of Colin Campbell, the Earl of Argyll, and had a baby son, Donald Dubh. There was no question of leadership of Clan Donald going at this time to this child or reverting to John II. In any case, it appears that Donald Dubh was taken at this time by his mother to live with her father's family.[75] Instead, Alexander MacDonald of Lochalsh, John II's nephew, emerged as the new Clan Donald strongman. He was described in Irish sources as John II's deputy.[76] Alexander mounted a devastating raid into Ross in the early 1490s at the head of a coalition of clans including the MacDonalds of Clanranald, Camerons, Macintoshes and the Roses of Kilravock, partially aimed at strengthening the MacDonald grip on the earldom and at taking revenge on the MacKenzies. Inverness and its castle were destroyed. This was no doubt the main reason for the final forfeiture of John II in 1493. Although he may not have sanctioned the raid, and probably had little influence on his clan, he was held personally responsible. He became a pensioner at the court of James IV, dying in Dundee in 1503.[77]

King James IV was determined that there would never again be a Lordship of the Isles to challenge him or his successors, or cause disturbances in the West. In the summer and autumn of 1493 he went to Argyll to receive the submission of many of the leaders of Isles' society. They were given crown charters of those lands they had held of the Lord of the Isles, and Alexander of Lochalsh, far from being punished for his raiding in Ross, was knighted. So was John Mor of Dunyvaig and the Glynns, son of Donald Balloch. The creation of these two Islesmen as knights was more than a sign of royal favour. It was an attempt to establish a personal relationship with them, to instil in them some of the values and status of this dignity as long understood in courtly circles.[78] In 1494 King James returned to the West and proceeded to build a new castle at Tarbert, guarding the narrow isthmus between Kintyre and Knapdale, where boats could be taken across from West Loch Tarbert to the Firth of Clyde. He also put a garrison in Dunaverty Castle at the south end of Kintyre.

Clearly this royal interest in Kintyre, long dominated by the MacDonalds of Dunyvaig, was most unwelcome to the then chief, John Mor, who had lost title to them, but presumably not possession, by the first forfeiture of John II in 1475. He is said in a late and unreliable source to have stormed the castle in 1494 and hanged its royal governor from the walls within sight of the king as he passed in his fleet. Certainly, he was summoned that September to answer a charge of alleged treason in Kintyre.[79]

Whatever the truth of this colourful tale, it seems from later events that John Mor broke with King James – or rather the king with John Mor – soon after he was knighted in 1494. The *Annals of Ulster* identified him as 'King of Innse Gall' (Lord of the Isles) and it may have been his assumption of this title, or election to it by the leaders of Clan Donald, that brought royal opprobrium. As noted above, only a role of deputy to John II had been claimed by Alexander of Lochalsh. The leaders of Clan Donald may now have agreed to depose John II. About the same time, Alexander of Lochalsh was murdered on Oronsay, possibly by John Mor's son, John Cathanach and John MacIan of Ardnamurchan.[80]

The MacIans of Ardnamurchan, with their main stronghold at Mingary on the Sound of Mull, were a senior branch of Clan Donald descended from Angus Mor, Lord of Islay in the thirteenth century. They also had a foothold on Islay, lands granted them by Alexander Lord of the Isles, and were baillies of Islay, at least from the time of John II, probably with their main residence on Islay on the crannog of Eilean Mhurreill in Loch Finlaggan, within site of the lordly residence on Eilean Mor. That John MacIan should have been allied with the MacDonalds of Dunyvaig is not surprising. What is, is that a few years later he turned against his own kinsmen, perhaps after pressure from James IV when the latter visited Mingary on another expedition to the Isles in 1495.[81]

In 1499 the king granted a charter to MacIan at Tarbert Castle as a reward for capturing Sir John, his son John Cathanach and their accomplices, and also for handing over the lands of mid Kintyre with the office of steward. The *Annals of Ulster* record that in 1499 John Mor, King of the Isles, his son John Cathanach and two others were hanged by James IV. From the Book of Clanranald and Hugh MacDonald's *History* we learn that John Cathanach and two or three sons were treacherously taken prisoner on the island of Finlaggan and taken to Edinburgh where they were executed. Perhaps Sir John was captured in different circumstances than John Cathanach. There may be a clue in the MacIan charter of 1499 in the requirement for MacIan to give up the lands of Mid Kintyre. He could have acquired these, along with Sir John, as a result of a military campaign through the MacDonald of Dunyvaig territories in that peninsula.[82]

The capture of the MacDonalds at Finlaggan by treachery is intriguing. Archaeological excavations have demonstrated that at that time neither Eilean Mor nor Eilean na Comhairle was fortified. They were not properties that had belonged to the Dunyvaig family, they and the neighbouring land of Portaneilean to which they were attached almost certainly being demesne land retained by the Lords of the Isles for themselves. Perhaps, however, the MacDonald chiefs, including MacIan, were there for a council meeting when MacIan struck. The archaeological evidence also suggests that at some time about the end of the fifteenth century there were dramatic changes on Eilean Mor, with the great hall and other buildings being dismantled and replaced by the more humble houses and barns of a farming township. It is possible that MacIan had instructions from his royal master to destroy Finlaggan, to prevent it ever again being the administrative and ceremonial centre of a Gaelic Lordship of the Isles.

The thoroughness of King James's efforts to eliminate any future threats from the Isles is suggested by the creation of a line of defences on the Kintyre peninsula protecting the Lowlands. Apart from Dunaverty and Tarbert there was Kilkerran Castle erected by James at the site of the future burgh of Campbeltown about 1498; Airds Castle at Carradale, granted in 1498 to an Ayrshire laird, Sir Adam Reid; Saddell Castle, erected about 1508–12 by David Hamilton, Bishop of Argyll, a loyal supporter of the king; and Skipness Castle, a MacDonald stronghold granted in 1493 to Sir Duncan Forrester, an officer of the royal household. Castle Sween in Knapdale was already in the hands of the Earl of Argyll, as was the royal castle at Dunoon in Cowal. Argyll also had another stronghold at Carrick on Loch Goil.[83]

MacIan, as James IV's trusted agent in the West, built up a considerable landholding in Islay, largely at the expense of the MacDonalds of Dunyvaig (Fig. 4.2). A royal confirmation of 1505 shows he had been granted Dunyvaig Castle itself. Information extracted from the grants to MacIan and the Islay rental of 1507 indicates that he held land there with an extent of £130 at a time when the total for the lands on the island listed in the rentals was computed at £212 5s 4d[84] These £130 lands un- doubtedly included the 60 merk (£40) lands that had been granted to the founder of the house of Dunyvaig in the fourteenth century.

In June 1506 MacIan submitted an account of the rents of the island to the king's commissioners at Dunadd in mainland Argyll. A large part of the meeting appears to have been taken up with defusing possible conflict over land between MacIan and Lachlan MacLean of Duart, another major Islay landholder.[85]

Lachlan MacLean's father, Hector, had been one of the followers of John II at the Battle of Bloody Bay and may have been rewarded with lands on Islay for his support. In 1542 Lachlan's son Hector persuaded King James V to grant him lands on Islay, with an extent of over £20, on the basis that they had belonged to his grandfather but that the documents to prove this had been destroyed in the time of deadly feud with Angus Og. These lands were in three groups, in geographical terms. Firstly, there were lands in the Rhinns, including Coull, Sunderland and Foreland. By 1540 there was a castle in Loch Gorm that belonged with the land of Sunderland, and this island may have been the main MacLean residence on Islay in the time of the Lordship of the Isles. Secondly, there were lands on the east side of Loch Gruinart and along the north coast of the island, including Corsapol, Killinallan and Bolsa. And thirdly, there were lands in the glen up the middle of the island, including Daill, Robolls, Kepolls and

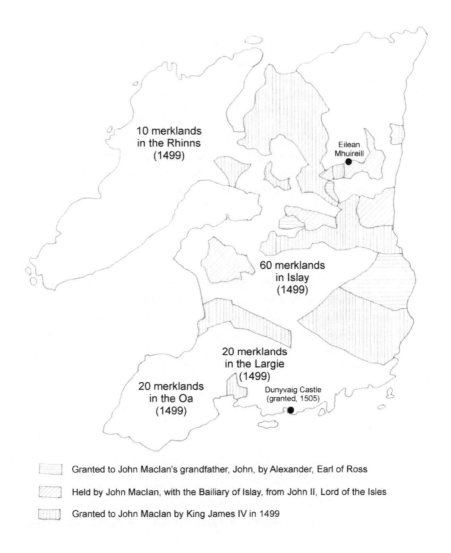

10 merklands
in the Rhinns
(1499)

Eilean
Mhuireill

60 merklands
in Islay
(1499)

20 merklands
in the Largie
(1499)

20 merklands
in the Oa
(1499)

Dunyvaig Castle
(granted, 1505)

Granted to John MacIan's grandfather, John, by Alexander, Earl of Ross

Held by John MacIan, with the Bailiary of Islay, from John II, Lord of the Isles

Granted to John MacIan by King James IV in 1499

Figure 4.2 John MacIan's Islay lands, using MacDougall's map as a template.

Scanistle. The last three were included among the lands granted by James IV to John MacIan, and were no doubt the cause of the MacIain/MacLean squabbling in 1506. While the MacLeans certainly had a considerable presence on Islay in the later sixteenth century it is not clear how successful they were in preserving what they regarded as their rights before then in the face of MacIan opposition. Lachlan was in trouble with the government in 1516 and 1517 for uplifting the king's rents in Islay and elsewhere, a clear indication that he was then trying to establish or maintain his rights to lands on the island by force.[86]

Lachlan was given a charter by James IV in 1496 of lands in Mull, Tiree, Jura, Knapdale, Lochaber and elsewhere, which he had held hereditarily, all then to be incorporated in a free barony to be known as the Barony of Duart. Included in these lands was Torlissay on Islay, which then gets listed in all succeeding grants of the Barony of Duart down to the seventeenth century. Torlissay has never been satisfactorily identified and it can not be credited that the MacLeans had possession of it throughout the sixteenth century. One possibility is that it was a regional name for some or all of the lands held by the MacLeans on Islay in the fifteenth century, but if so, they must have forgotten this by the late sixteenth century.[87]

The MacNeills of Gigha, who were constables of Castle Sween in Knapdale on behalf of the Lords of the Isles, also held lands in Islay in the time of the Lordship. These were the five-merk land estate in Kildalton parish of Knockrinsey and other neighbouring lands. They had belonged to Malcolm MacNeill who died c.1494, but it appears that his heir, Torquil, did not gain entry to his father's lands until several years later.[88] The Knockrinsey estate must be included in a holding of twenty-merk lands, along with MacDonald lands about Dunyvaig, listed in the 1507 rental as the land of Largie.

The 1506 Islay rental lists the relatively modest holdings of eight local gentlemen and officials (of which more in Chapter 7), including a Hugh MacKay, identifiable as the Coroner of the Rhinns, and 'Gilcristo McVaig, surrigico', the then head of the Macbeths of Ballinaby. 'Angusio filio Angusii' (Angus the son of Angus), with a holding of ten-merk lands, cannot be identified. It is just possible that he was a descendant of the Brian Vicar MacKay granted lands in perpetuity in 1408, still holding on to some of them. That estate appears in the 1507 rental as the twenty-merk lands of the Oa and the ten-merk lands of Kintra.

The 1507 rental also lists £42 5s of church lands, many being recognisable as the possessions of Iona Abbey listed in the papal letter of 1203 discussed above. The island dwelling in Loch Lossit, now known as Eilean Mhic Iain (MacIan's Island), may have been the administrative headquarters of these lands in Islay. The 33s 4d land of Kilmeny is known from other sources to have belonged to the Bishop of the Isles. It is described in 1580 as a grange, and the medieval chapel, of which there are fragmentary remains, would have served the bishop's tenants. The bishop also had land at Innerloskin, a now-lost name, but perhaps the chapel site at Laggan was part of it.[89] Two chapels are specifically mentioned with the lands provided for the support of their chaplains: the chapel of St Columba (Keills) with the 33s 4d lands of Knocklearoch and Baloshin; and the chapel of Finlaggan with the 33s 4d land of Ballachlaven. These generous provisions probably result from the chaplains of both places being in the service of the Lords of the Isles. The chapel at Keills, on architectural grounds, is of about the same date as that at Finlaggan. The island of Texa, dedicated to Our Lady, had lands on that island as well as on Islay to the value of 41s 8d. There are the ruins of a chapel on Texa that must have served the lords of nearby Dunyvaig Castle. It appears to be of similar date to the chapels of Finlaggan and Orsay. Lands belonging to the priory of Oronsay are identified including Sandak (Sanaig?) and 'Superior' (Over) Sandak, and Gruinart, with a total extent of 48s 4d.

The 'cella' of St Columba of 'Arrobollis' (Nerabus, in the Rhinns) is included with a value of £4 3s 4d. The use of the word 'cella' indicates that this was the daughter-house of a monastic establishment, known from other sources to have been the Augustinian Abbey of Derry in Northern Ireland. Nerabus was due to pay yearly sixty ells of cloth – white, black and grey – or 8d for each ell. This provides a clue that the Augustinians ran Nerabus as a sheep farm. There are the foundations at Nerabus graveyard of what may have been a substantial medieval chapel or grange with another building alongside.[90]

By the end of the fifteenth century Islay was clearly well provided with churches. Apart from the three parish churches of Kildalton, Kilarrow and Kilchoman there were chapels on Orsay, Nave Island and Texa, and others at Finlaggan, Keills, Nerabus and Laggan. The substantial churches at Kilnaughton, Kilchiaran and probably Kilmeny, might have served as alternative parish churches for the parishes of Kildalton, Kilchoman and Kilarrow respectively. The relatively large church on the Abbey of Iona's estates at Kilnave would have been used by more than the abbey's tenants.[91]

None of the parish churches of Islay were appropriated to religious houses, but Kilarrow and Kilchoman remained in the patronage of the Lords of the Isles while Kildalton was in the patronage of the bishops of the Isles. The clergy were mostly local men, sometimes son succeeding father. As elsewhere, the clergy often held more than one benefice, an apt excuse here being their low value. Kilchoman had a vicar for the cure of its souls, meaning that the bulk of the teinds could be appropriated to support a parson, presumably an absentee. In 1428 Angus Bishop of the Isles successfully petitioned the Pope to hold it in commend (that is along with his bishopric) because of his poverty. Angus was a son of Donald, Lord of the Isles.[92]

Apart from the MacDonalds of Dunyvaig, the MacIans of Ardnamurchan, the MacLeans of Duart, the Church and the other landowners mentioned above, the rest of Islay in the years before John II's forfeiture in 1493 may have been held by John himself, or usurped by his son Angus Og. Some land would have been held in demesne, directly for the Lord's support when residing at Kilchoman or Finlaggan. Beyond Islay there were other extensive lands in the Lordship retained by the Lords, and castles, including Ardtornish in Morvern and Aros in Mull. Prior to 1475 there was Skipness Castle in Kintyre, Dingwall Castle, which was the caput of the Earldom of Ross, and, at times, the castle of Inverness, and Urquhart Castle on the shores of Loch Ness. This was a rich heritage, which the Islemen clearly believed should, and would, be enjoyed by a new Lord of the Isles.

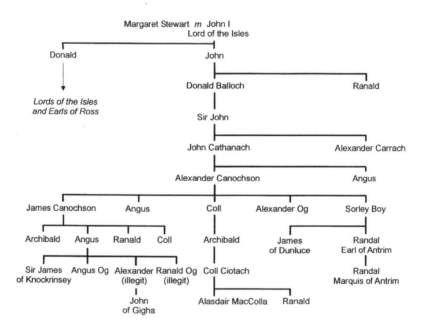

Clann Iain Mhoir

Lords of Islay

The history of Islay in the sixteenth century is largely to do with the efforts of Clann Iain Mhoir to retain its heritage and restore the status of Clan Donald. John MacIan had not totally eliminated the MacDonalds of Dunyvaig in the 1490s. Two sons of John Cathanach, Alexander and Angus, had escaped to Ireland and MacIan, despite expending much effort and money, failed to root them out there. Alexander was not immediately in a position to return to Scotland to exercise any authority in the Isles or take revenge for the death of his kin.[1]

Meanwhile in Scotland the eclipse of the Lords of the Isles left Archibald Earl of Argyll as the major power in the West Highlands and Islands, solidly a supporter of the king and much favoured by him. In 1500 he was appointed to head a royal commission to set the lands in the Lordship, excepting Kintyre and Islay, and he was also made royal lieutenant for the same area. The king required Argyll to pacify the region and produce rents for the royal coffers, but he clearly did not live up to royal expectations. There is no evidence that he made any serious attempt to corner any of the considerable assets of the Lordship for himself or any of his kin.[2]

Argyll's failure may largely be explained by a natural reluctance to turn against men who were allies, friends and even relatives. Included in this latter category was his teenage nephew Donald Dubh, the heir of Angus Og. In 1501 Donald Dubh exchanged residency with the Campbells for a home with another uncle, Argyll's brother-in-law, Torquil MacLeod of Lewis.[3] Donald Dubh became a figurehead for Gaelic resistance in the West to attempts by royal agents, especially the Earl of Huntly, to impose order. By 1503 there was widespread insurrection in the West Highlands with raids by Islesmen from Bute to Badenoch. Apart from Torquil MacLeod, the main rebel was another of Argyll's brothers-in-law, Lachlan MacLean of Duart. Both were accused of promoting Donald Dubh as Lord of the Isles. Another royal naval expedition was sent to the West in 1504, resulting in the surrender of MacLean's castle of Cairn na Burgh in the Treshnish Islands, and in 1506 Huntly captured MacLeod's castle of Stornoway in Lewis. Donald Dubh was captured and put in royal custody. The rebellion was effectively over.[4]

In the next few years MacIan consolidated his position in Islay at the expense of Clann Iain Mhoir. There was further rebellion in the West Highlands in the aftermath of King James IV's death at Flodden in 1513, with various clan chiefs acting in their own interests. They had not, however, given up on re-establishing the Lordship of the Isles. To that end, a meeting took place at the Point of Ardnamurchan about 1518. The place surely suggests that MacIan was instrumental in calling the meeting, presumably in an attempt to bolster his own position and, somehow, neutralise the forces that had good reason to seek revenge on him. In the absence of Donald Dubh in royal custody, the main contenders to be recognised as Lord of the Isles – the MacDonald – were Alexander 'Canochson'[5] and Donald Gallda, the son and heir of Alexander of Lochalsh who had been brought up at the court of King James IV. The Book of Clanranald claims that Donald Gallda was nominated 'MacDonald of this side of the Point of Ardnamurchan' (i.e. to its north). This suggests that there was no agreement, and that Alexander would at least have claimed to be overall lord of the islands and lands to the south of the Point of Ardnamurchan, including Ardnamurchan itself. Irish sources are certainly clear that he was the MacDonald, Lord of the Isles and chief of his name, and English sources also refer to him as 'Lord of the Out Isles'. The most significant outcome of this meeting, however, was the murder of MacIan and his sons at the hands of Alexander and Donald Gallda. Hugh MacDonald believed that Alexander slipped away secretly in the night time after this, fearing that Donald Gallda would next turn on him, not least for his part in the murder of his father.[6]

Donald Gallda, who was identified by the regency government as the main troublemaker, died shortly after in 1519, leaving no male heirs.[7] This should have meant that Alexander's position as overall chief of Clan Donald would have been recognised by all the Isles' chiefs, but Alexander's power base, still largely confined to his lands in the north of Ireland, was not extensive enough for him to pursue this with any vigour, and perhaps he was discouraged by a patron, who now emerged to help him re-establish his position in his family's ancestral Scottish estates. The patron in question was Colin, 3rd Earl of Argyll. As early as 1516, Alexander was described in an official document as one of Argyll's familiars and servants. The earl was made Lieutenant of the Isles and adjacent mainland in 1517 for the express purpose of bringing order to this region. Among his instructions was one enjoining him to win over Clann Iain Mhoir by offering them land in the Isles so that they could live there without plundering the king's lieges, they now being without heritage owing to the forfeiture of Sir John Cathanach. Argyll had petitioned for this commission and it appears that all or most of its terms conformed to his request. The accounts that Argyll submitted as chamberlain of Kintyre indicate that he had been authorised in 1522 to give Alexander lands there, with an extent of over £90, that had been held by his grandfather, Sir John Mor.[8]

Argyll was granted ward, nonentries and relief of the murdered MacIan's possessions along with the marriage of his son and heir, Alexander – thus allowing Argyll to supervise and enjoy the MacIan inheritance until Alexander MacIan came of age. A bond of gossipry (friendship) in 1520 between John Campbell of Cawdor and Alexander of Dunyvaig indicates that actual control of some of the MacIans' Islay lands was quickly passed to Alexander Canochson, for he was given a five-year tack of lands, including Colonsay and forty-five merk lands in Islay, in return for the support of Clan Donald South by land and sea. Cawdor, as in many other affairs at this time, was acting on behalf of his brother the Earl of Argyll. Cawdor was four years later given a royal remission for burning Colonsay, an event thought to relate to fighting in the aftermath of Cawdor's murder of Lachlan MacLean of Duart. Alexander Canochson may have supported the MacLeans' efforts to get revenge, but if so, there may have been no great falling out with the Earl of Argyll at this stage.[9]

There is also the matter of Alexander's marriage to Catherine, daughter of John MacIan, to consider. Hugh MacDonald claimed that it was the outcome of a deal with John MacIan when he surrendered Islay to Alexander after the latter had invaded it, captured Dunyvaig Castle, and forced the surrender of MacIan in the castle of Loch Gorm.[10] A more likely explanation is that Colin Earl of Argyll engineered the marriage after MacIan's death.

It should not be forgotten that Clann Iain Mhoir, with its possession of the Glynns of Antrim, remained a significant landholder in Ireland. Alexander was seen by native Irish dynasts as a potential source of men for fighting their own wars because he could call on men from his ancestral lands in Scotland and act as a contractor for supplying men from a wider area of the Highlands and Islands of Scotland. In 1522 many of the MacDonalds in Ireland, led by Alexander Carrach, a younger brother of John Cathanach, joined a coalition put together by Conn Bacach O'Neill to oppose Sir Hugh O'Donnell, Lord of Tyrconnell. Alexander Carrach appears to have been the leader of the MacDonalds in Ireland at that time, presumably with his base in the Glynns. The campaigning of that year ended with the disastrous defeat of O'Neill's forces in a night attack on his camp at Knockavoe near Strabane.[11]

The MacDonalds, however, had traditionally been friends and allies of the O'Donnells rather than the O'Neills. In 1523 Sir Hugh's son, Manus, is said to have visited Scotland and it was probably as an outcome of this, and his marriage to a niece of Alexander Canochson, that we find that in 1524 Alexander provided his support to the O'Donnells, leading not just the gentlemen of Clan Donald in Scotland, but also MacDonald Galloglass based in Ireland, and other chieftains from Scotland. The O'Donnell army met up with the forces of O'Neill and the Lord Justice, the Earl of Kildare, at Drumleen in Donegal, but instead of the two sides fighting, Kildare managed to arrange a conference at which O'Neill and O'Donnell made peace.[12] The reputation and standing of Alexander and his clan depended more at this time on their activities in Ireland than in Scotland. It may also have been as a result of this campaign in 1524 that Alexander established his ascendancy over the MacDonalds in Ireland.

King James V began his personal rule in 1528 and, as was customary, grants made in his minority were annulled. This, of course, removed the legal basis for land occupancy in Islay and Kintyre by Clann Iain Mhoir. Alexander MacIan was given sasine (possession) of his Islay lands in February 1529. The MacDonald response to these developments was the traditional one of rising in rebellion. Alexander Canochson was summoned to court in April 1530 to answer charges of insurrection, plundering and slaughter while Archibald, the new Earl of Argyll, was commissioned to raise an army to deal with any further trouble. The MacDonalds failed to make an appearance and now targeted the royal lands of Rosneath, the chamberlain of which was the Earl of Argyll, and when the other clan chiefs of the Isles volunteered to come to court a few weeks later, it was on condition that some leading gentlemen of Clan Campbell were warded as a guarantee of the earl's good behaviour towards them.[13]

King James planned an expedition to the Isles in 1531 to be led by himself, but the threat of this caused Alexander Canochson to come and submit. Remarkably, not only was he not punished, but he was pardoned and had the lands in Kintyre restored to him during the king's will. Among the conditions imposed upon him were that he should establish good rule in the region, see that rents were paid, and he should release all the prisoners he had pertaining to the Earl of Argyll. There is no specific mention of the forty-five Islay merk lands, but it is improbable that he did not continue to hold them despite Alexander MacIan's sasine. Meanwhile, the Earl of Argyll was, at least for a period of a year, stripped of his hereditary office of Chamberlain of Kintyre, this going instead to the Comptroller, James Colville.[14]

Part of the explanation for Alexander of Dunyvaig's behaviour at this time must be disenchantment with the new Earl of Argyll. While the former must have made a good impression on the king, the latter was humiliated by his royal master, and the poor quality of administration exercised by him and his father over the royal estates in Kintyre was exposed. Later that year, while he was still detained in Edinburgh to answer charges brought against him by Argyll, Alexander submitted articles to the Lords of Council which denied he had done wrong and blamed Argyll. He also claimed that he could, and would, raise more men to support the king in his wars than Argyll.[15]

It may be this claim, very probably true, that more than anything else endeared Alexander to his king. It probably suited James that Alexander was allied with Sir Hugh O'Donnell, one of the most powerful native Irish lords and a thorn in the flesh to the English administration in Ireland. In

1528 Alexander again joined O'Donnell, this time in an invasion of Moylurg, the territory of the McDermots in Roscommon, and yet again in 1532, when it was reported in Edinburgh that Alexander had taken a force of 4,000 Scots to Ireland. The following year, along with MacLean of Duart, he plundered the Isle of Man. The most notable outcome of this raid was the capture of an English ship, the *Mary Willoughby*, which was handed over to King James. It was MacLean, however, that got the credit for this.[16]

Alexander of Dunyvaig died in 1536 with charges of piracy, against ships belonging to a Glasgow merchant, outstanding against him. According to a later Campbell writer he had been imprisoned in Dunoon Castle by the Earl of Argyll but escaped. Why he should then, as the same source maintains, have made his way to Dublin is not explained, but it was there, we are told, that he died, and was buried in St Patrick's Cathedral.[17] His son and heir, James Canochson, had been at court since 1531, no doubt with the intention that he should be educated in good Lowland ways. He was allowed to return to the Isles after his father's death to claim his heritage. The situation in Islay presented opportunities with the death of Alexander MacIan sometime between 1534 and 1538, leaving no adult male heir. There were also difficulties.[18]

From 1538 Hector MacLean of Duart was chamberlain of the royal lands of Islay, and the MacLeans still nursed claims to Islay lands that were part of the heritage of Clann Iain Mhoir. Hector's father, Lachlan, as noted in the previous chapter, had been in trouble with the government in 1516 and 1517 for uplifting the king's rents in Islay and elsewhere, presumably of those lands he claimed. Whether the MacLeans managed to retain any presence in Islay in the years after that is not known. Writing in 1549, Donald Monro, the Dean of the Isles, tells us that the castle of Loch Gorm of old belonged to Clan Donald but had been usurped by MacLean. It is possible that this usurpation took place between the death of Alexander Canochson and the return of his son James from Edinburgh.[19]

In 1540 Hector's son and heir, Hector, received from the king a new grant of lands including Torlissay in Islay,[20] and two years later Duart himself, probably while James Canochson was in royal custody (see below), was granted lands in Mull and Islay. The king had been informed that they had belonged to Hector's grandfather, but the deeds for them had been destroyed in the time of deadly feud between the latter and Angus Og so that Hector's father, Lachlan, had been unable to obtain heritable entry to them.[21] The Islay lands in question included the contiguous properties of Coull, Sunderland and Foreland in the Rhinns. Loch Gorm Castle was on the land of Sunderland though there is no mention of it in the charter, possibly because it continued to have a royal garrison in it. The grant also included the lands of Daill, Robolls, Kepolls and Scanistle in the parish of Kilarrow (and Kilmeny). The substantial

island dwelling in Loch Ballygrant was part of the estate of Scanistle, and is
the island dwelling mentioned by Monro (Plate XIX).

Hector MacLean must also have used his position as chamberlain to
secure a gift for his brother Alan (Ailean nan Sop) of the nonentries of the
lands of the MacNeills of Gigha, including the estate of Knockrinsey on
Islay. The grant was revoked the following year, the Lords of Council
having discovered that Niall, the chief of the MacNeills, with sixty of his
clan, had been killed in royal service fighting against the rebels of the Isles,
and the principle perpetrator of these slaughters was none other than Alan
MacLean. This must have happened about 1530. The lands were therefore
regranted in 1542 to Niall, the natural son of the MacNeill chief killed by
Alan MacLean.[22]

The relationships between MacDonalds, MacLeans and Campbells at
this time are difficult to interpret on the basis of contemporary documentary sources. The MacDonalds must surely, however, have been
uneasy about the way the MacLeans were, with royal backing, improving
their position on Islay while they, and to a lesser extent the Campbells,
were not highly regarded at court.

It is possible to see the role of Archibald, Earl of Argyll, in a good light as far
as Clann Iain Mhoir is concerned. Documents of 1538 and 1540 chronicle a
process by which the MacIans' heritage was granted to a sister, Mariota, of
Alexander MacIan, only to be resigned in favour of the Earl of Argyll. The
earl may have been trying to engineer a permanent settlement of the MacIan
lands on James Canochson. The falling out between the earl and James's
father was mended at some stage and James married the earl's base sister,
Agnes Campbell.[23] Argyll's attempts, however, were to come unstuck with
the purchase by King James V of the MacIan inheritance in 1541.[24]

King James not only wanted to bring order to all parts of his kingdom,
he was also determined to maximise his revenues. In the summer of 1540
he sailed in a well-armed fleet round Scotland visiting the principle
Western Isles. The main chiefs came to meet him, and several hostages
were taken to guarantee good behaviour. The highest-ranking prisoner,
sent to custody in Dunbar Castle, was James Canochson. He was clearly
not in royal favour, and the king now required him out the way so that he
could take control of Islay. The castles of Dunyvaig and Loch Gorm were
placed in the keeping of Archibald Stewart and his brother, and commissioners were installed in Dunyvaig to make up a new rental of the island
and issue tacks. In 1542 Archibald Stewart was appointed Justice and
Governor of Islay with the authority of a sheriff. James and the other
Highlanders may have remained captive for a long time if King James V
had not died at the end of 1542. They were, however, released in the
summer of 1543 on giving bonds to the governor, the Earl of Arran, for
their good behaviour.[25]

Arran may also have been responsible for the release of another prisoner,
Donald Dubh, in 1543. Donald had been held captive since 1506, at least

from 1525 in the care of first, Colin, Earl of Argyll and then his successor as earl, Archibald, to both of whom he was distantly related. Expenses for four servants for Donald were allowed to be deducted from the accounts of Cowal and Rosneath, which may suggest that Donald was confined in Dunoon Castle. While it was reported in May 1543 that Argyll was labouring to put together an army to go against this 'Earl of the Isles', Governor Arran could still see fit to make a payment of £4 8s to Donald in January 1544. Perhaps Donald had been released because Arran wanted to keep Argyll in the West rather than at court. He may not have foreseen that Donald would immediately be courted by his rival, the Earl of Lennox, and signed up to support King Henry VIII's attempts to acquire the young Mary Queen of Scots for marriage to his son Edward.[26]

James Canochson would not have viewed the reappearance of Donald Dubh with great enthusiasm. While MacLean of Duart offered Donald wholehearted support in his bid to be recognised as Lord of the Isles and Earl of Ross, James stood back, recognising the threat to his claims to be the MacDonald. Donald Dubh followed Lennox in rebelling against the Scottish government of the Earl of Arran and became a subject of Henry VIII. That monarch had in the spring of 1544, as part of a larger invasion strategy, intended that a fleet under the command of Lennox, including 180 ships and 4,000 Scots provided by Donald Dubh, should enter the Firth of Clyde and take Dumbarton Castle.[27] Although this invasion came to little, thanks to English mismanagement, James must have felt that his lands on the Clyde were at risk. Perhaps only when this danger appeared to have past, James and his brother Coll took a force over to Ireland to support the MacQuillans against the O'Kanes, keeping conveniently away from Donald Dubh.[28]

Nevertheless, James did not – probably could not – keep himself totally aloof from Donald Dubh's proceedings. His answer was to have another brother, Angus, take part with Donald, and we find that Angus was one of those that attended the Council of the Isles in July 1545 that appointed commissioners to deal with Henry VIII. Angus, with the rest of Donald's supporters, then took an oath at Carrickfergus in Ireland in August of that year to be a subject of the English king. The council meeting actually took place on Islay at 'Ellencarne', the island in Loch Ballygrant that belonged to the MacLeans of Duart (Plate XIX). Curiously, it has a small artificial island connected to it by a causeway, mimicking the Council Island of the Lords of the Isles at Finlaggan.[29]

Lennox's efforts in Scotland on behalf of his English master petered out. Donald Dubh died of a fever at Drogheda late in 1545 and his Scottish supporters returned to their homes. James Canochson appears to have remained loyal in 1543 and 1544 to the Scottish government and to have maintained his friendship with Argyll. He may even have been encouraged by the government to burn Saltcoats on the coast of Ayrshire, possibly in 1545. Saltcoats belonged to the Earl of Glencairn, a supporter of Lennox and the English.[30]

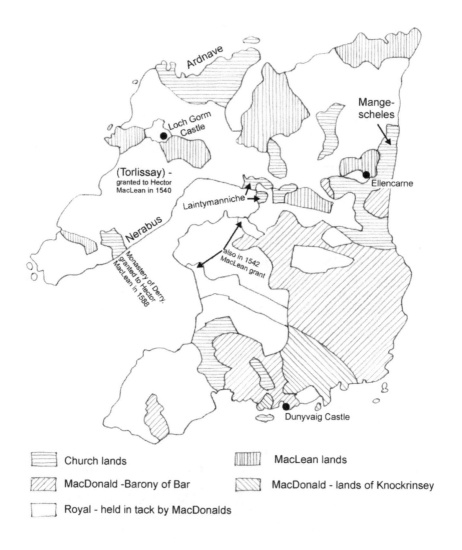

Ardnave

Mange-
scheles

Loch Gorm
Castle

Ellencarne

(Torlissay) -
granted to Hector
MacLean in 1540

Laintymanniche

Nerabus

Monastery of Derry,
granted to Hector
MacLean in 1588

also in 1542
MacLean grant

Dunyvaig Castle

Church lands

MacLean lands

MacDonald -Barony of Bar

MacDonald - lands of Knockrinsey

Royal - held in tack by MacDonalds

Fig. 5.1 Map of Islay in the late sixteenth century, showing the lands of the
MacDonalds, MacLeans and the Church; using MacDougall's map as a template.

As a reward for his loyalty in helping the governor to resist the old enemy of England, James was given a charter in April 1545 of lands in Kintyre, Colonsay, Islay, Uist, Sunart and Morvern, along with the Island of Rathlin, all erected into the free barony of Bar (in North Kintyre) to be held by him and his heirs hereditarily (Fig 5.1).[31] The lands in Kintyre, Colonsay and Islay were those forfeited by his great grandfather to which the family had had no secure title since the 1540s. In the charter James is, significantly, given the territorial title 'of Dunyvaig and the Glynns', a recognition of his new status in government eyes as a baron rather than the clan chief descended from John Cathanach. The grant included the five merk lands of Dunyvaig, the royal garrison of which may well have packed its bags when James was released from prison in 1543.

More was to follow. At Rothesay Castle the following summer, in the presence of the earls of Arran and Argyll, Hector MacLean was forced to renounce his lands in the Rhinns of Islay, including some given in tack to him since the death of James V, in favour of James of Dunyvaig. This can hardly have played well with the MacLeans, who evidently were not prepared in practice to be budged from the Rhinns and Loch Gorm Castle. We are not aware, however, of open hostilities between the two clans until January 1561 when Archibald 5th Earl of Argyll attempted, without success, to bring the two to agree in a two-week convention in Glasgow. Three years later the dispute over possession of the Rhinns was set to be resolved by the Privy Council, which it was, in James's favour, primarily because he appeared on the appointed day but his rival did not.[32]

In the following years James was to receive several more marks of royal favour. He was made Baillie of South Kintyre and granted other Kintyre lands, including those at Carradale given by James IV to the Reids from Ayrshire. The Earl of Argyll sold him the eighty merk lands of Ardnamurchan with the castle of Mingarry (former MacIan possessions), and from the Earl of Arran he acquired forty-eight merk lands in Kintyre (former church lands), including the hereditary captaincy of Saddell Castle. In 1562 Queen Mary gave him a tack of further lands in Kintyre with an extent of almost 100 merks, and over 160 merks' worth of land in Islay. He also bought the estates of the MacNeills of Gigha and further lands in Uist.[33] Thus by the early 1560s James was a trusted baron of the realm in possession of many of the MacDonald ancestral lands, especially in Islay, Colonsay and Kintyre. His ability to buy so many estates indicates considerable wealth.

To what extent, however, was there an awareness at court of his double dealing with the English after the death of Donald Dubh? In January 1546 he wrote from Ardnamurchan to the English administration in Ireland describing himself as apparent heir of the Isles. He was ready with his following, Alan MacLean of Gigha (Duart's younger brother), Clanranald, Clan Cameron, Clan Ian and 'our own surname, both north and south', to take part with Lennox to further the English cause. He required the same rewards as Donald Dubh and would be ready about St Patrick's Day, should Henry send forces to meet him at the island of Sanday off the south end of Kintyre. A few days later the English received a letter from Cameron of Lochiel saying that James was worthy to succeed as Lord of the Isles, being a forward young man with a large clan and many friends, and nearest heir to the house of the Isles. Then in February it was reported that James now claimed the title of Lord of the Isles by consent of the nobility of the Isles.[34]

James's overture was not taken up by the English, nor does he appear to have provoked the Scottish government by openly using the title of Lord of the Isles. James V had permanently annexed it to the Crown by Act of Parliament in 1540, and it has remained a royal title ever since, one of those that goes with the Dukedom of Rothesay, held by the heir to the throne.[35]

It is possible that a reconciliation between James and Argyll, staged before the Privy Council at Ardrossan in June 1546, marked his return to the fold. His relationship with his brother-in-law seems to have remained good from then on until the latter's death in 1558. James joined with Argyll to help Governor Arran deal with the English invasion in the summer of 1547, and together they formed the left wing of the national army defeated at Pinkie on 10 September. The Queen Dowager, Mary of Guise, is said to have attempted in 1559 to provoke James into action against the new Earl of Argyll. Instead James brought 700 men to Leith to support the Protestant lords, of whom Argyll was one, against the queen.[36] This surely indicates that James had accepted the teachings of the Protestant Reformers.[37]

If the English administration in Ireland was doubtful about James and his standing in 1546, they were soon to learn that he was a force to reckon with. In 1551, along with his brother Coll, he repulsed an English invasion of Rathlin. The English commander, Bagenal, was captured and exchanged for James's brother Sorley Boy, then held prisoner in Dublin.[38]

Six years later, the English Lord Deputy in Ireland was reporting to his king and queen that James had held much of the north of Ireland since overrunning it with his force of 7,000 Scots in 1553, and this despite campaigning by the English in 1555. That year, the Earl of Argyll and James appear to have combined their efforts in support of Calvagh O'Donnell, newly married to the earl's daughter. It may have been Argyll's brass ordnance that helped in the capture of several castles which were then retained by the Scots, while an area sixty miles across was ravished. Three years later James was back with two pieces of ordnance and seemed likely to threaten the main English stronghold in the north, Carrickfergus Castle. On his withdrawal to Scotland the English sent a fleet over from Ireland to ravage his lands there. They picked on the south of Kintyre, and also despoiled Arran and the Cumbraes, but failed to hit Islay, their main target. It was in 1558 that Sorley Boy was put in charge of the Route, the lands to the east of the Glynns, with the castle of Dunluce, captured from the MacQuillans. According to Shane O'Neill in a letter to the English Lord Justice and Council in September 1564 the Scots (meaning James and his brothers) had by then also usurped territories in Clandeboye, Dufferin, Lecale and O'Cassidy's country.[39]

MacDonald expansion and ambitions in Ireland not only worried the English administration there but clearly threatened the O'Neills, from 1559 under the leadership of Shane O'Neill who was seeking to be the main power in Ulster and be recognised by the English as Earl of Tyrone. Shane was clearly intimidating Sorley Boy by the spring of 1563, and in the autumn of 1564 launched an attack against the Scots in Ulster. More fighting followed in May 1565 with Shane invading Clandeboye, the Route and the Glynns. He was opposed at Glenshesk near Ballycastle by a large MacDonald army under the command of James, newly arrived from Scotland with reinforcements. The MacDonalds were heavily defeated, losing about 700 men, among them James's brother Angus. James and Sorley Boy were both captured, and James died soon afterwards in captivity from his wounds.[40]

James's achievements had been remarkable. He had totally turned round the fortunes of his family in Scotland, and had greatly expanded his power base in Ireland. The latter appeared to be totally undone by his defeat and death, with the very real possibility that the lordship of the MacDonalds of Islay was now finished in Northern Ireland. The English had attempted in 1561 to bring James, the Earl of Argyll and the O'Donnells together to help them oppose Shane.[41] Now Shane had achieved another long-term policy for them by expelling the MacDonalds of Islay from Ireland. With the passing of James, the Earl of Argyll lamented the loss of a friend and supporter while the annals by the pro-O'Donnell 'Four Masters' eulogised him as 'a paragon of hospitality and prowess, a festive man of many troops, and a bountiful and munificent man'.[42]

James left as his successor his son Archibald, apparently still a minor. His uncle, Alexander Og, acted as his tutor and had not only to re-establish his nephew's position in Ireland but had to keep the family's grip on their Scottish lands. Hector MacLean of Duart had opportunistically ravished Gigha, part of the jointure lands of James MacDonald's widow, and Alexander Og only felt able to return to Ireland in May 1567, safe in the knowledge that his ally, the Earl of Argyll, had been appointed to proceed against MacLean.[43]

Alexander Og was cynically being encouraged by the English to take revenge against Shane O'Neill although it was their policy that no Scots should be allowed to be residents of Ireland. His opportunity came soon after his landing, when Shane O'Neill, hard pressed by the English and recently defeated by the O'Donnells, remarkably turned to Alexander Og for help. At a feast at Cushendun in the summer of 1567 the MacDonalds turned on their guest and cut him to pieces.[44]

Alexander Og would have wished to carve out a territorial base for himself in Ireland but it was his younger brother, Sorley Boy, that was to achieve this. Despite ongoing English hostility, and numerous setbacks, he succeeded in 1586, four years prior to his death, in having his conquest of the Route recognised by the English and was received as an Irish citizen.[45] This was a by-product of negotiations at national level that resulted in a league between Scotland and England in that year.

The young Archibald of Dunyvaig was dead by 1569 and was succeeded by his brother Angus who was active on his own behalf by 1579.[46] He was to preside over the total loss of his family's lands in Scotland and Ireland. Although Elizabeth I of England recognised his claim to the Glynns in an indenture of 1586,[47] his ability to invest enough time and effort in maintaining his affairs in Ireland was circumscribed by the threat to his position in Scotland by the MacLeans of Duart. After the death of his uncle Sorley Boy, his sons, firstly James and then Randal, undermined his position. The latter had not only usurped the Route from his brother James's children but also took the Glynns. He was confirmed in possession of both in 1603. More politically adept than other members of his clan he crowned a successful career with being made Earl of Antrim in 1620.[48]

Randal had learnt how to be a courtier and ingratiate himself with King James VI and I. The main business for his Scottish relatives throughout the sixteenth century was the provision of mercenary forces to fight in Ireland, essentially for whoever made them the best offer. Irish chiefs were dependent on such forces for their wars and the MacDonalds of Dunyvaig and the Glynns were the main suppliers. Turlough Luineach O'Neill married James MacDonald's widow Agnes Campbell in 1569, and Hugh O'Donnell married her daughter Finola because of the access these ladies could provide to mercenaries from their Scottish relatives.[49]

Angus of Dunyvaig's nemesis was Lachlan MacLean of Duart. The feud between the two men that was to dominate events in the West Highlands in the second half of the sixteenth century was rooted in the struggle between their father and grandfather, respectively, over lands in Islay.[50] The picture was further complicated by the extensive lands in Islay of the Bishopric of the Isles and Abbacy of Iona, including the estates of Laintymanniche, Mangescheles and Ardnave, which also seem to have changed hands between the MacDonalds and MacLeans, depending on which clan was in the ascendancy.[51]

Perhaps a struggle between their clans was largely inevitable as Mac-Donald power weakened and the MacLeans' increased. Angus, however, had the powerful support of Archibald, 5th Earl of Argyll and Colin the 6th Earl. The latter entered into a contract of maintenance, protection and manrent with Angus in February 1574. This may have been in the aftermath of Angus's failure to take Loch Gorm Castle by siege. Four years later the earl contributed a force of 200 men to help Angus take it.[52]

In 1584 Angus received a tack of those Islay lands that had first been given to his father in 1562.[53] Early the following year, when, on the pleading of Queen Elizabeth I, he was recalled from Ireland by King James VI, he was well received. A proclamation was issued charging the lieges in the West to support him in defence of his lands because he was being harassed by quarrelsome neighbours – undoubtedly the MacLeans.[54] There was, however, to be a dramatic turning point in the MacDonald–MacLean feud later in 1586. The story, as recounted by Sir Robert Gordon, goes as follows.

Angus made an unannounced visit to Lachlan at his castle of Duart in Mull, hoping to mediate in a quarrel between Lachlan and Donald Gorm (MacDonald) of Sleat in Skye. Instead he was imprisoned, and in return for his freedom, was obliged to renounce the Rhinns of Islay to Lachlan, leaving his eldest son James and his brother Ranald as pledges. James at this stage was still a boy and, it should be noted, Lachlan's nephew, since the latter was married to Angus's sister. When Lachlan duly turned up to take possession of the Rhinns he was persuaded to accept Angus's hospitality at his house at Mulindry. Lachlan, not totally devoid of fear and suspicion, came with a force of eighty-six of his kinfolk and friends, and Angus's son James, hoping that his hold on the latter would be the ultimate guarantee of his safety. After much feasting Lachlan and his men were lodged that night in a separate house, along with James MacDonald. The house was then surrounded by Angus's men, and when Lachlan appeared with James 'between his shoulders' as protection, he was imprisoned. So were all the rest of his men apart from two against whom Angus had a particular grudge. They were burnt to death in the house.

A false rumour reached Islay soon afterwards that Ranald had been put to death by the MacLeans, and in revenge, another of Angus's brothers, Coll, commenced beheading the MacLeans at Mulindry at the rate of two a day. News of these events having got to the Earl of Argyll, he was instrumental in securing the release of Lachlan in return for Ranald. That, however, was by no means the end of the hostilities, for Lachlan soon returned to Islay, while Angus was in Ireland, and burned a great part of it. Inevitably Angus then invaded Mull and Tiree, and Lachlan went on to waste the MacDonald lands in Kintyre. A cessation of hostilities was only brought about after King James summoned Angus and Lachlan to Edinburgh in 1591. Despite assurances, they were both imprisoned in the castle, but released soon afterwards on paying remissions.[55]

Some aspects of this account may seem too fantastic to be believed, but there is no doubting that major conflict broke out at this time between Clann Iain Mhoir and the MacLeans of Duart. The accusation prepared against Angus by the king's advocate mentions only two prisoners beheaded without any due process of law.[56] Angus was persuaded by the king to release Lachlan in return for a remission for his crimes and seven hostages, including Lachlan's son and apparent heir (Hector), Alexander brother of William MacLeod of Dunvegan, Lachlan and Neill the sons of

Lachlan MacKinnon of Strathordell, John and Murdo the sons of Rory MacNeill of Barra, Allan the son of Ewin MacLean of Ardgour, and Donald the son of Hector MacLean the Constable of Carnburgh.[57] The remission to Angus and his supporters, apart from his immediate kin, included Donald Gorm (MacDonald) of Sleat, Alexander MacAlister of Loup, Murdoch MacFie of Colonsay and John MacIan of Ardnamurchan.[58] Clearly the feud involved many clans in the West Highlands and Islands.

Despite an assurance of good behaviour given by Lachlan to Argyll, the records of the Court of Justiciary show that in 1589 the MacLeans ravished the islands of Oronsay and Gigha, and the church lands of Ardnave on Islay. The latter were presumably then held by the MacDonalds. He had also, treacherously, imprisoned MacIan, and with the aid of the ship and crew of the Spanish Armada that had fetched up in Mull, overran the islands of Rum and Eigg, belonging to the Clanranald, and Canna and Muck, possessions of MacIan. Meanwhile, Angus was charged with pursuing Lachlan with a force including Englishmen – perhaps from Ireland – and with harrying in Mull, Tiree and Coll.[59]

Support for the MacDonald cause appears now to have been ebbing away in favour of the MacLeans. It is possible that those in power perceived that the MacLeans were less barbarous or more trustworthy than their adversaries. The events alleged to have taken place at Mulindry, if true, would not have played well with many erstwhile MacDonald backers. It may have been the case that support was flowing towards the latter because they seemed to be in the ascendancy. In March 1588 Lachlan's son and heir, Hector, was granted a charter of lands in Islay and elsewhere of the abbeys of Iona and Derry, including Ardnave and Nerabus in the Rhinns. It was claimed that Lachlan's father, Hector Og had previously been infeft in them.[60] This was a massive boost to MacLean power and status at the expense of Angus.

A contributory factor in the downturn of MacDonald fortunes was their loss of support from the house of Argyll. Colin the 6th Earl had died in 1584 leaving as his heir Archibald, still only a child. In March 1586 Lachlan signed a bond of friendship with two of the young earl's trustees, Duncan Campbell of Glenorchy and James Campbell of Ardkinglass. Lachlan was soon involved in Campbell plots and in 1594, after the new earl had come of age and was tasked by King James VI with leading an army against the Earl of Huntly, Lachlan and his clan were part of that army that met defeat at Glenlivet.[61] Meanwhile, Angus had entered into a bond of friendship with a rival trustee of the earl, John Campbell of Cawdor, and his son and heir, James, was married to Cawdor's daughter Mary. Cawdor was murdered in 1592 on the instigation of Glenorchy and Ardkinglass, an act in a wider conspiracy that also resulted in the death of the Earl of Moray and came dangerously close to tearing Clan Campbell apart.[62]

Angus now had no close allies among the leaders of Clan Campbell apart from Cawdor's relatively young and inexperienced successor, also named John. The unfriendliness from the house of Argyll is reflected in a report on the Western Isles written about 1595 for the English government by the Dean of Limerick, an illegitimate son of the 5th Earl of Argyll. He not only drew attention to the way his clan had risen to prominence in the West Highlands through the ruin of the MacDonalds, but also labelled them as being very odious to the house of Argyll.[63]

From the perspective of Parliament and the Privy Council in Edinburgh a power vacuum had been created in the West by the death of the 6th Earl of Argyll and the succession of a minor. It was now perceived that there was a Highland problem, one that required greater monitoring and attention from the centre of government. Although there was to be little consistency in royal policy it was generally underlain by the desire to increase royal revenues from the area.[64] Angus's behaviour did not endear him to many at court, least of all the king, who was frustrated of the money and dues promised by Angus to obtain his release. The king had again recognised Angus's hold on all of Islay, including the Rhinns, but a note in the Exchequer Rolls indicates that his failure to pay had a knock-on effect in halting the programme of work on the royal residences.[65]

For non-compliance with the terms of his release in 1591 he was summoned to Edinburgh and, in his absence, was forfeited by Parliament in June 1594 along with other West Highland chiefs.[66] Under threat of a royal military expedition to the West, all the chiefs but Angus submitted, so that the force that did go to Kintyre in 1596 under the command of an experienced soldier, Sir William Stewart, Commendator of Pittenweem, was targeted at Angus alone.

His son James had been held as a hostage in Edinburgh for his father's good behaviour since 1591, but in early 1596 he was released to try and persuade his father to surrender. He duly returned with a letter, read to the Privy Council on 8 October, in which Angus proposed to surrender his lands in favour of James. This offer was rejected out of hand, and the king gave instructions that he wanted James detained at court. Angus, and all his family, servants and friends who were not actually tenants were to vacate Kintyre and Gigha, and Angus had to maintain good order in Islay, Colonsay, Jura and Gigha. Lastly, Angus, or else his natural son Archibald, were to appear before the king alongside James by 25 December, and Dunyvaig Castle was to be handed over. Only then would King James consider what lands Angus and his kin would retain, and on what terms. Meanwhile Angus submitted to Pittenweem in a court held on 1 November on the site of present-day Campbeltown.[67]

Soon after James's return to Edinburgh a letter was received by King James from James MacDonnell of Dunluce. He made a bid for the Scottish lands of Clann Iain Mhoir, claiming that he had a better right to them than Angus (since the latter, he alleged, was illegitimate), and reported that Angus had in any case offered him the most part of these lands in return for his support against the royal army and garrison in Kintyre. He added that he utterly refused to accept this offer – at least until he heard from King James whether he would give him a royal grant of some of the lands. It is difficult to see why such a letter should have suggested that James would be a better prospect than Angus, but a few months later Dunluce was in Edinburgh, presenting his case for the Scottish lands to the Privy Council and clearly creating a good impression on the king. He was knighted but not given the lands he craved.[68]

It is possible that the king was deliberately playing James of Dunluce off against James, son of Angus, who, it was noted, was off hunting with the king while his father, having been obliged to come to Edinburgh, had returned home. He had indeed been forced to relinquish his hold on Kintyre and Dunyvaig Castle, and accept that Lachlan MacLean should hold the lands in the Rhinns.[69] His son may have been knighted about this time, taking the designation 'of Knockrinsey' from the Islay estate of that name in the parish of Kildalton.

A contemporary account of proceedings noted that James of Dunluce showed no respect to the Earl of Argyll and that the latter was supporting Angus against Dunluce. It is possible that Argyll only viewed Angus as the lesser of two evils. There is no evidence of any conspiracy at this stage to oust the MacDonalds in favour of the Campbells.

The king again allowed Sir James to go west in 1598 to persuade his father to keep to the terms of his submission. By now James must have been exasperated by his father's conduct and the likelihood that all his inheritance would be lost. His rival, James of Dunluce, had made another visit to Edinburgh in December 1597 at the request of King James and had again been well received, and there was talk at court of a consortium of Fife lairds bidding to settle Lewis, and others from Lothian taking on Skye.[70] All this may also have encouraged Sir James to pursue a course of action that would put him at the head of Clann Iain Mhoir in place of his father.

Having burned Angus out of the house of Askomil in Kintyre and imprisoned him in irons, Sir James crossed to Islay to oppose the occupation of the Rhinns by Lachlan MacLean, his father-in-law. Perhaps he was prepared to reach an accommodation with Lachlan without resorting to violence, but the forces of the two men met at Tràigh Ghruineart at the head of Gruinart on 5 August 1598, and the MacLeans were decisively beaten.[71] Lachlan lost his life, and it is said that 80 of the chief men of his kin and 200 hundred common soldiers also died, out of a force that was 600 strong. Sir James MacDonald, the victor, was also seriously wounded, but survived.

There is very little reliable information on the battle itself. Initial reports reaching Edinburgh, inimical to James, claimed that Lachlan had been killed treacherously at a tryst – 'under trust', but since James was not accused of such a crime when the Privy Council was desperate to bring him to trial a few years later, this should probably be viewed as calumnious.[72] The MacDonalds are said to have feigned a retreat in order to secure the high ground and have the sun behind them. The fleeing MacLeans were chased to their boats, and later tradition claims that a party of them which took shelter in Kilnave Church was burnt alive by their enemies. The spot where Lachlan fell is marked by a cairn, replacing an earlier stone, near the farmstead of Aoradh. His death was predicted by witches and the instrument of his death was an arrow shot by a Shaw from Jura, known as Dubh-Sìdh. A medieval cleric's grave-slab in the burial ground at the old parish church of Kilchoman is now pointed out as his place of burial.

Perhaps also of dubious veracity is the account in a MacLean history of how revenge was gained soon afterwards by the rout of Sir James at Beinn Bheigier – surely an unlikely place for a battle. This otherwise unrecorded success was achieved by the new MacLean chief, Hector, accompanied by Cameron of Lochiel, the chief of the MacKinnons, MacLeod of Dunvegan and MacNeill of Barra.[73]

King James may not have been unhappy to have Lachlan MacLean eliminated. There was no condemnation of Sir James for his death, though contemporary suspicions that this resulted from a conspiracy, possibly even involving the king, are probably far-fetched. The king was also ready to give Sir James a post-dated warrant authorising the capture of his father and exonerating his behaviour. Sir James was eventually persuaded to hand him into royal custody. In September 1599 the Privy Council approved proposals by Sir James, effectively to take leadership of Clann Iain Mhoir and restore peace to Kintyre. He would accept that Dunyvaig Castle along with sixty merk lands should be held by a royal garrison, and requested that he should have the remaining 300 merk lands in feu ferme at forty shillings per merk land a year. He would also provide for his father, giving him a yearly pension of 1,000 merks.[74] Nothing came of this, and the king, instead of dealing firmly with Angus, had him released after a short space of time.[75] The king's proposal to bring both father and son to the negotiating table in 1601, on neutral ground away from the court (probably the island of Cumbrae), with a new lieutenant for the South and West Isles, the Duke of Lennox, never got off the ground.[76]

By 1601, with O'Neill's uprising in Ireland in full swing, both Angus and Sir James were negotiating to supply troops, the former to the English, the latter to the Earl of Tyrone. Sir James, on going to Ireland was opposed by James of Dunluce, defeated and imprisoned in Dunluce Castle. Not for the last time in his remarkable career he soon escaped his prison, this time by suborning the constable and taking over the castle for himself. Despite this, and ongoing support from King James for the possession of the Glynns by himself and his father, Sir James's continued stay in Ireland appears to have been unsustainable. Returning to Scotland his father turned the tables on him and had him put in custody in 1603.[77]

In fact, Angus handed his son over to the Earl of Argyll who produced him before the Privy Council. It ordered his detention in Blackness Castle on the Forth near Linlithgow. It is clear that the earl was seriously offended by the death of his ally Lachlan MacLean, and one of his agents was reported in 1601 as saying that Sir James was his master's greatest enemy.[78] With King James's succession to the throne of England and removal to London in 1603 Argyll was left to pacify the West Highlands and Isles. In return for coming down heavily on the MacGregors he was given a grant of the MacDonald lands in Kintyre and south Jura in 1607, and shortly after brought in Lowland families to the former area. This followed on from a second attempt in 1605 to colonise Lewis with Lowlanders. In 1610 Argyll also got the MacDonald lands of Colonsay.[79]

Meanwhile Angus of Dunyvaig, in order to retain possession of Islay, was forced to seriously contemplate abiding by the laws of Scotland, paying his rents and dues, and helping with 'the reformation of the barbarity' of the Isles. His offers to that effect got no response from the Privy Council or king, nor did other offers from his captive son James, who was so depressed by his imprisonment and prospects that he contemplated banishment as an alternative.[80]

From his new centre of power in London, King James, having now inherited the problem of pacifying Ulster, knew that a key to this was stopping support to his Irish rebels from the Western Isles. He was therefore now more determined, and more able, than ever, to either bring the likes of Angus of Dunyvaig to heel or else have him replaced by someone who would be loyal and reliable. His immediate solution was to send a force, including English contingents, under the command of Lord Ochiltree, to the Western Isles in 1608. Angus and his son Alexander surrendered Dunyvaig Castle and the fort of Loch Gorm to him. Ochiltree installed a garrison of twenty-four soldiers in the castle and destroyed the fort. He also acceded to a request from Hector MacLean of Duart, to meet with him. Hector came with his cousin, the Laird of Coull,[81] and 'McKynnell'.[82]

Ochiltree sailed on for Mull where he arranged a meeting with all the main Isles chiefs. Not without the strong suspicion of bad faith on Ochiltree's part they were detained and taken back to Edinburgh as prisoners. Angus of Dunyvaig alone, perhaps because he was sufficiently co-operative or contrite, was allowed to go home, temporarily, before turning himself in before the Privy Council on 12 May 1609.[83]

The very next day his son James was brought to trial for treason and condemned to be beheaded. Although he had been imprisoned for the murder of Lachlan MacLean under trust he was not charged with this crime, presumably because it was by then well known not to be true. Instead he was tried for burning down Askomil and capturing his mother and father, and for breaking ward. He had, in fact, made two unsuccessful attempts to escape his imprisonment. He did not deny that he had captured his parents but the king's letter exonerating him was ignored, as presumably, the mitigating circumstance that he had sought, and been granted, his parents' forgiveness for his behaviour towards them.[84]

Surviving documents of the time fail to give a clear indication of the motivation behind Sir James's trial. It is possible that the Earl of Argyll pressed for it. It would certainly have suited him to have Sir James's head as revenge for the death of Lachlan MacLean. It is even possible that Argyll was already scheming to acquire Islay, the only remaining Scottish lands of Clann Iain Mhoir.

No place or time for Sir James's execution were set, perhaps indicating that there was a strong body of support for him from Privy Councillors unhappy with Argyll and his methods. Some clue is provided to this, for instance, by remarks in a letter written by Sir Alexander Hay in December 1615, commenting on the earl's activities in the West. He indicates that it was a view then widely held that many of the troubles had been exacerbated by the Campbells and they were the chief benefactors from them. The letter was a private one to John Murray, gentleman of the king's bedchamber, but perhaps Hay hoped that this might be a circumspect route to influencing the king.[85] Sir James was returned to imprisonment in Edinburgh Castle for several more years.

All the other Isles chiefs were released from their jails and a new expedition sent west under Andrew Knox, Bishop of the Isles, in July 1609. He held a court at Iona that month with the Isles chiefs, including Angus of Dunyvaig, at which the famous Statutes of Iona were drawn up and agreed. These covered such issues as supporting the Reformed faith and its ministers, curbing the number of men maintained by the chiefs (for service in war), limiting the consumption of alcohol, teaching English to the eldest sons of the gentry, banning firearms and discouraging 'bards and other idlers of that class'. The underlying remit for the bishop was, no doubt, to persuade the clan chiefs to pay their rents and obey the laws, but these statutes may also genuinely have been a well-meaning attempt at restructuring local society, turning the chiefs into government agents and administrators while weakening the bonds of the clan system. The alternatives to the adoption of such progressive ways notably included displacement in favour of the Campbells, who had long ago embraced the new ways.[86]

Clann Iain Mhoir, under their aged chief Angus of Dunyvaig, managed to live in relative peace over the next few years – leastwise not drawing attention to any deeds that would have annoyed King James or his Privy Council in Edinburgh. Their Irish lands were now firmly in the possession of James of Dunluce's younger brother Randal. The opportunities to fight in Ireland, either for the native lords or the English administration, had disappeared with the flight of O'Neill and other Ulster leaders in 1607. Ulster was being settled by Lowland Scots and English incomers. In May 1610 Bishop Knox of the Isles was appointed Steward of the Isles with his headquarters at Dunyvaig Castle, until then held by a garrison installed by Lord Ochiltree.[87]

Angus of Dunyvaig, however, was by now an old man and the future of his remaining lands, especially Islay, was at stake. His condemned son, Sir James, still in prison in Edinburgh Castle, clearly did not appear to be a very likely contender. The two front-runners were Sir James's brother-in-law, Sir John Campbell of Cawdor, and Randal MacDonnell of Dunluce. Legally, Angus of Dunyvaig had not been the feudal holder of these lands since his forfeiture in 1594, but it appears that he was now prepared to sell his interest in Islay to Cawdor. It is not known what his relationship was at this time with his son James, but it was probably part of the deal that an excambion (exchange of land) should also be arranged so that James would acquire some of Cawdor's northern estates. When this was put to the imprisoned James by Cawdor's agent in July 1612, he bitterly accused his brother-in-law of being drawn from his friendship with him by the Earl of Argyll.[88] It has been suggested in recent times that the advancement of Cawdor was part of a Campbell plot to compensate him for the murder of his father in the Clan Campbell feuding in 1592.[89]

This Campbell deal, however, was quickly undone by the intervention of Sir Randal MacDonnell who apparently provided the money to have the tack of Islay lands redeemed. There was a meeting between Cawdor's agents, Sir Randal and Angus in St Giles Church in Edinburgh about September 1612 at which the money and documents were to be exchanged. By their own admission, Cawdor's agents could not produce the necessary paperwork but Randal and Angus got the backing of the Privy Council for the completion of the business in their favour.[90]

Angus must have died soon afterwards.[91] There is no sense that he was a man lacking in energy but so many of his efforts appear to have been ineffectual. He failed to adjust to the changing politics in both Ireland and Scotland, and did not know when to temporise, or how to deal with the increased interest in his affairs by the king. Perhaps he displayed foolishness rather than just misplaced trust when he allowed himself to be taken by Lachlan MacLean in 1586, and his revenge taking for this insult did not strengthen his position or his reputation. Clearly in old age he lost the respect of his son, Sir James, and the fact that both were at loggerheads was another contributory cause in the collapse of the family fortunes.

On Angus's death Sir Randal appears to have been offered a heritable grant of Islay, provided he appeared in person before the Privy Council to satisfy the lords about the conditions under which it was to be held and his future conduct.[92] The tenants, however, were not happy with their new MacDonnell lord because he introduced burdens, exactions and impositions they were not used to, and wished to subject them to the laws of Ireland. When they complained to the Privy Council in 1614 the lords of that institution were sympathetic and ordered Sir Randal to desist from these practices.[93]

Might it have been Sir James that put the tenants up to this? They had already, about 1600, been persuaded to write to the Privy Council in support of the continuing lordship of the MacDonalds in the person of Angus, and thereafter Sir James.[94] Sir James may now have been behind a new initiative designed to re-establish his position in Islay, although he was later to deny it in a series of private letters to other nobles.[95] In the spring of 1614 the bishop's garrison in Dunyvaig Castle was surprised and evicted by one Ranald Og, who claimed to be a bastard son of Angus of Dunyvaig. He may have been put up to this by Sir James's illegitimate son, Donald Gorm. Ranald and his men climbed the walls of the castle in the early morning, and then hid in the outer courtyard till the main gate was opened. It was then a reasonably simple matter to rush it and take the rest of the castle.[96]

This gave an excuse to Sir James's younger brother, Angus Og, who was staying within 6 miles of the castle, to send round a fiery cross to raise a force to besiege the castle, ostensibly to return it to the proper authorities. Ranald Og and his companions escaped in the night by boat after six days of Angus Og investing the place. The Privy Council was duly informed of all this by Sir James, and Angus Og's offer to redeliver the castle to the bishop's men. At the same time Sir James made a new plea that he should be released from his imprisonment.[97]

The Privy Council was not unnaturally suspicious of these turns of events and resolved to seek advice from the Earl of Argyll and Bishop Knox. The latter was deeply embarrassed about the inadequacy of his preparations for holding the castle and was propelled into going to Dunyvaig that September without the forces and artillery under the Earl of Caithness that would have allowed him to dictate terms, and without the support he had sought from other Isles chiefs.

This turned out to be a bad mistake because the bishop found that he was no match for a determined Angus Og, backed by other leaders of Clann Iain Mhoir including Coll Ciotach, a distant cousin who was to acquire a reputation for being a 'most warlike man'.[98] His Gaelic sobriquet means either 'left-handed', or perhaps in his case more appositely, 'cunning'. In order to preserve his own freedom the bishop was forced into a humiliating deal by which he promised to set to Angus Og the church lands previously held by his father, and was to do his best to secure a seven-year tack of all the royal lands in Islay for Angus, along with Dunyvaig Castle. He also had to hand over his son and nephew at Lossit as hostages for his delivering on his promises.

Interestingly, it seems evident from this that Angus Og was setting himself up not only as a contender to Sir Randal but also to his brother Sir James, for control of Islay. The only sign of any attempt by Sir Randal to rescue the situation for himself was an offer to the Privy Council by his Islay tacksman, Sir George Hamilton, to lead a royal expedition to the island to sort matters out. The council, however, forbore acting upon his offer, and this may effectively have marked the last chance of his master Sir Randal retaining his hold on Islay.[99]

About this time Sir James wrote another plea from his prison offering, if given his freedom, to take Islay in hand. He only sought a seven-year tack, paying 8,000 merks yearly. In his desperation to be free he was alternatively prepared to settle for removing himself and his clan from Islay, or even banishment abroad. That he was out of touch with what was really happening is suggested by the fact that the cautioners he proposed for delivery of his promises included Sir Randal of Dunluce and Sir John Campbell of Cawdor. The latter, however, was given a commission on 22 October to suppress the rebellion in Islay, and on 21 November was granted a charter under the Great Seal of all the lands of Islay, including the lands claimed by the MacLeans, but excluding the church lands and the estates of Ballinaby and Knockrinsey. Sir Randal MacDonnell was forbidden from returning to the island.[100]

Angus Og claimed that he had instructions from the Earl of Argyll to hold on to Dunyvaig Castle rather than hand it over to the bishop, and in return the earl would seek to secure Islay for him.[101] This unlikely story was, unsurprisingly, not given much credence, although the earl might well have viewed more opportunities for himself and his clan in dealing with a rebellion under the likes of Angus Og. That the activities of Ranald Og and Angus Og had brought about the removal of Sir Randal of Dunluce was a considerable bonus.

Certainly it was the Campbells who capitalised on the Islay uprising. Bishop Knox, writing on 11 October, was in no doubt that all the trouble that had befallen him and his friends resulted from the Earl of Argyll's determination to secure Islay for Cawdor. He added bitterly that it was neither good nor profitable to king and country to root out one pestiferous clan and replace it with one little better.[102]

There are signs, however, of an anti-Campbell, if not pro-MacDonald, plot in government circles that, perhaps, aimed to deny the Campbells their prize. This revolved around the activities of one George Graham, secretly commissioned by the Lord Chancellor, the Earl of Dunfermline, to go to Islay and attempt to secure the release of the bishop's pledges. This, remarkably, Graham achieved by presenting himself to Angus Og as on an official mission from the Privy Council. In the process he gave Angus Og written instructions to hold the castle on behalf of the king and the council. In this, Graham undoubtedly exceeded his instructions, and left the chancellor with some awkward explaining to his royal master. Graham potentially, however, caused double trouble for Cawdor's efforts to secure Islay. Firstly, by removing the bishop's pledges to safety he took away part of the justification for attacking Dunyvaig. Secondly, he stiffened the resolve of the MacDonalds to hold out against what they might now reasonably perceive to be an unjust assault. Perhaps the chancellor really hoped that this meddling might undermine Cawdor's attempt. Any suspicions that he was attempting to create opportunities for himself to acquire Islay seem rather far-fetched.[103]

Indeed Cawdor's efforts must at first have seemed unlikely to succeed. Despite a commission allowing musters for his invasion of Islay mostly from the mainland areas of Argyll, he found it difficult to raise men, and the guns and soldiers he was promised from Ireland did not turn up. He remained in Islay for some of December, achieving nothing before retiring to the mainland again. Presumably James Anstruther, encouraged by the Privy Council to try out his petard on Dunyvaig Castle, had failed in this task.[104]

An Irish force turned up soon after he left, not the 6 cannon and 200 trained soldiers that the king had sanctioned but 2 cannon and a culverin with 150 soldiers. They were, however, under the command of the experienced Sir Oliver Lambert. Cawdor now returned with his meagre force of 200 men, later augmented by 140 more, rendezvousing with Lambert off Jura on 5 January.[105]

In the first few days of the expedition Cawdor took steps to secure the island, marching his force to Portaneilean (Finlaggan), Laggan, Ballyneal and Balynaughton. On 21 January, Angus Og's brother, Ranald surrendered the fort in Loch Gorm and several other leading MacDonalds turned themselves in.

Meanwhile, in stormy winter weather, Lambert had found it difficult to keep his ships safe and find a place to disembark the artillery. He eventually found a suitable port at Loch Leòdamais, the site of present-day Port Ellen. The guns were in position and started firing at the castle walls on 1 February (Plate XX). That day the guns battered a tower guarding the gate to the outer courtyard and a good part of the wall of the inner courtyard. This exposed the 'poart of the castle', meaning probably the accessway to the main house, to fire from musketeers entrenched round about.[106] Lambert had supposed that the castle walls would be strong enough to withstand a sustained artillery bombardment and, given his meagre supply of powder, he would have to contrive to get his men up to the base of the walls to attack them with picks. Good progress on this first day gave him the confidence to keep shooting apace on the second.

Soon after firing commenced that day, Angus Og sought a parley with Cawdor. The latter attempted to persuade him that his instructions from George Graham were not valid. Angus was prepared to surrender, but not Coll Ciotach, and so the garrison held out against the bombardment until that evening. By this time the inner courtyard was largely reduced to rubble and Lambert reckoned he could lodge a force in the outer courtyard ready for an assault on the rest of the castle. Angus, his family, and some of the garrison now came out to submit unconditionally to Cawdor, but Coll Ciotach, not being inclined to give in, managed to launch a boat from the castle and make his escape with a handful of other desperadoes.[107] Angus Og appears to have been neither a great war leader nor an adept politician.

For his troubles, he and five others who surrendered with him were taken to Edinburgh, tried and sentenced to be hanged.[108]

There was yet to be one last attempt by Clann Iain Mhoir to retain some vestiges of their inheritance. In May 1615 Sir James MacDonald escaped from Edinburgh Castle with the help of MacDonald of Keppoch and the son of Clanranald. Given the strictness of Sir James's confinement consequent on previous attempts to break free it may be wondered if his escape now was encouraged or eased by the anti-Campbell faction in government. He certainly believed that Cawdor had acquired a warrant for the sentence of death against him to be carried out and used this to justify his breaking ward.[109] Pursued through the Highlands with a price on his head, he made for Skye where he was given a large boat by Donald Gorm MacDonald of Sleat. He was then able to rendezvous at Eigg with Coll Ciotach who had turned pirate since his escape from Dunyvaig.

Although Sir James did not get much overt or direct help from other chiefs in the Highlands and Islands, apart from Keppoch, he still, nevertheless, started attracting a large band of followers. The Earl of Argyll was later to seek guidance from the Privy Council on whether or how the inhabitants of Kintyre, Islay, Colonsay, Jura and Gigha should be punished because all of them had turned out in support of Sir James. There is mention also of men from Skye and MacIans from Ardnamurchan. MacLean's people on Islay even helped with expelling Cawdor's supporters. At the height of the rebellion Sir James may have mustered 1,000 men.[110]

In July Sir James, with a force of several hundred men, reached Colonsay, and there erected a fort. A few days later he made for Islay, and took Dunyvaig Castle with comparative ease. The following account (with modernised spelling) is Sir James's own:

> We lay in a bush about the house, till the captain and twelve of his best men came out. We pursued over rashly before they came far from the house. The captain's men fled, but himself and three or four were slain. We went in at the outer barmkin [courtyard] with the rest, but they closed the yette [gate] of the inner barmkin. Before twelve hours we took the water, the outer tower, and the two barmkins from them, and set fire to the yette of the inner barmkin, burnt it, killed and hurt some of their men with our shot; for we shot from four in the morning till after twelve. Two of mine were killed, a soldier and a boy; two lightly hurt. The house was promised to yield before ten hours in the morning. And so the Prior [Campbell of Ardchattan] and all that came out got their life and their clothes.[111]

Sir James then had all Cawdor's followers expelled from the island. The island in Loch Gorm was refortified and a new fort erected at Dunand in the Oa. He was not content, however, to sit tight in Islay and await developments but opted for spreading his rebellion to Kintyre in the expectation of appealing to the folk there who until recently had been MacDonald tenants and clansmen.

Sir James's activities caused alarm in government circles and produced a determination to counter his rebellion. Cawdor was not to be trusted to lead a counteroffensive and, in any case, his resources were too slender to make much of an impression. As so often before with troubles in the West, the Earl of Argyll, on the king's instructions, was to take matters in hand. He had been living in London and there was some delay before he could return to his homeland and take charge of the forces that were mustering at Duntroon on the Argyll mainland. This was in September, by which time Sir James was in Kintyre with most of his forces. Argyll sent Cawdor by sea to attempt the destruction of the enemy's ships, actually on the island of Cara, adjacent to Gigha. He sent the Laird of Auchenbreck south to Tarbert and went there himself with other forces from Cowal by sea. Sir James had intended that the narrow isthmus between Tarbert and West Loch Tarbert should be defended by a force of 300 or 400 under the command of his uncle, Ranald MacRanald, but no stand was made. Realising that he was facing a large-scale attack by both land and sea, Sir James, with some of his followers, fled rather ignominiously to Rathlin Island for two nights before returning to Islay. He now set up base at the south end of the Rhinns. His force was now reduced to 500 men, which in numbers were no match for the army of over 1,000 being led against him by Argyll, including the fencibles not only of Argyll but also the shires of Ayr, Renfrew, Dunbarton, Bute and Inverness. He also had 400 hired soldiers.

Argyll, his forces now augmented by three ships with siege artillery sent by the king from England, was quick to pursue Sir James to Islay. The earl landed his men and artillery at Loch Leòdamais. Sir James tried, without success, to negotiate for time, but Argyll mounted an attack against him by sea. He received warning of this through his supporters lighting beacons in the Oa, and he was forced to flee for Ireland. Shortly afterwards he disbanded his army. Coll Ciotach, who had been left in charge, surrendered the fort of Loch Gorm and Dunyvaig Castle on terms favourable to himself without the royal artillery being brought into play. The fort of Dunand was either ungarrisoned or unfinished.[112]

This rebellion, which had the makings of a serious threat to peace and the status quo in the west, had collapsed remarkably quickly and easily. Sir James and Keppoch soon made their way to Spain, the former a spent force as far as his clan and Scottish politics were concerned.

Archaeological evidence for Cawdor's invasion and the MacDonald uprising can be found at the castle of Dunyvaig and the fort of Dun Athad, evidently the Dunand mentioned in contemporary sources. At Dunyvaig a terrace some 180 m north-east of the castle is likely to be the remains of the gun platform constructed for the siege by Lambert in January 1615. The upstanding portion of the east wall of the castle's outer courtyard is badly defaced, the result of a heavy bombardment rather than weathering. The inner courtyard is choked with the rubble from its own walls and from the demolition of the hall above it. This destruction ties in with Lambert's own account of the siege with an artillery barrage of two days.[113] Although the castle was garrisoned as late as 1647, it is possible that only the outer courtyard was maintained as a place of residence after the events of 1615.

Two small pointed bastions have been added to the ends of the landward side of the outer courtyard. They are now reduced to their foundations, or possibly never completed. They seem to show some awareness of 'state of the art' bastions on artillery fortifications but, unlike them, show no understanding of the principle of providing covering fire for each other. It is unlikely that they pre-date the siege of early 1615 since they are not mentioned in the accounts of it, but they might represent the efforts of Sir James MacDonald to make the castle secure again after he took it later that year.

Sir James's work as a military engineer is evident at Loch Gorm Castle. Here he was reported in the summer of 1615 to be refortifying the castle with a bawn or enclosure of turf, said to be twenty feet thick. The castle as it now survives consists of a rectangular turf platform, 20.5 m by 17 m, with a circular bastion at each corner. All the exterior walls are faced with stone. The platform incorporates a hall, possibly of earlier date, and there are the foundations of two other buildings on its surface, which may be more recent work. This bastioned fort is comparable to another in Loch an Sgoltaire on the neighbouring island of Colonsay, which can also be identified as Sir James's work. Here there is a five-sided fort, 33 m by 30 m, with semicircular bastions, constructed with dry-stone walls, 2 m thick and now little more than 1 m high. This encloses a smaller stone structure of earlier date.[114]

Another fort or gun bastion on Islay, at the head of Loch Gruinart, has been associated with the Battle of Tràigh Ghruineart in 1598. There is no mention of it in contemporary accounts of the battle and it would seem more likely to be the work of Sir James in 1615. It is similar in type to his forts in Loch Gorm and Loch an Sgoltaire, and could have served to protect his line of communications between them. It is positioned where he might have been expected to beach his ships. The earthwork in question is known as A' Chrannag. It is a small platform about 16 m square with small circular bastions at each corner. It is surrounded by a ditch.[115]

Dun Athad is an impressive promontory near the Mull of Oa, bounded by sheer cliffs. Access is by a narrow path across a gulley at the landward side that is squeezed between the cliff edge and the end of a massive stone rampart, 90 m long and 5 m or more thick, presumably the work of Sir James.[116]

There was a surprising sequel to Sir James's engagement with the Earl of

Argyll. In 1619, the earl was declared a traitor for going to Spain the year before without permission. Argyll had married a Catholic wife, converted to that religion and entered the service of the King of Spain. There was a fear that he might combine with Sir James and Keppoch in a new, more dangerous, rebellion. Largely because of this, Sir James and Keppoch were recalled by the king in 1620 and Sir James spent the last six years of his life as a pensioner in London. King James would have had him return to Scotland but the Scottish Privy Council refused to countenance this.[117]

Sir James comes across as a man caught between two worlds. He had a Lowland education and a love of books, and seems to have fitted in well with the court in Edinburgh. Perhaps he would have enjoyed his enforced stay in London in the last few years of his life. At the same time, he was the child that his uncle Lachlan MacLean attempted to use as a human shield at Mulindry, and he was later responsible for Lachlan's death in battle. His attempts at escaping from prison and his own account of his recapture of Dunyvaig suggest a man of adventure, but also one lacking in patience, with near-disastrous consequences in his treatment of his parents at the taking of Askomil. He could clearly command the support of his clansmen, and there are elements in the 1615 uprising, like the construction of forts and moving his campaign to Kintyre, that suggest careful thought and an understanding of strategy. Nevertheless, his uprising collapsed with surprising ease – surely an indictment against his ability as a leader.

His was the melancholy fate of being the last MacDonald Lord of Islay after a run of over three centuries. Sir Randal MacDonnell, from 1620 Earl of Antrim, long maintained an aspiration to reunite the Scottish lands of Clann Iain Mhoir with his own territories in Ireland, but a proposal to purchase Islay from the Campbells of Cawdor in 1627 came to naught.[118] The last Clan Donald laird on Islay was, in fact, John MacDonald, Laird of Gigha, the barony of which included the estate of Knockrinsey. He was the son of Alexander, the bastard son of Angus of Dunyvaig. In 1627 he sold Knockrinsay to John Campbell, Fiar of Cawdor, promising as part of the deal to remove his tenants, including Alexander MacDonald of Largie and Donald Gorm MacDonald. The latter was still on Islay in 1631, as Cawdor's tenant in Balynaughtonmore, Over Leorin and Texa.[119]

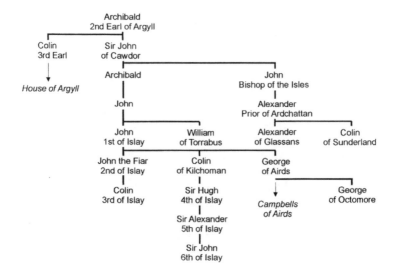

The Campbells of Cawdor, Lairds of Islay

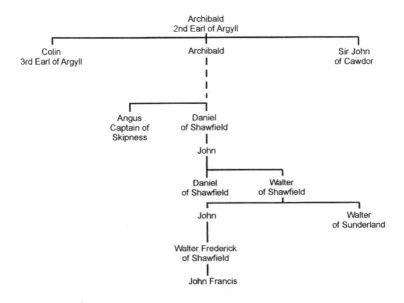

The Campbells of Shawfield

Campbell Lairds and Later Proprietors

The new lord, or laird, of Islay from 1614, Sir John Campbell of Cawdor, was the great grandson of John, a younger brother of Colin, 3rd Earl of Argyll. He had made a fortunate marriage in 1511 with Muriel, the heiress of the Thane of Cawdor, thus acquiring extensive estates in the north-east in the vicinity of Nairn. Throughout its long history, continuing to the present day, the interests of this branch of Clan Campbell have largely been concentrated in the north-east. In the sixteenth and seventeenth centuries, however, Cawdor lairds did maintain landed interests in Argyll and created networks of support there. The acquisition of Islay propelled Sir John into the first rank of Argyll landowners and confirmed his status as one of the key figures in Clan Campbell. It also brought him a great deal of trouble – a hostile population and expense that took him to the verge of financial meltdown.

By 1618 he was 'put to the horn' (proclaimed an outlaw) for non-payment of the feu duties of Islay, amounting to the sum of £12,000, for the two previous years. He was unable to purchase the church lands of Islay when they were offerd by the bishop in 1617. They were only secured in 1626 to consolidate the Cawdor hold on the whole island. He was fortunate that his escheat was acquired by his trusty agent, the Edinburgh lawyer, James Mowat, rather than a rival who might have used it as leverage against him. His debts are said to have climbed to a staggering 100,000 merks and he had to sell some of his lands in the north-east.[1]

The 1614 grant of Islay required Cawdor to pay 9,000 merks (£6,000) yearly, by common consent, a high price, especially when compared with the offer made by Sir James MacDonald in 1599 which would have required an annual payment of only £720.[2]

Sir John won little credit for failing to take a firm grip on Islay and being too weak to nip the MacDonald rebellion of 1615 in the bud. His conversion to Catholicism by Irish Franciscan missionaries brought, at best, suspicion. To avoid the consequences of forfeiture and excommunication on his family fortunes for his continued adherence to the Catholic faith, he was obliged to dispone his lands to his son John in 1626. The latter, as fiar, was required by the Privy Council in July 1626 to seek out

Jesuits in his lands, and hand over his Uncle William, another convert, for examination by the council.[3] Meanwhile Sir John was required to go to St Andrews to receive instruction in religious matters from the Archbishop and other learned men. He remained obdurate in his beliefs, living on to 1642.[4]

There was no easy acceptance by many of the people of Islay that their allegiances lay with the Campbells. John the Fiar petitioned the Privy Council in 1631 for permission to knock down Dunyvaig Castle. He feared that it would be captured in one of his absences and held against him by the rebels of the island, as had almost happened the previous year. He now had enough of his own people on Islay to feel secure enough without the castle. Permission was granted, but the castle stayed, in the event John demonstrating that he did not feel as safe as he had boasted to the council.[5] Indeed, a history of the Campbells of Craignish, written in the late seventeenth or early eighteenth century, says of Islay that 'the Family of McDonald . . . was and is still the chief of the inhabitants'.[6]

Events in the civil wars of the mid seventeenth century were to lead to an escalation of hatred between the two clans and opportunities to demonstrate their anger in action, not just on the field of battle but in atrocities, and the cold-blooded murder of prisoners. At a national level, the main focus of attention during the First Bishops' War, in 1639, was in the East Borders. MacDonald–Campbell animosity, and the prospect of an invasion of Argyll by the royalist MacDonnells of Antrim, led to trouble in the west. The new Earl of Argyll, Archibald the eighth, captured Coll Ciotach and two of his sons, perhaps treacherously, and Colin Campbell of Ardesier mounted a devastating raid on Colonsay, Coll Ciotach's territory, killing all the cattle and taking much spoil. This Colin was a younger brother of John the Fiar and had just been appointed his tutor owing to John being declared a lunatic. Argyll now gave Colonsay and Oronsay in feu to Colin.[7]

Coll Ciotach's sons, Alasdair and Ranald, were meanwhile in Ireland, but during the hostilities that marked the Second Bishops' War, in 1640, they raided Islay with a small force of eighty men, perhaps with the intention of taking leading Campbells prisoner so they could be exchanged for their own father and brothers. George Campbell, another of John the Fiar's brothers, narrowly escaped them.[8]

In 1641 the Scottish Parliament was encouraged by both King Charles I and the English Parliament to send an army to Ireland to help put down the rebellion of the native Irish. This Scottish Covenanting force was backed by the Campbells, and included among its officers was John the Fiar's brother, George. While the Campbells of Cawdor were being blamed for not supplying their full quota to the army, some Ilich, including MacKays from the parish of Kildalton, had actually gone to Ireland to fight with the rebels.[9]

Meanwhile, according to the history of the Campbells of Craignish, a wicked woman of the family of Dunstaffnage (Janet, wife of George Campbell), who was then in command of Islay, made a practice of seizing followers of the MacDonalds in the night, binding them hand and foot, and transporting them to deserted rocks and islands where they were left to die. Donald Campbell of Ellister, who kept a birlinn for trading to Ireland and the North Isles, was able to rescue them and land them on Rathlin or the coast of Ireland.

The context for the story must be the period from George Campbell going with the army to Ireland in 1641, and his return to Islay late in 1642 to take over as tutor of John the Fiar on the death of his brother Colin. On 4 July 1642, George wrote to Colin from Ballycastle, obviously concerned about reports he had heard that his lands on Islay had been wasted and his wife threatened. This was only weeks before Colin died, and perhaps illness had brought him to a state in which he could not do much about the troubles that surrounded him. The story of the wicked Janet taking matters into her own hands has probably been exaggerated in the telling, but the main point is that supporters of the MacDonalds were being forcibly evicted, and that can hardly be doubted.[10]

Alasdair MacColla (that is Coll Ciotach's son) again raided in the islands, late in 1643, capturing Colonsay and Rathlin. In the following spring some of his forces fled to Islay and Jura to escape Campbell retaliation under Campbell of Ardkinglass. The Scottish Parliament passed an Act in 1647 relieving Campbell of Cawdor from payment of his feu duties for the previous three years and until the rebels be expelled from his lands. There is a telling gap from 1643 to 1649 in the accounts kept by George Campbell as Tutor of Cawdor. This indicates that the Campbells had lost control of Islay for most of that period, starting in 1643.[11]

That summer, Alasdair MacColla left for Scotland again with an even larger force of three regiments, mixed Irish and Scots. This was an army, sponsored by the Marquis of Antrim, sent to aid the royalist commander in Scotland, the Marquis of Montrose. It included many MacDonalds and MacDonald sympathisers, and was to form the backbone of the army that was to win a remarkable string of victories over Covenanting forces in the following months – Tibbermore, Aberdeen, Inverlochy, Auldearn, Alford and Kilsyth. It gathered support from many other clans in the West Highlands and Islands, with as much interest in wreaking revenge on the Campbells as supporting the cause of King Charles I. The devastating defeat at Inverlochy on 2 February 1645 of Argyll (since 1641 elevated to a marquisate) was particularly sweet, and was followed by the ravaging of Campbell territories throughout Argyll.[12]

While Montrose (without Alasdair) was decisively beaten at Philiphaugh on 13 September 1645, Alasdair again headed west with his force of Irish and Highlanders, including many who joined specifically to take revenge on the Campbells. He spent most of 1646 in Lorne, Knapdale and

Kintyre, and looked set to re-establish Clann Iain Mhoir in Scotland under his own leadership. Campbell pockets of resistance were reduced to a handful of castles.

In April or May 1646, Argyll's regiment, one of those defeated at Inverlochy, attempted a landing on Islay to aid the Campbell garrison in Dunyvaig Castle, then under siege by Alasdair's forces. The castle was relieved, but the regiment had to withdraw hastily to Ireland on the arrival in the island of forces under the Captain of Clanranald. Archibald MacAlaster, Minister of Kilchoman and Kilarrow, later reported that all his congregation had gone over to Alasdair and he himself had to join Clanranald for his own protection.[13]

About the same time, a new force under the command of the Marquis of Antrim arrived in Kintyre to reinforce Alasdair's army. Instructions from King Charles, however, reached Antrim and Alasdair soon afterwards that they should disband their forces as a consequence of his surrender to the Scottish Covenanting army in England. Antrim withdrew with some of his men to Ireland later that year, leaving Alasdair defiantly holding on to his Scottish gains. The following year an experienced Covenanting army was sent against him under the command of David Leslie.

Alasdair evidently never intended to defend Kintyre, but withdrew his forces to Islay, and then to Ireland, perhaps hoping to gather new forces with which to return to Scotland. He never did, meeting his death at the Battle of Knockanauss in County Cork on 13 November 1647.[14]

Before departing Scotland he had installed a garrison in Dunyvaig Castle, under the command of his aged father Coll Ciotach, and another in the fort in Loch Gorm under a brother. David Leslie's army landed on the island in late June 1647 and immediately invested the castle, which withstood a few days siege before surrendering. Leslie did not have a train of large siege guns and the castle, perhaps little repaired since its destruction in 1615, may have had a force of 200 in it. Its surrender may have been precipitated by lack of water.

Most of the garrison were allowed to depart with their lives. Coll Ciotach, however, had been taken prisoner a few days beforehand when he left the castle, without having taken adequate assurance for his safety, apparently intending to speak with the Captain of Dunstaffnage, an old friend, in the besieging force. He was tried by Argyll's sheriff depute, none other than George, the Tutor of Cawdor, who had suffered so much animosity from his Islay neighbours and tenants, and was not surprisingly sentenced to be hanged. The fort in Loch Gorm surrendered to the Campbells some time after the departure of Leslie's army, and the Tutor was empowered by Parliament in 1649 to continue the garrison he had hitherto been maintaining at his own expense. It was to be under his command and consist of a lieutenant, a sergeant, two corporals, a drummer and thirty soldiers. It may have been lodged in Loch Gorm rather than Dunyvaig.[15]

Islay was probably devastated by Alasdair's forces, the Clanranald, Leslie's army or all three. It was still described as altogether wasteland in 1651.[16] Depopulation, and a determination to get a firm grip on the island, led George Campbell of Airds, who administered the Cawdor estates until 1661, to plant army officers and men with Covenanting convictions from the south-west of the country. The evidence comes from the 1654 rental, which lists new tenants including Majors Robert Kilgour and Stewart, and Captain John Wallace. Others with English or Lowland names, like John Osborne, Archibald Muir, Robert Blair, George Stewart and Hugh, Alexander and Thomas Montgomery, probably belong to this colony.[17]

The leader was Lieutenant Colonel James Wallace, who had already acquired land in the Lowland plantation in Kintyre. Wallace was a professional soldier who had served in the Scottish army in Ireland and went on to have a colourful career. He was captured at the Battle of Kilsyth on 15 August 1645 and had a spell as Governor of Belfast in 1649. He was appointed lieutenant colonel of His Majesty's Life Guard of Foot and, as such, was captured at the Battle of Dunbar on 3 September 1650. He is notorious for his part in the Covenanting uprising in 1666. He led the army that suffered defeat at Rullion Green outside Edinburgh that year and spent his last years as an exile in the Low Countries, dying there in 1678.[18]

The effect of this plantation of Covenanters on the island is not known. Some may have left after a few years and others been absorbed into the local population. Clearly, George Campbell would have hoped they would have helped 'civilise' the islanders, but after all the horrors of several years of war perhaps the Ilich were finally prepared to accept the new Campbell order. George seems to have been careful to avoid drawing Islay and the other Cawdor possessions into conflict with the Cromwellian Regime in Scotland in the 1650s, refusing to side with the Marquis of Argyll in attempting to resist payment of reparations for the losses sustained by the English army on campaign in Argyll in 1652.[19] Neither was he guilty of overt or active support for the regime. After the downfall and execution of the marquis in 1661, following on from the Restoration of Charles II in 1660, several of the chiefs of Clan Campbell were excepted from an Act of Indemnity and severely fined. The £5,000 required of George was one of the largest, and seems to have been particularly vindictive.[20]

There was also the matter of religion. Archibald, 7th Earl of Argyll, Sir John Campbell of Cawdor and his brother William of Torrabus were exceptional among their clan in becoming staunch Catholics. The Campbells were otherwise strong supporters of the Reformed Church, and the Covenanting movement prior to 1660. Protestantism had probably made little headway in Islay, and Catholic missionaries reported relatively easy successes in reviving a dormant interest in their faith and making new converts. There is record of an Irish Jesuit, Fr David Galwey, visiting Islay in 1619 and making forty converts.[21] A particular effort was made by the Irish Franciscan Mission in the years from 1624 to 1629. Patrick Hegarty claimed to have won over 119 Ilich to the Catholic faith, baptised 18 and exorcised 4, in a visit in 1624. Two years later, Cornelius Ward noted that almost all the inhabitants of Islay had converted. Some of this was due to another visit by Hegarty in 1625 when he converted 518, including Sir John Campbell and several of his relatives, and baptised 48. These missionaries claimed similar success in Kintyre and elsewhere in the Isles.[22]

Meanwhile, the Kirk experienced difficulties in finding reliable ministers who were fluent in Gaelic. There is little information on the early provision of ministers to Islay. One of the priests, Charles MacLean of Kilarrow, conformed to the new religious order from the 1560s and kept his living. In 1615 it was reported that there was only one minister on the island and the people were inclined to papist ways. In the following year, after the suppression of the MacDonald uprising, Bishop Thomas Knox could report that the island was served by two ministers, Patrick MacLachlan and Duncan MacEwan.[23]

The Synod of Argyll saw fit in 1651 to order the building of a new church at Kilbride, near Dunyvaig, but the minister of it had not only to cover the old parishes of Kildalton and Kilnaughton (the Oa) but also Jura as well. The minister in question, Martin MacLachlan, had fled the island in 1646 to avoid Alasdair MacColla's forces, and was only ordered back to the island in 1650. Meanwhile Kilarrow and Kilchoman were a joint charge, still with no minister since the suspension of Archibald MacAlaster for siding with Clanranald in 1646, and he had since got into further trouble for a drunken brawl. Nevertheless the Synod desired that the two parishes be separated, and the care of Colonsay and Oronsay added to Kilchoman. They made no provision for ministers at that time, but at their meeting in October 1652 had to accept that MacAlaster should again take over Kilchoman, basically because nobody else would have him. Kilarrow was added to the enormous area already covered by MacLachlan.[24]

These arrangements, not surprisingly, did not turn out to be satisfactory. It was reported in 1652 that many Ilich were going to Ireland to get married or have their children baptised, in many cases to avoid the censure of the Kirk in Scotland. The following year, the Synod refused to listen to the complaint of Martin MacLachlan that he had too large a parish to handle. By 1654 Islay and Jura were notorious as places of shelter for fugitives from Church censure, and in 1659 the island was reported to be in a sad condition through ignorance and scandalous enormities.[25]

Nevertheless, the Reformed faith must have been winning ground, and those who adhered to Catholicism must have found it increasingly difficult to maintain and practise their beliefs. Since the efforts of the Irish Franciscans in the 1620s, Islay is only known to have enjoyed the presence of the priests with Alasdair MacColla's forces in 1646. An Irish Vincentian, Dermot Duggan, visited Islay in 1652,[26] but there is not much

evidence for missionary activity after that. The case of one Nicholas
Dunbar, then in Islay, first reported to the Synod of Argyll in 1657 as a
professed papist, is of interest. Rather than excommunicate him outright,
the Kirk was prepared to engage him in debate, until the Synod finally
tired of his obstinacy in 1661. It is not improbable that this Nicholas was
the father of three brothers from Nerabus who were at the Scottish
Benedictine monastery of Ratisbon in Bavaria in the 1670s, one of them,
George, taking vows in 1674.[27] Another Islay Catholic, Donald MacLachlan, even had his expenses paid by the Synod so that he could stay in
Inverary in 1660 and receive instruction from the ministers there.[28]
Catholicism totally died out in Islay soon afterwards, and a Protestant
people was more likely to find common cause with its firmly Protestant
laird.

John the Fiar died in 1654. His son Colin had predeceased him in 1647
while a student at Glasgow University, and he was succeeded by his cousin
Hugh, who only came of age in 1661. He was the son of Colin the Tutor,
Laird of Ardesier on the coast of the Moray Firth. Colin had possessed
Kilchoman on Islay, and this was, presumably, where Hugh lived, when he
visited Islay, until the erection of Islay House at the head of Loch Indaal.
Hugh had a remarkably long spell as laird during which the Ilich forgot
their enmity to the Campbells and became an important part of the
Campbell empire in Scotland. Some of this was no doubt due to the
careful and moderate policies followed by Hugh.

The erection of Islay House in 1677, a considerable investment in
money and effort, marked the progress of Islay from hostile, undeveloped
territory to a settled estate that paid its way. This house, now modified and
incorporated in a much larger, rambling structure (Plate XXI), was a
typical L-planned structure of the period, similar to others built by
prosperous Lowland lairds.[29] Although, as built, it would have had a
fashionable castellated appearance, with turrets and battlements, these
would not have been expected to have been militarily functional.

Even so, there were political troubles ahead that could so easily have
undone the progress being made on Islay, and ironically, the main danger
came from the head of Clan Campbell himself, Archibald, 9th Earl of
Argyll, who had gone into exile in 1682 rather than accept the religious
policy of King Charles II. This put all of Clan Campbell under suspicion,
and in 1684 the Marquis of Atholl, newly appointed Lieutenant of Argyll,
invaded Argyll, intent on subduing it and disarming the population.
Several Campbell gentlemen were required to give bonds to appear before
the Privy Council within ten days of being cited, including Donald
Campbell, wadsetter of Daill and Archibald Campbell of Sunderland.[30]

The Privy Council's concerns were not ill-founded, for in 1685, after
the succession of Charles's Catholic brother, James (VII of Scotland, II of
England), Argyll returned to raise a rebellion to coincide with another led
by the Duke of Monmouth in England. With his small force he sailed

around the north of Scotland, making for Islay, hoping to raise a force of 600 men there before going on to recruit in his own lands. Argyll arrived in the Sound of Islay on 16 May, after the island had been disarmed by a force of Atholl's men. Meanwhile, Archibald Campbell of Octomore, Bailie of Islay, had come from Edinburgh and was doing his best to discourage any show of support for the earl. The next day Argyll landed a force of men who marched to Kilarrow. They narrowly missed capturing Octomore, and despite the latter's efforts eighty men offered to sign up for the rebellion. When the bailie was captured the next day Argyll issued a threat that he would hang him unless 300 men presented themselves for service with him. Neither seems to have happened, and the earl sailed on for Kintyre on the 19th. By the 24th, at Campbeltown, of the eighty Ilich, all but twelve had deserted. The rebellion collapsed soon afterwards in ignominious failure and Argyll was hustled off to Edinburgh for execution.[31]

Government retribution soon followed on those who had supported the earl. Hugh Campbell of Cawdor, as Lieutenant Depute of Islay, summoned several Ilich to stand trial at Kilarrow on 1 September 1685, but only two of those cited actually appeared. One of them, a drover called Gilbert MacArthur, was sent for trial to Edinburgh and eventually transported to North America, despite, like many others, claiming that he had been strong-armed into joining the rebellion and deserted it as soon as he could.[32]

In 1688, Sir Hugh's son and heir, Alexander, married a Welsh lady, Elizabeth Lort, and Sir Hugh resigned the islands of Islay and Jura to the young couple, reserving Cawdor Castle for his own use. Alexander took up residence in Islay House, but still maintained an interest in the family's northern estates, not least by succeeding his father as Member of Parliament for Nairnshire in 1693. He died in 1697, nineteen years before his father, and his son John succeeded to all the estates in 1716.[33]

At that time Islay had been administered for several years by an Edinburgh lawyer, James Anderson. Anderson remained in Edinburgh, relying on his son-in-law, John Allan, Bailie of Islay, to look after business on the island. His son, Patrick Anderson, also sent reports to him on island conditions. James Anderson had had to deal with the effects of poor crops, cattle disease, smallpox among the human population, and the uncertainties and dangers of rebellion in 1715 with the Jacobite Uprising in that year. It was reported in March 1715 that a considerable number of Islay men were in camp at Inverary as part of government measures to oppose the rebellion. There was apparently by that time no inclination by the islanders to support the cause of the exiled house of Stewart, despite the Jacobite leanings of the elderly Sir Hugh Campbell of Cawdor. Meanwhile, 'an unlucky crew of ye name of Mcgregor' (Rob Roy and his associates) was threatening the safe delivery of the Islay drove to Lowland markets.[34]

In January 1718 it was reported that the state of Islay was very melancholy, the islanders having lost upwards of 6,000 cattle through the 'traick' (cattle disease), besides most of their grain, which had been fed to weak cattle to keep them alive. The resulting lack of grain almost occasioned a famine, and excessive prices were being charged for imported meal. Many were reduced to poverty and it was with the utmost difficulty that any money could be got to pay taxes and feu duties. The rent arrears were enormous.[35] The following July the bailie, John Allan, convened a committee of Islay gentlemen to agree on the amount of money that had to be paid by each quarterland to cover payment of the cess (land tax) for the island, and then in November at a further meeting, this group decided not just on the level of this stent to pay the cess, but also what had to be raised to cover such things as the salaries of the surgeon and the Kildalton schoolmaster, and the building of a schoolhouse for that parish. Whether this Stent Committee was the idea of John Allan, James Anderson or the new laird is not known. It was clearly deemed a good thing, and met regularly from then on, normally twice a year.[36]

John Campbell of Cawdor had spent most of his childhood in England and Wales where the family now had estates. He also inherited large debts and considerable financial liabilities. He, therefore, as part of a process of rationalisation, disposed of Islay. In 1723 he granted a wadset (mortgage) for £6,000 of Islay and Jura lands to Daniel Campbell of Shawfield (Plate XXII). Daniel also bound himself to pay a further £6,000 for the right of reversion of other lands on Islay already held by wadsetters. He acquired Islay and the south part of Jura outright in 1725 by paying the full amount of money. The cash for this deal came from the inflated compensation the City of Glasgow was forced to pay him for the sacking of his town house earlier that year by the Glasgow mob. This was because, as the city's first Member of Parliament at Westminster, he had supported the imposition of an unpopular malt tax. Given that the Islay rent by 1716 was nearly £16,000 Scots – about £1,332 sterling – it appears that Daniel Campbell got a good deal, an estate that, even without improvement, should repay its purchase price within a few years.[37]

Daniel Campbell was a younger son of the Captain of Skipness in Kintyre. He had made his fortune as a merchant engaged in transatlantic trade, and as a banker and entrepreneur.[38] Prior to his purchase of Islay he had bought two estates in Lanarkshire, Shawfield and Woodside. Daniel was clearly a canny, indeed ruthless, businessman and politician, with cosmopolitan tastes and experience. He was close to the Whig Prime Minister, Robert Walpole. At first sight his interest in Islay might seem surprising, but perhaps he had been severely rattled by the systematic and thorough destruction of his Glasgow house. It clearly demonstrated a deep-seated hatred for him by more than a fickle mob. Islay offered him the security of remoteness from mob violence, and an opportunity to play his part as a laird of Clan Campbell. The Duke of Argyll was his main patron in Scotland.

Daniel clearly expected to run Islay as a business, introducing new ideas and farming methods from the Lowlands. Improvements, however, were slow in taking root, as he had to deal with the resistant, well-established wadsetters and tacksmen from the Cawdor regime. Daniel intended to redeem the wadsets, break up the largest holdings into their constituent farms, and lease them to men who could persuade him or demonstrate that they were able and prepared to adopt new, improved methods of farming. Many of the wadsets were due for redemption in 1741, but rather than rush in to make drastic changes before he fully understood the local situation, and had knowledge of who would be model tenants, he decided to postpone the redemption of the wadsets until 1760. He gave plenty of advance notice of his intentions, publicly, as early as 1747. Part of his strategy was to charge wadsetters hefty grassums or entry fees to compensate for the repayment of the wadsets.[39] He did not live long enough to carry out this policy, but was committed enough to Islay to add substantially to Islay House. Islay, of course, was only one of his many concerns, including his other estates and his work as an MP that took him to London.[40]

A unique Islay development that Shawfield had the good sense to retain was the Stent Committee, which went from strength to strength as a business committee, deciding on what money should be raised, not only to pay government taxes and impositions but on good works. As time went on the committee took an interest, among other things, in the provision of roads, bridges, schooling, ferry services and postal services. It survived until 1843.[41]

The fateful year 1745 came and went with apparently very little direct effect on the island. There is no evidence that the uprising in favour of the exiled Stewarts attracted any support from Ilich. The concerns of the Stent Committee in that year were focused on theft.[42] Shawfield raised a body of Ilich to join the government forces, fitting them out with his own money. They were no doubt commanded by his son John, and with the rest of the Argyll militia, saw service at the Battles of Falkirk and Culloden.[43]

Daniel Campbell was succeeded in 1753 by his grandson, also called Daniel, still then a teenager. He too became an MP, in his case for Lanarkshire, from 1761 to 1768. He also maintained his grandfather's interest in developing Islay and improving the quality of farming, though he did not carry out his grandfather's proposed redemption of the wadsets. He was responsible for founding the village of Bowmore and had schemes for fishing, linen manufacture, trade, the improvement of communications, religion, education, and law and order. He died unmarried, aged forty, in 1777, leaving his estates to a younger brother, Walter, then an advocate in Edinburgh.[44]

Walter also inherited the estate of Skipness from his brother John, and considerable debts from Daniel. He sold off Shawfield and his lands in Jura, and divided his attentions between Islay, Skipness and Woodhall. In

1778 he finally did what his two predecessors had intended, and redeemed the remaining large wadsets – Ballachlaven, Killinallan and Lossit. A 'day book', started by his brother Daniel, contains memos about Islay business, illustrating his commitment to the island and the progress he made in turning it into an estate, efficient and prosperous by the standards of the day, one admired by others, including James MacDonald, the writer of a general view of agriculture in the Hebrides. He believed that Islay was the best managed of the Hebrides, though the 1s 10d that each acre paid in rent could easily be increased to 3s. The development of Islay House Farm with its impressive, large square surrounded by ranges of farm buildings was, probably, down to Walter. In 1788 he purchased the Sunderland Estate and conveyed it to his third son, Walter, in 1814. This son had previously been a captain in the East India Company's Shipping Service, and in 1815–16 captained one of the ships that accompanied Lord Amherst's diplomatic mission to the court of the Chinese emperor.[45]

Walter died in 1816 and his teenage grandson, Walter Frederick, succeeded to Islay and Woodhall (Plate XXIII). He also became an MP, for Argyllshire, from 1822 to 1832 and from 1835 to 1841, and continued the family tradition of investing time and energy in the improvement of Islay. Farming, roads, ferries and the creation of new villages were some of the things he turned his attention to. Islay House was expanded in size and the gardens and planned landscapes at the head of Loch Indaal, started by Daniel Campbell the Younger, now covered a large area. A house (*cottage ornée*) was built at Ardimersay for shooting parties.[46] Walter Frederick, however, was not a sound administrator of his own finances, and other factors beyond his control, including a dramatic rise in population, national and international economic matters, and the potato failure of 1845, conspired to bring about his ruin.

The increase in the island's population had largely been made possible by the adoption of the potato as the main element in the diet for the majority from the late eighteenth century. Potatoes were nutritious, easy to grow, and could thrive reasonably well in poor soil. So when the crop failed, the results were devastating. Potato disease was prevalent across northern Europe in the 1840s, and in the case of Islay, spread northwards from Ireland. Walter Frederick reported that the disease was first observed in Islay in a field near Port Ellen in August 1845. Withering of the leaves and stems here indicated that the tubers were diseased. Elsewhere, the disease was not spotted until the potatoes were lifted. The rot spread very rapidly.[47]

Steps were taken by the British government to alleviate this crisis, most severe in parts of Ireland and of considerable consequence in many parts of Scotland. Perhaps on Islay the problems would have been less severe if Walter Frederick had admitted sooner that there was a predicament that was beyond his resources to deal with. Instead of applying to the Highland Relief Committee for aid, he tried to manage the crisis by expending his own limited financial resources on job-creation schemes, principally the road from Port Ellen to Bridgend, in order to provide the poverty-stricken with wages to buy food. In practice, many villagers got the money rather than poor farmers who had meanwhile consumed the grain crops which should have paid their rents.[48]

Despite the miseries suffered by many islanders, and the fact that Walter Frederick was responsible for some evictions, he seems to have been respected and generally well liked by the Ilich. This comes across from the writings of the journalist and political activist, John Murdoch, and the diary of a schoolmaster, Donald Sinclair, even though he was reduced through poverty to working on the road from Port Ellen to Bridgend and receiving handouts. Indeed, it was his actions to alleviate the lot of his poorer tenants, after their potato crops failed, that precipitated his insolvency. He and his family left Islay in 1847 for exile in France. He died at Avranches in Normandy in 1855.[49]

Walter Frederick's son, John Francis Campbell (Iain Òg Ìle), was disappointed in his efforts to rescue the family property. Denied his inheritance, he was destined for a greater future than mere lands could bring, as he achieved fame as a folklorist and Gaelic scholar, primarily for his four-volume work recording *Popular Tales of the West Highlands*. A monument was erected to his memory by the Glasgow Islay Association (Plate XXIV). It stands on Cnoc na Dail, at Bridgend.[50]

From January 1848 Islay was administered on behalf of Walter Frederick's creditors by an Edinburgh accountant, James Brown. The factor, William Webster, saw to matters on Islay, and was clearly disliked by many. He had the best house on the island (Daill) and personally held farms that previously supported thirty-seven substantial farmers. He was accused of turning against even those whom he first encouraged, and of being vindictive in dispossessing tenants.[51]

A purchaser for the whole island was finally found in August 1853 in the person of James Morrison, one of the wealthiest Englishmen at that time, from 1841 to 1847, Liberal MP for the Inverness burghs. His surname indicates probable Scottish roots, and he is said to have had a liking for the west coast of Scotland. Morrison's was a classic rags to riches story. He was the younger son of an innkeeper in Middle Wallop, Hampshire who went to work for John Todd, a wholesale haberdasher in London. He was made a partner in the business, married his boss's daughter and went on to turn the business into an enormous financial success. From 1836 he developed a large Anglo-American merchant banking business. Prior to acquiring Islay he had already bought the estates of Fonthill in Wiltshire and Basildon Park in Berkshire.[52]

James Morrison only briefly visited Islay once, in 1849, prior to his death in 1857. He was succeeded by his son, Charles, who made an even greater fortune as a banker and financier than his father. On his death in 1909 his estate is said to have been bigger than that left previously by any other British businessman.[53] In his long spell as laird he was able to take much more interest in Islay than his father, but, nevertheless, spent relatively little time there. Islay House was only used by the family from 1892, by Charles's nephew, Hugh Morrison, who eventually succeeded to Islay on his uncle's death.[54]

When James Morrison made his reconnaissance of the island in 1849 he had the opportunity to discuss local matters with John Ramsay, the proprietor of Port Ellen Distillery, confidant and friend of Walter Frederick Campbell. The outcome was a deal, on the successful purchase of Islay by Morrison, for some of it to be sold on to Ramsay. Thus in 1855 Ramsay became proprietor of Kildalton, an estate extending from Proaig on the Sound of Islay across the south of the island to include Port Ellen. By 1861 Ramsay had also acquired the Oa and land extending northwards to include Laggan.

John Ramsay was born in 1814 into a Stirling-based family of farmers, businessmen and tradesmen. His uncle, Ebenezer Ramsay, a distiller in Alloa, had an interest in the Port Ellen Distillery, and in 1833 sent the young John there to report back on business. By 1840 John was proprietor of the distillery, and held the farms of Cornabus and Kilnaughton. He was involved in the international drinks trade, was a ship-owner and also an MP – for the Stirling burghs in 1868, and for the Falkirk burghs from 1874 to 1880, and from 1880 to 1885. He took a great interest in education, a fact reflected in the provision of schools and schooling on Islay, but saw the Gaelic language as an obstacle to progress in the Highlands.[55] He replaced Ardimersay Cottage as his island residence in 1870 by the nearby Scots baronial style Kildalton House, now a sad ruin. Ramsay, however, was much criticised for evictions on his estate, especially in the Oa (see Chapter 11). The diary he kept of a visit to Canada in 1870, to visit Ilich whom he had encouraged to emigrate, evinces a desire to justify his actions through the resulting happiness of these ex-tenants in a new country.[56] He was opposed to the introduction of the Crofters' Act in 1886, since it encouraged the population to stay on the land and did not provide facilities for migration and emigration. When the bill was debated in Parliament he introduced an amendment to have Islay, along with Jura and Colonsay, excluded from its provisions.[57]

Another substantial chunk of Islay, the estate of Lossit (now known as Dunlossit), was sold on by Charles Morrison in 1860. It was purchased by an English banker, Sir Smith Child. He built Dunlossit House in 1865, a large Scottish baronial pile, extensively remodelled after a fire in 1909 (Plate XXV).[58]

There have been several changes to the ownership, size and number of Islay estates since 1860. Charles Morrison's grandson, the second Lord Margadale, still owns much of Islay today, though not Islay House. Kildalton passed from the Ramsays in 1922. Dunlossit is now owned by the banker, Bruno Schroder, and there are other estates, including those based on Ardtalla, Island House, Sunderland and Foreland, and Kinnabus. Although farming still plays a significant part in the island economy, many estates are retained primarily for sport – shooting and fishing. John Ramsay was arguably the last laird for whom Islay was a powerbase.

The People of Islay

Our knowledge of changes in the make-up of the population of Islay, and fluctuations in its size, is very imprecise until we reach the Modern Period. It is probably safe to assume that neither remained totally static for any length of time. We might guess that Islay's population prior to the eighteenth century was generally in the range from 3,000 to 6,000. War, famine and pestilence were ever potential threats. Islay must have been affected by the Black Death, which reached Scotland in 1349–50 and is known to have caused a devastating loss of life. Perhaps deaths would have been fewer in the Highlands and Islands than the Lowlands, but the national average might have been as much as 33 per cent of the population.[1]

The population was, according to Webster, 5,344 in 1755, and census data at ten-yearly intervals from 1801 to 1951 (excluding 1941) shows it rose to a peak of almost 15,000 in 1841, thereafter decreasing to 4,269 in 1951.[2] It is now less than 4,000.

By the twelfth century the mix was predominantly of people with Scandinavian and Celtic roots, and it is probable that the arrival of Somerled and his dynasty would have occasioned an influx of his supporters, awarded land for their services. If they came from the mainland of Argyll they would have had more Celtic blood than Scandinavian flowing in their veins. They would have been instrumental in establishing Gaelic as the sole language of Islay until Scots English started taking a hold in the seventeenth century. The bulk of the population stayed Gaelic-speaking through much of the nineteenth century, many knowing no other language.

In the twelfth and thirteenth centuries, numbers of Anglo-French and Flemings were settled in other parts of Scotland as landlords, churchmen and burgesses. These people made little progress in penetrating the Islands and West Highlands, whether by conquest or invitation. Indeed, it must be viewed as deliberate policy on the part of the Lords of the Isles in the fourteenth and fifteenth centuries to keep their lordship Gaelic. It was possibly only after the acquisition of Islay by the Campbells of Cawdor in 1614 that there was a considerable infusion of Lowland genes into the Islay pool.

Prior to the Campbell takeover there may have been significant movement of people between Islay and other parts of the West Highlands and
Ireland. Certainly, many of the surnames that occur on Islay are also to be
found elsewhere, and sometimes the actual relationships can be traced.
When the Bryces gave a bond of manrent (an undertaking to provide
assistance) to Angus MacDonald of Dunyvaig and the Glynns in 1575, they
agreed that he could place them in any of his lands he pleased.[3] Although a
preparedness to move may not normally have been spelled out so clearly in
such agreements, we cannot doubt that it was a reality, and for supporters of
Angus might have meant relocation to Islay, Kintyre or Ulster.

Not all relocation, however, was voluntary. The fortunes of many
tenants and clansmen would have been affected by those of their lords and
chiefs. It is probable that the aftermath of an event like the MacDonald
victory over the MacLeans at Tràigh Ghruineart in 1598 would have
meant the exodus from the island of MacLean supporters, or at least those
that remained losing status.

It is only in the fifteenth century that we can start distinguishing some
of the gentlemen, tacksmen or substantial tenants who formed the
backbone of Islay society. In rentals from the seventeenth century onwards
we get down to the level of the tenants who jointly farmed the lands of
Islay. We have no real evidence for the bulk of the population, the
subtenants and cottars, the womenfolk of all classes, prior to the census
returns of the nineteenth century.

Until the collapse of the Lordship of the Isles at the end of the fifteenth
century, the people of Islay would have been seen by outsiders as part of
Clan Donald, although, as already mentioned, MacDonald was not
adopted as a surname outside the core family. Where the names of Ilich
are given, in early rentals and other documents of seventeenth-century and
earlier date, they sometimes appear to be patronymics rather than
surnames. It is not always possible to be sure that a name like Ian MacIan
is Ian surnamed MacIan, or Ian the son of Ian. A name like 'Gillychreist
McCanzoucht Vcbrethuin' (1631) can, on the other hand, be read as
'Gilchrist, the son of Kenneth Macbrayne'.[4] Sometimes clarity is provided
as, for instance, with the additional information that Neil Campbell, feuar
of Torrabus in 1629, was also known as 'McAlister vic Patrick'.[5]

Some Islay kindreds could be regarded as clans in their own right. These
included the MacKays, the Macbraynes and the MacFarquhars, the leaders
of which subscribed bonds of obedience in 1618 with the new Laird of
Islay, Sir John Campbell of Cawdor, admitting that they had previously
been favourers of Clan Donald but would now be dutiful servants and
tenants of Sir John.[6]

A characteristic of medieval society in the Lordship of the Isles was the
way it was geared for war and able to support a class of warriors. Many
families on Islay, however, owed their status and lands to the provision of
other services to the MacDonalds, as poets, musicians, smiths, physicians,

judges and land officers. Remarkably, these professions remained unique to particular kindreds, the offices being provided from generation to generation on a hereditary basis. An early instance of a Lord of the Isles surrounding himself with such office-holders or courtiers is provided by an Islay charter of 1408 by Donald Lord of the Isles.[7] The charter itself is noteworthy because it is in Gaelic instead of Latin, the only medieval Gaelic charter to survive from Scotland, and because it provides some of our earliest surviving information on Islay people. It records the grant of lands to Brian Vicar MacKay. The witnesses included a Macbrayne, a Macbeth and a MacKay, who, as we will show below, can reasonably be identified, respectively, as the Islay judge, Donald's doctor and the coroner of the Rhinns. Macbeth probably wrote the charter, but the other two signed with their marks, suggesting that they were illiterate. This should not fool us into thinking they were unskilled in their professions. All three Islay land officers in 1606 could write. This is indicated by their signatures on a document drawn up in Canongate (Edinburgh) by which Angus MacDonald of Dunyvaig agreed to pay the expenses of a royal garrison installed in Dunyvaig Castle.[8] Angus clearly felt the need of these men, two MacKays and a MacIan, to advise him on the necessary financial arrangements.

The Hearth Tax return of 1694 provides a slender clue that the Campbell lairds might in the seventeenth century have continued to foster some Islay professional families. Or is it just a coincidence that there is a surprising concentration around Dunyvaig Castle of two MacVurrichs (poets?), a 'Mckeard' (smith?) and a Brown (judge?)?[9]

The clergy were another body of men who provided services and scholarship to the Lords. Celibacy was not an invariable rule among them, and so we find that son did sometimes succeed father in benefices. It is also interesting to note that clerics were sometimes drawn from the ranks of other learned families.

MacIans, MacLeans and MacNeills

A royal rental of Islay prepared in 1541[10] gives little indication of lasting MacIan influence. It is not possible to detect from it that there was any large influx of MacIan followers from Ardnamurchan or elsewhere. Nevertheless branches of the family do seem to have hung on in Islay. An Ane McKane is listed as tenant of Kintour and Tallant, while Allestar McKane had Proaig and Baleachdrach. Alester McRanald McCane had both Stremnishmore and neighbouring Ballychatrigan in the Oa, both still held by MacIans in the 1630s. A MacIan was master of the household to Angus MacDonald of Dunyvaig (died c.1612), possibly the Ranald McEane who was 'coronell of the Harrie' (i.e. officer or maer of Kilarrow) in 1606.[11]

The grave-slab of a MacIan, perhaps of the family at Proaig, is in the old parish church at Kildalton (Plate XXVI). He is shown wearing a protective, quilted leather coat known as an actoun, and on his head he has a pointed iron basinet or helmet. This was the typical fighting gear of West Highland warriors in the sixteenth century and the Medieval Period. He is in the act of fastening his sword belt, and underneath his feet is the depiction of a galley. Unfortunately his name cannot now be deciphered though the inscription on the slab indicates that he was a great-grandson of John MacIan.

There is also little evidence of an influx of MacLeans and their supporters from outside Islay, though it appears that the MacLeans could count on Islay-based supporters. These included the MacFarquhar and MacMay kindreds in the Rhinns (see Appendix 1 for both of these families). The rental of 1541 only notes two MacLeans, a Johnne McClane who was given the tenancy of the land of Clagenoch (Claggain), then bordered on both sides by lands described as 'waste', and a Marioun McClane, tenant of Nosebridge and Roskern. When Lord Ochiltree visited Islay in 1608 he received a MacLean delegation, led by Hector MacLean of Duart, including 'his cousin', the Laird of Coull, presumably Hector, son of Ailean nan Sop, Bailie of the Rhinns.[12] It would appear from this that the MacLeans had managed to retain a foothold in the Rhinns, despite their defeat at Tràigh Ghruineart ten years previously. With the loss of the castle or fort of Loch Gorm to the MacDonalds, and presumably the neighbouring lands of Sunderland and Foreland, they may have been confined to Coull on the west coast. The ruined house in the fort of Am Burg may have been the residence of this MacLean Laird of Coull.

Changing times and allegiances even meant that MacLean's people on Islay helped with expelling Cawdor's supporters during the MacDonald uprising in 1615.[13] The MacLeans, however, were, like the MacDonalds, dispossessed by the 1614 grant of the island to Sir John Campbell of Cawdor, although their Islay holdings continued to be listed in the lands of the Barony of Duart when it was regranted in the seventeenth century. They clearly did not have actual possession. By the early seventeenth century, MacLean had all but disappeared as a surname in Islay, only reappearing, probably as the result of an influx of new people, in the eighteenth century.

There were several substantial tenants called MacNeill on the island in the late seventeenth century, but there is nothing to connect them with the landholding of the MacNeills of Gigha prior to 1554. On the other hand, the tenant surnamed McBreatnich on the land of Ardmenoch in 1693, was probably related to the family of that name on Gigha. They had been a family of hereditary harpers, but there is no need to jump to the conclusion that this Islay man had any musical ability.[14]

Clan Donald gentlemen

The earliest evidence for many Islay surnames is the rental made in 1541 after King James V had purchased the MacIan inheritance. The lands were set for a period of three years and the payments were high, typically 4 marts (oxen or cows fattened for slaughter), 4 wedders (lambs), 10 shillings, 30 stones of cheese, 30 stones of meal, 4 geese and 4 hens yearly for each quarterland. The payments in kind are excessive when compared with later rentals, but the tenants in 1541 were technically now tenants in chief with no intermediaries between them and the Crown. The royal commissioners who set the rents were probably required to squeeze as much money as possible out of the island. Their royal master evidently believed that it was there to be taken. As Chamberlain of Islay in the preceding years, MacLean of Duart had only remitted £40 a year to the royal coffers. The new rental of 1541 would have produced £158 besides about 365 marts, 353 wedders, 2,688 stone of meal and the same of cheese, 356 geese and 356 hens.[15]

All the new royal tenants were probably those who already held the lands in question. They were men who mostly owed allegiance to the MacDonalds of Dunyvaig and who would have been recognised as the *daoin-uaisle* – gentlemen – of Clan Donald. They thus not only had to pay the royal rents but were probably bound to make payments for hospitality and pay calps (a form of death duty) to James of Dunyvaig as protection money and in recognition of his role as chief. These calps may have been the tenant's best cow or other beast.[16] In any case, when the officers of the south part of Islay (Kildalton) and the Middle Ward (Kilarrow) rendered up their accounts for the year from October 1540, they had to record substantial sums from the Crown's rents intrometed with (taken illegally) by James MacDonald of Dunyvaig.

Many of the tenants probably had an association with their lands extending back through their fathers and grandfathers to the days of the Lordship of the Isles. These tenants were not the sort of men renowned for getting their hands dirty in tilling the soil, but for what were then regarded as more manly pursuits. A report on the Western Isles written in the 1590s states that each unit of land on Islay valued at one merk – of which there were 360 – was required to support one household man, free from any work on the land, for service whenever required by his lord.[17] The MacDonalds had need of what amounted to a professional fighting force to pursue their ambitions, especially in Ireland. These tenants, along with others, were that fighting force.

Among the most prominent of them were the MacKays, a family based in the Rhinns, the head of which acted as hereditary coroner or officer of the Rhinns (Fig. 7.1). He is also said to have been a member of the Council of the Isles. There was another branch of the MacKays in Kildalton Parish.[18] The Macbraynes were also an important Islay kindred.

Their chief held the lands of Laggan and was the hereditary Islay judge, or brehon (hence the surname), for the Lords of the Isles. The Donald MacGillespie who was crown tenant of Finlaggan in 1541 may have been descended from a family that played some role in looking after this residence of the Lords of the Isles prior to their forfeiture. There is a fine representation of him on a grave-slab at Finlaggan, wearing typical West Highland armour, and a representation of a galley (Plate XXVII).[19] The MacDuffies or MacFies were based in the neighbouring island of Colonsay, but had spread to Islay by the sixteenth century.

The MacFarquhars, or MacErchars, held lands in the Rhinns and appear in the sixteenth century to have been supporters of the MacLeans. The same may have been true of another kindred with lands in the Rhinns, the MacMays, for when they agreed in a bond of manrent in 1592 to accept Angus MacDonald of Dunyvaig as their only lord and master, they specifically excepted Lachlan MacLean of Duart.

Professional families

Several families in Gaelic society had relatively high status on account of professional skills, passed from generation to generation. They included musicians, poets, metalworkers and physicians. Their position in society was bolstered by hereditary appointments to serve chiefs and landlords.

The Lords of the Isles retained a family of hereditary harpers, a family named MacIlschenoch, with lands in Kintyre. The Duncane McGillehaanich listed as a crown tenant in Islay in 1506 might possibly be one of them. Traditions associated with musicians on Islay, however, are to do with pipers. One tells of how a ploughman – 'the Big Ploughman' – of the Lord of the Isles, was working with a boy at 'Knockshainta'. No sooner had he told the boy he was very hungry than an old grey-haired man appeared by the side of the hill, with a table spread with food. He invited the ploughman and his boy to come and eat but only the ploughman took up the offer, the boy being too frightened to do so. When the ploughman had finished eating the old man gave him a black chanter to try. Although he had never played before, the ploughman discovered that he could play as well as any piper had ever done on Islay. Soon after this, MacDonald in his palace at Finlaggan heard the ploughman playing and had him appointed as his piper.

MacDonald brought back a young man called MacCrimmon from a trip to Skye, and he took a fancy to the ploughman's daughter. She gave MacCrimmon the black chanter, and once he had tried it, he discovered that he could play as well as the big ploughman. He took it off to Skye with him and thus the music went from Islay to the Isle of Skye. The MacCrimmons were, of course, hereditary pipers to the MacLeods of Dunvegan in the eighteenth century.[20]

Figure 7.1 Map, with some of Islay's main kindreds,
based on the rental of 1541, and using MacDougall's map as a template.

One of the best-known piping stories from Islay is a variant of a legend that crops up elsewhere in Ireland and the Highlands of Scotland. It tells how a piper, playing his pipes, and his dog, entered the cave at Bolsa near the northern tip of the island. Some three weeks later the dog emerged at a well near Duisker, with not a hair on his body. Of the piper there was no trace, though sometimes the faint sound of his bagpipes could be heard.[21]

Then there is the tradition, associated with Dunyvaig Castle, about the piper playing a warning to his master. The year was 1615, and Coll Ciotach had made a daring escape by boat from the castle prior to its surrender to government-backed forces. Unaware that the castle had fallen, Coll returned with reinforcements, but his piper, still in the castle, played a tune in such a way that his master was warned off. We might add, however, that this is not the only version of this story nor the only occasion for it![22]

So there should be no surprise that a family of hereditary pipers to the Lords of the Isles on Islay has been identified. These were the MacArthurs of Proaig on the Sound of Islay. When the Finlaggan Visitor Centre was opened in 1989, Pipe-Major MacArthur, a descendant of this family, was there to play his pipes. There is no evidence, however, that the tradition of great Highland families having their own pipers can be pushed back any earlier than the sixteenth century.[23] The earliest record of them being used in warfare to inspire the troops comes from a French account of the siege of Haddington in 1548. The troops in question on this occasion were Highlanders led by the Earl of Argyll, and so most probably included the contingents from Islay and Kintyre of his brother-in-law, James MacDonald of Dunyvaig and the Glynns.[24]

All this material, legend and history, provides a reassuring background for the supposed importance of the MacArthurs of Proaig as hereditary pipers, if not of the Lords of the Isles, then of the MacDonalds of Dunyvaig, by the mid sixteenth century. MacArthurs are famed in the annals of Scottish music as pipers to the MacDonalds of Sleat on the Isle of Skye in the eighteenth century. Unfortunately, the tradition that the MacArthurs of Proaig were a piping family cannot be substantiated, and there is no evidence for MacArthurs in Islay prior to the seventeenth century.

The Lairds of Cawdor maintained an interest in piping. Among the Cawdor Muniments there is a precept for a pension granted by Sir Hugh Campbell to Ranald MacDonald, piper, who was engaged to be one of pipers of the laird's son on Islay. Other Islay pipers turn up in later sources – John McMicheall in Glenegedale in 1741, and Neil Macaffer in Carnain in 1841[25] – and Walter Frederick Campbell retained a piper in the early nineteenth century. This was John Campbell, who the laird's son, John Francis, later described as his 'kilted nurse'.[26]

The MacVurichs, a famous bardic family, can be traced in Islay from the early sixteenth century onwards, although it is not known that any of them practised this craft. In the eighteenth century, many MacVurichs changed their name to Currie. Sir John Campbell of Cawdor was clearly very interested in maintaining the Gaelic tradition of poetry as the Irish Catholic missionary, Cornelius Ward, disguised himself as one in 1624 to gain access to him. Ward composed a poem in praise of Cawdor and, accompanied by a singer carrying a harp, was graciously received and provided with hospitality at Muckairn on the Argyll mainland for three days or more.[27]

According to tradition, the hereditary armourers or smiths of the Lords of the Isles were based on Islay. There is a thirteenth- or fourteenth-century grave-slab at Finlaggan that is uninscribed, but has had a fine representation of an anvil added at a later date. It is possible that it commemorates one of these armourers.

The earliest information on these craftsmen is provided by the minister of Lismore, Donald MacNicol, writing, originally, in 1817. He states that the smith of MacDonald of the Isles lived near Finlaggan. In his day the locals could point out the site of his watermill, the stone where he knapped his ore, and the rock out of which he dug it. He gives the smith's name as Maccregie (son of the rock) and ventures the opinion that he and his descendants made complete suits of armour, helmets, swords and coats of mail, as well as the 'Isla hilt for the broadsword', so well known and famous as to have become proverbial.[28]

The folklorist, John Francis Campbell of Islay, was the first to record in print the story of the smith and the fairies. The smith's surname was MacEachern, and he lived in Crosprig near Kilchoman. Campbell notes that the walls of the smith's house were still standing in his day in a place called Caonis Gall.

The story tells how the smith discovered that the fairies had taken his own son, leaving a changeling as a substitute. With advice from a wise man, he was able to rescue his son from the fairies in the fairy hill at Borraichill. For a year and a day after his rescue the boy did or spoke very little, but then, seeing his father making a sword he asked if he could take over, and produced the most beautiful sword that had ever been seen. From then on father and son worked together. Their fame spread, and they became swordsmiths to the Lords of the Isles.[29]

It is clear that there was a particular type of sword hilt that could be identified as the work of Islay smiths, but it has not been possible to establish what they were like. If they were basket hilts, the earliest date that could be assigned to the type would be the late sixteenth century.

There are no surviving medieval documents with the names of Maceachern smiths. Indeed the only smith on Islay surnamed Maceachern that can be traced is John McEachern in Kilarrow, given a tack in the late eighteenth century.[30]

An early eighteenth-century history of the Campbells of Craignish says that this family of hereditary smiths were at that time commonly called

Clan Gowan (from Gaelic *gobhainn*, a smith or blacksmith), and incidentally, says there was another branch of them long established in Morvern, in mainland Argyll.[31] It is possible that the Malcolm McGown who appears as the tenant of Tighcargaman in the parish of Kildalton in 1541 is one of them. Donald MacGuin of Esknish was one of the men of Islay who petitioned the Privy Council, about 1600, in support of Angus MacDonald of Dunyvaig and his son James.[32] Tighcargaman and Esknish still had Macgowan tenants in 1631, and there were others elsewhere on the island at Kilbride (Kildalton Parish), Tiervaagain and Ballighillan. Gillycreist Gow Smyth, tenant of Carnbeg, might be a practising smith, and possibly of the same kindred. It is likely that many Islay folk of the eighteenth and nineteenth century, surnamed Smith, were descendants of the Maceacherns and Macgowans.

There is another Islay family of interest in this context, the Macnocards. Their name is derived from the Gaelic for the son of the *ceard*, meaning a smith or metalworker, often with the sense of someone who worked in copper and silver, rather than iron. There was a Gilcrist McNarkerde in Brade in the Rhinns in 1541, and several tenants with this surname occur in later rentals on various Islay lands, including Gearach in the parish of Kilchoman (Donald McNokard in 1733 and 1741).[33] It is believed that at a later date, MacNokards in Argyll generally adopted the name Sinclair,[34] and Sinclairs do indeed turn up in Islay rentals of the eighteenth century.

The lands of Brade and Gearach are adjacent to each other, and the former possibly included, or was certainly near, Caonis Gall, said to have been the home of the Maceachern smiths. There is also a small valley called the Gleann na Ceardaich (glen of the smiddy) less than a mile to the north. It is possible that the Macnocards were also descended from the Maceachern smiths of the Lords of the Isles. It is worth pointing out that the tenants of Gearach in 1733 included Donald McNokard, Archibald McKecheran and Donald Smith, perhaps all distantly related.

Another possible Islay professional family, associated with the manufacture of weapons, are the Macinleisters, recorded as early as 1541. The Fletchers that appear in rentals from the late eighteenth century onwards may be descendants.

The Macbeths were a family of hereditary doctors or physicians that originated in Ireland. The ancestor of the Scottish branch of the family is said to have been in the retinue of the Irish lady, Aine Ni Cathan, when she married Angus Og, chief of Clan Donald in the early fourteenth century.[35]

The surname Macbeth is derived from the Gaelic for 'son of life'. Other versions of the name include McVay and McVeig, but not all the family adopted these as a surname. Some were named for their profession, for example Gilbert Leich (leich being an old Scottish term for a doctor – compare Gaelic *liaigh*) who was one of the temporary sheriffs appointed to give sasine of Islay lands to John MacIan in 1506.[36] The Gaelic word for a physician, *Ollamh*, was also used, thus Fergus Oldowe (*Ollamh dubh*, the black physician) in the 1541 Islay rental. To add to the confusion, the family began to adopt the surname Beaton from the late sixteenth century. Beaton is ultimately of French origin, and there were well-established families in Scotland with that name in the sixteenth century that had no relationship whatsoever to the medical families.

An inscription on the magnificent cross that stands beside the old parish church of Kilchoman records that it was erected by a doctor (*medicus*) Thomas, the son of Patrick, in memory of his parents and his wife (Plate XXVIII). Below the crucifixion scene there are two small images of Thomas and Patrick, side by side, both holding books. The cross can be dated on stylistic grounds to the fourteenth or fifteenth century, but perhaps a late-fourteenth-century date is preferable. King Robert Bruce had a doctor called Patrick Macbeth, rewarded with lands on the Scottish mainland for his services to the king. Could he be the Patrick commemorated on the cross? This is all the more possible when it is recalled that the king, as a fugitive, sought shelter with the Macbeths' patron, Angus Og, in 1306–07, and the said Angus was to be one of his staunchest supporters. The Thomas who commissioned the cross then might be the Thomas MacBethson who was bailie of Forfar in 1361. If so, it demonstrates this branch of the family maintaining its roots with their relatives back on Islay.

A Fergus Macbeth was one of the signatories of the charter granted in 1408 by Donald Lord of the Isles to Brian Vicar MacKay. Indeed, it is thought that he was the man who wrote it. It is not unreasonable to suppose that he was the head of the family on Islay at that time, and to identify him with the Fergus Fionn identified in a seventeenth-century genealogy as the progenitor of several other branches of the family. Using contemporary records and sixteenth- and seventeenth-century Macbeth family genealogies, it is possible to reconstruct a line of descent for the Macbeths of Ballinaby.[37]

Ballinaby in the Rhinns of Islay is the place that has long been associated with the original branch of the family in Scotland, and was presumably the home of Fergus Fionn and his immediate ancestors. His son appears as Gilcristo McVaig, *surrigico* (surgeon) in the Islay rental of 1506, holding lands with an extent of £3 6s 8d. This was the value of Ballinaby, along with the adjacent land of Leek, listed in the following year, and the rental of 1541 specifically links Fergus Ollamh with Ballinaby.

In 1609 King James VI confirmed Fergus Macbeth (presumably Fergus Ollamh's grandson) the chief physician within the islands of Scotland, in possession of Ballinaby and other lands in the Rhinns, with an extent of £3 6s 8d. The superiority of these lands was therefore not acquired by the Campbells of Cawdor when they got Islay a few years later. Further royal support for Fergus Macbeth is manifest in 1616 when King James issued a formal protection for him, presumably an indication that he and his family were not viewed in Edinburgh or London as recalcitrant supporters of the MacDonalds, but potentially at danger from them.[38]

By the seventeenth century there were branches of the family throughout the West Highlands and elsewhere in Scotland, maintaining their medical traditions. The Scottish kings from Robert Bruce, in the early fourteenth century, through to James VI, in the early seventeenth century, were served by physicians from this family.

There was another branch on Islay that also practised medicine. It was based at Kilennan in the parish of Kildalton, and was represented in 1541 by Neill Og Leich. At the same time, there was Doctor Nigel (Neil) McMorquhar, holding the land of Mulindry in the parish of Kilarrow as his fees. He was possibly related to the MacMurachies, a family associated with Kilberry in Knapdale.[39] He witnessed a band by Archibald MacDonald of Dunyvaig and the Glynns to Archibald the Earl of Argyll at Glasgow in 1566. He is there described as a 'leich' and burgess of Stirling. He was probably related to the 'Johne Oig McMurquhie, leiche in Ilay' who witnessed a band by Ranald, son of Sir James MacDonald of Dunyvaig, in 1615.[40]

At least in the 1540s, there was a doctor available in each parish of the island. Sir Murdoch McMoroquhy, tenant of Arrihalich in the Rhinns in 1541, was probably also a relative, the 'sir' in this case denoting that he was a cleric. The name later crops up in the late seventeenth and eighteenth centuries as MacMurchie. The Ewin Mcmurchie and Mun' Oig Mcmurchie in Arrihalich in 1631 might well be descendants of Sir Murdoch.

In 1629 John Macbeth, who had just succeeded to Ballinaby on the death of Fergus, gave up his lands to Archibald Campbell, Lord of Lorn, and there were no Macbeths at Kilennan by 1631. Beatons are to be found on the island at a later date but there is no evidence that any of them continued to practise medicine. Indeed, when there was a need for a doctor on Islay in 1638 to attend John, the second Campbell Laird of Islay, large sums were paid to bring a doctor all the way from Edinburgh. It appears just to be a coincidence that he was called James Beatoune.[41]

Several Gaelic manuscripts survive that belonged to, or were the work of, members of this family in Islay and elsewhere. They demonstrate that they had access to the main classical and Arab texts, including Hippocrates, Galen, Avicenna and Averroes, and that their practice and understanding of medicine was wide, if rather conservative. Most of the manuscripts are in the National Library of Scotland.

The Campbells and other incomers

After the acquisition of Islay by the Campbells of Cawdor in 1614, new blood was introduced to the island, most obviously in the form of

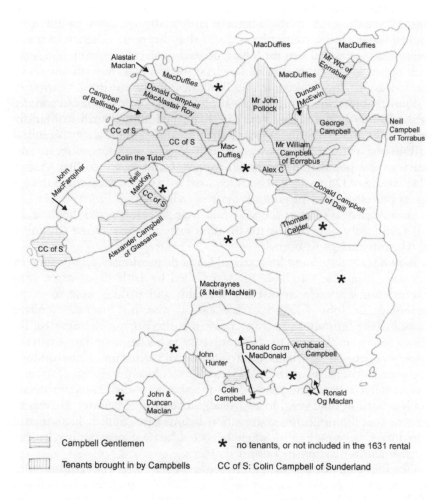

Figure 7.2 Map showing early settlement by the Campbells,
using MacDougall's map as a template.

Campbell lairds and tacksmen to supplant the Clan Donald and its supporters (Fig. 7.2). The Campbells of Cawdor were essentially landlords rather than Clan leaders. The bonds of obedience, extracted from the chiefs of the MacKays, Macbraynes and MacFarquhars in 1618, provide some evidence for an attempt to build up their power base on the island.

The new lairds and many of their supporters came from the same cultural background as the islanders, and many of them would have spoken Gaelic, but it cannot be doubted that they were different in many ways. Clan Campbell had for long espoused close collaboration and links with the court, government and Lowland society, and the main estates of the Lairds of Cawdor were in the Lowlands of Nairnshire.

Remarkably, religion might have been a means to bring the old and the new inhabitants closer together. The Reformed Church had made little progress in much of the West Highlands and Islands after the initial enthusiasm of the 1560s. It was difficult to find ministers to serve, and much of the population continued to have Catholic sympathies. Angus MacDonald of Dunyvaig had been required with other island chiefs to sign up to professing and promoting the true religion (i.e. Protestantism) at Iona in August 1609, but the Islay folk were still considered 'Popishe' in 1615, and the zealots among the invasion force that year found a number of religious images to burn.[42]

Islay was fertile ground for renewed Catholic missionary activity, and in the years from 1624 to 1629, it was visited by Irish Franciscans, who claimed much success in reviving the faith and making new converts, including Sir John Campbell of Cawdor, and his brother, William Campbell of Torrabus. In July 1626 the Privy Council required Sir John's son, John the Fiar, to seek out Jesuits in his lands, and to detain his uncle William of Torrabus (and Geddes in Nairnshire), 'ane obdurit obstinate papist [that] hauntis and frequentis within the bounds of Ila, and by reasoning and otherwayes corrupts the ignorant inhabitants of the said bounds both in thair religion and alledgeance to his Majestie'. He was to be sent to Edinburgh for examination before the Council. He was still noted as a 'fervent Papist' when he was lifted for questioning by the English administration in Ireland in 1639.[43]

The first Campbell gentleman to settle on Islay after the acquisition of the island by Cawdor is said to have been Colin Campbell, a natural son of the Prior of Ardchattan in Lorn. It is claimed that as a young boy he served with Sir James MacDonald at the Battle of Tràigh Ghruineart. He may have been one of the two sons of the prior, along with the prior himself, captured by Sir James MacDonald in Dunyvaig Castle in 1615, and given their liberty. He was given a feu of the land of Cladville in the Rhinns in 1624, and four years later, a feu of Sunderland, Foreland, Coull and other lands in the Rhinns. This family remained in possession of this estate until 1786 when it was purchased by Walter Campbell of Shaw-field.[44]

George Campbell, a younger brother of Sir John, the first Campbell Laird of Islay, had a feu by 1628 of a large estate in the region of Finlaggan, including Staoisha, Portaneilean (Finlaggan), Mulreesh, Mullinmadagan and Margadale. Although he had to return to Islay in 1642 to become tutor for his lunatic brother, his direct interest in Islay landholding may have ceased because he unexpectedly succeeded his uncle, Sir Donald Campbell of Ardnamurchan, becoming founder of the Campbell family of Airds, with substantial lands in Appin and Lismore.[45] He remained in control of the Cawdor estates, including Islay, until 1661.

In 1628 Kepollsbeg and Kepollsmore, along with the neighbouring lands of Ayen, Eorrabus, Balole, Duisker and Ballimartin, and Keirreishlaraich (unidentified) were feued to Mr William Campbell. This Mr William was sometimes described as 'of Eorrabus'. His title 'Mr' indicates he had a university degree, and he may also be the same William Campbell who was a servitor of the first Campbell Laird of Islay, perhaps retained for his skills with documentation. John Campbell had succeeded to this estate by 1654, but the lands reverted to the Laird of Islay sometime after that.[46]

In 1629 the superiority of the Ballinaby estate, consisting of the lands of Ballinaby, How, Saligo and Erasaid, was bought from Fergus Macbeth by Lord Lorn (later Earl and 1st Marquis of Argyll) and feued to the Campbells of Ballinaby, a family that remained in possession until the end of the eighteenth century. Ballinaby House was totally destroyed by a fire in June 1933, but a photograph of about 1915 shows it as a substantial five-bay house of two stories and an attic with a nepus gable. It had lower wings added at both ends and a porch. It probably dated to the mid eighteenth century.[47]

Other Campbells who received feus of Islay lands included Neill Campbell who got Torrabus and Persabus in 1629, lands previously held by William, the laird's brother. Neill's alias is given as McAlister Vic Patrick. His descendants, Alexander and son Neil, resigned Persabus to the Laird of Islay in 1695, but about the same time became wadsetters (holders of a mortgage) of the adjacent lands of Ardnahoe, Overnag (Cove) and Bolsa, stretching northwards up the Sound of Islay and round to the north coast of the island. The feu of Torrabus was acquired by the mining entrepreneur, Sir Alexander Murray of Stanhope, after 1727.[48]

Two early feuars were not Campbells – Duncan McEwin and his son John, granted the lands of Baile Tharbhach and Octocorrich by 1628. These lands were still held by the heirs of the late Duncan McEwin in 1654, but thereafter reverted to the lairds of Islay. One of the three joint tenants of Baile Tharbhach in 1686, however, was a Duncan McEwin, probably a relative.

Feus gave security and permanence to their holders, as well as increasing financial benefit as time went on and inflation reduced the value of the feu duties. It is not surprising that the lairds of Islay were reluctant to grant them. An alternative arrangement, that offered a significant amount of protection and status, was the granting of wadsets. The wadsetter lent a sum of money to the laird in return for a holding of land at a favourable rent for as long as the loan remained unpaid. Many wadsetters would have anticipated that the lands thus acquired would eventually be theirs or their descendants'. The parlous financial situation of the Cawdor Campbells also made wadsets attractive to them as an occasional source of large sums of ready cash.

Colin Campbell of Ardersier (Nairnshire), a younger son of the first Campbell Laird of Islay, had a wadset of Kilchoman prior to 1631, and as tutor to his lunatic elder brother from 1639 to his own death in 1642. Other wadsetters at this time were the progenitors of important Islay families, including the Campbells of Ballachlaven, Ellister and Daill.

George Campbell – a different George from the one who was brother to John the Fiar – was the ancestor of the Campbells of Ballachlaven, a family that remained in possession of that land well into the eighteenth century. George entered into contracts of wadset for the lands of Ballachlaven, Kepolls and Robolls in 1627 and 1628, and two further agreements were drawn up by George's grandson, John, in 1678 and 1695. The family still held Ballachlaven in 1778. George also rented Sean-ghairt, a property adjacent to Ballachlaven on Loch Finlaggan. The marriage contract of his daughter, Margaret, with Mr John Darroch, minister of Gigha, was signed at Kilarrow and Sean-ghairt on 29 and 31 October 1632, suggesting that George might have had a residence at Sean-ghairt.[49]

There were at least two separate Campbell families that successively wadset Daill in the Parish of Kilarrow. Donald Campbell already had a wadset of this land by 1631. In 1684, however, Donald Campbell (a son or grandson?), wadsetter of Daill, was one of the Argyllshire gentlemen who gave a bond to the Marquis of Atholl that he would appear before the Privy Council within ten days of being cited. Duncan Campbell of Ellister acted as his cautioner, under a penalty of £1,000. It is clear from this that Donald was suspected of being a supporter of the exiled Earl of Argyll, and may have joined his rebellion the following year. It may not be a coincidence that later in 1685 Sir Hugh Campbell of Cawdor gave a new wadset of the land of Daill, along with three others in Kilarrow – Sorn, Kilbranan and Octinfrich – amounting in all to three quarterlands, to Lauchlan Campbell, son of the late Colin Campbell of Clunes (younger brother of the first Campbell Laird of Islay). Daniel Campbell of Shawfield attempted to force Lauchlan's son Colin, presumably then of some considerable age, out of these lands in 1749 by redeeming the wadset, but three years later granted him sasine.[50]

Most of the Campbell gentlemen on Islay were neither feuars nor wadsetters, but holders of tacks – hence tacksmen. Their holdings might be a single quarterland or two or more. They did not have the same security of tenure as feuars and wadsetters but set their holdings to their own tenants. Many would have lived off their rents rather than undertake any extensive farming on their own behalf.

The majority of Ilich, too humble or poor to be considered gentlemen, either farmed their lands as joint tenants of the laird or other gentlemen, or were subtenants or cottagers, working as servants or labourers for other tenants. Some of these combined a trade or craft with the growing of a few crops and the raising of a few animals. Among these tenants and subtenants were other families of incomers in the seventeenth century, including Pyotts, Stewarts, Dallases, Frasers, MacNabs and Hunters, all of whom could have come from the estates of the Campbells of Cawdor in the north-east of Scotland. The presence of two tenants in 1631 with names from the East Border – James Ker and James Chirnside – is harder to explain.

After the acquisition of the island by Daniel Campbell of Shawfield in 1726, yet other families crop up in the rentals and other sources on Islay life. It is no surprise to see MacAlisters and MacNeills brought in from Kintyre to be tacksmen. Thus in the first surviving rental, dating to 1733, produced for the new owner, we find that Charles MacAlister of Tarbert rented Proaig, Storakaig, Ballyneal and Arivoichallum. Another MacAlister, Coll, with family connections in Kintyre and Arran, was appointed Bailie of Islay, and rented extensive, choice, lands, including Portaneilean (Finlaggan) and Eallabus. He left no children when he died in 1747.[51] Malcolm MacNeill of Tarbert and Donald MacNeill of Knocknaha, two Kintyre lairds, also feature in the 1733 rental.

Other new names that figure in Islay rentals and documents in the years after 1726 include MacFadyens, Taylors, Bells, Keiths, Grahams, Carmichaels, Simsons, Hyndmans, Johnstons and Wilkinsons. Some of these could be hitherto unrecognised old Islay families. Bell may be a name adopted by some MacMillans,[52] and Johnson an Anglicised version of MacIan. Nevertheless, there may be evidence here, which must be scrutinised in more detail, of new people brought in by the Shawfield Campbells, partly to raise standards in farming.

There may also have been a need to raise the population. Islay suffered badly in the years about 1717 and 1718. Contemporary reports describe an epidemic of smallpox, thousands of cattle dying of disease, no grain, famine and arrears of rent.[53] It is known that several hundred left Islay for North America in the 1730s and '40s (see Chapter 11), but perhaps there were many more leaving in the previous twenty years.

This pattern of population loss as a result of adverse conditions, including crop failure, change of landlords, and the immigration of new tenants with new skills, was to be repeated again in the nineteenth century. From the eighteenth century onwards we are increasingly aware of the arrival on the island of skilled workers and other professionals to help develop the new industries, improve farming and provide services as doctors, lawyers, etc. Not all put down roots, like John Ramsay, the distillery manager who became one of the island's main landowners in the nineteenth century (see Chapter 6).

At the other end of the social scale was a cooper from Edinburgh who got a job at Bunnahabhain Distillery in 1912. Although he only stayed a few years, his sojourn is of interest because his young son, James Whittaker, has left us an account of growing up there, of his schooling and schoolboy exploits. The school had only one room and teacher and yet provided the young Whittaker with a good basis for later life. He describes how the children would 'tickle' fish, trap rabbits and gather hazelnuts, roasted over a fire in a nearby cave.[54]

Continuity and Change –
Place-Names and Extents

Prior to the mid nineteenth century the majority of Ilich lived on the land, growing crops and raising animals to feed themselves and pay their rents to the lords, lairds or proprietors who held the island. From the late eighteenth century the properties they rented, individually or jointly, were normally known as farms. Prior to that, they were generally called lands, while the actual settlements occupied by them might be called townships or wintertons, since they were only permanently occupied by the whole community in the winter months. In recent times their ruins have often, rather misleadingly, been called villages.

An important characteristic of pre-modern farming was the use of shielings (Gaelic *airigh*), pasture grounds away from the growing crops where the beasts were taken in the summer months. Although on Islay the shielings were rarely any considerable distance from the main settlements, temporary huts were erected to avoid the need to return home every night (Plate XXIX). Often it was just the women and young folk who went off to the shielings. The animals were milked for making butter and cheese.

The origins of the shieling system are unknown, but very probably belong in prehistoric times. Shielings were certainly part of the early Scandinavian way of life. When exactly the summer move to the shielings came to an end on Islay is not known. Marginal notes in the 1722 rental, and listings of shielings in eighteenth-century sasines, suggest that they were still an important part of farming life until the mid eighteenth century.

The early settlement pattern

There is evidence of settlement in historic times in most of Islay. The distribution of duns, forts and crannogs, which may or may not have been occupied into early historic, or even medieval times, shows three main clusters: firstly, in the Rhinns; secondly, in a broad swathe up the central valley from the head of Loch Indaal to Port Askaig; and thirdly, along the south coast, extending inland for over a mile to the edge of higher ground. They are clearly grouped within reach of land that is suitable for growing crops. In the Rhinns and Kildalton parish many are on the coast or have easy access to the sea.

The lack of such settlement sites adjacent to the light sandy soils along Laggan Bay and around Loch Gruinart is not necessarily an indication that their value as easily cropped arable land was not recognised from early times. Although there are few place-names of Norse origin in these localities, it is known that Scandinavian settlers, when they arrived in the ninth century, chose such land, not just on Islay, but elsewhere in the Hebrides. As mentioned above, many of Islay's Viking artefacts have been recovered from machair at Cruach Mhor and Machrie on Laggan Bay.

With so little archaeological work on historic sites on Islay the main source for understanding the development of settlement is place-names.[1] While the majority of these are Gaelic in origin, language experts believe that very few of them can be dated to the period prior to the Scandinavian *adventus*.[2] A significant minority can be considered to be Norse. The introduction of names such as Olistadh (ON *Óla(fs)staðir*, 'Óli's/Ólaf's farm'), Campa, a rocky knoll on the coast to the north of Coull (from ON *Kambr*, 'comb, crest or ridge'), and Stremnish (from ON 'headland of the current'), can be traced to the Viking Age. What they represent in terms of settlement history is not certain.

Previous studies have concentrated on the relative numbers of Norse and 'native' farm-names on the island. Thomas, writing in 1881–82, considered that it was 1:2. As this is considerably lower than Orkney, where almost all farm-names are Norse, or Lewis, where the ratio is greater than 4:1, Islay's Norse nomenclature is usually attributed to seasonal exploitation by transient Vikings, or their assimilation into an otherwise stable Gaelic-speaking society. Where the possibility of independent Norse settlement has been entertained it has been assumed to have been economically, or spatially, peripheral to that of the Gaelic-speaking majority.[3]

When, however, the location and relative agricultural potential of Islay lands are examined in detail, it is clear that Norse names are no more indicative of poor quality land than their Gaelic counterparts. Neither are they restricted to coastal, regional or any other enclaves. The implantation and survival of so many Norse names points to the existence of a stable, Norse-speaking population spread over the whole island. An island-wide incidence of Gaelic place-names containing Norse *ex nomine* onomastic units – for instance Glenegedale (from G 'the valley of *Egedale*', derived from ON *Eika(r)dalr* 'oak valley') and the waterfall on the river flowing from Loch Allan into the Sound of Islay, Eas Forsa (from G 'the waterfall of *Forsá*', derived from ON *Forsá*, 'waterfall river') – suggests, moreover, that widespread Norse language use only gave way to Gaelic at a later date. By way of contrast, the absence of Norse names containing Gaelic *ex nomine* onomastic units points to a lack of linguistic transition at the beginning of Islay's Norse Period. Given the fundamental connection between land and status in early Gaelic society and the central place of ethnic delineation in Viking Age Europe generally, the most straightforward explanation of the place-name evidence on Islay is a process of 'ethnic cleansing' by an incoming Norse-speaking population, followed by their (eventual) adoption of Gaelic speech.

When the Gaelic place-names containing Norse *ex nomine* onomastic units are taken into account, it is clear that Norse names must have been much more prevalent than is initially suggested by the supposed ratio of Norse to Gaelic place-names of 1:2. This statistic was derived from late-nineteenth-century valuation rolls, which obviously excluded many names not linked directly to human habitation. When Islay's place-names are examined individually there are indications that many Norse names have been translated or otherwise adapted by speakers of Gaelic. For example, Beinn Tart a' Mhill in the Rhinns appears to be derived from G *Beinn*, 'hill', added to ON **Hartafjall*, 'stag hill'.

Other Norse names can be teased out from later naming processes. For instance, the Gaelic name for the settlement which preceded the village of Port Wemyss was Bun Abhainne, meaning 'mouth of the river'.[4] The river in question, the Abhainn Gleann na Rainich, virtually bisects the southern end of the Rhinns before entering the sea opposite the Island of Orsay. The land of Orsay, valued at 16s 8d in the 1507 rental, must have included some of the adjacent mainland. Given too, the local pronunciation of Orsay, it seems likely that the original form of this island-name was ON **Áróssey*, 'the island by the mouth of the river'. This would mean that Bun Abhainne is a later Gaelic translation for a settlement called in Norse **Áróss*.

Other Gaelic names that are likely to represent the outright replacement of Norse forms include those formed with *baile-*, 'enclosure' or 'township'. There is no evidence for its use anywhere in settlement-names prior to the middle of the twelfth century.[5] It occurs in 18 out of the 178 farm names shown on MacDougall's map of Islay (Fig. 8.1). Possibly it reflects a period of administrative reorganisation and renaming following the arrival of Somerled and his descendants in the twelfth century. In the case of three lands with *baile-* names, all in Kilmeny parish, there is possible evidence that they are replacing ON names with *-bólstaðr*. Ballimartin first appears in the 1631 rental, apparently replacing an earlier Stanepoll. There is a Dun Chollapus and a Goirtean Bholsa on the land of Baile Tharbhach, and a Gortean Bólsach on Balole. This kind of onomastic realignment could have been even more prevalent in the case of topographic names prior to the stabilisation provided by their appearance on maps.

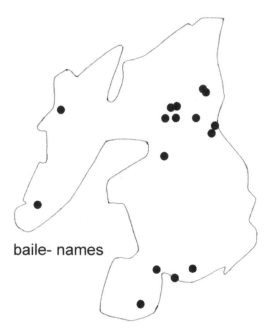

baile- names

Figure 8.1 Distribution of farms on MacDougall's map of Islay
with *baile-* names, after Macniven, The Norse in Islay.

Norse settlement of Islay may have been swift and thorough but that
does not mean that it remained static in terms of population and land
units.[6] Place-names hold the key to how settlement developed during the
time that the Norse language held sway. Many are formed with Norse
habitation elements, including *-staðir*, *-land*, *-býr*, *-bólstaðr*, and *-setr*,
which may represent different phases or circumstances of land-division.

There are ten *-staðir* names on Islay (counting Easter and Wester Ellister
as one), of which six are in the southern Rhinns – Ellister, Coultorsay,
Glassans, Greamsay, Kelsay and Olistadh. Comparative studies of this
name-type elsewhere in the Norse world suggest the Islay examples might
represent an initial apportionment of Islay after its conquest. Six lands have
Norse names with *-land* suffixes – Grulin, Sunderland, Foreland, Tallant
(Kilarrow parish), Tallant (Kildalton parish) and Ardtalla. Such *-land* names
are common in south-west Norway and Orkney but rare in the Hebrides.
Their presence in Islay might, therefore, suggest that Islay was subject to
earlier, more intensive settlement than elsewhere in the Hebrides.

Conisby, Ballinaby and Nereby all include either the Norse *-bær* or *-býr*.
If the former, links with west Norwegian and Icelandic usage would seem
likely. It can, however, be deduced, on the basis of the early forms of these
names and local pronunciation that they are more likely to incorporate -
býr, suggesting links with East Norway. A tentative conclusion from this

might be that they result either from the expedition of King Harald Hárfagr (or other East Norwegian chieftains) in the late ninth century, or else the expansionist activities of another King of Norway, Ólaf Tyrggvason, in the late tenth century.

The most common Norse generic in Islay settlement names is *bólstaðr*, producing in modern usage either *-bus* or *-bols* suffixes. There are more farms (18) with this form of name on MacDougall's map than any other (Fig. 8.2). Islay's twenty-six *-bólstaðr* names are mostly grouped into three distinct clusters. The first is confined to the western extremity of the parish of Kilarrow, to the north of the River Sorn, on some of the best farmland on the island. The second group lie along the northern bank of the Sorn from Kepolls to Persabus, and are also in an area of relatively good arable land, much of it on limestone. The third group occupies a strip through the centre of the Oa where underlying limestone also provides good arable ground.

The use of *bólstaðr* as an element in place-names is widespread in the Hebrides, the far north of Scotland and the Northern Isles. The lack of Christian personal names among the specifics, and on Islay the lack of forms including 'kirk' or 'cross', suggests that these names all pre-date the Norse conversion to Christianity at the end of the tenth century. The three Islay clusters could represent a systematic division of large farms into smaller units, perhaps within a very short space of time, and possibly not that long after the initial land-taking.

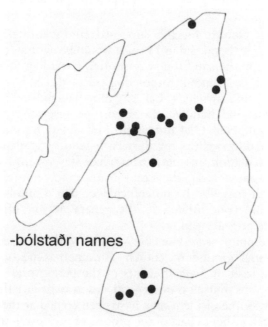

-bólstaðr names

Figure 8.2 Distribution of farms on MacDougall's map of Islay with *-bólstaðr* names, after Macniven, The Norse in Islay.

Finally, there are two Norse -*setr* names on Islay, represented today by the farm names of Staoisha and Erasaid. Since such names generally indicated shieling sites, the absence of any more on Islay may at first sight seem surprising. The explanation lies in the early adoption by Norse-speaking settlers of the Gaelic word *airigh*. An example of this may be the farm name Corary in the parish of Kilarrow. It is perhaps more likely to be a Norse coinage containing the ON generic *erg* (shieling) rather than Gaelic *airigh*, because of the word order. If Gaelic *airigh* were the generic, this term would have prefixed the specific. It might also be noted that Corary must be an early example of a shieling ground being turned into a permanent farm.

Norse was probably giving way to Gaelic as the spoken language of the people of Islay in the eleventh century, but the impetus for a whole new wave of place-names, in Gaelic, possibly only came with the acquisition of Islay by Somerled in 1156. Of the 178 farms on MacDougall's map, 18 include the element *baile*, making it one of the commonest types of farm names on the island. The fact that some of these incorporate Norse elements and personal names indicates that they do date to the period immediately after the domination of the Norse language. Whether or not, as suggested above, some *baile*- names replaced ones with -*bólstaðir*, their appearance on Islay might relate to another phase or incidence of land-granting, *baile* perhaps being the local vernacular term for Latin *villa*, in the sense of a townland, the term that might have been recorded in legal or fiscal documents.

The obvious context for this supposed land-granting would be the takeover of Islay by Somerled in 1156. It would be natural for him to place several of his supporters in his new territories, rewarding them with grants of land. Thus *baile*- names incorporating personal names may actually be recording their first owners – Ballachlaven, Ballighillan, Ballychatrigan, Ballyneal, Balole and Balulive, the townships, respectively, of Clement, Gillan, Chatrigan, Neil, Olaf and Uilbh. This situation would parallel that well documented in twelfth- and thirteenth-century Scotland where there is often documentation that place-names like Stevenston, Lamberton and Riccarton do commemorate the recent incomers to whom these lands had been granted. It may also be no coincidence that a number of the Islay *baile*- names are concentrated in the general region of the medieval lordship centre at Finlaggan.

Almost as common as *baile*- names are those with the Gaelic generic *cill*, meaning a burial ground or church. Although some of these names commemorate Irish or Scottish saints of the period prior to the arrival of the Vikings, this of itself is not a good reason to believe that all of them date that early. Some of them may have been coined at the same time as the *baile*- names, either as part of the process of organising the Church, or else to establish the credentials of the MacSorleys as supporters of local traditions.

Other Gaelic generic settlement elements found in Islay place-names include *tigh*, house. There are only three *tigh-* farm names on MacDougall's map – Taynornock (now Tayandock), Tighandrom and Tighcarmagan – surprisingly few if there really were any continuity of Gaelic language and tradition spanning the Norse period. After all, the earlier version of this word, *tech* (pl.), was used to quantify land holdings in the *Senchus fer nAlban*. *Gart*, 'field', and *goirtean*, 'enclosure', appear likely to be relatively late coinages, indicating the subdivision of existing holdings, or the creation of new from land previously considered marginal. Finally, we might note here some farm names like Airigh Ghuaidhre, Airigh re Abhaine and Airigh Sgallaidh, which are indicative of shieling grounds being occupied permanently and turned into new farms.

Land divisions and extent

Islay's settlement pattern compares well with circumstances in much of Scotland prior to modern times, but in one important respect the situation on Islay was anomalous – its system of land units. It is important to gain some understanding of this since, locked away in the nomenclature and valuations, are keys to the island's early history.

Islay lands were measured not in terms of their area, but their 'extent', the sum of money the tenants of each were to produce each year for the landholder. These extents, or valuations, became a convenient way of describing the worth of different lands. They are often provided not as pounds, shillings and pence but as merks. A merk was a unit favoured in accountancy, equivalent to 13s 4d, or two-thirds of a pound. Whereas the extent for many holdings remained the same from the sixteenth to the eighteenth century, the actual rent paid by the tenants increased with time and inflation. Thus the tenants of Sean-ghairt, a land with an extent of £1 13s 4d, were by 1722 required to pay £120 17s 4d Scots (£10 1s 5d sterling).

The earliest surviving extent of the island dates to 1507 when it was assessed in a Crown rental at £212 5s 4d Scots (a bit over 318 merks), including both the church lands and those in lay hands. It is clear, however, that some of the lands of Islay are missing from this rental, for instance those granted by Donald, Lord of the Isles, to Brian Vicar Mackay in 1408. Another estimate of Islay made at the end of the sixteenth century assesses it as 360 merks, that is £240. On the other hand, by 1733 the Stent Committee for Islay reckoned the island amounted to 135 quarter-lands, equivalent to an assessment of £225.[7]

The variations in these figures should teach some caution in interpreting fluctuations in the extent of individual lands over time. We should accept that individual farms might have their assessment changed because they were deemed more or less profitable, and not just because segments of land have been added or subtracted. It should also be said that rentals do not always include some of the lands for reasons including they were wadset (mortgaged), in different ownership, or not currently rented.

The 1494 charter by King James IV, awarding John MacIan of Ardnamurchan Islay lands and the office of bailie, provides the earliest evidence of what is known as the Islay quarterland system. A quarterland was a unit of land with an extent of $2\frac{1}{2}$ merks, or £1 13s 4d, and the evidence from rentals from 1507 onwards indicates that many lands were quarterlands or halves, quarters, etc. Half a quarterland was an auchten-part, or 16s 8d land, and quarter of a quarterland was a leorthas, or 8s 4d land. Even smaller fractions are occasionally found in later documents – a cota-ban, or groat land, with an extent of 4s 2d, and a Dha Sgillin, valued at 2s 1d.

The concept of a quarterland is not unique to Islay, but is found either explicitly, or implicitly, in the fiscal systems of large parts of Scotland and Ireland, albeit with different names. In Ireland four quarterlands made a *bailebiataigh*, while in other parts of Scotland the equivalent 'four-quarter-land' units were 'ouncelands', particularly in areas settled by Scandina-vians, and *davochs*, especially in former Pictish areas. There are no references whatever to any such parent denomination in Islay. Attempts, however, to link the Islay system of land extents to those in Ireland, or to see some continuity with an earlier system of land divisions, as reflected in the *Senchus fer nAlban*, have not been totally convincing.[8]

It is striking that 'quarterland' in its Gaelic form, *ceathramh*, is not found in Islay place-names, with one possible exception, Keirreishlaraich, a now-lost land, probably in the parish of Kilmeny, and not attested prior to the seventeenth century.[9] There are also seven place-names containing the Gaelic element *Ochdamh*, eighth, of which three are still current – Octofad, Octomore and Octovullin.[10] The limited number of these names suggests that they were coined comparatively late, certainly after the names for the larger units of land had stabilised. They may all belong to a relatively short period of time.

The Crown charter of 1499, granting extensive lands on Islay and elsewhere to John MacIan, does not value any of them as quarterlands. The smallest, and most common extent in this charter, comprising ten of the fifteen Islay holdings, is five merks, that is the equivalent of two quarterlands. The remaining holdings, with extents of 10, 20 and 60 merks, are all multiples of five merks. Is it possible that the fundamental settlement unit on Islay had an extent of five merks, and the quarterland terminology was an introduction, either by MacIan or royal clerks, to replace a system or terminology they disliked, or did not fully understand? The rental prepared by MacIan in 1507 does not give any information on tenants, but it may represent an attempt to portion pre-existing land-holdings among his own clan and supporters.

Out of 110 land-holdings in the 1507 rental, 63 have an extent of £1

13s 4d (2½), and of these 23 consist of two units of land, presumably each valued at 16s 8d. Later rentals indicate that auchtenpart, or 16s 8d lands, were typical single holdings. A system of five-merk units quartered into 16s 8d lands would make sense, and in terms of value, would compare reasonably well with the valuation of six merks often put on ouncelands and davochs elsewhere in Scotland.

'Ouncelands' were also prevalent on the Isle of Man, where they were known as treens, and divisible into four quarterlands called kerroo. Elsewhere in the West Highlands and Islands the ounceland was known in Gaelic as *tirunga*, and the quarterland as *ceathramh*. The Manx terms are clearly closely related to these Gaelic words.

The name implies a taxation system in which each ounceland was required to pay an ounce of silver, but whether rated at six or five merks, the medieval extent of these lands would have amounted to rather more in silver coinage than an ounce. The explanation for this appears to lie in a revalorisation, referred to in rentals and other documents as 'the old extent'. This is believed to have been conducted for the Scottish Crown soon after the acquisition of the Hebrides through the Treaty of Perth in 1266.

It is possible, using the evidence of early charters and rentals, and other information on boundaries, principally those for parishes, to produce a tentative map (Fig. 8.3) showing how Islay could have been divided into five-merk land units. If the Islay five-merk units were equivalent to ouncelands, then the auchtenpart lands would originally have been quarterlands.[11]

In the West Highlands and Islands there is yet another type of land unit, the pennyland (Gaelic, *peighinn*), which is of relevance to our study of Islay. In terms of extent, there were twenty pennylands to one ounceland. Remarkably, however, there are no pennylands in either the Isle of Man or Islay.[12] Might this be because lands in these islands, as possessions of the kings of the Isles, were exempt from paying a money tax? Or has all evidence for a pennyland assessment on the island also been wiped away by the changes made by John MacIan?

There may be no evidence for pennylands on Islay, but seventeenth- and eighteenth-century rentals provide evidence for cowlands of 3s 4d. There were therefore, twenty cowlands in a five-merk land unit. The equivalence of Islay cowlands to pennylands is difficult to resist. Cowlands are unknown elsewhere in Scotland, but do occur in Ireland, mostly in north-west Ulster.[13] The earliest reference to them on Islay is in a charter of 1506 which describes Proaig as consisting of six cowlands. This land had an extent of 20s in the rental of 1507.

A series of grants by Ranald, son of Somerled, his son Donald and Angus Mor of Islay, recorded in the register of Paisley Abbey, are made in terms of a penny from each house on their lands from which smoke exits, or else a total of eight cows.[14] Perhaps these grants reflect in some way an earlier taxation system, which required pennies or cows, and gave rise to lands called penny-lands and cowlands.

Figure 8.3 Map of Islay with hypothetical early parishes
and 5-merk units, after Macniven, The Norse in Islay.

There are no compelling reasons to see any links between any of these land units – five-merk land units, quarterlands/auchtenpart lands, cowlands – and the earlier house system of the *Senchus fer nAlban*. It is more likely that these units were introduced, probably severally, between the arrival of Scandinavian colonists and the annexation of the island by Somerled.

There was also a need to group these land units into larger administrative areas. It may be highly speculative on the basis of surviving evidence, but certainly not unlikely, to imagine that Islay had at one time a hierarchical system of districts similar to that established on the Isle of Man.[15]

Early rentals provide the information that the island had three wards – the Rhinns, the Herreis or Midward, and the Largie or Southward, and each ward had an officer, or coroner, to act as the lord's or laird's agent (see Chapter 7). These wards corresponded to the medieval parishes, respectively, of Kilchoman, Kilarrow and Kildalton, well documented from the fourteenth century onwards. It is possible, however, that when the parochial structure was established on Islay in the twelfth century, that there were six, the other three being centred on Kilchiaran in the Rhinns, Kilnaughton in the Oa, and at Kilmeny. At all three of these locations there are the ruins of relatively large medieval chapels, though admittedly none appear to be any older than the fourteenth century.

Parishes were primarily about the provision of church services to the population at large, but underlying their divisions it may be possible to detect an early system of secular administration. There are eighteen lands on Islay, including those that provide their names to the putative six medieval parishes, that are all formed with a *cill-* prefix, in most cases followed by the name of a recognisable early Irish or local saint. These names, like Kilslevan and Killelegan, would originally have identified particular churches and burial grounds, in these two cases, the dry-stone chapels of Slébhine and Findlugán, respectively, but clearly these names became of much greater significance when they were applied thus to lands or districts.[16]

An analysis of these *cill-* names demonstrates that they are spread fairly evenly throughout the island. With the passage of time, some place-names may have been lost or others added, and the lands or districts they identify will have changed in shape and importance. Nevertheless, underlying this distribution of *cill-* names there is a suggestion of an original pattern that had some meaning, perhaps one in which there were three *cill-* units in each of six parishes.

One explanation is that the *cill-* names represent an original parish structure; perhaps one imposed in the first half of the twelfth century by the Manx king, Olaf Bitling. He is credited with establishing parishes on the Isle of Man, of which there are seventeen, perhaps originally sixteen.[17] There may then have been a rationalisation of this structure on Islay into fewer, larger parishes in the time of Ranald, son of Somerled. In Figure 8.3, the evidence for '5-merk units' is combined with a modified version of this data on *cill-* names to suggest a possible early structure of eighteen parishes.

Units of land, whether parishes, estates or farms, had physical boundaries. It was probably always the case that the boundaries of the larger, administrative units respected those of the smaller estate or farm boundaries, so that, for instance, individual lands were not bisected by parish boundaries. How the boundaries of these lands were known or recorded before modern times is not altogether clear. Until the eighteenth century, the boundaries between neighbouring lands were probably not defined by dykes or fences, although the tenants of each farm would have been well aware of the boundaries of their land.

Farmers from earliest times may have been less concerned about the marches of their lands than the divisions between their own fields, or rigs of arable, and securing their crops from depredations by cattle. The rough pasture beyond the head dykes was certainly undivided, although there were agreements or understandings in place as to the shielings for the exclusive use of individual farms or townships. For many Islay farms, the shielings were fairly close to the arable land and the beasts must have been herded to prevent them from straying on to the crops or neighbouring farms where there were no dykes or fences to hold them in. More than one late-eighteenth-century writer commented on the lack of dykes or fences.[18]

Stephen MacDougall's surveys of Islay dating to 1749–51 mark a significant new step as they were not just about building up an overall map of the island for Daniel Campbell of Shawfield. They were primarily about establishing the acreage of each farm. It was probably MacDougall who computed a table giving the areas of each farm on the island.[19] The total area for the whole estate (almost all of Islay) was given as 110,787 Scots acres (about 56,960 hectares), and the 171 farms varied in size from 4,695 Scots acres (about 2,414 hectares) to 40 Scots acres (about 20.6 hectares).

The boundary lines drawn by MacDougall on his map were, for the most part, not on the ground in the form of walls, dykes or fences. Daniel Campbell the younger was determined that they should be. The standard leases for Islay farms issued from the 1770s required the tenants to build proper march dykes. They not only had to straighten the marches in the process, but also exchange pieces of ground with neighbouring farms, all for the improvement and good order of the country.[20] Since the dykes that the tenants then had the resources to build themselves were traditional-style ones of turf and stone, we might expect that many such march dykes, particularly relatively straight and distinct ones, were first laid out in the late eighteenth century. The professionally built dry-stone dykes, many of Galloway type, also encountered as march dykes, may for the most part, only date to the nineteenth century when, it is said, dry-stone dykers were brought in from Durham, Northumberland and Galloway.[21]

MacDougall's map, and the accompanying surveys, mark a logical conclusion to centuries of development. They show the island divided up into farms, each with a share of arable and pasture for animals. There is no land that is outwith this grand scheme, and by definition, all the islanders were included in it, each with a share of the land and its produce, whether as tacksmen, tenants or subtenants. MacDougall was no doubt recording considerable improvements and rationalisations encouraged or imposed by Daniel Campbell of Shawfield, but it would not be long before this scheme would be seen as traditional and not capable of incorporating improvements in land management being developed elsewhere – generally an impediment to progress.

Living on the Land

Climate and land quality, neither of which were constant, even in historic times, were major factors in creating continuity in the type of farming undertaken on Islay. Until the introduction of potatoes it is difficult to imagine that viable alternatives to oats and barley as staple crops could have been adopted. Much of the land was not suited for agriculture, only for grazing animals, whether cattle, horses, sheep or goats. It would still have been possible, however, within these basic restrictions, to vary practices and produce quite considerably. Perhaps for much of the period under consideration the Ilich were more interested in following traditional practices than introducing changes. When the latter came, they appear to have been imposed or introduced from outside by the lairds rather than innovations developed locally and spread from the bottom of society upwards.

Farming prior to the arrival of the Campbells

Surviving documents offer little information on medieval farming and only a little can be deduced from the archaeological evidence. An observation of relevance here is that the Islay landscape contains many remains of field systems consisting of small, irregular, contiguous fields. They are defined by turf and stone dykes and contain cultivation rigs. The rigs are normally narrow, 2 m to 3 m wide, and were dug with spades. Some of these systems clearly belong to prehistoric times, like those at An Sithean, dated as a result of radiocarbon dates from samples taken in recent archaeological excavations. At An Sithean the fields are associated with clearance cairns and hut circles, also of prehistoric date; but these traces were adapted and overlain at a later date by rather similar fields enclosing rigs, believed by the archaeologists who investigated the site to be of medieval or post-medieval date. Pennant passed this way in 1772 and mentioned 'some cairns, and some ancient fences on the heaths', perhaps indicating that the fields were long since out of use at that time.[1] Several other groups of enclosed fields with rigs show no obvious traces of a

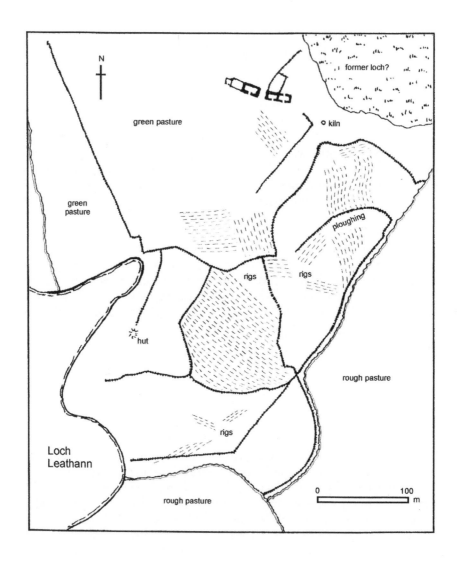

Figure 9.1 Sketch plan of old field system at NGR NR 412 634,
possibly the farm of Arivuine. The kiln and houses to the north
are of eighteenth- or nineteenth-century date.

prehistoric past, like those around Loch Finlaggan on the lands of Sean-ghairt, Portaneilean (Finlaggan) and Robolls.

Elsewhere on the island there are concentrations of these enclosed field systems in the parish of Kildalton. In the Oa they can be found on the lands of Stremnishbeg and Stremnishmore. Further east there are other systems on the lands of Kilbride, Balynaughtonbeg and Balynaughton-more, and Ardtalla. A group to the east of Loch Leathan on the land of Eacharnach, possibly representing the old farm of Arivuine, contain broad, s-curved rigs characteristic of early ploughing (Fig. 9.1). Although these field systems may be of medieval origin, they undoubtedly remained in use much more recently. Until the seventeenth century, many of these field systems would have appeared like islands in a sea of moor and unimproved pasture. There were probably no march dykes.

It can be assumed, on the basis of evidence from other parts of the country and our knowledge of farming practices at a later date, that the main crops grown were barley and oats, both mostly for human con-sumption. The 1541 rental required a quarterland to pay yearly 4 marts (oxen or cows ready for slaughter), 4 wethers (castrated rams), 10 shillings, 30 stones of cheese, 30 stones of meal (presumably either oats or barley), 4 geese and 4 fowl (hens, etc.). The balance of produce suggests a mixed farming economy aimed at providing subsistence for the island's popula-tion. The relatively high quantity of cheese probably reflects the fact that sheep as well as cows were being milked. That tenants were expected to pay a part of their rent as cash suggests there must have been a limited money economy at the time.

These tenants had practically no security of tenure and may have been subject to removal on a yearly basis. In practice, most may have been left in possession for long periods of time, provided they paid their rents and supported their chiefs. The royal rental of 1541, in that it specified that the lands were being set for three years only, may even have introduced a level of uncertainty not hitherto understood.

Although the documentation for the cattle-droving business from Islay concerns the period from the very end of the sixteenth century onwards, there is reason to think that it may be of greater antiquity. The land quality maps produced by the Macaulay Institute clearly show that most of Islay, despite its reputation as one of the most fertile of the Hebrides, now contains little land that would be deemed suitable for crops of cereal. There are, on the other hand, extensive pastures, and mild winters, and it is likely that the island has always been of more value for cattle than corn. It may not be unreasonable to assume that there would have been cattle available for export in the Medieval Period.

It does seem significant that in 1506 there were ninety-six marts and their followers at Ross in Knapdale, having just been taken by sea from Islay.[2] This represents the Crown getting to grips with the rents of the lands of the Lordship of the Isles in the aftermath of the forfeiture of John

II in 1494, but are we to believe that such shipments from Islay and the other Isles were a relatively new phenomenon? Traditional Highland lordship involved the conspicuous consumption of produce,[3] but there could still have been a significant surplus of cattle for export. Stock-raising must have made a contribution to the wealth of the Lordship of the Isles, and helped underpin the economy of the Scottish burghs and the country's export business in cattle products.

In 1609 Angus MacDonald of Dunyvaig was one of the West Highland chiefs who successfully petitioned the Privy Council to rescind a recent proclamation forbidding the purchase of cattle and horses in the Isles. The chiefs persuaded the Council they would be unable to pay their rents to the Crown if they could not sell their beasts.[4] It is evident that the trade in cattle must then have been a business of some extent. The record of a deal in 1599 between Angus's son, Sir James of Knockrinsey and a merchant burgess of Perth, Andrew Donaldson (a MacDonald?) survives. By it Donaldson was to take delivery in Islay of 120 marts, for which he was to pay in Edinburgh 1440 merks (equivalent to £960, or £8 each).[5]

The archaeology of medieval stock-raising has been little sought, and there may indeed be little to see but the extensive areas of moorland where cattle were pastured in the summer months. Some possible medieval shieling huts can, however, be identified, particularly the remains of four circular houses in the vicinity of the large nineteenth-century sheepfold at Airigh Ghuaidhre (Fig. 10.3). They are represented by rings of turf collapsed from their walls. All are 7 m to 7.5 m in overall diameter, and three of them are cut into gently sloping ground, with their entrances facing down-slope. Traces of these houses have only survived because they are beyond the limits of once cultivated ground. They may date to a time before the colonisation of this pastureland, a development prior to 1494 when it was one of the lands granted to John MacIan. Since Airigh Ghuaidhre is sited in the moor beyond the fort of Dun Guaidhre (on the land of Kilmeny), it is likely that it was originally the shieling ground for there.

Shieling grounds might be developed into farms as the land around these temporary summer settlements was improved by manure, and as shielings were turned into arable land, new shieling grounds had to be found. Such developments were always likely to be happening, and might be accelerated from time to time by factors such as periods of improved weather and population growth. Equally, less productive and more remote arable plots might be abandoned as permanent habitation centres when the climate deteriorated or there was less population pressure.

Doodilmore, in the parish of Kilmeny, is another example of a shieling ground being developed into a permanent farm, this time in the sixteenth century. It is first recorded as a separate farm in 1541. It resulted from a division of Doodil sometime after 1509 into Doodilbeg and Doodilmore.[6] Doodilmore appears to this day like an island of green, formerly cultivated ground in the moors. It is not without significance that a piece of adjacent moorland is called Airigh Mhic Dhomhnaill (MacDonald's shieling). Doodilmore was deserted by the middle of the nineteenth century.

Colonisation of shieling grounds in the sixteenth century is probably also represented by the adjacent lands of Upper and Lower Leorin, misnamed the two lands of Lennynes in the grant of the Barony of Bar to James MacDonald in 1545. As planned in the early nineteenth century, Lower Leorin appears as a model, unimproved farm, with arable fields surrounding the township and a large tract of pasture beyond (Fig. 9.2). The old road from Dunyvaig to Laggan Bay and beyond runs to the east of the township, and to the west of the road lies Upper Leorin, which does not appear to have developed such a strong arable base as its neighbour. An early nineteenth-century plan indicates that there was still an expanse of 'common muir' to its east.[7]

Upper and Lower Leorin may have developed contemporaneously as two contiguous but separate settlements. It is probable, however, that the splitting of a land into an upper and a lower, or a 'more' and a 'beg', has generally resulted from a medieval expansion of arable activity at the expense of shieling grounds. Apart from Doodilbeg and Doodilmore, likely examples include Balynaughtonmore and Balynaughtonbeg, and Stremnishbeg and Stremnishmore. Such processes would have created farms with no, or limited, access to shieling grounds, including some along the south coast of the island and others along the north bank of the River Sorn.

The rental of 1507, with its pairing of several lands to make up quarterlands, may be demonstrating the requirement for each agricultural unit to have access to adequate grazing. Thus Eorrabus was coupled with neighbouring Esknish, the latter adding moorland to the largely arable Eorrabus. In many cases the pairings were of contiguous lands, but in others they were separate. Such was the unit composed of Bolsa and part of Scanistle. Scanistle was relatively fertile land hemmed in by other agricultural units, whereas Bolsa was primarily land for grazing. Other lands retained shielings as pendicles – detached portions. This was the case with Nosebridge, which had Allallaidh as a pendicle, and Ballyneal, which had Arivoichallum as its shieling. Conas-airigh (NR 365 497 – by the early nineteenth century, part of Upper Leorin) is probably the 'shielding in the muir' of Torradale and the 'sheltering in the muire' for Ardmenoch was possibly a good six miles away in Gleann a' Chromain. None of these arrangements are recorded prior to the eighteenth century but all are likely to be of some antiquity.

Other examples of an expansion of arable land in the sixteenth century at the expense of shielings probably include such small holdings as Ellay, Galtak and Margadale in the parish of Kilmeny, each with an extent of 8s 4d or less; Leatur, valued at 6s 8d, in the parish of Kildalton; and Skelrioch, valued at 8s 4d, in the parish of Kilarrow. Of these, Ellay and

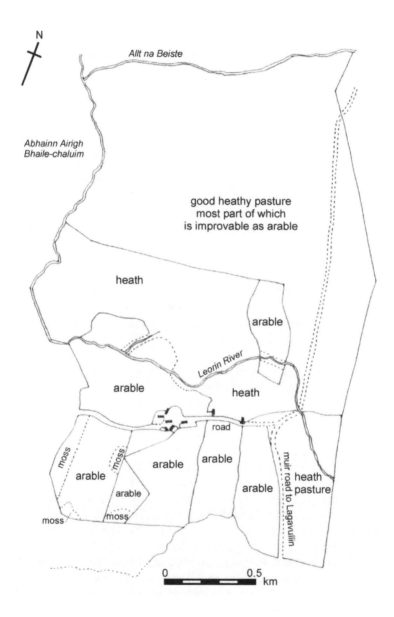

N

Allt na Beiste

Abhainn Airigh
Bhaile-chaluim

good heathy pasture
most part of which
is improvable as arable

heath

arable

Leorin River

arable

heath

road

moss

moss

arable

arable

arable

arable

arable

moss

heath
pasture

muir road to Lagavulin

moss

moss

0   0.5
km

Figure 9.2 Plan of the farm of Lower Leorin about 1830,
redrawn from the original William Gemmill map
in the Ramsay of Kildalton Papers (ML, TD 1284/9/12).

Galtak are not recorded after 1654, and Skelrioch disappears after 1686. There may be a clue here that these were not sustainable in the long term as arable units.

A more important consideration prior to the Campbell takeover than the carrying capacity of the land for animals was its ability to support fighting men. A report on the Isles written in the 1590s says that each merk land on Islay supported one household man, free from any work on the land, for service whenever required by his lord.[8] This is clearly a continuation of the system that allowed the Lords of the Isles to raise large forces for warfare. The fact that it was based on merk lands rather than quarterlands raises some interesting issues. It indicates it was a system of considerable antiquity.

Farming on Islay in the Post-Medieval Period

Field evidence on Islay indicates that a type of farming, known as an infield–outfield system of agriculture, was widely practised. This was widespread throughout Scotland prior to the introduction of improved methods of farming in the late eighteenth and nineteenth century. In an infield–outfield system, crops were grown in rotation yearly on the infield, land that was regularly manured or fertilised and which lay around the farm settlement itself. The outfield was land beyond the infield, which was not normally fertilised. Crops would be sown in parts of it for a couple of years or so and then left fallow for several years to recoup. In the summer months, the farm beasts would be removed to the shieling grounds in the hills to benefit from the summer grass and to keep them well away from damaging the crops around the farm. The infield can often be distinguished from the outfield by the density of rigs, and in any case, they were often separated, one from the other, by turf dykes.

Groups of unenclosed rigs – or open fields – whether in the infield or outfield, imply a 'runrig' system of farm management in which the tenants' rigs were intermingled and reallocated from time to time in proportion to the extent of their holding. Lord Teignmouth recorded in 1836 that runrig was then still prevalent in Islay with rigs being exchanged at three-yearly intervals.[9]

These systems of agriculture were rarely static, so often what appears on the ground, in areas where all evidence has not been obliterated by modern ploughing, is a palimpsest of remains, sometimes including prehistoric houses, traces of small irregular enclosed fields, groups of unenclosed rigs and different phases of head dykes, pushing outwards to enclose more and more pasture that could be made to give up crops of corn or potatoes.

At Goirtean an Uruisge, at the head of Glen Logan, there is an example of an abandoned farm operated on the infield–outfield model, little obscured by earlier or later activity (Fig. 9.3). There are three ruined

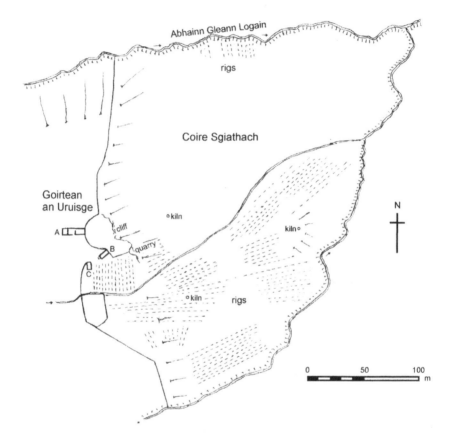

Figure 9.3 Sketch plan of the field system and settlement
at Goirtean an Uruisge (NR 420 624).

houses, the largest of which has been rebuilt as a sheepfold. Their walls are mostly of locally quarried blocks of limestone and phyllite, set in clay mortar. Against the end of one of these houses is a small secondary semicircular pen. There is an irregular shaped enclosure, bounded on one side by cliffs, which may have been a stack-yard, and across a stream to the south is a garden enclosed by a stone-and-earth dyke.

On lower ground to the east of the houses is Coire Sgiathach, a flat, approximately triangular, area contained between the confluence of the Abhainn Gleann Logain and a tributary. It is protected from the unwanted intrusion of beasts by a line of dykes from main river to tributary, connecting the garden and houses. These dykes, the river and stream define an area of relatively fertile, once-cultivated ground, surrounded by rough pasture.

Coire Sgiathach is divided in two by another, smaller stream flowing from the south of the houses, north-eastwards. To the south of it there has been intensive agricultural activity with groups of unenclosed rigs, each about 6 feet (1.83 m) wide. This was the infield. The outfield to the north contains much less evidence of rigs. The underlying geology is limestone, and there are two small circular limekilns, both less than 4 m in overall diameter. A substantial stone platform with a diameter of 5 m may either be another kiln, or else, perhaps, the base for corn-stacks.

Goirtean an Uruisge may tentatively be identified as the land called Gortan, paired with Eacharnach, in the rental of 1507, and also Skeag, mentioned in seventeenth-century rentals. The remains described, as suggested by the presence of the limekilns, would appear to relate to occupation from the late eighteenth century when 'Gartaninuisk' was recorded as a property detached from Airigh Ghuaidhre. Like the latter, it must have been cleared for sheep in the middle of the nineteenth century.[10]

Segments of head dykes can be traced on the ground in many parts of Islay. In most cases the arable land of a farm was contiguous to that of others and so head dykes progressed across the boundaries of more than one property. This is the case with dykes, originally marking the edge of rough pasture, that traverse the lands of a group of farms in the valley formed by the upper reaches of the River Laggan and the Barr River. The farms in question are Nosebridge, Cattadale, Roskern, Barr, Storakaig and Airigh Ghuaidhre. Only fragments of the dykes can readily be traced on the ground today but fieldwork observations are in this case backed up by the evidence of a series of farm plans for all of these farms, except Storakaig, dating to the 1820s or '30s. Another series of early nineteenth- or eighteenth-century plans, for the farms of Balole, Duisker, Baile Tharbhach and Ballachlaven, helps establish the line of head dykes marking the upper edge of cultivation along the north-west side of the valley formed by the River Sorn.[11]

Head dykes played an important role in infield–outfield systems of agriculture, and on Islay there appears to be no good reason to posit that any might be of earlier date. It is notable that shieling huts sometimes occur just outside the line of head dykes. Small groups of them are to be found near the head dykes of Ballachlaven (Plate XXIX) and Sean-ghairt. It is possible that these represent a phase before the erection of the head dyke, and the line of the head dyke consciously abuts a zone of shielings. These shielings could mark the nearest point to the arable land that beasts would be tolerated in the growing season. For what it is worth, the Ballachlaven head dyke appears to incorporate a shieling hut, perhaps of earlier date. Whether or not these shieling huts pre-date the head dyke they may represent a phase in the summer flitting of the beasts. There is plenty of evidence for other groups of shieling huts further out on the moors. Those that may have been occupied by the tenants of Ballachlaven and Sean-ghairt are at Airigh na Creige (NR 363 693), Airigh Ruadh (NR 369 689), Airigh an t-Sagairt (NR 368 698), Airigh an t-Sluic (NR 363 699), and Airigh nan Sidhean (NR 366 715). The nearest, Airigh Ruadh, is about half a mile away from the head dyke while the furthest, Airigh nan Sidhean, is over two miles away. It is likely they were not all in use at the same period.

On Islay, there is a plethora of *airigh* names, many still marking the location of groups of little collapsed turf-and-stone circular shieling huts. The type site published by the Royal Commission is at Margadale, where some twenty-five huts are strung out along the banks of a stream, probably at the boundary between the farms of Margadale and Ardnahoe.[12] In the Oa, just to the south of the road between Risabus and Lenavore, is another group, just where the boundaries of most of the lands in the Oa came together. Although many of these shieling sites may go back to the Medieval Period or earlier, most of the huts visible nowadays probably date to post-medieval times. In some cases they are mounded quite high, suggesting rebuilding over many seasons. An engraving published by Pennant in 1774 shows such huts in use on the neighbouring island of Jura. They were dome-shaped or conical, with walls of turf supported on a framework of branches.[13]

A later development may be represented by single, rectangular houses on the moorland, like one 5.65 m by 6.65 m at Cachlaidh Chreagach (NR 389 700) on the farm of Portaneilean, and another larger one (9 m by 9.25 m) represented by low, turf-covered walls and a yard, on the head dyke at Robolls (NR 392 673). They may be for all-the-year-round occupation by herdsmen. All-year occupation of the moorland grazings is also indicated by a small cottage on an early nineteenth-century plan of Ballachlaven Moor. It is labelled 'Herds cot', with a sizeable patch of 'ground improved by the herd and soil fine red'.[14] If these houses represent a move from joint herding of a farm's livestock by the tenants to the employment of professional herdsmen, we are probably seeing a development that took place only from the eighteenth century onwards.

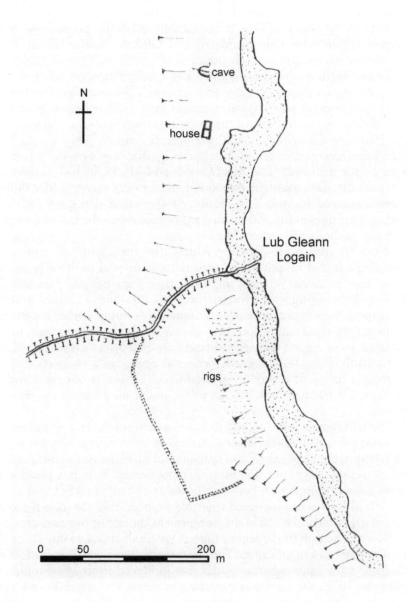

Figure 9.4 Sketch map of house and rigs
at Lùb Gleann Logain, on the Sound of Islay.

Some shieling sites, often using caves for shelter, were located around the coast, allowing for fishing as well (Plate XXX). A series of ruined eighteenth- or early-nineteenth-century houses with associated rigs and gardens on the Sound of Islay at the mouths of Gleann Logain (Fig. 9.4), Gleann Ghaireasdail (An Claddach) and Gleann Choireadail represent permanent occupation of such sites.

Infield–outfield agriculture goes back to medieval times in other parts of Scotland but its dating on Islay and relationship to early enclosed fields is not well understood.[15] Its development may well have taken place over several generations, but one of the main impetuses behind it was probably the incoming Campbells in the seventeenth century. They would have been introducing practices, including runrig, that they were more familiar with on the mainland. The MacDonalds and MacLeans had notoriously not paid the rents and feus they owed the Crown, except under duress. Now continued Campbell possession of the island depended on them paying these dues in full and making a profit for themselves. A shake-up in farming methods was part of the solution.

It can be seen from surviving rentals that the Campbell lairds were requiring a higher proportion of their rents to be paid to them in money rather than produce. Whereas in 1541 a typical quarterland paid only 10 shillings Scots, along with 4 marts, 4 wethers, 30 stone of cheese, 30 stone of oatmeal, 4 geese and 4 hens, in seventeenth-century rentals the money element rises significantly and the rent in kind drops. For instance, in the rental of 1654 a good quarterland paid over £60 Scots, a wether, a sheep and a lamb, some butter, geese, hens and eggs, and a proportion – for example a half – of a stirk (a young bullock). Meal is only included as multure, the payment in kind due to the miller for grinding the tenant's grain.

The rent money is most likely to have come from the raising and selling of stock, principally cattle. Young cattle were driven from Islay every year for sale at mainland markets and fattening on Lowland or English pastures before being slaughtered for meat. Unfortunately, it is not possible to make a direct comparison between the value of cattle in 1541 and 1654, but it is likely this had increased eightfold or more.[16] In that case the silver rent of a quarterland in 1654 might represent the sale of five or more cows and oxen. The shift in the rentals from payment of cheese to butter, by the 1630s, may be of significance. The cheese was almost certainly made from sheep or goats' milk whereas butter was produced from cows' milk.

In the 1630s the laird was exporting between 100 and 200 cattle per year. By 1688 the laird was hoping to sell 1,200 or more head of cattle from that year's drove to an Edinburgh merchant, John Hall. It is not clear if these were all his or included the beasts contributed to the drove by Islay gentlemen, but there is no reason to think that this was an exceptional quantity of cattle for the period. A financial account of two years later indicates the payments due to eleven Islay gentlemen from beasts sent on the drove of that year.[17] In the 1760s the number exported annually could be as high as 2,800, while in 1772 the travel writer, Thomas Pennant, was told that 1,700 cattle were exported yearly. Actual figures for this export business show that over 2,300 beasts were being transported from the island yearly between 1801 and 1807, and as many as 3,498 in 1801.[18] These figures perhaps represent a peak for the unimproved Islay black cattle.

Cattle, mostly stots (young oxen), were only exported when they were three years old. In 1695 the tenants of Islay agreed with Alexander Campbell, younger, of Cawdor, that from 1697 they would give him one three-year-old stot out of each quarterland on 10 July yearly. This was instead of the one- or two-year-old stirks they had previously paid, which the laird had difficulty looking after till they were ready for market, especially as he was not resident on the island.[19] It will be noted that this also seems to represent an increase in the number of cattle paid since the rental of 1654.

These cattle were driven to Port Askaig where they were kept in a fank (enclosure) until they could be ferried over to Feolin in Jura. This fank is first recorded in 1686. On Jura they were driven up past Loch a' Bhaile-Mhargaidh, said to be a place where cattle were bought and sold, to Lagg, or sometimes Kinuachdracht, from where they were shipped to the mainland. Some were sold at the cattle fair at Kilmichael Glassary near Lochgilphead. Most were taken on to the fair at Dumbarton, or increasingly from the 1770s, to the market at Falkirk. They were sold on for fattening on Lowland or English farms before being slaughtered for meat.[20]

Writing about Islay in the 1760s, the Revd Dr John Walker considered that the greatest defect in the agriculture of the island at that time was the lack of sown grass.[21] Haymaking was not much practised and there was thus little food to feed the animals over the winter months. Only the milk cows, however, were kept indoors. In most years the climate was mild enough for the rest of the beasts to survive outside, foraging for themselves.

Of considerable importance in the development of this cattle business were the drovers, who not only took the beasts from Islay to market but who often also acted as middlemen, buying and selling them. Some became very rich in the process. An Islay-based drover was Hector McNeill of Ardbeg (and perhaps previously of Portaneilean), described in the accounts of the Chamberlain of Islay for 1684 to 1687 as a drover, paid for driving Islay cattle to Falkirk. Falkirk was one of the main trysts (markets) for cattle from soon after 1707 onwards, and well into the nineteenth century.[22] Duncan McLauchlan, who had a house in Kilarrow by 1722, was another Islay drover. He was, by 1733, also renting the lands of Duisker and Ballimartin, no doubt convenient for gathering cattle on their way to the ferry at Port Askaig. Coll MacAlaster, the Bailie of Islay, had clearly built up a considerable network of commercial contacts with lairds, farmers, drovers and others on Islay, Jura, Colonsay and the mainland, prior to his death in 1747.[23] Other drovers came from the mainland to buy Islay cattle, like Archibald Campbell, Laird of Knockbuy (Minard in Knapdale) in the 1730s and '40s.[24]

It was noted in the 1760s that Islay farmers had for the last twenty years concentrated more on the raising of oxen (stots) at the expense of milk cows, resulting in a considerable rise in the price of butter. Nevertheless, in 1810 a third of the cattle on the island were reckoned to be milk cows.[25] More cattle meant more manure. It would also have meant that it was feasible not just to manure the infield but also parts of the outfield by folding the cattle in areas of it where it was intended to take a crop. Indeed, it is likely that the development of infield–outfield cultivation on Islay depended on an increase in the number of cattle.

The rental of 1722 gives the soum (grazing limits) imposed on each toun or land. This could vary considerably from one land to another, irrespective of their extent, but the island as a whole, excluding the Ballinaby Estate, could carry 6,685 cows and 2,220 horses. To these figures should be added the produce of each beast, that is animals of two years or less, and two sheep with their lambs for each cow.[26] These figures can be compared with those for the breeding stock of the island in the early 1980s – 5,700 beef cows, 1,196 dairy cows and 24,164 ewes.[27]

The evidence from testaments shows the importance of beasts to all Ilich. Alexander McDugald, probably with only an eighth share of the 16s 8d land of Kilbride, had in 1737 2 tidy (pregnant) cows, 1 farrow cow (that is a cow giving milk), 2 two-year-old stots (oxen), 1 three-year-old stot, 1 plough horse, 1 mare and 2 fillies, and 6 sheep with their lambs.[28] This seems to square reasonably well with his share of the soum for Kilbride which, overall, is given in 1722 as 30 cows and 16 horses. Testaments for other tenants seem to indicate that their stock was less than they may have been entitled to carry.[29] There are many possible reasons for this, including poverty and a climatic downturn. The testament of Lachlan Campbell, tacksman of Cladville, died 1737, notes that it does not include 10 big cows, 3 stots, 19 two-year-olds, 6 horses and 4 mares with their followers, that had all died in the spring of that year through the severity of the weather.[30]

On the other hand, William Campbell in the quarterland of (Easter) Ellister in 1733 had 14 tidy cows, 13 farrow cows with their stirks, 14 three-year-old cows and stots, 3 other stirks, 12 two-year-olds, a bull, 4 plough horses, 2 mares with their foals, 8 other mares, some with followers, 61 sheep and lambs, and 35 yeld (barren) sheep and wethers.[31] Easter Ellister's soum in 1722 was only 40 cows and 16 horses, so possibly some of these animals were pastured elsewhere on lands where the full soum allowance was not being utilised. This was probably also the case for other big-time farmers like John Campbell, the wadsetter of Killinallan, who at the time of his death in 1728 had 263 assorted cattle and 32 horses against a soum of 80 cows and 24 horses. The 1722 rental does indicate that he was then renting other neighbouring lands as well.[32] James Campbell, tacksman of Ardmore, had 134 assorted cattle and 14 horses, excluding followers, at his death in 1728, and Colin Campbell, wadsetter of Ellister, 251 cattle and 61 horses when he died in 1729, in both cases well above the carrying capacity of their main lands because they were renting others from the laird.[33] Mr John McVicar, the minister of Kildalton, was living on the land of Surnaig in 1720 where he kept some cattle and horses and grew oats and barley. He also held the lands of Ardinistle, Auchnacarrin and Torradale, where his animals were in the hands of his bowmen, that is, tenants who had hired grazing rights. Perhaps this was a common situation at that time.[34]

Islay cattle were smaller than modern breeds, hardy, and mostly black. By the end of the eighteenth century demand for them had outstripped cattle from other islands so that they fetched a higher price. In the first decade of the nineteenth century the average price for them was £8 10s, whereas cattle from Skye and Mull were only fetching £6.[35]

It is noteworthy that the inventories in these testaments never include pigs, and seldom goats. Rare examples of the latter are the eighteen goats listed among the goods of the deceased Lauchlan Campbell of Cladville and Tockmal in 1737 and Bailie Coll MacAlaster had nineteen when he died in 1747. Poultry are not mentioned either, although payments of geese, hens and eggs were required as part of the rent of most farms. The Revd John Walker bemoaned the fact that in the 1760s there were 4,000 to 5,000 geese wintered on the island but that their potential for providing quills and feathers was largely ignored. A note in the 1722 rental records that one of the attractions of Duich was that it had a rabbit warren, and about 80 dozen rabbit skins were being exported to Glasgow annually in the 1760s.[36]

Sheep were kept primarily for their wool and a supply of mutton. Horse rearing was, however, of some importance, not just for providing beasts of burden, for pulling ploughs and for riding, but also for export. The minister of Kilchoman mused in the 1790s that perhaps there were too many horses being kept, instead of cattle, but they brought a lot of money in sales, particularly to the Irish. In the early nineteenth century between 250 and 300 were being exported annually, as many as 120 to 180 of these being sold to Irish dealers.[37]

In the middle of the eighteenth century Daniel Campbell of Shawfield commissioned the surveyor, Stephen MacDougall, to map his Islay estate. Very few of the individual maps of lands survive but an overall plan of the island showing farm boundaries does (Fig. A2.1). It shows that almost all the rough pasture and moorland has been parcelled up and assigned to adjacent farms, no doubt preserving traditional links with shielings. It is probable that this rationalisation of boundaries remained, largely, a paper exercise, and would not have been demonstrable on the ground in the form of dykes. It was probably done in anticipation of Daniel's planned redemption of the Islay wadsets in 1760 and a massive exercise in issuing new leases for new tenants. He died, however, before he could carry this out.[38]

The minister of Kildalton Parish noted in 1794 that part of the extensive mountainous area of the parish was common to all the tenants, and no doubt the same would still have been perceived as being true at that time in the rest of the island.[39] Dykes marking the boundaries between farms probably only became necessary, or of importance, with the introduction of the infield–outfield system, but traditional understandings between neighbours on the location of shielings, and the imposition of soums, made the extension of dykes across the moors an unnecessary effort.

An accompanying statistical survey by MacDougall not only gives overall areas but also figures for the arable, green pasture and 'heathy pasture' of each. This threefold division reflected the infield–outfield system of farming then universally practised across the island. The area of arable on most farms was above 50 Scots acres (about 25.7 hectares) and might represent half or more of the total area. Many farms had relatively little green pasture, perhaps because this had, by MacDougall's time, been turned into permanent arable. A few farms, on the other hand, like Proaig, Bolsa and Cove, were almost entirely rough pasture, suitable only for stock raising.[40]

As important in the farming economy as access to rough pasture was the availability of bogs for cutting peat for use as fuel, a task still practised by some islanders today. Old peat cuttings can be found all over the island. Eighteenth- and nineteenth-century leases were concerned to ensure that cuttings were made in an orderly fashion.

The staple crops remained oats (often just listed as corn) and barley. A note in the 1722 rental says, however, that the inhabitants also sowed yearly peas, rye and potatoes. At that time, and in later years, much more oats were sown than barley, typically five to eight times the quantity of the former to the latter. This was probably not always the case, with as much barley as oats being sown in the seventeenth century. In the 1760s there was a surplus of potatoes, which were being exported for sale. It was also noted that not only was the planting of potatoes good for helping to reclaim ground for agricultural purposes but also for encouraging the local linen industry. The reasoning behind the latter statement was that they were cheaper and growing them required much less effort than grain. By the early nineteenth century it was reported that potatoes were being grown in a fifth of the cultivated land on the island.[41]

The Islay corn was the 'small grey oat' rather than the 'white oat' which was grown in the Lowlands. The small grey oat (bristle-pointed) was slow in ripening but could stand up to high winds. Its grains were much smaller than the white variety.[42] The barley being sown in the 1760s and much later was actually bere, a four- or six-row variety of barley which was hardier and coarser than the two-row barley grown in the Lowlands and elsewhere. The bere was said to give as much as an elevenfold return, the oats sixfold.[43] Since the grain was often still damp when it was harvested, it had to be dried in a kiln before it could be ground into meal. There are numerous ruins of these kilns all over the island, small circular structures, lined with stones (Plate XXXI).

The bere by the eighteenth century was increasingly being used for brewing and distilling while the oats were consumed in the form of bannocks, porridge and gruel. The inventory of the possessions of Neil Smith in Esknish, died 1739, details the utensils used to prepare his corn for food. He had a knocking stone (stone tub or mortar) for pounding it and a mill (quern) for grinding it into meal. There was a griddle for baking his bannocks and a sowan kit – a wooden tub for fermenting sowans, a dish made from oat husks and fine meal.[44]

Although querns were commonly used from prehistoric times onwards, tenants were thirled to mills provided by, or approved by, their landlords, and were obliged to have all their corn ground there, paying a proportion of their corn as a multure. The multures due from each land are recorded in rentals. The first mills with upright waterwheels were probably only replacing the earlier clack-mills in the late seventeenth century. By 1733 there were nine of the new mills, operated by professional millers, spread through the island, at Dunyvaig, Kintour and Killeyan in the parish of Kildalton; at Breakachey, Glassans (Skiba) and Octofad in the parish of Kilchoman; and Ballygrant and Kilarrow in the parish of Kilarrow. Other meal mills were erected later in the century at Glengeoy (Eallabus) and Ardnish (Nerabus), and at Glenastle in the Oa in the nineteenth century.

A major factor in improving crop production by the eighteenth century was the increasing use of fertilisers other than manure, the household midden and old thatch. Farms with access to the shores would have availed themselves of seaweed and sand. It is also probable that old midden deposits were cleared from the more accessible caves around the coast. The biggest difference was made by the practice of liming, introduced in the middle of the century. Islay was fortunate in having extensive deposits of Dalradian limestone that could readily be quarried, and there are several ruins of small, circular kilns in which it was burnt, in many parts of the island, often several to a farm.[45]

Encouragement to improve farms and farming was provided by the leases introduced by the Campbells of Shawfield from the early 1750s, normally for nineteen years. They gave security of tenure but also forced would-be tenants to bid against each other for desirable farms. Conditions imposed upon tenants in the tacks issued from the 1770s included the taking in and cultivation of pieces of moorland or bog, extending to four acres for each quarterland each year. Alternatively, they were to plant potatoes in this same extent of previously uncultivated ground.[46] Presumably the intention was not only to bring more ground into cultivation and thereby increase the crops grown, but also to, gradually, break down the old system of infield–outfield farming.

Much land was prepared for cultivation with spades. This is evident by the survival of systems of narrow rigs in areas which have not been subjected to modern ploughing. The rigs shed excess water which was allowed to drain away in the furrows. Eighteenth-century testaments, however, show that even the poorest tenants had horses, often specified as plough horses, and ploughs and their associated equipment appear in the inventories of the richer farmers.

Some early nineteenth-century plans of Islay farms show how old methods of farming were being transformed in this way – for instance, the farm of Airigh Ghuaidhre (Fig. 9.5), where it is possible to distinguish the old infield as an area of arable lying immediately to the west of the township. To the south of this arable is the old outfield, together with the infield forming an oval area contained by a head dyke. The outfield is marked as either arable or pasture, depending on whether it was then lying fallow. The surrounding areas of heath (pasture) and moss (bog) appear to be in the process of being improved, some being described as pasture, or even arable. A new head dyke has been created to the east, separating off an extensive area of 'heathy pasture'. At Lower Leorin, at the same time, it

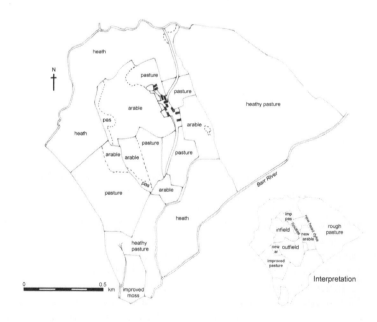

Figure 9.5 Plan of the farm of Airigh Ghuaidhre about 1830
with an interpretation of its field system. The main plan is redrawn
from the map by William Gemmill (NAS, RHP 11082).

appears that the outfield has all been upgraded to arable, and much of the old rough pasture is marked as 'good heathy pasture most of which is improvable as arable' (Fig. 9.2). This confidence in what could be achieved is demonstrated by other contemporary farm plans, but, as at Lower Leorin, was often shown to be misplaced optimism.

A rather idyllic picture of life for small farmers on joint tenancy farms is given by the journalist, John Murdoch, remembering his childhood on Islay in the 1820s. Speaking specifically of Kilchiaran in the Rhinns, he describes how it had the homes of twenty-five families. Six of these families were the 'regular farmers' or tenants holding directly from the proprietor, the rest being cottars who had houses, and enjoyed certain privileges, from the chief tenants. The arable land was fenced off into six portions, indicating allocations for the length of the lease rather than a yearly redistribution through a system of runrig. A rotation was practised of oats, potatoes manured from the farmyard and from the shore with seaweed and shell sand, barley, oats, and then fallow for one or two years. The oats were chiefly eaten in the form of porridge and oatcakes, while the barley was used to pay the rent. Beyond the arable land was unreclaimed upland or common where the farmers' animals were grazed. Sheep and cattle were mostly kept outside all year round, except the milk cows and working horses.

Murdoch further makes the point that

> [few of them] had attempted the raising of wheat, rye-grass or turnips; and, on the whole, the system of husbandry was far from being what would meet with a commendation from an agriculture committee of the Highland Society. Still, these men lived comfortably; brought up large families in plenty; exercised generous Highland hospitality towards all comers; paid their rents regularly and well and could have found a whole year's rent in advance without selling a head of stock or a sack of grain for the purpose. Every one of them had more than that amount to his credit in the bank at Inverary.[47]

Homes

There are substantial remains of the residence of the Lord of the Isles at Finlaggan, but of their house at Kilchoman there is no trace. The homes of lesser folk in the Medieval Period have so far eluded discovery. Possible candidates include the foundations of two barrel-shaped houses, one with turf walls near the chapel on Nave Island,[48] and the other, about 15 m by 3 m, defined by orthostatic slabs on a hill terrace at NR 413 659 near the broch of Dun Bhoraraic. They may be compared with other similar-shaped medieval houses excavated at Finlaggan.

The residences of some of the chief men of Islay prior to the arrival of the Campbells can be identified. They may be divided into those sited on rocky outcrops and those on islands, mostly artificial in origin. In all cases there is reason to believe that use of the sites extends back in time at least to the Medieval Period. Foremost in the first category is the MacDonald castle of Dunyvaig on the south coast of the island. It includes an outer and inner courtyard, both overlooked by a small rock stack crowned by a hall. Almost all of the work is of medieval date.[49]

The MacLeans were probably the builders of a house on the fort of Am Burg on the land of Coull (Plate XXXII). The fort is a coastal rock stack, its summit at least partially surrounded by a rubble wall. It was only accessible by a steep path from the shore below. The house is now represented by turf-covered foundations indicating a building about 12 m by 7 m overall with opposed entrances, and at one end a smaller, narrower chamber. This is the 'vestiges of various habitations, the retreat of the ancient natives in times of irresistible invasion' viewed by Pennant, the Welsh travel writer, in 1772,[50] and may represent the MacLeans' last toehold on Islay after they were evicted from Loch Gorm Castle in 1578.

A much smaller coastal stack, Dunan Mor, on the land of Laggan, has a flat, triangular summit defended by a wall of boulders, and is reached by a stepped path from the seaside. This may be the medieval and later residence of the Macbraynes. On the land of Lossit in the Rhinns, a triangular dry-stone enclosure, about 10 m by 8 m, overlies the outworks of a dun (small Iron Age or Early Historic fort) on a rocky summit overlooking Lossit Bay (Plate XXXIII). It may mark the residence of the chief of the MacFarquhars. A rectangular stone enclosure about 10 m by 12 m, on the summit of the dun, Dun Mideir, on the land of Greamsay, can be identified as the residence of the chief of the MacKays.

On the land of Mulindry, on the shoulder of a hill rather than a separate outcrop, is Caisteal Mhic Dhomhnuill (MacDonald's castle), defined by a ruined wall or bank of stones enclosing a circular space about 20 m in diameter. The interior is obscured by stones and quarry pits. This monument is difficult to assess in its present condition but its name and position suggest that it is the residence, with more than one house, where Angus MacDonald of Dunyvaig is said to have persuaded a reluctant Lachlan MacLean of Duart to stay with him in 1586.

One of the island settlements is recorded along with Dunyvaig in a written source of 1549 as one of the 'strynthie castells' on Islay. This is the castle of Loch Gorm on the land of Sunderland in the Rhinns. The only structure likely to pre-date 1615 that can be traced is a hall of dry-stone construction, measuring 7.5 m by 4 m internally, the work either of the MacDonalds, or the MacLeans. Since it was buried in a later earthwork its walls survive almost to full height, enough to show that it was a single-storey structure with a cruck-framed roof.

Eilean Mhic Iain in Loch Lossit belonged to the Church and is specifically listed in early sixteenth-century rentals. The name suggests it was occupied by MacIan of Ardnamurchan, but later in the century, perhaps in the 1570s, it was granted by the Bishop of the Isles to Hector ('Allansoun') MacLean, Bailie of the Rhinns for MacLean of Duart. It was presumably the principle messuage of the tenandry of Lossit described in legal language in a sasine (seisin) of 1692 as 'the tour fortalice and mannour place of Losset'. This need not be taken as an exact description, or evidence that it was still occupied at that time – the then abandoned castle of Dunyvaig is given in the same document as the principle messuage of the barony of Islay. A defensive wall encloses an oval area about 35 m by 38 m containing the foundations of two substantial rectangular houses at right angles to each other. Both are about 11 m by 6 m. A third house, less regular in plan, is clearly of later date since it partially overlies one of the others.[51]

There are four other crannogs or island dwellings, probably all of considerable age but with buildings which appear likely to date to the sixteenth century. All have traces, or substantial remains, of perimeter walls which would have been defensive in nature. They typically have two buildings each, one presumably a dwelling, the other a barn. Eilean Mhuireill in Loch Finlaggan, belonging to the land of Robolls, was a MacIan possession, perhaps his official residence as Bailie of Islay. In 1542 Hector MacLean of Duart was awarded Robolls, and it was later in-corporated into the Barony of Duart. The crannog in Loch Laingeadaill in the Rhinns appears to have been on lands of the Abbey of Iona recorded in the rental of 1561 as being held by Clan Donald. The other two crannogs, Loch Corr, either on the land of Sanaigbeg or Kindrochit, and Loch nan Deala on the land of Keills, were lands leased by the Crown to the MacDonalds of Dunyvaig from 1562.[52]

The homes of the lesser tenants and other people in the sixteenth century have not been traced anywhere on Islay, with the notable exception of Eilean Mor in Loch Finlaggan. The island is of some size, with an area of over 7,000 square metres, and excavations have demonstrated how a farming township was built in and over the ruins of the substantial complex of medieval buildings. The only medieval building that remained in use was the chapel, along with its burial ground.[53]

The settlement included at least twelve sub-rectangular or oval houses with rubble walls, either of dry-stone construction or held together with clay mortar. They had earth floors and probably pitched roofs of thatch and turf. Several of them had opposed entrances. Not all were necessarily houses as distinct from barns or byres, but at least one had a central fireplace. There were also two kilns, presumably for drying corn. The main building was a rectangular structure, 7.3 m by 6.4 m with gable walls, still largely upstanding (Plate XXXIV). It has a ground-floor chamber and an upper storey contained in the roof space. The walls are of coursed random rubble in lime mortar and are partially of medieval date. It would appear to have been the residence of somebody of some status locally, and the obvious candidate is Donald MacGillespie, crown tenant of Portaneilean in the 1540s. There are no local parallels for 'MacGillespie's House'.

An arrangement of four large post settings and a spread of nails were discovered in excavations near the highest point on the island. These may tentatively be identified as evidence for a wooden watchtower about 3 m square. A plinth of stones might have been a step providing access, or supporting a ladder. Such timber towers are shown in English views of Inisloughan Fort and a crannog under siege in Ulster in 1602.[54] Inisloughan was a stronghold of the O'Neills and had a square timber tower with gun-loops below a flat top surrounded by a wooden handrail. The unidentified crannog may be that of Lough Roughan, County Tyrone, captured by the English in 1602. It had a wooden tower shown only as a framework of timbers – four corner posts braced together at top and bottom by cross-beams. Perhaps it was erected hurriedly in anticipation of the siege, but left incomplete.

There is no archaeological evidence for how long the township on Eilean Mor remained occupied. The complete lack of common, typical seventeenth-century artefacts like copper coins, Throsk-type pottery and glass bottles suggests that it did not survive long into that century. The adjacent crannog, Eilean na Comhairle (the Council Isle), does not appear to have been occupied as late as the sixteenth century.

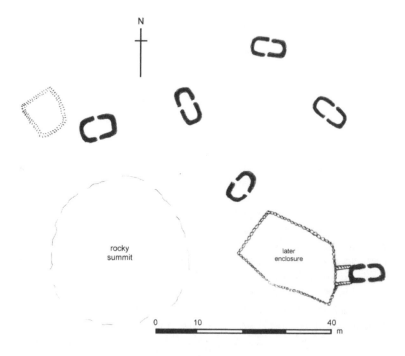

Figure 9.6 Sketch plan of the settlement of Ballore, NR 455 521.

I. (*above*) Geese flying over Mulreesh, with the snow-covered Paps of Jura in the distance. Photograph by the author.

II. (*left*) Medieval grave-slab of a lady, in the old burial ground at Kilarrow, near Bridgend. She appears to be holding a book and a rosary, and there is a pair of shears beneath her feet. From Graham, *Carved Stones*, pl. VIII, no. 26.

LI. Kelp kiln, on the shore at NR 396 782, near Bolsa. All that remains is a rectangular arrangement of stones. Photograph by the author.

LII. Caol Ila Distillery. In its present form, the distillery is a rebuilding of the 1970s. Photograph by the author.

I. (*above*) Geese flying over Mulreesh, with the snow-covered Paps of Jura in the distance. Photograph by the author.

II. (*left*) Medieval grave-slab of a lady, in the old burial ground at Kilarrow, near Bridgend. She appears to be holding a book and a rosary, and there is a pair of shears beneath her feet. From Graham, *Carved Stones*, pl. VIII, no. 26.

III. (*above*) The Toothache Stone, in a small valley at the back of Port Charlotte, at NR 233 584. It is a large boulder with several nails driven into cracks in its surface. Photograph by the author.

IV. (*right*) Two Ilich standing in the ruins of Kilchiaran Church in the 1890s, with a medieval grave-slab of a priest. They would both have been Gaelic speakers but their dress would not have distinguished them from Scots in the Lowlands. From Graham, *Carved Stones*, pl. XVIII.

V. Chambered cairn, Ballynaughton More (NR 390 464). The long cairn has mostly gone, leaving exposed this segmented, now roofless, chamber. Photograph by the author.

VI. Dùn Nosebridge. This impressive fort, with three concentric ramparts, is sited at NR 371 601 in the lower valley of the River Laggan. Photograph by the author.

VII. Cross slab, near Kilchoman old parish church, on a stretch of bank which probably represents the boundary of an early monastery. Photograph by the author.

VIII. The Kildalton Cross, beside the ruined, medieval parish church of Kildalton. The cross is a superb example of early Christian sculpture, dating to the late eighth century. Photograph by the author.

IX. Cill Tobar Lasrach, the church of St Lasair, at NR 373 457 in Kildalton Parish. There are the ruins of a small, rectangular, dry-stone chapel with a small burial ground enclosed by a turf and stone bank. Photograph by the author.

X. The Carragh Bhàn, a standing stone, probably set up in prehistoric times, but identified as the burial place of Godred Crovan. It stands beside the road to Kintra, at NR 328 478. Photograph by the author.

XI. Dunyvaig Castle, one of the key lordly residences on Islay, from the late fourteenth through the sixteenth century, the main seat of the leaders of Clann Iain Mhoir. It is possible that occupation of this site goes back to the time of Somerled. Photograph by the author.

XII. Creag an Airgid, the rock near Port Ellen Distillery where, it is said, the rents in kind were paid 'while the Isle of Man was part of the kingdom of the Isles'. Photograph by the author.

XIII. Excavations on Eilean na Comhairle, Finlaggan. The horizontal scale (in half metres) rests on one of the walls of the early keep, dismantled, perhaps, in the fourteenth century. The wall over it belongs to the Council Chamber. Photograph by the author.

XIV. The old parish church, Kildalton, perhaps dating to the time of Ranald, son of Somerled. Photograph by the author.

XV. Aerial view of Finlaggan showing Eilean na Comhairle (The Council Isle) and the larger Eilean Mor beyond it. Photograph by Prof. Mick Aston.

XVI. Aerial view of Eilean Mor, Finlaggan. The foundations of the great hall can be seen in front of the upstanding gable of 'MacGillespie's House'. To the right of it there is a piece of upstanding masonry belonging to a wall that separated off the tip of the island, and beyond it can be seen the foundations of another, smaller, hall, probably for the private us of the Lords and their family. Photograph by Prof. Mick Aston.

XVII. Medieval grave-slab, in the chapel on Eilean Mor, Finlaggan. It is West Highland work, probably of the fourteenth century, and may have been commissioned for a child. From Graham, *Carved Stones*, pl. III, no. 8.

XVIII. Cross shaft of Ranald of Islay, from the burial ground beside the chapel on Texa, but now in the collections of the National Museums Scotland. On one side is a representation of Ranald as an axe-wielding warrior. On the other side is a hunting scene and a fine representation of a West Highland galley. From Graham, *Carved Stones*, pl. XXX, no 105.

XIX. Island dwelling, Loch Ballygrant, probably the 'Ellencarne' where Donald Dubh met with his Barons and Council of the Isles in 1545. Photograph by the author.

XX. Aerial view of Dunyvaig Castle. The ruined hall can be seen on the summit of the rock adjacent to the sea. To the left of it is the small inner courtyard, and then the large outer courtyard containing the foundations of buildings. The sea-gate, with a cleared stretch of shore in front of it, is also discernible. At the top left the modern house is sitting on a level piece of ground which represents the platform where Lambert sited his siege guns in 1615. Crown copyright © RCAHMS.

XXI. Islay House, the main Islay residence of the Campbells of Cawdor and later lairds and proprietors. The original house of 1677 is included in the main block, to the left in this view. Photograph by the author.

XXII. (*right*) Daniel Campbell of Shawfield, who acquired Islay in 1726. From an etching in Russell, *Three Generations of Fascinting Women*.

XXIII. (*below*) Walter Frederick Campbell and his wife, Lady Ellinor, landing on Islay. The painting is by George Sanders, and shows Walter Frederick's love of Highland dress. Photograph courtesy of the Scottish National Portrait Gallery; painting the property of Francis David, 12th Earl of Wemyss and March, KT.

XXIV. John Francis Campbell, a portrait bust on the monument erected to his memory at Bridgend. Photograph by the author.

XXV. Dunlossit House, overlooking Port Askaig and the Sound of Islay; originally built in 1865, rebuilt 1909, in Scots baronial style. Photograph by the author.

XXVI. (*right*) Sixteenth-century grave-slab in the old parish church of Kildalton with the effigy of a warrior, a great grandson of John MacIan of Ardnamurchan. From Graham, *Carved Stones*, pl. XXVIII, no. 90.

XXVII. (*far right*) Grave-slab of Donald MacGillespie in the chapel on Eilean Mor, Finlaggan. Donald is dressed in typical West Highland armour, and there is a galley beneath his feet. Part of he inscription has gone missing since this photograph was made. From Graham, *Carved Stones*, pl. II, no. 3.

XXVIII. (*below*) The Kilchoman Cross. This outstanding example of late fourteenth-century West Highland sculpture commemorates members of the Macbeth family of Ballinaby. An inscription indicates it was set up by Thomas, and the images of two men below the Crucifixion must represent him and his father Patrick, the doctor. From Graham, *Carved Stones*, pl. XIII, no. 39.

XXIX. Shielings at Ballachlaven. They are represented by the mounds lower left. Beyond them, the turf dyke is the head dyke for Ballachlaven. Photograph by the author.

XXX. Cave on the Sound of Islay. Note the wall across the entrance. This is one of several caves around the coast in which there is evidence for human occupation in post-medieval and modern times. It may have been used during the summer by fishermen. Others may have served as shielings, or for clandestine distilling. Photograph by the author.

XXXI. Corn-drying kiln, Sean-ghairt, overlooking Loch Finlaggan at NR 381 678. It is built into an outcrop of rock. Photograph by the author.

XXXII. House on the fort, Am Burg, near Coull, possibly a residence of the MacLeans. Photograph by the author.

XXXIII. Dun at Lossit, in the Rhinns. In the foreground is the rampart forming one side of the triangular enclosure, possibly a residence of the MacFarquhars. Photograph by the author.

XXXIV. 'MacGillespie's House', Eilean Mor, Finlaggan. This house, with an upper storey, was created in the sixteenth century from the ruins of a medieval structure. As the only substantial house on the island at that time it can be identified as the home of Donald MacGillespie, the crown tenant. Photograph by the author.

XXXV. Lower Cragabus in the Oa in the late nineteenth or early twentieth century, showing traditional houses with thatched roofs. Photograph courtesy of the Museum of Islay Life.

XXXVI. Ballinaby House, about 1915. It was destroyed by fire in 1933.
Photograph courtesy of the Museum of Islay Life.

XXXVII. (*above*) Risabus, showing the Parliamentary Church of 1828, now roofless, and the former school and schoolmaster's house. Photograph by the author.

XXXVIII. (*left*) Rhuvaal Lighthouse, erected between 1857 and 1859 for the Northern Lighthouse Board, to designs by David and Thomas Stevenson. Photograph by the author.

XXXIX. (*right*) Islay House Farm – the late eighteenth-century entrance to the steading. Photograph by the author.

XL. (*below*) The Islay and Jura Agricultural Show, about 1890. Photograph courtesy of the Museum of Islay Life.

XLI. Braigo Farmhouse and steading in the Rhinns, a new farm created in the 1860s.
Photograph by the author.

XLII. Bowmore on Fair Day, about 1830, painted by William Heath. Photograph courtesy of the
Museum of Islay Life.

XLIII. Aerial view with the island of Orsay in the foreground and beyond, the houses of Portnahaven arranged around a sheltered harbour. To the right is the planned village of Port Wemyss.
Crown copyright © RCAHMS

XLIV. Garden at Airigh an t-Sluic, a nineteenth-century attempt to grow crops on the moors.
Photograph by the author.

PORT-ELLEN PIER, ISLAY, AT GLASGOW FAIR

XLV. (*above*) The *Pioneer* at Port Ellen pier, disgorging holiday-makers during Glasgow Fair. She provided a service to Islay from 1905 to 1939. Duckworth and Langmuir, *West Highland Steamers*, pp. 75–76. Photograph courtesy of the Museum of Islay Life.

XLVI. (*left*) The American Monument on the Mull of Oa. It was erected by the American Red Cross to commemorate those lost, mostly US troops, in the sinking by a German U-boat of the *Tuscania* on 5 February 1918. Photograph by the author.

XLVII. (*above*) A Sunderland flying
boat in Loch Indaal, during the Second
World War. Photograph courtesy of the
Museum of Islay Life.

XLVIII. (*right*) South Ardachie Mine
showing a trench or trial cut by a later
shaft. Photograph by the author.

XLIX. The engine-house at Mulreesh, built by the Islay Lead Mining Company Ltd to contain the engine, installed in 1873 for pumping out the mines. Photograph by the author.

L. The Woollen Mill at Redhouses, near Bridgend, built in 1883, and still in business. Photograph by the author.

LI. Kelp kiln, on the shore at NR 396 782, near Bolsa. All that remains is a rectangular arrangement of stones. Photograph by the author.

LII. Caol Ila Distillery. In its present form, the distillery is a rebuilding of the 1970s. Photograph by the author.

There are the ruins of seven stone houses on an island in Loch Ballygrant, identified in Chapter 5 as the 'Ellencarne' where Donald Dubh convened a meeting of the Council of the Isles in 1545 (Plate XIX). Through comparison with the excavated evidence from Finlaggan, these houses can be identified as another sixteenth-century township. The island, belonging with the land of Scanistle, was by 1549 another residence of the MacLeans. At Ballore, near the deserted township of Creagfinn in Kildalton parish, there is a group of six stone houses like those at Finlaggan, nestling on a low rise overlooked by a rocky outcrop (Fig. 9.6). This too may be a sixteenth-century settlement.

The sites of other early nucleated settlements may yet be discovered under the ruins of farming townships abandoned in the nineteenth century. There are other sub-rectangular or oval houses which may date to the sixteenth or seventeenth century. They include a house at Cill Eileagain (NR 402 694) in Kilmeny parish, probably of dry-stone construction, with opposed doors, 9.3 by 5.6 m. Nearby is a small enclosure containing vestigial remains of a building, possibly of the same date. In the sixteenth and seventeenth centuries Cill Eileagain (Killelegan) was a separate farm and these buildings may date to that time. Two stone houses adjacent to a dun, near the chapel of Cill a' Chubein, Trudernish, might also be considered.

The outer courtyard of Dunyvaig Castle contains the turf-covered foundations of four rectangular houses, an open-ended structure – possibly a smithy – and a well. One of the houses contains an oven. The two largest houses are only 13 m by 6 m overall and appear unicameral. If these houses sheltering in the shattered and patched-together courtyard of the fortress do represent Sir John Campbell's main base on the island, they can hardly be said to demonstrate confidence in the immediate future, or adequate resources to impose his will on Islay. The Cawdor Campbells only started to build a substantial house, Islay House, in Lowland style in 1677 (Plate XXI). It is difficult to identify any other seventeenth-century gentlemen's residences in Islay.

There are some possible reasons for this. Perhaps the houses have not been recognised or have all been replaced by later structures. There is no trace of 'the choice mansion house' at Kilchoman that is said in a note in the 1722 rental to have been the main Campbell residence on the island. It had apparently gone by that date.[55] Some of the new Campbell gentry also had lands on the mainland and may not have spent much time on Islay. They may therefore not have seen a need to build substantial houses there for themselves. They were apparently also reluctant to be buried on the island. There are eight burial grounds with medieval and post-medieval grave monuments, but it is possible to identify only four monuments that date to the seventeenth century. One in the parish church of Kildalton is dated 1696 and commemorates Charles MacArthur, tenant of Proaig. The other three are in the burial ground of old Kilchoman Church. Two of them are actually medieval grave-slabs re-carved with near identical inscriptions commemorating Alexander Campbell and his wife Mary, 1681. The other is the grave-slab of Lachlan Campbell of Daill, died 1689. It dates to that time.

There are some remains of houses which might have belonged to the lesser tenants of Islay in the seventeenth century. These are sub-rectangular or oval houses constructed with walls of turf. They have been recognised in several places on Islay. At Kilslevan and Druim a' Chùirn (Sean-ghairt) there are possible examples surrounded by the ruined stone houses of townships abandoned in the nineteenth century.

Limited excavation of a turf-walled house (B) at Rudh' a' Chròcuin (NR 386 681) on the shore of Loch Finlaggan was initiated by Channel 4's *Time Team* in 1994 and completed under the writer's supervision. The house is 7.5 m by 5.5 m and there are the remains of another larger turf-walled structure (A) lying adjacent and at right angles to it. The excavation of house B demonstrated that it had a central hearth and an earth floor. A stake-hole, probably for supporting wattling, was traced on the inner edge of its turf wall.

These Islay turf-walled houses were probably similar to others, some-times called creel houses, known from the mainland, especially the Highlands. A good description of such a house is given by an English army officer, Edmund Burt, based in Inverness in the 1720s and '30s. The skeleton of the 'hut' was formed of small crooked timber with a large beam for the roof. The walls were about four feet high, lined with sticks 'wattled like a hurdle', built on the outside with turf. Thin 'divets' of turf were also used for covering the roof, and the floor was of earth. There was a small peat fire in the centre with a small hole in the roof to let the smoke escape.[56]

Many of the shieling huts occupied in the summer months also appear to have been erected in a similar fashion. These huts are circular or oval in shape, varying in diameter from about 5 m to 10 m. None have been excavated but there is an illustration and account of some still in use on the neighbouring island of Jura in Thomas Pennant's *Tour* of 1772. Jura was in the hands of other branches of the Campbells from 1614. A relatively large but poor island, it was heavily influenced by developments in Islay. Pennant's illustrator shows huts with a superficial resemblance to North American wigwams. The accompanying description is worth giving in full:

Land on a bank covered with sheelins, the inhabitants of some peasants who attend the herds of milk cows. These formed a grotesque group; some were oblong, many conic, and so low that entrance is forbidden, without creeping through the little opening, which has no other door than a fagot of birch twigs, placed there occasionally: they are con-structed of branches of trees, covered with sods; the furniture a bed of heath, placed on a bank of sod; two blankets and a rug; some dairy vessels, and above, certain pendent shelves made of basket work, to hold the cheese, the produce of the summer. In one of the little conic huts, I spied a little infant asleep, under the protection of a faithful dog.[57]

A hypothesis worthy of further testing is that the tradition of building turf-walled houses was brought to Islay by the Campbells of Cawdor and their tenants in the seventeenth century and, with the exception of shieling huts, had died out by the late eighteenth century. The houses of Islay tenants of that time were said by Pennant to be of stone, and another late-eighteenth-century writer on Argyll, Dr John Smith, a minister in Campbeltown, also described houses in the region as of stone.[58] Turf or creel houses had spread elsewhere in the West Highlands and Islands by the eighteenth century, but the presence of shielings of the type observed by Pennant has still not been demonstrated elsewhere in this region.[59] In several locations on Islay there are small woods of oak and hazel that have been coppiced at some time in the past. These are the residue of the numerous coppices noticed by an agricultural writer, the Revd Dr John Walker, in the late eighteenth century. The need for them, it may be supposed, was largely occasioned by their use in house building.[60] It is a moot point whether the coppices were developed to provide the materials for house building or a move to building creel houses could have been motivated by a change in land management, involving the exploitation of coppices.

Opposed doorways continued as a design feature of some houses on Islay in the eighteenth and nineteenth centuries. At Sean-ghairt, Kilslevan, and on the farm of Portaneilan at Cul a'bhaile (name supplied by farmer – NR 396 690) and (unnamed) on the farm of Balulive at NR 3986 6958, examples have been found, of dry-stone construction, or with clay bonding (Fig. 9.7 A, C). These traditional houses are all rectangular, vary in length from about 10 m to 12 m, and are about 6 m to 7 m wide. Where well preserved they can be seen to have end gables with no flues. Two late eighteenth-century paintings of Islay cottages, at least one by John Frederick Miller who accompanied Thomas Pennant to the island in 1772, show windows, thatched roofs and the upper parts of the gables finished in turf (Fig. 9.8).[61] There were still houses of this type occupied in the 1830s, as in the following contemporary description:

. . . An extensive hamlet consisting of hovels, or rather shapeless tumuli of sod and stone. They contain a single apartment furnished with a door on each side, an important point in the construction of a Highland cottage, to allow of ingress and egress on the side not exposed to the wind: with a hole in the roof, which, in several, served for window, as well as chimney, whilst others were furnished with a single pane in a side-aperture. To some was attached a rudely-constructed byre: but most of them shared their dwellings with their cattle, separated by no

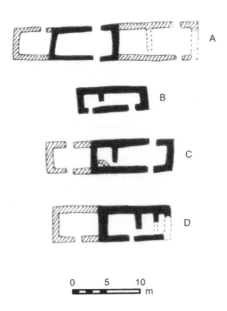

Figure 9.7 Plans of four typical traditional Islay houses, at the
abandoned settlement of Sean-ghairt, on the west side of Loch Finlaggan.

other partition than by some stone flags. I saw no cottages on the
mainland as wretched as these.[62]

The ruins of such houses can be traced in many deserted townships,
sometimes with barns or byres added at one or both ends. There may have
been a tendency for earlier stone houses to be narrower than later ones,
since their builders may have been slow to take advantage of the relative
ease of spanning wider spaces from load-bearing walls.[63] Certainly ruined
houses can be found on Islay which clearly incorporate narrower gables in
their rebuilt walls, for instance at Druim a' Chùirn (Sean-ghairt) to the
south-west of Loch Finlaggan, at Cill an Ailein (Claggain), and at
Tornabakin (Lower Glenastle) in the Oa. Many earlier stone houses were
constructed with boulders and blocks gathered from the fields, sometimes
split to provide a flat face. Those built of quarried, but undressed stone,
may mostly be later, say from the late eighteenth century onwards.
Examples can be found of extensions in quarried stone being added to
houses built of field stones, but never vice versa. There is clearly much
more work to be done on surveying and interpreting the many ruins of
early houses in the Islay landscape. There are considerable differences in
plan which are as yet little understood (Fig. 9.7).[64]

Some evidence can also be gleaned from testaments about doors and

Figure 9.8 A late eighteenth-century Islay cottage, an engraved version of
a 1772 painting by John Frederick Miller, published in Pennant's *Tour*, 205.

windows. When Nichol McCalman died in 1732 he had four door
leaves with their checks (door-frames) in his house, barn and byre. Neil
Smith in Esknish, who died in 1736, had five door leaves and two
locks. McCalman lived in Kilfinan (otherwise unknown) in the parish
of Kilmeny, and as a weaver, was relatively wealthy. Smith, on the
basis of the Islay rental of 1733, had a reasonably sized holding on a
good farm. Most eighteenth-century inventories, however, do not
specifically mention doors, and many may have consisted of hides
stretched over a frame or wickerwork. The change-house kept by Neill
McLergan at Machrie Coull at the time of his death in 1753 evidently
had two glass windows, noted presumably because they were then an
unusual luxury.[65]
   Thatched roofs have all but disappeared on Islay although they were the
normal covering for all houses until the nineteenth century (Plate XXXV).
The couples that supported them were a valuable commodity on an island
lacking stands of mature trees. They were the property of the tenants who
flitted with them when their leases ran out. These timbers can be found in
the inventories included in their testaments. That of Dugald Taylour and
his wife, Christian McGee, when the latter died in 1725, specifies four
couples, sufficient for roofing a reasonably sized single-storey cottage of the
period, perhaps including a byre at one end. Dugald was at that time one

of the tenants of the farm of Barr in Kilmeny parish, with rather limited resources.[66]

Turf houses and many stone houses did not have walls sturdy enough to take the weight of a roof directly. In these cases the roof couples were supported on crucks bedded on, or in, the ground. The wall-slots for these crucks can be seen in some Islay ruins, for example a house at Lurabus in the Oa and byres at Smaull and Grulinbeg. The majority of Islay stone houses probably had couples supported on their wall tops.

It is noteworthy that the standard leases on the Islay Estate from the 1750s make much of the obligation on tenants to maintain 'the whole houses and biggings' on their land and leave them in a fit state for occupation by succeeding tenants. Outgoing tenants were now encouraged to leave house timbers in place and claim payment for them from their successors.[67]

Although they are now viewed as 'traditional' to distinguish them from the 'modern' cottages and houses introduced in the nineteenth century, the impetus for the erection of stone houses may largely have come from the new laird, Daniel Campbell of Shawfield, who would have been familiar with rectangular, gabled houses on his Lowland estates. He would have seen these houses as an improvement on the creel houses which were probably prevalent when he first acquired the island. Many would still have housed cattle at one end during the winter, the byre being separated from the kitchen by a wooden partition and box beds (Fig. 9.9, older plan).[68]

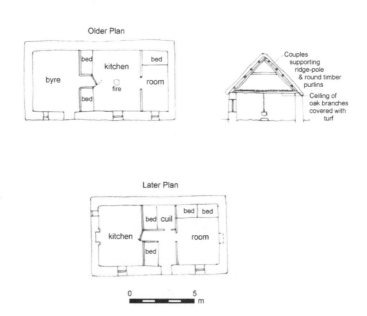

Figure 9.9 'Dailriadic Type' houses, after Sinclair, *Thatched Houses*, 71.

MacDonald could write in 1811 that houses had recently been greatly improved in Islay.

> They are now composed of stone and clay, harled with lime, and roofed with heath, fern or straw . . . The inside has in general a family room, divided by a deal partition from the kitchen, and cellar or store-room. The garret is allotted to lumber of different kinds. Such a cottage costs c £20; the cottar himself furnishing the stones, mortar and carriage.[69]

Such simple cottages can be found listed in a survey of Islay houses prepared for the new Morrison laird in the 1850s. Typically they had two rooms, described as a room and kitchen, divided by a wooden partition combined with a press and shelves, or else box beds, and perhaps a 'cuil' or scullery (Fig. 9.9, latter plan). Each had a mantelpiece, indicating a (kitchen) fireplace in a gable wall. There was one or more windows, and separate external doorways to the two rooms. Some had a loft.[70] Reminiscing about his youth on Islay in the 1820s John Murdoch recorded that such cottages were built by the prospective occupiers with help from their neighbours, and sometimes by the main tenants for their cottars. He reckoned that a day might be expended quarrying stone, and that a house could be built – roofed, thatched, floored, inhabited and 'warmed' – in a week or two.[71]

Two early visitors have left accounts of their visits to Islay homes, no doubt houses like those described above. In the 1830s Lord Teignmouth visited 'an extraordinary specimen of a farm-house' on the west coast of the island:

> It consisted of a single but large apartment, without a loft. The vent for the smoke was an aperture in the wall, at a height of some feet above the fire, apparently knocked out without reference to shape: and capable, from its size, of admitting a gale of wind. A bed was placed at each corner of the apartment; and chests, and various utensils, were scattered about the floor, mingled with as many sheep as the place would contain, lying, their feet tied together, whilst a girl was shearing them as fast as she could. An old woman sat near the fire; and in front of it stood a tall, gaunt-looking female, attending to the boiling of a pot, clad in a blue jacket and red petticoat, a pipe in her mouth, looking, and with a loud voice uttering, apparent defiance, whilst she in reality afforded me a welcome to a seat. I visited some other poor hovels, and found among the inmates only two who could speak English: they had a singularly wild appearance, and stared at me like savages.[72]

Then in the 1860s the journalist 'Gowrie' sought shelter overnight in the home of George Clark (at Killinallan?):

Having obtained an entrance, I at once made myself at home before a glorious peat fire, and Mr Clark arriving shortly after, I had every attention paid to my comfort that the dwelling could afford; the kindness with which it was paid making up for any deficiency in its character. A great pot of potatoes, plenty of milk, and a few fish – a mixture, under the circumstances, which I did not stop to criticise – made amends for the want of a dinner; and the agreeable conversation of Mr Clark, a pleasant little old man, and evidently a character, passed the evening until bed-time.

That we might see to finish our evening repast, a wick was extemporised for the 'cruisy', and a little girl stood by us picking it out with a pin as fast as it burned down, which kept her constantly employed. The house – which was roofed with saplings twined over the rafters, covered with turf and then thatched – was much out of repair, the landlords caring little for the convenience of the smaller farmers. Their good table could scarcely stand on the uneven earth floor, and the window was by no means weather proof, but that did not prevent the thatch covering much true kindness and hospitality.

The number of inhabitants I am unable to give. Besides himself, his kindly dame, and a fine-looking daughter grown up, I could see that his quiver was well filled with smaller shafts. Any number of chickens, three or four collies, two or three cats, and a grumphy [pig] that ran under my bed and could not be dislodged, helping to keep things lively. And yet I was accommodated with sheets pure and fresh as snow, while the parents, and I know not how many children, were sleeping in another bed in the same room – the daughter coming in and waking me in the morning as a matter of course, the other occupants having cleared out at cock-crow. Such is a notion of an Islay cottar-farmer's dwelling of the better class.[73]

At least one tacksman, Coll MacAlaster, Bailie of Islay, had erected a 'slate house' (that is one with a slate, rather than a thatched roof) in the early eighteenth century – prior to his death in 1747. It was at Glengeoy (Eallabus), and although it cannot be traced on the ground today, it is reasonable to assume it was a house of some substance.[74] The Campbell lairds of Ballinaby built themselves a substantial house, probably in the mid eighteenth century. It was totally destroyed by a fire in June 1933, but a photograph of about 1915 shows it as a substantial five-bay house of two stories and an attic with a nepus gable. It had lower wings added at both ends and a porch (Plate XXXVI).[75] The representation of a substantial two-storey house at Coull with an adjacent park, shown on the plan of that land made about 1750 by MacDougall, should perhaps be taken seriously.[76] It was on the site of the present house and steading, which appear to be no earlier than the nineteenth century. A more substantial drawing, that by Moses Griffiths of Mr Freebairn's house and smelter at Freeport

(Caol Ila) in the 1770s, shows that the mine manager, despite being an architect, settled for living in a cottage with an attic and outbuilding. It had a slate roof and fireplaces with chimneys in the gable ends.[77]

MacDonald wrote in 1811 that tacksmen's houses in Islay had been much improved in the last twenty-five years, being now mostly built of stone and lime, two stories high, furnished with kitchens and other accommodation, and roofed with slates.[78] These houses are now difficult to spot on the ground in relatively unaltered form, but good examples include the farmhouse at Ardnave and Foreland House. Other tacksmen probably continued to live throughout the eighteenth century in houses little different from the more substantial tenants.

The image in most people's mind of the interior of a traditional Islay house is provided by Pennant's illustration of a weaver's cottage. The weaver sits at his loom while the rest of his family sit on stools or the earth floor around an open fire with a pot-hook hanging over it. There is a small table, and utensils including staved tubs, two large jugs and a basket. In the background is what may be a box bed.

The testaments of several Ilich who died in the eighteenth century list their household goods and plenishings. We learn from these that many houses of tenants and cottagers did contain items of furniture including chests, chairs and presses. The inhabitants either slept in box (enclosed) beds, standing beds or 'long sadle beds'.[79] There were often spinning wheels, sometimes a big one and a small one. The former, spun by hand, would have been used for wool. The latter, operated by a foot treadle, were required for flax. An essential piece of equipment for cooking was a crook (hook for hanging pots over the fire), and typically there was a big and a small pot – probably of cast iron – for cooking, and sometimes a griddle for baking and a kit (wooden barrel or tub) for making sowans (a dish made from oat husks and meal, steeped in water). Prior to the mid eighteenth century, when there is evidence for imported vessels of earthenware, most plates, dishes, water and milk stoups and drinking vessels were probably of wood. The drinking vessels are sometimes listed as cogs (staved vessels), methers (rectangular vessels carved from solid blocks of wood) and noggins (small mugs).[80]

An emigrant to New Zealand who left Islay in the 1860s, later wrote about the houses he knew in his youth. They were divided into two, a 'but' and a 'ben', by two box beds placed back to back. There was a meal girnel (chest), a table, and a few sparred chairs and three-legged stools. The main item of furniture, however, was a dresser, on which all the art of the household was concentrated.[81]

At the upper end of the social scale in the 1730s was Lauchlan Campbell, Commissar Depute of Islay. At the time of his death in 1737 he had his house, presumably Cladville, furnished with tables and chairs, beds, chests and presses. He also had pewter plates, trenchers and flagons.[82] In 1713 John Campbell of Ballinaby also had a gardevine (case) of glasses, silver spoons, a silver dram piece and a silver dram tumbler.[83] The 1733 inventory of the possessions of William Campbell in Ellister, and his wife Margaret, lists sheets, table clothes, napkins and blankets valued at £50 Scots, and 5 feather beds with bolsters and 24 pillows at £48 Scots. Among the utensils was a large copper still.[84]

Moving on to the late eighteenth century the papers of Robert Campbell of Sunderland provide the information that, at the time of his death in 1780, his possessions included a still, silver tableware, 2 copper coffee pots, knives and forks, 5 crystal decanters (some of them broken), 9 pictures of little value and 36 books (some in more than one volume), some historical, others religious.[85]

Townships and farms

Seventeenth- and eighteenth-century rentals demonstrate that most lands were set to groups of tenants, from two to six or more, each with a specified share. Unrecorded in these rentals are many servants and cottagers who sublet from the main tenants. Included among them would have been various craftsmen like wrights, shoemakers and weavers. Also, for the most part, unrecorded are the tenants on the lands that were set to tacksmen or in the hands of wadsetters. Farming was very labour-intensive and there were advantages in farmers being grouped together to undertake such tasks as ploughing, harvesting and erecting dykes.

Settlement on pre-improvement farms was often clustered into townships, the ruins of which can be traced all over the island. In their present form these settlements appear to date to the late eighteenth or nineteenth century, but at some, like Kilslevan on the Dunlossit Estate, the quantity and relationship of the ruins suggests a sequence extending back in time. It is possible that future fieldwork and excavation will demonstrate that some of these townships have origins in medieval times. It is noteworthy that Kilslevan is adjacent to a dry-stone chapel and burial ground, probably of Norse date.

At Tockmal in the Oa the township buildings were arranged with some measure of regularity around a long central area. There were three main house complexes, out-buildings, a corn-drying kiln, and behind the main house complex a structure that may have been a water mill. All probably date to the late eighteenth or early nineteenth century. More typically, these townships may be described as clusters of houses and other structures. Sometimes there were two or more clusters of houses on the one land, such as at Grasdale, Sean-ghairt and Mulreesh. There were sometimes also individual cottages well away from the main settlements.

The place-names of these settlements may have gone back hundreds of years, and their extents have remained the same since first recorded, but it would be a mistake to think of them as unchanging. Tenants came and went, houses were rebuilt, and farming methods did change. In the nineteenth century, however, pressure from the landlords, and other factors like the failure of the potato crops, brought this way of life to an end, and replaced it with radical new solutions.

Improving Ways

Islay's role as the centre of a Gaelic state left a legacy that has perhaps never quite been shaken off. There was no easy transition from the consciously cultural separateness of the Lordship of the Isles to fully embracing the alien ways of Lowland Scotland. Real progress, if that is how we must see it, only became evident from the eighteenth century, picking up pace in the nineteenth century. Key indicators of improving ways are the establishment of villages, improved communications and the adoption of new, more efficient ways of farming. These improvements, as we will show later, were not immediately of benefit to all. Nevertheless, there were clearly increasing opportunities for even the poorest of Ilich to better themselves, either on the island or by moving to the mainland or further afield.

Education

Education played no small part in this. There was a legal requirement for a school in each parish from as early as 1616 though we have no information on how seriously the provision of schooling was taken on Islay prior to the establishment of the Stent Committee in 1718. In the following year it was concerning itself with the building of a schoolhouse in Kildalton parish and paying the Kildalton schoolmaster's salary.[1] The schools of all three parishes continued to be looked after by the committee until the 1830s. There were several other schools by the end of the eighteenth century, some run by charities, others small private affairs. The total tally of schools recorded by the island's ministers in the New Statistical Account of 1845 was thirty-seven, including schools run by the Society in Scotland for Propagating Christian Knowledge and the Gaelic Society of Edinburgh. There was a school for girls near Bridgend, partly funded by the laird's wife. The 'Disruption' in the Church of Scotland in 1843 led to the minister and congregation that formed the Free Church at Port Wemyss establishing their own school there.[2]

The Scottish Education Act of 1872 brought in free, compulsory education for all children from the age of five to thirteen years. Provision was in the hands of parochial school boards, and led to the erection of new school buildings at Gortan (on Loch Indaal, to the north of Bruichladdich), 'Kilchoman' (actually on the B8017 between Lochs Gorm and Gruinart), Glenegedale, Kintour, Port Ellen, Risabus (in the Oa) (Plate XXXVII), Bowmore, Kilmeny (Ballygrant) and at Newton (near Bridgend). Other schools at Port Charlotte, Portnahaven, Ardbeg, Keills and Mulindry were transferred to the control of the school boards. With the exception of Bowmore and Port Ellen, these schools were small, with fewer than 100 pupils and only one or two teachers.

The teaching no doubt varied in quality but clearly could often have been of a very high standard. Perhaps the most famous of the island's teachers was Hector MacLean (1818–93) brought up and schooled in Ballygrant. He became tutor to the laird's children in his early years, later collaborating with one of them, John Francis Campbell, to produce *Popular Tales of the West Highlands.* He was a scholar with an international reputation, but spent most of his career as schoolmaster at Ballygrant.[3] Remarkably, MacLean's own teacher, and predecessor as schoolmaster at Ballygrant, was Neil MacAlpine who published in 1832 a highly regarded *Gaelic–English Dictionary.*[4]

How different from MacAlpine and MacLean appears an unnamed Islay teacher of the nineteenth century, an incomer to the island, who denounced Gaelic song and language. On hearing some of his schoolgirls singing in that language after they had left his classroom, he called them back and belted them until the blood trickled from their fingers.[5] Unfortunately, this dominie was only expressing views that were too prevalent amongst educated circles, that English was the future and Gaelic had to be discouraged at all costs. As noted in Chapter 6, one of the main Islay lairds in the nineteenth century, John Ramsay of Kildalton, saw discouragement of Gaelic as part of his undoubted drive to improve education.

It was always possible for clever boys, and much later girls, to go to Scottish universities. Often they were encouraged and given special tuition by the local teachers. 'Gowrie' noted four local boys on holiday from Glasgow University, drinking in a Bowmore inn during his visit in the 1860s.[6] Formal, free education on Islay until the age of eighteen only came in 1978 when Bowmore School was upgraded. It is the only secondary school on the island, fed by several primary schools. Prior to 1978, pupils who wished to stay on to eighteen went to Oban for their last three years' schooling, staying in a school hostel along with several others from the Western Isles. A few went to Dunoon. Glasgow University has remained a favourite destination for those going on to do a degree.

In 2002 *Ionad Chaluim Chille Ìle* (The Columba Centre, Islay) opened in the rebuilt fever hospital outside Bowmore. It is affiliated to the University of the Highlands and Islands, and its prime function is to maintain and promote Gaelic culture and language. It offers Gaelic courses at all levels, from beginners to higher education.

The Church

Inextricably linked with education before modern times was the Church. From the institution of Presbyterian church government in 1690 until the early nineteenth century, there was no effective or significant challenge to the established church in Islay, or for that matter, in many other parts of the country. At the end of the seventeenth century, Martin Martin recorded that there were churches (presumably then in use?) at Keills, Kilchoman, Kilchiaran, Laggan (that is the church at Kilbride near Dunyvaig), Nave Island (chapel) and Killinallan.[7] Kilarrow remained without a minister, its parishioners being expected to trudge over the moors to the church at Kilbride or the medieval parish church at Kildalton, which may have remained in occasional use until the end of the seventeenth century.[8] This no doubt explains the presence on Martin's list of churches at Keills and Killinallan, perhaps providing occasional services in those areas of the parish furthest away from Kilbride. The church at Keills was a medieval chapel and may have continued to act as the church for Kilmeny, which was described in documents of the 1740s and '60s as a parish then joined with that of Kildalton.[9] The medieval church of Kilmeny, identified by the Dean of the Isles in 1549 as a parish church,[10] was presumably by then in ruins. There is no other evidence for the church at Killinallan.

Patrick MacLachlan, the incumbent of Kilchoman at the time of the Revolution, was succeeded in 1692 by David Simson. The parish of Kildalton may have been served by MacLachlan until 1693. The Presbyterian settlement was clearly not to his taste, and he accepted a charge in the Church of Ireland in 1693. Kildalton then remained vacant until James McVurrich (or Currie) took it on in 1698. From then on there was a continuous succession of ministers in both parishes of Kilchoman and Kildalton, one or other also serving the needs of Kilarrow. Although the old parish church of Kilarrow remained unused and was allowed to fall into ruin, the two Islay ministers had their manses at Kilarrow along with their glebes.[11]

Daniel Campbell of Shawfield was not content to suffer this rather inadequate provision for his island estate, and in 1747 proposed to the Synod of Argyll that he would create a new church structure with three parishes, supplying the ministers with stipends, communion money, manses and glebes, in return for the synod transferring to him the valued teinds of Islay and feu-duty payable the Church, and Queen Anne's bounty, specifically given for the building and repair of churches, education, etc. Although Daniel's offer was accepted, it was left to his grandson

Daniel to see the business through in the 1760s, despite a last-minute hitch, which saw him taking the synod to court in 1769 to clarify the details of their agreement.[12]

The new erection provided for a new joint parish of Kilarrow and Kilmeny with churches at Bowmore and Kilmeny, a parish of Kilchoman with a church at Kilchoman, and a parish of Kildalton with a church at Lagavulin. All the above churches, apart from that of Kilmeny, were to be new-built. Modifications were made to the medieval boundaries of these parishes, with the lands of Coullabus and Corsapol being disjoined from Kilarrow and added to Kilchoman, and Duich and Proaig also being taken from Kilarrow and given to Kildalton.

The most obvious sign of the Shawfields' determination to improve the religious experience of the islanders is the church erected in 1767 to serve as the parish church of Kilarrow. It is the famous round church that stands at the head of their new planned village of Bowmore. It was also to serve as the family mausoleum, with impressive monuments to Daniel the Younger's successor, Walter, and to Walter Frederick Campbell and his wife, Lady Ellinor Campbell.[13] There is no evidence of other significant new work or renovation of older churches by Daniel Campbell as a consequence of the new erection of parishes. The church at Kilbride had been replaced in the early 1730s by a new parish church for Kildalton, nearer Lagavulin, on the land of Ballynaughtonmore, and it is apparent that there was a church at Kilmeny by the end of the eighteenth century that had replaced the chapel at Keills.[14]

The considerable increase in the island's population led to a renewed drive in the 1820s to improve church provision. The medieval parish church at Kilchoman was replaced by a new, larger church, on the same site, in 1827. The incumbent, the Revd John McLiesh, noted in 1794 how he went on occasion to the extremities of his parish to preach, but in mentioning other, older, places of worship, indicates that they were by then all in ruins.[15] The church at Lagavulin was replaced in 1825 by yet another on the land of Surnaig to the west of Lagavulin Bay. The church at Kilmeny was rebuilt in the late 1820s and 'parliamentary churches' (that is those required by the Parliamentary Commissioners appointed to build additional places of worship in the Highlands and Islands) were erected at Portnahaven and Risabus in the Oa (Plate XXXVII) to a design prepared by the great engineer, Thomas Telford. The status and high regard in which ministers were held is indicated by the impressive manses that were built for them, for example those at Kilchoman (1825–26) and Kilmeny (1828).[16]

All, however, was not well in the Church of Scotland at national level, and many years of acrimonious argument on policy and doctrine led to the Disruption of 1843, which resulted in many ministers and congregations leaving the Kirk to form the Free Church, one which would be free from the influence of heritors in appointing their clergy. Free churches were established at Gruinart (a mission house), Port Charlotte, Port Ellen, Bowmore and Skerrols (later Church of Scotland). The United Presbyterian Church, a body founded in 1847, had a church in Port Ellen. The Baptists also established a congregation in Bowmore in the 1840s, followed by another church in Port Ellen in 1910. The Scottish Episcopalian Church built St Columba's at Bridgend in 1888.

The Church of Scotland itself was in need of reorganisation. This led in 1849 to extra *quoad sacra* (for religious maters only) parishes being established – Kilmeny, the Oa (with its church at Risabus) and Portnahaven. Population shifts led to the building of new churches, St John's in Port Ellen in 1898, and St Kiaran's between Port Charlotte and Bruichladdich in 1899, to serve those two communities.

The Church, in all its branches, was undoubtedly very influential in improving the islanders, clearly not just in a religious sense. Prior to the Poor Law Act of 1845 it was responsible for distributing poor relief and took a great interest in education, supporting local schools. The clergy were leaders of local opinion, and in many cases must have offered a model of how it was possible to be Gaelic-speaking as well as civilised and cultured. The decline in religious beliefs and the influence of the church in the twentieth century is only too obvious today, with fewer churches and services, and often pitifully small congregations. Now the Church of Scotland only has services in St Kiaran's, Portnahaven, St John's, the Round Church in Bowmore, and Kilmeny. The Episcopal Church still has St Columba's in Bridgend, also used by a small Catholic community, and the Baptists maintain their two churches in Bowmore and Port Ellen.

Health

Detailed information on the health of the inhabitants of Islay prior to modern times is largely non-existent. Epidemics and famine were clearly recurrent problems, and even at the best of times, there was a lack of healthy variety in the diet of most. At the end of the seventeenth century, Martin Martin had noted how the inhabitants of Islay were prone to a variety of diseases and put this down to the land being low and the air unwholesome through the lack of fresh breezes.[17] Martin's reasoning now appears to us to be absurd. Rather, the problem lay in the very houses occupied by many, with livestock under the same roof as humans. This induced respiratory diseases, especially tuberculosis, for long among the main killers of the Ilich.

An infectious diseases hospital was built at Gartnatra beside Bowmore in 1900 (now remodelled as the Gaelic College) to isolate sufferers and prevent them passing the disease on.

Poverty and poor diet were generally to blame for much illness. Pennant recognised this in 1772, and cited dropsy and cancer as major problems.[18]

By the late eighteenth century the staple diet for many had shifted from oats and barley to potatoes, eked out with fish, caught in the summer and dried for consumption in the winter. Since much casual work, for example helping at harvest time, was paid for in kind, there was little access for many to money to purchase other comestibles, though bartering commodities like eggs remained a way of life well into the twentieth century. There were, however, some other potential sources of protein, like berries and nuts in season, and some of the more enterprising islanders would eat cormorant, seaweed (dulse and carragheen) and soup made from limpets.[19] A sixteenth-century midden at Finlaggan with large quantities of limpet shells may be evidence for this latter dish at that time.

Soup kitchens, operating January to March 1906–11 in Bowmore, Port Charlotte and Port Wemyss, were a well-meaning effort funded by the Morrisons to provide much-needed sustenance, free in the case of the children.[20] The fact they were needed gives a poor impression of the Islay diet of that time. Starvation can hardly be viewed as a problem for the times since then, though, as with the rest of Scotland, there may be valid, ongoing concerns about the healthiness of much that is eaten.

Prior to the mid nineteenth century the responsibility for dealing with the poor lay with the Church, and cash payments were issued by the kirk sessions to those in need. In 1812 the Stent Committee proposed that the ministers issue tickets to the deserving poor in their own parishes. There was a concern that they should be distinguished from impostors and outsiders. No beggars were to be allowed to keep dogs.[21] It was also clearly the case that those in need were often helped out by their neighbours. The Poor Law Act of 1845 passed responsibility for the poor on to a combined Parochial Board for the whole island and Jura, and a poor house was built in the 1860s at Gortonvoggie, near Bowmore, to house them. A letter written by John Ramsay to Charles Morrison in November 1859 clearly shows his concern that the number of paupers was getting out of hand, well above the national average. He supposed there were then over 600 in a population of 11,000, meaning one for every sixteen self-supporting members of society, compared with the national average of 1:23.[22] The 1881 census, however, indicates that there were then only eighteen residents of the poor house, seven of them staff, including the governor, Archibald McIntyre. A lot had undoubtedly changed in the island since 1859, and it is more than likely that Ramsay was exaggerating the extent of the problem then, but nevertheless, underlying the disparity in the figures is the determination by most to avoid the poor house at all costs. Life in such institutions was not intended to be an easy, pleasant option, and was only ever seen as a last resort.

The Islay Combination Poor House developed after 1930 into the Gortonvoggie House Poor Law institution with accommodation for sixty inmates, including ten medical beds. It was replaced in 1965–66 by the present hospital and eventide home.

The fine tradition of Islay-based medical doctors extending back to the Macbeths or Beatons of Ballinaby was maintained by the Stent Committee. One of its first acts in 1718 was to sanction a yearly fee to the surgeon based on the island. A surgeon continued to be supported throughout the rest of that century. By 1834 three doctors were also being paid retainers to provide a service for the poor, and in 1839, a midwife as well.[23] This laudable effort came to an end with the Stent Committee itself.

There are now medical practices in Bowmore, Port Ellen and Port Charlotte, with a dental practice based at the hospital. Access to more specialist services on the mainland is becoming increasingly important as medical knowledge and skills expand and improve. Here the provision of an air ambulance service is of the utmost importance. The first emergency evacuation of an islander by air took place in 1933. The service has ever since been a great success, literally providing a lifeline. The tragic loss in bad weather, however, of an incoming plane in 1957, with its crew of two and a nurse, is well remembered.

Early villages and trade

Great lords in the Medieval Period often had burghs erected on their lands. A burgh was something rather more than a town or village. It was a settlement with considerable privileges, legally defined, for trade and manufacturing. It was a population centre and a base for local administration. The Lords of the Isles controlled the burghs of Inverness and Dingwall in the fifteenth century, and visited and did business in other Scottish burghs. There were, however, no burghs in Islay or the rest of the Lordship of the Isles, a fact that can only be explained as policy by the Lords. They must have perceived they were unnecessary or contrary to the way of life in the Lordship.

The charter of Islay granted to Sir John Campbell of Cawdor in 1614 included the erection of a burgh that was to be built anywhere on the island of Sir John's choosing. The name given to it was Laggan, and, undoubtedly, Sir John intended that it should be adjacent to the castle of Dunyvaig.[24] Merchants and all sorts of skilled craftsmen would be appointed burgesses and freemen with freedom to buy and sell, and bailies and councillors would be elected – all under the supervision or control of Sir John and his heirs. There was to be a weekly market every Friday and a free fair, lasting eight days, every Michaelmas (29 September), when outsiders could come and set up stall. A market cross would provide a focus for the markets and a tolbooth (townhouse) for the business and administrative affairs of the burgh.

No burgh was erected by Sir John, or by any of his descendants or successors once peaceable possession of the island had been gained. This meant that craftsmen working as smiths, weavers, shoemakers, etc.

remained unregulated, and until the nineteenth century, lived on farms as tenants or cottagers, combining their trades with a bit of farming for themselves, or labouring for their neighbours. For instance, Archibald McNeill, a wright living on the land of Keills, at the time of his death in 1735 left a testament indicating that he was a man of modest means. He not only had his work looms (tools), nails and dales (planks) but also eight cows, two stots, a mare with a two-year-old follower, and ten sheep. Similarly, Nichol McCalman, a weaver in Kilfinan in the parish of Kilarrow when he died in 1732, had his weaving equipment, cloth and yarn, but also a number of animals, seed-corn, an iron spade, grape and fork. He also had a barn and a byre.[25]

Several surviving testaments list the debts due to tradesmen, typically tailors and shoemakers, but also, for instance, a builder, Patrick McAulay, who was still owed money for building the dwelling house of William Campbell, tacksman of Kelsay, some time prior to the latter's death in 1745.[26] The sums of money involved are invariably given in Scots, prior to 1750, even though the Scottish coinage was replaced by sterling in 1708, at which time the exchange rate was 20:1, Scots to sterling. The continued use of Scots money for accounting purposes may indicate that there was only a limited money economy on the island until well into the eighteenth century. There is a note in papers belonging to the Campbells of Sunderland to the effect that John MacNicol, shoemaker in Sunderland in 1780, got a yearly payment of a boll of meal or barley for providing his services as shoemaker to Coull.[27] This may have been a fairly typical arrangement for the period.

Coll McDugald was described in his testament, after his death in 1754, as a merchant in Tayndrom. His business was to peddle cloth, buttons, lace, ribbons, etc. around the farms, mostly in the parish of Kildalton. He had two chests for carrying his ware and a set of scales with weights.[28] The majority of Islay merchants, or at least those with substantial businesses, prior to the 1760s seem to have been located in either Lagavulin or Kilarrow, probably the only two settlements which could have been counted as villages as distinct from touns or townships.

Of these, Lagavulin was the older. As a place-name it is only known from the seventeenth century, the land previously being part of Dunyvaig, but perhaps the village had its roots in the seventeenth century. There were nine inhabitants of Dunyvaig with eleven hearths listed in the Hearth Tax return of 1693. There was a meeting house at Lagavulin, which the Stent Committee accepted was their responsibility to repair in 1718, presumably the same as the courthouse listed in the 1722 rental. That rental, unusually, noted three houses, belonging to Duncan Carmichael, the Reids and Dugald Campbell, along with the (meal) mill of Dunyvaig. The parish church of Kildalton was also at Lagavulin after 1763 when, as part of a new plan for a parochial structure on the island, Daniel Campbell the younger undertook to build a new church there. It had been at Kilbride since the 1650s. The receiving house for the mail of the parish of Kildalton was at Lagavulin from 1802 until it was removed to the new village of Port Ellen in 1836.[29]

There were at least two merchants based in Lagavulin in the mid eighteenth century, Archibald Campbell and Archibald MacDonald. Included in the latter's stock, listed in his testament after he died in 1762, was distilling equipment, buttons, stockings, fine linen cloth, spurs, bottles of claret and castor oil, and hand lines (for fishing).[30] Although Lagavulin was supplanted by Port Ellen as the centre of the parish of Kildalton the development of a whisky distillery in the nineteenth century meant it survived as a small settlement.

Kilarrow would only have developed as a village from 1677 when the lairds erected Islay House nearby at the head of Loch Indaal. The 1693 Hearth Tax return lists nine occupants with ten hearths. In 1722 there was a meal mill, brew houses and eight houses, two of them with gardens, one also with a kiln. An eighteenth-century painting shows thatched houses, some with attics or upper stories, on both sides of a street.[31] The medieval parish church of Kilarrow remained in use, and both Islay ministers had their glebes here. There was a tolbooth by the end of the seventeenth century where the Bailie of Islay appointed by the lairds would have done business, including conducting trials for minor offences. The small hill of Cnoc na Croiche (Gaelic, 'hill of the hanging') may have been the site of the gallows in earlier days[32] but when islanders were tried for capital offences in the time of the Campbell lairds they were sent to Inverary, like 'John McVeir alias McDonald in Elistererrarich' (Easter Ellister) accused in 1699 of the murder of Christian MacMillan, wife of Donald MacKenzie in Ellister by pushing her off a rock into the sea while they were both gathering shellfish. He did this to try and cover up the murder of the widow 'Moir NcIlchenich' in Ellister, committed in the previous year out of mere avarice and covetousness by Christian herself acting along with her husband, John McVeir's wife 'Efferick NcKenzie' (sister of John McKenzie) and 'Katharin NcInughlassie'. They entered her house by night, strangled her in bed and then threw her body into the sea. Not only was John McVeir sentenced to hanging, but also the three others he sought to protect. The sentence was carried out on 12 June at Inverary and their right hands were cut off for affixing to the tollbooth in Kilarrow as a warning to others.[33]

Prior to the establishment of Bowmore, Kilarrow became the main base for Islay merchants. In 1693 Alexander Campbell, younger, of Cawdor, received a parliamentary grant to hold weekly markets here on Thursdays and two free fairs annually, each for two days, on 14 July and 15 August.[34]

One of these merchants, Archibald Maclauchlan, had, at the time of his wife's death in 1723, £600 Scots of merchantware in his shop, a further £600 in cash in his house, and was owed £1,108. He had several cattle and sheep and his house appears to have been relatively well furnished. Another merchant, Archibald Campbell, who died in 1746, operated on a much larger scale, supplying casks of rum and brandy, bottles of white wine and claret, to customers as far away as Colonsay, Oban and Dalmally. He had a sloop for shipping his goods and two guns and a side pistol for his own personal protection.[35] Cases brought before the Vice-Admiral Court of Argyll suggest that several other Islay residents and merchants may have owned, or part-owned ships in the eighteenth century. For instance, in 1755 Alexander Campbell, merchant in Balole, bought a half share of a brigantine of 50 tons named the *Mary of Glasgow* which was engaged in transatlantic trade.[36]

Other residents of Kilarrow in the 1740s included the merchant, John Simson, a barber, William Smith, a weaver, John MacMillan, and a bleacher, Daniel Campbell.

Although the village of Kilarrow was abandoned in the 1760s in favour of the new settlement at Bowmore, the nearby Bridgend Hotel has remained a focus of activity, with shops and the estate office for the Islay Estate. It was here that the first branch of a bank was established on the island, the National Bank of Scotland in 1843.[37] Bridgend has also remained to the present day the place for cattle auctions and the annual show of the Islay, Jura and Colonsay Agricultural Association.

Communications

Routeways connecting Islay settlements, one with another, there must always have been. By an Act of Parliament of 1669 for repairing roads and bridges responsibility had fallen on tenants and cottars within each parish to provide the necessary tools and equipment and six days' work for a man and horse yearly, for the first three years, and then four days yearly thereafter. They were paid for this work. Its supervision and planning was taken up by the Stent Committee, and it might be supplemented through government grants for improvements which the lairds were successful in acquiring in the 1760s and 1780s.[38]

MacDougall's map shows that by the middle of the eighteenth century there was a rudimentary system of roads. One route connected the ferry port of Port Askaig with Kilarrow. This road diverged so that the traveller had the choice of going round by Eorrabus, Ballimartin, Sean-ghairt and Portaneilean, or else by Esknish and Ballygrant, which is more or less the line of the modern road. This latter route was chosen in preference to the former from 1753.[39]

From Kilarrow another road headed by Coullabus up the west side of Loch Gruinart to Breakachey (Ardnave), and one around the shore of Loch Indaal all the way to Portnahaven at the south end of the Rhinns. A road branched off this one going via Foreland and Sunderland and branching to Coull and East Kilchoman (Rockside). Also from Kilarrow a road headed via Corary and Island (House) to Laggan Bay and then along the sand to Kintra and down to Kilnaughton on the south coast. A road extended from Kilnaughton along the south of the Oa via Lurabus to (Upper) Killeyan, and eastwards along the south of the island by Lagavulin and Kildalton to Proaig. Finally there was a road branching off this one at Lagavulin heading north-west via Kilbride to join the road along Laggan Bay at Knockangle where there was an inn or change-house.

The Stent Committee had accepted responsibility for maintaining roads and bridges on the island, but in 1775 this duty was taken out of its hands by the Argyllshire Road Act, which gave authority to the shire's Commissioners of Supply (local government) to levy money for this purpose and appoint district committees and surveyors.[40] The Stent Committee, however, continued to look after local matters since the commissioners had little interest in most roads on the island. The Stent Committee provided money from time to time for the building of bridges across the main rivers. It seems that bridges already existed over the River Sorn at Kilarrow and the River Laggan at Corary. In 1776 the decision was made to build a wooden bridge over the River Duich. This was to result in maintenance problems until, remarkably for this early date, it was replaced by a bridge of cast iron.[41]

Langlands' map of 1801 shows the road from Port Askaig to Bowmore, via Kilmeny, and the road along the south coast from Killeyan in the Oa to Trudernish as major routes, presumably suitable for carriages. It also represents a network of other lesser routes, perhaps little more than paths, including one around the coast from Killinallan at the head of Loch Gruinart by Bolsa and Ardnahoe to Port Askaig, and thence down the Sound of Islay to Proaig (Fig. 1.1). This never developed into a road for wheeled transport.[42]

In 1812 the Trustees under the Act of Parliament (of 1775) for making and repairing roads and bridges in Argyllshire commissioned a report from a surveyor, Samuel Crawford, on the state of the roads and bridges in Islay. He reported that there had been no regular meetings of a roads committee on Islay for several years and no district clerk had been appointed to oversee the business. The tenants and cottars of the parishes of Kildalton and Kilchoman had been in the habit of performing their annual statute labour, but those of Kilarrow and Kilmeny had mostly, for several years, commuted their service to a money payment. Those who continued to provide their service personally had been working on a new road to Glen Cattadale, presumably the present one from Bridgend to Cluanach. Another new road was being created through the Oa from Cornabus towards Kinnabus. Crawford also noted recent work on repairing and rebuilding several bridges. Direct responsibility for looking after the island's roads and bridges was only lifted from the inhabitants a few years later. A new Act of Parliament of 1843 for making and maintaining roads in Argyll resulted in a charge on the rates for funding work from then on.[43]

Nevertheless, the present 'high' road from Port Ellen to Bridgend was started in 1846 largely at the expense of the laird in order to give employment to the poor of the island suffering from the effects of the potato famine. The road was later finished by John Ramsay and Charles Morrison after they acquired Islay in the 1850s, and Ramsay was responsible for having the road from Port Ellen to Bowmore constructed as well. The last Campbell laird had left unfinished the road from Bridgend via Mulindry to Ballygrant and the locals had to petition in 1858 for the last section from Ardachie to Barr to be completed. The 'low' road from Port Ellen to Bowmore was constructed for John Ramsay. It had to be floated across the peat on birch faggots.[44]

There is little concrete information on the state of Islay's roads prior to modern times. Most would have travelled any distance by horse, but the Stent Committee received a report in 1788 that the bridge over the River Duich had been clayed and gravelled, and was sufficiently strong for foot passengers as well as horses and carriages. At least the intention was there at that time for such modes of transport. On the other hand, an account of 1825 describes how forty-five years previously there were no carriage roads on the island and only about two or three carts, whereas by 1825 there were 90 miles of carriage road and over 500 carts. By the 1860s there was a stagecoach service which connected Bowmore with Port Askaig and Port Ellen. This main route way, at least, must have been reasonably well maintained by that time. A traveller's account of 1890 describes leaving the Bridgend Hotel by the coach at six in the morning, in order to catch the eight-thirty ferry from Port Ellen. Although the writer was seated on the top of the coach the journey was comfortable and only took two hours.[45] In 1915 a motor mail-bus service was started between Port Askaig and Port Ellen, and local bus services have been operating ever since.[46]

A ferry service from Port Askaig, undoubtedly across the Sound of Islay to Feolin on Jura, is first documented in the rental of 1541, where it is listed immediately after Dunyvaig, possibly because it also was in the hands of the captain of the castle there. This service probably goes back to much earlier times, and has been provided continuously ever since. Another ferry service from Lagg in Jura would have provided access to the mainland through Keills in Knapdale. The present Port Askaig Hotel has its roots in the seventeenth century though the present building is mostly of nineteenth-century date. It has always provided a service for travellers. The multitude of animals driven off the island annually was in earlier times accommodated in a fank behind Port Askaig, first recorded in 1686. After complaints from the drovers about the difficulties of keeping cattle here while they were waiting to cross the water, a request was made to the laird in 1787 for sixty or eighty acres of land to create a 'proper' fank. Attempts by the inhabitants of Port an-draighion (on the land of Carnbeg), Gleann Choireasdail and Proaig in 1821 to encroach on the rights of the Port Askaig service were to be firmly resisted.[47]

In the years after World War II a small boat called the *Rothesay Castle* provided a ferry service from Islay to Jura. The route was taken over by Western Ferries from 1969 to 1998 with their *Sound of Gigha*, and since then the *Eilean Dhiura*, operated by Argyll and Bute Council. Both of these ferries are landing-craft type vessels capable of taking cars or lorries. A fast and frequent service can be provided between the two islands, and there has been much debate in recent years on whether the road through Jura from Feolin to Lagg could be greatly improved and another ferry service provided from Lagg to Keillmore in Knapdale, thus offering an alternative route to these two islands than the relatively long sea voyage from Kennacraig. Proponents of this 'overland route' point out that it would provide a quicker service with better access to Oban and the north, as well as Glasgow, and that the ferries could provide a turn-up-and-sail service. Obvious disadvantages include an increased flow of traffic, including lorries, through an otherwise 'unspoiled' Jura. A feasibility study, however, commissioned in 2005, was not totally enthusiastic about the viability of this option, and since then, the enhancement of the facilities at Port Askaig for the operation of the ferry service from Kennacraig will mean that the overland route will probably not be viewed as an option again for some time to come.

The establishment of a 'packet' – ferry service – providing a direct communication from Islay to West Loch Tarbert, dates to 1764, and was another initiative of the Stent Committee. It part funded it, and appointed a subcommittee to run it, though the boats used successively for this service were contracted to the committee. They not only carried passengers, the better-off ones in a cabin, and the mail, but could also take animals and other freight. The return sail to West Loch Tarbert was to be made at least once a week.[48] This was a uniquely ambitious venture for Argyll and the Western Islands at that time, giving Islay remarkably good communications with the outside world.

In 1822 the Stent Committee expressed its willingness to subsidise the running of a steam boat in place of the sailing ship used for the packet up to that time, should Campbell of Shawfield and others contract to supply one. A steam-boat service commenced two years later.[49] The boat in question was a wooden paddle-steamer built in Port Glasgow in 1815, renamed *Maid of Islay*. She was joined in 1827 by another paddle-steamer named *Maid of Islay No. 2*, and the two supplied a service connecting not just Islay with West Loch Tarbert but also Oban, Mull, Skye, Greenock and elsewhere. These sailings tied in with others provided by other companies. Later Islay proprietors, including Charles Morrison and John Ramsay, provided steamer services which were taken over in 1876 by David Hutchison & Co., a company that was to develop into (Caledonian) MacBrayne (CalMac), still operating today.[50]

MacBraynes' ferries remained small in the post World War II years, with limited capacity to take vehicles. A separate cargo service was provided by boats sailing direct from Glasgow. Then in 1968, an alternative ferry service was provided by a newly formed, rival company, Western Ferries, with a 'roll on, roll off' ship, the *Sound of Islay*, soon replaced by the larger *Sound of Jura*, sailing from Kennacraig to Port Askaig, capable of taking container lorries. MacBraynes was forced to compete, and being the recipient of large government grants, was better able to come out on top. Western Ferries was forced to give up its Kennacraig–Port Askaig service in 1981, and CalMac took over Kennacraig as its mainland base, in place of its jetty further up West Loch Tarbert, and commenced the alternate runs to Port Ellen and Port Askaig that are a feature of its service today.

To aid with navigation, seven lighthouses were erected around the coasts of Islay. The earliest was erected on the island of Orsay at the south end of the Rhinns for the Commissioners of Northern Lighthouses in 1824–25. Then in 1832 the lighthouse at Port Ellen was built by Walter Frederick Campbell to aid shipping using the harbour of his new village. Other lighthouses followed at Ruvaal at the northern tip of the island in 1857 (Plate XXXVIII), at MacArthur's Head on the Sound of Islay in 1861, the Loch Indaal Light near Port Charlotte in 1869, the lighthouse on Eilean a' Chuirn off the south-east corner of Islay in 1907, and Caraig Mhor Lighthouse on the Sound of Islay near Port Askaig in 1928. They did not lead to the total elimination of shipwrecks around Islay's coasts, but no doubt the known toll of well over 100 would have been much higher without them.[51]

The first aeroplane to land on Islay, a small private one that took off from Renfrew Airport, touched down near the Machrie Hotel in July 1928. Five years later the first scheduled passenger service was started by Northern and Scottish Airways with daily flights from Renfrew to Campbeltown and the airport at Glenegedale on Islay, now known as Port Ellen Airport.[52] There are now daily flights from Glasgow, although they are sometimes cancelled or delayed by bad weather.

The development of a postal service for Islay followed improvements in other means of transport. The first receiving office for mail on the island was established at Port Askaig in 1767. Mail was taken by runner from there to Bowmore, and from Feolin on Jura up to Lagg where it was ferried to Keills on the mainland. The service developed considerably with the coming of the steamers and the establishment of other offices elsewhere on the island, including Port Ellen and Bridgend.[53]

Islay was connected by a telephone service to the mainland in 1935, fifty-six years after the first establishment of telephone exchanges in Britain. Since 1973 the island has had its own newspaper, the *Ileach*, issued every two weeks by the Islay Council of Social Service. It is avidly read by both islanders and exiles, and is now one of the main communications for all Islay news and business.

Improved farming

Improved communications and trade were only two of the factors that were opening up Islay to an increasing pace of change from the late eighteenth century. One of the main drivers for this was the determination by successive proprietors to improve the farming of the island, to bring this into line with the advancements made on their Lowland estates, and thus to bring in more rent. A key feature of the desired changes was to be the introduction of new tenants from elsewhere and the encouragement of a small group of Islay-bred farmers to take on farms as single tenants. There was an ongoing expectation that new methods and hard work would turn much of the island into productive arable land.

Daniel Campbell the younger built upon the efforts of his namesake, the first Shawfield laird, and applied for money from the Commissioners of the Forfeited Estates for financial support to introduce improvements. His second application in 1777 shows that he wanted to bring in qualified farmers from other areas of the country in order to introduce the best farming practices. He also proposed sending some of his tenants to Northumberland and other parts of England to gain training and experience in agriculture. In order to encourage the growing of a greater variety of crops, including wheat, turnips and clover, he intended to offer premiums. The assessor for his application, however, politely dismissed the efficacy of these proposals and only recommended those that would encourage fishing.[54]

Daniel's views on the state of agriculture on the island are also given in a proposal, dated 1776, on how to introduce improvements from 1779 when most of the tacks of Islay lands would come to an end.[55] Campbell was clear that lack of progress in improving Islay farming was due to the fact there were two classes of tenants, neither of whom were greatly minded to improve their husbandry. The great or gentlemen tenants possessed several quarterlands, which they set on a yearly basis to poor people they called their farmers. While these gentlemen tenants were only concerned with their rents, their farmers could only take a short-term approach to what returns they could get from the land. The small tenants, in groups of four to eight, farmed a single quarterland jointly and lived in 'indolence and debate'.

The solution to these defects was to limit the holdings of the gentlemen tenants to such an extent of land that could readily be managed by a good improver, and to remodel the farms of the small tenants so that each had their own holding. The proposal also expressed the belief that there was much land that could be improved, and also mosses and bogs that could be drained and turned into fertile land, but only on the issue of new leases once the current ones ended.

The main critic of the Shawfield methods of estate management, John Murdoch, writing in the 1850s, saw the use of leases as a means of controlling what tenants could and should do, as the start of the decline of Islay. Murdoch was perhaps even more optimistic than the Shawfield lairds about the amount of ground on the island that could be reclaimed for agricultural purposes, but his vision of a population of 40,000, apparently living off the land, was not only counter to all reasonable trends of the period in streamlining farming and investing much more in industrial development and trade, it was hopelessly unrealistic.[56]

Daniel II had little chance to implement his proposals prior to his death in 1777. He had, however, started draining the salt marshes at the bottom of Loch Gruinart (the Gruinart Flats)[57] and may have been responsible for planning the Islay House Farm. This impressive, large steading at the back of Islay House dates to the later eighteenth century and is the earliest farm steading on the island (Plate XXXIX). His tenants could not aspire to anything like it, but they would have been expected to learn from the farming practised there. Daniel's brother and successor, Walter, was growing wheat on the home farm by 1784.[58]

By the end of the eighteenth century all the remaining wadsetters of Islay lands had been bought out and the Sunderland estate had been acquired as well. Neither the leases nor tacks, however, issued by Daniel Campbell in 1775 or those of Walter Campbell in the years from 1777 to 1802, demonstrate any considerable movement to improve farming by cutting the size of the holdings of the gentlemen tenants or tacksmen. Nor is there much evidence for the remodelling of the holdings of the small tenants.[59] Indeed, joint tenancy farms were to remain a feature of the Islay landscape throughout the nineteenth century. There was, however, a significant rise from the end of the eighteenth century onwards in the number of tacks to individual farmers, some of local stock, others from elsewhere, who were clearly improvers.

Cattle-ranching had been the preserve of some of the Islay gentry, wadsetters and feuars, but it seems it was also taken up by incoming gentlemen farmers. By 1799 Neil McGibbon, a writer in Inverary, and Shawfield's factor for Islay and Jura, held the tenancies of Goirtean an Uruisge, Lossit, Baleachdrach, Ballyclach, Eacharnach and Arivuine – a sizeable holding of lands, all contiguous. It is probable that McGibbon rented these lands for raising cattle for the growing markets in Scotland and England. Certainly they would have provided an abundance of pasture rather than arable. The minister of Kildalton parish wrote in 1794 that the gentlemen farmers employed almost all their time in rearing good black cattle, laying out their fine arable land for feeding them. They had large parks, seldom, if ever ploughed, retained for feeding their young cattle in the winter. He possibly had the surgeon, Dr Samuel Crawford in mind. Another probable cattle ranch was created for him in the late eighteenth century by adding the seaward end of Storakaig to Proaig, creating a large area of rough pasture bordering on the Sound of Islay. At Ballyclach there is a large, irregular enclosure, bounded by a dry-stone wall and overlying the ruins of earlier houses, which may have been created by McGibbon for wintering cattle in the manner described by the minister.[60]

Even by the early 1820s a visitor could report of Islay that it was not very interesting to a traveller, unless he should take pleasure in witnessing the rise and progress of agricultural improvement and wealth. He felt that the island had lost most of its distinctiveness, and was just like the Lowlands. It had opulent tenants, Lowland agriculture, good houses and roads.[61]

It is probable that in some cases the rearing and breeding of beasts, and the cultivation of crops undertaken by these improvers was not signifi-cantly better than that of the better tenants on joint tenancy farms, but the improvers had the advantage of scale, greater control over their farming operations, and wholehearted support from the proprietors – Walter Campbell of Sunderland and Campbell of Ballinaby as well as the Shawfield lairds. The fifty-eight Ilich who formed the Islay Association in 1838 would clearly all have regarded themselves as improvers, but only thirteen of them were then single tenant farmers. They included some farmers relatively new to the island, like George Chiene, the factor, in Eallabus; Colin McTavish, the surgeon appointed by the Stent Commit-tee, in Springbank; James Telfer in Skerrols, and William Webster, overseer for Islay and factor of the Campbells' Woodhall Estate, in Daill. Malcolm MacNeill in Lossit (Kilmeny parish) was the brother of Lord Colonsay, a noted improver. Colin MacLean in Laggan had until recently been the commander of the *Marquis of Hastings* for the East India Company.[62] Fourteen other of the founder members of the Association were joint tenant farmers, and several of the others were residents of the villages of Portnahaven and Bowmore.

The object of the association was the improvement of the Highland breed of cattle and sheep on the islands of Islay, Jura and Colonsay, and this was to be encouraged by the holding of an annual competition at Bridgend (Plate XL). Other worthy farming aims soon followed, including the improvement of crops and ploughing. The association still survives today as the Islay, Jura and Colonsay Agricultural Association, and over the 170 years of its existence has had a large and positive influence on farming and life on Islay.[63]

The Highland breed of cattle remained a preoccupation of Islay farmers throughout the nineteenth century and in the 1930s John Granville Morrison of Islay (from 1964 Baron Margadale of Islay) built up a herd of Highland cattle that was much admired. Farmers who came to the island from Ayrshire and the Lowlands in the second half of the eighteenth century were more interested in dairy farming, and Ayrshire and Friesian cows, bred for their capacity to deliver milk, from which cheddar and Dunlop type cheeses were made, were a feature of Islay life until relatively recent times. The 'draft' left over from the production of whisky in the distilleries has long been found to be a good winter feed for cattle. Islay farmers also bred Clydesdale horses, an essential part of farming life, providing the pulling power for ploughs, carts and other farm equipment prior to the general use of tractors after World War II. At some farms, like Cladville, Tallant, Torradale and Sleiverin, can still be seen the open-air horse-gangs where horses turned the mechanisms for operating threshing mills. The abandoned barn of lot 52, Glenmachrie, still contains a threshing mill by J. & T. Taylor of Ayr. Adjacent to the barn is the horse-gang that powered the threshing mill, its turning mechanism by J. & T. Young, also of Ayr. Horses were listed among the main exports of the island in the late 1870s.[64]

Essential assets for improving farmers were a substantial lime-mortared farmhouse with a slate roof, and a farmsteading, often laid out as ranges around a court. The ranges included such buildings as a barn, byre, stable, cart shed and milking parlour. An impressive early example, little changed since it was erected in about 1826 for a Fife farmer, George Whyte, is the large steading at Kilchiaran in the Rhinns, built on a semicircular plan.[65] More typical of prosperous farms are rectangular steadings like those at Balulive, Eorrabus, Coullabus, Ballachlaven and Knockdon. At Torony in the Rhinns such a steading has been created incorporating two earlier dry-stone houses. By the late nineteenth century two-storey farmhouses with slate roofs and steadings were a feature of the Islay landscape (Plate XLI).

Lord Teignmouth noted how Campbell of Sunderland had erected cottages of stone and mortar, slated with chimneys and fireplaces 'in the English manner' (that is incorporated in the gable walls) for the tenants on his estate. Their byres stood separately.[66] Such houses replaced more primitive dry-stone houses all over the island as the century progressed.

There is an architect's plan in the Ramsay of Kildalton Papers of a farm servant's cottage, annotated to say it could be built for £90, exclusive of carriages and excavations (Fig. 10.1). It appears to be fairly typical of the houses being provided for farm workers in the late nineteenth century. It is 32 feet by 18½ feet overall (9.75 m by 5.64 m), with a concrete floor, gable walls, slate roof and attic lit by skylights. Entrance is by a centrally placed doorway, opening on to a lobby, behind which is a pantry, under the stair to the attic, and a bed closet with its own window in the back wall of the house. The lobby gives access, left, to a room with a fireplace and window, and right to a kitchen, similarly sized and provided. The bed closet opens off the kitchen. Often, in such houses, an out-shot was added at the back, with a back door and a sink.

A priority for single tenant farmers was to create a new landscape of regular enclosed fields with below-ground drainage. Drystane dykers were brought in from Durham, Northumberland and Galloway in the nine-teenth century to build, and encourage the locals to build, these walls in preference to the traditional turf dykes. Many of these still stand, several of them demonstrating the characteristic Galloway loose upper structure that was intended to discourage animals from jumping them. A plan of Skerrols

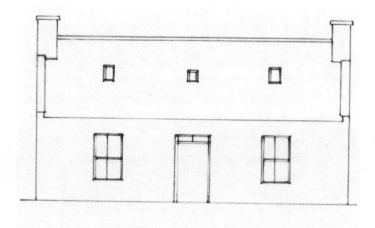

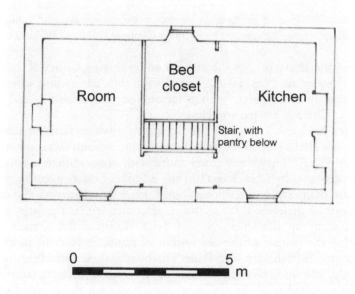

Room

Bed closet

Kitchen

Stair, with pantry below

0   5
        m

Figure 10.1 Plan and elevation of a farm servant's cottage,
from a drawing in the Ramsay of Kildalton Papers (ML, TD 1284/9/39).

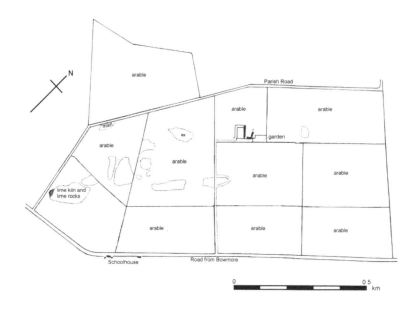

Figure 10.2 Plan of the farm of Skerrols in the early nineteenth century,
redrawn from the original by William Gemmill (NAS, RHP 11024).

dating to the 1820s or '30s shows what an improving farmer of the period
expected to create (Fig. 10.2). The farm is divided up into eleven neat
fields, mostly rectangular, with a farmhouse and steading, and also a
limekiln. There is no pasture land.[67]

Walter Frederick Campbell commissioned a whole series of new farm
plans in the 1830s and 1840s from the surveyor, William Gemmill, many of
which survive.[68] They show many farms with rather different boundaries
than represented by MacDougall in the middle of the eighteenth century.
There are many changes resulting from further rationalisation and straigh-
tening out of marches, but the major difference is that the large areas of
moor containing the shielings have been detached from many farms,
indicating the demise of the old system of transhumance. In some cases,
for instance Ballachlaven and Baile Tharbhach, these have been planned
separately, and show how the old shieling grounds were being cultivated.[69]
The optimistic view of the time may have been that these would develop
into new improved farms. It was not to be in either of these cases
though such a process did make more progress elsewhere, for instance
on the land of Airigh Ghuaidhre. The mid-eighteenth-century map shows
that it then extended from its core area, a low hill now crowned by a
sheepfold, eastwards down Glen Logan to the Sound of Islay (Fig. 10.3).
The Gemmill survey of c.1830 shows the farm minus the extensive tract of

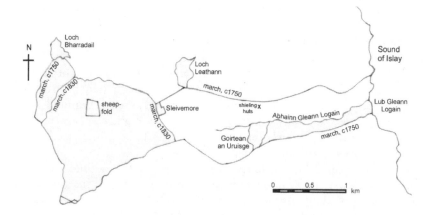

Figure 10.3 Sketch map of Airigh Ghuaidhre,
compiled from the MacDougall map and later surveys.

Glen Logan with its, probably by now abandoned, settlement of Goirtean an Uruisge. The 1841 census lists four families settled at Sleivemore beyond the new eastwards boundary of Airigh Ghuaidhre, and there was one family there in 1861, probably occupying a fine new house (now abandoned and in ruins) set in an extensive garden. Its development into a new farm may only have been curtailed by the creation of a large sheep run in the 1850s, into which it was presumably incorporated.

By the time the first-edition Ordnance Survey Maps of Islay were published in 1878, new field systems had swept away earlier infield–outfield systems with their unenclosed rigs, all over the island. These are for the most part the fields that can be seen today, the old rigs and dykes ploughed flat, and drainage provided, not by surface run-off between the rigs, but by subsoil drains.

Not long before his sequestration in 1847, Walter Frederick Campbell had secured a grant of £30,000 from the Enclosure Commissioners for drainage works. This was probably the impetus for the erection of the tile-works at Foreland, responsible for providing many of the necessary drainage tiles for creating these drains.[70] The Islay rental for the year to Whitsunday 1853 records drainage interest paid by tenants across the whole island.

With the end of transhumance, cattle were herded in the new enclosed fields and milking parlours were provided for the milk cows. Crops of turnips and grass were now grown for cattle-feed in the winter months. The circular stone stances for haystacks, erected in the nineteenth century, can be seen on the farms of Kilbride and Torradale. It was, however, noted in the late 1870s that, although the area of arable land in the island had been greatly increased, not as much progress had been made as had been expected. Apart from corn (barley and oats) the main crops were turnips and potatoes. In many years there was a large surplus of potatoes for export.[71]

The new farms still required large labour forces but the labourers were not now to have their own stake as subtenants on the farms where they worked. They were often provided with accommodation or cottages, or may have walked to work from the villages where many may have settled. They were a work force taken on and relinquished as needs required. They advertised their availability for work at the annual market in Bowmore for horses and lambs, or the May market in Bridgend. They were feed by the farmers for six months at a time.[72]

The journalist, John Murdoch, writing in 1850 at a time when the sequestrated estate of Walter Frederick Campbell was still in administration, came up with an ambitious scheme which he believed would cancel the debt on the Islay Estate, improve the soil, better the condition of the inhabitants, restore such land as would be sold to its 'natural owners', its cultivators, and leave the residue to Walter Frederick Campbell, whose plight he viewed with considerable sympathy. The basis of his scheme was to divide the island into 3,000 lots for outright sale. He hoped that many of them would be acquired by natives, or those with Islay ancestry, but needless to say Murdoch's idea was ignored. It is interesting, however, for its insight into contemporary problems, and for Murdoch's desire to sweep away a system where the tillers of the ground reaped very little benefit for themselves, and the farmers who employed them were at the mercy of proprietors and their factors.[73]

A change to the Islay landscape, as radical in its implications for much of the population as that proposed by Murdoch, emerged from the Brown administration of the years from 1848 to 1853. That was the introduction of large-scale sheep farming, which required little land management and relatively few workers. Leicester, Cheviot and Blackface sheep replaced the smaller and more delicate local animals. The results for the Ilich were the opposite of what Murdoch sought. The rentals from 1843 to 1856 show William Webster, the Islay overseer, creating an ever larger land-holding for himself, including several adjacent farms in the parish of Kilarrow and Kilmeny – Daill, Kilbranan, Druiminduich, Airigh Ghuaidhre, Storakaig and Roskern. Much of this was made into a large sheep run. One of its large fanks (sheepfolds) at Airigh Ghuaidhre is still a prominent feature in the landscape (Fig. 10.4). It is built over the site of the township of that name.[74]

On many farms sheep were kept as part of a mixed farming economy. Kilennan, however, was noted in 1881 as a sheep farm in the hands of John McKellar, who also farmed extensively on the mainland and in Ireland, and the first edition Ordnance Survey Maps demonstrate that, by the 1870s, much of the island had been given over to them. The evidence

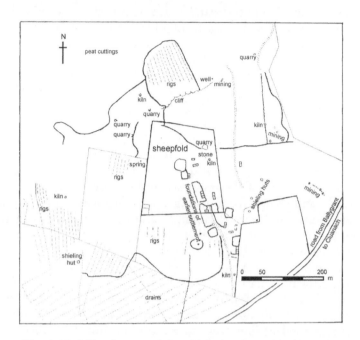

Figure 10.4 Sketch map of the old farm of Airigh Ghuaidhre,
with a sheepfold erected over its ruins in the mid nineteenth century.

is provided by fanks, some with sheep dips added in the twentieth century, and the remains of metal fence-lines straddling the moors to separate the runs. Out on the moors can be found smaller, makeshift enclosures, many created in the ruins of earlier houses, for providing shelter, particularly protection for ewes and their lambs from predators at lambing time. At Gortantaoid are the ruins of a barn for storing the fleeces prior to them being sold. It was reported in the late 1870s that a considerable number of cross lambs were sent to Glasgow early in the season and that the hill districts were covered with thriving flocks of Blackface and Cheviot sheep.[75]

Some large sheep farms survived into the second half of the twentieth century, and sheep are still raised by several Islay farmers.[76] The boom in sheep farming, however, was apparently over by the 1890s, local farmers being unable to compete with foreign competition. John Nicolls, mine manager, Robolls, reported in an interview at Bridgend in 1894 to the Royal Commission (Highlands and Islands, 1892) that he had lived on the island for the previous eighteen years and in that time the present system of large sheep farms had proved rather disastrous for the island and the community. He said he had been told by the farmer of Finlaggan and Robolls (Alexander or James Greenlees), at the time he sold up, that after fifteen years he had not made a brown penny.[77]

After the acquisition of the island by the Morrisons in the middle of the nineteenth century, and the creation of other estates, more and more of the old pasture grounds and outlying areas of cultivation were viewed primarily as shootings for stalking deer. Writing about 1859, John Murdoch was aware of these traces of previous farming activity on the moors. He deplored a system that extolled the virtues of 'high and large farming' and which banished the people to make a solitude for game.[78] From the 1960s some moorland has been covered with conifer plantations for commercial exploitation, including large areas in the Laggan Valley, the Oa, the southern Rhinns, Finlaggan and Staoisha.

Farming remains an important source of income on the island down to the present day, most of the business still being concerned with raising stock, cattle and sheep, for fattening up by mainland farmers prior to slaughter. Dunlossit Estate is currently also experimenting with raising pigs, in the expectation that their foraging activities will encourage woodland regeneration. The high costs, however, involved in importing fertilisers, animal feed, etc. and shipping beasts to the mainland and then transporting them to market, are clear disadvantages to Islay farmers, and many are diversifying into other areas of business including holiday accommodation. Many farmers receive compensation from Scottish Natural Heritage for allowing geese to graze undisturbed on their land in winter, although there is often much unhappiness about the level of compensation and how it is calculated. European Union subsidies are a major source of income, but reform of the Common Agricultural Policy will clearly lead to smaller and smaller sums of money for Islay farmers. At present the future does not look bright for this long-standing industry.

There are now few opportunities for a younger generation to enter this profession. Dunlossit Estate has recently done away with its tenant farmers, and now controls its farming operations centrally. There are relatively few farms owner-occupied, these including the farms of the former Foreland Estate in the Rhinns which was sold by Charles Morrison in 1978. Generally, it appears to be the continuing policy of the Morrisons (Islay Estate) to retain the rest of their land in the hands of tenant farmers. These tenants may pay relatively low rents but there appears to be little or no money for maintenance and improvements to their houses and steadings. Islay House has been sold off by the Morrisons, but not other houses surplus to requirements. One of the features of the Islay landscape today is derelict farmhouses, allowed to deteriorate beyond likely renovation, rather than put on the market.

Planned villages of the eighteenth and nineteenth centuries

From the point of view of successive lairds in the late eighteenth and nineteenth century a key consideration in improving their Islay estates was to reduce the population on the land so that single tenancy farms could be created for improving farmers. The deliberate creation of villages was one ploy for taking the surplus population. The villagers would provide a pool of labourers for hire, and otherwise could turn to commerce or other industries to make a living.

Bowmore is an early example of a Scottish planned village. Its establishment on the land of Ardlarach in 1768 owes much to Daniel Campbell the younger's desire to clear the inconvenient settlement of Kilarrow out of the way of his ambitious planned landscape around Islay House. From his point of view it would also have made sense to encourage a settlement where there could be port facilities and a population including craftsmen and other specialists (Plate XLII).

One of the first steps in creating the new settlement was the building at the laird's expense of the new church at Bowmore for the newly created parish of Kilarrow and Kilmeny. It was erected by 1767. It is still the focal point of the village, its distinctive round shape for long only challenged by the distillery in defining the character of the place. The settlement that grew up around the church had a regular grid pattern of streets with houses built by the inhabitants themselves, of lime and stone, with fireplaces incorporated in their gable walls. Early leases indicate that inhabitants also had three acres of land nearby and the right to graze animals on the common moor. Many also probably had their own brew-houses in their backyards.[79]

By 1793 there were 500 inhabitants in Bowmore living in 110 houses, 50 of which had slate roofs, 20 tiles, and the rest thatch. The concern expressed by the Stent Committee in 1804 to do something about the destructive crowd of pigs running up and down the streets, which were also graced with the dunghills of the villagers, does not paint a very flattering picture of village life at that time.[80]

Such nuisances must have been removed prior to the 1830s when it was noted that Bowmore was well provided with shops, while twenty or so years later this 'metropolis of Islay' had a population of from 900 to 1200.[81] The Andersons wrote in their travel guide that

the plan has been but indifferently observed, houses being permitted to be erected of any size, shape or material suited to the means and views of the builder. A principal street, ascending a pretty street hill, is terminated at the west by the school-house . . . Another wide and also ascending street crosses this at right angles, beginning at the quay, which is a substantial edifice, admitting common coasting vessels to load and unload, and terminates at the summit . . . by the church . . . A third street runs parallel to the one first described, along which the houses present so poor an appearance as to leave the popular designation it has received in the village, of the 'Beggar Row', far from being a misnomer.[82]

Gartnatra, described as 'a continuation of tile-roofed cottages extending partially along the shore from Bridgend', was effectively a suburb of Bowmore. Another travel writer in the late 1860s noted several churches, Free, Baptist and Established, and the building, then in progress, of a large poorhouse. By then, however, several houses were empty, their former occupants having emigrated to America, and the pier appeared not to be much used.[83] Although Bowmore could never develop into a port suitable for modern shipping, the town thrived in the longer term as Islay's capital and largest settlement.

The origins of the village of Portnahaven on a creek at the south end of the Rhinns lie in a settlement of fishermen encouraged by Walter Campbell of Shawfield in the late eighteenth century. The houses of the inhabitants, however, were later said to have been miserable hovels, many apparently cut into the side of a bank with a built wall across the front. After it became part of the estate of Walter Campbell of Sunderland in 1814 this proprietor created a new planned settlement around the creek and encouraged the inhabitants to build new cottages (Plate XLIII). These were described in the 1830s as having slate roofs, windows and fireplaces, and included among them were the shops of smiths, grocers and other tradesmen, as well as a public house. A parliamentary church was erected in 1828 to serve the southern portion of the parish of Kilchoman. By the 1860s there were about sixty houses and in 1881 a population of 361.[84]

In 1833 Walter Frederick Campbell of Islay erected the village of Port Wemyss, named for his father-in-law, the Earl of Wemyss, about 300 metres south-west of Portnahaven. The plan is D-shaped, and to the back of the settlement the long narrow plots of land offered to the inhabitants can still be traced. This was also a settlement of fishermen. It had a population of 263 in 1881.[85]

Walter Frederick was also responsible for founding the island's two main villages after Bowmore – Port Ellen and Port Charlotte, respectively in Kildalton parish and the Rhinns. Port Ellen was named for his wife, Lady Ellinor Charteris, while Port Charlotte commemorated his mother, Lady Charlotte Campbell.

Port Ellen was founded in 1821 on the sheltered Loch Leòdamais on the land of Tighcargaman. Already by the 1830s several tradesmen had settled, but apart from the masons and wrights employed in building there was not enough business for them to thrive. Lord Teignmouth particularly noted a baker from Glasgow, tempted over by an advertisement. He was struggling because the locals' staple was oatcakes, baked by themselves, whereas the wheaten bread he could offer was considered a luxury for special occasions. One of the main imperatives for the erection of the town had been the expectation that it would become a herring station but this failed to materialise.[86] Instead the village became a centre for distilling.

Port Ellen had a population of 673 by 1845.[87] 'Gowrie' describes it in 1868 as 'row of white-washed, plain, two-storey houses, running round the harbour, built so near the water that the southerly winds of water coat all the windows with sea-salt, and a street behind the shelter of a rock continued to the open bay.'[88] 'Gowrie' also noted the unoccupied houses resulting from an exodus of several inhabitants to America a year or two previously. There were few opportunities for employment locally apart from in the distilleries. A feeling of gloom was accentuated by a heatwave which had robbed the village of its water supply, forcing the people to draw their water from the stream beside the distillery, where they were also washing their clothes. On the other hand, there was then a branch of the City of Glasgow Bank, situated at Port Ellen Distillery, and a reading-room supplied with magazines and papers.[89] The latter had been set up in 1858 by some locals, and soon developed into a library, and a place for educational talks and soirées. A resolution was wisely taken early on to allow nothing relating to 'total abstinence' to be introduced into the news and reading-room lectures.[90] Port Ellen developed into the largest village on Islay after Bowmore, an important distilling centre and ferry port.

Port Charlotte was founded in 1828 at Skiba on the land of Glassans. Here there was a mill and change-house, where the Lochindaal Distillery was established from 1832, becoming one of the main sources of employment for the villagers. As with Port Ellen, Port Charlotte was a planned settlement with two-storey houses. Prospective inhabitants were encouraged by relatively large grants of four acres of land on plots laid out to the south-west of the village. Indeed, if Lord Teignmouth is to be believed, the generous provision of land could have held back the development of the village as a centre of trade and industry. He feared that the inhabitants would settle for an existence as small-time farmers on their plots rather than develop other skills or make themselves available as day labourers.[91] Certainly, Port Charlotte never developed to the same extent as the main villages in the other two parishes, Bowmore and Port Ellen, and is noted more for being picturesque than a centre for shops and services.

Other small settlements or villages grew up in the nineteenth century adjacent to the distilleries, with houses, and sometimes other facilities for the workers. The most notable of these continues to be Bruichladdich in the Rhinns which now rivals Port Charlotte as the main centre in Kilchoman parish. Indeed, when a new parish church was erected in 1899, it was placed halfway between the two villages in an attempt to keep both communities happy. Ballygrant, on the road between Bridgend and Port Askaig, uniquely developed as a mining village adjacent to an earlier meal mill and change-house. A row of miners' cottages is still occupied. The village of Keills, between Ballygrant and Port Askaig grew out of a settlement of weavers encouraged by Walter Frederick Campbell in 1828.

Much of the housing stock of Islay's villages remains nineteenth century, mostly considerably renovated and well maintained. As with other settlements throughout Scotland there are now significant numbers of houses, built from the 1930s by the local authority and housing associations for rent, and more up-market developments erected by local builders for sale.

Islay's villages turned out only to be a partial solution to the problems of an increasing population and the need to diversify the economy away from a total dependency on farming. The only industry that grew really big in the villages was whisky distilling, but it never created a need for large work forces.

Improvements to the quality of life followed developments elsewhere on the mainland. Piped water was introduced from the 1890s. Electricity did not make an appearance in Islay homes until after World War II. The Air Force had brought its own generators during the war and the North of Scotland Hydro Electric Board (created in 1943) inherited some of these in 1946 and developed its power station on the eastern edge of Bowmore. Islay was only linked by a submarine cable to the National Grid in 1961. There has also been since 2000 a pioneering wave power station at Portnahaven contributing electricity to the island's users.

The majority of Ilich live in the island's villages. Bowmore, with a population of about 1,000, is the main shopping and business centre, closely followed by Port Ellen. There are village stores in Port Askaig, Ballygrant, Bridgend, Bruichladdich, Port Charlotte and Portnahaven. Some businesses, like Alexander Currie's Bakery in Bowmore and Port Ellen, and David Harkness's general store in Bowmore, used to send carts or vans around the island to make sales to the rural community. There is a continuing reliance on shopping trips to the mainland and on mail-order catalogues. Nevertheless, the island offers a wide range of facilities and comforts.

The Museum of Islay Life, based in the former Free Church in Port Charlotte, opened its doors to the public in 1977, and is a much-admired local museum with displays on local life extending back to Mesolithic times, and an important library and archive of local material. The Finlaggan Trust opened its visitor centre in a restored cottage in 1989 and since then has greatly improved access to Finlaggan and understanding of this important site. There are displays of finds from the excavations, and ready access to Eilean Mor thanks to the bridge-building skills of the Army. At the time of writing an ambitious scheme to expand the centre's facilities is about to be realised. The Islay Family History Society was founded in 1991 and is providing a valued service to those, here and abroad, keen to trace their ancestry.

There is no cinema, although the 'screenmachine', a mobile one, occasionally visits the island, as do touring performances, singers, musicians, etc. Local societies, events and impromptu parties make up for the lack of professional entertainment. Since 1986 *Feis Ile*, the Islay Festival of Malt and Music, has been attracting large audiences from the local area and further afield. It takes place for a week each year, starting on the last weekend of May, and includes concerts, ceilidhs, children's shows, distillery open days, etc. There is also now a very successful, yearly Jazz Festival.

These events are the result of local initiative, nowhere seen better than in the fundraising campaign to have a swimming pool so that the children of Islay and Jura could learn to swim. The splendid MacTaggart Leisure Centre opened in 1991 in a converted bonded warehouse in the centre of Bowmore, gifted by Bowmore Distillery, and the water is kept to temperature as a by-product of the distilling process.

Emigrants and Visitors

There is considerable evidence for population shifts affecting Islay from the eighteenth century onwards. Many islanders moved off the land, often off the island altogether, and improved communications opened the place up to outside influences and, to a certain extent, settlers from elsewhere. Islay has not significantly been left behind by the increasing pace of change in modern times, but has in recent times found its distinctive identity challenged and difficult to maintain.

Clearance and emigration

A sense of adventure, the belief that life could be better, motivated many from the 1720s onwards to seek their fortune elsewhere. The move off the land in the eighteenth and nineteenth centuries in many cases took Ilich beyond the shores of their island, a step aided by improved communications. Many went to the developing industrial centres on mainland Britain, especially to Glasgow and the surrounding area, as they still do today. In 1862 Ilich based in Glasgow founded *An Comunn Ileach* (The Glasgow–Islay Association), which continues to this day to encourage and help islanders in that city. Emigration to regions of the world beyond Britain, especially North America, has attracted much more attention.

Often those who left the island were reacting to fears of possible or actual changes that would undermine their livelihood on the island. Improved farming, and other events like the potato famine, meant that the desires of many to carry on a traditional way of life on the land were bound to be thwarted. The 1824 rental shows that there were over 60 joint tenancies shared by over 700 tenants. By 1863 joint tenancies had halved in number since 1824, and had all but disappeared by the end of the nineteenth century.[1]

Many of these tenants would have moved voluntarily, sought better opportunities elsewhere, but others were torn unwillingly from what they regarded as their heritage. All were aware that they were required to pack up and move on when their leases expired, but as more land was turned into improved farms, there were fewer opportunities for the smaller farmers to find tenancies for themselves. From at least the time of Daniel Campbell the Younger they had to submit offers to take on new tenancies in competition with others.[2]

This provided an opportunity for the proprietors in the nineteenth century to reduce the numbers on the land by accepting offers from smaller, rather than larger, groups of tenants. It then became easier for these smaller groups to agree on consolidation of their holdings, moving from a runrig system of periodic allocation of rigs to clearly defined holdings, for as long as their tenancy lasted, including a share of the former infield, outfield and heath or common pasture land. The tenants' houses, barns and byres normally continued to cluster together in townships, but in some cases the tenants' homes were on their own holdings. Examples of the latter include Ballitarsin and Eorrabus (Fig. 11.1). There are plans of both dating to the 1820s or '30s by William Gemmill.[3] They both depict a regular system of fairly large fields overlying earlier systems of 'old dykes not inserted'. The individual steadings are approached by their own roads. It is not clear if this settlement pattern resulted from the consolidation of the individual holdings or, at least in some cases, reflected trends extending back into the earlier settlement histories of these farms.[4]

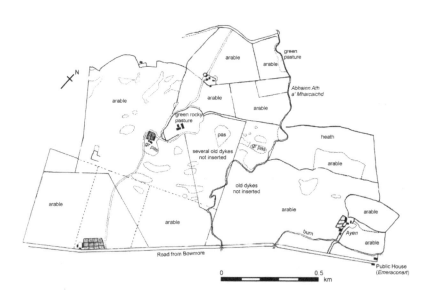

Figure 11.1 Plan of the farm of Eorrabus in the early nineteenth century, redrawn from the original by William Gemmill (NAS, RHP 10987).

In much of the West Highlands and Islands, crofting was developed in the nineteenth century, in place of joint tenancies, as a means of releasing land for sheep farming, stalking and other uses. Tenants had access to common pasture but held small plots of arable land or crofts individually, and these were often grouped, side by side, around crofting townships. The Crofters Act of 1886 gave crofters security of tenure. On Islay, crofting failed to develop, the settlement at Claddach at the south end of the Rhinns, being an exception. There were, however, several other individual small holdings by the end of the nineteenth century, including those originally provided in the 1820s for weavers at Keills, which Islay Estates had to recognise might be crofts in terms of the Act of 1886.[5]

As a means of satisfying the aspirations of cotters of good character, Walter Frederick Campbell came up with an alternative to crofting in 1829 – the lotting of holdings that were meant to provide self-sufficiency for individual families through growing crops and raising animals. Sixty-three lots in all, equal squares of twenty Scots acres of peat, were surveyed on the moorland of Duich, Torra, Glenegedale and Glenmachrie. There was an expectation that the holders would clear the land themselves. 'Spirited men' would apply fertilisers and grow vegetables. The land was very wet moss producing nothing but the most stunted heather, but there was gravel lying underneath the peat that could be thrown up to make an excellent top dressing, and shell sand and seaweed could be got from Laggan Bay.

The laird's report on this experiment in estate management, published in 1834, gives a glowing account of its success in encouraging the reclamation of ground for arable use, and how, by making the occupiers of the lots lairds, they were all contented and happy.[6] Twenty acres was, however, only half the size Murdoch had expected would be enough for any industrious family,[7] and whereas he expected that twelve acres of each lot would be arable, census returns suggest that two or three acres of arable was about all that most managed to create in each lot.

There is reason to think that the lots were at least partially intended as a dumping ground for problem tenants. For instance, the 1828 rental of Portaneilean contains a note about the multitude of disorderly cottars and the removal of some of them to 'the muir'. It was reported in 1846 that the region with the lots was known as Canada because the tenants there were shut out from more fertile land elsewhere.[8] The lots never developed into a thriving community, though a few have remained occupied up to the present day.

The lots only regularised and increased a move to the moors already being undertaken through their own initiative by Ilich, desperate to retain a foothold on the land. The rise in the island's population to nearly 15,000 in 1841 was only possible through the adoption of potatoes as the mainstay of the diet. Potatoes could thrive in poor quality peaty soil. The encourage-ment given by the Shawfield lairds, indeed the requirement, written into leases, to reclaim land from the moor for agricultural purposes, probably led some of the more enterprising or energetic subtenants to carve out farms for themselves. Such appear as pendicles on some early-nineteenth-century farm plans, like Diranea (Doir' an Fhèidh) on the land of Coullabus and Slevuha (Sliabh a' Chatha) on the land of Gartloist.[9]

The Revd John McLiesh of Kilchoman parish, writing in 1794, believed that Shawfield's rents had more than doubled in the previous dozen years through reclamation of moorland for arable.[10] Maybe at that time such processes were responsible and sustainable, but as time went on, it appears that too much was being expected of land that was too poor to provide a reliable return in crops for human consumption.

The ruins of late eighteenth- or early nineteenth-century houses can be found well out on the moors with associated systems of lazy-beds. Such is the house (later converted into a sheepfold) at Goirtean Bholsa at the mouth of Gleann Airigh an t-Sluic, on the farm of Baile Tharbhach. It is shown on Gemmill's plan of the 'Muir of Balliharvey'.[11] There are clearance cairns and a limekiln as well. This represents colonisation of shieling ground, and indeed, there is a shieling hut on top of a small knoll near the house.

Gemmill's plan of the neighbouring 'Muir of Ballichlavan' has a herd's house adjacent to ground improved by him.[12] This can now be traced as a plot of lazy-beds by the Abhain Airigh an t-Sluic (Plate XLIV), near a later sheepfold. It is difficult to believe that such settlements could have been sustainable in the longer term. The land may have grown potatoes in good years, but was hardly up to producing much else. In the aftermath of the failure of the potato crop in the 1840s many of these plots were abandoned and their cultivators must have been forced off the land, many of them overseas.

Other tenants later in the century had land to grow crops, but felt excluded from the moor, like Neil MacArthur in Mulreesh, who appeared before a hearing of the Royal Commission on the Highlands and Islands in 1892 because he wanted more grazing for raising cattle. Mulreesh, 'a small park which was at that time overgrown with rushes, heather, and rough grass, with a lot of lime rock jutting through here and there', was detached from the neighbouring single tenancy farm of Finlaggan in 1885, to be turned into eight small holdings. By 1892, these were shared between six tenants. Three of them had one or two cows each, and there was one horse and no sheep. More cattle were needed to dung the land, but those the tenants had, had to be sent away to be grazed elsewhere at considerable inconvenience and cost. The Mulreesh tenants were probably by no means alone in being caught in this type of insufficiency trap, and there is no evidence that anything was done for any of them. There was no long-term future on Islay for small-time farmers like them.[13]

In some cases, tenants were actually forced to move before their leases ran out. Such was the case at Kilchiaran where twenty-five families in all

were removed about 1826, by Walter Frederick Campbell, to make way
for George Whyte and the new steading built at the former's expense.[14]
How often this happened in the time of the Shawfield lairds is not known.
In his contribution to a parliamentary select committee on emigration in
1826, Walter Frederick Campbell endorsed the idea of subsidising 'the
redundant population' of the West Highlands and Islands to emigrate,
otherwise, proprietors like himself ended up having to support these
people rather than receiving rent from them. He had had some success in
getting some of them off his land into villages, but would have liked to be
able to force others to go abroad.[15]

The activities of William Webster in creating his sheep farm in the
Glen, in the 1840s and 1850s, were reported to the Royal Commission
(Highlands and Islands) by Duncan MacIndeor, one of the tenants
displaced from Airigh Ghuaidhre about 1854–55:

> I was a farmer and carried on farming in Airidh-Ghuairidh successfully
> for twenty-three or twenty-four years. I was always able to pay my rent,
> as my receipts will show. Mr Webster, the under-factor at this time, had
> put out a lot of small farmers and had taken the land into his own hands.
> He wanted my farm as well at the time, promising me another if I would
> give it up quietly. I refused to do so, and then he noticed me out of the
> farm. Nevertheless I had paid my rent, I protested against such unjust
> actions. He compelled me to leave my farm. I next wrote Mr Dickson
> [James Morrison's factor], and laid my case before him, but he was too
> late in taking steps in this line of action. Mr Webster had so falsified
> matters to Mr Dickson that before he knew the truth of the whole case
> the lease had been signed and Webster got the farm. Notwithstanding
> his fair promises about giving me another farm when he got possession
> of mine, I could not get another worth anything under him. Moreover,
> after my corn was sown and just coming through the ground, he sowed
> rye grass seed, and in harrowing it spoiled my corn crop, and I could not
> get compensation from him for it. There were many others as well as
> myself put out or deprived of their farms about this time to make way
> for Webster. Four tenants got notice to leave Airidh-Ghuairidh; six or
> seven got notice to leave Strongaig [Storakaig]. At or about that time.
> Rostern [Roskern] contained four who had to be moved from their
> holdings. Nosebridge had eight tenants who were also moved; Con-
> egarry [Kynagarry] also contained eight tenants; Benveridle [Beinn
> Bharra-dail] also contained seven tenants; and four farmers got notice
> to quit Kilbranan and three to quit Dranich; in other words no less than
> forty-four or forty-five had to leave their holdings to give scope to
> Webster and sheep.[16]

Whether for grazing sheep or cattle, the improving farmers, once established, acquired more and more of the land of joint tenancy farms. The

clearance of these was rarely recorded, but the process of abandonment by the tenants can be traced in the census. The townships and cottages were left to fall into ruin, or were sometimes superseded by sheepfolds. The first-edition Ordnance Survey maps of 1878 provide a comprehensive overview of these abandoned settlements.

Not all those who gave up their land and left Islay in the late 1840s and '50s were paupers, forced out by the failure of their potato crops. Some more enterprising or well-off islanders emigrated primarily because they could see economic advantage in doing so. Many of those went to North America, but at least some went as far as the goldfields of Australia and New Zealand.[17]

In 1862 and 1863 the new lairds of Islay, Charles Morrison, John Ramsay and Smith Child found about 400 willing to emigrate to Canada. Ferry fares were paid as an encouragement for these people, many of whom had been settled in the Oa, to go.[18] It has been reckoned that Islay's net out-migration in the 1860s may have amounted to as much as a quarter of the population.[19] It is clear that many Ilich left before they were pushed, or they were reduced to absolute penury.

These lairds may genuinely have thought they were doing a good thing in 'encouraging' poverty-stricken Gaelic speakers on to boats bound for a far country. It was certainly a good option for them in removing a financial burden that would have fallen largely on their shoulders as a result of the Poor Law Act of 1845. A letter written by John Ramsay to Charles Morrison in November 1859 clearly shows his concern that the number of paupers was getting out of hand, well above the national average. He supposed there were then over 600 in a population of 11,000, meaning one for every sixteen self-supporting members of society, compared with the national average of 1:23.[20]

Much contemporary opinion doubted that the lairds' actions were altruistic. John Ramsay in particular was accused in the press of enforced removals. William Livingston (Uilleam MacDhunlèibhe), an Ileach who had emigrated to Glasgow and become a fine poet in his native language, published a poem, *A Message for the Poet*, on the subject. It showed how 'injustice, Foreigners and taxes have triumphed', and how

> The district of the Oa has been stripped bare,
> The beautiful Lanndaidh and MacKay's Rinns;
> Sunny Largie with its many hollows
> Has a pathetic remnant on its slope;
> The Glen has become a green wilderness,
> Owned by men of hatred without tenants or crops.[21]

When Ramsay read a paper on 'Periodical Destitution in the Highlands and its Remedy' to the National Association for the Promotion of Social Science in Edinburgh in October 1863, he concluded that 'the remedy as plainly appears to be the local development of industry, so as to provide a greater supply of remunerative employment'.[22] It is difficult to make a good case that, in this regard, Ramsay, or the other proprietors, practised what he preached.

Sometimes the exodus consisted of the odd family or individual, leaving to better themselves, like Alexander Campbell, wadsetter of Lossit (Kilmeny) who settled in Jamaica, from at least 1757.[23] The minister of Kildalton parish complained in 1794 that there were more females than males in his charge since so many of the young men had left for the Lowlands or America.[24]

In some cases, large groups left together. An early documented example of this was the emigration of 472 Ilich to New York Colony in the years 1738, 1739 and 1740, at the instigation of Captain Lachlan Campbell, tacksman of Upper and (Nether) Leorin. Campbell apparently persuaded his party to go on the basis that each family would be given 200 acres, a share in the 100,000 acres offered by the governor of the colony in a proclamation of 1734 to families of loyal Protestants who should transport themselves from Europe. It appears, however, that Campbell deliberately misled his fellow settlers, knowing, in fact, that the 100,000 acres had long since been settled, and what was on offer was land at a rate of £3 per hundred acres. Campbell's dealings with the New York authorities were complicated by their realisation that what he actually wanted was to establish a kind of feudal lordship with himself as lord and the others as his tenants. This was a state of affairs that many of his party were trying to escape. It did not square with the ideals of the provincial officials with whom he had to deal, and they resisted his efforts to establish his lordship. Some Ilich went off and found land for themselves. Others were eventually given land, but no thanks to Campbell, who returned to Scotland to fight for the government against the Jacobites in 1745. In 1764 a certificate and letters patent were issued in the name of King George III to 145 survivors or descendants of those who left Scotland with Lachlan Campbell, giving them 'The Argyle Patent', a grant of 47,450 acres in Washington County for a yearly rent of two shillings and sixpence sterling per hundred acres.[25]

At the same time as Lachlan Campbell's party was heading for New York, other Ilich were making for Cape Fear in North Carolina. Encouragement for them to go was provided by the offer of tax exemptions for Protestant settlers, and favourable reports brought back by traders and early settlers. 'Highlanders' may have settled here as early as 1729, and others followed throughout the 1730s, many taking up North Carolina's offer to provide each with fifty acres. Those that could not afford the passage, and had no financial reserves to get them started in the New World, could go as indentured servants, and, after a few years, hope to save enough to set themselves up.[26] A party of around 350, including some from Islay, settled in Bladen County (later renamed Cumberland), 100 miles inland from the port of Wilmington, in 1739.[27] The main settlement at Cross Creek developed into the county town, Campbelltown, now known as Fayetteville. Others from Islay followed in 1755 on the brigantine, *Mary of Glasgow*, which belonged to Neil Campbell, possibly one of the party that had left for New York Colony with Lachlan Campbell.[28]

Soon North Carolina was to be the favourite destination of emigrants from the Western Isles. An open letter published in 1773 by 'Scotus Americanus', apparently an Islay man, painted a glowing picture of the benefits of settling in North Carolina. By 1776, there may have been as many as 12,000 of these Highlanders, able to provide 3,000 fighting men to support the Loyalist cause in the War of Independence. Several of these were evidently from Islay, like the sixty-two discovered on the brigantine *Carolina* when she was driven back to Campbeltown by bad weather in December 1774.[29]

Alexander Campbell, wadsetter of Balole, spent twelve years in Jamaica, extending his business interests to the islands of St Vincent and Grenada before finally settling with his family in North Carolina in 1775. He died four years later in the West Indies where he had gone to try and transfer his wealth, including negro slaves, to his new American home. He may have been the gentleman of wealth and merit of Islay descent who, it was reported in 1771, was about to lead a group of 500 from Islay and the adjacent islands to America. He can possibly be identified as the writer, 'Scotus Americanus', and was certainly the author of another letter that circulated in Skye encouraging emigration to North Carolina from that island. It confirms the availability of land at two shillings and sixpence a year per hundred acres, talks favourably of the climate and the quality of life of those already settled there. It alludes to a gentleman of Islay who went there two years previously, only returning a year ago to sell his wadset and stock in this country.[30]

Most of the Highlanders in North Carolina were loyal to Britain in the War of Independence, and many moved on to Canada after the British defeat. Canada thereafter supplanted North Carolina as a goal for emigrants, many of whom were encouraged by agents touting for business for shipping companies. One such was Archibald McNiven of Islay, who claimed to have been responsible for 12,000 Highlanders going to Cape Breton, Nova Scotia, Prince Edward Island and Upper Canada in the years from 1821 to 1832.[31]

Many Ilich who emigrated in the 1860s went to Ontario in Canada, where they joined others who had emigrated there in the early 1830s. John Ramsay of Kildalton paints a glowing picture of how happy and successful they were when he paid a visit in 1870. Others went to Australia, and one, W. N. Blair, who went to New Zealand, left reminiscences of life in Islay.[32] There was also a settlement of Islay people in southern Peru in the nineteenth century, resulting in a province of that name, and a now-abandoned town called Islay. More research is needed, however, on who was behind this initiative and why.

Visitors in peace and war

Much use has been made of the observations on Islay and its inhabitants by early travellers, like Martin Martin at the end of the seventeenth century and Thomas Pennant in 1771. Others visited on official business, like the Revd Dr John Walker, who came in the 1760s to make a report for the Commissioners of the Annexed Estates.

The establishment of steamboat services connecting Islay to the mainland, and increasing prosperity, encouraged a flow of tourists to the island. Friends and relatives of the proprietors had opportunities to fish and shoot, and the Morrisons let the shootings on their lands from their acquisition of Islay in 1853. An Islay guidebook, printed in the 1930s, noted that the shootings of Islay House covered over 70,000 acres, two thirds of which were moor. The covers were also fairly extensive and well stocked with pheasants. Snipe shooting was said to be excellent, and for woodcock these shootings were unsurpassed by anywhere else in Scotland. Several lochs and rivers were noted for fishing.[33]

Middle-class visitors could also, from 1891, amuse themselves by playing golf on the golf course at Machrie. There was another course at Gartmain, between Bridgend and Bowmore, from 1907 to 1938.[34]

By the 1870s, a few hundred tourists would come to Islay from Glasgow during that city's annual fair fortnight (holiday).[35] Many would have been working-class people, some with Islay roots (Plate XLV). The Islay villages, being some distance from the major population centres in the Scottish Lowlands, never developed into popular resorts of the type that fringed the Firth of Clyde. In the latter part of the twentieth century the island's increasing flow of tourists included many who pursued interests in whisky, birds, archaeology and so on as hobbies. Passengers on the CalMac ferry service to Islay rose from 28,489 in 1973 to 120,731 in 1997, with an increase in cars and caravans over the same period from 8,355 to 36,835. Much of this can be explained as increased tourism. A number of outsiders have acquired houses or cottages as holiday homes, and other properties have been inherited by a younger generation no longer resident on the island. The result of these changes in ownership is that some settlements, especially Portnahaven, can appear like ghost towns in the winter months.

Several unfortunates visited Islay accidentally as a result of their ships being wrecked, over 250 vessels since the late eighteenth century.[36] The majority turned up lifeless on the shore. Prior to the twentieth century, unidentified bodies were often buried where they were found. Such graves can be found at Saligo Bay, where there are three marked by stone slabs, one with the date 'DEC AD 1818'. In a gulley near Coull another sailor's grave can be located by two small slabs, one still upright.[37]

A well-documented Islay wrecking was that of the *Exmouth of Newcastle* on 28 April 1847. This was a two-masted brig which had just left Derry with a crew of 12 and a cargo of 240 men, women and children, looking for a better life in Canada. In a dreadful stormy night she struck the coast near Geodha Ghille Mhóire, on the coast of the Rhinns, two miles west of Sanaigmore. Only three of the crew managed to get ashore with their lives. A group of Ilich, including John Francis Campbell, Colin Campbell of Ballinaby and John Murdoch, recovered 108 bodies, among them 63 children and 9 infants, which were buried at Traigh Bhàn near where they were washed ashore. There is now a memorial cairn there and a monument at Sanaigmore.[38]

A monument on the Mull of Oa, a prominent landmark visible from many parts of the island, commemorates the nearby sinking of the *Tuscania* on 5 February 1918 (Plate XLVI). She was torpedoed by a German U-boat while transporting US troops to the war in Europe. One hundred and sixty-six lost their lives. Later that year, on 6 October, another troop carrier, the SS *Otranto*, sank off Machir Bay after colliding with another ship, with yet more loss of life to US troops on their way to fight. The destroyer, HMS *Mounsey*, managed to take off 596 men, but about 400 lost their lives. Only 16 managed to swim to shore.[39]

Less-welcome visitors included the French squadron of three ships that anchored in Claggain Bay on 15 February 1760, at a time when Britain and France were at war. The ships were commanded by François Thurot, a notorious privateer who had already cruised in adjacent waters in 1758. Thurot was badly in need of supplies but was under instructions not to make hostile landings in Scotland since his political masters supposed there might still be Jacobite sympathies that might be nurtured in French interests. He therefore negotiated the sale of several bullocks, oatmeal and some flour. He left on 19 February to meet his death on the 28th of that month, in the Irish Sea, at the hands of a British force that captured all his ships.[40]

Further scares were occasioned by the presence in Scottish waters of the American privateer, John Paul Jones, in 1778. News reached Whitehaven in Cumbria that, at Laggan on 10 May, guns were heard firing out at sea for about an hour.[41] Two years later, on 14 October, the Islay packet was captured by a French privateer, the *Fear Nought*, commanded by William Kane.[42]

To counter a perceived threat of further activities of this sort from Napoleon's forces, a Militia Company was raised on the island in 1798, and put under the command of the laird's eldest son, John, who had been in the Guards. Probably about the same time, four towers were erected, three overlooking Loch Indaal from Bowmore, Carnain and Cnoc na Croiche at Bridgend. Only the last two of these survive. They may have been intended primarily to beautify the policies of Islay House, but could also have mounted guns and been useful lookout posts. The summit of Cnoc na Croiche is surrounded by an earthwork, and there are still some pieces of artillery lying abandoned on rotten carriages. There was another tower at Port Askaig with pieces of artillery, and a gun was also positioned on top of Cnoc Rhaonastil on the south coast.[43]

None of this prevented, during the war with the United States, an American 26-gun man-of-war, the *True Blooded Yankee*, under the command of Captain Duplait, looting, burning or stranding some twenty or thirty ships sheltering at Skiba on 4 October 1813. The losses sustained are said to have amounted to £600,000.[44]

Islay was never seriously threatened by enemy invasion the rest of the nineteenth century, but public-spirited islanders continued to take an interest in defensive measures. 'Gowrie' noted in 1868 how the end of the principal rock at Port Ellen harbour was crowned by a flagstaff rising over two cannon, and there was a target on a dilapidated pier near the distillery.[45] In 1887 the 6th Company of the 1st Argyll and Bute Volunteer Corps acquired land for a gun battery at Pennycraig, overlooking Loch Indaal, between Bowmore and Bridgend, and later erected another at Bowmore.[46]

The twentieth century brought new and greater threats to the islanders. War Memorials, at Port Ellen, Port Charlotte and Portnahaven, provide evidence of the ultimate sacrifice made by some of the many Ilich who served in World War I (1914–18) and World War II (1939–45).[47] There was probably never any serious thought of a possible invasion of Islay in the first of these conflicts, but things were very different in the second. While no enemy succeeded in gaining a foothold, many servicemen and -women from other parts of Britain were based on the island.

The fall of France in June 1940, and the imminent threat of the invasion of Britain, was taken very seriously. Although, with hindsight, it seems slightly comical that the German army would ever have attempted an invasion of Islay, stranger things have happened. Certainly, there were many points considered suitable as landing grounds, such as Laggan Bay, Machir Bay, Saligo Bay, Kilnaughton Bay, Claggan Bay, the northern sweep of Loch Indaal and the mouth of Loch Gruinart.[48] How the German navy would have transported large numbers of troops and landed them in these areas is another matter.

What was, perhaps, much more plausible, was the possibility of a commando-style raid launched from a U-boat or two. Indeed, it was known to at least some islanders how a U-boat commander during World War I boasted of using the inlet at Glas Uig, between Ardmore and Aros Bay, as a hideaway and an opportunity to get fresh mutton. The large expanses of flat ground across Islay would have been perfect for paratroop landings, and the ground around the aerodrome at Glenegedale was considered ideal for glider landings.[49]

The formation of the Local Defence Volunteers (later renamed the Home Guard) in Argyll on 20 May 1940 saw part of No. 2 Company of the 1st Argyll Battalion responsible for the defence of Islay (the rest of the Company covering Knapdale, Kintyre, Jura and Colonsay). In July 1940 this Local Defence unit was reorganised, and Islay was put in the hands of the South Argyll Battalion. In February 1942 the Home Guard was reorganised again with 'C' Company, 3rd Argyll Battalion being responsible for Islay[50] and located as shown in Table 11.1.

Table 11.1 Headquarters of 'C' Company, 3rd Argyll Battalion, February 1942

Unit	Normal Headquarters	Battle Headquarters
'C' Company	Port Ellen	Bridgend Hotel
No. 1 Platoon	Port Ellen	Cairmore
No. 2 Platoon	Drill Hall,	Bridgend Bridgend Hotel
No. 3 Platoon	Bruichladdich	Bridgend Hotel
No. 4 Platoon	Bowmore Island House	Bowmore

(No. 5 Platoon: Jura and Colonsay)
(No. 6 Platoon: Gigha)

The senior officers of 'C' Company were listed as follows at the start of each year:

1 January 1942
Major G. Blaine, MC Officer Commanding
Captain D. N. Stuart Second in Command
Lieutenant A. MacNab O/C No. 1 Platoon
Lieutenant J. H. Cranston O/C No. 2 Platoon
Captain D. N. Stuart O/C No. 3 Platoon
Lieutenant C. S. Sandeman O/C No. 5 Platoon

1 January 1943
Major G. Blaine, MC Officer Commanding
Captain D. N. Stuart Second in Command
Lieutenant A. MacNab O/C No. 1 Platoon
Lieutenant W. Jaffray O/C No. 2 Platoon
Captain F. G. J. Sherwin O/C No. 3 Platoon
Lieutenant C. S. Sandeman O/C No. 5 Platoon

1 January 1944
Major A. MacNab Officer Commanding
Captain J. Chalmers Second in Command
Lieutenant D. Johnston O/C No. 1 Platoon
Lieutenant J. R. B. Hepburn O/C No. 2 Platoon
Lieutenant J. Binnie O/C No. 3 Platoon
Lieutenant R. C. Hodkinson O/C No. 4 Platoon
(Lieutenant C. S. Sandeman O/C No. 5 Platoon)
(Lieutenant M. Allan O/C No. 6 Platoon)

The primary role of the Islay Home Guard was the general defence of Islay from an invading force. It was, however, to particularly focus on the defence of the important military targets on the island. Thus Glenegedale aerodrome was to be defended through control of the road approaches; help was to be given to the defence of the radar stations at Saligo and Kilchiaran, and assistance was also to be provided in the defence of the Embarkation Section at Port Ellen, as well as the port there.[51]

The occupation of France was to have even greater consequences for Islay than the somewhat distant threat of invasion. Transatlantic shipping in and out of west coast ports, such as Liverpool and Bristol, had previously sailed south of Ireland, but with the German forces occupying the Channel coast, this was no longer safe. Consequently, convoys were routed north of Ireland and through the North Channel. This basically brought all Atlantic convoys across Islay's doorstep, and meant that the waters around Islay were a favourite haunt of German U-boats, and even bombers. It was to counter these threats that several bases were established on Islay by the Royal Air Force. Instead of a German assault, the island enjoyed an incursion of British forces, somewhere between 1,500 and 3,000 at any one time.

Principal among these establishments were the aerodrome at Port Ellen and the flying-boat base at Bowmore. From these locations, aircraft took off for long patrols over the Western Approaches. RAF Bowmore was a satellite station to the much larger base at Oban, but even so, a number of different types of flying boat were based at Bowmore between September 1940 and July 1945. Primarily these were Short Sunderlands (Plate XLVII), the main flying boats used by Coastal Command, and so heavily armed that they were nicknamed the 'Flying Porcupines'. However, two Short S.23 C Class flying boats, named *Clio* and *Cordelia* operated from Bowmore, as did the three S.26 G Class flying boats, *Golden Fleece, Golden Hind* and *Golden Horn*.[52]

RAF Bowmore's main claim to fame is as Port Ferry Bay, its fictitious name for its starring role in the film *Coastal Command*, produced by the Crown Film Unit and premiered on 16 October 1942 in London. The film tells the fictional story of a Sunderland (call-sign 'T' for Tommy) and its crew, and their involvement in the hunt for a German battleship, the *Düsseldorf*, which had broken out into the Atlantic and threatened Britain's Atlantic convoys. Although fiction, the story parallels the hunt for the *Bismarck* in 1941, and the film used RAF aircrew as actors.[53]

Another waterborne unit that was based on Islay was No. 67 Air Sea Rescue Marine Craft Unit, formed in June 1943 with two 73-foot Vosper High Speed Launches, HSL 2564 and HSL 2567. It was based at Port Ellen prior to a move to Bowmore in July 1945 (at the same time that RAF Bowmore closed down as a flying-boat base). It closed down in the spring of 1946.

The aerodrome at Glenegedale, which still operates as Islay's airport, opened as RAF Port Ellen in August 1940, with the station headquarters established in Port Ellen Distillery on 21 August.[54] That must have been a most pleasant location for the RAF officers! Construction of runways and buildings began in 1941, and the RAF Embarkation Office at Port Ellen (renamed c.December 1941 as No. 30 RAF Embarkation Unit) was formed on 17 March 1941 to carry out the unloading of supplies at Port Ellen, and their delivery to Glenegedale for the building work on the aerodrome.[55] The runways had been completed by 1 August 1942, with the maintenance hangar 95 per cent complete at that date. It was not until 31 October 1942 that the main workshops, main stores, officers' bath block, squash court, educational block, airmen's dining hall, by-produces store, small-arms ammunition stores, parachute store and gymnasium were handed over to the RAF.[56] This was a massive construction programme.

Even before RAF Port Ellen was completed, flying from it was taking place. The main unit using the aerodrome was No. 48 Squadron; although based at Aldergrove in Northern Ireland, a detachment from the squadron operated at Port Ellen. The detachment flew Avro Ansons primarily for convoy escorts, but also for anti-submarine patrols and searching for missing aircraft. These operations were flown until September 1941 and, in conjunction with the flying boats from Bowmore, played an important role in attempting to protect convoys entering and leaving the North Channel, and trying to keep the waters around Islay free from U-boats.[57]

A change of role came to Port Ellen in February 1943 with the formation of No. 304 Ferry Training Unit. This unit was set up to train crews how to fly and navigate Bristol Beaufighters on long-distance ferry flights over the open sea. This was not easy, and many crews crashed into hills in and around Islay; some simply disappeared and were never found.[58] It must be remembered that these crews were still learning, and navigation over open water, with no landmarks as reference points and no electronic navigational aids or beacons, was extremely difficult. It was all too easy for a crew to get lost or disorientated and run out of fuel before returning to land. This training continued for almost a year, until the unit moved away in January 1944. RAF Port Ellen then reverted to care and maintenance.[59]

Another thread in the defences against German attacks on Allied shipping were the two radar stations built on Islay, at Saligo and Kilchiaran.[60] Saligo was a Chain Home radar station providing long range early warning of aircraft. It had transmitting aerials slung between 325-foot-high steel masts, and receiving aerials on 240-foot wooden towers. It was primarily looking for German bombers either trying to attack Allied shipping directly, or laying mines in the shipping lanes. The station began passing plots in January 1941, but although there were rarely any hostile aircraft to plot, the station played an invaluable role tracking the flying boats from Bowmore, providing vectors to some aircraft to help them reach base.[61]

On 24 January 1943, Saligo assisted Short Sunderland III DV979 of No. 246 Squadron to reach its home base at Bowmore. Tragically, the aircraft touched the ground at Blackrock on its landing approach, and crashed. After escaping, the crew discovered the rear gunner was trapped. Returning to rescue him, the depth charges on the aircraft exploded, killing nine in the worst loss of life on Islay during World War II.[62]

The airmen working at Saligo were originally billeted in the Port Charlotte Distillery warehouse, but a camp was eventually built at Coille, nearer the technical site. RAF Saligo was placed on care and maintenance in March 1945.[63]

Kilchiaran was the other wartime radar station on Islay, and it too began passing plots in January 1941. Kilchiaran was a Chain Home Low station and its aerials were mounted on a frame which rotated above the transmitter and receiver huts. As well as plotting aircraft, the station was able to plot shipping, both single vessels and large convoys. In February 1943 new equipment was added to the station which operated on a much shorter wavelength and was therefore much more accurate. This set gave good ranges on ships, and plotted one convoy in March 1943 out to a range of 56 miles. Kilchiaran closed down in July 1945. A more extensive radar station was built at Kilchiaran during 1955 as part of a new radar system intended to defend against faster aircraft operated by the Soviet Union. This was never fully operational and closed down in 1958.[64]

Industries

The major employment for Ilich until the twentieth century was farming, followed in the years of MacDonald domination by armed service. Industries like mining may have been of considerable importance in the Medieval Period, but sadly the evidence does not survive to substantiate this. Other activities like the manufacture of textiles and fishing were greatly encouraged by the lairds in the eighteenth and nineteenth centuries. Although there was often an ambition that industries should expand into significant money earners, with products being exported off the island, for the most part this never happened. It has been distilling alone that has grown into a major industry, which, indeed, has been responsible more than anything else for putting Islay on the map and giving the island an international reputation.

Mining

Galena – lead ore – has long been known to occur on Islay, in several narrow veins in the limestone region in the general vicinity of Ballygrant. The limestone, which occurs along with dolerites and phyllites, is metamorphosed, and dates in geological terms to the Dalradian of about 600 million years ago.

The travel writer Thomas Pennant believed it likely that the early Scandinavian settlers of Islay mined lead, and such speculation has continued to this day, unsubstantiated by any real evidence.[1] Archaeological research by Mike Cressey has, however, allowed the date for lead mining in the vicinity of Knocklearoch (Glasco Beag) and Ardachie to be pushed back at least to the 1360s. He analysed sediments from Lochs Finlaggan, Lossit and Bharradail, identifying the influx of lead and other minerals as a result of mining activity. Those from Loch Lossit provided the earliest date using the ^{210}Pb radiometric dating method.[2] In the Middle Ages there was much need of lead for the roofs and plumbing of prestigious buildings, like large churches, for making trinkets and for alloying with other metals for making bronze and pewter vessels, etc. It is possible that lead, exported to the

mainland and beyond, was a major source of income for the Lords of the
Isles.

A much quoted documentary account of the presence of lead on Islay
comes from Donald Monro, Dean of the Isles, who in 1549 wrote that
there was much lead ore in 'Moychaolis'. This is the area of land that
belonged to Iona Abbey, bordering the Sound of Islay, stretching from
Torrabus southwards to Kilslevan and Lossit.[3]

Earlier references to lead mining which have previously escaped attention appear in the *Accounts of the Lord High Treasurer of Scotland* for 1512.
A royal servant, William Striveling, submitted his expenses for assaying the
lead mined in Islay, transporting it, for building a house for the mine on
Islay, for charcoal and other expenses made on tools, etc., from 23 August
to 1 September 1511. These expenses amounted to the not inconsiderable
sum of £11 4s 8d. The following March, Striveling had lead transported
from Dumbarton to Edinburgh, and that April a 'finour' (smelter) called
Gray was paid for following the king to Dumbarton to smelt lead.[4]

In 1511 Islay was probably only just coming under effective royal
administration. It was possibly only now practical to send Striveling to see
if anything could be made of mines operated for the Lords of the Isles. The
house erected by Striveling may have been no more than a store for his
tools. The lead smelted at Dumbarton and transported to Edinburgh was
surely from Islay.

There was renewed interest in the potential for mining on Islay after its
transference from MacDonald to Campbell hands. Archibald Primrose,
an Edinburgh burgess, then held the post of Clerk of the Mines, and in
1616 he received a patent from the Privy Council of the copper and lead
mines in Islay, Mull, Skye and Lewis.[5] Nothing may have come of this, at
least as far as Islay was concerned. Instead an offer was made in 1619 to
an entrepreneur, called Mr Nathaniell, to take a nineteen-year tack of the
mines, and either he, or another, was in Islay to assess the prospects. This
'Mr Nathaniell' may be identified as Nathaniel Udwart, son of a previous
provost of Edinburgh, who that year set up a manufactory in Leith for the
exclusive production of soap. He had a royal patent for this, and in 1626
was to acquire others for the making of iron ordnance and for taking 'oil
fish' in the Greenland Sea. Meanwhile, the new Campbell laird was
taking steps, perhaps as an alternative course of action, to employ Irish
miners.[6] The story of lead mining on Islay is one of fits and starts, with
long gaps of inactivity. Perhaps, however, there was always a significant
amount of unrecorded small-scale activity being undertaken by the locals
prior to the late eighteenth century.

Anxious to raise money, Sir Hugh Campbell, the fourth Campbell Laird
of Islay, was treating with a Mr Wanbruch (Vanbrugh), a mining
adventurer, in 1677. Three years later, he had two offers to take over
all mining on the island, one from Mr John McKay of Mults, the other
from Squire Dobs. The laird decided to accept the offer from Dobs.[7] The

only documentary indication of the location of mining activity at this time comes in a much later report by the Revd Dr John Walker, prepared on the basis of a visit to Islay in 1764. He remarks that about eighty or ninety years previously, lead mines were discovered at Ballygrant and worked for some time. The 1693 Hearth Tax return lists six hearths for Robolls which seems an unusually high number, unless it reflects this mining activity.[8]

A tack of the lead mines of Islay was granted by the Laird of Islay to Robert Cassie, Esq., of Ireland and John Pollock, gentleman, of Dublin, on 27 December 1704. Possibly this was a renewal of an existing lease as it was noted that there was already a considerable quantity of lead ore raised and ready to be taken away.[9]

Pollock alone acquired a new 21-year lease of all the lead mines of Islay in 1707 from Elizabeth Campbell, the widowed mother of the then laird, having, perhaps, bought out Cassie. Pollock had, however, to raise capital for his venture by taking on partners. It was probably at this point that he contacted the London (Quaker) Lead Company to see if it was interested. This resulted in an experienced English miner, John Taylor, being sent to Islay from their operations at Blackhills in Durham to report on the mines, but his masters apparently did not take up the offer to expand into Islay. Taylor himself returned in 1709 as Pollock's overseer. The source for this and later details of Taylor's involvement is a fascinating, but not necessarily totally accurate, biography of his life written when he was well over a hundred years old.[10]

Pollock found Scottish partners to aid him in his venture, and Taylor recruited miners in the north of England. By 1720 there were only four partners – John Bowman, merchant in Glasgow and at that time Provost of that city, William Thomson, a Glasgow surgeon, William Baxter, merchant in Glasgow, and James Littlejohn, stabler in Edinburgh. In that year Littlejohn was bought out by the others, and the following year Bowman acquired Baxter's share. The business on Islay was being managed on behalf of the partners by Colin Campbell, tacksman of Daill. The partners were obliged to pay to the laird the seventh part of all clean-washed lead ore they mined. The miners had their dwellings near Knocklearoch, at a place later known as Glasco Beag (Little Glasgow), an indication that the main mining activity at this time must have been nearby at Ardachie.[11]

An account of the Islay lead mines by John Williams, a mineral surveyor, published in 1789, is quite disparaging of the work carried out by the 'company of Glasgow merchants'. He was informed that the principal way of procuring ore was by paying the locals to dig for the ore at so much a bing, a fact confirmed by a note in the Islay rental of 1722 indicating that each bing was worth about twenty shillings sterling. In consequence, the whole area of the mines was criss-crossed with shallow trenches. Since the country folk had no pumps, or other drainage equipment, they could not work to a greater depth than about two or three fathoms – that is a maximum of about 5.5 m.[12] It is certainly the case that such trenches or trials, often following the edge of geological dykes, can be traced today in many places from the east side of Loch Finlaggan, on the old farms of Keppolsmore, Robolls and Portaneilean, to the high ground adjacent to the road from Ballygrant to Cluanach, on the farms of Ardachie (Plate XLVIII) and Airigh Ghuaidhre.

This may be the reason why, on 16 April 1722, the Laird of Islay was persuaded to agree a further contract, letting the mines and minerals of brass, lead, potter's ore, copper and tin on Islay, this time with Alexander Murray, the younger of Stanhope, a Scottish mining entrepreneur who, about the same time, was developing mining enterprises in North Argyll, at Strontian and elsewhere. His Islay contract was to be without prejudice to the lead mines already discovered, and then being worked by Bowman.[13]

Murray was evidently prepared to enter into a partnership with Bowman, and understood that the latter was making losses through the failure and mismanagement of his partners, but in the event nothing came of this. How Bowman's tack was to operate alongside Murray's is not clear, but there is a hint that Murray was prepared to adopt underhand ways to gain an advantage. In an undated letter from Donald Campbell of Octomore to Murray of the 1720s or '30s, there is mention of the discovery of copper veins at Kilslevan and the need to mine them under the pretence of extracting marl.[14]

The issuing of the new contract to Murray certainly had an electrifying effect on Bowman. Within weeks he had decided to have the ineffective Colin Campbell replaced as sole factor and administrator by John Bowman junior (his son?), despite the opposition of the other partner, William Thomson. Bowman junior was instructed to go to Islay immediately to audit Campbell's accounts and to send back, as soon as possible, a report on the mill and other houses belonging to the enterprise, the tools and materials, with an estimate of their value. He was also to reappoint those of the workforce that were capable of raising ore, call them to account for their outstanding debts, and generally sort out problems and get the business up and running more efficiently.[15]

Bowman's lease was due to end in 1728, though according to Bowman's overseer, John Taylor, their work came to an end in 1730, at which point he, Taylor, had to leave the island. A later report on mining schemes in Islay suggests that the last few years were largely spent in extracting lead from existing waste material and slag.[16]

As for Murray's enterprises, little is known. He acquired a feu of the land of Torrabus on the Sound of Islay, sometime before 1741, and it may be significant that the smelter operated by the lead mines in the 1770s (see below) was on this land. Might it have been erected in the first place by Murray? Murray's tack of the mines was extended up to 1762 although he himself died heavily in debt in 1743. His main mining interests, however, lay elsewhere, and he is accused of never being on the island, but leaving the business to be managed by an unskilled local gentleman, perhaps Donald Campbell of Octomore. His estates, including Torrabus, passed about 1770 to the Riddell family.[17]

Meanwhile, Islay had been acquired by a new laird, Daniel Campbell of Shawfield, an entrepreneur who by 1733 was involved in a partnership for producing iron at works on the mainland.[18] Shawfield must have been dissatisfied with the continuing state of affairs on Islay – poor management and disturbance of the countryside to little purpose. A report of about 1760 mentions various expedients and initiatives, including a tack given to Squire Haily, and another in 1745 to an Englishman, Captain William Thynne. None of this turned out well as reference is made to the smelting mill being stopped and all the tools belonging to the work being laid up in the girnel (storehouse) in Glasco Beag prior to July 1745.[19]

On the ending of Murray of Stanhope's lease the laird, Daniel the Younger of Shawfield, granted a new 31-year tack of the lead mines of Islay to an Edinburgh architect, Charles Freebairn, on 8 July 1762. A report by him, compiled in 1770, mentions 1,000 trials, in a 40-square-mile area, left by his predecessors in surface digging of lead veins. He goes on to describe his own workings at Ardachie, Gartness, Mulreesh and Sean-ghairt, mentioning the shafts and levels by which he was able to extract lead from the veins, to a depth of as much as 24 fathoms (c.44 m) in the case of Mulreesh.[20]

These shafts or bell-pits, sunk vertically, are evident today at many mining sites, including the ones listed by Freebairn, normally as circular depressions surrounded by heaps of grassed-over waste material, as at Ardachie. Sometimes they have been sunk through earlier trials or trenches as at Robolls on the side of Loch Finlaggan. Galleries or levels were dug from the bottom of these shafts, following the veins of galena. Some levels or adits were designed to drain water away from the workings. The entrances to such adits can be seen at Mureesh and Robolls.[21]

A more detailed report on the mines, written the same year by Alexander Shirriff, the manager of the mines at Leadhills in Lanarkshire, lists seven lead mines: Mulreesh, Portaneilean, Sean-ghairt, South Arda-chie, North Ardachie, Ballygrant and Gartness, along with the copper mine at Kilslevan. Shirriff was concerned to assess the viability of these workings, and where engines might be erected to improve their drainage. His conclusion was that there was enough evidence for mineral wealth in the veins already discovered, and that if they were worked well, and engines properly placed, the mines would have a long life, producing considerable profit both for the proprietor and the undertaker of the work.[22]

Underlying these 1770 reports by Freebairn and Shirriff it is possible to detect a problem that had probably bedevilled mine-working on Islay since its inception – a lack of investment. A report on Islay written in 1780 for the laird is quite disparaging of Freebairn, who had shown an inability to work the mines properly at any period. Freebairn was clearly desirous of an injection of hard cash. He had already borrowed money in 1765 and 1766 from William Hogg and Son, bankers in Edinburgh, and pressure was being brought to bear for repayment. In 1776 and 1777 the mining operations were being funded by a Glasgow merchant, Ronald Crawford, who had moved into Freebairn's property of Persabus by 1780, presumably to look after his investment.[23]

In 1772 Thomas Pennant was entertained by Freebairn at his house at Freeport, near Port Askaig. Freeport is now the site of the Caol Ila Distillery on the Sound of Islay but the 'air furnace' there was drawn by Moses Griffith for Pennant, though not included in the book giving an account of his tour.[24] It is noteworthy that Griffith's illustration shows the smelter with two chimney-stacks, suggesting the presence of two sets of hearths. Were this to be the case, then one would have been the primary smelter (first smelt), and the second for refining the slags of the first smelt. Interestingly, there also seems to be some form of chute leading from the top of the hill down into the smelter building. This would have saved carting heavy loads of dressed ore down the steep incline to the foreshore. Another document of 1770, assessing the damage caused by mining activities at Ardachie and Portaneilean, provides the information that there was a washing house at Ardachie, probably one of two ruined buildings surrounded by dumps and other mine workings at NGR NR 398 633. This was where the ore was washed and crushed, the water to do the washing and, probably, power a crushing mill, being channelled from Loch Fada.[25]

Silver was a valuable by-product of lead mining that was extracted in this period by cupellation. According to Pennant, the Islay lead veins provided 40 ounces of silver from a ton of metal. Lead ore was the major source of silver at this period, and there is a silver goblet of c.1780, made by the Glasgow goldsmith Adam Graham solely from metal from Islay. It is now in the collections of Glasgow Art Galleries and Museums.[26]

Useful statistics concerning lead and its production on Islay between the years 1769 and 1774 are recorded in Table 12.1.

Table 12.1 Lead output statistics between 1769 and 1774.

Item	Tons	Cwt
Bar lead	260	1
Ore	72	6
Slag of lead	90	–

These statistics are after Wilson and Flett, *Memoirs of the Geological Survey, xvii*, 65–73. Compare what Freebairn told Pennant in 1772 – that since 1763 the lead he had smelted at Freeport had brought a return of £6,000 (Pennant, *Tour*, 207).

Freebairn's hold on the lease of the mines came to an end in ignominious circumstances in 1779 when Hogg's creditors forced its voluntary roup and sale within the Exchange Coffee House in Edinburgh. Freebairn died in August the following year. He was by then tenant of the farm of Persabus and also Glasco Beag.[27]

In 1786, Walter Campbell of Islay agreed a new lease with Robert Hodgson of Congleton, Thomas Smyth of Liverpool and Edward Hawkins of Macclesfield. The area of their operations was defined as a circle with a diameter of six miles, the centre to be chosen by the lessees and marked with a fixed pillar with an inscription on it. They were also to have a lease of the farm of Persabus. Work was evidently undertaken at Gartness and Mulreesh, but by July 1790 they had given up, and in 1803 they agreed to remove themselves, their people and possessions from the area.[28]

There then seems to have been a cessation of mining activity on Islay for several years, until 1836 when the laird signed a new lease with John Arthur Borron. Borron was an industrialist who had a glass works in Warrington. From 1828 he was agent (manager) of the lead mines at Leadhills, and of the nearby lead mines at Wanlockhead from 1831. His son, William, took over the management of the mines in 1834. The father's lease on Islay gave him the right to mine for gold, silver, quicksilver, zinc, copper, tin, lead, cobalt and manganese, and generally all other metals, ores, earths, fossils, paints, minerals and mineral waters, for a period of thirty-six years. Again the concession was defined as a circle with a diameter of 6 miles, its centre this time set as the meal mill at Ballygrant. This included all known workings apart from those at Ballitarsin. Barron also bound himself to employ daily and continuously at least twenty-four able pickmen or miners, and to carry on the work at Ballygrant. A tourist guide published in 1863, however, says that the lead mines had then been abandoned for many years.[29]

The new Morrison owners of Islay initiated a final phase of lead mining in 1862 when they gave a 42-year lease to John Thomas Campbell of London, and William Jeffrey, a mining captain from Colbeck in Cumberland. From 1869 they took on Robolls House (now the Ballygrant Inn) as the home for their manager, and they had a row of cottages (Miners' Row – still occupied) in Ballygrant village for their workers. The main centre of operations seems to have shifted to Mulreesh. It was visited by the travel writer 'Gowrie' in the 1860s. He tells how the machinery at the mines, hitherto worked by water, was being supplied with a steam engine.[30]

The business was reformed in 1871 as the Islay Lead Mining Company Ltd with its head office at 9B New Bond Street in London. The new company only took possession of the mine on 23 September 1872, but at the first Ordinary General Meeting the following month an optimistic series of messages was delivered to the assembled shareholders by the chairman, Walter Sandell Mappin.

Workmen were already employed clearing the watercourse, and an engine and two boilers had been purchased in Ireland and were on their way to Islay. The old pumps would be at work in a few days, as also the water-wheel, and the engine, hopefully, by Christmas. Mappin conveyed surprise about the amount of equipment the company was inheriting with the mine, and was also hopeful that there might be a return from bog iron ore.[31]

Mappin's statement was indeed more optimistic than the turn of events warranted, since by 1874 the company was in liquidation. There is a sense in the documents preserved in the Islay Estate Papers of a lack of resources, and not the happiest of relationships with the estate factor and neighbouring farmers. There was an acrimonious dispute over the cutting of peats, and the company was accused of damaging a crane at Port Askaig when their engine was unloaded early in 1873, rather later than the chairman had predicted. The lease was acquired by a Mr Headley, and the company continued in business. In 1876 it was reported that a quantity of dynamite was imported for use at the lead mines where a rich and thick lode had been discovered on the farm of Finlaggan.[32]

Data from Home Office tax returns provide records of ore extracted and lead produced on Islay in the years from 1872 to 1896 (Fig. 12.1). The output data reflects a rise in lead production to 1867, and then a decline in the early 1870s, followed by another peak in 1878. Silver production followed the same trend as lead output (Fig. 12.2). The silver was probably extracted as a litharge from the lead, a by-product of the primary smelting operation. No records survive detailing where this operation took place but it is possible that secondary processing was undertaken elsewhere on the Scottish mainland.

The returns note that the company was not working in 1886, and had discontinued in 1887, 1890–95. The breaks in yearly production may reflect the vagaries of the lead market, operational difficulties or financial troubles within the company. In 1896, the last year of recorded production, there were eight workers underground, and eight above ground.[33]

The installation of a beam engine and two boilers, along with other work, represented a considerable investment in the industry at a time of falling world prices and increasing competition from the mainland. The argentiferous quality of the Islay ore may well account for such outlay.

The company's lease of the Islay lead mines came to an end in 1904, and the following year the job of dismantling the works and salvaging equipment was subcontracted to a Glasgow firm, Clyde Salvage Company. A letter of 14 December 1905 from Thomas Archer, a consulting engineer based in Gateshead-on-Tyne, to the Islay Estate factor, contains the following, perhaps fitting, epitaph:

The Mining Co. lost well on to £20,000 . . . As for myself God only knows what a loss the place has been to me, spending the best time of my life over the place and neglecting my interests at Home, all for good to the owner & the workmen of the Mines & others.[34]

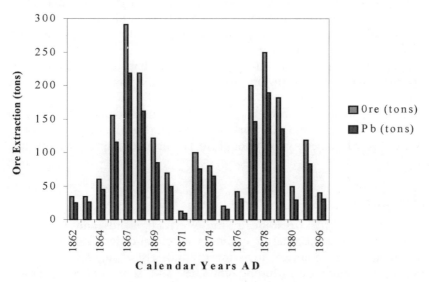

Figure 12.1 Ore extracted and Pb
produced between 1862 and 1896 (after Burt et al. 1981).

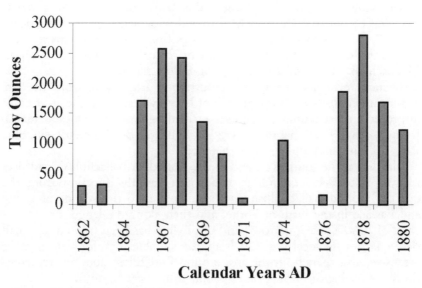

Figure 12.2 Silver produced between 1862 and 1880 (after Burt et al. 1981).

There are considerable remains at Mulreesh of mining activities extending back at least as far as the seventeenth century. Most obvious are some of the structures associated with the Islay Lead Mining Company in the late nineteenth century, including the building that housed the steam engine for pumping water out of the workings (Plate XLIX), and the reservoir, opposite the Finlaggan road end, that supplied the water to operate a hammer for crushing the ore and to separate the galena from the rock.

Sporadic interest has been taken in the mineral resources of Islay in the century since the ending of work at Mulreesh, but the economic conditions have never been good enough to favour a resumption of activity.

Slate quarries

There is very little freestone in the West Highlands and Islands. In medieval times sandstone for quoins, window and door surrounds, was imported from quarries in Kintyre and elsewhere for the more prestigious buildings including churches and some of the buildings at Finlaggan. Otherwise local stone has been the main building material, sometimes quarried and roughly dressed, but often as unaltered boulders gathered from the fields. Islay does, however, have rock that is suitable for the manufacture of roof slates and there is evidence that this has been used since the thirteenth century. Both the chapel and great hall at Finlaggan had slate roofs, the slates including Dalradian phyllites and Easdale types probably quarried nearby.[35] When, however, Coll MacAlaster, the Bailie of Islay, had a house at Glengeoy and the Eallabus Mill roofed with slates, prior to his death in 1747, he appears to have got the slates from quarries at Croy, to the north-east of Glasgow. His testament records a debt to Duncan MacLachlan, there, of £80 Scots for 8,000 slates.[36]

There is evidence for a slate industry on Islay again from the late eighteenth century when the growth of Islay's villages, and the erection of improved farm steadings and houses, created a considerable local demand. It was noted in 1779 that there were 110 houses in Bowmore, 50 with blue slate, 20 with tiles and the rest thatched.[37]

Islay lies at the south-west end of the Dalradian Ballachullish and slate islands 'Slate Belt', extending in a south-westerly direction from the quarries around Ballachullish on the mainland to the islands of Luing and Easdale in the Firth of Lorne, and then along the length of the east coast of Jura. There a narrow band of phyllite has been utilised for small slate quarries for local use. On Islay, the suitable rock for slate is more extensive, and apart from the area around Port Ellen, does not represent the same geological formation as found in the slate islands.

Geologically on Islay, the oldest 'slate' rock is found at Kilchiaran. It belongs to the Colonsay Group, a suite of rocks thought to be slightly earlier that the Dalradian Supergroup. In north-east Islay, the slate quarries at Emeraconart and nearby Esknish, coupled with numerous small quarries around Mulreesh, Finlaggan and Ballygrant, belong to the Mullach Dubh Phyllite Formation, part of the Appin Group of the Dalradian Supergroup. The Appin Group lies about midway in the Dalradian succession and is slightly older than the 'Slate Belt' quarries.

The major minerals of slate from the Ballachulish and slate islands 'Slate Belt' comprise quartz, white mica and chlorite. Secondary minerals often deleterious to the weathering of the slate include pyrite, pyrrhotite, graphite and carbonate. Luckily the pyrite is in cube form and is less prone to oxidation but over time can fall out from the face of the slate. Sometimes the carbonate is in the form of the mineral dolomite, which is more resistant to weathering. The amount of quartz and its grain size influences the durability of the slate, while the mica and chlorite content influence the ease with which a slate can be split. The production of slate is very wasteful and large waste tips accumulate at the quarries. It has been estimated that only 15 to 20 per cent of the material excavated is made into slate products.

Islay Estate Records indicate that from 1861 into the early years of the twentieth century there were major efforts across the island to replace thatch roofs with slate.[38] These initiatives largely depended on local quarries opened up in the nineteenth century. One was reported near the harbour of Port Ellen in 1845. 'The quality of the slate is very good, and there seems to be a considerable body of it.'[39] This must be the quarry at Carraig Fhada near the Port Ellen lighthouse. It is of limited extent, set into the former cliff line, but access by both sea and road was possible so that the slates could be taken to roof the houses of Port Ellen. It was disused by 1907. Geologically speaking, these slates are phyllites of the Jura Slate Member, the lowest member of the Scarba Conglomerate Formation, which, in turn, is the lowest formation of the Easdale Subgroup of the Argyll Group. They appear colour-banded, grey and bluish. Carraig Fhada slates can be identified on several houses in Port Ellen and some in Bowmore.[40]

Around Kilchiaran Bay in the Rhinns there are the remains of several slate quarries, especially two large ones on the north side of the bay, known as Cul Leac and Rudha Liath. They produced a rough inferior slate, geologically forming part of the Colonsay Group, of base Dalradian age. The finished Kilchiaran slate has a unique shape and texture, being generally narrower in width and longer in length when compared with other Scottish slates, and generally thicker. The grain of the slate runs along the length of the slate and is easily split. This characteristic gives the slate a clean vertical edge but leaves the bottom edge with a rough finish.

There is evidence in the fabric and roof of the Kilchiaran farm and outbuildings, built not long after 1826, that slate was being used, not only for the rubble stone walls of the building but for slating the roofs. The *Statistical Account* of 1845 records that 'Slate of good colour and quality are made at Kilchiaran. The quarry is now wrought to a great extent.'[41]

Accounts survive for quarrying operations at Kilchiaran from 1887 to 1899. It appears that there was a handful of workers under a foreman. Workers could earn from 1s to 1s 6d per day, while slates sold at the quarry in December 1896 cost 1s for twenty large slates or fifty small slates. Lintels and steps were also produced.[42] Another use for the stone was fences. Pieces of thick slate, with holes bored for wire, were positioned at intervals in dry-stone walls. An example of this type of fence can be seen on the road from Kilchiaran to the radar station in the hills near Creag Bealach na Caillich. Roofs with Kilchiaran slates can be seen in the villages of Portnahaven and Port Wemyss, and further afield on the smithy roof at Pennycraig on the shore of Loch Indaal between Bridgend and Bowmore (until the mid 1990s). The quarries were apparently still working in 1907.[43]

The Morrisons developed a slate quarry at Esknish, near Ballygrant, from the late 1870s or 1880s. Its slates can be seen on roofs in Bowmore. The rock at Esknish belongs to the Mullach Dubh Phyllite Formation, the middle of the three formations that form the Blair Atholl Subgroup of the Dalradian Supergroup. The slates themselves show surface colour-banding, and often contain large cubes of iron pyrites. The Morrisons clearly had ambitions to develop it for more than local use. The slate quarries at Easdale were in full production at this time, though their vulnerability had been demonstrated in 1881 by a tidal wave that flooded many of them.[44] The Morrisons got an estimate from Dempster, Moore & Co. of Glasgow in 1888 for building a light railway 'for quarry and other purposes'[45] and commissioned a survey of the quarry from J. Menzies, a civil engineer connected with the slate quarrying industry in Wales.

Menzies noted that the quarry was situated on the slope of a hill about 3 miles from Bridgend and within 200 yards of the highway from Bridgend to Port Askaig. The excavation was on the side of the hill and was about 150 feet long, 40 feet wide and 24 feet deep. The slate vein itself was about 300 yards in width, bounded on both sides by limestone rock. He considered that the rock was well formed, comparatively free from disturbances and produced a blue slate of excellent cleavage. It would always command a ready market provided the metal contained nothing which would on exposure become discoloured, a thing that could be tested by having samples of the rock analysed.

A return of the results of working the quarry, for the months of May and June 1888, indicated that 23,000 slates were produced at a cost of £51 9s 7d for labour and materials. These were saleable locally for £62 10s. The proportion of full-sized slates manufactured was 70 per cent of the make. These results from top rock were considered extremely satisfactory, comparing favourably with the two largest Scottish quarries, Ballachulish and Easdale, where the full-sized slates were produced in the proportion of 50 per cent at Ballachulish and 44 per cent at Easdale.

The slates hitherto manufactured at Esknish were sold at the quarry for local use at 65s per 1,000 for full-sized, and 30s per 1,000 for undersize, but these prices were considerably in excess of what would be realised in the open market. A serious fall in the price of all qualities of slates had occurred during the last ten years. Scottish slates were now only valued at 62s 6d and 22s 6d per 1,000, full and undersized respectively, when delivered in Glasgow, from which had to be deducted the cost of conveyance, merchants' profits and other charges, leaving the net value of the two sizes of slates at the quarry as 51s and 17s 6d.

Menzies was of the opinion that the quality of the slate, the cleavage of the rock and the facilities of working the Esknish Quarry compared favourably with those at Ballachulish and Easdale. The only unfavourable feature was the difficulty of conveyance to the shipping port, as to effect delivery cheaply it would be necessary to construct a tramway to Bruichladdich, a distance of about eight miles. There appeared to be no engineering difficulties of any kind in so doing. There would be few cuttings or embankments and the gradients would be easy throughout. Menzies reckoned from his own experience that the tramway would cost £750 per mile.

Prior to embarking on the construction of the tramway, Menzies recommended further testing of the quality of the slate and the extent and depth of the vein. It would be necessary to purchase a steam crane and a pulsometer, or pump, for draining water from the workings.[46]

Unfortunately, the quarry did not live up to expectations. No tramway was built and the quarry, though quite extensive for its time, declined in use. A note by James Forbes, factor, on 16 January 1896 stated that the quarry had not been worked for some years.[47] It is also evident from Islay Estate Records that from 1896 the majority of slates used from then were imported from Wales.[48]

Tiles

There are the ruins of a tile works at Foreland on the Sunderland Estate (NGR NR 272 646) consisting of a kiln, engine-house and drying-shed. It was erected, probably in the 1840s, about the time Walter Frederick Campbell got a drainage grant for the manufacture of drainage tiles, though bricks for chimneys and pantiles for roofing may also have been produced. The pantiles on the boathouse of Kildalton are said to have been manufactured here.[49] Walter Frederick Campbell was described in the documents relating to his sequestration in 1847 as a manufacturer of tiles and bricks on Islay.[50] It appears that these works must have been operated for him, and manufacture may not have carried on after his financial ruin.[51]

Textiles

Woollen cloth, woven on Islay from local wool, must have been the basis for clothing for most islanders down to the eighteenth century. This requirement for wool was the main reason why tenant farmers kept sheep, just enough for their own use, though as noted in Chapter 4, it appears that the Abbey of Derry ran its estate of Nerabus specifically for the production of cloth. There may also have been large-scale cloth production involving professional clothiers on some of the MacDonald estates on Islay and elsewhere in the fourteenth and fifteenth centuries. This can be deduced for Kintyre or Knapdale from two grave-slabs at Kilmory Knap, decorated with cropping shears, one of which commemorates a certain Henry Tulloch. Tulloch is not a local name. Also, when the Earl of Douglas came to meet Alexander, Earl of Ross, in Knapdale in 1452, bearing gifts of wine, clothes, silver, silk and English cloth, he was given mantles in return. These mantles were presumably locally produced plaids, tartan cloths that could double as cloaks and blankets. They were worn over linen shirts. James of Dunyvaig's wife presented Queen Mary with a 'marvellously fair Highland apparel' prior to a royal expedition to hunt in Argyll in 1563.[52]

In 1658 Hugh Campbell of Cawdor entered into a contract with a miller, James Riddoch, for the construction of a 'touk myln' for fulling cloth. Riddoch was to cut and square the timber for the mill in the woods of Sunart and Ardnamurchan, and Cawdor was to supply the boat and men for transporting it to Islay. The mill was clearly to be a substantial building with adjoining house. It was probably the first mill on the island with a vertical water-wheel, and was presumably intended to process all locally produced woollen cloth. It seems to have been erected on the River Sorn near Bridgend, where later woollen mills were established. It was tenanted as late as 1741 by James Cargill.[53]

Islay would have been affected by the banning of Highland dress after the failure of the Jacobite uprising of 1745, though it is probable that many islanders for some time before then would have dressed little different from contemporaries in the Lowlands. The 'Highland plaid' among the possessions of William Campbell, tacksman of Kelsay, who died in 1745, was exceptional. Other inventories of Islay gentlemen of that period list coats and waistcoats, sometimes matching, and breeches. When the proscription of Highland dress was lifted in 1782 there was no move in Islay to adopt it. In the 1790s the Ilich were described as being 'more clad in the long coat, hat, and breeches, than the inhabitants of any of the

Hebrides'.[54] Walter Frederick Campbell, however, was described in the 1830s as being fond of old Highland customs, including the ancient dress (Plate XXIII), and had encouraged his tenants to imitate his example. About sixty of them were said to wear Highland dress on public occasions. In 1845 Walter Frederick is said to have taken 300 retainers fully equipped in the Highland garb to Inverary for the marriage of the Marquis of Lorn, and two years later another contingent for the visit there of Queen Victoria.[55]

It is probable that many made a living as handloom weavers of woollen textiles. The testament of Nichol McCalman in Kilfinan (otherwise unknown) in the parish of Kilarrow, died 1732, demonstrates that he was a weaver. He had his loom, loom yarn, lint and wool, 6 ells of fine plaid and 7 ells of grey cloth, and two spinning wheels, one of them big. Household equipment included a brass candlestick, two tubs, a pair of cans (drinking vessels) and a pair of creels, a big and a little pot, and a crook and tongs. The only items of furniture listed are three beds, and two chests, one wooden, the other of steel. Apart from his house he had a barn and byre, perhaps all conjoined, a spade, fork and graip. He had some seed-corn and barley and some animals, including an old mare which may have been for riding since he also had a saddle.[56]

Weavers were not always viewed sympathetically by the lairds and gentlemen of Islay. In 1725 they had the Bailie pass an act to limit their alleged profiteering, representations having been made that they, and other tradesmen, were taking extravagant wages. The weavers were from henceforth to take the meal of the country, at the rate of the country, for their work, and were to be fined if they refused.[57] Perhaps some had had the temerity to demand money for their work. In 1792 the Stent Committee, no doubt mindful of the spirit of revolution elsewhere in Europe, was concerned about unlawful combinations and meetings being held by the weavers, although the weavers' main crime at the time seems to have been a desire to replace the Islay ell as a unit of measurement with the English yard.[58]

Pennant's *Tour* is famously illustrated with an engraving of the interior of a weaver's cottage on Islay, showing the weaver working on his upright loom while his family crowd round the adjacent open fireplace.[59] Nine-teenth-century censuses indicate that there were a number of men who gave their profession as weavers, and where more detail is given, woollen handloom weavers. This activity may have peaked in the 1850s. The census of 1851 records over eighty of them, mostly living as cottagers on joint tenant farms.

Flax for making linen may always have been grown on a small scale for local use, but clearly by the eighteenth century the encouragement of flax growing was one of the main elements of the Shawfield lairds' policy for improving farming. This chimed in with government policy through the Board of Trustees for Manufactures and Fisheries with what was happen-

ing elsewhere in Scotland. The moving force behind the British Linen
Company, incorporated in Edinburgh in 1746 to facilitate the manufacture and trade of linen, was the Duke of Argyll, who two years later
established a linen manufactory at Inverary.[60]

Daniel Campbell, the first Shawfield laird, was said by his grandson to
have spent more than £2,000 sterling on building lint mills and bringing
manufacturers, hecklers and weavers to Islay. The rental of 1741 indicates
that there was then a weaver, John McMillan, and a bleacher, Daniel
Campbell, both living in the village of Kilarrow. It was necessary to bleach
linen cloth to whiten and purify it, but neither the weaving nor bleaching
of linen developed into an industry of even local significance on Islay.
Indeed, it was reported in 1811 that there were then no bleachfields
anywhere in the Hebrides, although a good site for one was where the
stream runs out of Loch Finlaggan.[61]

Dr Walker, who visited Islay in 1764, noted in his report that one of the
conditions of tacks given to tenants was that they should sow half a boll of
foreign (American, but imported from Ireland) linseed for each quarterland. Such a tack of 1752 survives. It is for Sanaigmore, Scarrabus and
Staoisha, issued to Archibald Campbell, and further required, as later
surviving tacks, the use of the laird's lint mills for processing the flax
grown. The strategy had many advantages from the laird's point of view,
including the development of trade and improved farming through a wider
range of crops. It also encouraged the production of a crop that could be
processed and sold for cash to pay the rents. The minister of Kilchoman
noted in the 1790s that farm labourers might be paid with the use of plots
of ground for growing their own flax. It is clear that those with land
generally sowed quantities of their own home-produced linseed over and
above what was required by the laird. Travelling merchants went round
the island selling linseed and buying up the linen yarn that was produced
from it. Pennant was told in 1772 that about £2,000 worth of linen yarn
was being exported for sale. In 1775 the Stent Committee established a
market for yarn to be held in Bowmore on the first Tuesday of March,
yearly. In the early nineteenth century the output was worth up
to £10,000 a year and was the main means for many families of paying
their rents.[62]

Flax grew well in Argyll.[63] When the crop had ripened it had to be
pulled and the stems retted (soaked) for some time in order to soften them.
A series of rectangular banked enclosures at Toranore near Ballinaby may
be retting ponds. The process of scutching (pounding) the stems, to release
the fibres from the woody core of the stems, was then done in a mill. The
heckling or carding of the fibres was done by hand prior to spinning.
Spinning was a cottage industry, mostly done by women.

There were lint (flax) mills at Lagavulin and Skerrols. The former was,
presumably, on the site of the present distillery, and may not have
remained in operation for many years. The latter was on the River Sorn,

upstream from the Islay Woollen Mill. It was leased in 1773 to John Taylor, probably an experienced incomer, for three years. There is a note on the back of his missive of 1773 to the effect that his lease should not be extended. It was, ultimately to the regret of the islanders. The Stent Committee felt obliged to petition Shawfield in 1811 to do something about the very bad order that the mill was kept in. It could not even deal with the lint produced by the parish, never mind that of the rest of the island which it seems to have been expected to do.[64]

The laird got a grant from the Board of Trustees for Manufactures and Fisheries, which administered a fund specifically for encouraging and improving the manufacture of linen in the Highlands, to provide forty wheels and twenty reels for distribution on Islay, and these were duly given out in 1799.[65]

The lint mill at Skerrols ceased business sometime between 1828 and 1836.[66] A linen mill was, however, established at Sunderland in the 1840s by the new owner of that estate, Alexander McEwan, a Glasgow merchant. It was only in operation for a few years. By that time it was impractical for a mill in Islay to compete with those in Glasgow and its surroundings, and spinning became limited to producing supplies of yarn for local use.

No great effort was ever put into the development of a linen weaving industry, though some linen was woven for home use. When the Laird of Islay recruited weavers from Glasgow to come and settle and encourage the development of weaving by the natives, the product in question was book-muslin, that is a cloth made from imported cotton specifically for use in binding books. By 1828, ten semi-detached cottages had been built at Keills, alongside the road from Port Askaig to Bridgend, for these weavers and their families: William Walker, John Stewart, John McLellan, Andrew Young, Robert Crauford, William McLellan, Robert Whyte, William Brownlie, Patrick Hamilton and John Stewart. The houses are still there, now interspersed with late twentieth-century houses, but only two of the weavers, John McLellan and Robert Whyte, can be identified in the 1841 or 1851 census, both living elsewhere on the island. It was by then too late for a small-scale weaving industry on Islay, whether producing cotton or linen, to compete with larger industrialised concerns elsewhere. Flax growing and the production of linen yarn had all but disappeared on Islay by the 1840s.[67]

The development of sheep farming in the nineteenth century meant that there was a new interest by the lairds in the production of woollen cloth. There was a carding mill on the Sorn near Bridgend by 1851 when Donald McGeachy is listed in the census as a wool carder and waulk miller. The building survives today as a derelict structure adjacent to Islay Woollen Mill. The mill had apparently been erected by the estate, and its water-wheel, a spur wheel and shafting for drawing the cards, belonged to the laird. McGeachy owned the stove and the machinery in the mill, perhaps including the scribbler, carder, slubbing-billy and spinning-

jennies which are now in the Islay Woollen Mill. McGeachy resigned the
mill in 1874 and the estate brought in a wool spinner, James Christie,
from Machrihanish in Kintyre, to take over the business. Much of it may
have been carding wool for local women to spin. There were still many
doing this in the early twentieth century.[68] An 1881 advertisement by
Christie, however, announces that he 'cardes, spins, weaves, dyes and turns
out wool finished into tweeds, winceys, druggets, blankets, plaidings,
flannels, sheetings, bed-covers, rugs, etc', and touts for business in
Colonsay, Jura and the Small Islands as well as Islay.[69]

In 1883 the estate built a new, much larger, mill for Christie, not just to
replace the carding mill, but so that woollen cloth, especially tweeds,
blankets and rugs, could be produced (Plate L). The Christie family kept
up this business until Mr William B. Christie, the third generation, retired
in 1979. In 1981 the Islay Woollen Mill Company Ltd was formed with
Gordon Covell as manager, later owner. It has since operated successfully
as a family business, producing tweeds for the estates and the film industry,
amongst others, and a range of woollen garments, blankets and rugs, and
items for the tourist market. Until 1983, the water-wheel installed in 1928
by D. H. and F. Reid of Ayr was in use to provide power.

The two spinning-jennies are nineteenth-century versions of James
Hargreaves' famous invention. The slubbing-billy, a type of machine
introduced in the mid nineteenth century, was for piecing together wool
into continuous strips for weaving, work previously done by hand. It is a
unique survival. The carding and piecing machine, a 'Devondale no. 6' of
the mid nineteenth century, was in use until 1963, and now appears to be
the only such piece of equipment remaining *in situ* in a mill. Two
nineteenth-century looms are still in operation.

Kelp

Kelp is a name given to seaweeds that grow in abundance in the seas
around the Western Isles. When dried and burnt, they were a source of the
alkali – often also referred to as kelp – that was used in the manufacture of
glass and soap. The processing of kelp for the glass industry in Scotland
goes back to the early seventeenth century. There is evidence for the
growth of a considerable industry in Argyll and the Western Isles in the
eighteenth century as industrial production of glass took off in Lowland
Scotland, Ireland and England.[70] It was also possible to make similar alkali
from the burning of bracken, but, by and large, this was not done in
Scotland. Perhaps if Daniel Campbell the Younger had not died so young
he would have encouraged this business, as the load of 'fern ashes' shipped
to Liverpool for sale in September 1778 may have been produced through
his initiative rather than that of his brother Walter who had by then
succeeded him.[71]

Seaweed was collected in the summer, dried in the sun and then burned, at a high temperature, in simple rectangular kilns or pits. The outline, formed of boulders, of a such a kiln can still be seen next to the shore on the farm of Bolsa, at NR 395 781 (Plate LI). These kilns produced a fused mass of sodium carbonate and potash which was then broken up into smaller lumps for transporting to the glass-houses.

Kelp was being exported from Islay by the 1760s. In 1768 James MacDonald, change-keeper at Port Askaig, had to go to law over payment for 42 tons of kelp owed him by John Weir, a Campbeltown merchant.[72] In 1780 Donald McColl, farmer in Acharanich, Mull, appears to have had a lease for gathering or producing kelp on Islay as he had 16 tons of it in various locations. He had entered into a contract with Messrs Ewing and Stevenson in Glasgow to supply it all to them. Arrangements were made to ship it on the *Sally* of Greenock, commanded by Archibald Brown, but Brown had not uplifted all of it, because to have done so would have overloaded his ship. Sixteen tons, however, was not a great quantity, and indeed, Islay's annual export of about 200 tons, noted in 1811, was not great at a time when the Hebrides as a whole were producing as much as 15,000 to 20,000 tons.[73]

The lack of production was not necessarily due to indifference by the laird or his tenants but rather to the availability of the weed. This can be deduced from a detailed report on kelp on Islay prepared in 1821 by James Murray. He recommended that 'industrious families' should be trans-planted along some parts of the coast, particularly the most productive stretches on the Sound of Islay, and along the north coast, so that they could double production and make a profit for the laird. He reckoned that each family, on average, would provide three labourers, each producing a ton a year at £5 a ton. This money was all for the laird's benefit with no indication of what the industrious labourers would get for their troubles.

He divided the coastline into sections and estimated their potential total productivity as 310 tons. Going anticlockwise his sections are as follows:

1 Port Askaig to Rhuvaal, 60 tons
2 Rhuvaal to Gortantaoid, 30 tons
3 Ardnave to southern boundary of Sanaig, 60 tons
4 Portnahaven to Bowmore, 15 tons
5 Bowmore to the Laggan boundary, 20 tons
6 Ballychatrigan and Lurabus (in the Oa), 6 tons of 'black tang'
7 Ballychatrigan and Lurabus, 3 tons of 'yellow tang'
8 Tighcargaman (by Port Ellen), 1 ton
9 'Gergar' and Ballyneal (The Ard), 4 tons
10 Ardinistle (Laphroaig), 2 tons
11 Texa, 4 tons
12 Lagavulin, 2 tons
13 Ardbeg, 3 tons

14 Ard Imersay, 12 tons
15 Ardilistry, including Loch a Chnuic, 20 tons
16 Ardmore, 40 tons
17 Kintour ('good for planting')
18 Truddernish (lots of 'redware')
19 Ardtalla, 3 tons
20 Proaig, 4 tons
21 Proaig to Port Askaig, 20 tons.[74]

In fact, there is no evidence that the laird acted upon Murray's report. Preserved in the Islay Estate Papers is a report of the Kelp Committee of the Highland Society of Scotland held in Edinburgh on 10 January 1810.[75] The committee was concerned about improving the quality of kelp production since it was aware that it was one of the main sources of income for a significant number of people in the Highlands and Islands. It recognised that this indigenous industry was under threat from the importation of barilla. This was alkali made from burning a plant of that name that grows in Spain and elsewhere. The £5 a ton reckoned by Murray in his report of 1821 was a far cry from the £20 to £22 a ton that kelp could fetch at the beginning of the century when supplies of barilla virtually ceased as a result of war with Spain and France. Indeed, even £5 may have been a rather optimistic estimate in 1821 as barilla was flooding the market as a result of the removal of high import duties.[76]

The medieval chapel on Nave Island was re-roofed and extended in size at some unknown date in the early nineteenth century. A furnace with a tall brick chimney was erected inside it. This initiative may have stemmed from the efforts of the Highland Society to encourage improved efficiency and standards of production, but it probably rapidly proved to be uneconomic. It represents the last fling of the kelp industry on Islay.

Fishing

The seas around Islay abound in fish and other food resources. It appears, however, that these have never been utilised by the local population to the fullest extent. In the Medieval Period the Church encouraged the eating of fish on the numerous fast days, including Fridays, when meat was prohibited. Fish bones have been recovered from a waterlogged midden at Finlaggan dating to the thirteenth century. These have all been identified as cod bones, perhaps cod fished commercially and salted for preservation. Soil conditions at the site may not have favoured the survival or recovery of the bones of other fish like trout and salmon. The tradition, recounted in Appendix 1, about one of the Macbraynes being buried with his salmon spear and their ownership of the fishings of the River Laggan demonstrate that salmon were valued as a source of food in the seventeenth century and earlier. Martin Martin particularly notes in his late seven-teenth-century account of the island the rivers and freshwater lochs stocked with salmon, trout and eels.[77]

Salmon fishing was of particular interest to later lairds as a recreation. Daniel Campbell the younger of Shawfield commissioned a report on the fisheries of Islay in 1776 from William Moffet and James Black. This looked at the scope for encouraging the fish to enter and spawn in the River Sorn, Laggan and the 'River of Ardnahow' – presumably the Margadale River – but there was also interest in the potential of netting the fish in Loch Gruinart and Loch Indaal. A seventeenth-century account of Islay had claimed there was a great store of salmon in Loch Gruinart, but now it would be necessary to get rid of the seals to make net fishing worthwhile.[78]

We have little knowledge of sea-fishing in the seventeenth-century. In 1619 the legal adviser, John Mowat, of the new Campbell laird, passed on advice to him from 'the Duke', that he should bring in Englishmen to develop the fishing.[79] There is no evidence that Cawdor acted upon this advice. A clue that Sir Hugh Campbell intended to encourage a fishing industry is provided by the steps he took to establish saltpans at Ardlarach in 1693, under the direction of James Scott. The most likely explanation for this initiative is that it was proposed to use the salt for preserving fish. The pans are commemorated by the place-name Saltpan Point at Gart-breck. The mention of salt pans on Islay, 'sett up here not long agoe' in the description of Islay in Sir Robert Sibbald's manuscripts, appears to relate to earlier, seventeenth-century works.[80]

Fish were a major element in the diet of the Ilich throughout the eighteenth and nineteenth centuries. Many who lived around the coast kept their own small boats for inshore fishing. Fish were caught on lines strung with hooks, baited with limpets and other shellfish. Some of the caves around the coast have middens largely consisting of periwinkle, whelk and limpet shells. These may represent the activities of other islanders occupying the caves on a seasonal basis to catch their own supply of fish (Plate XXX). A sherd of 'white gritty' pottery from the midden in a cave at Kilnaughton Bay may indicate that this activity extends back to the thirteenth century, and very probably earlier. The relative ease with which fish could be got for home consumption was one of the main factors in inhibiting the devel-opment of fishing on a commercial basis.

Several commentators on conditions in Islay lament this lack of any development of a fishing industry or any trade. In 1764 the Revd Dr John Walker was concerned to note how the stocks of mullet in Loch Gruinart and the cod off the north and east coasts of Islay were not fished. He stated that there were neither nets nor long lines on Islay, nor anybody who made fishing their employment.[81]

In 1777, not long before his death, Daniel Campbell the Younger applied to the Commissioners of the Forfeited Estates for a grant for improvements on Islay, both for agriculture and fishing. He received a matching grant of £500 for the latter, and his brother and successor, Walter, was able to report back in 1779 on how the money had been spent. The pier at Port Askaig had been improved and a fishing smack purchased, as well as two yawls. A cargo of cod, ling and salmon had been sent to Liverpool in the previous year. Pursuant to instructions from the Board of Commissioners, two experienced fishermen from the county of Nairn, David and John Mains, had been employed in 1777 to search for fishing banks and make experiments with long-line fishing around the coasts of the island.[82] The minister of Kilarrow noted in the 1790s how twenty years previously some fishing smacks from Liverpool would come and fish for cod and ling off Islay, but their owners soon gave up the business owing to the bad conduct of the fishermen.[83]

Portnahaven was established as a fishing village in the late eighteenth century with the laird, Walter Campbell of Shawfield, providing boats, land and timber for houses, to encourage the development of cod fishing. This may not, immediately, have come to very much, but a new impetus was provided after 1814 by a new laird, Walter Campbell of Sunderland. Writing in the 1830s, Lord Teignmouth described how conditions had been greatly improved. The fishermen had been induced to acquire larger boats with a keel of from 20 to 25 feet (about 6 m to 7.6 m). There were about twenty of these and they used them to catch stainlocks (skate) and cod on lines on banks to westward. The laird wanted to construct a pier for the boats but they were small enough to be readily drawn up on the shore. The fish were dried on the rocks, salted in barrels, and then taken to be sold in Ireland. A salt-house had been erected in the village and the laird was keen to encourage the locals to specialise either in fishing or the processing of fish. He also wanted the trade of the cured fish to be concentrated in fewer hands with the provision of a smack for carrying the collective produce of the fishery to Ireland. At the time of Teignmouth's visit not much headway had been made with these ambitions.[84]

By the 1860s the fishermen of Portnahaven were sailing down the coast of Ireland in search of fish. By 1881 they were fishing off Barra and selling their catch of stainlocks and cod at the annual Ballycastle Fair in Ireland. Line fishing continued into the early twentieth century. Until 1915 the Islay hand-line fishermen set up base in the summer at Glemanuill Port, the south end of Kintyre. Here they lived in thatched stone-and-turf huts.[85]

Evidence is limited for the proprietors of the other main estates in the nineteenth century encouraging sea-fishing. An offer to Walter Frederick Campbell in 1840 for a three-year lease of the fishings off the coast of Islay makes mention of an ice house at Laggan for preserving the fish before being sent to market. The fish in question may have been mackerel.[86] The development of a herring fishery, using drift-nets, however, was seen as a lucrative opportunity.

There were four herring busses based in Islay in 1763, ten by 1766, going to the fishery in the Firth of Clyde from the rendezvous at Campbeltown. Government bounty schemes were at this time a great encouragement to the development of the industry. Busses were substantial, three-masted boats of 70–100 tons that might remain at the fishing for the full three months of the season, starting on 1 September. The rest of the year they were employed in taking kelp from the Highlands to Liverpool, Belfast, Derry and other Irish ports, though Daniel Campbell the younger wanted to encourage them to fish for other species of fish in the other nine months of the year. The herring were salted and packed in barrels for export. Campbeltown was then the centre for the Scottish herring fishery.[87] The government had introduced a bounty scheme to encourage herring fishing, paying, from 1757, 50s a ton. The Islay merchant, David Simson, noted in an undated letter of the 1770s that he was waiting to be paid his bounty of about £230. This represented a catch of 92 tons of fish, though there is no indication of whether this was for one or more seasons.[88]

The Scottish herring fishery was to develop into a major industry in the nineteenth century, but the direct involvement of Islay boats may not have been long-lasting. There are no comments on it by any of the three Islay ministers who contributed to the first *Statistical Account* in the 1790s, or indeed in any later surveys of the island prior to the late nineteenth century. The Islay fishermen notably resisted the use of ring-nets or trawl-nets which were seen to be too destructive of the fish stocks, and instead continued to fish with drift-nets from small boats of Irish type, obtained in Portrush in Northern Ireland. Trawling involved the rounding up of shoals of fish within a large net rather than waiting for the fish to get caught in the mesh of a drift-net. One of the Port Wemyss fishermen, Donald Anderson, who tried out a trawl-net in Loch Indaal in 1874, was threatened with death and the destruction of his gear by a local mob.[89]

For a period of nine years from 1886 herring appeared in numbers around Islay, prompting the arrival of fishermen from further afield in Argyll, the Islands and the Clyde. By 1893 it was recorded that there were 309 boats crewed by 1,082 men along with nine steamers for taking the catch off to market. In 1888 a herring station was established on the shore of Loch Gruinart, at Tayovullin, perhaps largely for steam trawlers. It was only in use for a few years, but a report notes that in 1891 about 22,000 crans of herring were caught there, valued at upwards of £18,500, which was 'a great deal in such an out of the way place'. Islay Estate planned a village in 1892 with lots for fishermen and others connected with the fishing industry at Gruinart, but the Islay fishermen had not lost their abhorrence of trawling and agitated, with success, to have Loch Gruinart closed to trawlers that very year.[90]

The second edition Ordnance Survey map shows a row of half a dozen houses, a slip and a complex of buildings, presumably the sheds where the

fish were cured and stored, and there is a photograph of the complex taken
about 1910.[91] The Tayovullin station possibly did not impact greatly on
the Islay economy. Many such small stations around the coasts of Scotland
were closed down as the industry became more concentrated in a few larger
ports.

In the twentieth century inshore fishing continued to occupy a number
of fishermen on Islay. From the 1960s a considerable business grew up,
catching lobsters, crabs, scallops and winkles, mostly for export to Europe.
Oysters are also farmed at Craigens on Loch Gruinart.

Cheese-making

Islay rentals demonstrate the importance of cheese in the local economy
from early times. Cheese could be made in the summer months from the
milk of cows, sheep and goats, and preserved as a food for consumption all
year round. It was only from 1942 that cheese making was undertaken on
a commercial scale with the establishment of the Islay Creamery in Port
Charlotte by the Milk Marketing Board, keen to support those farmers
who were turning to dairying as a means of making money. Production
was at first carried out in part of the old Loch Indaal Distillery, but in 1981
a new factory, painted the same orange colour as the product, was built
adjacent to the Museum of Islay Life. The creamery ran into difficulties in
May 1996 and had to be closed down, but the local dairy farmers, facing
the loss of their herds and livelihoods, took the creamery over and re-
started production in August 1997. The creamery produced a Dunlop-
style cheese, latterly 25 tons of it each month with milk from eight dairy
herds. It was marketed widely through the UK, but had strong competition from creameries producing a similar product on the mainland where
costs, especially transport, were rather lower. To be viable after 1997 the
Islay Creamery had to come up with an extra-high-value product, but the
proposed production of a mature cheese never got off the ground and the
creamery was finally closed in 2000, and the factory dismantled soon
afterwards. Twenty-five jobs, directly or indirectly involved in the industry, were lost, and 700 cows had to be sent off the island for slaughter.

Whisky distilling

The distillation of whisky has brought Islay great fame. At the present time
there are seven distilleries in operation – Bunnahabhain, Caol Ila, Ardbeg,
Lagavulin, Laphroaig, Bowmore and Bruichladdich – a remarkable concentration. They all rely on local water and peat, and at one time barley. The
latter, however, is now all imported. Most of it is turned into malt at the Port
Ellen maltings and supplied to all the Islay distilleries, though Bowmore and

Laphroaig still produce some of their malt, in the traditional way, on their own malting floors. After being steeped in water, the barley is spread out on these floors where it germinates, thus producing the sugars from which the alcohol is extracted. The grain is then dried in a kiln and ground to a coarse grist. In Islay distilleries, peat is used as a fuel in the kiln-drying process, thus imparting to the finished products their distinctive Islay flavour.

The malt grist is then mixed with hot water and stirred in large mashtuns in order to produce wort, a sweet liquor that is drained off from the spent grist or draft. Yeast is added to the wort to encourage fermentation, and it is this mixture which is then boiled in wash stills (Fig. 12.3). The alcohol evaporates off, is cooled in a condenser and liquefied. The process of distillation is in practice quite complex, and involves careful measurement of the spirit produced so that the correct excise duties can be paid. The whisky is then aged in casks for a number of years before being used for blending or bottled as single malts. These casks are normally either reused American bourbon or Spanish sherry casks which also impart some of the flavour to the whisky.[92]

Islay malts are recognised as one of the four key groupings of Scotch malt whisky, alongside those of Campbeltown, the Lowlands and the Highlands. Different editions of Islay malts are keenly sought after by connoisseurs the world over. From personal observation, any bar or restaurant anywhere in the world with malt whisky on offer is as likely

Figure 12.3 The Still House of Bowmore Distillery in the 1880s,
a light and roomy building with five copper stills. Note the peat fuel
in the foreground. From Barnard, *Whisky Distilleries*, 101.

to have an Islay malt as any other. Much Islay whisky, however, is destined for blending, and most blended whiskies contain some Islay malt. Caol Ila, the largest distillery with the newest plant, sends almost all its whisky for blending in Johnnie Walker, Black Bottle and Bells.

The importance of peat in the production of Islay whisky came to the attention of the world in 1983 when a planning application by Port Ellen Maltings to cut peat on Duich Moss was opposed by some of the most high-profile conservationists of the day on the grounds that it would adversely affect the white-fronted geese that roosted there. The conservationists overstated their case and failed to consult with islanders. In a stormy meeting at Bowmore they were heckled and felt obliged to rely on the police to escort them from the meeting. Duich Moss was made into a National Nature Reserve and the distillers were obliged to do their peat-cutting at nearby Castlehill, with funding from the Nature Conservancy Council (the predecessor of Scottish Natural Heritage).

Present-day production for the seven distilleries together is approaching 12 million litres of pure alcohol per year. Caol Ila produces by far the most, 3.5 million litres, followed by Lagavulin with 2.3 million and Laphroaig with 2 million litres. Bruichladdich, recently reopened after a period of closure, is only producing 320,000 litres. The workforce of each distillery numbers fewer than twenty-five, and in this things do not seem to have changed significantly over the years. For instance, a staff photograph for Laphroaig in 1934 shows twenty-one, whereas the workforce now is twenty-four. This relatively small workforce, however, is responsible for a manufacture that brings millions in revenue to the British Exchequer.[93]

The distillation of spirits was introduced to Scotland in the Middle Ages. Sherds from a pottery alembic have been identified among the finds from Jedburgh Abbey and there is a worm (condenser) from the Campbell castle of Carrick on Loch Goil. The excavators were able to demonstrate that it must date prior to the bombardment of the castle in 1685, and it could well be part of a still that was in use as early as the fifteenth century.

The term normally used in early documents for whisky is aquavite, from the Latin for 'water of life'. The Gaelic *uisge beatha*, hence whisky, means the same.

The Statutes of Iona of 1609 forbade the importation of wine and aquavite to the Isles, but also recognised the right of the islanders to 'brew' aquavite for their own use.[94] It was consumed as a drink in social circumstances, but may also always have been considered to have medicinal qualities. It would surely have been of interest to the Macbeths of Ballinaby, the hereditary physicians to the Lords of the Isles.

A possible clue to early distilling on Islay, on behalf of the Campbells of Cawdor, if not the MacDonald Lords before them, is provided by a place-name, Brewseat, first recorded in the rental of 1631. Brewseat is noted in the 1686 rental as being in 'Lagmullin' – an early form of the name Lagavulin, and is listed between the mill and the malt kiln of Dunyvaig, both of which may also have been located on the land of Lagavulin. Brewseat is a term in old Scots for a piece of land that supported brewing activity. Since it is adjacent to Dunyvaig Castle, and early documents do not distinguish between the brewing of beer and the 'brewing' of whisky, it is tempting to suggest that Lagavulin was already a centre of whisky production in the early seventeenth century.

A tax was first placed on whisky in Scotland in 1644, when the Scottish Parliament sought to raise money for its war effort by taxing various commodities including spirits.[95] Excise duties have been payable ever since. Much of the whisky produced in Scotland has always come from the Highlands and Islands. Until well into the nineteenth century many of those distilling it in these regions, for their own use or wider distribution, avoided paying the increasingly onerous duties levied by government. Whisky was growing greatly in popularity in the second half of the eighteenth century, with large quantities being exported to England. Since many stills were small and easily moved around, this did not encourage many involved in distilling to make their enterprises legal. In any case, government efforts to regulate distilling in the Highlands were generally unsympathetic or unhelpful to local producers. Illicit distillers in places like Islay could not only make whisky much cheaper than the legal distillers, but their product was generally recognised to be of superior quality.[96]

The minister of Kildalton noted in the early 1790s that, because there was no excise officer on the island, the Ilich felt at liberty to distil whisky without paying duty on it. The quantity produced was very great, and the minister considered that it was a cause of great evil, not only in encouraging excessive drinking but in consuming barley that should have fed the poor. He alleged that distillers would advance sums of money to struggling farmers on the promise of their barley crops at a fixed price, which was well below the market value at harvest time.[97]

The first excise officer did arrive in Islay later in the 1790s, and in 1795 over ninety stills were seized, only to be replaced by tinkers invited over from Ireland for the purpose. In 1798 it was reported that no licences had been taken out on the island nor any revenue paid (since 1784). The islanders were neither able to pay nor prepared to give up their distilling. More distilling than ever before was being undertaken with spirits being exported to Argyll, Inverness-shire, Mull, Lewis, Galloway and Ireland.[98]

In 1801, all grain distilling was banned by the government because of a disastrous harvest. This resulted in 233 Ilich being charged with distilling or malting privately. Included in the list were Hugh Currie in Octovullin, Duncan and Duncan Johnston in Tallant, Neil McCallum in Scarrabus, Alexander and Alexander McDougall in Lagavulin, Donald McEachan (McEachern) in Ballachlaven, Neil McEachan in Bridgend and John McLachlan in Sean-ghairt.[99] These appear either to be the same people as, or relatives of, those legal distillers on a list of 1818 (see below). The

1801 action demonstrates just how prevalent distilling was on Islay at that time and also the roots of the industry that developed in the nineteenth century.

The task of the excise officers based on Islay was not an easy one in a society which liked whisky but disapproved of taxation. John Murdoch, himself an excise officer, recorded the tradition that Cnoc na Croiche (Gallows Hill) at Bridgend got its name because it was there that the 'good people' of Islay erected gallows specifically to hang the first excise officer on the island. The unfortunate man was rescued by an influential gentleman who provided a horse for him to escape to the nearest port.[100] The grave monument at Kilnaughton of one early excise officer from Banff, John Nicol, who died at Bowmore in 1833 aged thirty-one, is quite revealing. His surviving relatives felt it was necessary to inscribe on it that 'in private live he was endeared to all who knew him and deservedly respected for the correctness of his motives and the unostentatious benevolence of his heart'.

There are several stories told on Islay concerning the illicit distilling of whisky. When Alfred Barnard visited Lagavulin in the 1880s, he was informed that in 1742 there had been ten small, separate smuggling 'bothys' for the manufacture of 'moonlight'. One of them must have belonged to Donald Galbraith, died 1750, whose still with its furniture was valued at £7 7s sterling.[101] Eighteenth-century testaments demonstrate that it was by no means unusual for better-off farmers, tenants and merchants to have their own distilling equipment, and probably all the keepers of change-houses distilled whisky for sale. Indeed the title change-keeper may sometimes have been a euphemism for (illegal) whisky distiller. Such would appear to have been the case with Angus McFee, died 1738, in Glenavulin (a clack mill? – with associated malt kiln) on the land of Kinnabus in the Oa.[102]

There is a tradition that whisky was made at Nerabus in the Rhinns, in an old clack mill up the glen from the present-day settlement, and it is also said to have been made in several caves, including one at Allt na Goibhnean near Lower Killeyan in the Oa. It was here in 1850, with the help of the customs cutter ss *Chichester*, that the Excise finally discovered some distillers. Although they all made off, they were known faces and were soon caught and jailed in Inverary for three months – Alexander McCuaig in Upper Killeyan, Donald McGibbon in Lower Killeyan and Neil McGibbon his brother. From the point of view of the customs and excise staff in Port Ellen, this must have been more satisfying than having poor grocers in town fined for, apparently unwittingly, selling coffee adulterated with chicory.[103]

Well remembered are the activities of Baldy Mhorachaidh, a crofter fisherman who lived at An Cladach, at the mouth of Gleann Ghaireasdail on the Sound of Islay, in the late nineteenth century.[104] Here there are the ruins of three houses, one recently restored as a bothy, traces of cultivation and a small inlet for pulling up a boat. Baldy's still was apparently housed in a cave about a mile to the north at Lùb Gleann Logain. There is a small

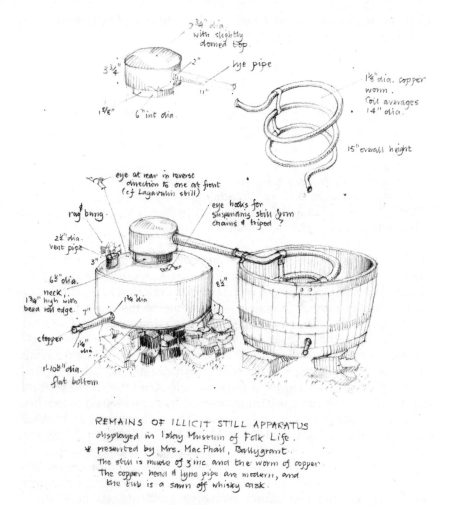

Figure 12.4 Drawing of an illicit still in the Museum of Islay Life. Copyright, The Royal Commission on the Ancient and Historical Monuments of Scotland.

pot still with its worm (condenser) in the Museum of Islay Life in Port Charlotte, which is thought to have been used illegally in the hills behind McArthur's Head on the Sound of Islay (Fig. 12.4).

The first legal distillery on Islay was established in the new village of Bowmore in 1779 by the merchant, David Simson, who had apparently been distilling at Bridgend in the years beforehand. Simson owned the business outright, having acquired a feu of the land from the laird. The Simson family had the business until 1837 when they sold it to William and James Mutter, Glasgow merchants of German extraction. It was several years before Bowmore was joined by any other legal distilleries on the island, but an excise account of Scottish distillers producing for home consumption, for the period November 1818 to April 1819, provides the information that there were then:

Neil McEachern & Co., Daill
George Montgomery & Co., Octomore
Hugh Currie & Sons, Octovullin
John McLachlan & Co., Keppolsmore
John McDougall & Co., Ardbeg
Archibald Campbell & Co, Lagavulin
John Johnson, Lagavulin
John McDuffie & Co., Kintour
Donald McEachern & Co., Bridgend
Neil McCallum & Co., Ballygrant
Donald & John Johnston, Tallant[105]

Many of these businesses would have arisen as a result of new legislation in 1816, which allowed the use of stills of as small a capacity as 40 gallons.[106] This made it easier for distillers, especially in the Highlands, to set up small-scale businesses producing malt whisky. Some of those listed here, like McLachlan at Keppolsmore, McDuffie at Kintour and the Curries at Octovullin may never have got off the ground as viable commercial concerns.

Some of the others had relatively short lifespans, and only ever operated on a modest scale. Such was the McEachern distillery at Bridgend. This business was established in 1818 and sequestrated in 1821. It was probably attached to the inn (now the Bridgend Hotel) where Donald McEachern was listed as merchant and innkeeper in Pigot's *Directory* of 1825. Daill, operated by the McEacherns from 1814 to 1834, had an annual output by 1827 of a little over 6,000 gallons. The nearby distillery at Newton was run from 1819 to 1837 by Thomas Pattison who then moved on to distil at Octomore. Octomore had been run by the Montgomery family from 1816 to 1840 with production exceeding 3,500 gallons in 1826–27. Pattison's efforts at Octomore could not have lasted long since the lease was relinquished to the new laird, James Morrison, in 1854.[107] Distilling at Daill and Octomore probably took place in the farm-steadings. The present Newton House may be where the Newton Distillery was located.

Tallant, a farm a couple of miles south-east of Bowmore (not the farm of the same name near Kildalton), was the home of the Johnson family, which was also heavily involved in distilling in the early days of the industry. A distillery was operated here from 1821 to 1852. Neil McCallum & Co., Ballygrant, may be our earliest evidence for the Lossit Distillery that is recorded as late as the 1860s. It was operated from 1826 by Malcolm MacNeill in Lossit, and its building survives as a private house called the Kennels, between Lochs Ballygrant and Lossit. It, and its distilling apparatus ('utensils'), belonged to the Laird of Islay, and was set to George Stuart in 1840 for ten years. He was still there in the following decade.[108]

The real winners in this list of 1818 were Ardbeg and Lagavulin. Ardbeg is said to have been founded in 1815 by the McDougall family who were tenants of this farm from at least 1798. As the list shows, there were at first two distilleries at Lagavulin. The Archibald Campbell who had one of them was probably related to the Duncan Campbell who was tacksman of half of Lagavulin and the (lint) mill by 1780. A 1784 inventory of the possessions of Duncan Campbell includes whisky and distilling equipment. Possibly it was this mill that was developed into the distillery. John Johnson was tenant of the other half of Lagavulin as early as the 1790s. He is believed to have been related to the Johnstons who were at Tallant. By 1837 there was only one distillery at Lagavulin.[109]

Legal distilling was given a boost by the Excise Act of 1823 which more than halved the duty on spirit and made the production of malt whisky more cost-effective. It enabled small distilleries to make malt whisky that could compete in taste with that produced by the smugglers, and opened up the trade with England which had previously been monopolised by two large Lowland distillers. At the same time, the Excise was being encouraged to clamp down much more rigorously on illicit operations.[110]

These developments may have encouraged the establishment of a handful of new Islay distilleries and the improvement of pre-existing ones in the 1820s and 1830s. The laird, Walter Frederick Campbell, was apparently keen to encourage these developments, though this interest, with one exception, did not extend to feuing any more land for the purpose. Instead, long tacks were offered – fifty years for Loch Indaal in 1832, fifty-seven years for Ardinistle in 1834 and fifty-seven years by the estate administrator for Ardbeg in 1848. The exceptional case was Port Ellen Distillery, founded in 1825, where particular encouragement was given by the laird to James Ramsay after he acquired it in 1836. In 1840 Walter Frederick granted a lease of the distillery along with the nearby farms of Cornabus and Kilnaughton. This was the basis of Ramsay's rise to power as a successful businessman, landowner and politician (see Chapter 6).[111]

Laphroaig was founded in 1826 by another member of the Johnson family, Donald the son of John Johnson, the distiller at Lagavulin. The neighbouring, less successful, distillery of Ardinistle was eventually merged with Laphroaig in the 1860s.[112] Lochindaal Distillery was established on the east shore of the loch of that name in 1825, adjacent to the village of Port Charlotte that was founded a few years later. It was based on a meal mill and change-house at Skiba. Although it was closed in 1929, many of its buildings still survive, now partially occupied by a youth hostel and field centre. The original agreement for its erection was made between Walter Frederick Campbell and Colin Campbell of Surnaig in 1825, but nothing may have got underway until the property was leased for fifty years in 1850 to George McLennan, a spirit merchant in Glasgow, with approval to erect buildings for a distillery.[113]

Figure 12.5 Caol Ila Distillery in the 1880s.
From Barnard, *Whisky Distilleries*, 108.

Caol Ila is said to have been founded by a Glasgow distiller, Hector Henderson, in 1846 (Fig. 12.5). It is situated on the site of the lead smelter at Freeport. The 1848 Islay rental indicates that Freeport Distillery was then set to William Campbell, and in 1850 he was given a ten-year lease of the land on which the Caol Ila distillery was built, with right of renewal.[114]

Less successful than these distilleries was one at Mulindry, erected by John Sinclair in 1826. Its production was less than 5,000 gallons a year, and probably closed with Sinclair's bankruptcy in 1831.[115] There is little trace of it now. Mulindry is inland, and it is no accident that all the successful distilleries on Islay are on the coast, thus making transport of supplies and the finished product much easier in the days before the development of good roads and road haulage. It was only with the advent of a roll-on–roll-off ferry service to Islay in 1968 that location by the sea became less important, since it was now possible for large container lorries and tankers to be shipped to and from the island.

There was a final flurry of distillery founding on Islay in the early 1880s, reflecting an expansion of malt whisky distilling in the country at large at that time. More Islay malt whisky was needed by the whisky blenders who by now had achieved a worldwide market for their products. Bunnahabhain was founded in 1880 by a partnership including William Robertson and John Marshall, both wine and spirit brokers of Glasgow, James Ford, a merchant in Leith, and James Greenlees, a distiller in Campbeltown. Bruichladdich was set up in the following year by three brothers from a

Glasgow distilling family, Robert, William and John Gourlay Harvey. Both distilleries retain, to a considerable extent, their 1880s form and appearance, with buildings grouped around rectangular courtyards. A third distillery was planned in 1883 for Rubha Bhachlaig, on the Sound of Islay to the north of Bunnahabhain, but it never materialised. All three were on the Islay Estate of Charles Morrison and he was content to grant feus for the land they were built upon.[116]

A fascinating snapshot of Islay's distilleries in the 1880s is provided by the journalist Alfred Barnard who wrote of his visits to the nine then in operation – Ardbeg, Lagavulin, Laphroaig, Port Ellen, Bowmore, Lochindaal, Bruichladdich, Caol Ila and Bunnahabhain.[117] Barnard considered Ardbeg to be picturesque, and noted how its site had been chosen for the softness and purity of the water supply, obtained from Lochs Arinambeast and Uigidale (Lochs Iarnan and Uigeadail). Fifty years before his visit, it was among the largest works, although only producing 500 gallons per week, but then it was making 250,000 gallons a year – a tenfold increase.

Lagavulin was then producing 75,000 gallons a year, and although much of this went for blending, some was bottled as a single malt which was held in high regard. Laphroaig was turning out 23,000 gallons a year, while Port Ellen supplied 140,000 gallons. The works at Port Ellen were more up to date and mechanised than those at Lagavulin and Laphroaig.

Barnard noted that the lade or watercourse which conducted water from the River Laggan to the Bowmore Distillery was said to be the longest to any Scottish distillery, nine miles in total. It allowed the distillery to achieve an annual output of 200,000 gallons. Lochindaal Distillery in Port Charlotte was still contained in the original buildings built earlier in the nineteenth century. Much of its output of over 120,000 gallons per year was then floated out to ships in Loch Indaal in casks, lashed together in groups of ten. Some of Lagavulin's whisky was exported from the distillery in a similar fashion.

Bruichladdich and Bunnahabhain were both only a few years old at the time of Barnard's visit. Both were purpose-built and had piers for shipping their whisky. The former was producing 94,000 gallons annually, the latter 200,000 gallons. The distillery at Caol Ila was not only situated in the wildest and most picturesque location viewed by Barnard, but was also arranged in the most modern style with the most up-to-date appliances. It was, however, totally demolished and replaced by a brand new edifice in the 1970s (Plate LII). In Barnard's time it was turning out 147,000 gallons a year.

The whisky industry has gone through many vicissitudes since the 1880s, with the distilleries in Islay showing remarkable resilience and success. At the present day, Lagavulin, Caol Ila and Port Ellen belong to the large international drinks consortium, Diageo. The distillery at Port Ellen was closed in 1983, but the maltings there, which were erected in 1973 to supply other Islay distilleries, are still in production. Laphroaig is now part of Allied Distilleries after, famously, in the 1950s and 1960s being run by a woman, Bessie Williamson. She was the secretary of the previous owner, Ian William Hunter, and inherited it on his death in 1954.

Bunnahabhain was from 1887 until a few years ago part of Highland Distilleries, but has recently been acquired by Burn Stewart Distillers Ltd. Bruichladdich has recently reopened after a short period of closure. Since 2000, it has belonged to Murray McDavid and is experimenting with new production methods and products. Ardbeg was closed in the late 1970s and '80s, but since its acquisition by Glenmorangie in 1997 has had a new lease of life.

The equipment of Lochindaal Distillery was removed in 1929 leaving no hope that it could be reopened. At the time of writing, however, there is some prospect that the owners of Bruichladdich will open a new distillery in Port Charlotte. Another interesting development of recent times has been the establishment of a small-scale distillery at Rockside Farm. This Kilchoman Farm Distillery was started in 2005 by Anthony Wills and its first output is eagerly awaited. Finally, we might note the establishment of the Islay Ales Company Limited in 2003, the island's only microbrewery.

Some Islay Surnames

Beaton
See Macbeth.

Bell
See MacMillan.

Brown
See Macbrayne.

Campbell of Ballachlaven
George Campbell, a younger son of John Campbell of Barrichbeyan and brother of Ronald, the Bailie of Jura, was the progenitor of the Campbells of Ballachlaven, a family that remained in possession of that land until 1778. George entered into contracts of wadset for the lands of Ballachlaven, and others. He was succeeded by his son John, and he by his nephew John, who in 1681 married Marie Campbell, daughter of John Campbell of Ballinaby. The last of this line that held Ballachlaven was James, probably a son of John and Marie.[1]

Campbell of Ballinaby
In 1629 the superiority of the Ballinaby estate, consisting of the lands of Ballinaby, How, Saligo and Erasaid, was bought from John Macbeth by Lord Lorn (later Earl and 1st Marquis of Argyll), and feued to the Campbells of Ballinaby, who remained in possession until the late eighteenth century. The family was descended from Donald, the third son of Sir John, the first Campbell Thane of Cawdor, through a natural son, Alasdair Roy. John Campbell of Ballinaby and his eldest son Donald entered into a contract of wadset with Sir Hugh Campbell of Cawdor in 1671 for the lands of Corsapol and others, and rentals show the family often held tacks from the Lairds of Islay for other lands in the Rhinns as well. They were thus one of the most substantial families on Islay in the seventeenth century.[2]

Donald Campbell of Ballinaby supported, or was suspected of supporting the Earl of Argyll's rebellion in 1685. John Campbell of Ballinaby and his wife, Anna Campbell, were two of the emigrants that sailed to New York in 1738 with Captain Lauchlan Campbell. They were both dead by 1763.[3]

This family of Campbells retained Ballinaby until 1778, when Donald Campbell of Ballinaby, Captain in the Argyllshire Highland Regiment, sold the estate, extending to five merk lands of old extent, to Colin Campbell, tacksman of Carnbeg, for the sum of £3,500. Colin also got other substantial lands, including Gruinart, Leek, Sanaigbeg and Corsapol, Coultoon and Calumsary, all wadset lands held of the Campbells of Shawfield.[4]

Campbell of Daill
There were at least two Campbell families that successively wadset Daill in the parish of Kilarrow. Donald Campbell already had a wadset of this land by 1631. In 1684, however, Donald Campbell (a son or grandson?), wadsetter of Daill, was one of the Argyllshire gentlemen who gave a bond to the Marquis of Atholl that he would appear before the Privy Council within ten days of being cited. In 1685 Sir Hugh Campbell of Cawdor gave a new wadset of the land of Daill and others amounting to three quarterlands, to Lachlan Campbell, son of the late Colin Campbell of Clunes (younger son of John, 3rd of Cawdor). Lachlan's grave-slab is in the burial ground at the old parish church of Kilchoman, indicating he died on 12 December 1689. Daniel Campbell of Shawfield attempted to force Lachlan's son Colin, presumably then of some considerable age, out of these lands in 1749 by redeeming the wadset, but three years later granted him sasine. By 1723 he had apparently sublet Daill to Colin Campbell, son of George Campbell of Octomore.[5]

Campbell of Ellister
Duncan Campbell (Donach McCallan), first of Ellister, was second son of Colin of Sunderland. In 1672 he entered into a contract of wadset with Sir Hugh Campbell of Cawdor for the lands of Ellister Wester and others. Duncan married Elizabeth, daughter of Archibald Campbell, son of Ronald, Bailie of Jura. He was succeeded, between 1696 and 1704, by his son Colin, married to a daughter of Archibald Campbell, the third of Sunderland. He died in 1729. George Campbell of Ellister married Mary, daughter of Ferqhard Campbell of Lagganlochan (mainland Argyll) in 1769.[6] There are three eighteenth-century grave-slabs in the burial ground of the old parish church of Kilchoman commemorating members of this family, including Colin who died in 1730.

Campbells of Killinallan and Ardnahoe
Alexander, a younger son of John Campbell of Ballinaby, entered into a contract of wadset in 1672 with Sir Hugh Campbell of Cawdor for the land of Killinallan. His son Alexander had succeeded by 1686, and he was

followed by his son, John, who died around 1728. His testament indicates that he owned 263 cattle of various sorts, including 7 bulls, and 32 horses excluding followers. The 1733 rental shows that John's eldest son and heir, Alexander, held Killinallan and Ardnahoe, and all the coastal farms in between, that is a vast sweep of Islay from Loch Gruinart round the headland of Rhuvaal and down the Sound of Islay. He also had Margadale, inland from Ardnahoe, and Ardnave on the west side of Loch Gruinart.[7]

This third Alexander died in 1741, and was succeeded by his brother Donald. Donald was a man 'very weak and facile, and who is often troubled with fits of madness', and so in 1742 he voluntarily renounced control of his lands and affairs and put them in the hands of a group of interdictors, including his younger brother, Colin, who by then held the wadset of Ardnahoe and others. Daniel Campbell (the elder) of Shawfield had intimated that he intended to redeem the wadset in 1760, and Colin surreptitiously did a deal with the laird to have a lease of Killinallan. When this was found out, it led to a bitter dispute in the Court of Session. The wadsets were not redeemed in 1760 and Colin held both until Walter Campbell of Shawfield finally redeemed them in 1778. He then left the country. The Mrs Campbell of Killinallan, and her son Angus, who were listed as tenants of Killinallan and other lands in the 1780 rental, were probably the widow and son of Donald.[8]

Campbell of Kinnabus
This family is descended from Duncan Mor, the illegitimate son of Captain Alexander Campbell, son of George Campbell of Airds, tutor of Cawdor.[9] Several generations of tacksmen are recorded on grave monuments at Kilnaughton, including Duncan (died 1731) and Colin (died 1755). Colin, recorded in the rental of 1780, also held Stremnish-more, and his son George (died 1858) by 1799 had added the Mill of Oa. The family had lost these lands by 1848.

Campbell of Lossit (Kilmeny)
The first member of this family to hold Lossit was John Campbell of Kirktoun (Taynuilt, in mainland Argyll), an illegitimate son of Donald of Ichterachyn, third son of Sir John Campbell, first of Cawdor. John had Donald, who is included in the 1722 rental of Islay as wadsetter of six quarterlands, including the lands of Lossit, Gartnatiber, Gortenanloss, Baleachdrach, Ballyclach, Eacharnach, Arivuine, Kilslevan, Kilmeny and Tiervaagain. Donald's grave monument is in the churchyard of the parish church at Muckairn in Lorn, with an inscription indicating that he was also Bailie of Muckairn and died in 1729, aged seventy-seven.

His son, John Campbell of Lossit and Bailie of Muckairn, was succeeded by his son Donald, who served as a lieutenant in the 60th Royal Americans in the French Indian Wars (1756–63). There he was captured by the Indian chief, Pontiac, at Detroit, and met a grisly end.[10] In

1751 he had sold Lossit to his half-brother Alexander, son of John and his second wife Jean, daughter of the Revd John Campbell of Knockamilly, Minister of Kilarrow. Alexander was a prosperous merchant in Jamaica. He continued to live there, and in 1776 gave over the estate to his younger brother, Colin Campbell, tacksman of Carnbeg (formerly tacksman of Daill), provided he paid all rents and duties, including annuities to Florence MacNeill, the widow of his other brother James, and James's daughter, Ketty.[11]

Soon after succeeding to Islay in 1777 Walter Campbell of Shawfield redeemed the Lossit wadset, and the 1780 rental shows these lands leased to several new tenants. As noted above, in the entry on Campbell of Ballinaby, Colin purchased the Ballinaby estate in 1778.

Campbell of Octomore

George Campbell, first of Octomore, was a younger son of George Campbell of Airds, son of Sir John Campbell the first Laird of Islay. George was Bailie of Islay. In 1663 Archibald Campbell in Octomore made a contract of wadset with Sir Hugh Campbell of Cawdor for the quarterland of Octomore, the quarterlands of Coultorsay and Lorgba, the quarterland of Greamsay, the lands of lewirheis of Doodilmore and the cowland of Gyline. This Archibald was also Bailie of Islay, and was captured by the Earl of Argyll in May 1685 when he was attempting to raise men for his rebellion.[12]

Archibald's son, George Campbell of Octomore, does not appear to have been infeft in the family's estate. Instead, by a disposition of 1694, they were to be divided among three of Archibald's grandsons, including Donald, the eldest son of George. In 1737, Alexander, a younger son of George, received sasine of the whole estate, the heirs of Archibald, specified in the disposition of 1694, having been bought out.[13]

Campbell of Sunderland

The first Campbell gentleman to settle on Islay after the acquisition of the island by Sir John Campbell of Cawdor is said to have been Colin Campbell (Colin McIphryar), a natural son of Alexander, the Prior of Ardchattan in Lorn. He was given a feu of the land of Cladville in the Rhinns in 1624, and four years later a feu of Sunderland, Foreland, Coull and other lands in the Rhinns, with remainder to his natural brother, Alexander Campbell of Glassans.

Colin was succeeded sometime prior to 1665 by Alexander. Alexander Campbell got sasine of the Sunderland Estate in November 1683. The following year, Archibald Campbell of Sunderland was one of the leading men of the island from whom the Earl of Atholl took a bond, and he married Alice, daughter of Donald Campbell of Craignish.[14]

This family remained in possession of this estate until the late eighteenth century. Robert Campbell of Sunderland died in 1779 leaving a widow, Bland Campbell, who remarried in 1782, and only one child, then under legal age, a daughter called Jean. The estate was sequestrated and the cattle sold off by the factor on behalf of the heiress. The estate was purchased by Walter Campbell of Shawfield in 1788 and disponed to his younger son Walter in 1814.[15]

Campbell of Torrabus

Neill Campbell got a feu of Torrabus and Persabus in 1629, lands previously held by William, a younger brother of Sir John Campbell of Cawdor. Neill's alias is given as McAlister Vic Patrick. His descendants, Alexander and son Neil, resigned Persabus to the Laird of Islay in 1695, but about the same time became wadsetters of the adjacent lands of Ardnahoe, Overnach (Cove) and Bolsa, stretching northwards up the Sound of Islay and round to the north coast of the island. The feu of Torrabus was acquired by the mining entrepreneur, Sir Alexander Murray of Stanhope, after 1727.[16]

Currie

See MacVurich.

Fletcher (MacInleister)

The Fletchers were among the joint tenants of Kepollsmore from the early nineteenth century, all the way through to the twentieth century. This was probably quite remarkable continuity for Islay. Alexander Fletcher was a tenant in Kepollsmore from 1817, and one of the founder members of The Islay Association in 1838.[17] He was one of four tenants of Kepolls-more rouped in 1863 since they were in desperate arrears. His nephew, Hugh Fletcher, was born in 1790 and was a tenant of Kepollsmore by 1833. In 1881, a year before his death, he is recorded as a farmer of 200 acres. His son Edward also took on the tenancy of Robolls from 1885.

This family was probably originally surnamed MacInleister or MacLe-ister ('son of the arrowmaker), only adopting the name Fletcher in the eighteenth century since it had a more acceptable English form. Possible MacInleister ancestors can be traced in Islay rentals of 1541 and 1686. In 1686 there were two Macinleisters in Kildalton parish, another in the Rhinns, and a third in the parish of Kilarrow.

Johnson

This surname, first recorded on Islay in the late seventeenth century, is likely to be a translation of the Gaelic MacIan, but no direct links can actually be traced between Johnsons and MacIans on Islay. One family of Johnsons is well known because of its involvement in whisky distilling. It is descended from Ronald Johnson, tacksman of Corrary, who died in 1790. His son John established the Lagavulin Distillery, and John's sons, John and Donald respectively, distilled at Tallant and Laphroaig. The Laphroaig

Distillery remained in the family until the death of Dugald, Donald's son, in 1877.[18]

MacArthur

A Charles McArthoure was joint tenant of Largybrecht in the parish of Kildalton in 1631, and there was also a Gillycallum McArtherson at Nereby in the parish of Kilarrow. They may have been ancestors of the MacArthurs of Proaig.

There is no sound basis for the tradition that the MacArthurs of Proaig were pipers to the Lords of the Isles, and there is no evidence that such a position existed. Many of the MacArthurs on Islay seem more likely to have been brought in by the Campbells of Cawdor in the seventeenth century.

The MacArthurs were at Proaig by 1654. The rental of that year indicates that Proaig, and the nearby land of Trudernish, were set to Donald Mcarthur, while Jon Mcarthur's widow, Jen, had Clagincarroch (Claggan). The tenant of Proaig in 1686 was Charles McArthour, and his grave-slab is in the old parish church at Kildalton. It is decorated with a Scottish long gun, a powder-horn and a hunting dog, and the inscription informs us that he died on 15 February 1696. There is no evidence for any MacAthurs at Proaig after that. Charles MacArthur's grave-slab gives no clue that he was a member of a distinguished family of pipers, and probably he was not. As for the Angus Dubh MacArthur, said to be piper to Islay in the seventeenth century, there is no trace in contemporary documents.[19]

More important than the MacArthurs of Proaig in terms of status were the MacArthurs of Coultoon in Kildalton parish. Finlay MacArthur was tenant of Lossit and Coultoon in the Rhinns in 1654, and was probably the same Finlay to whom Sir Hugh Campbell of Cawdor wadset the lands of Coultoon and Calumsary in 1672–73. Alexander MacArthur is listed in the Hearth Tax return of 1693. Duncan Campbell of Coultoon married Muriel Campbell in 1684, but in 1702 gave his lands to another Duncan MacArthur as security for a loan.[20] Coultoon was being held as a wadset by a John Campbell in 1722, but MacArthurs remained strongly represented in the Rhinns in the eighteenth and nineteenth centuries.

There are plenty more MacArthurs to be found in Islay from the late seventeenth century onwards, including Gilbert, a drover, transported for taking part in the Earl of Argyll's rebellion in 1685.[21]

MacAvish

MacAvish means the son of Thomas. A family with this surname was prominent on Islay in the sixteenth century. In 1541 Donald McCawis, Ewin McCawis and Gilcallen McCawis were all tenants in the Mid Ward, while Donald McCarle McCawis had Conisby in the Rhinns. Hectour MakCaus in Kinnabus was one of the tenants of Islay that petitioned the

Privy Council about 1600 in support of Angus MacDonald of Dunyvaig. In 1615 he is to be found in the service of Angus Og, going to Glasgow on his business.[22] There is little evidence for the family after the early seventeenth century.

Macbeth (Beaton)

The Macbeths of Ballinaby were a family of hereditary doctors, or physicians, that originated in Ireland. The ancestor of the Scottish branch of the family is said to have come to Scotland with Aine Ni Cathan, when she married Angus Og the early-fourteenth-century chief of Clan Donald.[23]

The family began to adopt the surname Beaton from the late sixteenth century. A Fergus Macbeth was one of the signatories of the charter granted in 1408 by Donald Lord of the Isles to Brian Vicar MacKay.[24] He was probably the head of the family on Islay at that time, the 'Fergus Fionn' identified in a seventeenth-century genealogy as the progenitor of several other branches of the family.

In 1609, King James VI confirmed Fergus Macbeth, the chief physician within the islands of Scotland, in possession of Ballinaby and other lands in the Rhinns, with an extent of £3 6s 8d.

By the seventeenth century there were branches of the family throughout the West Highlands and elsewhere in Scotland, maintaining their medical traditions. The Scottish kings from Robert Bruce in the early fourteenth century through to James VI in the early seventeenth century were served by physicians from this family.

There was another branch on Islay that practised medicine. It was based at Kilennan in the parish of Kildalton, and was represented in 1541 by Neill Og Leich.

In 1629 John Macbeth, who had just succeeded to Ballinaby on the death of Fergus, gave up his lands to Archibald Campbell, Lord of Lorn, and there were no Macbeths at Kilennan by 1631. Beatons are to be found on the island at a later date but there is no evidence that any of them continued to practise medicine. Indeed, when there was a need for a doctor on Islay in 1638 to attend John, the second Campbell Laird of Islay, large sums were paid to bring a doctor all the way from Edinburgh. It appears just to be a coincidence that he was called James Beatoune.[25]

Macbrayne (Brown)

One of the signatories of the 1408 charter was Patrick McAbriuin, who was probably an ancestor of the Macbraynes. The name also appears early on without the 'Mac', as Brihoune in the case of Donald, one of the 'sheriffs in that part' (substitute for a sheriff) instructed by King James IV in 1499 to give sasine of lands in Islay to John MacIan.[26] The Sir Angus Macbreochane who had been chaplain of Keills and Finlaggan prior to his death in or before 1503 must have been a close relative.[27] The 1541 rental shows that

Gilpatrik Bryon then had several contiguous lands to the south of Loch Indaal, including Laggan.

The family, as indicated by their name, provided the hereditary brehons – brieves or judges – of Islay. They had their judgement mound, the Torr a' Bhreitheimh, a natural hillock now largely quarried away, beside the road from Port Ellen to Bowmore. A MacDonald history of the late seventeenth century says that, in the time of the Lordship of the Isles, there was a judge in each island. For undertaking this task they were granted lands and entitled to the eleventh part of every action decided. It was possible to appeal their decisions to the Council of the Isles.[28]

Contemporary evidence for the existence and activities of these judges is difficult to find. One 'Donaldo breyff' was with John II Lord of the Isles and his court on the island of Cara (within a day's sail of Islay) in June 1456, as he was a witness to documents there. He might well be the same man as Donald the judge (*iudex*) who witnessed a document of Alexander Lord of the Isles at Dingwall in November 1447, and the Donald Mcgillemore *iudice Insularum* (Judge of the Isles) with John II Lord of the Isles at Dingwall in November 1457.[29] It is possible that this was another of the Islay Macbraynes.

There was a tradition, recorded at the end of the seventeenth century, that one of the brehons was buried, by his own wish, standing on the brink of the River Laggan with a salmon spear in his hand. This may reflect in some way the requirement for Irish kings – and hence possibly also the Lords of the Isles – to give their judge a salmon out of every abundant catch, and all their salmon heads. The fishings of the River Laggan were identified as a right which belonged with the lands occupied by the family as early as 1614.[30]

A Soirll (Sorley) Mcbraine, and a Ronald McSoirll, possibly both Macbraynes, were among the supporters of Ranald Og MacDonald withholding the castle of Dunyvaig from the Bishop of the Isles in 1614, and four years later the Macbraynes (Clan Breghoun) made a bond of obedience with the Laird of Cawdor, protesting that they had only supported His Majesty's rebels, the Clan Donald, through fear for their lives. The Macbrayne chief is given as Patrick Breghoun in Laggan, and his son as Donald. Others are named as Gillecreist McBreghoun and Gormyk McBreghoun.[31]

Macbraynes – Gillychreist McCanzoucht VcBrethuin and Gillicallum McBrechoun – were still at Laggan in 1631, mere tenants of part of it and Nether Duich. By 1654 they had been replaced or superseded by tacksmen brought in by the Campbells of Cawdor. Macbraynes did not, however, entirely disappear from the island. Donald Og McBrihon was the tenant of Margadale and part of Staoisha in 1686, and a Donald McBrayan was one of the tenants of Kepolls in the same year. The tenant of the malt kiln at Dunyvaig was called Donald Browne.[32] This is the earliest indication that the name was being changed to a form more acceptable to English speakers.

MacCuaig

This name, meaning 'son of Blackie', is particularly associated with Islay. It is first recorded in 1686 when there were MacCuaigs in the lands of Stremnishmore and Cragabus in the Oa.

MacDougall

The minister of Kildalton in the late sixteenth century was Alexander MacDougall, but most MacDougalls on Islay probably descend from settlers that came in the wake of the Campbells of Cawdor, perhaps from their other lands in Argyll. Three MacDougalls are listed on joint tenancy farms in Kildalton parish in the 1654 rental. One Duncan, son of John MacDougall in Tayndrom, was by 1799 tenant of Ardbeg, half of Lagavulin, Airigh nam Beist and Ardinistle. His son, John, established the Ardbeg Distillery in 1815, and the family continued a connection with the distillery down to the twentieth century.[33]

MacDuffie or MacFie

The home of the MacDuffies or MacFies was the neighbouring island of Colonsay, and they also were followers of Clan Donald. This surname is apparently from the Gaelic personal name, *Dub-shíde*.[34] Some MacDuffies are to be found on Islay as substantial tenants in the sixteenth and seventeenth centuries. One Archibald McKofee was set £5 worth of land in Islay by the Crown in 1506, possibly honouring a tenure that dated back to the years before the forfeiture of John II Lord of the Isles in 1493. This was a relatively substantial landholding. In 1541, Doule McIlfee, Bailie of the Midward of Islay, was tenant of Kepollsmore, Kepollsbeg and Baile Tharbach, all near Finlaggan. It is possible that he was a descendant of Archibald Mckoffee and that the family had remained on these lands in the intervening years. The presence of a branch of the MacDuffies here beside Finlaggan may not be unconnected with their traditional role as hereditary keepers of the records of the Lordship of the Isles.[35]

There were other MacFies or MacDuffies who were substantial tenants in 1541. The rental of 1631 indicates that MacFies, including the widow of the last chief, held most of the north coast of the island – Sanaigmore, Ardnave, and all the land from the mouth of Loch Gruinart round to Rhuvaal. They still had Ardnave in 1654. Mac-Duffie and MacFie have remained typical Islay surnames down to the present day.

Maceachern

'Aichane McCauchrane' is listed as tenant of Killeyan, Stremnishbeg, Cragabus and Glenastle (Upper), all in the parish of Kildalton, in 1541. Other MacEacherns, probably the main branch, were settled at Killellan in Kintyre in the Medieval Period. The smiths or armourers of the Lords of the Isles are said to have been MacEacherns who lived in Crosprig, near Kilchoman. The only documented Islay smith, surnamed Maceachern, is John McEachern in Kilarrow, in the late eighteenth century.[36]

Neil and Peter MacEachern, merchants in Islay, held Daill by 1802. It was probably this Neil that established the distillery at Daill from 1814. Donald MacEachern senior and Donald MacEachern junior operated a distillery at Bridgend from 1818.[37]

MacErchar
See MacFarquhar.

MacFarquhar, or MacErchar
Less is known about the MacFarquhars than the two previous kindreds. The name commemorates an (unknown) *Fearchar*, the 'very dear one'. The earliest on record is probably the Donald Ferquharsone, chosen as a 'sheriff in that part' to give sasine of lands in Islay to MacIan of Ardnamurchan.[38] At first sight it does not appear that any lands were rented to them by the Crown Commissioners in 1541. In the rental of that year, however, there is one Tarloch McDonald Glass McClane holding three lands in the Rhinns, including Easter Ellister. In the following year Charles McDonald McFerquhar was let off paying the rent of Easter Ellister. It seems clear that this was the same man. It is possible that the Johnne Dow McIncarroch who rented Lossit and Coultorsay, both in the Rhinns, was another of the MacFarquhars. Certainly Lossit was occupied by the chief of the clan in 1618, Archibald McKearchar, when he gave a bond of obedience to the new Campbell laird on behalf of himself and his 'brethern', Johne McWyle McKearchar, Ewin McKearchar, Farlach McKearchar, Eachin McKearchar, etc.[39] The first of these brethren appears in the 1631 rental as Johnne Mowle McvcKearchar, the tenant of Lossit.

Thereafter the family seems to disappear from the records – unless the Finlay MacArthur who was tenant of Lossit and Coultoon in the Rhinns in 1654 was really a member of the same family. Sir Hugh Campbell of Cawdor wadset the lands of Lossit and Coultoon to Finlay McArthur in 1672,[40] and MacArthurs were still there in 1693. There is an obvious similarity between the names MacFarquhar and MacArthur in terms of sound. Confusion might initially have been caused by the incoming Campbells and their supporters, unfamiliar with the local dialect. Lossit and Coultoon were tenanted by Campbells by 1733 but MacArthurs remained strongly represented in the Rhinns in the eighteenth and nineteenth centuries.

MacgilleCainnech or MacIlschenoch (Shaw)
It is known that the Lords of the Isles had hereditary harpers, the MacIlschenochs, with lands in Kintyre. Excavations at Finlaggan have

led to the recovery of four harp pegs of medieval date leaving little doubt of the importance of harpists as entertainers. Two early Highland harps or clarsachs are preserved in the collections of the National Museums of Scotland. One of them, known as the 'Queen Mary Harp', has decoration linking it to the decoration on medieval West Highland sculpture.

A member of this family may be one of the crown tenants listed in the rental of 1506 – Duncane McGillehaanich – holding land with an extent of £5 0s 4d. On the other hand, it is probably more likely that he was a member of a family more commonly associated with Jura, that later adopted the name Shaw. The name would then be Mac-gille-Cainnech, the son of the servant of (Saint) Kenneth.

Neil Makilanich, probably a descendant of Duncan, was the tenant of Carabus in 1541, a land valued at £1 5s. He may have held some of the land not listed in this rental. Certainly, in 1631, Archibald McGilvinok and Duncan McGillyvanok were listed as the tenants of Eallabus and Kinnabus as well as Carabus. Thereafter there is no trace of the family on Islay, although several Shaws are recorded from the eighteenth century onwards.

MacGillespie

Donald MacGillespie is listed in the 1541 rental as the tenant of 'Ellenynegane' (Finlaggan), Staoisha and Balole, lands with a total extent of £5 16s 8d. His grave-slab is still at the ruined chapel at Finlaggan and demonstrates his status. He is dressed in typical West Highland armour, including a basinet and an actoun, and has a representation of a galley beneath his feet. It was with such galleys that Clan Donald maintained its dominance in the seas around Islay and across the North Channel to Ireland.

Donald MacGillespie's father is given on his grave-slab as Patrick, otherwise unrecorded. The family's links with Finlaggan prior to the 1540s are suggested by the fact that one sir Malcolm MacGillespie was chaplain of Finlaggan from February 1503 until his death sometime before 24 September 1508.[41] His father was Dungal, possibly the same person as Dougald MacGillespie, who witnessed a charter of the Lord of the Isles on Islay in 1479, and was one of the temporary sheriffs appointed in 1499 to give sasine of Islay lands to MacIan of Ardnamurchan.[42]

It is tempting to speculate that the MacGillespies might have been keepers of Finlaggan in the days of the Lordship. It is probable that Donald MacGillespie lived in a small two-storey house rebuilt from the ruins of the residence of the Lords, and surrounded by the barns and houses of a farming township. The Angus McConil Vcgillesbie on record in 1538 as a witness to the granting of sasine of Islay lands was probably a son.[43] There were still MacGillespies at Finlaggan in the 1630s, but then reduced to the rank of joint tenants.

MacGillies
MacGillies means 'the son of the servant of Jesus'. The 1541 rental provides the information that there was a Donald McIlleis in Ballachlaven, Doule McIlleis in Laoigan, and Gilcrist McGilleis in Ardnahoe, Balligh-illan and Balulive. In 1580 Gillechrist Og McCuleis in Ardnahoe was one of those accused of intrometing with the rents of the Bishopric of the Isles and Abbey of Iona. Ardnahoe is adjacent to the lands of Iona Abbey, 'Magenburg and Mangecheles', along the Sound of Islay.[44] A probable descendant, Donald Mcoleis, still held Ardnahoe in 1631.

MacGowan
The history of the Campbells of Craignish says that the MacGowans were hereditary smiths of the Lords of the Isles.[45] It is possible that the Malcolm McGown who appears as the tenant of Tighcargaman in the parish of Kildalton in 1541 is a descendant. Donald MacGuin of Esknish was one of the men of Islay who petitioned the Privy Council in about 1600, in support of Angus MacDonald of Dunyvaig and his son James.[46] Tigh-cargaman and Esknish still had Macgowan tenants in 1631, and there were others elsewhere on the island at Kilbride (Kildalton parish), Tiervaagain and Ballighillan. Gillycreist Gow Smyth, tenant of Carnbeg, might be a practising smith, and possibly of the same kindred. It is likely that many Islay folk of the eighteenth and nineteenth centuries, surnamed Smith, were descendants of the Maceacherns and Macgowans.

MacIlschenoch
See MacgilleCainnech.

Macindeor
A Gillespie Macindeor was the tenant of Ardtalla in 1541. The name means 'son of the dewar' in Gaelic. A dewar was a secular custodian of a saintly relic. Angus Macindeor was one of four tenants in Kinnabus and Eallabus in 1686, and several others with this surname are to be found on the island in the eighteenth and nineteenth century, for example in Kilennan, Blackrock and Balole. Angus Macindeor, a surgeon/doctor, practised at Bridgend in the late nineteenth century, and acquired Balinaby and Coull prior to his death in 1921. It is thought that some Macindeors changed their name to MacArthur.[47]

Macinleister
See Fletcher.

MacKay
The MacKays were one of the most important families on Islay in the Middle Ages. The surname signifies 'Son of Aodh (Hugh)'. The first recorded MacKay on Islay is one Odo (Hugh) MacKay who was parson of

Kilchoman by 1393.[48] It is likely that he was related to the Brian Vicar MacKay to whom Donald Lord of the Isles granted a charter in 1408, and the Hugh Mackay that witnessed it. The latter may well have been the chief of the family.

The MacKays of Islay, who do not appear to be related in any way to the clan of that name in the North of Scotland, are thought to be related to the MacKays of Ugadale in Kintyre, an early ancestor of whom appears to have been the Gilchrist, son of Ivor MacKay, to whom lands in Kintyre were confirmed by Crown charter in 1329.[49] In Islay there were two main branches of the MacKays, the better known of which was based in the Rhinns.

A MacKay of the Rhinns is said in a seventeenth-century source to have fought at the Battle of Inverlochy in 1431 with the forces of the Lordship under Donald Balloch of Dunyvaig, routing a royal army led by the Earl of Mar. MacKay of the Rhinns is listed as one of the members of the Council of the Isles.[50] The post of officer, or coroner, of the Rhinns that the family held at the beginning of the seventeenth century was a hereditary appointment, going back to medieval times, with responsibilities for administering the area on behalf of the Lords of the Isles. It is of significance that the MacKays of Ugadale held a comparable post, that of maer or coroner of North Kintyre.

The shaft of a cross of the fourteenth or fifteenth century, from the burial ground at Nerabus in the Rhinns, commemorates Neil MacKay (Nigelli Odonis), perhaps a priest, and there is a mortuary house identified as belonging to a member of the family, 'a famous prophet', at the chapel on the island of Orsay, off the tip of the Rhinns.

The earliest surviving rental for Islay, that for 1506, lists only eight crown tenants (apart from MacIan of Ardnamurchan) and one of them was Odoni (Hugh) McKy.[51] The lands in the Rhinns held by members of the family can be traced in the rental of 1541. These included Grimsay, occupied with other lands by Neill MacKay, possibly then clan chief. In 1592 Neill McKwoy, officer of the Rinnis, witnessed a bond of manrent by a local family, the MacMays, to Angus MacDonald of Dunyvaig, and in 1618 the MacKay chief appears to have been called Neil, and also in possession of Grimsay.[52] Clearly one or more Neil is involved here – Neil was obviously a favourite family name.

There was still a Neill McKay at Grimsay in 1631, but in 1654 George Campbell of Airds, the tutor for the lunatic laird, took the tenancy of Grimsay for himself. The land was then described as waste.[53] MacKays, presumably descendants of this branch of the family, are to be found in the Rhinns through the seventeenth and eighteenth centuries.

The 1408 grant of lands in the Oa to Brian Vicar MacKay might mark the foundation of another, Kildalton, branch of the family. The vicar element in his name may indeed signify that he held that ecclesiastical rank, though being in holy orders was not necessarily a bar to procreation.

Thus, the Alester McKay who was renting extensive lands in the Oa and Kildalton in 1541, including the island of Texa, is likely to have been a descendant, as also the Donnald McCay who is described as coroner of the Oa and the Largie (i.e. Kildalton) in 1606.[54] He may not have been the first MacKay to hold this post.

The lands in the grant of 1408 were given to Brian and his heirs 'to the end of the world'. It is not known if such grants were exceptional, or if Islay families like the MacKays generally had security of tenure under the Lords of the Isles. Legal title to them would have been lost in 1493 as a result of the forfeiture of John II, Lord of the Isles, or in the following year through the forfeiture of Sir John MacDonald of Dunyvaig. Only one of these properties, Cragabus, was included in the lands rented to Alastair MacKay in 1541. It is clear that after the forfeiture in 1493 they had at best a status as kindly tenants, that is, a right based only on continuous or long occupation of the land. Ballyneal was held by Alastair Mackay as his fee as coroner.

Other MacKays had the lands of Ballynaughton in 1541, and the Donald Gorm MacDonald who held the lands of Ballynaughtonmore, Upper Leorin and Texa in 1631 may have been the chief of this branch of the family at that time. Thereafter, the Kildalton branch of the MacKays disappears from sight in Islay. The explanation may relate to the war in Ireland in the early 1640s when many Ilich went to fight with the native Irish. Among these was Donald Gorm MacDonald (Donald Gorrum McRanichcholl), who, according to a report from Ireland by the laird's brother, George, was one of the men of the Irish force killed in battle in the summer of 1642. Other Ilich that died with him included Johne McRanich Gorume McKy, tenant of Ballyneal (coroner?), Donald McEan VcKy and Donald McGillespick Og VcKy.[55] Others not killed in the fighting may be among the ancestors of the MacGees of Northern Ireland.[56]

MacLinlagan
MacLinlagan is a particularly interesting Islay name, meaning the servant of St Findlugán, the Columban monk from whom Finlaggan takes its name. The earliest the surname is attested is 1541, in the person of Neill McKinlahan, tenant of Corsapol. Three of the four tenants of Stremnishbeg in the Oa in 1631 had Mcelinlagan for a surname, and Stremnishbeg was set to Archibald McLinlagan in 1686. Thereafter the name disappears from the records.

MacMath
See MacMay.

MacMay or MacMath (Mathieson)
The MacMays were a family particularly associated with Islay. 'May' was a diminutive for Mathew. Sometimes the name takes a form like McMatha for 'son of Mathew'. For what it is worth, there are two lands on Islay

which are also named for a Madagan ('little Mathew') – Tiervaagain (Madagan's land), near Ballygrant, and the now-lost Mullinmadagan (Madagan's mill) that was nearby. There is also Druim nam Madagan (Madagan's ridge) with a standing stone at NR 382 459 near Torradale in Kildalton parish.

A Gillonane McMoy appears as the tenant of Corsapol in 1541, and there were others in the Rhinns – Gilnewland McMay in Sunderland and Mealand. The family might well have escaped attention had it not been for the survival of two bonds with Angus MacDonald of Dunyvaig and the Glynns. The first is dated at Kilchoman on 30 June 1575 and records that Angus McMaye, Molmorie McMaye, Gilcollim McMay, his brothers, and Gilcollim McMaye, his son and their heirs and successors will pay calps to Angus for his support. The second is a bond of manrent dated at Mulindry, 19 January 1592. By it Gillicallum McMatha, Gilpatrick McMatha and the remanent of their kin accept Angus as their lord and master above all manner of men in the world, Lachlan MacLean alone excepted.[57] Perhaps they did support Lachlan MacLean against the MacDonalds at the Battle of Traigh Gruineart in 1598 and lost their lands and/or their lives as a result. MacMays are, however, to be found in rentals from the late seventeenth century onwards, the normal form by the early nineteenth century being MacMath. The name was then changed by some holders of it to Mathieson. For example, one Alexander McMath, a tenant of Kynagarry, is noted in the rental of 1833–34 as also being called Mathieson.[58]

MacMillan (Bell)
Archibald MacMillan is recorded as the tenant of Lossit and other lands in Kilmeny parish in 1654. He was probably descended from the MacMillans long settled in Knapdale. The name is derived from the Gaelic for 'son of the bald or tonsured one'. Other MacMillans can be found in later seventeenth- and eighteenth-century rentals. It is believed that many MacMillans later adopted the name Bell. Bells appear in Islay documents from the second half of the eighteenth century onwards.[59]

MacMurachie
Nigel (Neil) McMorquhar was holding the land of Mulindry in 1541 as his fees for being a doctor. He was probably the same as the Neill Oig McMorquhy that witnessed a band by Archibald MacDonald of Dunyvaig and the Glynns to Archibald the Earl of Argyll at Glasgow in 1566. He is there described as a 'leich' and burgess of Stirling. Islay-based relations appear to have included the cleric, Sir Murdoch McMoroquhy, listed as tenant of Arrihalich in the rental of 1541, and 'Johne Oig McMurquhie, leiche in Ilay' who witnessed a band by Ranald, son of Sir James MacDonald of Dunyvaig, in 1615.[60] There was a family of MacMurachies associated with Kilberry in Knapdale, possibly the origin of the Islay MacMurachies.[61]

The name later crops up in the late seventeenth and eighteenth centuries as MacMurchie. The Ewin Mcmurchie and Mun Oig Mcmurchie in Arrihalich in 1631 might well be descendants of Sir Murdoch.

MacNeill

There were several substantial tenants in Islay with this surname from the early seventeenth century onwards. It is possible that they all came to the island from Kintyre after the Campbell takeover. Neill MacNeill held Laggan and Over Duich in 1631. Neil Og MacNeill and Hector MacNeill had Portaneilean by 1654. That Hector, still holding Portaneilean in 1686, may have been the same Hector listed under Kildalton for the Hearth Tax return of 1693, and described as 'of Ardbeg' on a receipt concerning Sir Hugh Campbell's drove of cattle. He was himself a drover in the 1680s.[62]

In the 1830s and 1840s Lossit (Kilmeny) formed part of a large holding including the neighbouring farms of Ardachie, Baleachdrach, Ballyclach, Eacharnach, Airigh re Abhain and Knocklearoch that was rented to Malcolm McNeill, brother of Lord Colonsay. He was one of a small group of Islay gentry regarded by the young John Murdoch. Malcolm McNeill ran the Lossit Distillery and was also the first chairman of the Islay Association when it was founded in 1838.[63] He was succeeded in his farms by Charles McNeill, whose grave-slab in Port Charlotte graveyard indicates he died in 1870.

MacNerlin

A fourteenth- or fifteenth-century commemorative cross from Kilchoman, now in the collections of the National Museums of Scotland, has an inscription informing us that it was set up for the souls of Duncan 'Mecinnirlegin' (MacNerlin) and Mary and Michael. The surname means 'son of the *fer léginn*', that is the head of a monastic school. Another member of this family, described as Donald Dominici Macanerelegwi or Donald Dominicii, was provided to the vicarage of Kilchoman in 1426, a post he held along with the vicarage of Gigha and the prebend of Kilcolmkill in Kintyre. In this case the 'Dominicus' may be representing the Gaelic 'Donnchad' (Duncan). Thus the vicar might be the son of the Duncan commemorated on the cross. The vicar's son Dominic (Duncan?) was appointed parson of Kilchoman in 1462.[64] The name is not in evidence at a later date.

Macnocard (Sinclair)

This surname is derived from the Gaelic for the son of the *ceard*, (smith or metalworker). There was a Gilcrist McNarkerde in Braid in the Rhinns in 1541 and several tenants with this surname occur in later rentals on various Islay lands, including Gearach in the parish of Kilchoman (Donald McNokard in 1733 and 1741).[65] It is believed that at a later date MacNokards in Argyll generally adopted the name Sinclair,[66] and Sinclairs do indeed turn up in Islay rentals of the eighteenth century. Donald Sinclair (1792–74) was a schoolmaster who kept a journal, giving fascinating insights into life on Islay from the 1830s to the 1870s.[67]

MacQueen
See MacSween.

MacSween or MacQueen
Two MacSweens (McSuyna), Lachlan and Maurice, were crown tenants in 1506 of lands with an extent of £5 each and therefore of some local importance. The MacSweens were a family that traced their descent from Suibhne, a twelfth-century Lord of Knapdale. While the branches that rose to prominence in Ireland adopted the form MacSweeney, in Scotland the name became MacQueen. MacQueens are to be found in rentals from the end of the seventeenth century, but it is not clear whether they had any direct connection with the two crown tenants of 1506.

MacTaggart
This surname is from the Gaelic for 'son of the priest', and is likely to have arisen in several locations at different times. A Duncan MacTaggart was accused of the theft of sheepskins from Nauchtane McKeith in Killeyan in 1629, and other MacTaggarts were tenants of farms in the Oa from the early eighteenth century, including Giol and Lower Killeyan.[68]

MacVurich (Currie)
The MacVurichs are famous in Gaelic society as a bardic family, tracing their ancestry in Scotland to an Irish poet of the early thirteenth century, and beyond that to the bardic family of O'Daly, descended from an eighth-century Irish king . They served the Lords of the Isles and the 1507 rental of Kintyre notes they held their land there by virtue of their office.[69]

A Donald McMureich was one of the temporary sheriffs appointed in November 1506 to give MacIan sasine of Islay lands, and a Cristin McVirich and Ewar McVirich witnessed the giving of sasine of Islay and Jura lands in 1538. It is likely that all three were natives of Islay. A seventeenth-century history of the MacDonalds, however, claims that one of the concubines of Angus Mor in the thirteenth century was a daughter of MacMurich of Arpun (Ardfin) in Jura, suggesting the possibility that there was a branch of this family established on that island.[70]

MacVurichs can be traced on Islay in the rental of 1686 and the Hearth Tax return of 1693. At that time there was a concentration of them in the Rhinns, including Lachlane McWurie in Ardnave and Angus McWurie, one of three tenants in Leckgruinart. Another was a tenant in Wivernock (Cove) at the north tip of the island, and there was a John McWurie, one of four tenants in Ballitarsin. A further two, John and Donald McVyrie, were at Dunyvaig. In more recent times the name MacVurich on Islay has been Anglicised as Currie. The rentals of 1733 and 1741 provide the transitional forms, McCurrie and McCurich.

There is no evidence that any of these Islay based MacVurichs were professional poets.

Mathieson
See MacMay.

Montgomery
Hugh Montgomery is listed as a tenant of Nereby, and Alexander and Thomas Montgomery as joint tenants of Coultorsay and Lorgba, in 1654. Montgomery is a Lowland name, prevalent in Ayrshire and Renfrewshire. These Montgomeries in Islay appear to belong to the group of Covenanting army officers introduced by George Campbell the Tutor. Probable descendants include George, the tacksman and distiller at Octomore, who died in 1833.

Shaw
See MacgilleCainnech.

Simson
The first recorded Simson on Islay was David, minister of Kilchoman from 1692 to his death in 1700. He had previously been minister of Southend in Kintyre, succeeding his father, also called David, in that charge. David, senior, had been exiled to New Jersey in 1685 for his dissident Presbyterian beliefs. David, junior, married Isabel, a daughter of Lachlan MacNeill of Lossit, their children including John, merchant in Kilarrow, who was renting Grobolls by 1733. The David Simson active on the Stent Committee from 1750 was, possibly, John's son. He was a merchant, taking on the responsibility for running the packet in 1769. He was also postmaster for Bowmore from 1784, and, most importantly, the founder of Bowmore Distillery. He was renting Ardinistle by 1774, and Gartmain by 1799. Other members of the family thrived in Islay in the late eighteenth century, including Dugald in Cullabus, Hector and William in Coultorsay, and Lilly and her sister, proprietors of the Ship Inn in Bowmore.[71]

Sinclair
See Macnocard.

Islay Lands, Recorded Prior to 1722[1]

Airigh Ghuaidhre, Kilmeny
NR 398 627
The traditional explanation of this name is G *Àiridh Ghutharaidh*, Godred's shieling. Could the Godred in question have been Godred Crovan? Prior to colonisation in the Medieval Period, this may have been a shieling associated with the fort of Dun Ghuaidhre, now on the land of Kilmeny.

1494   33s 4d land granted to John MacIan
1499   with Barr and Storakaig, a 5-merk land granted to John MacIan
1507   a 16s 8d land
1722   16s 8d land
1878   a small portion of pasture land which some time ago was inhabited.

By the eighteenth century Airigh Ghuaidhre included Goirtean an Uruisge (G, the Urisk's croft[2]), first recorded as such in the rental of 1798–99, but possibly the 'Gortane' paired with Eacharnach in 1507. See also *Skeag*.

Airigh nam Beist, Kildalton
NR 416 475
G animal shieling.
1686   first recorded, jointly with Drumchurran
1722   paired with Ardimersay to make a quarterland (with Ardimersay and Solam), a tolerable possession for stock
1878   a house and small portion of ground.
Perhaps originally the shieling for Ardimersay.

Airigh Sgallaidh (Arrihalich), Kilchoman
NR 190 556
The first word means shieling; the second, Sgallaidh, is probably derived from ON *skalli*, meaning bald head or summit, the hill in question being the treeless top of Beinn Cladville.
1507   with Almond, a 33s 4d land
1541   16s 8d land

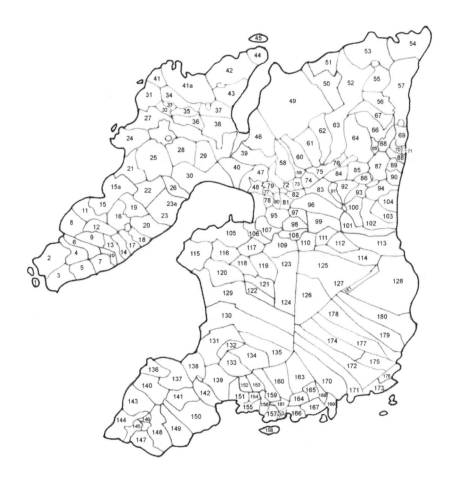

Figure A2.1 Map of Islay farms about 1750,
redrawn from a map by Stephen MacDougall.

Key to farm names on Fig. A2.1:

Airigh Ghuaidhre, 101
Airigh Sgallaidh, 6
Airigh nam Beist, 165
Allallaidh, 127
Almond, 10
Ardachie, 100
Ardbeg, 167
Ardilistry, 171
Ardimersay, 169
Ardinistle, 157
Ardlarach, 105
Ardmenoch, 176
Ardmore, 173
Ardnahoe, 57
Ardnave, 44
Ardtalla, 180
Arivoichallum, 132
Assabus, 146
Avinlussa, 119
Avonvogie, 121
Baile Tharbhach, 62
Baleachdrach, 104
Ballachlaven, 63
Ballighillan, 68
Ballimartin, 75
Ballimony, 4
Ballinaby, 27
Ballinaby, Pendicle of, 33
Ballitarsin, 98
Ballivicar, 139
Ballychatrigan, 149
Ballyclach, 103
Ballygrant, 86
Ballyneal, 155
Balole, 60
Balulive, 66
Balynaughtonbeg, 160
Balynaughtonmore, 161
Barr, 112
Bolsa, 53
Brade, 15a
Breakachey, 42
Carn, 18
Carnbeg, 89
Carrabus, 47
Cattadale, 114
Cladville, 2
Claggan, 179
Conisby, 30
Corary, 116
Corsapol, 46
Coull, 24
Coullabus, 39
Coultorsay, 23a
Cove, 54
Cragabus, 141
Craigfad, 14
Creagfinn, 177
Coultoon, 12
Curilach, 118

Daill, 96
Dluich, 97
Doodilbeg, 51
Doodilmore, 52
Duich, 129
Duisker, 61
Eacharnach, 102
Eallabus, 79
Eilean na Muice Duibhe, 120
Ellister, Easter, 5
Ellister, Wester, 3
Eorrabus, 74
Esknish, 83
Foreland, 29
Gartachara, 26
Gartachossan, 95
Gartloist, 107
Gearach, 19
Giol, 143
Glassans, 20
Glebe, 80
Glenastle, 140
Glenegedale, 130
Gortantaoid, 50
Grasdale, 137
Greamsay, 22
Grobolls, 106
Gruinart, 38
Grulin, 35
Keills, 88
Kelsay, 9
Kepollsmore, 84
Kilarrow, 78
Kilbranan, 99
Kilbride, 159
Kilchiaran, 15
Kilchoman, East, 25
Kilchoman, West, 21
Kildalton, 172
Kilennan, Nether, 123
Kilennan, Upper, 126
Killeyan, 144
Killinallan, 49
Kilmeny, 92
Kilnaughton, 142
Kilnave, 43
Kilslevan, 90
Kindrochid, 34
Kinnabus (Kilarrow), 48
Kinnabus (Oa), 145
Kintour, 175
Kintra, 138
Knocklearoch, 93
Knockrinsey, 170
Kynagarry, 125
Lagavulin, 166
Lagbuie, 77
Laggan, 115
Leckgruinart, 37
Leek (Kilmeny), 59

Leek (Rhinns), 36
Leorin, Lower, 133
Leorin, Upper, 134
Lossit (Kilmeny), 94
Lossit (Rhinns), 8
Lurabus, 150
Lyrabus, 40
Machrie, 131
Margadale, 55
Mulindry, 109
Mulreesh, 65
Nave Island, 45
Nerabus, 13
Nereby, 108
Nosebridge, 110
Octofad, 7
Octomore, 23
Octovullin, 72
Olistadh, 16
Orsay, 1
Persabus, 70
Portaneilean, 64
Port Askaig, 71
Proaig, 128
Robolls, 85
Rosquern, 111
Sanaigbeg, 41
Sanaigmore, 41a
Scanistle, 87
Scarrabus, 58
Sean-ghairt, 76
Skerrols, 82
Smaull, 31
Solam, 163
Sorn, 81
Staoisha, Nether, 67
Staoisha, Upper, 56
Stoine, 174
Storakaig, 113
Stremnishbeg, 147
Stremnishmore, 148
Sunderland, 28
Surnaig, 162
Tallant, 117
Taynanock, 73
Texa, 158
Tiervaagain, 91
Tighandrom, 154
Tighcargaman, 151
Tockmal, 136
Tormisdale, 11
Torra, 124
Torrabus, 69
Torradale, 156
Torony, 17
Trudernish, 178
Unnamed (common moor),
  32, 122, 135, 152, 153, 181

1542   with Foreland, a 33s 4d land granted to Hector MacLean on the basis it had belonged to his grandfather
1563   'Eilistrie [Ellister] vek Archare', included in tack to Sir James MacDonald
1722   wadset to Campbells of Ellister. A very good possession
1878   an elevated portion of land.

By 1686 'Anscallaige' (presumably a misreading for Ariscallaige) was part of the estate held by the Campbells of (Wester) Ellister. Another land, 'Arrihalich', valued at 25s, is listed separately. 'Arichallich' was part of the Ellister estate in 1722. The explanation for all this may be that the land of *Airigh Sgallaidh* was temporarily divided in the late seventeenth century.

Allallaidh, Kilarrow
See *Nosebridge.*

Almond, Kilchoman
NR 222 554
ON the confluence of rivers, referring to the joining of the stream from Gleann Amaind with Abhainn Ardnish.
1507   with Àirigh Sgallaidh, a 33s 4d land
1541   16s 8d land
1722   16s 8d land

Altgaristill, Kilarrow/Kilmeny
NGR Unknown, but possibly in the locality of Sgairail (NR 361 757).
1614   8s 4d land
1686   wadset to Campbells of Killinallan

Ard, Kilchoman
See *Ardmulane.*

Ardachie, Kilmeny
NR 402 635
G *àird* + *achadh*, the high land of the field.
1499   with Baleachdrach and Ballyclach, a 5-merk land granted to John MacIan of Ardnamurchan
1507   33s 4d land
1562   included in tack to Sir James MacDonald
1686   set to Archibald Campbell of Octomore

Ardaright, Kildalton
See *Ardilistry*

Ardilistry, Kildalton
NR 441 490
G *àird* (headland), attached to ON **Hellastaðir,* farm of the flat rock.
1494 (prior to) 'Ardaright', part of the estate of Knockrinsey on Islay,
      belonging to the MacNeills of Gigha
1631 16s 8d land
1722 (with Knockrinsey) a good possession for stock; and has one small
      isle annexed to it
1878 a small farmsteading

Ardimersay, Kildalton
NR 437 475
G *àird* (headland), attached to ON **Himbrimisey,* island of the great
northern diver.
1631 first recorded
1722 paired with Airigh nam Beist to make a quarterland (with Airigh
      nam Beist and Solam) a tolerable possession for stock

Ardinistle, Kildalton
NR 391 450
ON name that has been Gaelicised and had G *àird* (height) added as a
prefix. The original name may have been ON **Askdalr,* ash-tree valley, or
ON **Eskidalr,* valley with the clump of ash-trees.
1494 prior to, part of the estate of Knockrinsey on Islay, belonging to
      the MacNeills of Gigha. See *Knockrinsey*
1722 3 cowlands. (with Barr, Surnaig and Craignagour) being alike
      good both for the increase of sowing and cattle both for milk and
      gendering of cattle, as good as any so much in the country, lying
      upon the shore side
1878 a farm dwelling house and steading

Ardlarach, Kilarrow
NR 293 586
G promontory of the site of a building or ruin. The promontory in
question is Rubha an t-Sàile, which juts into Loch Indaal to the immediate
north of the farmbuildings.
1507 33s 4d land
1562 included in tack to Sir James MacDonald
1722 33s 4d, a tolerable good possession, very good for stock and
      exposed to much improvement in sowing
1878 a farmhouse and offices

Ardmenoch, Kildalton
NR 465 510
G mid height or promontory
1541   16s 8d land
1545   included in Barony of Bar
1722   16s 8d land. A good little possession, enclosed almost by the sea.
        Good for sowing and stock; and a sheltering in the moor (in
        Gleann a' Chromain?)
1878   a shepherd's dwelling house

Ardmore, Kildalton
NR 465 505
G great headland.
1541   16s 8d land
1545   included in Barony of Bar
1722   (with Kildalton) a very good possession for sowing and pasturage
        and increase of cattle, and has both shore and moor and three
        islands belonging to it
1878   a farmsteading with offices attached

Ardmulane, Kilchoman
NGR Unknown
G height of the mill.
1507   'Ard' with Lossit, a 33s 4d land
1563   16s 8d land included in tack to Sir James MacDonald
1614   with Lossit, a 33s 4d land

Ardnahoe, Kilmeny
NR 423 616
G *àird*, height or promontory + ON **haugr*, mound. 'The promontory of
the mound' seems an apt description for the site of the present-day farm
buildings.
1507   with Ballulive, a 33s 4d land
1562   16s 8d land included in tack to Sir James MacDonald
1878   a farmhouse and offices

Ardnave, Kilchoman
NR 283 713
The name is probably a conflation of G *àird*, promontory, with ON **Nef*,
meaning the same.
1507   two church lands valued at 5 merks
1561   £8 13s 4d land of the Bishopric of the Isles, held by the Clan
        Donald
1588   5-merk land (2 quarterlands of Ardnave called the eighth land of
        Mee, the middle tenement commonly known as Ballevannych,

and the island of Ardnave), formerly belonging to Abbey of Iona, granted to Hector, son and heir of Lachlan MacLean of Duart

1617   a 5-merk land, part of Tenandry of Lossit
1722   including Nave Island, a quarterland and 2 cowlands. A noble possession (with Breakachey), an extraordinary fine going for cattle
1878   a farmhouse and offices

See *Breakachey* and *Kilnave.*

Ardtalla, Kildalton
NR 466 545
G *àird* (headland), attached to ON **Háland*, high farm.
1541   two lands of Ardtalla appear in the rental of this year, one with an extent of 33s 4d, the other waste
1545   33s 4d land included in Barony of Bar
1614   two lands valued at 33s 4d each
1722   very good for pasturage and fattening and for grain
1878   a substantial dwelling house with garden and offices attached
Ardtalla is not included in the rental of 1631, and thereafter is listed as one 33s 4d land.

Arigearie, Kildalton
See *Knockrinsey.*

Arivoichallum, Kildalton
See *Ballyneal.*

Arivuine, Kilmeny
NR 412 634 (?)
1507   'Aremungane', a 16s 8d church land
1617   16s 8d land of Iona Abbey, included in Tenandry of Lossit
1686   set with Eacharnach
Langlands' 1801 map shows 'Arivain' near Eacharnach and well to the north of Airigh Ghuaidhre, suggesting that it was the settlement and field system lying to the north-east of Loch Leathann.

Aros, Kildalton
NR 461 519
ON mouth of the river. The river in question is the Kintour River.
1654   first recorded
1722   (with Kintour and Stoine) a spacious quarterland, very good for stock, being in three separate divisions
1878   the ruins of two small houses
Aros was possibly, originally, a quarter of Kintour with an extent of 8s 4d

Arrihalich, Kilchoman
See *Àirigh Sgallaidh*.

Assabus, Kildalton
NR 304 426
ON ridge farm, the ridge in question being Cnoc Seunta
1878   a house and ruin
This is an ON *bólstaðr* farm name, first recorded on MacDougall's map.
Assabus was probably part of Stremnishmore prior to that. There is a Port
Asabuis only 600 m ENE of Stremnishmore.

Avinlussa, Kilarrow
NR 351 581
G *abhainn,* river + ON **Laxá,* Salmon River.
1562   16s 8d land included in tack to Sir James MacDonald
1722   16s 8d land
1878   a farmhouse and offices built of stone and thatch

Avonvogie, Kilarrow
NR 360 563
G river of the muddy or boggy place.
1631   first recorded
1878   a handsome and commodious stone building with garden and
       extensive offices attached

Ayen, Kilmeny
NR 368 653
1631   first recorded
1654   last record in rentals

Baile Tharbhach (Ballyharvey), Kilmeny
NR 362 674
G *baile* + *airbhe,* the farm by the boundary.
1499   with lands of Duisker and Ballimartin, a 5-merk land granted to
       John MacIan
1507   with Sean-ghairt, a 33s 4d land
1562   included in tack to Sir James MacDonald
1722   a good quarterland both for sowing and stock, the moor thereof
       being among the best in the island
1878   a shepherd's house (once a farmhouse)
At Goirtean Bholsa at the mouth of Gleann Airigh an t-Sluic is a patch of
previously farmed land enclosed in an earth dyke. Goirtean is Gaelic for a
small enclosure. There are clearance cairns, a limekiln, and a long house
converted into a sheepfold at NR 354 689. This represents colonisation of
shieling ground in the eighteenth or early nineteenth century, and indeed

there is a shieling hut on top of a small knoll near the house. Bholsa may commemorate the presence here of a Scandinavian settlement with an ON *bólstaðr* farm name. Its name may be preserved in Dun Chollapus a kilometre to the south, a conical hill 164 m high crowned with the remains of a dun of Iron Age or Early Historic date, overlooking Goirtean Bholsa. The name Chollapus seems to be derived from ON *Kollabólstaðr*, meaning Kolli's steading.

Baleachdrach, Kilmeny
NR 422 652
G *baile* + *iochdarach*, meaning netherton. The name points to the separation of this farm from a larger holding. That holding may have been the five-merk land that included Baleachdrach with the neighbouring lands of Ballyclach and Eacharnach, granted to John MacIan in 1494. Baleachdrach is lower than the other two and may represent an expansion of farming and occupation down the valley of the small stream, now called the Abhainn a' Bhail' Iochdaraich, towards the Sound of Islay. In a second charter of 1499 to MacIan, Baleachdrach appears again, this time grouped with Ballyclach and Ardachie as a 5-merk land.
1545   16s 8d land included in the Barony of Bar
1722   wadset to Campbells of Lossit
1878   the ruin of a dwelling

Ballachlaven, Kilmeny
NR 422 652
G Clement's township.
1507   33s 4d land belonging to the Chapel of St Findlugán
1614   included in charter to Sir John Campbell of Cawdor
1722   wadset to Campbells of Ballachlaven
1878   a farmhouse and offices

Ballenish, Kilarrow
NR 32 73
Now lost land, but its general location is indicated by the place-name Tràigh Baile Aonghais, to the east of the mouth of Loch Gruinart. G Angus's township.
1499   with Carrisay, Killinallan and Lag a 5-merk land granted to John MacIan
1507   with Lag, a 33s 4d land
1562   included in tack to Sir James MacDonald
1722   33s 4d land let (along with Gortantaoid) to Killinallan, which is undoubtedly the best possession in the country

Ballephersoun, Kildalton
NGR Unknown, but probably near Kilnaughton.

G the parson's township.
1614   with Kilnaughton and Ballivicar, a 25s land
It also appears in the rentals of 1631 and 1654.

Ballevannych, Kilchoman
See *Ardnave*.

Ballighillan, Kilmeny
NR 408 696
G Gillan's township.
1507   16s 8d land
1562   included in tack to Sir James MacDonald
1878   hamlet of three thatched cottages with ruins

Ballimartin, Kilmeny
NR 370 661
G Martin's townland, first appears in the rentals in 1631 when it seems to
take the place of a now-lost Stanepoll, from ON *Steinabólstaðr*, stony
farm. As 'Stanelous', it is grouped with the adjacent lands of Duisker and
Baile Tharbhach as a 5-merk land, granted in 1499 to John MacIan.
1507   25s land
1562   included in tack to Sir James MacDonald
1722   a good possession, although a small holding
1878   a substantial farmhouse and steading

Ballimony, Kilchoman
NR 195 550
In this form the name appears to be G boggy townland. Versions of the
name prior to the mid eighteenth century, including Ballydale (1507) and
Ballygallie (1562), suggest an earlier form combining G *baile* with ON
dalr, valley.
1507   33s 4d land
1562   included in tack to Sir James MacDonald
1722   wadset to Campbells of Ellister
1878   a farmhouse with offices attached

Ballinaby, Kilchoman
NR 221 670
The name is best interpreted as a combination of Gaelic and Old Norse, *Baile
na Býr*, 'the farm of the farm'. The widely held explanation that it is the
townland of the abbot does not square with the etymological evidence, and
there is no historical evidence that the land ever belonged to an abbot or abbey.
1507   £3 6s 8d land
1541   36s 8d land set to Ferguis Oldowe
1562   33s 4d land included in tack to Sir James MacDonald

1609   £3 6s 8d land confirmed to Fergus Macbeth, the chief physician within the islands of Scotland[3]

1629   superiority of Ballinaby purchased by Lord Lorne[4]

1722   £2 3s 4d land

1878   a neat mansion, the residence of William Campbell Esq.

Ballitarsin, Kilarrow

NR 355 611

G *baile* + *tarsuinn*, the township on the slope.

1506   33s 4d land granted to John MacIan in recognition that his father had held it from Alexander Earl of Ross

1545   included in the Barony of Bar

1562   included in tack to Sir James MacDonald

1878   a small district comprising of three small houses

Ballivicar, Kildalton

NR 343 468

G townland of the vicar.

1408   granted to Brian Vicar MacKay

1722   25s land. A very good pennyworth of land, alike for sowing and pasturage as any in the parish, and a good soil for sheep

1878   a substantial farm steading

Ballore, Kildalton

See *Creagfinn*.

Balloshin, Kilmeny

NGR Unknown, but perhaps in the region of Tobar a' Chinn (NR 393 651).

1494   'Kinbeloquhane' (?), a 16s 8d land granted to John MacIan

1507   with Knocklearoch, a 33s 4d church land belonging to the chapel of St Columba (Keills)

1542   granted to Hector MacLean on the basis it had belonged to his grandfather

1686   with Knocklearoch, a 25s land

Ballychatrigan, Kildalton

NR 323 419

G *baile*, township + ON **Kattahrygginn*, the ridge of the cats. The ridge in question would be Cnoc a'Mhacain, some 100 m north of the Ballychatrigan farm buildings.

1541   33s 4d land

1562   included in tack to Sir James MacDonald

1722   amongst the foremost quarterlands in the whole island, if not the very best

1878   a few houses and ruins

Ballyclach, Kilmeny
NR 416 642
G *baile* + *clach*, stone farm. Some earlier forms of the name are clearly for
Baile chlachach, stony farm.
1494   with Baleachdrach and Eacharnach, a 5-merk land granted to John
       MacIan
1499   with Baleachdrach and Ardachie, a 5-merk land granted to John
       MacIan
1545   16s 8d land included in Barony of Bar
1722   wadset to Campbells of Lossit

Ballydale, Kilchoman
See *Ballimony*.

Ballygallie, Kilchoman
See *Ballimony*.

Ballygrant, Kilmeny
NR 395 662
G **Baile Ghrànna*, townland of the corn, or store town.
1507   16s 8d land
1562   included in tack to Sir James MacDonald
1654   meal mill first recorded
1722   a good compact auchtanepart, alike good for sowing and stock,
       and has now erected a change-house in it
1878   a small village situated on the road leading from Bridgend to Port
       Askaig.

Ballyneal, Kildalton
NR 370 450
G, Neil's townland.
1541   33s 4d land
1545   included in Barony of Bar
1722   a very good quarterland, having a good park and a small island in
       the sea, and a good shieling in the moor called 'Arwaolchallim'
       annexed to it
This shieling, Arivoichallum (G, Malcolm's shieling), is at NR 349 499. In
the rental of 1733, its extent is given as 1 cowland. It remained paired with
Ballyneal as late as 1780.

Balole, Kilmeny
NR 355 661
G **Baile Ola*, Ola's township. This personal name derives from ON *Óláfr*.
About 700 m north-west of the farm steading is a hill, named Cnoc
Goirtein Bhólsach, the hill of the little enclosure of 'Bólsach', and an

enclosure identified as Gortean Bólsach, the little enclosure itself. The final unit common to both these names appears to contain the ON farm name, *bólstaðr*, perhaps with the G locative suffix *–ach*.

1507   33s 4d land
1722   a very good possession for sowing and stock and hay
1878   a substantial farmhouse with offices attached

Balulive, Kilmeny
NR 405 699
G **Baile Uilbh*, Uilbh's township. This personal name is derived from ON *Úlfr*. Two standing stones on the farm (one now fallen over) are known as Ulvr's Stone and Olaf's Stone.

1507   paired with Ardnahoe
1562   16s 8d land included in tack to Sir James MacDonald
1686   with Killelegan, a 33s 4d land
1722   33s 4d land
1878   a substantial stone and slate farmhouse and offices

Balynaughton, Kildalton
Balynaughtonbeg, NR 394 468; and Balynaughtonmore, NR 393 465.
G Nechtan's townland, with the prefixes *-beag* (lesser, or less important) and *-mór* (greater or more important).

1408   'Baile Neaghtoin' was included in the grant to Brian Vicar MacKay, but Lamont argues that this was Kilnaughton.[5]
1541   two lands of 'Ballenachtane', each with an extent of 33s 4d
1545   5-merk land included in Barony of Bar
1722   Balynaughtonbeg and Balynaughtonmore, each valued at 16s 8d
1878   Balynaughtonbeg, a ruin of old dwelling; and Balynaughtonmore, a farm dwelling-house with steading attached

Barr, Kilarrow
NR 391 608
ON *mörk*, boundary or border. The valley of the Barr River, in which Barr is situated, forms a stretch of the eastern border of the parishes of Kilarrow and Kilmeny. It is overlooked by Beinn Bharradail, and nearby is Loch Bharradail at the boundary of seven farm districts. Perhaps underlying these Gaelic names is ON **Markadalr*, the valley of the boundaries or borders, an appropriate name for the valley of the Barr river.

1499   with Airigh Ghuaidhre and Storakaig, a 5-merk land granted to John MacIan
1507   36s 4d land
1562   33s 4d land included in tack to Sir James MacDonald
1878   a farmhouse with offices attached

Barr, Kildalton
NR 401 453 (Barr an t-Seann Duine)
1686   set with Drumhunst and Creagnagouer
1722   set with Surnaig, Drumhunst and Creagnagouer
See also *Ardinistle*.

Bolsa, Kilmeny
NR 386 775
ON *bólstaðr*, farm. The earliest version of the name in the rental of 1507 is
Spulse, suggesting the possibility that the name was originally more
complex.
1507   with part of Scanistle, a 33s 4d land
1542   granted to Hector MacLean on the basis it had belonged to his
       grandfather
1878   the ruin of an old dwelling

Brade, Kilchoman
NGR Unknown
G brae.
1507   'Brakilkerane', with Crosprig and Saligo a 38s 4d land
1541   25s land
1562   'the braid of Kilkerran', included in tack to Sir James MacDonald
1722   a very good tenement

Brae, Kildalton
NGR Unknown
1541   with Tighandrom, a 16s 8d land
1614   with Tighandrom, a 16s 8d land
1878   a dwelling house and steading, stone and thatched
Perhaps this was Brahunisary (NR 376 464), G *bràighe*, upper part, added
to ON **Hundsœrgi*, shieling of the dog. It is on MacDougall's map, but
not named.

Brahunisary, Kildalton
See *Brae*.

Branapols, Kildalton
NR 338 473 (Cnocan Bhrannabuis)
ON burnt farm.
1541   10s land
1686   last recorded

Breakachey, Kilchoman
NR 275 725
G speckled field.

1507   33s 4d church land
1561   presumably included in the £8 13s 4d land of the Bishopric of the Isles held by the Clan Donald
1722   including Nave Island, a quarterland and 2 cowlands. A noble possession (with Ardnave), an extraordinary fine-going for cattle. There is also a mill of Breakachey

MacDougall's map apparently shows Breakachey on the site of the present Ardnave House, with the settlement of Ardnave further to the north.

Brewseat, Kildalton
See *Lagavulin*.

Callumkill, Kildalton
NR 408 465
G (St) Columba's Church. Early forms of the name include Kilcallumkill.
1541   16s 8d land held by Captain of Dunyvaig
1558   included in Barony of Bar when it was regranted in this year
1562   included in tack to Sir James MacDonald
1722   listed as 35s, but described as 3 leorthas
1878   a good two-storey farmhouse with extensive outbuildings
See *Dunyvaig*.

Calumsary, Kilchoman
NGR Unknown
ON Callum's shieling.
1507   with Coultoon, a 33s 4d land
1541   16s 8d land
1563   included in tack to Sir James MacDonald
1722   wadset to Campbells of Ballinaby

Carn, Kilchoman
NR 245 572
G cairn, referring to the prehistoric burial monument on Cnoc a' Chuirn.
1507   with Gartachara, a 33s 4d land
1541   16s 8d land
1563   included in tack to Sir James MacDonald
1722   'Carneglassans', a compact little tenement
1878   a small group of houses

Carnbeg, Kilmeny
NR 416 678
G little cairn.
1507   'Ochtokerne', a 16s 8d church land
1617   'Carnbeg', a possession of Iona Abbey, included in Tenandry of Lossit

1722   a very small compact good possession for stock and sowing
1878   the ruins of dwellings with a sheepfold attached

Carrabus, Kilarrow
NR 314 639 (for Mid Carrabus)
ON *Garðabólstaðr*, Gari's farm, or the farm of the enclosures.
1499   with Octovullin, a 5-merk land granted to John MacIan
1507   25s land; and also a 6s 8d church land
1722   25s land
1878   divided into three: West Carrabus (NR 308 637), Mid Carrabus
       and East Carrabus (NR 321 640). Mid and West are both
       described as a small farmhouse with offices attached
See also *Grobolls*.

Carrisay, Kilarrow
NGR Unknown
1499   with Ballenish, Killinallan and Lag, a 5-merk land granted to John
       MacIan
1507   with Killinallan, a 33s 4d land
1542   granted to Hector MacLean on the basis it had belonged to his
       grandfather
1631   last mentioned. Perhaps subsumed in Killinallan

Cattadale, Kilarrow
NR 386 601
ON *Kattadalr*, the valley of the cats.
1545   16s 8d land included in Barony of Bar
1722   16s 8d land
1878   a substantial farmhouse with offices attached, partly slated and in
       good repair

Cill Bhraenan, Kilarrow
See *Kilbranan*.

Cladville, Kilchoman
NR 178 541
ON bright hill. The hill in question is Ben Cladville.
1507   'Cladepele', a 33s 4d land
1507   'Ochtocladsell', with Octofad, a 33s 4d land
1541   50s land
1562   40s land included in tack to Sir James MacDonald
1614   50s land
1878   a substantial farmhouse with offices and garden attached

Claggain, Kildalton
NR 460 533
G field of the best land.
1541   'Clagenoch', a 16s 8d land
1545   included in Barony of Bar
1562   included in tack to Sir James MacDonald
1722   'Clagincarroch', a 16s 8d land. A very good toun for pasturage and
       fattening, and gendering of cattle
1878   an old farmhouse now in ruins

Clagnish, Kilchoman
NGR Unknown
1507   'Clagenach', with Over Kilchiarian a 33s 4d land
1541   16s 8d land
1722   part of estate of Kilchoman, and perhaps later subsumed in it

Cnoc Rhaonastil, Kildalton
See *Knockrinsey*.

Conisby, Kilchoman
NR 262 618
ON king's farm. The king in question is said, traditionally, to have been
Godred Crovan. The beach at Tràigh an Luig (G, the strand of the hollow)
falls within the bounds of Conisby as shown on MacDougall's map.
According to Pennant, this was where the 'great MacDonald' had his
harbour. While no traces of this structure remain, Pennant surmises that it
once had 'piers with doors to secure . . . shipping; a great iron hook, one of
the hinges, having lately been found there'.[6]
1507   33s 4d land
1541   33s 4d land
1562   included in tack to Sir James MacDonald
1722   a large good quarterland, very good for stock and also for sowing
1878   a small hamlet consisting chiefly of small crofters

Cornabus, Kildalton
NR 334 464
ON corn farm.
1408   included in grant to Brian Vicar MacKay
1541   10s land
1722   (with Kilnaughton) a compact pretty little possession for holding
1878   a substantial farmhouse and steading
See also *Cornaschil*.

Cornaschil, Kildalton
NGR Unknown
1654　listed with Kilnaughton and Cornabus; possibly a shieling for the latter, the name being a new coinage by the tenant (since at least 1631), John Hunter, including the Scots *shiel,* shieling
1686　'Cornaschalvag'

Corra-ghoirtein, Kilarrow
NR 314 696
1617　'Carro', an 8s land belonging to Iona Abbey, included in Tenandry of Lossit
1751　with Bun-an-uilt, divided off from Corsapol
1878　the ruins of an old farmhouse and outhouse

Corrary, Kilarrow
NR 312 571
Perhaps ON **Káraerg, Kári's* shieling, rather than G **Corr àirigh,* the shieling on the round hill.
1494　with Cùrlach, a 33s 4d land granted to John MacIan
1507　with Island, a 33s 4d land
1562　16s 8d land included in tack to Sir James MacDonald
1878　a substantial stone building with garden and offices

Corsapol, Kilarrow/Kilchoman
NR 299 665
ON *kross + ból,* farm at the crossroads. The routes in question are one from the north coast down the east side of Loch Gruinart to Loch Indaal, and another linking Kilarrow with the north of the Rhinns.
1499　with 'Keirbous' (Lyrabus?) a 5-merk land granted to John MacIan
1541　33s 4d land
1686　wadset to John Campbell of Ballinaby
1751　Bun-an-uilt and Corra-ghoirtean recorded as separate farms in the northern portion of Corsapol
1878　a farmhouse and offices. By that time another farm, Craigens (NR 297 671), had been carved out of Corsapol. It was then described as a farmhouse and extensive offices. It may have replaced an earlier holding called Gartnagaul
See also *Gruinart* (1878).

Corse, Kilarrow
See *Gartloist.*

Coull, Kilchoman
NR 200 646
ON knob-like hill.

1507   33s 4d land; and Coull and Lorgbaw, with an extent of 33s 4d
1541   33s 4d land
1542   granted to Hector MacLean on the basis it had belonged to his
        grandfather
1628   becomes part of the estate of the Campbells of Sunderland
1878   a large farmhouse with offices and garden attached

Coullabus, Kilarrow/Kilchoman
NR 298 658
ON **Kúlaból'staðr*, hilly farm.
1507   with Lyrabus, a 33s 4d land
1722   16s 8d land, a good possession for stock and sowing
1878   a farmhouse and offices

Coultoon, Kilchoman
NR 200 572
ON the farm by the hill. The generic, 'toon', may be a later Scots
addition.
1507   with Calumsary, a 33s 4d land
1562   16s 8d land included in tack to Sir James MacDonald
1722   33s 4d land, a good wadset (belonging to Campbells of Ballinaby)
1878   a dwelling house and offices

Coultorsay, Kilchoman
NR 258 604
The name probably reflects two separate holdings, Cul and Torsa, which
have been conflated – ON *Kúla*, knob-like hill, and ON **þól'staðir*, þórir's
steading.
1541   16s 8d land
1562   included in tack to Sir James MacDonald
1722   wadset to Campbells of Octomore
1878   a handsome stone building, formerly a farmhouse, but now
        occupied by the servants of the farm

Cove (Overnag), Kilmeny
NR 40 78
Cove first appears in the mid eighteenth century as a farm name, clearly
representing the renaming of a property called Overnag, first recorded in
1541. The location of this holding at the northern extremity of the island
points to derivation from ON **Yfirvík*, the upper bay. The sandy bay of
Bàgh an Dà Dhoruis (G the bay of the two doors), the largest and most
accessible landing point in this holding, is also the most northerly in Islay.
Given that this name contains the ON loanword *vágr*, and therefore post-
dates the Viking Age, it is likely to be the G replacement for **Yfirvík*.
    The renaming as Cove (Scots, cave) draws attention to the best-known

feature on this land – Uamh Mhor (G the great cave), often now known as the cave of Bolsa. There is a small enclosure[7] at NR 402 789 defined by a bank of earth and stone on a rock stack west of Bàgh an Dà Dhoruis, which may represent the main settlement of Overnag prior to the late seventeenth century, by which time it may have shifted to Uamh Mhor. Martin Martin records a visit to it at that time, calling it 'Vah Vearnag' (Uamh Fhearnaig), the largest cave that he had ever seen, one that could contain 200 men. He describes seeing a corn-drying kiln on its east side and on the west a wall built close to the side of the cave which was used as a bedroom. Apart from a bed there was a fireplace and some chairs; also a stone outside the entrance 'about which the common people make a tour sunways'. In Pennant's time (1770s) it was occupied all year round by three families, and fourteen or fifteen families used it in the summer months as their shielings. It now contains a sheepfold that was in use in the 1860s for rounding up, clipping and smearing sheep.[8]

1541   'Overnag', with Bolsa a 25s land
1542   'Owo', 8s 4d land granted to Hector MacLean on the basis it had
       belonged to his grandfather
1722   'Uaberneik', wadset to Campbells of Killinallan

Coyne, Kilarrow
NGR Unknown
1562   'Gone', 8s 4d land included in tack to Sir James MacDonald
1631   'Goyan'
1654   'Coyne'

Cragabus, Kildalton
NR 326 451 (Middle Cragabus)
ON crow farm, or possibly, Kraki's farm.
1408   granted to Brian Vicar MacKay
1541   two lands, each with an extent of 16s 8d, one of them belonging to
       the chapel on Texa.
1562   16s 8d land included in tack to Sir James MacDonald
1631   listed as Over and Nether Cragabus
1722   33s 4d land, a very good pennyworth of land, very good for sowing
1878   Lower Cragabus (NR 330 452), three farmhouses and steadings
       attached; Middle Cragabus, houses; and Upper Cragabus (NR 322
       445), a farmhouse and steading

Craigens, Kilarrow
See *Corsapol.*

Craigfad, Kilchoman
NR 229 558
G long rock or cliff.
1694   first mentioned
1722   16s 8d land, a good tenement
1878   a farmhouse with offices attached

Creagfinn, Kildalton
NR 453 522
G white rock. This name would apply more appropriately to the ruined settlement, identified in 1878 as Ballore, on a low hill at NR 455 521. Its houses may be sixteenth- or seventeenth-century in date. The ruined settlement identified as Creagfinn may be its successor.
1541   8s 4d land
1545   included in Barony of Bar
1722   16s 8d land
1878   a shepherd's dwelling house and ruins of several buildings

Creagnagouer, Kildalton
NGR Unknown
1631   first recorded
1722   (with Barr, Surnaig and Ardinistle) being alike good, both for the increase of sowing and cattle, both for milk and gendering of cattle, as good as any so much in the country, lying upon the shore side

Croash, Kilchoman
1654   'Crwech'
1722   part of estate of Kilchoman

Crois Mhòr, Kilarrow
NR 296 702
G great cross.
1631   set with lands of Killinallan, Corsapol and Altgaristill
1686   wadset to Campbells of Killinallan
1878   a small promontory

Crosprig, Kilchoman
NR 211 623
The name is Gaelic, but includes a metathesised form of ON *borg*, fort – hence, Fort of the cross(es).
1507   with Brade and Saligo, a 38s 4d land
1541   6s 8d land
1562   included in tack to Sir James MacDonald
1878   a piece of pasture land and ruins

Cruach, Kilarrow
NR 324 584
G stack-like hill.
1654 first recorded
1722 2 cowlands, included with Ardlarach
1878 a small district comprising of a few scattered houses, arable and
moorland

Cùrlach, Kildalton
NR 328 567
1494 with Cùrlach, a 33s 4d land granted to John MacIan
1562 8s 4d land included in tack to Sir James MacDonald
1878 some ruins and a stretch of pasture land

Daill, Kilarrow
NR 363 657
ON *dalr*, valley, rather than G *An Dàil*, focal-point, place/chief centre.
1507 with Kilbranan and Octinfrich, a 5-merk land
1541 'Dalbeg' and 'Dalmoir' with 'Gorthe', a 50s land
1542 'Dall', a quarterland granted to Hector MacLean on the basis it
had belonged to his grandfather
1722 wadset to Campbells of Daill. The most of it (with other lands)
lying exposed for good improvement
1878 a substantial farmhouse with garden attached. The offices are
situated a little to the north of the dwelling house

Dluich, Kilarrow
c.NR 35 62. There is an Allt Dluich forming a tributary of the Daill River.
G *dlùbh* + *faiche*, the close or near field.
1494 with Octinfrich, a quarterland granted to John MacIan
1541 8s 4d land
1722 with Gortanilvorrie, a 25s land, a very good possession for holding
and sowing

Doodil, Kilmeny
Doodilbeg, NR 345 748; and Doodilmore, NR 367 741.
These two farms are, respectively, the small and large Doodil. The
etymology of Doodil is ON *dúfa* + *dalr*, pigeon or dove valley.
1507 Doodil, with 'Tyd', a 25s land
1541 Doodilmore, an 8s 4d land
1562 Doodilbeg and Doodilmore, both 8s 4d lands, included in tack to
Sir James MacDonald
1722 Doodilmore, wadset to Campbells of Octomore
1878 Doodilbeg, a ruin; and Doodilmore, the ruins of a hamlet

Downan, Kilchoman
NGR Unknown
1563   16s 8d land included in tack to Sir James MacDonald
1654   set with Kilchoman and other lands to the Tutor of Cawdor
1722   part of estate of Kilchoman

Drumalla, Kilarrow
NR 353 636 (Druim Aladh)
1507   with Octovullin, a 33s 4d land
1541   'Drumhalden', a 16s 8d land
1562   included in tack to Sir James MacDonald
1722   with Octovullin, a 50s land

Drumchurran, Kildalton
NR 419 473 (Druim a' Churrain)
1541   8s 4d land set to Captain of Dunyvaig
1654   set with other lands, including Surnaig, to the Tutor of Cawdor
See also *Drumhunst*.

Drumhunst, Kildalton
NGR Unknown
1631   first record
1686   set with Barr and Creagnagouer
1722   set with Surnaig, Barr and Creagnagouer
See also *Ardinistle*. Drumhunst might be the same place as Drumchurran.

Duich, Kilarrow/Kildalton
NR 319 545
G *dubh* + *faiche*, black meadow.
1507   with Kilcallumkill, a 33s 4d land
1541   33s 4d land
1542   with 'Garbols' (Grobolls, rather than Carrabus?), a 33s 4d land
        granted to Hector MacLean on the basis it had belonged to his
        grandfather
1562   33s 4d land included in tack to Sir James MacDonald
1722   a good quarterland, very good for stock, with a 'conning warrant'
        [rabbit warren] belonging to it

Duisker, Kilmeny
NR 361 669
ON *dúfa* + *sker*, dove rock.
1499   with Baile Tharbhach and 'Stanelous' (Ballimartin) a 5-merk land
        granted to John MacIan of Ardnamurchan
1507   33s 4d land
1562   included in tack to Sir James MacDonald

1722 16s 8d land, a good possession
1878 a farmhouse substantially built without offices

Dunyvaig, Kildalton
NR 405 454
G *dùn*, fort, attached to ON **Útvík*, outer bay.
1541 33s 4d land in hands of Captain of Dunyvaig
1545 5-merk land included in Barony of Bar
1722 41s 8d land including a mill, the court house of Lagavulin, and
    houses belonging to Duncan Carmichael, —— Reid and Dugald
    Campbell. A good possession
Dunyvaig at its fullest extent probably included the lands of Lagavulin,
Solam, Ardbeg and Callumkill.

Eacharnach, Kilmeny
NR 410 642
G place of the horses.
1494 with Baleachdrach and Ballyclach, a 5-merk land granted to John
    MacIan
1507 with 'Gortan' (Goirtean an Uruisge?) a 25s land
1617 16s 8d land of Iona Abbey included in Tenandry of Lossit
1686 set with Arivuine
1878 a dwelling house

Eallabus, Kilarrow
NR 336 632
ON *áll*, eel + *bólstaðr*, farm.
1507 16s 8d church land
1588 16s 8d land, formerly belonging to Abbey of Iona, granted to
    Hector, son and heir of Lachlan MacLean of Duart
1617 16s 8d land of Iona Abbey included in Tenandry of Lossit
1722 with Kinnabus, a 33s 4d land, a good quarterland, alike good for
    stock and sowing
1878 the estate factor's dwelling, with farm offices, corn mill, etc
The corn mill was previously known as Glengeoy. At the time of his death
in 1747, Coll MacAlester, Bailie of Islay, held Glengeoy, and also the Mill
of Eallabus.[9] The latter was later renamed the Mill of Glengeoy, with the
land of Glengeoy presumably being subsumed within Eallabus.

Eilean na Muice Duibhe, Kilarrow
NR 307 567
G island of the black pig.
1494 included in grant to John MacIan
1507 with Corrary, a 33s 4d land
1562 16s 8d land included in tack to Sir James MacDonald

1878   Island House, a handsome dwelling house built in an ancient style of masonry; has garden and offices attached

Now known as Island (House).

Ellay, Kilmeny
NGR Unknown
1617   6s land of Iona Abbey included in Tenandry of Lossit
1654   last recorded

Possibly a shieling land. In the 1631 rental it is listed after Keills, and in 1654 is paired with it

Ellister, Kilchoman
Easter Ellister, NR 202 535; and Wester Ellister, NR 188 522
ON *hella* + *staðir*, flat rock farm.
1541   two lands ('Ilistik Arrarauch' and 'Alester Etrach'), each with an extent of 33s 4d
1562   the two lands of 'Aclisty', each with an extent of 33s 4d, and 'Oclisty', with an extent of 16s 8d, included in tack to Sir James MacDonald
1563   'Eilistrie Erirath', a 33s 4d land; and 'Eilistrie vek Archare', a 33s 4d land, included in tack to Sir James MacDonald
1614   'Ilystick Arrarauch' and 'Alester Etrach', each with an extent of 33s 4d
1722   Ellister Easter, a good quarterland; Ellister Wester, along with Ballimony and Àirigh Sgallaidh, wadset to Campbells of Ellister, a very good wadset, and has a good isle [Orsay] annexed unto it
1878   Easter Ellister, a farmhouse with offices and garden attached; and Wester Ellister, a substantial stone building with garden and offices attached

Eorrabus, Kilarrow
NR 359 646
ON *Efribólstaðr*, upper farm.
1499   with Esknish, a 5-merk land granted to John MacIan
1507   with Esknish, a 5-merk land
1541   33s 4d land
1722   50s land
1878   a district

Erasaid, Kilchoman
NR 294 652
ON *Ari* + *setr*, Ari's steading.
1541   6s 8d land set to Ferguis Oldowe
1563   included in tack to Sir James MacDonald

1629   included in the estate of Ballinaby, the superiority of which was
        purchased by Lord Lorne[10]
1878   a dwelling house with barns attached

Erphill, Kilchoman
NGR Unknown. The name is now lost, but it may, like Nerabus, contain
ON *Eyrar*. A place labelled 'Erueil' appears on Blaeu's map adjacent to (to
the north of) Nerabus.
ON *Eyrar* + *fell*, the hill by the gravel bank.
1541   16s 8d land
1562   included in tack to Sir James MacDonald
1686   set to Duncan Campbell of (Wester) Ellister

Esknish, Kilmeny
NR 367 647
ON *Áskellsstaðir*, Askill's farm.
1499   with Eorrabus, a 33s 4d land granted to John MacIan
1562   a 33s 4d land included in tack to Sir James MacDonald
1722   a 33s 4d land
1878   a district comprising of several farmhouses and offices
See also *Mullinmadagan*.

Finlaggan, Kilmeny
See *Portaneilean*.

Foreland, Kilchoman
NR 269 643
ON farm producing fodder or hay.
1507   with 'Camkilane' [Keanchyllan] a 33s 4d land
1541   16s 8d land
1542   with Àirigh Sgallaidh, a 33s 4d land granted to Hector MacLean
        on the basis it had belonged to his grandfather
1722   part of estate of Campbells of Sunderland
1878   a substantial mansion house surrounded by a small portion of
        ornamental ground

Galtak, Kilmeny
NGR Unknown
1562   8s 4d land included in tack to Sir James MacDonald
1654   last mention
See *Ballighillan*.

Gartachara, Kilchoman
NR 253 613
G field of the standing stone. The stone in question is at NR 252 613, a
little to the west of the farm steading.

1507   with Carn, a 33s 4d land
1541   16s 8d land
1562   included in tack to Sir James MacDonald
1722   a very good possession, and of an easy rent
1878   a small farmhouse

Gartachossan, Kilarrow
NR 344 609
G field of the footpath.
1507   33s 4d land
1562   included in tack to Sir James MacDonald
1722   31s 8d land
1878   a small district

Gartloist, Kilarrow
NR 333 609
G *Gart loisgte*, scorched or burnt field; or, possibly, G *gart* + *loiste*, the fertile enclosure.
1507   with 'Corse' a 25s land
1878   a few small thatched houses

Gartnagaul, Kilarrow
See *Corsapol*.

Gearach, Kilchoman
NR 223 593
ON an enclosed plot of land.
1507   with Octomore, a 33s 4d land
1541   2 lands of 'Garrebege' and 'Garremoir', each with an extent of 16s 8d
1563   both lands included in tack to Sir James MacDonald
1722   33s 4d land, a good possession
1878   one dwelling house and offices

Giol, Kildalton
NR 284 439
ON ravine or gulley.
1541   25s land
1562   with Glenastle (part of), a 33s 4d land included in tack to Sir James MacDonald
1722   25s land
1878   ruins

Glassans, Kilchoman
NR 240 570
ON glaring headland.

1507   33s 4d land
1562   included in tack to Sir James MacDonald
1722   a very good possession, the mill, kiln and change-house thereof
       being a very good pennyworth

Glenastle, Kildalton
Upper Glenastle, NR 302 449; and Lower Glenastle, NR 289 457
G *glean*, valley, attached to ON **Assdalr*, the valley of the ridge.
1408   the two Glenastles included in the grant to Brian Vicar MacKay
1541   Upper Glenastle, a 13s 4d land, and Lower Glenastle, a 10s land
1562   Upper Glenastle, a 8s 4d land, included in tack to Sir James
       MacDonald; also Glenastle and Giol, with a combined extent of
       33s 4d
1614   Upper Glenastle, a 13s 4d land, and Lower Glenastle, a 10s
       land
1722   Upper Glenastle, 4 cowlands, a very cheap pennyworth of land,
       very good for holding and sowing; and Lower Glenastle, 3 cow-
       lands, a good little possession for stock and sowing
1878   Glenastle, a farmhouse with outbuildings attached; and Lower
       Glenastle, ruins

Glenegedale, Kildalton
NR 333 517
G *Gleann*, valley, attached to ON **Eikadalr*, valley of the oak trees.
1499   with Tighcargaman, a 5-merk land granted to John MacIan
1507   with Tighcargaman, a 5-merk land
1562   included in tack to Sir James MacDonald
1722   a spacious quarterland, moor and shore alike, good for holding and
       sowing
1878   a small hamlet

Glengeoy, Kilarrow
See *Eallabus*.

Goirtean an Uruisge, Kilmeny
See *Airigh Ghuaidhre, Skeag* and *Eacharnach*.

Goirtean Bholsa, Kilmeny
See *Baile Tharbhach*.

Gortanilivorrie, Kilarrow
G Gilmour's field.
NR 358 622
1541   'Gorthe', with Daillbeg and Daillmore, a 50s land
1631   'Gortengillymorie'

1722   with Dluich, a 25s land, a very good possession for holding and
       sowing
1878   a substantial stone building with garden and offices attached

Gortantaoid, Kilmeny
NR 339 732
The name in this form first turns up in the rental of 1631. Prior to that it
was Tyd, or something similar. It appears to be G *Gortan Taoid*, field of
cords. The cords in question might be cultivation rigs, or perhaps a specific
cord is meant, a prominent large hump of land which runs northwards
from the current farm buildings. These are on the Gortantaoid River about
half a mile upstream from where it flows into the large sandy bay, Tràigh
Baile Aonghais, to the east of Loch Gruinart.
1507   Tyd with Doodil, a 25s land
1562   Tyd, a 8s 4d land included in tack to Sir James MacDonald
1722   16s 8d land let (along with Ballenish) to Killinallan, which is
       undoubtedly the best possession in the country
1878   a shepherd's house

Gorthe, Kilarrow
See *Gortanilivorrie*.

Grasdale, Kildalton
NR 300 475
ON grassy valley.
1408   included in grant to Brian Vicar MacKay
1541   with Kintra, a 33s 4d land
1562   16s 8d land included in tack to Sir James MacDonald
1722   with Kintra, a 41s 8d land, very good for sowing and stock, the
       best pennyworth in the whole parish
1878   a shepherd's house

Greamsay, Kilchoman
NR 226 605
ON Grim's steading.
1507   33s 4d land
1541   16s 8d land
1722   wadset to Campbells of Octomore
1878   a small dwelling

Grobolls, Kilarrow
NR 338 598
ON *kró*, a small pen or fence, or perhaps, *Gró* (female personal-name) +
bólstaðr, farm.
1507   33s 4d land

1542 'Garbols' (or perhaps Carrabus?), with Duich, a 33s 4d land granted to Hector MacLean on the basis it had belonged to his grandfather
1562 included in tack to Sir James MacDonald
1722 25s land
1878 a small district comprising of a few small farmhouses and a number of ruins

Gruinart, Kilchoman
NR 278 682
ON shallow firth.
1507 25s land, and a 8s 4d church land mortified anew to Oronsay Priory by John MacIan
1562 33s 4d land included in tack to Sir James MacDonald
1722 wadset to Campbells of Ballinaby
1878 a district situated at the south end of Loch Gruinart. It comprises of farms of Gruinart Flats, Aorodh, Graineal, Gruinart Farm, Gruinart Cottage, schoolhouse, post office, a Free Church Mission House and the farms of Craigens and Corsapol
See also *Leckgruinart*.

Grulin, Kilchoman
NR 241 681
ON Gró's farm. Gró is a female name.
1654 Nether Grulin recorded
1751 appears as one property on MacDougall's map
1878 Grulinbeg (NR 239 680), a number of dwelling houses comprising two farm dwellings, houses and steadings; and Grulinmore (NR 242 666), two dwelling houses

Gyline, Kilchoman
NGR Unknown
1686 a cowland, wadset to Archibald Campbell of Octomore
1722 a cowland, wadset to Campbells of Octomore.

How, Kilchoman
NGR Unknown
1541 16s 8d land, of which 8s 4d belongs to Oronsay Priory
1614 16s 8d land

Innerloskin, Kildalton
NGR Unknown
1507 two church lands with a total extent of 33s 4d
1617 16s 8d land of Bishopric of the Isles, included in Tenandry of Lossit

1631   set with Largibreck
Innerloskin may have been in the region of Glenmachrie.

Island, Kildalton
See *Eilean na Muice Duibhe*.

Keanchyllan, Kilchoman
NGR Unknown, but possibly now represented by Kilellan on the West-
side of Loch Gruinart, at NR 285 719.
1507   with Foreland, a 33s 4d land
1541   16s 8d land
1562   6s 8d land included in tack to Sir James MacDonald
1614   16s 8d land
1686   with Kindrochit, a quarter and a cowland. Also 'kowland of
        Keanchyllane in Machoroshinis' [Machrie] wadset to John Camp-
        bell of Ballinaby

Keills, Kilmeny
NR 415 684
Until the eighteenth century the name was generally Kilcallumkill – G *cill*
+ *Callum-Chille*, (St) Columba's Church. The church in question is a
now-ruined, late-medieval chapel, formerly under the patronage of the
Lords of the Isles. The lands of Knocklearoch and Balloshin (see under
Knocklearoch) belonged to the chapel.
1506   25s church land
1617   16s 8d land of Iona Abbey included in Tenandry of Lossit
1722   25s land, a good possession
1878   a village comprising a school, shop and private dwellings (seven
        buildings in all), situated on both sides of the public road leading
        from Port Askaig to Bridgend

Keirreishlaraich, Kilmeny
NGR Unknown. Other forms include Keirreish Laich (1631) and
Kerowbhyachie (1654).
1628   feued to Mr William Campbell of Eorrabus
1654   last record

Kelsay, Kilchoman
NR 192 560
ON *Kjell staðir*, keel steading.
1507   with 'Kintesane' (Kilcavane?), a 33s 4d land
1562   with Kilcavane, included in tack to Sir James MacDonald
1722   33s 4d land, a very good possession
1878   a farmhouse, garden and outbuildings attached

Kentraw, Kilchoman
NR 267 628
G head of the strand.
1507   33s 4d land
1562   included in grant to Sir James MacDonald
1686   paired with Conisby
1878   a few houses

Kepolls and Kepollsmore, Kilmeny
NR 373 653, NR 383 681
ON *Kappi*, either a man's name, or a man's by-name meaning champion, or else ON *kjappi*, a billy-goat + *bólstaðr*, farm. The name has also been Gaelicised as *Ceapasadh*, as in the name of the fort, *Dun Ceapasaidh Mor*.

At least three different lands of Kepolls are listed in early documents: Kepollsmore, Kepollsbeg and Kepolls Mckeorie, according to the 1614 charter of Islay to Campbell of Cawdor. Kepollsmore is consistently reckoned in documents as a quarterland, and Kepollsbeg and Kepolls Mckeorie both auchtenpart lands, giving a total extent of 5 merks for a greater Kepolls. The Kepollsbeg or Little Kepolls of early documents is now known as Kepolls. Kepolls Mckeorie, or just plain Kepolls, is now part of Robolls. Little Kepolls and Kepolls were granted to John MacIan in 1494. He was then granted the two Kepolls in 1499, identifiable as the land of Kepollsmore, along with the Little Kepolls and Kepolls already given him in 1494.

1542   with Robolls, a 33s 4d land granted Hector MacLean on the basis it had belonged to his grandfather
1562   Kepollsbeg, a 16s 8d land, and Kepollsmore, a 33s 4d land, were included in the tack given to Sir James MacDonald
1614   Kepollsbeg, a 16s 8d land, Kepolls Mckeorie, a 16s 8d land, and Kepollsmore, a 33s 4d land
1722   Kepolls, with an extent of 50s
1878   Kepollsmore, a district

Kilarrow, Kilarrow
NR 332 628
G church of (St) Máel Rhubha.
1507   'Kilmacow', a 16s 8d church land
1617   16s 8d land of Iona Abbey included in Tenandry of Lossit
1722   an auchtenpart land, given as glebes to the two ministers. There was also a mill, brewhouses, and the houses of eight named individuals.

Kilbranan, Kilarrow
NR 374 623
G church of (St) Brendan.

1494   with Little Kepolls, a 33s 4d land granted to John MacIan
1507   with Daill and Octinfrich, a 5-merk land
1541   16s 8d land
1562   included in tack to Sir James MacDonald
1722   wadset to Campbells of Daill, the most of it (with other lands) lying exposed for good improvement
1878   'Cill Bhraenan', a small farm

Kilbride, Kildalton
NR 383 467
G (St) Bride's church.
1541   Kilbride Over, a 8s 4d land; and the two Kilbrides, with an extent of 16s 8d, belonging to Texa Chapel
1614   Kilbride, a 8s 4d land; Kilbride Over, a 8s 4d land; and the two Kilbrides, a 16s 10d land
1722   16s 8d land
1878   a number of small farm and cottar houses, stone and thatched

Kilcallumkill
See *Callumkill*, Kildalton and *Keills*, Kilmeny.

Kilcavane, Kilchoman
NGR Unknown
1507   'Kintesane' (?), with Kelsay a 33s 4d land
1541   with Kelsay, a 33s 4d land
1614   with Kelsay, a 33s 4d land
1631   'Killaghan' with Kelsay and Orsay
1686   'Kiltechmes', last record
The best form of this name is difficult to establish, but it does appear to include G *cill*, church. It is possible that the generic commemorates a saint called Kevin (Caomhán), as Kilkivan in Kintyre. There is an early church and burial ground (unrecorded by RCAHMS) at NR 194 560, near the Kelsay farm steading. This may be the church in question.

Kilchiaran, Kilchoman
NR 207 603
G (St) Ciarán's church. The saint in question is probably St Ciarán of Clonmacnois, whose obit is recorded in *AU* 549.[11]
1507   with Kilchoman, a church land with an extent of 8s 4d; Kilchiaran, a 33s 4d land; and Over Kilchiaran with Clagnish, a 33s 4d land
1541   Kilchiaranbeg, a 16s 8d land; and Kilchiaranmor, a 33s 4d land
1562   Kilchiaranbeg and Kilchiaranmor included in tack to Sir James MacDonald
1722   58s 4d land, a very good possession, alike good for sowing and holding

1878   a large group of houses. Kilchiaran House, a handsome stone
       building of considerable size with offices, etc., attached

Kilchoman, Kilchoman
NR 216 632
G (St) Choman's church. The Choman in this dedication is probably the
Presbyter honorabilis mentioned in Adomnan's Life of Columba, a son of
the sister of the fourth abbot of Iona.[12]
1507   £6 13s 4d lands with pertinents; with Kilchiaran, a 8s 4d church
       land
1541   a 10 merk land
1562   a 5 merk land included in tack to Sir James MacDonald
1722   including Kilchoman, Clagnish, Downan, Croash and Kynaskeill,
       a £4 5s land; Also the Mill of Kilchoman. A choice, large, good
       possession, having many parks and enclosures in it; wherein was
       once the choice mansion house of Cawdor in this country, and
       always possessed by Cawdor or his Tutor until Sir Archibald
       Campbell of Clunes, Tutor, his removal from this country . . .
       (He) built a large malt kiln and change-house, and a good corn
       mill upon it, and many other improvements
1878   a small collection of houses including the parish church, manse
       and school
Kilchoman was split in two between 1722 and 1733, the two portions later
being called West and East Kilchoman. West Kilchoman is the settlement
by the church. East Kilchoman was renamed Rockside in the nineteenth
century.

Kildalton, Kildalton
NR 458 508
G church of the foster brother or disciple, e.g. St John the Evangelist.
1614   8s 4d land
1722   16s 8d land, paired with Ardmore with which it is described as a very
       good possession for sowing and pasturage and increase of cattle, and
       has both shore and moor and three islands belonging to it

Kilellan, Kilchoman
See *Keanchyllan*.

Kilennan, Kilarrow
Upper Kilennan, NR 356 581; and Lower Kilennan, NR 350 570
G (St) Finan's church. The saint in question is probably St Finan
Lobur (the diseased or infirm), c.550–600.[13]
1507   33s 4d land with the fishing of the 'Lessane'
1545   included in the Barony of Bar
1686   divided into Over and Nether Kilennan

1722   Over Kilennan, a 16s 8d land, a special good room for holding and fattening; and Nether Kilennan, a 16s 8d land, good for sowing and stock

1878   Kilennan – a shepherd's house . . . this name at one time was given to a small district formerly thickly populated but now only two dwelling houses remain . . . further south stands a large and commodious farmhouse which secures as a mark of distinction [the name] Kilennan House

Killelegan, Kilmeny
NR 403 694 (Cill Eileagain)
G the church of (St) Findlugán. There are the ruins of an early dry-stone chapel with a ruined house, possibly of sixteenth- or seventeenth-century date, nearby.

1507   with Ballighillan, a 33s 4d land
1541   16s 8d land
1542   granted to Hector MacLean on the basis it had belonged to his grandfather
1686   with Balulive, a 33s 4d land

Killeyan, Kildalton
Upper Killeyan, NR 281 419; and Lower Killeyan, NR 277 431
G (St) Aidan's church.

1541   41s 4d land
1562   included in grant to Sir James MacDonald
1722   41s 8d land, a very good possession, and the mill thereof the best pennyworth of a mill in the island
1780   split into Upper and Lower Killeyan
1878   Lower Killeyan, a hamlet; and Upper Killeyan, a few dwelling houses

Killinallan, Kilarrow
NR 313 718
G *cill* + *Faelan*, or **Allan*, the church of (St) Fillan or Allan. The latter is unattested.

1499   with Carrisay, Ballenish and Lag, a 5-merk land granted to John MacIan
1507   with Carrisay, a 33s 4d land
1541   with Carrisay, a 33s 4d land
1542   granted to Hector MacLean on the basis it had belonged to his grandfather
1722   33s 4d land wadset to Campbells of Killinallan, the very best wadset of so much in Islay
1878   a farmhouse and offices

Kilmacow, Kilarrow
See *Kilarrow*.

Kilmeny, Kilmeny
NR 391 653
G *Cille M'Eithne*, meaning 'My Eithne's Church', after Eithne, the mother of St Columba.
1507   33s 4d church land
1561   land of the Bishopric of the Isles
1694   Kilmeny and Over Kilmeny
1722   wadset to Campbells of Lossit. This wadset is very good for stock of all sorts, especially for sheep
1878   a hamlet consisting of a few dilapidated dwelling houses, two farm dwelling houses and offices

Kilnaughton, Kildalton
NR 344 451
G (St) Nechtan's church.
1507   25s church land
1722   16s 8d land. Kilnaughton and Cornabus, a compact pretty little possession for holding
1878   a small cottage situated beside Kilnaughton burying ground

Kilnave, Kilchoman
NR 283 731
G *cill* + ON *nef*, church of the nose-shaped promontory.
1722   33s 4d land
1878   a small district comprising several farmhouses
Kilnave was a church land, part of the estate of Ardnave which belonged to Iona Abbey. See *Ardnave*.

Kilslevan, Kilmeny
NR 421 673
G Slébhine's Church. Slébhine was an abbot of Iona who died on 2 March 767.[14]
1507   the two Kilslevans, a 33s 4d church land
1617   Over and Lower Kilslevan, each with an extent of 16s 8d, lands of Iona Abbey included in Tenandry of Lossit
1722   'Kilsleaveens', wadset to Campbells of Lossit. This wadset is very good for stock of all sorts, especially for sheep
1878   the ruins of a hamlet

Kinbeloquhane
See *Balloshin*, Kilmeny.

Kindrochid, Kilchoman
NR 232 687
G bridge end.
1507   33s 4d land; and 'Schannagangrig' (part of Sanaig) with Kindro-
        chit, a 40s land
1562   included in tack to Sir James MacDonald
1722   (with Smaull) has a good park annexed unto it
1878   a farmhouse with outbuildings detached

Kinnabus, Kilarrow
NR 31 63 (no longer extant)
ON **kona* + *bólstaðr,* the farm of the queen, or of the women. If the latter,
it might indicate ownership by nuns.
1507   33s 4d church land
1588   quarterland, formerly belonging to Abbey of Iona, granted to
        Hector, son and heir of Lachlan MacLean of Duart
1617   land of Iona Abbey included in Tenandry of Lossit
1722   with Eallabus, a 33s 4d land, a good quarterland, alike good for
        stock and sowing

Kinnabus, Kildalton
NR 294 424
ON *kinn* + *bólstaðr,* farm of the 'cheek' – in the sense of a steep hillside.
1878   a farmhouse with outbuildings and garden attached
Although the name is not recorded prior to 1722, it is clearly an old farm
name.

Kintour, Kildalton
NR 547 513
G towerhead. The tower may refer to the fort of Creagan na Ceardaich
Móire.[15]
1499   10-merk land granted to John MacIan
1541   33s 4d land
1545   included in Barony of Bar
1722   (with Aros and Stoine) a spacious quarterland, very good for stock,
        being in three separate divisions. Also a mill at Kintour recorded at
        this time
1878   a large farmhouse with garden and offices attached
Stoine, an 8s 4d land, first recorded in 1722, is shown on MacDougall's
map as if it has been carved out of the pasture land of Kintour.

Kintra, Kildalton
NR 320 483
G head of the strand.
1408   included in grant to Brian Vicar MacKay

1541   with Grasdale, a 33s 4d land
1562   16s 8d land included in tack to Sir James MacDonald
1722   with Grasdale, a 41s 8d land, very good for sowing and stock, the
        best pennyworth in the whole parish
1878   a large farm steading built of stone and slated

Knockane, Kilarrow
NR 334 636 (Knockanbearach)
1617   16s 8d land of Iona Abbey included in Tenandry of Lossit
1722   16s 8d land
1878   Knockanbearach, three attached dwelling houses substantially
        built of stone and slate

Knocklearoch, Kilmeny
NR 399 649
G hill of the clerics. Knocklearoch was church property and there are two
standing stones beside the steading which are known as *Na Clerrich*, the
clerics. These are said to mark the place where two clerics were hanged on a
particularly wet and windy day. Hence unusually wet and stormy days
became on Islay to be compared to the day they hanged the clerics.[16]
1507   with Balloshin, a 33s 4d church land belonging to the Chapel of St
        Columba (Keills)
1722   33s 4d land. In this place are the dwellings of the miners of the
        mines of Islay
1878   a farmhouse and outbuildings

Knockrinsey, Kildalton
NR 438 487 (Cnoc Rhaonastil)
G *Cnoc*, hill, attached to ON **Hreinssalr*, Hrein's hall or farm.
   The 5-merk lands of Knockrinsey, including Ardilistry, Ardinistle and
Arigearie, belonged to the MacNeills of Gigha prior to the forfeiture of the
Lordship of the Isles in 1494. The lands of the MacNeills of Gigha were
held briefly in the 1530s by 'Ailean nan Sop', the younger brother of
Hector MacLean of Duart, and were then granted to his son Hector in
1553. Nevertheless, Neill MacNeill sold the lands to Sir James MacDonald of Dunyvaig in 1554.[17] From him they passed to Archibald, a natural
son of Angus of Dunyvaig, but Archibald and Angus sold Gigha to Sir
John Campbell of Cawdor in 1590, retaining the Islay lands for themselves. Archibald's half-brother, Sir James, then adopted Knockrinsey as
his territorial designation when he was knighted, about 1597. Knockrinsey
was still in the hands of John MacDonald, son and heir of Archibald, after
the Campbell takeover of Islay. He sold it to Sir John Campbell in 1629.[18]
   The location of Arigearie cannot now be identified, but it was possibly a
shieling that belonged to Ardinistle.
1722   33s 4d land, a good possession (with Ardilistry) for stock; and has

one small isle annexed to it. There is a remarkable vision said to be seen about sixty years ago upon the top of a great hill above the house of Knock of a cripple on stilts and a young man also, a little halting, led by an old man, and all three lowping and skipping in the top of the hill crying 'Hei! Gilbert ho! Gilbert, Gilbert, mwo so, Gilbert, mwo shud!'

Kylladow, Kilmeny
NGR Unknown, but probably on east side of Loch Finlaggan, adjacent to Quenskerne.
1628   set with the lands of Portaneilean, Mulreesh and Quenskerne
1722   with Portaneilean and Quenskerne, a 42s 8d land

Kynagarry, Kilarrow
NR 377 589
It seems likely that the name reflects G *Caoingaradh,* the farm of the smooth place, the generic possibly representing the use of ON *garðr* as a loan-word in G, or the G adaptation of an ON precursor.
1507   33s 4d land
1562   included in tack to Sir James MacDonald
1722   a special quarterland for sowing and holding
1878   a small district

Kynaskeill, Kilchoman
NGR Unknown
1562   16s 8d land included in tack to Sir James MacDonald
1563   two lands of 'Kenisgillis' included in tack to Sir James MacDonald
1631   'Kinaskaillis'
1722   part of estate of Kilchoman

Lag, Kilarrow
NR 315 687 (Lag Odhar)
1499   with Carrisay, Killinallan and Ballenish, a 5-merk land granted to John MacIan
1507   with Ballenish, a 33s 4d land
1878   'Lag Odhar', a flat tract of pasture and rough heathy pasture

Lagavulin, Kildalton
NR 404 457
G mill hollow.
1631   brewseat
1686   'brewseat in Lagmullin'
1722   courthouse of Lagavulin (under Dunyvaig)
1878   a hamlet including Lagavulin Distillery and the residence of Captain Graham, part proprietor
See *Dunyvaig.*

Laggan, Kilarrow
NR 285 555
Perhaps a G adaptation of ON *Laxán,* the salmon river, rather than G, small hollow.
1507 33s 4d land
1562 included in tack to Sir James MacDonald
1722 with Torra and the salmon fishing, a 58s 4d land, more pleasant than profitable
1878 a large dwelling house with barns, out-offices and garden attached

Laichtcarlane, Kilmeny
NGR Unknown, but probably on west side of Loch Finlaggan
1507 with an eighth part of Portaneilean, a 33s 4d land
1562 16s 8d land included in tack to Sir James MacDonald
1686 with Sean-ghairt, set to John Campbell of Ballachlaven

Laoigan, Kilmeny
NR 406 685
1541 8s 4d land
1562 included in tack to Sir James MacDonald
1878 six scattered thatched cottages with other ruins

Largibreck (Machrie), Kildalton
NR 327 491
G, speckled slope (with Machrie, G for machair land).
1408 'Machaire Learga riabhoige', included in grant to Brian Vicar MacKay
1541 'Largebrak', in hands of Captain of Dunyvaig
1617 'Lagrivug', a16s 8d land of the Bishopric of the Isles included in Tenandry of Lossit
1694 'Legrebock'
1722 'Macharies', a 33s 4d land
1878 a farmhouse with outbuildings attached

Leatur, Kildalton
NGR Unknown
1541 'Iletor', 6s 8d land in possession of Captain of Dunyvaig
1722 with Mulindry, a 31s 8d land, a good possession, very good for sowing, and a competent holding

Leckgruinart, Kilchoman
NR 277 692
The name appears to be a conflation of the neighbouring farm-names of Leek and Gruinart.

1631   first recorded
1722   a 35s 4d land
1878   a small farmhouse and offices and several dwelling houses

Leek, Kilchoman
NR 223 678
Possibly from ON *lækr*, brook, rivulet, in reference to River Leoig; or else
G *leac*, rock.
1507   33s 4d land
1562   included in tack to Sir James MacDonald
1722   with Sanaigbeg, Gruinart and Corsapol wadset to Campbells of
       Ballinaby
1878   a small dwelling house and ruins

Leek, Kilmeny
NR 359 652
The etymology of this name is uncertain. Possible explanations include G
leac, a slab of stone, ON *leikr*, perhaps in the sense of a 'rutting place', or
else ON **Laekr*, a stream.
1507   with 'Stynypollis' (Ballimartin), a 33s 4d land
1541   8s 4d land
1562   with 'Knox', a 16s 8d land included in tack to Sir James
       MacDonald
1722   with Balole, a 50s land

Leorin, Kildalton
Upper Leorin, NR 360 492; Lower Leorin, NR 353 485
ON loamy or mud-banked river.
1545   probably the two 'Lennynes' included in the Barony of Bar
1631   Over and Nether Leorin
1722   Over and Nether Leorin, each a 16s 8d land
1878   Upper Leorin, a number of dwelling houses; and Leorin, a large
       dwelling farmhouse with commodious steading attached

Lorgbaw, Kilchoman
NR 251 593
1507   with Coull a 33s 4d land
1541   16s 8d land
1562   included in tack to Sir James MacDonald
1722   wadset to Campbells of Octomore
1878   a few houses and one dwelling house

Lossit, Kilchoman
NR 185 563
G kneading trough, in reference to the fertility of the land.

1507   with 'Ard' (Ardmulane), a 33s 4d land
1541   set with Ardmulane
1562   33s 4d land land included in tack to Sir James MacDonald
       (evidently including Ardmulane. In 1563 and 1564 Ardmulane
       is listed separately, and Lossit valued at 16s 8d.)
1614   with Lossit, a 33s 4d land
1722   a good quarterland, alike good for sowing and pasturage
1878   a farmhouse of considerable size with offices attached

Lossit, Kilmeny
NR 412 655
G kneading trough, in reference to the fertility of the land.
1507   with the island (Eilean Mhic Iain in Loch Lossit), a 33s 4d church
       land
1617   33s 4d land of Iona Abbey included in Tenandry of Lossit
1722   wadset to Campbells of Lossit
1878   a farmhouse with outbuildings attached

Lurabus, Kildalton
NR 337 435
ON loam or clay farm.
1541   33s 4d land
1562   included in tack to Sir James MacDonald
1722   33s 4d land
1878   ruins

Lyrabus, Kilarrow
NR 292 644
ON *leira* + *bólstaðr*, loam field farm.
1499   'Keirbous' (Lyrabus?) with Corsapol, a 5-merk land granted to
       John MacIan
1631   'Lerebols'
1722   a good auchtane part for stock and sowing
1878   a small district comprising a collection of crofters' houses occupied
       by crofters

Machrie, Kilchoman
NR 209 638
G, *machair* (low-lying land adjacent to sandy beach). Some early versions
of the name, like 'Masherrveolin' (1722), appear to include G, *Bheòlain*, as
in the name of the fort, Dun Bheòlain, at NR 210 689 (Smaull).
1631   first recorded
1722   part of estate of Sunderland
1878   a few small dwelling houses

Machrie, Kildalton
See *Largibreck*.

Margadale, Kilmeny
NR 394 744
ON *mörk* + *dalr*, valley of the boundary.
1562   6s land included in tack to Sir James MacDonald
1722   4s land or 2 cowlands
1878   ruins of old dwelling

Mealand, Kilchoman
NGR Unknown. Compare *Mee*
1541   8s 4d land
1614   8s 4d land
1683   'Machriemealanit', a 6s 4d land, part of estate of Sunderland[19]

Mee, Kilchoman
See *Ardnave*.

Migrim, Kilchoman
NGR Unknown. Blaeu's map shows it between Smaull and Coull
1562   33s 4d land included in tack to Sir James MacDonald
1722   a good quarterland, and has a very good winter park

Mulindry, Kilarrow
NR 358 596
G *muileann* + *treabh*, mill village.
1499   with Rosquern and Nosebridge, a 5-merk land granted to John
       MacIan
1507   with Rosquern and Nosebridge, a 5-merk land
1541   33s 4d land
1545   included in Barony of Bar
1722   with Leatur, a 31s 8d land, a good possession, very good for
       sowing, and a competent holding
1878   a district comprising three farm buildings and a board school, etc

Mullinmadagan, Kilmeny
NGR Unknown, but possibly adjacent to Tiervaagain
G *muileann* + *Mathagan*, meaning Mathagan's mill. Mathagan is a
diminutive of Matthew.
1507   33s 4d land
1562   two lands of Mullinmadagan, with an extent of 16s 8d, included in
       tack to Sir James MacDonald
1686   last recorded

Mulreesh, Kilmeny
NR 403 687
G *Maol Ris*, exposed hill-slope.
1628   set with the lands of Portaneilean, Quenskerne and Kylladow
1722   16s 8d land
1878   a hamlet comprised of Lead Mine Offices and dwellings (five
       buildings in all)

Nave Island, Kilchoman
NR 288 757
ON *Nef*, headland.
1507   13s 4d church land
1722   with Ardnave 36s 8d, Nave Island itself being reckoned as 2
       cowlands.
1878   a large rocky island
See also *Ardnave*.

Nerabus, Kilchoman
NR 226 551
The earliest versions of the name lack the initial 'N', for example
'Arrobollis' (1507), suggesting the possibility that the 'N' represents G
an, the. In that case, the name might originally have been ON *Eyr-
arbólstaðr*, the steading by the gravel bank.
1507   83s 4d land of the church of St Columba
1588   5-merk land, formerly belonging to Monastery of Derry, granted
       to Hector, son and heir of Lachlan MacLean of Duart
1614   with Tormisdale, a 5-merk land
1722   33s 4d land, a good tenement.
1878   a small collection of houses, numbering about 12
Nerabus was included in the Tenandry of Aros (Mull) as part of the
MacLean Barony of Duart, although seventeenth-century rentals of Islay
indicate it was enjoyed by the Campbells of Cawdor. The Earl of Argyll
was retoured there as late as 1695, but this was clearly a paper exercise with
no reality in fact, as far as the Islay land was concerned. Lack of knowledge
and interest in it is suggested by the careless way its name had by then
transmogrified into 'Morabulfadtie'.[20]

Nereby, Kilarrow
NR 361 604
ON *neðri* + *býr*, the lower, or more southerly, farm.
1507   33s 4d land
1545   included in Barony of Bar
1722   33s 4d land
1878   a large and commodious farmhouse with garden and offices
       attached

Nosebridge, Kilarrow
NR 372 602
ON *hnauss* + *berg*, turf fortress, referring to the impressive multivallate, Dun Nosebridge.
1499   with Rosquern and Mulindry, a 5-merk land granted to John MacIan
1507   with Rosquern and Mulindry, a 5-merk land
1545   included in Barony of Bar
1722   a good quarterland for stock and sowing.
1878   a district originally composed of small farms, now consisting of four distinct collections of ruins and the ancient fort called Dun Nosebridge
MacDougall's map shows Allallaidh (NR 480 580) as a pendicle of Nosebridge. It was presumably the shieling of that land

Ochtokerne, Kilmeny
See *Carnbeg*.

Octinfrich, Kilarrow
NGR Unknown
G eighth part of 'Freag'. It has been suggested that this refers to the district called Freag in the *Senchus fer nAlban*. It must have been adjacent to Daill.[21]
1494   with Dluich, a 33s 4d land granted to John MacIan
1562   16s 8d land included in tack to Sir James MacDonald
1654   set with Kilbranan
1722   wadset to Campbells of Daill

Octocorrich, Kilarrow
NGR Unknown
1507   16s 8d church land
1617   33s 4d land of Iona Abbey included in Tenandry of Lossit

Octofad, Kilchoman
NR 219 545
G long auchtanepart.
1507   with an eighth part of Cladville, a 33s 4d land
1541   16s 8d land
1562   included in tack to Sir James MacDonald
1722   33s 4d land
1878   a commodious dwelling house, two stories high, with garden and offices attached

Octomore, Kilchoman
NR 248 589
G great auchtanepart.

1507   33s 4d land; and, Octomore with Gearach, a 33s 4d land
1541   33s 4d land, and a 16s 8d land
1563   Ocotmore, a 16s 8d land, and 'Octomoir Gremsay', a 16s 8d land,
       included in tack to Sir James MacDonald
1722   wadset to Campbells of Octomore
1878   a farmhouse of considerable size with offices attached

Octovullin, Kilarrow
NR 347 641
G auchtanepart of the mill.
1499   with Carrabus, a 5-merk land granted to John MacIan
1507   with Drumalla, a 33s 4d land
1541   25s land
1722   with Drumalla, a 50s land
1878   a farmhouse and steading

Olistadh, Kilchoman
NR 218 583
ON Óláfr's steading.
1541   16s 8d land
1722   16s 8d land, a good convenient tenement
1878   a small collection of houses now in ruins

Orsay, Kilchoman
NR 163 515
This land unit, judging by its 16s 8d extent, must originally have included not
just the island of Orsay, but some of the adjacent land at the tip of the Rhinns.
The original form of the island name may have been ON *Aróssey*, the island
by the mouth of the river, with a putative parent settlement called ON *Aróss*,
mouth of the river. It is significant that the name for the settlement that
preceded Port Wemyss was Bun Abhainne,[22] which means the same in
Gaelic. The river in question is the Abhainn Gleann na Rainich.
1507   16s 8d church land of St Columba
1631   'Killaghan' [Kilcavane] with Kelsay and Orsay
1722   wadset to Campbells of Ellister
1878   a large island . . . the property of the Northern Light Commis-
       sioners who have erected a lighthouse and light keepers' residence
       on it

Overnag, Kilmeny
See *Cove*.

Persabus, Kilmeny
NR 417 690
ON *Prestabólstaðr*, the farm of the priest(s).

1507   25s church land
1617   25s land of Iona Abbey included in Tenandry of Lossit
1722   an auchtanepart land, with a change-house and malt kiln
1878   a substantial farmhouse and offices attached

Port Askaig, Kilmeny
NR 431 692
G *port*, bay, attached to ON **Askvik*, bay of the ash tree. Prior to the eighteenth century the name was just Askaig.
1507   3s 4d land
1541   'ferry boat of Eskcok', 3s 4d
1722   4s or 2 cowlands
1878   a small village consisting of a post office, shop, an hotel with dwelling houses, out-houses and stores.

Portaneilean, Kilmeny
NR 393 685 Renamed Finlaggan in the 1860s
G port of the island. The earliest version of the name, in the rental of 1507, 'Portalanynlagane', shows that it was the Port of Findlugán's Island. It appears in the crown rentals of 1541 simply as 'Ellenynegane' or 'Ellemyngane', the island of Findlugán.
1507   33s 4d land; and with Laichtcarlane, a 33s 4d land
1541   50s land
1562   included in tack to Sir James MacDonald
1722   with Quenskerne and Kylladow, a 42s 8d land, a large, good possession both for sowing and stock, adjacent to a large fresh-water loch
1878   Finlaggan, a farmhouse and offices

Portnahaven, Kilchoman
NR 168 521
1694   Mr Scott in 'Portnahavni', 2 hearths
1878   a small village . . .

Proaig, Kilarrow/Kildalton
NR 457 576
ON broad bay.
1506   6 cowlands granted to John MacIan in recognition that his father had held them from Alexander Earl of Ross
1507   20s land
1541   16s 8d land
1545   included in Barony of Bar
1722   16s 8d land, a toun very beneficial for pasturage, good for fattening and nourishing cattle
1878   a shepherd's house

Quenskerne, Kilmeny
NR 392 680 (Cuing-sgeir)
1628   set with the lands of Portaneilean, Mulreesh and Kylladow
1722   with Portaneilean and Kylladow, a 42s 8d land.

Robolls, Kilmeny
NR 396 668
ON *rá*, a nook or corner, + *bólstaðr*, farm.
1494   with Kepolls, a 33s 4d land granted to John MacIan
1542   with Kepolls, a 33s 4d land granted Hector MacLean on the basis
       it had belonged to his grandfather
1614   16s 8d land
1722   33s 4d land, wadset to Campbells of Ballachlaven
In the sixteenth century Robolls consisted of land on the east shore of Loch
Finlaggan. It was sometimes (e.g. 1631) called 'Tannach' Robolls, this
name now being represented by An Tamhanachd (NR 388 674) on
modern maps. Kepolls (Kepolls Mckeorie), centred on the present-day
Ballygrant Inn, became part of Robolls in the late seventeenth or early
eighteenth century.

Roskern, Kilarrow
NR 384 610
G **Ros a'chùirn* – perhaps 'wood of the cairn' rather than 'promontory of
the cairn'.
1499   with Nosebridge and Mulindry, a 5-merk land granted to John
       MacIan
1507   with Nosebridge and Mulindry, a 5-merk land
1541   16s 8d land
1545   included in Barony of Bar
1722   16s 8d land.

Saligo, Kilchoman
NR 209 662
ON, bay of happiness.
1507   with Crosprig and Brade, a 38s 4d land
1541   6s 8d land
1562   included in tack to Sir James MacDonald
1878   a house

Sanaig, Kilchoman
Sanaigbeg, NR 221 698; Sanaigmore, NR 237 707
ON sandy bay.
1507   two church lands, valued at 16s 8d. and 33s 4d, both belonging to
       Oronsay Priory; and 'Schannagangrig' with Kindrochit, a 40s land
1541   with Neanegane, a 16s 8d land

1562   Sanaigbeg (in 1563 'Sannage Nagrek'), a 16s 8d land included in tack to Sir James MacDonald
1722   Sannaigbeg, wadset to Campbells of Ballinaby; and Sanaigmore, a 33s 4d land, a very good possession
1878   Sanaigbeg, a ruin; and Sanaigmore, a farmhouse

Scanistle, Kilmeny
NR 407 676
ON *Skallastaðir*, Skalli's farm.
1494   quarter and eighth land granted to John MacIan
1507   a 33s 4d land; and with Bolsa, a 33s 4d land
1542   a quarterland; with Killelegan, another quarterland; and also a 6s 8d land – granted to Hector MacLean on the basis it had belonged to his grandfather
1614   4-merks 3s 4d land
1722   in the laird's hands
1878   a substantial farmhouse and offices

Scarrabus, Kilarrow
NR 348 652
ON Skári's farm.
1507   33s 4d land
1562   included in tack to Sir James MacDonald
1722   33s 4d land
1878   a substantial stone and slate farmhouse and offices

Sean-ghairt, Kilmeny
NR 380 675
G *Seanghart*, old field, in the sense of one that has been long cultivated, or else G *Seana-ghart*, meaning old in the sense of one that had formerly been cultivated.
1507   with Baile Tharbhach, a 33s 4d land
1722   33s 4d land
1878   the ruins of a small hamlet

Skeag
NGR Unknown
1588   2½ cowlands, formerly belonging to Abbey of Iona, granted to Hector, son and heir of Lachlan MacLean of Duart
1617   16s 8d land of Iona Abbey included in Tenandry of Lossit
1631   last record
The land at the deserted settlement of Goirtean an Uruisge in Glen Logan is called Coire Sgiathach, suggesting the possibility that Skeag is an alternative name for it.

Skelreioch, Kilarrow
NGR Unknown
1614   8s 4d land
1686   last record

Skerrols, Kilarrow
NR 351 638
ON *Haraldr* + *staðir*, Harold's farm.
1507   33s 4d church land
1617   33s 4d land of Iona Abbey included in Tenandry of Lossit
1722   a good quarterland, and the tuck mill upon it is a noble penny-
        worth, and a good croft annexed to it with some holding
1878   a substantial farmhouse and steading

Smaull, Kilchoman
NR 214 685
ON butter vale, pasture land.
1507   33s 4d land
1562   included in tack to Sir James MacDonald
1722   with Kindrochit, two very good quarterlands
1878   two farms

Solam, Kildalton
NR 411 482
ON sunny hill.
1631   first recorded
1722   16s 8d land (4 cowlands), set along with Ard Imersay and Airigh
        nam Beist, a tolerable possession for stock

Sorn, Kilarrow
NR 344 627 (Newton Cottage)
This land is named for the River Sorn, ON *Surn(á)*, referring to the noise
made by the water.
1507   25s church land
1588   7½ cowlands, formerly belonging to Abbey of Iona, granted to
        Hector, son and heir of Lachlan MacLean of Duart
1617   25s land of Iona Abbey included in Tenandry of Lossit
1722   wadset to Campbells of Daill

Stanepoll, Kilmeny
See *Ballimartin.*

Staoisha, Kilmeny
(Nether or Lower) Staoisha, NR 403 712; and Staoisha Eararach (Upper),
NR 399 724

ON *Steinnsetr, Steinn's farm.
1507   33s 4d land
1562   included in tack to Sir James MacDonald
1722   Staoisha Nether, a 16s 8d land, good for stock and sowing; and
        Staoisha Upper, a 16s 8d land, a very good possession for stock
1878   Staoisha, a shepherd's house; and Staoisha Eararach, the ruin of an
        old dwelling

Stoine, Kildalton
See Kintour.

Storakaig, Kilmeny
NR 405 619
ON *Stórákr, big field, with the addition of a G locative -aig.
1499   with Barr and Airigh Ghuaidhre, a 5-merk land granted to John
        MacIan
1507   16s 8d church land
1722   16s 8d land
1878   a small dwelling house, formerly used as a farmhouse, but now
        converted into a shepherd's house

Stremnish, Kildalton
Stremnishbeg, NR 306 407; and Stremnishmore, NR 311 408
ON, the headland of the current (with G suffixes for small and large).
1507   Stremnishmore, a 33s 4d land
1545   Stremnishmore, included in Barony of Bar
1562   Stremnishbeg, included in tack to Sir James MacDonald
1722   Stremnishbeg, a 16s 8d land; and Stremnishmore, a 33s 4d land
1878   Stremnishmore, several remains and ruins of old houses

Sunderland, Kilchoman
NR 246 645
Possibly from ON *Sjóvarþing, the assembly place by the lake. This
assembly place might be identified as the prominent natural mound at NR
240 648, overlooking Loch Gorm.
1507   33s 4d land
1542   granted to Hector MacLean on the basis it had belonged to his
        grandfather
1722   part of estate of Campbells of Sunderland
1878   a large and substantial farmhouse with offices and garden attached
Loch Gorm Castle or Fort is on the land of Sunderland.

Surnaig, Kildalton
NR 399 454
ON bay of the (River) 'Surn' – the Kilbride River.

1654   first recorded
1722   (with Barr, Ardinistle and Craignagour) being alike good both for
       the increase of sowing and cattle both for milk and gendering of
       cattle, as good as any so much in the country, lying upon the shore
       side
1878   a farm steading

Tallant, Kilarrow
NR 336 586
ON **Háland*, high holding.
1507   33s 4d land
1562   included in tack to Sir James MacDonald
1722   25s land, a compact room, well situated, good for sowing and stock
1878   a substantial farm steading with garden attached

Tallant, Kildalton
NR 453 508
ON **Háland*, high holding.
1541   8s 4d land
1545   included in Barony of Bar
1878   a dwelling house

Texa, Kildalton
NR 392 438
Clearly an island name, ending in ON *ey*, island, but the first part is
obscure.
1507   41s 8d church land
1541   8s land
1614   8s land
1722   8s 4d land
1878   a large island
The extent of the island itself was 8s. or 8s 4d. The rental of 1507 clearly
has other lands under Texa that belonged to the chapel. These must have
included at least some of the land of Kilbride.

Tiervaagain, Kilmeny
NR 381 647
G *tir* + *Mathagan*, Mathagan's land. Mathagan is a diminutive of
Matthew.
1506   granted to John MacIan in recognition that his father had held it
       from Alexander Earl of Ross
1507   16s 8d land
1545   included in Barony of Bar
1722   wadset to Campbells of Lossit
1878   farmhouse and offices

Tighandrom, Kildalton
NR 373 461
G house on the ridge.
1541   with Brae, a 16s 8d land
1545   8s 8d land included in Barony of Bar
1614   with Brae, a 16s 8d land
1722   16s 8d land, a very good pennyworth . . . for sowing and holding
       for so much
1878   a farm dwelling house and steading

Tighcargaman, Kildalton
NR 363 495
G Cargaman's house.
1499   with Glenegedale, a 5-merk land granted to John MacIan
1507   with Glenegedale, a 5-merk land
1545   33s 4d land included in Barony of Bar
1722   a good pennyworth of a quarterland, being very good for sowing
       and increase of corn, and a good soil for sheep
1878   a dwelling house

Tockmal, Kildalton
NR 300 472
ON Haukr's ridge, or the ridge of the hawks.
1408   included in grant to Brian Vicar MacKay
1541   8s 4d land
1562   with 'Tornobelsay', a 16s 8d land included in tack to Sir James
       MacDonald
1722   8s 4d land, a very good pennyworth of land
1878   several ruins
Tornobelsay is otherwise unknown, but there is a deserted farm
called Tornabakin at NR 292 454 in Glenastle, immediately to the
south.

Torlissay
NGR Unknown
1496   granted to Lachlan, natural son of Hector MacLean of Duart[23]
1540   granted to Hector, son and heir of Hector MacLean of Duart[24]
Torlissay may have been a district name for the lands in the Rhinns held
or claimed by the MacLeans. It continued to be listed in grants and
retours of their Islay lands in the sixteenth and seventeenth centuries,
alongside the individually named lands in the Rhinns, apparently with
no understanding of what and where it was.[25] The name of the farm of
Coultorsay in the Rhinns might possibly contain some memory of
Torlissay.

Tormisdale, Kilchoman
NR 193 587
Possibly from ON **Ormsdalr*, either Ormr's valley, or the valley of the snakes. If the latter, the name may describe the meandering path of the Allt a' Ghlinne.
1507   33s 4d land
1562   included in tack to Sir James MacDonald
1722   a good possession
1878   a small district including Carn and Thornasaig

Tornebelsay, Kildalton
See *Tockmal.*

Torony, Kilchoman
NR 236 561
G ferny hill.
1562   16s 8d land included in tack to Sir James MacDonald
1722   16s 8d land
1878   a cluster of houses, originally a farmsteading, but now occupied by cottars

Torra, Kilarrow/Kildalton
NR 345 547
ON **Horná*, river corner, perhaps referring to the prominent crook in the Duich/Torr River.
1541   6s 8d land
1562   6s land included in the tack to Sir James MacDonald
1722   with Laggan, a 58s 4d land, more pleasant than profitable.
1878   a number of ruins

Torrabus, Kilmeny
NR 422 703
ON *þorir* + *bólstaðir*, Thorir's farm (or possibly Thora's farm, from the female equivalent of Thorir).
1507   16s 8d. church land
1617   16s 8d land of Iona Abbey, included in Tenandry of Lossit
1722   16s 8d land
1878   a substantial stone and slate farmhouse and offices

Torradale, Kildalton
NR 380 401
ON greensward valley
1541   33s 4d land
1545   included in Barony of Bar

1722   a very good quarterland, alike good for sowing and milk, lying upon the shore, and a shieling on the moor
1878   a farm dwelling house and steading

Trudernish, Kildalton
NR 462 525
ON wild boar headland.
1541   with Artalla, a 33s 4d land, waste
1545   16s 8d land, included in Barony of Bar
1722   exceeding compact and convenient, with moor and dale
1878   a small farmsteading

Tyd, Kilmeny
See *Gortantaoid*.

Ugasgog, Kildalton
NR 314 478 (?)
1408   included in grant to Brian Vicar MacKay
1562   8s 4d land included in tack to Sir James MacDonald
1686   set with Grasdale and Kintra
Lamont suggests that the '-asgog' part of the name is of similar derivation to (Port) Askaig. The position of Ugasgog may be reperesented by the present-day Port Alsaig, or a ruined house a few metres inland.[26]

Notes

Chapter 1 The Queen of the Hebrides

1. MacDonald, *Sketches of Islay*, 1.
2. The rutter (sailing instructions) prepared for the king's voyage underlay other early accounts of Islay. See MacDonald, *General View of the Agriculture of the Hebrides*, 823; Adams and Fortune (eds), *Alexander Lindsay a rutter of the Scottish Seas*.
3. The NLS's copy of this map can be accessed at <http://www.nls.uk/maps/blaeu/page.cfm?id=98.html>. It is reproduced in Stone, *Illustrated Maps of Scotland*, pl. 40.
4. <http://www.nls.uk/maps/early/581.html>.
5. Dawson and Dawson, 'Holocene relative sea level change', 97.
6. Green and Harding, 'Climate of the Inner Hebrides'.
7. The following section on geology is by Nigel Ruckley. See also BGS maps, *South Islay* and *North Islay*, and Maltman et al., *A Guide to the Geology of Islay*.
8. Thompson, 'On the Geology of the island of Islay'. These tillites were previously known as boulder beds, and the term diamictite is now used for some of them.
9. Walker, *Report on the Hebrides*, 98. See also Alonzo Gray and Adams, *Elements of Geology*, 148; and Walker, 'The Islay-Jura Dyke Swarm'.
10. Wilkinson, 'The Geology of Islay', 64; Hole and Morrison, 'The differentiated dolerite boss, Cnoc Rhaonastil'.
11. Peacock, 'Quaternary geology of the Inner Hebrides'.
12. Dawson et al., 'Late Glacial Relative Sea Level Changes, Ruantallain-Shian Bay'.
13. Hudson and Henderson, 'Soils of the Inner Hebrides'.
14. The terminology for these landscape types is taken from Environmental Resources Management's report *Landscape assessment of Argyll and the Firth of Clyde*, 63ff.
15. *Shawfield's Day Bk*, 180.
16. Fraser Darling, *West Highland Survey*, 66.
17. Morton, *The Flora of Islay and Jura*. See also, Currie and Murray, 'Flora and vegetation of the Inner Hebrides'.
18. For a fuller, readable account of Islay's animal population, see Newton, *Islay*, 43–59. See also Berry, 'Evolution of animals and plants in the Inner Hebrides'.
19. Campbell and Williamson, 'Salmon and freshwater fishes of the Inner Hebrides'.
20. Booth, *Birds in Islay*; Reed, Currie and Love, 'Birds of the Inner Hebrides'; Elliott, *Birds of Islay*; Ogilvie, *The Birds of Islay*.
21. Ogilvie, 'Wildfowl of Islay'.
22. Bergin, 'An Address to Aonghus of Islay', 65; Thomson, 'The Harlaw Brosnachadh', 160–61.
23. For example in the 1860s, 'Gowrie', *Off the Chain*, 286–88.
24. See Newton, *A Handbook of the Scottish Gaelic World*, 121–23.
25. Macdonald, *Missions to the Gaels*, 27.

26. Campbell, *Popular Tales*.
27. Museum of Islay Life, *An Islay Miscellany*, 19–21.
28. Martin, *Western Islands*, 178–79; Pennant, *Tour*, 219–20.
29. For the toothache stone, see Caldwell, *Islay, Jura and Colonsay*, 215. The Kilchoman Cross is dealt with by Joseph Anderson in Somerville, 'Notice of an Ancient Structure', 139. See also Celoria, 'Notes on lore and customs in the district near Portnahaven'.
30. Pennant, *Tour*, 218–19.
31. Hunter, *For the People's Cause*, 13–14, 51–52; Reid, 'Shinty, Nationalism and Celtic Politics', 115–16.
32. *SA* (1794), xi, 287. See also Pennant, *Tour*, 218–19.
33. MacDonald, *Sketches of Islay*, 23.
34. NLS, MSS ACC 6223/14, bundle 2.
35. Edwards, *Seanchas Ìle*.
36. For a detailed analysis of Gaelic in Islay since the late nineteenth century, see Duwe, *Ìle, Diùra & Colbhasa*.

Chapter 2 Prehistory and Early History

1. This chapter is by Alan Macniven.
2. For a fuller account of Islay in prehistoric times, see Caldwell, *Islay, Jura and Colonsay*, 3–15, 95–113.
3. Edwards and Mithen, 'The colonization of the Hebridean Islands of Western Scotland'.
4. Caldwell, *Islay, Jura and Colonsay*, 99–101.
5. The Cragabus chamber, and part of the cairn façade, are beside the road at NR 329 451. The Port Charlotte chamber with remains of its cairn are next to the football pitch at NR 248 576. See also Caldwell, *Islay, Colonsay and Jura*, 106, 108.
6. Caldwell, *Islay, Colonsay and Jura*, 111–12.
7. The Coultoon Stone Circle is easily accessible from the road from Portnahaven to Kilchiaran, at NR 195 569. See Caldwell, *Islay, Colonsay and Jura*, 110–11.
8. Caldwell, *Islay, Colonsay and Jura*, 122–23.
9. For a fuller discussion of these early references see: Watson, *Celtic Placenames*, 23–34, 37; Rivet and Smith, *The Place-Names of Roman Britain*, 131–32, 140; MacBain, *Place-Names of the Highlands and Islands*.
10. See, for example, Forsyth, *Language in Pictland*; Sharpe, *Adomnán's Life of St Columba*, 32.
11. The provenance and significance of the *Senchus* and related documents are discussed at length elsewhere. See, for example, Dumville, 'Ireland and North Britain in the Earlier Middle Ages'; Sharpe, 'The Thriving of Dalriada'; Bannerman, *Studies in the History of Dalriada*; Anderson, *Kings and Kingship in early Scotland*; Ó Corráin, 'Book Review: Studies in the History of Dál Riata: John Bannerman'; Lamont, 'Old Land Denominations and the "Old Extent" in Islay; Thomas, 'On Islay Place-Names'.
12. Laing and Laing, *The Picts and the Scots*, 9–15.
13. See: Campbell, 'Were the Scots Irish?'; Lane and Campbell, *Dunadd*, 31–37.
14. For a modern translation with substantial introductory and explanatory notes see Sharpe, *Adomnán's Life of St Columba*.
15. For further discussion on the etymology of the island-name Islay, see: Watson, *Celtic Place-Names*, 87; Thomas, *On Islay Place-Names*, 248.
16. Sharpe, *Adomnán's Life of St Columba*, 172–73.
17. The legal sources for social structure in Early Medieval Ireland are set out at length in Jaski, *Early Irish Kingship and Succession*; Gerriets, 'Economy and Society: Clientship according to the Irish Laws', 42–61; Gerriets, 'Kingship and Exchange in Pre-Viking Ireland', 39–72; Byrne, *Irish Kings and High-Kings*. But, for a critical review of the Irish

laws on kingship and succession in a Dál Riatan context, see Sharpe, 'The Thriving of Dalriada', 47–61.

18. See Nieke, 'Settlement Patterns in the 1st Millennium AD: a case study of the Island of Islay', 95–115.

19. Macniven, The Norse in Islay, 49–50.

20. More specific details on Islay's archaeological heritage can be found in the RCAHMS inventory, *Argyll 5*, or on their online database, CANMORE, see <http://www.rcahms.gov.uk> (accessed 31 July 2007).

21. An asterisk (*) at the beginning of a word is used to indicate that it is a reconstruction, not attested in early sources.

22. For example, RCAHMS, Neg. no. D14304 (1997).

23. See references cited in note 4, above.

24. Thomas, 'On Islay Place-Names', 253; Maceacharna, *The Lands of the Lordship*, 31.

25. Thomas, 'On Islay Place-Names', 252; Lamont, 'Old Land Denominations' (Part 2), 97; Maceacharna, *The Lands of the Lordship*, 30.

26. Maceacharna *The Lands of the Lordship*, 31.

27. Thomas, 'On Islay Farm-Names', 252; Lamont, 'Old Land Denominations' (Part 2), 97; Lamont, *The Early History of Islay*, 8.

28. It first appears as Ochtownwruch in a royal grant of 1494 to John MacIan. Later versions from rentals include Ochtinfrich (1507) and Octonafreitch (1722).

29. Thomas, 'On Islay Farm-Names', 250–1; Maceacharna, *The Lands of the Lordship*, 20.

30. Thomas, 'On Islay Farm-Names', 251–2; Maceacharna *The Lands of the Lordship*, 30.

31. Thomas, 'On Islay Farm-Names', 250; Watson, *Celtic Place-Names*, 92; Bannerman, *Studies in the History of Dalriada*, 107; Maceacharna, *The Lands of the Lordship*, 30–1.

32. See, for example: Bannerman *Studies in the History of Dalriada*, 136–9; Nieke 'Settlement Patterns in the 1st Millennium AD'; Lamont, 'Old Land Denominations' (Part 2).

33. Dumville, 'Ireland and North Britain in the Earlier Middle Ages', 202; Bannerman, *Studies in the History of Dalriada*, 49.

34. See Macniven, The Norse in Islay, Chapter 8.5, and below, Chapter 8.

35. Caldwell, *Islay, Jura and Colonsay*, 23.

36. See Etchingham, *Church Organisation in Ireland*.

37. Anderson, *Kings and Kingship in early Scotland*, 8.

38. For a recent discussion making the case that Hinba is Jura, see Marsden, *Sea-Road of the Saints*, 101–27. For Nave Island and Kilchoman, see Caldwell, *Islay, Jura and Colonsay*, 23–24, 145–46, 151–52. The Early Christian disk-headed slab at Kilchoman stands on a surviving section of a massive bank with ditch, no doubt representing part of the early monastic enclosure. Its extent appears to be reflected in an early-nineteenth-century farm map for Kilchoman in the Islay Estate Papers. There is a photostat of the map in the NAS. Compare with RCAHMS, *Argyll 5*, nos 366, 383.

39. NMRS:NR27SE 1.00 (Kilnave Chapel and Cross); RCAHMS, *Argyll 5*, no. 374/1; Fisher, *Early Medieval Sculpture*, no. 374.

40. NMRS:NR45SE 3.00 (Kildalton Chapel and Cross); RCAHMS, *Argyll 5*, no. 367/1; Fisher, *Early Medieval Sculpture*, no. 367.

41. Swift, Irish Influence on Ecclesiastical Settlements in Scotland, 338–41; McEacharna, *The Lands of the Lordship*, 41–53; Watson, *Celtic Placenames*.

42. NMRS:NR36NE 2; RCAHMS, *Argyll 5*, no. 353.

43. Swift, Irish Influence on Ecclesiastical Settlements in Scotland, 310–12, 319–20.

44. *AU* 795.3; *AU* 798.2. Unless otherwise stated, all annalistic references have been taken from CELT (Corpus of Electronic Texts), the online resource for Irish history, literature and politics. A Project of the History Department, University College Cork – <http://www.ucc.ie/celt/> (accessed 6 June 2005).

45. See, for example, Smyth, *Warlords and Holy Men*, 142–3; Smyth, 'The effect of Scandinavian raiders on the English and Irish churches', 17–22; Dumville, *The Churches of Northern Britain in the First Viking Age*, 12–15.

46. For typically florid examples of Victorian scholarship on this topic, see Howarth, 'The Columban Clergy of North Britain and their harrying by the Norsemen'; Goodrich-Freer, 'The Norsemen in the Hebrides'.

47. Shetelig, 'The Viking Graves', 67–111; Skre, 'The Social Context of Settlement in Norway in the First Millennium AD'.

48. Charles-Edwards, 'Irish Warfare before 1100'; Ó Corráin, 'Viking Ireland – Afterthoughts'.

49. Pálsson and Edwards, *Eyrbyggja Saga*, 25–26.

50. See, for example, Smyth, *Warlords and Holy Men*; Jennings, 'Historical and linguistic evidence for Gall-Gaidheil and Norse in Western Scotland'.

51. The historical details of Lochlainn and the Viking Age *Gàidhealtachd* are dealt with in Ó Corráin's 'The Vikings in Scotland and Ireland' and 'Viking Ireland – Afterthoughts'.

52. *AU* 853.2.

53. Power, 'Scotland in the Norse Sagas'.

54. Woolf, 'The Age of Sea-Kings: 900–1300', 94, 98.

55. Nelson, *The Annals of St-Bertin*, 65.

56. Woolf, 'Dun Nechtain, Fortriu and the Geography of the Picts'.

57. *AU* 740.3.

58. *Chron. Man*, f33v.

59. Brooks, 'Gall-Gaidhil and Galloway'. Oram and Stell, *Galloway: Land and Lordship*, 97–116.

60. *FA* 856 (§247); *AU* 856.3; *AU* 856.6; *AU* 857.1; *FA* 858 (§260); *FA* 858 (§263).

61. See, for example, Nicolaisen, 'Norse Settlement in the Northern and Western Isles: Some Place Name Evidence'; Nicolaisen, *Scottish place-names*, 122–24.

62. Stewart, 'Lexical Imposition: Old Norse vocabulary in Scottish Gaelic', 406.

63. Smyth, 'Scandinavian raiders', 4–9.

64. Smyth, 'Scandinavian raiders', 21–22; Holm, 'The Slave Trade of Dublin, Ninth to Twelfth Centuries'; Hudson, 'The changing economy of the Irish Sea province: AD 900 – 1300'.

65. Thomas, 'On Islay Farm-Names', 273; Thomas, 'Did the Norsemen Extirpate the Inhabitants of the Hebrides in the Ninth Century', 503.

66. NMRS:NR26NW 4.0–4.05, 22; RCAHMS, *Argyll 5*, no. 293.

67. NMRS:NR36SW 2; RCAHMS, *Argyll 5*, no. 301.

68. NMRS:NR35SW 1; RCAHMS, *Argyll 5*, no. 296.

69. Stevenson, *Sylloge of Anglo-Saxon Coins*, xxi.

70. These Úi Ímar dynasts were descended from the ninth-century Ívarr Ragnarsson, said to have been king of the Norsemen of all Ireland and Britain (*AU* 873.3). See Woolf, 'The Age of the Sea-Kings', 95–96.

71. Duffy, 'Irishmen and Islesmen in the Kingdoms of Dublin and Man 1052–1171'; Woolf, 'The Age of Sea-Kings'.

72. Maghnus/Maccus son of Harald/Aralt is encountered in a military expedition to Ireland in *AFM* 970.13. His brother Gofraidh mac Arailt is dignified *rí Innsi Gall* ('king of the islands of the foreigners – i.e. The Hebrides') on his death in *AU* 989.4.

73. *AFM* 960.14; *AFM* 970.13.

74. Munch and Goss, *The Chronicle of Man and the Sudreys*, 50, no 2.

75. Monro's *Western Isles*, 299–346, 310.

76. Martin, *The Isles of Scotland*, 148.

77. *AFM* 979.5.

78. NMRS:NR34NE 18; RCAHMS, *Argyll 5*, no. 351; Fisher, *Early Medieval Sculpture*, no. 351.

79. Megaw, 'Norseman and Native in the Kingdom of the Isles'.

80. Smyth, *Warlords and Holy Men*, 141.

81. Woolf, 'The Diocese of the Sudreyar'.

82. Earl, *Tales of Islay*, 18.
83. Lamont, *The Early History of Islay*, 16.

Chapter 3 Somerled, the MacSorleys and Islay

1. *Chron. Man*, fol. 37v. The sea battle is thought by many, on no good authority, to have taken place off the coast of Islay. The details of the partition are not given in the *Chronicles* but are reconstructed from what is known about the land-holdings of Somerled's descendants. Woolf, 'The Age of the Sea-Kings', 105, suggests that it would have been Ranald rather than Dugald who was offered the kingship.
2. *Chron. Man*, fol. 37v–38r, 39v.
3. Sellar, 'The origins and ancestry of Somerled', 123–42.
4. Woolf, 'The origins and ancestry of Somerled'.
5. Sykes, *Adam's Curse A Future Without Men*, 203–25.
6. For Malcolm and his son Donald, see Ross, 'The Identity of the "Prisoner of Roxburgh"'. This Malcolm has wrongly been identified as 'Malcolm MacHeth'.
7. For Somerled's career in general, see McDonald, *The Kingdom of the Isles*, 39–67; Marsden, *Somerled and the Emergence of Gaelic Scotland*. Duncan and Brown, 'Argyll and the Isles in the earlier middle ages', 203, suggest that Bute may have passed from Somerled to the Scottish Crown, and thence to the Stewart family, as a result of the peace between Malcolm IV and Somerled in 1160.
8. *ES*, ii, 254; *Chron. Man*, fol. 39r; Marsden, *Somerled*, 98–101. For clues on the size of ships of the period and the number of men that rowed them, see Rixson, *The West Highland Galley*, 64–78.
9. Pennant, *Tour*, 215.
10. Maceacharna, *The Lands of the Lordship*, 69; Earl, *Tales of Islay*, 15.
11. Duncan and Brown, 'Argyll and the Isles', 198; McDonald, *The Kingdom of the Isles*, 70.
12. Cameron, *Reliquiae Celticae*, ii, 157.
13. Cowan and Easson, *Medieval Religious Houses*, 59, 151.
14. Cowan and Easson, *Medieval Religious Houses*, 59, 77, 151; *Registrum de Passelet*, 125; *HP*, i, 12.
15. Reeves (ed.), *Life of Saint Columba*, 353–55; *ES*, ii, 363.
16. *Monro's Western Isles*, 56. The lands are specified in a charter by the Abbot of Iona to MacLean of Duart in 1588. See *Coll de Rebus Alban*, 178.
17. Caldwell, *Islay, Jura and Colonsay*, 150–52.
18. Cowan and Easson, *Medieval Religious Houses*, 235.
19. See Sellar, 'Hebridean Sea Kings', 187–218. The date for this event is as suggested by Thomson, *The New History of Orkney*, 126. For the saga account, see Pálsson and Edwards, *Orkneyinga Saga*, 221.
20. *Chron. Man*, fol. 40v.
21. *Registrum de Passelet*, 125.
22. *RMS*, ii, no. 3170; *Registrum de Passelet*, 149.
23. *Monro's Western Isles*, 57.
24. Woolf, 'The Diocese of the Sudreyar'; Watt, 'Bishops in the Isles before 1203', 118.
25. *Chron. Man*, fol. 41r; *ES*, ii, 393, 395; Duncan and Brown, 'Argyll and the Isles', 199–200. Garmoran included the districts of Moidart, Arisaig, Morar and Knoydart.
26. Cameron, *Reliquiae Celticae*, ii, 157; Sellar, 'Hebridean Sea Kings', 200. In this paper Sellar suggests (p. 201) that Ruairi son of Ranald was the MacSorley killed at Ballyshannon, rather than Donald as given here, following the suggestion of Duffy, 'The Bruce Brothers and the Irish Sea World', 56. Compare also Duffy, 'The Lords of Galloway, earls of Carrick, and the Bissets of the Glens', 47; and Woolf, 'A dead man at Ballyshannon', which also favours Ruairi.

27. *HP*, i, 13–14.
28. Dunbar and Duncan, 'Tarbert Castle', 13–14.
29. Johnsen, 'The payments from the Hebrides and Isle of Man to the crown of Norway'.
30. McDonald, *The Kingdom of the Isles*, 89–91; *Chron. Man*, fol. 44v.
31. *ES*, ii, 548–9, 554.
32. Stevenson and Wood, *Scottish Heraldic Seals*, iii, 483; *ALI*, lxxx–lxxxi, 280.
33. Bergin, 'An Address to Aonghus of Islay', 65.
34. *CDS*, i, no 2041; Duffy, 'The Bruce Brothers and the Irish Sea World', 57. Compare Duffy, 'The prehistory of the galloglass', 16–18.
35. *ES*, ii, 605–42; Cowan, 'Norwegian Sunset – Scottish Dawn', 103–31.
36. *ES*, ii, 635, 649–57; *APS*, i, 109, 420–21, 447.
37. *APS*, i, 424.
38. Stevenson, *Documents*, i, 22–23, 337; *Charters of the Abbey of Crosraguel*, i, 12–13.
39. *HP*, i, 17.
40. Murray, 'A House Divided Against Itself'.
41. *CDS*, v, no. 152; *ALI*, 281; *Rot. Scot.*, i, 22, 40; Stevenson, *Documents*, ii, 187–91; Murray, 'A House Divided Against Itself', 222.
42. *AU*, ii, 393. I have followed Sean Duffy in making this identification. See his 'The "Continuation" of Nicholas Trevet', 311–12. Murray, 'A House Divided Against Itself', 222–23, argues that it was Angus Mor's son, Alexander Og.
43. *HP*, i, 15–16. The Alexander in question is here described as brother of Angus – presumably meaning Angus Og – Lord of the Isles.
44. *Rot. Scot.*, i, 21.
45. *CDS*, v, no. 472 (b); Dunbar & Duncan, 'Tarbert Castle', 16–17; *Registrum de Passelet*, 128; Barbour, *The Bruce*, 144–45.
46. *CDS*, v, no. 152.
47. Stevenson, *Documents*, ii, 435–7.
48. Duffy, 'The "Continuation" of Nicholas Trevet', 311–12.
49. Professor Duncan suggests that Rathlin is a mistake for Islay. Barbour, *The Bruce*, 148.
50. *Chron. Guisborough*, 370, 377–78; *Chron. Fordun*, ii, 335.
51. *Chron. Lanercost*, 179–80; *CDS*, iv, 489; Duffy, 'The Bruce Brothers and the Irish Sea World', 51–53.
52. *Chron. Lanercost*, 188. Fordun was presumably mistaken in having 'Donald of the Isles' as the Galwegian leader. *Chron. Fordun*, ii, 337; *APS*, i, 459.
53. Barbour, *The Bruce*, 420; *RMS*, i, app. 2, nos 56–58, 661. Compare Murray, 'A House Divided Against Itself', 224, which suggests that Angus Og did not hold Islay, and that that island had passed to Alexander, a son of Alexander Og.
54. Bannerman, *The Beatons*, 10. *HP*, i, 16. The description is actually said by MacDonald to be of Angus Mor. His history is notably confused at this point, and since he has Angus Mor as Bruce's supporter it may be logical to assume it is really of Angus Og.
55. I have followed McDonald, *The Kingdom of the Isles*, 187, in identifying this Alexander as Angus Og's son. It has to be recognised that this is little better than a guess. Others have suggested that he was Alexander the son of Angus Mor or Alexander the brother of Angus Mor. See, for instance, Lamont, 'Alexander of Islay, Son of Angus Mór'; *ALI*, 281. More recently, Murray, 'A House Divided Against Itself', 223–24, has argued that he was an otherwise unrecorded son of Alexander, the elder brother of Angus Og, and that this grant was based on an entitlement to these lands through marriage to Juliana of Lorn.
56. <http://www.ucc.ie/celt/published/T100A/> (Annals of Loch Cé) LC1318.7; *AI*, 429; Duffy, 'The "Continuation" of Nicholas Trevet', 314.
57. Duffy, 'The "Continuation" of Nicholas Trevet', 308, 314; Dunbar and Duncan, 'Tarbert Castle', 13–16; RPS, A1325.2, accessed 7 January 2008 (*APS*, i, 123). Murray, 'A House Divided Against Itself', 224, considers he may be another, otherwise unrecorded, son of Alexander Og and Juliana of Lorn.

Chapter 4 The Lords of the Isles

1. *Scotichronicon*, vii, 111; *ALI*, no. 1. The grant of Knapdale at this time has been described as abortive. See RCAHMS, *Argyll 7*, 259.
2. *Rot. Scot.*, i, 463–64, 515, 516, 535; *ALI*, nos 2, 3.
3. *AU*, iii, 19; *ALI*, nos 2, 3, 11.
4. *HP*, i, 21; Martin, *Western Islands*, 273; 'Caldwell, Finlaggan, Islay – stones and inauguration ceremonies', 61–75.
5. Monro's *Western Isles*, 56–57; Caldwell, 'Finlaggan – stones and inauguration ceremonies', 69–72. Monro's list of council members presumably relates to the late fifteenth century rather than the time of John I.
6. *HP*, i, 24–25, 27. See also Chapter 7 for more information on the MacKays, MacBraynes and MacDuffies.
7. *HP*, i, 25; MacLean-Bristol, *Warriors and Priests*, 18–30; *MacFarlane's Genealogical Collections*, v, 123; Major, *A History of Greater Britain*, 348.
8. *RRS*, vi, 505.
9. *Chron. Knighton*, ii, 25. John is here described as 'de Orgayle' (of Argyll).
10. *RRS*, vi, nos 72, 73.
11. *Rot. Scot.*, i, 677; *Foedera* (2nd ed.), v, 530–31.
12. *HP*, i, 73–75; *RMS*, i, no. 412.
13. *ALI*, no. 5.
14. *RRS*, vi, nos 148, 150 (pp. 174, 179, 185, 189–90).
15. Penman, *David II*, deals with the whole relationship between the king and the Lord of the Isles in the years from 1357 to 1371 in considerable detail, especially pp. 338–39, 352–53, 362, 368, 380–82, 391–92, 395. For John's submission, see *ALI*, no. 6.
16. *ALI*, xxix–xxxi; Boardman, *The Campbells*, 95–98, 184–90.
17. Cameron, *Reliquiae Celticae*, ii, 159–61.
18. Caldwell and Ruckley, 'Domestic Architecture in the Lordship of the Isles', 96–121; Caldwell, *Islay, Jura and Colonsay*, 163–75.
19. *Chron. Fordun*, ii, 39; *Islay Bk*, 541; Jameson, *Mineralogy of the Scottish Isles,* i, 162.
20. Cameron, *Reliquiae Celticae*, ii, 161. 1387 is the date of death preferred by the editors of *ALI*, 287.
21. *ALI*, no. 7; Cameron, *Reliquiae Celticae*, ii, 161. The shaft of Ranald's Cross on Texa is now in the collections of the National Museums Scotland.
22. Cameron, *Reliquiae Celticae*, ii, 161.
23. Cameron, *Reliquiae Celticae*, ii, 161.
24. *Rot. Scot.*, ii, 94–95; *ALI*, no. 15; *Foedera*, vii, 626, 639, 657, 716, 777, 824; *Scotichronicon*, viii, 29; *Chron. Wyntoun*, iii, 75–76. We have accepted the argument that the writer of *ALI*, no. 15, a letter from a John MacDonald to Richard II in 1395, was not John, brother of the Lord of the Isles, but a leading Irish Galloglas. See Nicholls, 'Anglo-French Ireland and after', 386–88.
25. *Rot. Scot.*, ii, 155–56; *Foedera*, viii, 146; Boardman, *The Early Stewart Kings*, 240–41.
26. Kingston, *Ulster and the Isles in the Fifteenth Century*, 49–53.
27. *HP*, i, 32; *RMS*, ii, no. 3085; Caldwell, *Islay, Jura and Colonsay*, 160–63.
28. *HP*, i, 32; *ALI*, no. 14; *Registrum Episcopatus Moraviensis*, nos 272, 303.
29. RPS, 1398/6–8, accessed 7 January 2008 (*APS*, i, 570, 571, 575). For the significance of the titles of the Dukedoms of Albany and Rothesay, see Boardman, *The Early Stewart Kings*, 207–08.
30. Thomson, 'The Harlaw Brosnachadh', 147–69.
31. Major, *A History of Greater Britain*, 348–49; *Scotichronicon*, viii, 75–77.
32. *Scotichronicon*, viii, 77; *ER*, iv, 213. The main pro-MacDonald account of the battle is given by Hugh MacDonald (*HP*, i, 28–31). For a recent detailed reconstruction of what happened in the battle, see Marren, *Grampian Battlefields*, 89–102. The ballad of *The*

Battle of Harlaw published in Child, *The English and Scottish Popular Ballads*, iii, 316–20, contains nothing of historical worth for this book. Other late and not totally reliable sources include *The Wardlaw Manuscript*, 92, 94–95.

33. Steer and Bannerman, *Late Medieval Monumental Sculpture in the West Highlands*. Edinburgh, 1977, 149–50, 205; *ALI*, no. 19.
34. Nicholson, *Scotland The Later Middle Ages*, 192–93, 462. The authority of the Bishops of Sodor based in the Isle of Man may have for long been minimal in the Isles. It was open to challenge, as in 1331 when the canons of Snizort sent a deputation to the Archbishop of Nidaros to persuade him – unsuccessfully – to have their election of Cormac as their bishop recognised. Cormac may have been a member of a local legal family. See Thomas, 'Political rift or ambitious cleric'.
35. Nicholls, 'Notes on the Genealogy of Clann Eoin Mhoir', 13: Cameron, *Reliquiae Celticae*, ii, 161, 163; *HP*, i, 34.
36. Cf. Oram, 'The Lordship of the Isles', 132. Oram does not see Donald as a 'Gaelic separatist' and views the acquisition of the title of earl as something that Donald should have valued.
37. *ALI*, no. 16 and pp. 299–300; Simms, *From Kings to Warlords*, 33–35; *CDS*, iv, no. 698.
38. *ALI*, nos 16 and 18. Bannerman, 'The Lordship of the Isles', 228, suggests that grants like that of 1408 may often have been delivered orally. The 1408 charter may only have been committed to vellum because the grantee was a churchman and therefore orientated towards the written word.
39. Cameron, *Reliquiae Celticae*, ii, 161; *ALI*, liii, no. 62, pp. 245–46.
40. *Scotichronicon*, viii, 245.
41. *Scotichronicon*, viii, 245; *AFM*, ii, 875. For James's stay in Ireland, see Kingston, *Ulster and the Isles*, 55–56, 68.
42. RPS, 1426/21, accessed 7 January 2008 (*APS*, ii, 11).
43. *HP*, i, 38; *Scotichronicon*, viii, 319; Brown, *James I*, 83.
44. *ER*, iv, 414; *Scotichronicon*, viii, 259, 261.
45. *HP*, i, 39; *Scotichronicon*, viii, 261.
46. *ER*, iv, 516; *AU*, iii, 875. See also Brown, *James I*, 74–76, 101–02.
47. *RMS*, ii, no. 163. This joint keepership was unusual. Montgomery may have been the obvious choice for the job. It is probable that he was fluent in Gaelic since his mother was Alexander's aunt, but this would also have been the reason why he could not have been trusted to hold the post alone.
48. *Scotichronicon*, viii, 261, 263. The supposition that the excursion into Knapdale and Kintyre was led by the king himself depends on a payment in the exchequer rolls for the repair of the king's crossbow (*balestarum regis*) while in transit towards the Isles by sea. *ER*, iv, 511.
49. *Scotichronicon*, viii, 261. A much fuller, though not necessarily very accurate, account of the battle and events surrounding it is given by Hugh MacDonald. See *HP*, i, 40–44.
50. *HP*, i, 45; *ALI*, no. 23 and p. 302.
51. *ALI*, nos 21, 22 and 105. Greenan was granted by John II Lord of the Isles in 1475 to John Davidson, and his charter (no. 105) can be read to imply the land was held prior to that by his father Gilbert. The Davidsons may have been a family of Ayr merchants. They held on to Greenan into the sixteenth century.
52. *CSSR*, iv, no. 105.
53. Watson (ed.), *Scottish Verse From The Book Of The Dean Of Lismore*, 81.
54. *HP*, i, 47.
55. Kingston, *Ulster and the Isles*, 102–03.
56. *ER*, v, 86, 167.
57. The source for these events is *The Auchinleck Chronicle*, McGladdery, *James II*, 167–68, 169. For the years they took place I have followed Grant, 'The Revolt of the Lord of the Isles and the Death of the Earl of Douglas', 169–74; and Boardman, *The Campbells*, 153–54.

58. The bond does not survive. I have followed McGladdery, *James II*, 63–66, in dating it to about 1450 or 1451. Cf. Kingston, *Ulster and the Isles*, 79–81, where the bond is dated to 1445 and the suggestion made that it was Donald Balloch rather than the Earl of Ross (Alexander) who was a party to it.

59. Thomson, *The New History of Orkney*, 194.

60. Boardman, *The Campbells*, 169.

61. *Chron. Auchinleck*, 231–32; Boardman, *The Campbells*, 174–79, 181; Thomson, *History of Orkney*, 196–97. John appears to have made no more appearances in person at Parliaments, prior to his forfeiture. He did, however, send procurators to the Parliaments in June 1455, October 1468 and May 1471. *APS*, ii, 77, 87, 98.

62. *ALI*, nos 74, 75.

63. Boardman, *The Campbells*, 187–88.

64. *Islay Bk*, 360; *RPC*, x, 347–48; McGladdery, *James II*, 167.

65. RPS, 1475/26, accessed 7 January 2008 (*APS*, ii, 111).

66. Macdougall, *James III*, 121–23. Donald Balloch's date of death is given as 1476 in an early-seventeenth-century Irish manuscript. Nicholls, 'Notes on the Genealogy of Clann Eoin Mhoir', 12. A. and A. MacDonald, *The Clan Donald*, ii, 509–10, claim Donald Balloch died on an island in Loch Gruinart on Islay at the end of 1476. This should be treated with caution.

67. RPS, A1476/7/1, accessed 7 January 2008 (*APS*, ii, 113); *ALI*, no. A24.

68. *RMS*, ii, no. 1246.

69. Macdougall, *James III*, 146; Boardman, *The Campbells*, 225–27.

70. *ER*, viii, 487; *HP*, i, 49, 51; Macdougall, *James III*, 122. The story of Atholl's capture is related in traditional histories as a separate episode, as revenge for Atholl's supposed kidnapping of Angus's son Donald Dubh. This, it seems to me, rather unlikely version of events can be read in Gregory, *History*, 53–54.

71. *ALI*, no. A37; Cameron, *Reliquiae Celticae*, ii, 163; *HP*, i, 47–50. Macdougall, *James III*, 146; *RMS*, iii, no. 2835.

72. *ALI*, no. 119, including the comment on p. 188.

73. Cameron, *Reliquiae Celticae*, ii, 163; *HP*, i, 51–52. The description of him as king of Islay comes from a poem on Diarmid O'Cairbre's head by the Dean of Knoydart. See Watson, *The Book Of The Dean Of Lismore*, 97. The MacKenzies at this time are dealt with by MacCoinnich, ' "Kingis rabellis" to "Cudich 'n Rìgh" ', 175–200. See especially 190 no. 73.

74. *ER*, ix, 404, 586.

75. I have followed here the interpretation offered by Boardman, *The Campbells*, 253.

76. *AU*, iii, 383, 1213.

77. Gregory, *History*, 55–58; *ALI*, 311; *ER*, x, 370.

78. Boardman, *The Campbells*, 262–63.

79. Gregory, *History*, 86–90, provides a useful account of the events of this period. The detail, however, of the governor of Dunaverty being hanged in sight of the king is based only on 'a tradition well known in the Western Highlands'. For the summons for treason, see *TA*, i, 238. No record survives of King James re-granting John Mor his ancestral lands in Kintyre and Islay.

80. Nicholls, 'Notes on the Genealogy of Clann Eoin Mhoir', 13; Boardman, *The Campbells*, 264.

81. *RMS*, ii, nos 2216, 3001; Boardman, *The Campbells*, 267.

82. *Islay Bk*, 28–30; Cameron, *Reliquiae Celticae*, ii, 163; *AU*, iii, 443; *HP*, i, 60–61.

83. For these castles, see the RCAHMS, *Argyll 1* and *Argyll 7*.

84. *ER*, xii, 587–90.

85. *ER*, xii, 709–10.

86. *RMS*, iii, no. 2835; MacLean-Bristol, *Warriors and Priests*, 70–71; *ADCP*, 81, 88.

87. *RMS*, ii, no. 2329; *RMS* (1620–33), no. 1610. The name of the farm of Coultorsay in the Rhinns might possibly contain some memory of Torlissay.

88. Steer and Bannerman, *Late Medieval Monumental Sculpture*, 147; *RSS*, ii, no. 3098.

89. *Coll de Rebus Alban*, 15: RCAHMS, *Argyll 5*, no. 378; Caldwell, *Islay, Jura and Colonsay*, 149–50.

90. *Islay Bk*, 89, 91; Caldwell, *Islay, Jura and Colonsay*, 152.

91. A papal letter of Clement VII of Avignon dated 1391 refers to the parish church of St Fynan on Islay, Argyll diocese. See *CPLS (1378–1395)*, 169. This evidently results from an error in transcription. For the church buildings themselves, see Caldwell, *Islay, Jura and Colonsay*.

92. Cowan, *The Parishes of Medieval Scotland*, 94, 97, 99; Barrell, 'The Church in the West Highlands in the late middle ages', 23–46; *CSSR* (1423–28), 197–98; *CSSR*, iv, no. 790.

Chapter 5 Lords of Islay

1. Cameron, *Reliquiae Celticae*, ii, 165; *HP*, i, 61–62.

2. Macdougall, *James IV*, 178–79; Boardman, *The Campbells*, 278–79, 281–83.

3. The version of events given by Gregory in his *History of the Western Highlands*, 96, that Donald Dubh was a prisoner of Argyll in the Castle of Innis Chonnell in Loch Awe and was released from there by the men of Glencoe, cannot be sustained on the basis of the documentary evidence. Gregory was no doubt influenced by his knowledge of later MacDonald–Campbell enmity. Government pronouncements that Donald Dubh was the bastard son of a bastard were clearly royal propaganda, lacking in truth, or at least relevance for the Gaelic world.

4. Macdougall, *James IV*, 179–90.

5. Viz., son of John Cathanach. This is how he is generally referred to in Scottish government sources though he signed himself 'of Dunyvaig'.

6. Cameron, *Reliquiae Celticae*, ii, 165; *HP*, i, 58–59; *ALI*, 285, 306; Nicholls, 'Genealogy of Clann Eoin Mhoir', 13; *Henry VIII L&P*, v, no. 1246. Compare Gregory, *History of the Western Highlands*, 114–26.

7. *ALI*, 306.

8. *RSS*, i, no. 2722; *ADCP*, 79–80: *ER*, xv, 165; 431–34; *ER*, xvi, 105. The lands were mostly in South Kintyre, but it appears that Alexander gave £8 8s of land in North Kintyre to his brother Angus.

9. *RSS*, i, no. 3048; *Cawdor Bk*, 133–35; MacLean-Bristol, *Warriors and Priests*, 95–96.

10. *HP*, i, 62.

11. *AU*, iii, 539–49; *AFM*, ii, 1353–63; *AC*, 641–45. *ALI*, 295, no. 12 misidentifies this Alexander Carrach. He has also been confused with Alexander of Dunyvaig, e.g. Hayes-McCoy, *Scots Mercenary Forces in Ireland*, genealogy table no. II. See Nicholls, 'Genealogy of Clann Eoin Mhoir', 19.

12. *AU*, iii, 549–55; *AFM*, ii, 1371; *AC*, 651.

13. *ADCP*, 326–29; *ER*, xv, 103, 675–76. The whole of James V's dealings with the Isles are dealt with in some detail in Cameron, *James V*, 228–48. The raiding extended to the Campbell lands of Craignish and the Lennox as well, and also involved the MacLeans. Both Alexander and Hector MacLean of Duart received remissions for this in 1531. See *RSS*, ii, nos 938, 939.

14. *ADCP*, 348–49, 356–58.

15. *ADCP*, 365–66.

16. *AFM*, 1395, 1413; *AC*, 669, 679; *AU*, iii, 587; *Henry VIII L&P*, v, no. 1246; vi, no. 610; *CSP Venice*, iv, no. 956: *ER*, xvi, 90, 566. See Cathcart, 'James V, king of Scotland – and Ireland?', which demonstrates the considerable interest that that king took in Ireland, and Gaelic Ireland in him.

17. *AU*, iii, 609; Pitcairn, *Criminal Trials*, I/i, 170–71; Campbell, 'Observations on the West Isles', 43.

18. *TA*, v, 432; vi, 212; vii, 159; *ALI*, 285.

19. *ER*, xvii, 90, 355, 485; *ADCP*, 81, 88; *Monro's Western Isles*, 56.

20. *Islay Bk*, 45–47.

21. *RMS*, iii, no. 2835.

22. *ADCP*, 482–83; Steer and Bannerman, *Medieval Sculpture*, 146–48.

23. She was unhappily married to the Sheriff of Bute when James is said to have abducted her. Campbell, 'Observations on the West Isles', 44.

24. AT, iv (26 Mar. and 11 Jul. 1538, 3 Dec. 1540); NAS RH6/1252, 1255, 1259; *TA,* vii, 470. Hill, *Fire and Sword*, 11–19, provides a recent account of Clann Iain Mhoir in the early sixteenth century, which takes the view that the Campbells were then out to oust the MacDonalds.

25. *TA*, vii, 323; *ER*, xvi, 278, 773; xvii, 296; *RSS*, iv, no. 4628; *Sadler Papers*, i, 266–67, 274–75.

26. *Sadler Papers*, i, 192, 214; *ER*, xv, 167, 430; xvi, 205; *TA*, viii, 247; *Henry VIII L&P*, XX, i, no. 865.

27. *Henry VIII L&P*, XX, ii, nos 120, 196–98, 293–94, 819, p. 217. For background on war with England at this time, see Merriman, *The Rough Wooings*.

28. *AFM*, ii, 1489; *AC*, 737.

29. *Henry VIII L&P*, XX, i, no. 1298; XX, ii, no. 42; Caldwell, *Islay, Jura and Colonsay*, 177. This would seem to be a more likely location for this Council Meeting than the island in the Sound of Islay suggested by Munro. See *Monro's Western Isles*, 58, 121.

30. *TA*, viii, 227, 308; *RSS*, iii, no. 1814.

31. *RMS*, ii, no. 3085; *Islay Bk*, 50–53. There was little justification for the Scottish government at this time to consider that Rathlin was its to grant.

32. Paton (ed.), *The MacKintosh Muniments*, no. 49; *Monro's Western Isles*, 56; *CSP Scotland*, i, nos 1066, 1072; *RPC*, i, 251, 272–73.

33. *RMS*, iv, nos 921, 1474, 1491; *RSS*, iv, no. 908; v, nos 1683, 1840, 2054; *MacKintosh Muniments*, no. 71; *Monro's Western Isles*, 76.

34. *Henry VIII L&;P* XXI, i, nos 114, 138, 219.

35. *RPS*, 1540/12/26, accessed 7 January 2008 (APS, ii, 360–61, 404–05).

36. *RPC*, i, 30; *Sadler Papers*, i, 431, 517.

37. *RPC*, i, 30; *CSP Scotland*, i, nos 19, 20; *Sadler Papers*, i, 517. For the part played by the Islesmen at Pinkie, see Caldwell, 'The Battle of Pinkie'.

38. *AFM*, ii, 1521; *CSP Ireland*, i, 116; Hill, *MacDonnells of Antrim*, 47–51.

39. *CSP Scotland*, i, no. 410; *CSP Ireland*, i, 136, 145, 146, 149, 245; *AFM*, ii, 1539, 1541.

40. *CSP Ireland*, i, 214, 254, 260, 261, 270, 271; *AFM*, ii, 1605.

41. *CSP Scotland*, i, nos 1018, 1066, 1166; *CSP Ireland*, i, 170.

42. *CSP Ireland*, i, 282; *AFM*, ii, 1605.

43. *Analecta Scotica*, no. cxv.

44. *CSP Ireland*, i, 324, 333, 335.

45. *C. Carew MSS*, ii, 427–28; Hill, *MacDonnells*, 181. For a recent biography of Sorley Boy, see Hill, *Fire and Sword.*

46. For the life and times of Angus of Dunyvaig and his son Sir James, I have depended heavily on Hayes-McCoy, *Scottish Mercenary Forces.*

47. Hill, *MacDonnells*, 171–72, no.162.

48. Hayes-McCoy, *Scots Mercenary Forces*, 324–38; Ohlmeyer, *Civil War and Restoration*, 19–28. James and Randal are often given the surname MacSorley in contemporary documents.

49. *CSP Ireland*, i, 363, 368, 415–20. For a recent overview of the part played by Clann Iain Mhoir in Ulster, see Morgan, 'The End of Gaelic Ulster'.

50. MacLean-Bristol, *Murder Under Trust*, 46–50.

51. *Coll de Rebus Alban*, 1–5, 12–18.

52. AT, vii (14 Feb. 1573–74, 12 Apr. 1575); viii (29 Sept. 1578). This siege was presumably successful as the castle is later described as ruinous.

53. *Islay Bk*, 78.
54. *CSP Ireland*, ii, 560; *RPC*, iii, 739.
55. Gordon, *Earldom of Sutherland*, 187–92. The same story is also given in slightly less detail in *The Historie and Life of King James the Sext*, 217–22.
56. Pitcairn, *Criminal Trials*, I, ii, 227.
57. *Islay Bk*, 86–88.
58. *Islay Bk*, 93–94.
59. Pitcairn, *Criminal Trials*, I, ii, 226–30.
60. *Coll de Rebus Alban*, 161–79.
61. Cowan, 'Clanship, kinship and the Campbell acquisition of Islay'; Campbell, *Clan Campbell*, ii, 91–117.
62. *HP*, i, 129–30; Cowan, 'Campbell acquisition of Islay'.
63. Campbell, 'Observations on the West Isles', 42.
64. Lynch, 'James VI and the Highland Problem'.
65. *ER*, xxii, 23, 28, 110, 157.
66. *The Historie and Life of King James the Sext*, 330; *Birrell's Diary*, 33.
67. *HP*, iii, 72–85; *RPC*, v, 321.
68. *Islay Bk*, 101, 103–05; *Birrell's Diary*, 43.
69. *Islay Bk*, 104.
70. *CSP Scotland*, XIII, i, no. 164. An expedition of several hundred settlers did indeed sail for Lewis in October 1598. See Macdonald, *Lewis*, 37.
71. Pitcairn, *Criminal Trials*, iii, 13. The battle and the traditions surrounding it are well covered by MacLean-Bristol, *Murder Under Trust*, 238–53. For an Islay traditional account, see Bruford and MacDonald, *Scottish Traditional Tales*, 429–34, 485–86.
72. *Birrell's Diary*, 47; *CSP*, xiii, no. 194.
73. Gregory, *History*, 285–86.
74. MacLean-Bristol, *Murder Under Trust*, 228, 245–52; Pitcairn, *Criminal Trials*, iii, 9; *CSP Scotland*, XIII, i, nos 126, 162; *RPC*, vi, 24.
75. *CSP Scotland*, XIII, ii, nos 497, 668.
76. *RPC*, v, 255–56; *CSP Scot*, XIII, ii, no. 497.
77. Hayes-McCoy, *Scots Mercenary Forces*, 324–25, 338.
78. Pitcairn, *Criminal Trials*, iii, 10; *CSP Ireland*, x, 352; *CSP Scot*, XIII, ii, no. 668.
79. *RMS*, vi, no. 1911; vii, no. 272; Cowan, 'Clanship, kinship and the Campbell acquisition of Islay', 151; McKerral, *Kintyre*, 25–26; Gregory, *History*, 309–10; Macdonald, *Lewis*, 40.
80. *HP*, iii, 86–88, 104–06.
81. Presumably Hector, son of Ailean nan Sop, Bailie of the Rhinns. See MacLean-Bristol, *Warriors and Priests*, 179–80.
82. *RPC*, viii, 174, 521–23; Gregory, *History*, 318–26. Angus's bastard son Alexander was also persuaded to seek a royal pardon for not surrendering Dunyvaig Castle the previous year. *RMS*, vi, no. 2092.
83. *RPC*, viii, 174, 751–52.
84. Pitcairn, *Criminal Trials*, iii, 1–11; Matheson, 'Documents Connected with the Trial of Sir James MacDonald of Islay'.
85. *HP*, iii, 302. MacGregor, Statutes of Iona, 152, suggests that Sir James may have owed his life at this time to Bishop Knox of the Isles intervening with the king on his behalf.
86. For the Statutes of Iona see, most recently, Goodare, 'The Statutes of Iona in Context' and MacGregor, 'The Statutes of Iona: text and context'.
87. *Islay Bk*, 144–48; *RPC*, viii, 761.
88. *Cawdor Bk*, 223–24, 226–27.
89. Cowan, 'Clanship, kinship and the Campbell acquisition of Islay', 153–54.
90. *Cawdor Bk*, 224–25.
91. Angus's death has been fixed as falling between 10 September 1612 and 17 March 1613. See MacGregor, Statutes of Iona, 167.

92. *HP*, iii, 132.
93. *Coll de Rebus Alban*, 160–166.
94. *Islay Bk*, 450–51.
95. *HP*, iii, 219–25.
96. *HP*, iii, 92, 141–43, 193–95, 206.
97. *RPC*, x, 695–97.
98. For Coll Ciotach, see Stevenson, *Highland Warrior*, 34–58.
99. *HP*, iii, 143–59.
100. *HP*, iii, 165–66, 168; *RPC*, x, 720–22; *RMS*, vii, no. 1137; *Islay Bk*, 199–230. The fact that the MacLeans seem to have taken their dispossession lying down is yet another indication that they had had no real presence on Islay for some time. The Islay lands they claimed did, however, continue to appear in grants and retours of the Barony of Duart, for instance, *RMS* (1620–33), no. 1610; and *Retours*, i, nos 16, 82, 93.
101. *HP*, iii, 155, 216.
102. *HP*, iii, 161–62.
103. *HP*, iii, 170–73, 178–79, 183, 187–88, 190–93. Cf. Gregory, *History*, 361; Stevenson, *Highland Warrior*, 40.
104. Gregory, *History*, 361–62; *RPC*, x, 726–27.
105. *RPC*, x, 717–18. An account of Lambert can be found in the *ODNB*.
106. For a description of the castle, see Caldwell, *Islay, Jura and Colonsay*, 160–63.
107. This account of the expedition to Islay and the siege of the castle is derived from a report by Archibald Campbell of Glencarradale, *HP*, iii, 177–86. There are two reports on the siege provided by Lambert, in *CSP Ireland*, xvi, 6–10 and *C. Carew MSS*, v, 287–88. See also Gregory, *History*, 362–64.
108. Pitcairn, *Criminal Trials*, iii, 363–65.
109. *HP*, iii, 219–25, 265–66.
110. Gregory, *History*, 367–69; *RPC*, x, 760–61; *HP*, iii, 273–74.
111. *HP*, iii, 267.
112. This account is largely based on the two reports given to the Privy Council for or by Argyll – *RPC*, x, 757–66.
113. *Islay Bk*, 240–6.
114. RCAHMS, *Argyll 5*, nos 405, 406.
115. RCAHMS, *Argyll 5*, no. 398.
116. RCAHMS, *Argyll 5*, no. 401.
117. Gregory, *History*, 399–402: *HP*, iii, 310–14.
118. *Cawdor Bk*, 270–71. There is evidence that James had two children, neither of whom inherited. See *RPC*, 2nd ser., i, 619.
119. *Islay Bk*, 376–77, 380–82.

Chapter 6 Campbell Lairds and Later Proprietors

1. *Islay Bk*, 353–66; *ODNB*, 'Campbell family of Cawdor'.
2. *Islay Bk*, 366; *RPC*, vi, 24.
3. *HP*, i, 130–33; Giblin (ed.), *Irish Franciscan Mission*, 79, 123; *RPC*, 2nd ser., i, 376–77, 389, 414; Hill, *MacDonnells of Antrim*, 58.
4. Giblin, *Franciscan Mission to Scotland*, 53–54; *RPC*, 2nd ser., i, 376–77, 414; 2nd ser., iii, 177–79.
5. *RPC*, 2nd ser., iv, 186.
6. *Scot. Hist. Soc. Misc.*, iv, 248.
7. Stevenson, *Highland Warrior*, 63–72; Hill, *MacDonnells of Antrim*, 57–58.
8. Stevenson, *Highland Warrior*, 73.
9. *Islay Bk*, 393–96.

10. *Scot. Hist. Soc. Misc.*, iv, 248–9; *Cawdor Bk*, 286–8.

11. *Islay Bk*, 296–97: *Cawdor Bk*, 302–03.

12. For a fuller treatment of these events, see Stevenson, *Highland Warrior*, 95–211.

13. MacTavish, *Minutes of the Synod of Argyll 1639–51*, 119–22.

14. Stevenson, *Highland Warrior*, 249–57; Ohlmeyer, *Civil War and Restoration*, 198–99.

15. Turner, *Memoirs*, 47–48; Stevenson, *Highland Warrior*, 238–40; *Islay Bk*, 401.

16. *Cawdor Bk*, 303.

17. There was already a John Kilgour a tenant in 1631.

18. *ODNB*, 'Wallace, James (d.1678), army officer'; McKerral, *Kintyre in the Seventeenth Century*, 97–98.

19. Dow, *Cromwellian Scotland*, 224.

20. Campbell, *History of Clan Campbell*, iii, 5–6.

21. Macdonald, *Missions to the Gaels*, 50–51.

22. Giblin, *Irish Franciscan Mission*, 33, 76, 79. There is a list of 101 Islay converts on pp. 40–41 of this work, including Sir John ('Joannes Dubuill, nobilis') and at least three other Campbells. See also Macdonald, *Missions to the Gaels*, especially chapter 2. Ward claimed to have gained access to Cawdor in his mainland home at Muckairn in 1624 by disguising himself as a poet, and then won him over by persuading him of the errors of the Reformed faith. Giblin, *Irish Franciscan Mission*, 53–54.

23. MacLean-Bristol, *Warriors and Priests*, 108–12; Macdonald, *Mission to the Gaels*, 22; *HP*, iii, 185–86; *Fasti*, iv, 73.

24. MacTavish, *Minutes of the Synod of Argyll 1639–51*, 123, 173, 177–78, 246; MacTavish, *Minutes of the Synod of Argyll 1652–61*, 21, 45. For the church at Kilbride, see Caldwell, *Islay, Jura and Colonsay*, 185–87.

25. MacTavish, *Minutes of the Synod of Argyll 1652–61*, 21, 35, 91, 192. See Macdonald, *Mission to the Gaels*, 113–14, for the Presbytery of Kintyre attempting in 1658 to suspend one Mr Adam Ritchie from acting as a minister in Islay. He was said to be a drunken, scandalous, fugitive from his presbytery in Ireland.

26. Macdonald, *Missions to the Gaels*, 144.

27. Dilworth, 'Benedictine Monks of Ratisbon and Wurzburg', 97–99; Macdonald, *Missions to the Gaels*, 140.

28. MacTavish, *Minutes of the Synod of Argyll 1652–61*, 150, 211, 228, 233–34, 238.

29. RCAHMS, *Argyll 5*, no. 411.

30. *RPC*, 3rd ser., ix, 325.

31. Erskine of Carnock, *Journal*, 117–18. For a recent account of the rebellion, see Campbell, *History of Clan Campbell*, iii, 27–54.

32. *Cawdor Bk*, 373; *RPC*, 3rd ser., xi, 114, 246, 308, 329.

33. *Cawdor Bk*, 375; Foster, *Members of Parliament*, 53; *HP*, i, 134–36; *DNB*, 'Campbell family of Cawdor'.

34. NLS, Adv. MS 29.1.2, fols 186–87; *ODNB*, 'Campbell family of Cawdor'.

35. NLS, Adv. MS 29.1.2, fols 50, 160.

36. *Stent Bk*, 2–3. The business recorded in the *Stent Book*, actually purchased for £3 in the latter part of 1719, starts in July 1718, but no committee is mentioned until July 1719.

37. *Shawfield's Day Bk*, 2. For a full account and analysis of the sale transactions, see Storrie, *Islay*, 65–68. In 1869 John Francis Campbell of Islay annotated the disposition of 16 July 1726 with his own calculation that the purchase price of the estates was actually £16,169, including previous loans to Campbell of Cawdor. The Jura lands were resold by Shawfield in 1738. See NLS, *Lamplighter and Story-teller*, 22.

38. Hill and Bastin, *A Very Canny Scot*.

39. All this is spelled out in the papers relating to a lawsuit over the wadset of Killinallan (see under Campbells of Killinallan and Ardnahoe in Appendix 1). See especially 'Answers for Colin Campbell of Ardnahow to the Petition of Donald Campbell of Killinalen, 1760', in NAS, CS230/C/5/9.

40. *ODNB*, 'Campbell, Daniel (1671/2–1753), merchant and politician'.

41. Jupp, *History of Islay*, 127–29, 136–41, 152–58, 171–87, 203–13, gives very full coverage of the activities of the Stent Committee.

42. *Stent Bk*, 30–31.

43. Hill and Bastin, *A Very Canny Scot*, 86.

44. *Shawfield's Day Bk*, 75–76; Storrie, *Islay*, 85–99.

45. *Shawfield's Day Bk*, 113–15, 124–79; MacDonald, *General View*, 64, 497, 549; Storrie, *Islay*, 102–17; Hill and Bastin, *A Very Canny Scot*, 114.

46. Storrie, *Islay*, 119–52; Storrie, 'Recovering the Historic Designed Landscape of Islay House'; Foster, *Members of Parliament*, 62.

47. Campbell, 'On the potato disease, crop 1845'.

48. Ramsay, *John Ramsay*, 22–27; ML, TD 1284/3/7/3.

49. Hunter, *For the People's Cause*, 14, 80; Sinclair, 'The Journal of Donald Sinclair'.

50. For a detailed account of his life and achievements, see MacKechnie, *Carragh-chuimhe*.

51. Hunter, *For the People's Cause*, 79–80; Royal Commission (Highlands and Islands), 836–37.

52. *ODNB*, 'Morrison, James'; Gatty, *Portrait of a Merchant Prince*, 288–92; Foster, *Members of Parliament*, 258.

53. *ODNB*, 'Morrison, Charles'.

54. Storrie, *Islay*, 165.

55. For Ramsay's views on Gaelic, see Cameron 'Poverty, Protest and Politics', 252.

56. For Ramsay's life in general, see the adulatory Ramsay, *John Ramsay*, by the wife of his grandson. Wilson, *The Island Whisky Trail*, 60–63; Foster, *Members of Parliament*, 293. For Kildalton House, see Walker, *Argyll And Bute*, 546–47.

57. Cameron, 'Poverty, Protest and Politics', 251–52. See also Ramsay, *Periodical Destitution in the Highlands and its Remedy*, 15–16.

58. Walker, *Argyll And Bute*, 550.

Chapter 7 The People of Islay

1. Jillings, *Scotland's Black Death*, 43, 88–89.

2. This data is tabularised by Fraser Darling, *West Highland Survey*, 83.

3. Paton, *MacKintosh Muniments*, no. 110.

4. Cawdor Castle, CM, bundle 655, Islay Rental of 1631, tenant of Laggan, etc. This document has a note on its cover indicating that it is the rental of 1633, but 1631 is clearly indicated in the body of the text.

5. CM, bundle 654, (d) no. 17.

6. *Cawdor Bk*, 242–3.

7. *ALI*, no. 16.

8. *RPC*, vii, 627.

9. NAS E69/3/1, 55–59.

10. *ER*, xvii, 611–20.

11. *RPC*, vii, 627; x, 721.

12. MacLean-Bristol, *Warriors and Priests*, 179–80. For Am Burg, see RCAHMS, *Argyll 5*, no. 125.

13. *HP*, iii, 273–74.

14. For the McBreatnich harpers, see Thomson, 'Gaelic Learned Orders', 69.

15. *ER*, xvi, 91, 485; xvii, 650. The figures for payments in kind are not exact since the rentals include fractions of marts, etc.

16. See Bannerman, 'The Lordship of the Isles', for a useful discussion on social organisation in the Lordship of the Isles, with relevance for later years; also Macinnes, *Clanship, Commerce and the House of Stewart*, 12–16 for traditional clan payments. A bond of 1575 made between James of Dunyvaig's successor, Angus, and a group of MacMays,

specifically refers to the latter's obligation to pay calps. Paton, *MacKintosh Muniments*, no. 109.

17. *Islay Bk*, 478.
18. For more details, and references, on this and the following families, see Appendix 1.
19. Steer and Bannerman, *Monumental Sculpture*, 123.
20. The source of this tale was Hector MacLean of Ballygrant, and it is recorded in Campbell, *Records of Argyll*, 337–38. 'Knockshainta' is identified as Cnoc Seunta (near the village of Keills), but might it have been Cnoc Seannda, the mound at the head of Loch Finlaggan adjacent to MacDonald's palace?
21. MacNeill, 'The Musician in the Cave'.
22. Haddow, *The History and Structure of Ceol Mor*, 38–55.
23. Sanger, 'The Origins of Highland Piping'.
24. Beaugué, *Histoire de la guerre d'Ecosse*, 62.
25. I owe this information on pipers to Keith Sanger.
26. MacKechnie, *Carragh-chuimhne*, 26.
27. Giblin, *Franciscan Mission to Scotland*, 53–54.
28. Macnicol, *Remarks on Dr Johnson's Journey*, 363.
29. Campbell, *Popular Tales*, ii, 57–62.
30. *Shawfield's Day Bk*, 107.
31. *Scot. Hist. Soc. Misc.*, iv (1926), 205.
32. *Islay Bk*, 451.
33. The 1733 and 1741 rentals of Islay are reproduced in *Shawfield's Day Bk*, 9–20, 37–44.
34. Black, *Surnames*, 552.
35. For a detailed account of this family, see Bannerman, *The Beatons*.
36. AT, iii, 46.
37. Our account of this family depends heavily on Bannerman, *The Beatons*.
38. *Islay Bk*, 141–42; *RPC*, x, 590–91.
39. Steer and Bannerman, *Monumental Sculpture*, 153.
40. *Cawdor Bk*, 234; AT, vi, 78.
41. Bannerman, *The Beatons*, 15, 124–5; *Cawdor Bk*, 295.
42. *RPC*, ix, 25–26; *HP*, iii, 185–6.
43. Giblin, *Irish Franciscan Mission*, 79, 123; *RPC*, 2nd ser., vii, 376–77, 389, 414; Hill, *MacDonnells*, 58.
44. CM, bundle 654 (d), nos 21, 22; bundle 656/8; *Scot. Hist. Soc. Misc.*, iv, 247–8; *HP*, iii, 257; *Shawfield's Day Bk*, 114.
45. Campbell, *History of Clan Campbell*, ii, 261.
46. *Islay Bk*, 240, 270, 391, 393. Note that the 'Extract Decree of Valuation of 1636' that lists Mr William as a heritor, as printed in *Islay Bk*, 388–90 and *Shawfield's Day Bk*, 57–59, mistakenly describes him as 'of Torrobollis' (Torrabus) instead of as 'of Eorobollis' (Eorrabus).
47. *Shawfield's Day Bk*, 127. The photograph is in the Museum of Islay Life, Port Charlotte.
48. CM, bundle 654, nos 13, 17; NAS RS 10/2 fols 479–80. *Islay Bk*, 421, provides a copy of the Procuratory of Resignation of Torrabus in 1695, printing '1620' instead of '1629' for the original sale of the lands.
49. *Scot. Hist. Soc. Misc.*, iv, 283, no. 104. The particular land of Robolls held by this family drops from the records since it was amalgamated with Kepolls.
50. *RPC*, 3rd ser., ix, 325; *Islay Bk*, 417–18, 433; *Shawfield's Day Bk*, 48–53.
51. *Shawfield's Day Bk*, 9–20; NAS CC 12/3/4 fols 62–68.
52. Black, *Surnames*, 67.
53. NLS, Adv. MS 29.1.2, vol. 5, fol. 162r.
54. Whittaker, *I, James Whittaker*, 61–88.

Chapter 8 Continuity and Change – Place-Names and Extents

1. The information that follows on place-names, land denominations and administrative units is largely derived from Macniven's thesis, The Norse in Islay, which should be consulted for more detailed analysis, information, and notes on sources.
2. Nicolaisen, *Scottish Place-names*, 122.
3. Thomas, 'On Islay Place-Names', 273.
4. Maceacharna, *The Lands of the Lordship*, 122.
5. Price, 'The Word *Baile* in Place-Names', 119.
6. The approach, however, by Maceacharna, *The Lands of the Lordship*, 72–82, to use place-name data as evidence for a phased takeover of the island is misguided.
7. *Islay Bk*, 111; *Stent Bk*, 1.
8. There is a detailed critique of previous attempts to come up with an understanding of Islay's system of land denominations in Macniven, The Norse in Islay, chapter 8. The main works in this field have been McKerral, 'Ancient Denominations of Agricultural Land'; and 'The Lesser Land and Administrative Divisions of Celtic Scotland'; and Lamont, 'Old Land Denominations'.
9. It appears in the 1631 rental as Keirreish Laich and in 1654 as Kerowbhyachie.
10. The others are Ochtocladesell (part of Cladeville), Octocorrich and Octinfrich (associated with Daill).
11. Lamont, in 'Old Land Denominations', and his later *Early History of Islay*, 80–84, made a valiant attempt to demonstrate that land denominations on Islay could be linked back to the house system of Dál Riata. A major plank in his thesis was that the quarterlands, with an extent of £1 13s 4d, represented a revalorisation of a smaller, earlier quarterland valued at 20s or £1. No amount of ingenious calculations can hide the fact that there is a singular lack of evidence for Islay units of land with an extent of 20s. The exception to the rule is Proaig, also known to have been reckoned as 6 cowlands.
12. *OP*, ii, 266 assigns 'the pennyland of Scar' to Islay on the basis of a misreading of a retour of 1662 of the Barony of Duart. See *Retours*, i, no. 67. There is also a property on the edge of Loch Indaal between Bowmore and Bridgend called Pennycraig. It is first recorded as a place-name in the nineteenth century and may be a coinage of that century.
13. McErlean, 'The Irish Townland System of Landscape Organisation', 317–22.
14. *Registrum Monasterii de Passelet*, 125–27.
15. This system of land divisions on the Isle of Man, which may have evolved over a long period of time after the direct political linkage between Man and Islay was broken, is described in detail by Reilly, *Computer Analysis of an Archaeological Landscape*, 8–44.
16. Appendix 2 lists them all. Included in this eighteen are Keills (an abbreviated form of Kilcallumcille), Callumkill (*recte*, Kilcallumcille), and Kilcavane, now lost.
17. Reilly, *Computer Analysis of an Archaeological Landscape*, 12–13.
18. Pennant, *Tour*, 215: Walker, *Report on the Hebrides*, 102.
19. *Shawfield's Day Bk*, 61–67.
20. *Shawfield's Day Bk*, 97.
21. *Shawfield's Day Bk*, 105.

Chapter 9 Living on the Land

1. Barber and Brown, 'An Sithean'; RCAHMS, *Argyll 5*, no. 237; Pennant, *Tour*, 213.
2. *ER*, xii, 709.
3. See Dodgshon, 'West Highland Chiefdoms'; and Shaw, *The Northern and Western Islands*, 154.
4. *RPC*, viii, 257–8.

5. Paton, *MacKintosh Muniments*, no. 188.
6. *ER*, xiii, 220; xvii, 548. Doodilbeg is first mentioned in a 1562 tack of Islay lands to James MacDonald of Dunyvaig and the Glens by Mary Queen of Scots (*RSS*, vi, no. 1112).
7. ML, TD 1284/9/11.
8. Skene, *Celtic Scotland*, iii, 437–38.
9. Teignmouth, *Sketches*, ii, 308.
10. *Shawfield's Day Bk*, 207–08.
11. These plans are in the possession of the Islay Estate Company. Photostat copies are available in the National Archives of Scotland (West Register House, Edinburgh), RHP series. Other plans of farms that became part of the Kildalton Estate can be found at ML TD 1284/9.
12. RCAHMS, *Argyll 5*, no. 425.
13. Pennant, *Tour*, pl. XV.
14. NAS, plan (photostat) RHP 10972.
15. In an overview of West Highland and Hebridean settlement the geographer, Dodgshon, has concluded that enclosed fields pre-date unenclosed rigs, and he links the latter to runrig and a move away from dispersed farmsteads to nucleated settlements. It should be noted, however, that at present Dodgshon's argument for a move from dispersed to nucleated patterns of settlement, corresponding to that from enclosed to open fields, does not appear to have relevance for Islay. See Dodgshon, 'West Highland and Hebridean settlement prior to crofting'.
16. The basis for this estimate is a comparison of the money prices for wethers, hens and geese in the 1542 and 1654 rentals.
17. *Cawdor Bk*, 351–52; CM, 590, nos 3, 25, 36, 41, 47, 70, 77, 78.
18. Walker, *Report on the Hebrides*, 100; Pennant, *Tour*, 217; MacDonald, *Agriculture of the Hebrides*, 623.
19. CM, 590/27.
20. *Islay Bk*, 519; *Stent Bk*, 59, 121, 151; Haldane, *The Drove Roads of Scotland*, 91–101.
21. Walker, *Report on the Hebrides*, 100.
22. CM, 590/41, 655/129; Haldane, *The Drove Roads of Scotland*, 138–43.
23. NAS, CC12/3/4, 128.
24. He is included among those who owed money to Archibald Campbell, tacksman of Ardnahoe, in 1737. NAS, CC12/3/4, 22; Cregeen, 'Recollections of an Argyllshire Drover', 144–45, 157–59.
25. Walker, *Report on the Hebrides*, 99; MacDonald, *Agriculture of the Hebrides*, 624.
26. *Islay Bk*, 521–44.
27. Grant and MacLeod, 'Agriculture in the Inner Hebrides', 571.
28. NAS, CC12/3/4, 5.
29. See NAS, CC12/3/3 for, for example, the testaments of Dugald Taylor in Bar, died 1725 (p. 7); John McKerash in Margadale, died 1715 (p. 9); and Patrick McEwan in Craigfad, died 1726 (pp. 13–14). Information on the (possible) size of their holdings and their shares of the soums of their respective farms is derived from the rentals of 1722 and 1733.
30. NAS, CC12/3/2, 99. Lachlan's testament indicates that he held Cladville in tack from Campbell of Sutherland at the time of his death, and also Tockmal in the Oa, where his brother, William Campbell of Auchindoun resided. Lachlan had also previously held Kintra, and he had been Commissar Depute of Islay since 1726.
31. NAS, CC12/3/3, 63.
32. NAS, CC12/3/3, 16–21.
33. NAS, CC12/3/3, 28–29, 38–39.
34. NAS, CC12/3/5, 23.
35. MacDonald, *Agriculture of the Hebrides*, 423–24.
36. NAS, CC12/3/2, 99; CC12/3/4, 73; Walker, *Report on the Hebrides*, 100.
37. *SA* (1794), xi, 279; MacDonald, *Agriculture of the Hebrides*, 622.

38. NAS, SC230/C/5/9, particularly 'Answers for Colin Campbell of Ardnahow to the Petition of Donald Campbell of Killinalen, 1760', and 'Petition For Donald Campbell of Killinalen, 1760'.

39. *SA* (1794), xi, 292.

40. *Shawfield's Day Bk*, 63–67. The survey is not signed or dated but can reasonably be assigned to MacDougall.

41. Walker, *Report on the Hebrides*, 101; MacDonald, *Agriculture of the Hebrides*, 629.

42. Walker, *Report on the Hebrides*, 100; Grant, *Highland Folk Ways*, 95–96.

43. Pennant, *Tour*, 215.

44. NAS, CC12/3/4, 53.

45. Without excavation it is often difficult to distinguish corn-drying kilns from limekilns. In limekilns the lime and fuel (peat) were combusted in the kiln itself whereas in corn-drying kilns hot air was drawn into the kiln along a flue from a fire placed outside.

46. See *Shawfield's Day Bk*, 222, for an example – Corary and Courilach, 1777. Many eighteenth-century tacks are recorded in the Islay Estate Papers (ML, TD 138/1/2), and the Kildalton Papers (ML, TD 1284/3/1 & 2).

47. Hunter, *For the People's Cause*, 109–10, reproducing part of NLS, MS 14986, 112–36.

48. It shows clearly in the aerial photograph on p. 225 of RCAHMS, *Argyll 5*.

49. Caldwell, *Islay, Jura and Colonsay*, 160–63; Caldwell and Ruckley, 'Domestic Architecture in the Lordship of the Isles', 103, 114. Cf. RCAHMS, *Argyll 5*, 268–75.

50. Pennant, *Tour*, 211; RCAHMS, *Argyll 5*, no. 125.

51. MacLean-Bristol, *Warriors and Priests*, 179–80; NAS, RS 10/2/360–63; RCAHMS, *Argyll 5*, no. 304.

52. *RMS*, iii, no. 2835; (1607–33), no. 1610; *Coll de Rebus Alban*, 3; *RSS*, vi, no. 1112. These four crannogs are inventoried as nos 305, 312, 311 and 313 in RCAHMS, *Argyll 5*.

53. The description and interpretation of the remains at Finlaggan offered here are based on the writer's own excavations in the 1990s. See also RCAHMS, *Argyll 5*, no. 404 and Caldwell, *Islay, Jura and Colonsay*, 163–75.

54. Hayes-McCoy, *Ulster and other Irish Maps*, 11–12, 20, plates VI, XI.

55. *Islay Bk*, 541.

56. Burt's *Letters*, 169–70. For more information on creel houses and attempts to reconstruct them, see Noble, 'Turf-walled Houses of the Central Highlands' and 'Creel Houses of the Scottish Highlands'.

57. Pennant, *Tour*, 204. The illustration of the Jura shielings is on p. 205, and has been reproduced, e.g. by Caldwell, *Islay, Jura and Colonsay*, 69.

58. Pennant, *Tour*, 217; Smith, *General View of the Agriculture of Argyll*, 15.

59. Dodgshon, 'West Highland and Hebridean settlement', 422. For descriptions of shielings elsewhere in the Western Isles, see Thomas, 'Beehive houses in Harris and Lewis'; 'Primitive Dwellings and Hypogea of the Outer Hebrides'; and Love, 'Shielings of the Isle of Rum'. MacSween and Gailey, 'Some Shielings in North Skye', gives an account of the excavation of a shieling mound on Skye.

60. Walker, *Report on the Hebrides*, 102.

61. Both paintings are reproduced in *Shawfield's Day Bk*, illus. 12, 13.

62. Teignmouth, *Sketches*, ii, 310.

63. Gailey, 'The Evolution of Highland Rural Settlement', 170.

64. For an attempt to classify Islay house forms, see Caldwell, McWee and Ruckley, 'Post-medieval settlement on Islay', 62–65.

65. NAS, CC12/3/3, 59; CC12/3/4, 53; CC12/3/5, 11.

66. NAS, CC12/3/3, 7.

67. *Shawfield's Day Bk*, 69, 223.

68. The name 'Dailriadic' was coined for traditional houses in Argyll, including Islay, by Sinclair, *Thatched Houses*, chapter 4. The term, however, is rather misleading.

69. MacDonald, *Agriculture of the Hebrides*, 93.

70. The source for this is a ledger valuing the wood in houses and offices on farms on the Morrison's estate. ML, TD 1338/2/2/34.
71. NLS, MS 14986, 126–27.
72. Teignmouth, *Sketches*, ii, 309.
73. 'Gowrie', Off the Chain, 286–88.
74. NAS, CC12/3/4, 149. Perhaps it is incorporated in Eallabus House which appears to be of late-eighteenth-century and later date.
75. *Shawfield's Day Bk*, 127. The photograph is in the Museum of Islay Life, Port Charlotte.
76. NAS, RHP 11034.
77. *Shawfield's Day Bk*, 95.
78. MacDonald, *Agriculture of the Hebrides*, 85.
79. 'Sadle' is a variant of settle, meaning a bench.
80. NAS, CC12/3/3–5, *passim*.
81. Blair, *Reminiscences of Islay*, 25.
82. NAS, CC12/3/2, 99.
83. NAS, CC12/3/3, 22–24.
84. NAS, CC12/3/3, 63.
85. NLS, MS ACC 6223/12, bundle 3.

Chapter 10 Improving Ways

1. *Stent Bk*, 2–3.
2. *SA* (1794), xi, 283, 296, 301; *SA* (1845), vii, 656–57, 666, 671; ICD, *s.v.* school.
3. MacKechnie, *Carragh-chuimhne*, 3–25.
4. There is an account of MacAlpine's life, along with a portrait, in later editions of his much reissued *Dictionary*.
5. This story was told to the great folklorist, Alexander Carmichael, by one of the victims. See Carmichael, *Carmina Gadelica*, 24.
6. 'Gowrie', *Off the Chain*, 252.
7. Martin, *Western Islands*, 275.
8. *SA* (1794), xi, 294–95. Note how there is a grave-slab, dated 1696, to Charles MacArthur in Proaig inside the medieval church. Proaig was then part of Kilarrow or Kilmeny parish.
9. *Shawfield's Day Bk*, 80, etc.
10. *Monro's Western Isles*, 57.
11. Scott, *Fasti*, iv, 71–77; *Shawfield's Day Bk*, 56.
12. *Shawfield's Day Bk*, 56, 75–94.
13. RCAHMS, *Argyll 5*, no. 360.
14. *SA* (1794), xi, 289–90, 301.
15. RCAHMS, *Argyll 5*, no. 366; *SA* (1794), xi, 283.
16. ICD, *s.v.* church; RCAHMS, *Argyll 5*, nos 412, 413.
17. Martin, *The Western Islands*, 267. Martin was actually contrasting the high level of disease in Islay and Colonsay on the one hand, with the healthiness of the inhabitants of Jura, on the other. It is not at all clear why such a difference should have been observable.
18. Pennant, *Tour*, 218.
19. *SA* (1794), xi, 294; Edwards, *Seanchas Ìle*, 127–35.
20. ML, TD 1338.
21. *Stent Bk*, 194.
22. ML, TD 1338/5/7/3/1; Ramsay, *John Ramsay*, 31–32.
23. *Stent Bk*, 1, 255, 266.
24. The Provincial Assembly of Argyll decided at a meeting in Inverary in 1642 that there should be a church at 'Lagan' beside Dunyvaig. This lends support to this supposition. Laggan seems soon to have been superseded, as a name, by Lagavulin. Less likely than this

explanation is that the burgh was to be erected at the mouth of the River Laggan on the land of Laggan. See MacTavish, *Minutes of the Synod of Argyll 1639–1651*, 55.

25. NAS, CC12/3/3, 59, 69.
26. NAS, CC12/3/4, 115.
27. NLS, ACC 6223/12, bundle 3.
28. NAS, CC12/3/5, 16.
29. NAS, E69/3/1, 55; MacTavish, *Minutes of the Synod of Argyll 1639–1651*, 246; *Stent Bk*, 1, 13, 160, 260. The church at Lagavulin is no longer, but the ruins of its predecessor can be traced at Kilbride. See Caldwell, *Islay, Jura and Colonsay*, 185–86; *Shawfield's Day Bk*, 76–83.
30. NAS, CC12/3/4, 163; CC12/3/5, 74.
31. This painting, the original of which is in the British Library, is reproduced in *Shawfield's Day Bk*, 158 (illus. 14).
32. But note the tradition, cited in Chapter 12, that the name arose from an attempt to lynch the first excise officer on the island!
33. Cameron, *The Justiciary Records of Argyll and the Isles*, i, 176–80.
34. Marwick, *List of Markets and Fairs*, 70.
35. NAS, CC12/3/3, 4; CC12/3/4, 145.
36. Bigwood, *The Vice-Admiral Court of Argyll*, 22, 23.
37. Anderson and Anderson, *Guide*, iv, 574.
38. *Shawfield's Day Bk*, 45–47.
39. *Stent Bk*, 45.
40. Jupp, *The History of Islay*, 156–57.
41. *Stent Bk*, 87, 118, 121, 152, 154, 156, 170, 174. 184; RCAHMS, *Argyll 5*, no. 432. The bridge has long since gone but is commemorated in the place-name An Drochaid Iaruinn at NR 303 554.
42. Langlands, *Map of Argyllshire*.
43. ML, TD 1338/5/1/1/25 and 47; *Shawfield's Day Bk*, 47.
44. Ramsay, *John Ramsay*, 23–24, 48; ML, TD 1338/5/1/1/31 and 32; Storrie, *Islay*, 168.
45. *Stent Bk*, 124; Booth, *An Islay Notebook*, 76–79; 'Gowrie', *Off the Chain*, 253.
46. Mackay, *Islay, Jura (Postal History)*, 18.
47. *Stent Bk*, 51, 121, 222.
48. *Stent Bk*, 64, 73, 100–01.
49. *Stent Bk*, 225, 231.
50. The development of steamer services to Islay is dealt with in detail by Duckworth and Langmuir, *West Highland Steamers*, especially pp. 41–43, 169.
51. For Islay wrecks, see Blackburn, *Dive Islay Wrecks*; and Moir and Crawford, *Argyll Shipwrecks*, 63–113.
52. Museum of Islay Life, *An Islay Miscellany*, 48; Mackay, *Islay, Jura (Postal History)*, 20.
53. For a detailed postal history of the island, see Mackay, *Islay, Jura (Postal History)*.
54. NAS, E727/60/1–2.
55. *Islay Bk*, 469–72; also Haldane, *Three Centuries of Scottish Posts*, 191–92.
56. NLS, MS 14986, p. 15.
57. The evidence for this are articles of agreement with Colin Campbell, tacksman of Carnbeg, for the latter to dig a canal from Uiskentuie to Coullabus. The work was still going on in the early nineteenth century. ML, TD 1338/3/4/1; MacDonald, *General View of the Agriculture of the Hebrides*, 382.
58. *Shawfield's Day Bk*, 168.
59. ML, TD 1338/1/1–2.
60. *Shawfield's Day Bk*, 206, 207, 208; *SA* (1794), xi, 287.
61. Macculloch, *The Highlands and Western Isles*, iv, 421.
62. NAS, NRA(S) 1277, bundle 5. The *Tourist's Guide*, 40, describes him as Captain Colin MacLean of Java.
63. For a history of the Association, see Storrie, *Continuity and Change*.

64. Groome, *Ordnance Gazetteer*, iv, 327.

65. RCAHMS, *Argyll 5*, no. 423; Hunter, *For the People's Cause*, 80, 113 (for the Fifeshire origin of the farmer – he is named in an 1828 list of tenants).

66. Teignmouth, *Sketches*, ii, 309–10.

67. *Shawfield's Day Bk*, 105; NAS, RHP 11024.

68. There are copies of several in NAS, the originals being still in the possession of the Islay Estate. Others can be found in the Ramsay of Kildalton Papers (ML, TD 1284/9).

69. NAS, RHP 10972, 11065.

70. NAS, GD 64/1/347.

71. Groome, *Ordnance Gazetteer*, iv, 327.

72. *Tourist's Guide*, 16, 23.

73. MacDonald, *Sketches of Islay*, 33–45.

74. *Royal Commission (Highlands and Islands)*, 836–37.

75. Groome, *Ordnance Gazetteer*, iv, 327.

76. See Storrie, 'Islay: A Hebridean Exception', fig. 6, for the pattern of land use in the early 1960s.

77. *Royal Commission (Highlands and Islands)*, 827.

78. NLS, MS 14986, p. 108.

79. ML, TD 1338/1/4/3/2; Mackay, *Islay, Jura (Postal History)*, 20.

80. *SA* (1794), xi, 301; *Stent Bk*, 167.

81. Teignmouth, *Sketches*, ii, 311; Anderson and Anderson, *Guide*, iv, 169–70.

82. Anderson and Anderson, *Guide*, iv, 584.

83. 'Gowrie', *Off the Chain*, 253.

84. Teignmouth, *Sketches*, 315–17; *SA* (1794), xi, 281; (1845), vii, 655; Anderson and Anderson, *Guide*, iv, 582; *Tourist's Guide*, 49.

85. *Tourist's Guide*, 49. For a plan of Port Wemyss and its lots, based on the 1833 survey by Gemmill, see Storrie, 'Land use and settlement history', fig. 3, or Storrie, *Islay*, 134.

86. Teignmouth, *Sketches*, ii, 312–14.

87. *SA* (1845), vii, 664.

88. 'Gowrie', *Off the Chain*, 239–40.

89. 'Gowrie', *Off the Chain*, 241–43. The villagers clearly had issues with the water supply, provided by means of stand pumps installed by the laird, John Ramsay. See Ramsay, *John Ramsay*, 46.

90. Booth, *An Islay Notebook*, 53–57.

91. Teignmouth, *Sketches*, ii, 312.

Chapter 11 Emigrants and Visitors

1. Storrie, 'Land use and settlement history', fig. 4; and *Islay*, chapter 10, 141–62. Compare the data on number of holdings and tenancies from 1733 to 1853 given by Storrie, 'Landholdings and Settlement Evolution', table 2.

2. For examples of typical missives and tacks dating from 1769 to 1802, see *Shawfield's Day Bk*, 214–42.

3. Storrie, 'Landholdings and Settlement Evolution', fig. 10, is a re-drawing of the plan of 'Ballitarson'.

4. Storrie, 'Landholdings and Settlement Evolution', 149, sees it as part of a 'revolutionary process' of reorganising small holdings. Caldwell et al., 'Post-Medieval settlement on Islay', 67, suggest that in some cases it may result from a previous history of ownership, but non-occupation, by tacksmen.

5. ML, TD 1338/1/3/89, no. 3.

6. Campbell, 'The improvement of waste land'.

7. MacDonald, *Sketches of Islay*, 36.

8. Ramsay, *John Ramsay*, 24.
9. NAS, RHP 10979 and 10990.
10. *SA* (1794), xi, 284.
11. NAS, RHP 11065.
12. NAS, RHP 10972.
13. *Royal Commission (Highlands and Islands)*, 835–36. MacArthur and his fellows are described in the report as crofters, though it is not clear that they would have been in the legal sense of the 1886 Crofters Act.
14. Hunter, *For the People's Cause*, 80, 109. Storrie, *Islay*, 129, demonstrates that six of the main tenants found new tenancies on the farms of Olistadh and Conisby while others settled in the villages.
15. Parliament, *Report of the Select Committee on Emigration*, 56–59.
16. *Royal Commission (Highlands and Islands)*, 836–37.
17. Hearn, 'Scots miners on the Goldfields', 82.
18. Ramsay, *John Ramsay*, 31–41, 141–45.
19. Storrie, *Islay*, 171.
20. Ramsay, *John Ramsay*, 31–32.
21. The translations are by Meek, *Tuath Is Tighearna*, no. 8.
22. Ramsay, 'Periodical Destitution', 18.
23. NAS, RS10/11, fol. 244–46.
24. *SA* (1794), xi, 293.
25. Pryde, 'Scottish Colonization in the Province of New York'; Patten, *The Argyle Patent*. Some of the documents in the latter are reproduced in *Shawfield's Day Bk*, 21–36.
26. Brock, *Scotus Americanus*, 80.
27. Dobson, *Scottish Emigration to Colonial America*, 110–11; Murdoch, 'A Scottish Document concerning Emigration'.
28. Bigwood, *The Vice-Admiral Court of Argyll*, 22–23.
29. Bennion, 'The Second Migration of Scots to North Carolina'; Meyer, *The Highland Scots of North Carolina*, 84–85; Graham, *Colonists from Scotland*, 99.
30. Murdoch in 'A Scottish Document concerning Emigration'. Alexander Campbell was also one of Pennant's main sources of information on Islay, acknowledged in his *Tour*, 2.
31. Dunn, *Highland Settler*, 18.
32. Ramsay, *John Ramsay*, 61–140; Blair, *Reminiscences of Islay*. For other Ilich in New Zealand, see Hewitson, *Far Off In Sunlit Places*, 204, 234.
33. MacNeill Weir, *Guide to Islay*, 48–51.
34. MacNeill Weir, *Guide to Islay*, 39–47.
35. Booth, *An Islay Notebook*, 97.
36. Storrie, *Islay*, 244–45.
37. Caldwell, *Islay, Jura and Colonsay*, 215.
38. Wiggins, *The Exmouth of Newcastle*.
39. Blackburn, *Dive Islay Wrecks*, 25–41, 66–69; Moir and Crawford, *Argyll Shipwrecks*, 99–101, 109.
40. Laughton, *Studies in Naval History*, 324–62; MacDonald, *Sketches of Islay*, 27–28.
41. Reported in the *Cumberland Chronicle and Whitehaven Public Advertiser*, 28 May 1778. Available online at www.pastpresented.info/cumbria/chron78mj.htm.
42. This event is often attributed, wrongly, to John Paul Jones. See Stewart, 'John Paul Jones and others'.
43. *Shawfield's Day Bk*, 114; RCAHMS, *Argyll 5*, 296.
44. This information on Duplait is derived from a letter written from Islay in 1848 by a well-informed American minister, Dr John Thomas of Richmond, Viriginia, who had come to visit John Murdoch. See www.angelfire.com/bc2/Bereans/Cornerstones/Pioneers/Herald/131.html, accessed 9 June 2007.
45. 'Gowrie', *Off the Chain*, 239–40.

46. ML, TD 1338/1/4/3/19/2.
47. This account of Islay in World War II is by Ian Brown.
48. TNA, WO 199/2859.
49. TNA, WO 199/2859. The activities of the World War I U-boat were reported by R. Hamilton in *The Scottish Field* (Oct 1975), 50.
50. NLS, MSS 3819.
51. TNA, WO 199/2859.
52. Smith, *Action Stations 7*.
53. Owen, *Royal Air Force Station Oban*.
54. TNA, AIR 28/644.
55. TNA, AIR 29/9.
56. TNA, AIR 28/644.
57. TNA, AIR 28/646.
58. Smith, *Action Stations 7*, 172; Museum of Islay Life, *An Islay Miscellany*, 58–59.
59. TNA, AIR 28/644.
60. For more information on Britain's radar defences in World War II, see Lowry, *20th Century Defences*, 36–47.
61. TNA, AIR 26/103.
62. TNA, AIR 26/103; Museum of Islay Life, *An Islay Miscellany*, 71–75.
63. TNA, AIR 26/103.
64. TNA, AIR 26/103, 2/12063.

Chapter 12 Industries

1. Pennant, *Tour*, 207.
2. Cressey, The Identification of Early Lead Mining: Environmental, Archaeological and Historical Perspectives from Islay, Inner Hebrides, Scotland. University of Edinburgh PhD, 1995, 233.
3. Monro's *Western Isles*, 55.
4. *TA*, iv, 274.
5. *RPC*, x, 525.
6. *RPC*, xii, 106–07, 503; 2nd series, i, 296, 375; *Cawdor Bk*, 247, 250–51; *Islay Bk*, 366–67.
7. *Cawdor Bk*, 338; *Islay Bk*, 456–57.
8. McKay, *Walker's Report on the Hebrides*, 106; NAS E69/3/1, 58.
9. NLS, Adv MS 29.1.1, vol. 7 fol. 33r.
10. ML, B10/15/3386; Anonymous, 'An account of old John Taylor'.
11. ML, B10/15/3386 and 3653; *Islay Bk*, 531.
12. Williams, *The Natural History of the Mineral Kingdom* 1789, ii, 327–28; *Islay Bk*, 531.
13. CM, 656/1; RCAHMS, *Argyll 3*, 250–55.
14. NLS, Adv MS 29.1.1 fols 118, 157.
15. ML, B10/15/3653. Although not specifically indicated in this document, Murray's papers show that Bowman's mill was for smelting lead (NLS Adv MS 29.1.1 fol. 118v).
16. Anonymous, John Taylor, 24; *Islay Bk*, 457.
17. *Shawfield's Day Bk*, 42; CM 656/1; *Islay Bk*, 457; NLS Adv MS 29.1.1 fols 136, 157.
18. Lindsay, 'The Iron Industry in the Highlands: charcoal blast furnaces', 57.
19. *Islay Bk*, 458; Smout, 'Lead-mining in Scotland', 117.
20. NAS, RD4/227 fol. 285 MacKenzie; *Islay Bk*, 462–64.
21. See Callender and Macaulay, *The Ancient Metal Mines of Islay*, for information and descriptions of mining locations. Detailed accounts and plans of the workings at Mulreesh, Robolls and Finlaggan/Portaneilean will appear in the *Finlaggan Archaeological Project Monograph*.
22. *Islay Bk*, 458–62.

23. NAS, RD4/227 fol. 285 MacKenzie; *Islay Bk*, 466; *Shawfield's Day Bk*, 181, 193; *Stent Bk*, 99, 100.

24. Pennant, *Tour*, 206–07. Griffith's picture of the smelter is reproduced in RCAHMS, *Argyll 5*, 322, and Ramsay, *Shawfield's Day Bk*, 95.

25. ML, TD 1338/3/4/1: Petition of Comprisement of Damages. For a plan of these workings, see Caldwell, *Islay, Jura and Colonsay*, 204 (fig. 79).

26. Pennant, *Tour*, 207; Storrie, *Islay* , 1997, 95.

27. NAS, RD4/227 fol. 285 MacKenzie; *Shawfield's Day Bk*, 108, 193, 196.

28. ML, TD 1338/1/6/1.

29. ML, TD 1338/1/6/2, Anderson and Anderson, *Guide to the Highlands and Western Islands*, iv, 162. For the Borrons' activities at Leadhills and Wanlockhead, see Harvey, *Lead and Labour*, part 2, chapter 7.

30. ML, TD 1338/1/6/3; 'Gowrie', *Off the Chain*, 256.

31. ML, TD 1338/1/6/9.

32. ML, TD 1338/1/6/9; Booth, *An Islay Notebook*, 95.

33. Burt, Waite and Atkinson, 'Scottish metalliferous mining', 18.

34. ML, TD 1338/1/6/14.

35. Caldwell and Ruckley, 'Domestic Architecture in the Lordship of the Isles', 97–121.

36. NAS, CC12/3/4, 73–75.

37. *SA* (1794), xi, 301.

38. ML, TD 1338/2/6/10–12.

39. *SA* (1845), vii, 662.

40. Wilkinson, *Memoirs of the Geological Survey, Scotland. The Geology of Islay, including Oronsay and portions of Colonsay and Jura.* (Explanation of Sheets 19 and 27, with the western part of Sheet 20); Emerton, *The Pattern of Scottish Roofing.*

41. *SA* (1845), vii, 647.

42. ML, TD 1338/1/6/23/6.

43. Emerton, *The Pattern of Scottish Roofing*, 72, 73.

44. Withall, *Easdale, Belnahua, Luing & Seil*, 9–10.

45. ML, TD 1338/1/6/2.

46. The above account paraphrases the report by Menzies, ML TD 1338/1/6/2.

47. ML, TD 1338/1/6/18/7.1.

48. ML, TD 1338/2/6/12. This is 'Slate Book no. 3'. There is, loose within it, a letter written by the store-keeper at Bruichladdich Pier to the factor listing the stock he had in his care, including about 47,400 Welsh slates and about 1,500 Highland ones.

49. RCAHMS, *Argyll 5*, no. 435; Caldwell, *Islay, Jura and Colonsay*, 206; *Shawfield's Day Bk*, 141.

50. NAS, CS280/40/29.

51. A report by the trustee of his sequestrated estate, issued in 1858, shows that sales of tiles and bricks were still being accounted for as late as 1853. NAS, GD 64/1/347/2.

52. Steer and Bannerman, *Late Medieval Monumental Sculpture*, 150; McGladdery, *James II*, 85, 167; *CSP Scot*, ii, no. 13.

53. CM, 656/9; *Shawfield's Day Bk*, 16, 42. There is mention in 1773 of a 'waulking mill' near the lint mill at Skerrols, possibly the same structure. ML TD 1338/1/9 no. 2.

54. NAS, CC12/3/4, 91 (William Campbell of Auchindoun), and 101 (William Campbell of Kelsay); *SA* (1794), xi, 280. Regrettably, there is little direct evidence for the clothing of women at this time.

55. Teignmouth, *Sketches*, ii, 332; MacDonald, *Sketches of Islay*, 4.

56. NAS, CC12/3/3, 59.

57. *Stent Bk*, 275–78.

58. *Stent Bk*, 133–34.

59. Pennant, *Tour*, 216, reproduced in Caldwell, *Islay, Jura and Colonsay*, 84 (Fig. 15).

60. Bremner, *The Industries of Scotland*, 214–69; McGeachy, *Argyll 1730–1850*, 141–42.
61. NAS, E727/60/1; *Shawfield's Day Bk*, 42; MacDonald, *General View of the Agriculture of the Hebrides*, 53–54.
62. McKay (ed.), *The Rev Walker's Report on the Hebrides*, 103; *Shawfield's Day Bk*, 71, 235; *SA* (1794), xi, 280, 294; Pennant, *Tour*, 215, 217; *Stent Bk*, 85; Lord Teignmouth, *Sketches*, ii, 323–34.
63. Smith, *General View of the Agriculture of Argyll*, 1798, 92–97.
64. ML, TD 1338/1/9 no. 2; *Stent Bk*, 191. Taylor was still tenant of the mill in 1780, not necessarily as late as 1811.
65. ML, TD 1338/1/9 no. 1.
66. The lint mill was tenanted by Dugald McLarty in 1828 but was unoccupied by the time of the 1836 rental. Thereafter it is referred to as the lint mill croft.
67. Lord Teignmouth, *Sketches of the Coasts and Islands of Scotland*, ii, 324; ML TD 1338/1/4/6 no. 2; *SA* (1845), vii, 658.
68. ML, TD 1338/1/9 nos 4, 6; Booth, *An Islay Notebook*, 72–73. The machinery listed here and other equipment in the mill is of the utmost importance as rare surviving examples of nineteenth-century technology.
69. *Tourist's Guide*, 28.
70. Turnbull, *The Scottish Glass Industry*, 9–10; McGeachy, *Argyll*, 60–61.
71. NAS, E727/60/3.
72. Bigwood, *The Vice-Admiral Court of Argyll*, 37.
73. McKay, *Walker's Report on the Hebrides*, 100; ML T-MJ 361; MacDonald, *General View of the Agriculture of the Hebrides*, 622. McGeachy, *Argyll*, 60.
74. ML, TD 1284/5/3/1.
75. ML, TD 1284/5/3/1. This document is in the Kildalton Papers but clearly must have been rescued from the papers of Campbell of Shawfield.
76. Stanford, 'On the Manufacture of Kelp'.
77. Martin, *Western Islands*, 272–75; *Islay Bk*, 488.
78. *Islay Bk*, 467–68, 481.
79. *Islay Bk*, 367.
80. CM 602; *Islay Bk*, 480, 482. The ruins of the saltpans at Gartbreck are depicted on Langlands' map of 1801. There are very slight traces of a building behind the present farmhouse which may be all that is left. The site was presumably chosen because of the ready accessibility of sea water at all states of the tide.
81. McKay (ed.), *Walker's Report on the Hebrides*, 103–04.
82. NAS, E727/60/1–3; Anderson, *Account of the Hebrides*, 154.
83. *SA* (1794), xi, 299.
84. Teignmouth, *Sketches*, ii, 315–17; *SA* (1794), xi, 281; (1845), vii, 655.
85. 'Gowrie', *Off the Chain*, 236; *Tourist's Guide*, 49; Martin, *Kintyre Country Life*, 168.
86. ML, TD 1338/1/13/1 and 6.
87. McKay (ed.), *Walker's Report on the Hebrides*, 103–04; Miller, *Salt in the Blood*, 62–67. Storrie, Islay, 94.
88. Miller, *Salt in the Blood*, 68; ML T-MJ 327.5.
89. ML, TD 1338/1/13/6; Martin, *The Ring-Net Fishermen*, 197.
90. ML, TD 1338/1/13/4; TD 1284/3/1/1; Martin, *The Ring-Net Fishermen*, 197–98.
91. The photograph is in the collection of the Museum of Islay Life, and has been published in that museum's booklet, *The Isle of Islay – looking back*, 1998, 61.
92. For detailed technical information on the manufacture of whisky on Islay, see Jefford, *Peat Smoke and Spirit*, 5–25 and Wilson, *The Island Whisky Trail*, 121–29.
93. These statistics are derived from Jefford, *Peat Smoke and Spirit*. The Laphroaig photograph is reproduced on p. 57 of Wilson, *Scotch and Water*.
94. *RPC*, ix, 28.
95. *APS*, VI, i, 76.

96. Distilling, legal and illicit, in Argyll in the period from 1730 to 1859 is dealt with in considerable depth by McGeachy, *Argyll*, 177–207, with particular reference to changes in legislation.

97. *SA* (1794), xi, 295–96. The Islay whisky industry has been well covered in other works. Of particular use are Barnard, *The Whisky Distilleries of the United Kingdom*; Moss and Hume, *The Making of Scotch Whisky*; Wilson, *Scotch and Water*; Wilson, *The Island Whisky Trail*; Craig, *The Scotch Whisky Industry Record* and Jefford, *Peat Smoke and Spirit*.

98. McGeachy, *Argyll*, 185–86.

99. Bigwood, *The Argyll Courts 3*, 88 and Appendix 4 (NAS, JP 36/5/46).

100. NLS, MS 14986, 52. Pennant, *Tour*, 209, however, viewed remains of the gallows here in 1772, and identified the place as where executions were carried out in the time of the Lords of the Isles.

101. Barnard, *Whisky Distilleries*, 93; NAS, CC12/3/4, 163.

102. NAS, CC12/3/4, 17.

103. NAS, CE81/6/2, 10–11, 95–96, 98.

104. MacDougall, *As Long as Water Flows*, 28–29.

105. Craig, *The Scotch Whisky Industry Record*, 541. The columns for spirits produced and amount of duty charged are unfortunately blank against these Argyllshire entries with just a note that returns had not yet been received. Bowmore is not included in this list, presumably because it was producing for export.

106. Craig, *The Scotch Whisky Industry Record*, 69.

107. ML, TD 1338/1/4/1; TD 1338/1/5/7/4 and 5; ICD (*s.v.* status/distiller); Wilson, *The Island Whisky Trail*, 130–33.

108. ML, TD 1338/1/5/7/6; Wilson, *The Island Whisky Trail*, 131–33.

109. Wilson, *Scotch and Water*, 46, and 48 for a reproduction of the 1784 inventory; Craig, *The Scotch Whisky Industry Record*, 443. John Johnston's grave monument is in Kilnaughton Graveyard (see ICD).

110. Moss and Hume, *The Making of Scotch Whisky*, 70–72.

111. The information on distillery tacks comes from the 1848 printed rental. Craig, *The Scotch Whisky Industry Record*, 461.

112. Wilson, *Scotch and Water*, 52–55.

113. ML, TD 1338/1/5/6/1; TD 1338/4/9/1.

114. Wilson, *Scotch and Water*, 79; ML TD 1338/1/5/4/1.

115. Wilson, *The Island Whisky Trail*, 132. See also Hunter, *For the People's Cause*, 52–53.

116. Moss and Hume, *The Making of Scotch Whisky*, 110; Wilson, *Scotch and Water*, 81; ML TD, 1338/1/5/2/1; TD 1338/1/5/7/8.

117. Barnard, *Whisky Distilleries*, 87–113.

Appendix 1 Some Islay Surnames

1. *Scot. Hist. Soc. Misc.*, iv, 243, 247, 283; CM, bundles 654 (d), no. 10, and 656, no. 10; *Scot. Hist. Soc. Misc.*, iv, 283, no. 104; NAS, RS10/11 fol. 433; ML, TD 1284/3/1/2 (no. 12).

2. NAS, RS1/27 fol. 129; CM, bundle 654 (d) no. 4; *HP*, i, 128. I am grateful to Alastair Campbell of Airds for information on Alasdair Roy.

3. *APS*, ix, 166b; *Shawfield's Day Bk*, 22, 25.

4. NAS, RS10/11 fols 222–23, 264, 368–74

5. *RPC*, 3rd ser., ix, 325; *Islay Bk*, 417–18, 426, 433; *Shawfield's Day Bk*, 48–53.

6. *Scot. Hist. Soc. Misc.*, iv, 246–49, 251; CM, bundle 654 (d), no. 8; NAS, RS10/11 fols 437–38; CC12/3/3 f38.

7. CM, bundle 654 (d), no. 6; NAS, RS10/8/329, CC12/3/3 f16.

8. NAS, CC12/3/4 fol. 22; NAS, CS230/C/5/9; ML, TD 1284/3/1/1 (Account of 8 Sept. 1777 between Shawfield and Colin Campbell of Ardnahoe); *Shawfield's Day Bk*, 195. This account differs from that given by Freda Ramsay in *Shawfield's Day Bk*, 103.

9. Information in a letter from Alastair Campbell of Airds, 13 September 2006.

10. Information in a letter from Alastair Campbell of Airds, 13 September 2006.

11. NAS, RS10/8 fols 222–23, 346; RS10/9 fols 109, 412; RS10/11 fols 244–46.

12. *Scot. Hist. Soc. Misc.*, iv, 248; *Journal of the Hon. John Erskine of Carnock 1683–1687*. Scot Hist Soc (1893), 118.

13. *Islay Bk*, 430–32.

14. *HP*, iii, 257n; CM, bundle 654 (d), nos 21, 22; bundle 656, no. 8; *Scot. Hist. Soc. Misc.*, iv, 247–8; *Shawfield's Day Bk*, 114; *RPC*, 3rd series, ix, 323–32; NAS, RS10/2 fol. 69.

15. NLS, ACC 6223, bundles 12–14, *passim*.

16. CM, bundle 654, nos 13, 17; NAS, RS 10/2 fols 479–80. *Islay Bk*, 421, provides a copy of the Procuratory of Resignation of Torabus in 1695, printing '1620' instead of '1629' for the original sale of the lands.

17. Storrie, *Continuity and Change*, 4.

18. ICD, *s.v.* Johnston* (*sic*); Wilson, *The Island Whisky Trail*, 28–29, 45, 53.

19. This Angus Dubh is listed in the manuscript Notices of Scottish Highland Pipers . . . compiled by J. MacLennan in the nineteenth century, with additions by others, including Major MacKay-Scobie. No sources are given. The original manuscript is in NLS, and there is a copy in the library of the National Museums of Scotland, Edinburgh.

20. CM, bundle 654, (d) no. 19; NAS, E69/3/1, 57; NAS, RS 10/3 fols 146, 322.

21. *RPC*, 3rd ser., xi, 114, 246, 308, 329.

22. *ER*, xvii, 616, 620; *Islay Bk*, 450–51; *HP*, iii, 203–05.

23. For a detailed account of this family, see Bannerman, *The Beatons*.

24. *ALI*, no. 16.

25. NAS, RS1/27 fol. 129; Bannerman, *The Beatons*, 124–25; *Cawdor Bk*, 295.

26. AT, ii (2), 599.

27. *RSS*, i, no. 911.

28. *HP*, i, 24–25.

29. *ALI*, nos 47, 63, 64, and p. 205.

30. Martin, *Western Islands*, 274–75; Kelly, *Early Irish Farming*, 291; *Islay Bk*, 488.

31. *RPC*, x, 721; *Cawdor Bk*, 242–43; *Islay Bk*, 364.

32. *Islay Bk*, 490–520 (Islay Rental of 1686).

33. ICD, s.v. MacDougall; Wilson, *The Island Whisky Trail*, 32–43.

34. Steer and Bannerman, *Monumental Sculpture*, 119.

35. *HP*, i, 25.

36. Steer and Bannerman, *Sculpture*, 157–58; *Shawfield's Day Bk*, 107.

37. ML, TD 1338/1/2/8, for 1802 tack of Daill; Wilson, *The Island Whisky Trail*, 130–31.

38. AT, ii (2), 599.

39. *Cawdor Bk*, 242–43; *Islay Bk*, 364.

40. CM, bundle 654, (d) no. 19.

41. Steer and Bannerman, *Monumental Sculpture*, 123.

42. *ALI*, 185; AT, ii (2), 599.

43. AT, iv, 48.

44. *Coll de Rebus Alban*, 13.

45. *Scot. Hist. Soc. Misc.*, iv (1926), 205.

46. *Islay Bk*, 451.

47. ICD, *s.v.* Macindeor. For the name change to MacArthur, see Black, *Surnames*, 516. We know of no other evidence for this.

48. Steer and Bannerman, *Monumental Sculpture*, 125 no. 6.

49. *RMS*, 1, app. 1, no. 99.

50. *HP*, i, 41, 24.

51. *ER*, xii, 709.

52. Paton, *MacKintosh Muniments*, no. 159; *Cawdor Bk*, 242–43.
53. CM, bundle 655, Islay Rental of 1654.
54. *RPC*, vii, 627.
55. *Cawdor Bk*, 288.
56. For another account of this family, the Mackays in Kildalton parish, see Lamont, 'The Islay charter of 1408'.
57. Paton, *MacKintosh Muniments*, nos 109, 159.
58. ML TD 1338/1/3/18.
59. ICD, *s.v.* McMillan; Black, *Surnames*, 67, 543–44.
60. *Cawdor Bk*, 234; AT, vi, 78.
61. Steer and Bannerman, *Monumental Sculpture*, 153.
62. CM, 590/41; 655/129.
63. Wilson, *The Island Whisky Trail*, 131–22; Hunter, *For The People's Cause*, 47; Storrie, *Continuity and Change*, 4: MacKechnie, *Carragh-chuimhne*, 62.
64. *CSSR (1423–1428)*, 127, 179; Steer and Bannerman, *Monumental Sculpture*, 123–24.
65. The 1733 and 1741 rentals of Islay are reproduced in *Shawfield's Day Bk*, 9–20, 37–44.
66. Black, *Surnames of Scotland*, 552.
67. Sinclair, 'The Journal of Donald Sinclair'.
68. ICD, *s.v.* MacTaggart. For some more recent MacTaggarts, see MacTaggart, 'The Mysterious Uncle Donald'.
69. For a detailed overview of this family, see Thomson, 'The MacMhuirich Bardic Family'.
70. AT, iii, 46; iv, 48; *HP*, i, 16.
71. *Fasti*, iv, 60, 66, 73; ICD, *s.v.* Simson.

Appendix 2 Islay Lands, Recorded Prior to 1722

1. The etymological information in this apprendix is derived from Alan Macniven's PhD, *The Norse in Islay*, which should be consulted for more detailed explanations and reasoning.
2. The Urisk were supernatural creatures, the offspring of unions between mortals and fairies. See Campbell, *Superstitions of the Highlands & Islands*, 195–99.
3. *Islay Bk*, 139–43.
4. Bannerman, *The Beatons*, 15.
5. Lamont, 'The Islay Charter of 1408', 177.
6. Maceacharna, *The Lands of the Lordship*, 90; Pennant, *Tour*, 209.
7. RCAHMS, *Argyll 5*, no. 453.
8. Martin, *Western Islands*, 273–74; Pennant, *Tour*, 223; 'Gowrie', *Off the Chain*, 282.
9. NAS, CC12/3/4, 73.
10. *Islay Bk*, 382–83.
11. Watson, *Celtic Placenames*, 278.
12. Watson, *Celtic Placenames*, 302.
13. Watson, *Celtic Placenames*, 285.
14. Watson, *Celtic Placenames*, 309.
15. RCAHMS, *Argyll 5*, no. 140.
16. Earl, *Tales of Islay*, 26.
17. Steer and Bannerman, *Medieval Sculpture*, 147–48.
18. *Cawdor Bk*, 191; *Islay Bk*, 380–81.
19. NAS, RS10/2/69.
20. *Retours*, i, nos 82, 93.
21. Maceacharna, *The Lands of the Lordship*, 29.
22. Maceacharna, *The Lands of the Lordship*, 122.
23. *Islay Bk*, 26–27.

ISLAY

24. *Islay Bk*, 45–47.
25. See, for instance, retour of Hector MacLean of Duart to the Barony of Duart in 1615. *Retours*, i, no. 16.
26. Lamont, 'The Islay Charter of 1408', 175.

Bibliography

Manuscript sources

Cawdor Castle, Nairn
Edinburgh, National Archives of Scotland
Edinburgh, National Library of Scotland
Glasgow, Mitchell Library
Glasgow University, Department of Scottish History

Unpublished works

Cameron, E. A., 'Poverty, Protest and Politics: Perceptions of the Scottish Highlands in the Era of the Crofters' War', forthcoming.

Cressey, M., The Identification of Early Lead Mining: Environmental, Archaeological and Historical Perspectives from Islay, Inner Hebrides, Scotland. University of Edinburgh PhD, 1995.

MacLennan, J., Notices of Scottish Highland Pipers. Manuscript, National Museums Scotland, n.d.

Macniven, A., The Norse in Islay. A Settlement Historical Case-study for Medieval Scandinavian Activity in Western Maritime Scotland. University of Edinburgh, PhD, 2006.

Murdoch., J. ('Finlagan'), The Queen of the Hebrides. NLS, MS 14986, c.1859.

Swift, C., Irish Influence on Ecclesiastical Settlements in Scotland: A Case Study of the Island of Islay. Department of Archaeology, University of Durham, MPhil thesis, 1987.

Electronic publications

<http://www.angelfire.com/bc2/Bereans/Cornerstones/Pioneers/Herald/131.html> Thomson, J., Excursion to Helensburgh and the Queen of the Hebrides (accessed 9 June 2007).

<http://www.finlaggan.com> The web-site of the Finlaggan Trust (accessed 1 January 2008).

<http://www.geo.ed.ac.uk/scotgaz> Groome, F. H. (ed.), *Ordnance Gazetteer of Scotland: A Survey of Scottish Topography, Statistical, Biographical and Historical.* Edinburgh, 1882–85 (accessed 1 January 2008).

<http://www.islayinfo.com> (accessed 19 November 2007).

<http://www.linguae-celticae.org/GLS_english.htm> *Gàidhlig (Scottish Gaelic) Local Studies vol. 16: Ile, Diùra & Colbhasa.* 2nd edition, May 2006 (accessed 30 November 2007).

<http://lists.rootsweb.com/index/intl/SCT/SCT-ISLAY.html> a site for those involved in genealogical research on Ilich (accessed 1 January 2008).
<http://www.nls.uk/maps/blaeu/page.cfm?id=98.html> Map of the *Isle of Ila*, from J. Blaeu's *Atlas Novus* of 1654 (accessed 9 June 2007).
<http://www.nls.uk/maps/early/581.html> Map of Argyllshire, G. Langlands. Campbeltown, 1801 (accessed 27 July 2007).
<http://www.oxforddnb.com> *The Oxford Dictionary of National Biography*. Oxford, 2004 (accessed 27 July 2007).
<http://www.pastpresented.info/cumbria/chron78mj.htm> Extracts from the *Cumberland Chronicle and Whitehaven Public Advertiser, 1778* (accessed 9 June 2007).
<http://www.rcahms.gov.uk> The Royal Commission on Ancient and Historical Monuments of Scotland, providing access to CANMORE, a database of archaeological sites and monuments in Scotland (accessed 31 July 2007).
<http://www.rps.ac.uk> The Records of the Parliaments of Scotland.
<http://www.ucc.ie/celt/> CELT (Corpus of Electronic Texts) – the online resource for Irish history, literature and politics; a project of the History Department, University College Cork.
<http://www.ucc.ie/celt/published/T100010A/> Annals of Loch Cé (accessed 27 July 2007).
<http://www.wsharvey.dial.pipex.com/leadandlabour> Harvey, W. S., *Lead And Labour. The Miners of Leadhills* (accessed 18 December 2007).

Paper publications

Adams, I. H. and Fortune, G. (eds), *Alexander Lindsay, A Rutter of the Scottish Seas circa 1540*. Greenwich, National Maritime Museum, 1980.
Alonzo Gray, A. and Adams, C. B., *Elements of Geology*. New York, 1859.
Analecta Scotica: Collections illustrative of the Civil, Ecclesiastical, and Literary History of Scotland. Edinburgh, 1834.
Anderson, A. O., *Early Sources of Scottish History, 500 to 1286*. 2 vols, Stamford, 1990.
Anderson, G. and Anderson, P., *Guide to the Highlands and Western Islands of Scotland*. 4 vols, Edinburgh, 1863.
Anderson, J., *An Account of the Present State of the Hebrides and Western Coasts of Scotland . . .* Edinburgh, 1785.
Anderson, M. O., *Kings and Kingship in early Scotland*. Edinburgh, 1973.
Anderson Smith, W. See 'Gowrie'.
Annals of Loch Cé, <http://www.ucc.ie/celt/published/T10001A/>.
Anonymous, 'An account of old John Taylor', *Scots Magazine*, 33 (1771), 24–26.
Arbuthnot, S. and Hollo, K., *Fil súil nglais. A Grey Eye looks Back: a Festschrift in honour of Colm Ó Baoill*. Ceann Drochaid, 2007.
Atkinson, J. A., Banks, I., and MacGregor, G. (eds), *Townships to Farmsteads. Rural Settlement Studies in Scotland, England and Wales*. British Archaeological Report, British series 293, Oxford, 2000.
Bain, J. (ed.), *Calendar of Documents Relating to Scotland*. Edinburgh, 1881–88.
————, *Calendar of Border Papers*. Edinburgh, 1894.
————, et al. (eds), *Calendar of the State Papers relating to Scotland and Mary Queen of Scots 1547–1603*. Edinburgh, 1898–1969.
Bannatyne Club, *Origines Parochiales Scotiae. The Antiquities Ecclesiastical and Territorial of the Parishes of Scotland*. 3 vols. Edinburgh, 1851–55.
Bannerman, J. W. M., *Studies in the History of Dálriada*. Edinburgh, 1974.
————, 'The Lordship of the Isles', in Brown (ed.) 1977, 209–40.
————, *The Beatons: A Medical Kindred in the Classical Gaelic Tradition*. Edinburgh, 1998.
Barber, J. and Brown, M. M., 'An Sithean, Islay', *PSAS*, 114 (1984), 161–88.

Barbour, J., *The Bruce*. See Duncan 1997.

Barnard, A., *The Whisky Distilleries of the United Kingdom*. Edinburgh, 2003.

Barrell, A. D. M., 'The Church in the West Highlands in the late Middle Ages', *Innes Review*, 54 (2003), 23–46.

Barrow, G. W. S., et al. (eds), *Regesta Regum Scottorum*. Edinburgh, 1960–.

Bartlett, T. and Jeffrey, K. (eds), *A Military History of Ireland*. Cambridge, 1996.

Beaugué, J. de, *Histoire de la guerre d'Ecosse: pendant les campagnes 1548 et 1549*. Maitland Club, 1830.

Bennion, L. F., 'The Second Migration of Scots to North Carolina', *The Argyll Colony Plus*, 19/2 (July 2005), 18–28.

Bergin, O., 'An Address to Aonghus of Islay', *Scottish Gaelic Studies*, 4 (1934–35), 57–65.

Berry, R. J., 'Evolution of animals and plants in the Inner Hebrides', in Morton Boyd and Bowes (eds), 1983, 433–47.

BGS, (map), *North Islay*. Scotland Sheet 27. Solid and Drift Edition. 1:50,000 Provisional Series, 1997.

————, (map), *South Islay*. Scotland Sheet 19. Solid and Drift Edition. 1:50,000 Provisional Series, 1998.

Bigwood, F. (ed.), *The Vice-Admiral Court of Argyll. Processes, etc (1685–1825)*. Privately printed, 2001.

———— (ed.), *The Argyll Courts 3. Justices of the Peace in Argyll Processes, etc of the JP Courts 1674–1825*. Privately printed, 2001.

Black, G. F., *The Surnames of Scotland*, New York, 1946.

Blackburn, S., *Dive Islay Wrecks*. Stoke-on-Trent, 1986.

Blair, W. N., *Reminiscences of Islay*. Museum of Islay Life, Port Charlotte, 1995.

Bliss, W. H., et al. (eds), *Calendar of Entries in the Papal Registers relating to Great Britain and Ireland: Papal Letters*. London, 1893–.

Boardman, S., *The Early Stewart Kings Robert II and Robert III 1371–1406*. East Linton, 1996.

————, *The Campbells 1250–1513*. Edinburgh, 2006.

———— and Ross, A. (eds), *The Exercise of Power in Medieval Scotland c.1200–1500*. Dublin, 2003.

Booth, C. G., *Birds in Islay*. Port Charlotte, 1975.

————, *An Islay Notebook*. Islay Museums Trust, n.d.

Bremner, D., *The Industries of Scotland*. Newton Abbot, 1969.

Brewer, J. S. (ed.), *Calendar of the Carew Manuscripts*. 6 vols, London, 1867.

————, et al. (eds), *Letters and Papers Foreign and Domestic of the Reign of Henry VIII*. London, 1864–1932.

Brock, W. R., *Scotus Americanus*. Edinburgh, 1982.

Broderick, G. (ed.), *Cronica Regum Mannie et Insularum Chronicles of the Kings of Man and the Isles*. Douglas, 1996.

Brooking, T. and Coleman, J. (eds), *The Heather and the Fern. Scottish Migration & New Zealand Settlement*. Dunedin, 2003.

Brooks, D., 'Gall-Gaidhil and Galloway' in Oram and Stell, (eds), 1991, 97–116.

Brown, J. M. (ed.), *Scottish Society in the Fifteenth Century*. London, 1977.

Brown, M., *James I*. Edinburgh, 1994.

Bruford, A. L. and MacDonald, D. A. (eds), *Scottish Traditional Tales*. Edinburgh, 2003.

Burns, C. (ed.), *Calendar of Papal Letters to Scotland of Clement VII of Avignon 1378–1395*. Scottish History Society, 1976.

Burt, E., *Burt's Letters from the North of Scotland*. Edinburgh, 1998.

Burt, R., Waite, P. and Atkinson, M., 'Scottish metalliferous mining 1845 to 1913: detailed returns from the *Mineral Statistics*. Part I', *Journal of Industrial Archaeology*, 16/1, 1981, 4–19.

Burton, J. H. et al. (eds), *The Register of the Privy Council of Scotland*. Edinburgh, 1877–.

Byrne, F. J., *Irish Kings and High-Kings*. Dublin, 2001.

Caldwell, D. H., 'The Battle of Pinkie', in Macdougall (ed.), 1991, 61–94.

————, *Islay, Jura and Colonsay: A Historical Guide*. Edinburgh, 2001.

————, 'Finlaggan, Islay – stones and inauguration ceremonies', in Welander, Breeze and Clancy (eds), 2003, 61–75.

———— (ed.), *Finlaggan Archeological Project Monograph*. Forthcoming.

———— and Ruckley, N. A., 'Domestic Architecture in the Lordship of the Isles', in Oram and Stell (eds) 2005, 96–121.

————, McWee, R. and Ruckley, R. A., 'Post-Medieval settlement on Islay – some recent research', in Atkinson, Banks and MacGregor (eds), 2000, 58–68.

Callender, R. M. and Macaulay, J., *The Ancient Metal Mines of the Isle of Islay, Argyll*. The Northern Mine Research Society, Sheffield, 1984.

Cameron, A., *Reliquiae Celticae*. 2 vols, Inverness, 1894.

Cameron, J. (ed.), *The Justiciary Records of Argyll and the Isles 1664–1705*, vol. 1. Stair Society, 1949.

Cameron, J., *James V. The Personal Rule, 1528–1542*. East Linton, 1998.

Campbell, A., A History of Clan Campbell. 3 vols, Edinburgh, 2000–04.

Campbell, Lord A., *Records of Argyll*. Edinburgh, 1885.

Campbell, D., 'Observations of Mr Dioness Campbell Deane of Limerick on the West Isles of Scotland', *Maitland Club Miscellany*, IV, i (1847), 35–57.

Campbell, E., 'Were the Scots Irish?', *Antiquity*, 75 (2001), 285–92.

Campbell, J. F., *Popular Tales of the West Highlands*. 4 vols, Hounslow, 1983–84.

Campbell, J. G., *Superstitions of the Highlands & Islands of Scotland collected entirely from oral sources*. Glasgow, 1900.

Campbell, R. N. and Williamson, R. B., 'Salmon and freshwater fishes of the Inner Hebrides', in Morton Boyd and Bowes (eds), 1983, 245–65.

Campbell, W. F., 'The improvement of waste land of a district in the island of Islay', *Transactions of the Royal Highland & Agricultural Society of Scotland*, 13 (1841), 232–35.

————, 'On the potato disease, crop 1845', *Prize Essays and Transactions of the Highland Society of Scotland*, new ser., 3 (1845–47), 460–62.

Carmichael, A., *Carmina Gadelica*. Edinburgh, 1994.

Carney, J. and Greene, D. (eds), *Celtic Studies: Essays in memory of Angus Matheson 1912–1962*. The Gaelic Society of Glasgow, 1968.

Cathcart, A., 'James V, king of Scotland – and Ireland?', in Duffy (ed.), 2007, 124–43.

Celoria, F., 'Notes on lore and customs in the district near Portnahaven, Rhinns of Islay, Argyll', Scotland, *Folklore*, 76 (1965), 39–47.

Chapman, J. and Mytum, H. C. (eds), *Settlement in Northern Britain 1000 BC – AD 1000*. BAR, Oxford, 1983.

Charles-Edwards, T. M., 'Irish Warfare before 1100', in Bartlett and Jeffrey (eds), 1996, 26–51.

Charters of the Abbey of Crosraguel. 2 vols, Edinburgh, 1886.

Child, F. J., *The English and Scottish Popular Ballads*. 3 vols, New York, 1965.

Clarke, H. B., Ní Mhaonaigh, M. and Ó Floinn, R. (eds), *Ireland and Scandinavia in the Early Viking Age*. Dublin, 1998.

Cowan, E. J., 'Clanship, kinship and the Campbell acquisition of Islay', *SHR*, 58 (1979), 132–57.

————, 'Norwegian Sunset – Scottish Dawn: Hakon IV and Alexander III', in Reid (ed.), 1990, 103–31.

———— and McDonald, R. A. (eds), *Alba Celtic Scotland in the Medieval Era*. East Linton, 2000.

Cowan, I. B., *The Parishes of Medieval Scotland*. Scottish Record Society, 1967.

———— and Easson, D. E., *Medieval Religious Houses Scotland*. London, 1976.

Craig, H. C., *The Scotch Whisky Industry Record*. Dumbarton, 1994.

Craigie, W. A. (ed.), *The Asloan Manuscript*. STS, 1923, ii, 215–44.

Cregeen, E., 'Recollections of an Argyllshire Drover', *SS*, 3 (1959), 143–62.

Curie, A. and Murray, C. W., 'Flora and vegetation of the Inner Hebrides', in Morton Boyd and Bowes (eds), 1983, 293–318.

Curle, A. O., Olsen, M. and Shetelig, H. (eds), *Viking Antiquities in Great Britain and Ireland*, Part 6. Oslo, 1954.

Dalyell, W. (ed.), *Fragments of Scotish* [sic] *History*. Edinburgh, 1798.

Dawson, A. et al., 'Late Glacial Relative Sea Level Changes, Ruantallain-Shian Bay, West Jura', in Dawson and Dawson (eds), 1997, 17–40.

Dawson, S. and Dawson, A. G. (eds), *The Quaternary of Islay & Jura Field Guide.* Quaternary Research Association: Cambridge, 1997.

———— and Dawson, A. G., 'Holocene relative sea level change Gruinart, Isle of Islay', in Dawson and Dawson (eds), 1997, 78–98.

Dickson, T., Balfour Paul, J., et al., *Accounts of the Lord High Treasurer of Scotland.* Edinburgh, 1877–.

Dilworth, M., 'Benedictine Monks of Ratisbon and Wurzburg in the Seventeenth and Eighteenth Centuries: Émigrés from the Highlands of Scotland', *Trans. Gaelic Soc. Inverness*, 44 (1964–66), 94–110.

Dobson, D., *Scottish Emigration to Colonial America, 1607–1785.* Athens, Georgia, 1994.

Dodgshon, R. A., 'West Highland Chiefdoms, 1500–1745: A Study In Redistributive Exchange', in Mitchison and Roebuck (eds), 1988, 27–37.

————, 'West Highland and Hebridean settlement prior to crofting and the clearances; a study in stability or change?', *PSAS*, 123 (1993), 419–38.

Dow, F., *Cromwellian Scotland.* Edinburgh, 1999.

Duckworth, C. L. D. and Langmuir, G. E., *West Highland Steamers.* Prescot, Lancashire, 1967 (3rd edit).

Duffy, S., 'The "Continuation" of Nicholas Trevet: A New Source For The Bruce Invasion', *Proc Royal Irish Academy*, 91 C, no. 12 (1991), 303–15.

————, 'Irishmen and Islesmen in the Kingdoms of Dublin and Man 1052–1171', *Ériu*, 43 (1992), 93–133.

————, 'The Bruce Brothers and the Irish Sea World, 1306–29', in Duffy (ed.), 2002, 45–70.

———— (ed.), *Robert the Bruce's Irish Wars.* Stroud, 2002.

————, 'The Lords of Galloway, Earls of Carrick, and the Bissets of the Glens: Scottish settlement in thirteenth-century Ulster', in Edwards (ed.), 2004, 37–50.

————, 'The prehistory of the galloglass', in Duffy (ed.), 2007, 1–23.

———— (ed.), *The World of the Galloglass. Kings, warlords and warriors in Ireland and Scotland, 1200–1600.* Dublin, 2007.

Dumville, D. N., *The Churches of Northern Britain in the First Viking Age.* Whithorn, 1997.

————, 'Ireland and North Britain in the Earlier Middle Ages: Contexts for *Míniugud Senchasa Fher nAlban*', in Ó Baoill and McGuire (eds), 2000, 185–211.

Dunbar, J. G. and Duncan, A. A. M., 'Tarbert Castle A contribution to the history of Argyll', *SHR*, 50 (1971), 1–17.

Duncan, A. A. M. and Brown, A. L., 'Argyll and the Isles in the earlier middle ages', *PSAS*, 90 (1959), 203, 192–220.

———— (ed.), J. Barbour, *The Bruce.* Edinburgh, 1997.

Dunlop, A. I., et al. (eds), *Calendar of Scottish Supplications to Rome.* Vols 1–3, SHS, 1934–70; vol. 4, Glasgow, 1983.

Dunn, C. W., *Highland Settler. A Portrait of the Scottish Gael in Nova Scotia.* Toronto, 1953.

Duwe, K. C., *Gàidhlig (Scottish Gaelic) Local Studies, vol. 16: Ile, Diùra & Colbhasa* (consulted on the Linguae Celticae website: <http://www.linguae-celticae.org/GLS_english.htm>).

Earl, P., *Tales of Islay Fact and Folklore.* Bowmore, n.d.

Edwards, D. (ed.), *Regions and Rulers in Ireland, 1100–1650.* Dublin, 2004.

Edwards, E. (co-ordinator), *Seanchas Ìle. Islay's folklore project.* Glendaruel, 2007.

Edwards, J. K. and Mithen, S., 'The colonization of the Hebridean Islands of Western Scotland: evidence from the palynological and archaeological records', *World Archaeology*, 26 (3) (1994–95), 348–365.

Elliott, R. E., *Birds of Islay.* London, 1989.

Emerton, G., *The Pattern of Scottish Roofing.* Historic Scotland, Edinburgh, 2000.

Environmental Resources Management, *Landscape assessment of Argyll and the Firth of Clyde.* Perth: Scottish Natural Heritage (Review no. 78), 1996.

Erskine, J., *Journal of the Hon. John Erskine of Carnock 1683–1687.* SHS, 1893.

Etchingham, C., *Church Organisation in Ireland AD 650 to 1000.* Maynooth, 1999.

Fisher, I., *Early Medieval Sculpture in the West Highlands and Islands.* RCAHMS, Edinburgh, 2001.

Forsyth, K., *Language in Pictland: The Case against Non-Indo-European Pictish.* Utrecht, 1997.

Foster, J., *Members of Parliament, Scotland.* London, 1882.

Fraser Darling, F., *West Highland Survey.* Oxford, 1955.

Freeman, A. M. (ed.), *Annála Connacht. The Annals of Connacht (AD 1224–1544).* Dublin, 1983.

Gailey, R. A., 'The Evolution of Highland Rural Settlement, with particular reference to Argyllshire', *SS,* 6 (1962), 155–77.

Gatty, R., *Portrait of a Merchant Prince. James Morrison 1789–1857.* Northallerton, n.d. [1977].

Gerriets, M., 'Economy and Society: Clientship according to the Irish Laws', *Cambridge Medieval Celtic Studies,* 6 (1983), 42–61.

————, 'Kingship and Exchange in Pre-Viking Ireland', *Cambridge Medieval Celtic Studies,* 13 (1987), 39–72.

Giblin, C. (ed.), *Irish Franciscan Mission to Scotland 1619–1646.* Dublin, 1964.

Goodare, J., 'The Statutes of Iona in Context', *SHR,* 77 (1998), 31–57.

———— and Lynch, M. (eds), *The Reign of James VI.* East Linton. 2000.

Goodrich-Freer, A., 'The Norsemen in the Hebrides', *Saga Book of the Viking Club,* 2/1 (1897), 51–74.

Gordon, R., *A Genealogical History of the Earldom of Sutherland.* Edinburgh, 1813.

'Gowrie', (W. Anderson Smith), *Off the Chain.* Manchester, 1868.

Graham, I. C. C., *Colonists from Scotland: Emigration to North America, 1707–1783.* Ithaca, New York, 1956.

Graham, R. C., *The Carved Stones of Islay.* Glasgow, 1895.

Grant, A., 'The Revolt of the Lord of the Isles and the Death of the Earl of Douglas, 1451–1452', *SHR,* 60 (1981), 169–74.

Grant, I. F., *Highland Folk Ways.* London, 1961.

Grant, J. W. and MacLeod, A., 'Agriculture in the Inner Hebrides', in Morton Boyd and Bowes (eds), 1983, 567–75.

Green, F. H. W. and Harding, R. J., 'Climate of the Inner Hebrides', in Morton Boyd and Bowes (eds), 1983, 121–40.

Gregory, D., *History Of The Western Highlands And Isles Of Scotland.* Edinburgh, 1836.

Groome, F. H. (ed.), *Ordnance Gazetteer of Scotland: A Survey of Scottish Topography, Statistical, Biographical and Historical.* Edinburgh, 1882–85. Consulted online at <http://www.geo.ed.ac.uk/scotgaz>.

Haddow, A. J., *The History and Structure of Ceol Mor.* 1982, 38–55.

Haldane, A. R. B., *Three Centuries of Scottish Posts.* Edinburgh, 1971.

————, *The Drove Roads of Scotland.* Edinburgh, 2002.

Hamilton, H. C., et al. (eds), *Calendar of the State Papers relating to Ireland.* London and Dublin, 1860–2000.

Hannay, R. K. (ed.), *Acts of the Lords of Council in Public Affairs 1501–1554.* Edinburgh, 1932.

Harvey, W. S., *Lead And Labour. The Miners of Leadhills.* <http://www.wsharvey.dial.pipex.com/leadandlabour>.

Hayes-McCoy, G. A., *Scots Mercenary Forces in Ireland (1565–1603).* Dublin, 1937.

————, *Ulster and other Irish Maps c.1600.* Dublin, 1964.

Hearn, T., 'Scots Miners on the Goldfields, 1861–1870', in Brooking and Coleman (eds), 2003, 67–85.

Hennessy, W. M. and McCarthy, B., (eds), *Annals of Ulster.* 3 vols, Dublin, 1887–1901.

Hewitson, J., *Far Off In Sunlit Places. Stories of the Scots in Australia and New Zealand.* Edinburgh, 1998.

Hill, G., *An Historical Account of the MacDonnells of Antrim.* Belfast, 1873.

Hill, J. and Bastin, N., *A Very Canny Scot. 'Great' Daniel Campbell of Shawfield & Islay 1670–1753.* Barnham, 2007.

Hill, J. M., *Fire and Sword: Sorley Boy MacDonnell and the rise of Clan Ian Mor, 1538–1590.* London, 1993.

Hole, M. J. and Morrison, M. A., 'The differentiated dolerite boss, Cnoc Rhaonastil, Islay: a natural experiment in the low pressure differentiation of an alkali olivine-basalt magma', *Scot. Journ. Geol.,* 28 (1992), 55–69.

Holm, P., 'The Slave Trade of Dublin, Ninth to Twelfth Centuries' *Peritia,* 5 (1986), 317–45.

Howarth, H., 'The Columban Clergy of North Britain and their harrying by the Norsemen', *Trans. Roy. Hist. Soc.,* 7 (1878), 395–444.

Hudson, B. T., 'The changing economy of the Irish Sea province: AD 900 – 1300', in Smith, (ed.), 1999, 39–66.

Hudson, G. and Henderson, D. J., 'Soils of the Inner Hebrides', in Morton Boyd and Bowes (eds), 1983, 107–119.

Hunter, J. (ed.), *For the People's Cause. From the writings of John Murdoch.* Edinburgh, 1986.

Ileach, The. See Islay Council of Social Service.

Imsen, S. (ed.), *Ecclesia Nidrosiensis 1153–1537.* Trondheim, 2003.

Innes, C. (ed.), *The Book of the Thanes of Cawdor, A Series of Papers selected from the Charter Room at Cawdor, 1236–1742.* Spalding Club, 1859.

Iona Club (ed.), *Collectanea de Rebus Albanicis, consisting of Original Papers and Documents relating to the history of the Highlands and Islands of Scotland.* Edinburgh, 1847.

Islay Council of Social Service, *The Ileach* (newspaper, issued every 2 weeks). Bowmore, 1973–.

Jameson, R., *Mineralogy of the Scottish Isles.* 2 vols, Edinburgh, 1800.

Jaski, B., *Early Irish Kingship and Succession.* Dublin, 2000.

Jefford, A., *Peat Smoke and Spirit. A Portrait of Islay and its Whiskies.* London, 2004.

Jennings, A., 'Historical and linguistic evidence for Gall-Gaidheil and Norse in Western Scotland', in Ureland and Clarkson (eds), 1996, 61–73.

Jillings, K., *Scotland's Black Death. The Foul Death of the English.* Stroud, 2003.

Johnsen, A. O., 'The payments from the Hebrides and Isle of Man to the crown of Norway 1153–1263', *SHR,* 48 (1969), 18–34.

Jupp, C. N., *The History of Islay from earliest times to 1848.* MIL, Port Charlotte, 1994.

Kelly, F., *Early Irish Farming.* Dublin, 1998.

Kingston, S., *Ulster and the Isles in the Fifteenth Century The Lordship of the Clann Domhnaill of Antrim.* Dublin, 2004.

Laing, D. (ed.), The Orygynale Cronykil of Scotland. 3 vols, Edinburgh, 1879.

Laing, L. and Laing, J., *The Picts and the Scots.* Thrupp, 1994.

Lamont, W. D., 'Old Land Denominations and "Old Extent" in Islay', *SS,* 1 (1957), 183–203; 2 (1958), 86–106.

————, 'The Islay Charter of 1408', *Proc. Roy. Irish Academy Archaeology,* 59–60 (1957–59), 163–87.

————, *The Early History of Islay.* Dundee, 1970.

————, 'Alexander of Islay, Son of Angus Mór', *SHR,* 60 (1981), 160–69.

Lane, A. and Campbell, E. (eds), *Dunadd: an early Dalriadic Capital.* Oxford, 2000.

Langlands, G. and son, *Map of Argyllshire.* Campbeltown, 1801. See <http://www.nls.uk/maps/early/581.html>.

Laughton, J. K., *Studies in Naval History. Biographies.* London, 1887.

Lindsay, J. M., 'The Iron Industry in the Highlands: Charcoal Blast Furnaces', *SHR,* 56 (1977), 49–63.

Livingstone, M., et al., *Registrum Secreti Sigilli.* Edinburgh, 1908–.

Love, J., 'Shielings of the Isle of Rum', *SS,* 25 (1981), 39–63.

Lowry, B. (ed.), *20th Century Defences in Britian. An introductory guide.* Council For British Archaeology, York, 1995.

Lumby, J. R. (ed.), *Chronica Henrici Knighton Vel Cnitthon Monachi Leycestrensis*, vol. 2. London, 1895.

Lynch, M., 'James VI and the "Highland problem"', in Goodare and Lynch (eds), 2000, 208–27.

Mac Airt, S. (ed.), *The Annals of Inisfallen*. Dublin, 1988.

MacAlpine, N., *A Pronouncing Gaelic–English Dictionary*. Glasgow, 1934.

MacBain, A., The Place-Names of the Highlands and Islands. Stirling, 1922.

MacCoinnich, A., '"Kingis rabellis" to "Cudich 'n Rìgh"? Clann Choinnich: the emergence of a kindred, *c*.1475–*c*.1514', in Boardman and Ross (eds), 2003, 175–200.

Macculloch, J., *The Highlands and Western Isles of Scotland*. 4 vols, London, 1824.

MacDonald, A. and A., *The Clan Donald*. 3 vols, Inverness, 1896–1904.

Macdonald, D., *Lewis. A History of the Island*. London, 2004.

Macdonald, F. A., *Missions to the Gaels. Reformation and Counter-Reformation in Ulster and the Highlands and Islands of Scotland 1560–1760*. Edinburgh, 2006.

MacDonald, J., *General View of the Agriculture of the Hebrides or Western Isles of Scotland*. Edinburgh, 1811.

MacDonald, W., *Descriptive & Historical Sketches of Islay, together with a new and ready way of disposing of that interesting island . . . by John Murdoch*. Glasgow, 1850 (reprint, Bowmore, 1996).

MacDougall, D., *As Long as Water Flows*. Bowmore, 2002.

Macdougall, N., *James III A Political Study*. Edinburgh, 1982.

———— (ed.), *Scotland and War AD 79–1918*. Edinburgh, 1991.

————, *James IV*. East Linton, 1998.

Maceacharna, D., *The Lands of the Lordship. The Romance of Islay's Names*. Port Charlotte, 1976.

MacFarlane's Genealogical Collections, vol. 1. SHS, 1900.

MacGregor, M., 'The Statutes of Iona: text and context', *IR*, 57/2 (2006), 111–81.

Macinnes, A. I., *Clanship, Commerce and the House of Stuart, 1603–1788*. East Linton, 2000.

Mackay, J. A, *Islay, Jura and the other Argyll Islands. Islands Postal History Series, no. 10*. Dumfries, 1979.

MacKechnie, A., *Carragh-chuimhne. Two Islay monuments and two Islay people. Hector MacLean and John Francis Campbell*. Bowmore, 2004.

MacLean-Bristol, N., *Warriors and Priests: The History of the Clan MacLean 1300–1570*. East Linton, 1995.

————, *Murder Under Trust: the crimes and death of Sir Lachlan Mor Maclean of Duart*. East Linton, 1999.

MacNeill, M., 'The Musician in the Cave', *Bealoideas*, 57 (1989), 109–32.

MacNeill Weir, L., *Guide to Islay*. Glasgow (1936).

Macnicol, D., *Remarks on Dr Johnson's Journey to the Hebrides . . .* Glasgow, 1852.

Macphail, J. R. N. (ed.), *Highland Papers*. 4 vols, SHS, 1914–34.

Macpherson, D., et al. (eds), *Rotuli Scotiae in Turri Londinensi et in Domo Capitulari Westmonasteriensi Asservati*. London, 1814–19.

MacSween, M. and Gailey, A., 'Some Shielings in North Skye', *SS*, 5 (1961), 77–84.

MacTaggart, K., 'The Mysterious Uncle Donald', *Scottish Life* (winter 2000), 52–57, 74–75.

MacTavish, D. C. (ed.), *Minutes of the Synod of Argyll 1639–1651*. SHS, 1943.

———— (ed.), *Minutes of the Synod of Argyll 1652–1661*. SHS, 1944.

Major, J., *A History of Greater Britain*. SHS, 1892.

Maltman, A. et al., *A Guide to the Geology of Islay including eight road descriptions*. Institute of Geography and Earth Sciences. University of Wales, Aberwystyth, 2000.

Marren, P., *Grampian Battlefields*. Aberdeen, 1990.

Marsden, J., *Sea-Road of the Saints. Celtic Holy Men in the Hebrides*. Edinburgh, 1995.

————, *Somerled and the Emergence of Gaelic Scotland*. East Linton, 2000.

Martin, A., *The Ring-Net Fishermen*. Edinburgh, 1981.

————, *Kintyre Country Life*. Edinburgh, 1987.

Martin, M., *A Description of the Western Islands of Scotland circa 1695*. Edinburgh, 1994.

Marwick, J. D., *List of Markets and Fairs now and formerly held in Scotland.* The Royal Commissioners of Market Rights and Tolls, 1890.

Matheson, A., 'Documents Connected with the Trial of Sir James MacDonald of Islay, *Trans. Gaelic Soc. Glasgow,* 5 (1958), 207–22.

Matthew, H. C. G. and Harrison, B. (eds), *The Oxford Dictionary of National Biography.* Oxford, 2004 (and online at <http://www.oxforddnb.com>).

Maxwell, Sir H. (trans and ed), *The Chronicle of Lanercost.* Glasgow, 1913.

McDonald, R. A., *The Kingdom of the Isles Scotland's Western Seaboard, c.1100–c.1336.* East Linton, 1997.

McErlean, T., 'The Irish Townland System of Landscape Organisation', in Reeves-Smith and Hammond (eds), 1983, 315–39.

McGeachy, R. A. A., *Argyll 1730–1850.* Edinburgh, 2005.

McGladdery, C., *James II.* Edinburgh, 1990.

McKay, M. M. (ed.), *The Rev Dr John Walker's Report on the Hebrides of 1764 and 1771.* Edinburgh, 1980.

McKerral, A., 'Ancient Denominations of Agricultural Land in Scotland: A Survey of Recorded Opinion, with Some Notes, Observations and References', *PSAS,* 78 (1943–44), 39–50.

———, *Kintyre in the Seventeenth Century.* Edinburgh, 1948.

———, 'The Lesser Land and Administrative Divisions in Celtic Scotland', *PSAS,* 85 (1950–51), 52–67.

Meek, D. E. (ed.), *Tuath Is Tighearna. Tenants And Landlords.* Scottish Gaelic Texts Society, 1995.

Megaw, B. R. S., 'Norseman and Native in the Kingdom of the Isles: A Re-Assessment of the Evidence', *SS,* 20 (1976), 1–44.

Merriman, M., *The Rough Wooings. Mary Queen of Scots 1542–1551.* East Linton, 2000.

Meyer, D., *The Highland Scots of North Carolina 1732–1776.* Chapel Hill, 1987.

Miller, J., *Salt in the Blood: Scotland's Fishing Communities Past and Present.* Edinburgh, 1999.

Mitchison, R. and Roebuck, P. (eds), *Economy and Society in Scotland and Ireland 1500–1939.* Edinburgh, 1988.

Moir, P. and Crawford, I., *Argyll Shipwrecks.* Wemyss Bay, Inverclyde, 1994.

Monro's Western Isles. See Munro, 1961.

Morgan, H., 'The End of Gaelic Ulster: a thematic interpretation of events between 1534 and 1610', *Irish Historical Studies,* 26 (1988), 8–32.

Morton, J. K., *The Flora of Islay and Jura (v.c. 102).* Printed as a Supplement to the *Proceedings of the Botanical Society of the British Isles,* 3/3 (1959).

Morton Boyd, J. and Bowes, D. R. (eds), *Natural Environment of the Inner Hebrides.* The Royal Society of Edinburgh (Proceedings, section B, vol. 83), 1983.

Moss, M. S. and Hume, J. R., *The Making of Scotch Whisky. A History of the Scotch Whisky Distilling Industry.* Edinburgh, 1981.

Munch, P. A. and Goss, D. R. (eds) *The Chronicle of Man and the Sudreys.* Manx Society Publication vols 22, 23 (1874).

Munro, J. and Munro, R. W. (eds), *Acts of the Lords of the Isles 1336–1493.* SHS, 1986.

Munro, R. W., *Monro's Western Isles of Scotland.* Edinburgh, 1961.

Murdoch, A., 'A Scottish Document concerning Emigration to North Carolina in 1772', *North Carolina Historical Review,* 67 (1990), 438–49.

Murdoch, J. See Hunter, *For the People's Cause.*

Murray, N., 'A House Divided Against Itself: a brief synopsis of the history of Clann Alexandair and the early career of "Good John of Islay" c.1290–1370', in Ó Baoill and McGuire (eds), 2002, 221–30.

Museum of Islay Life, *The Isle of Islay – looking back.* Port Charlotte, 1998.

———, *An Islay Miscellany.* Port Charlotte, 2002.

National Library of Scotland, *Lamplighter and Story-teller. John Francis Campbell of Islay 1821–1885.* Edinburgh, 1985.

Nelson, J., *The Annals of St-Bertin.* Manchester, 1991.

Newton, M., *A Handbook of the Scottish Gaelic World*. Dublin, 2000.

Newton, N. S., *Islay*. Newton Abbot, 1988.

Nicholls, K. W., 'Anglo-French Ireland And After', *Peritia*, 1 (1982), 370- 403.

————, 'Notes on the Genealogy of Clann Eoin Mhoir', *West Highland Notes & Queries*, series 2, 8 (Nov 1991), 11–24.

Nicholson, R., *Scotland: The Later Middle Ages*. Edinburgh, 1993.

Nicolaisen, W. F. H., 'Norse Settlement in the Northern and Western Isles: Some Place Name Evidence', *SHR*, 48 (1969), 6–17.

————, *Scottish Place-names*. London, 1989.

Nieke, M., 'Settlement Patterns in the 1st Millennium AD: a case study of the Island of Islay', in Chapman and Mytum, (eds), 1983, 95–115.

Noble, R. R., 'Turf-walled houses of the Central Highlands', *Folk Life*, 22 (1984), 68–83.

————, 'Creel Houses of the Scottish Highlands', in Owen (ed.), 2000, 82–94.

Ó Baoill, C. and McGuire, N. R. (eds), *Rannsachadh Na Gàidhlig*. Aberdeen, 2002.

Ó Corráin, D., Book review: *Studies in the History of Dálriada* by John Bannerman, *Celtica*, 13 (1980), 168–82.

————, 'Viking Ireland – Afterthoughts', in Clarke, Ní Mhaonaigh and Ó Floinn, (eds), 1998, 421–52.

O'Donovan, J. (ed.), *Annals of the Kingdom of Ireland By The Four Masters*. 3 vols, Dublin, 1848.

Ogilvie, M., *The Birds of Islay*. Bruichladdich, 1992.

Ogilvie, M. A., 'Wildfowl of Islay', in Morton Boyd and Bowes (eds), 1983, 473–89.

Ohlmeyer, J. H., *Civil War and Restoration in the Three Stuart Kingdoms*. Dublin, 2001.

Omand, D., *The Argyll Book*. Edinburgh, 2004.

Oram, R., 'The Lordship of the Isles: 1336–1545', in Omand (ed.), 2004, 123–39.

———— and Stell, G. (eds), *Galloway Land And Lordship*. The Scottish Society For Northern Studies, 1991.

———— and Stell, G. (eds) *Lordship and Architecture in Medieval and Renaissance Scotland*. Edinburgh, 2005.

Orkneyinga Saga. See Pálsson and Edwards 1981.

Owen, N., *Royal Air Force Station Oban 1939–45*. Privately printed, no date.

Owen, T. M. (ed.), *From Corrib to Cultra*. Belfast, Institute of Irish Studies, 2000.

Pálsson H. and Edwards, P. (eds), *Orkneyinga Saga: The History of the Earls of Orkney*. London, 1981.

———— and Edwards, P. (eds), *Eyrbyggja Saga*. London, 1989.

Parliament (House of Commons, Proceedings), The Report of the Select Committee on Emigration in 1826. London, 1827.

Paton, H. (ed.), The *MacKintosh Muniments 1442–1820*. Edinburgh, 1903.

Patten, J. M., *The Argyle Patent and accompanying documents* (excerpted from *History of the Somonauk Presbyterian Church*). Baltimore, 1979.

Payne, P. L. (ed.), *Studies in Scottish Business History*. London, 1967.

Peacock, J. D., 'Quaternary geology of the Inner Hebrides', in Morton Boyd and Bowes (eds), 1983, 83–90.

Penman, M., *David II 1329–71*. Edinburgh, 2004.

Pennant, T., *A Tour in Scotland and Voyage to the Hebrides 1772*. Edinburgh, 1998.

Pitcairn, R., *Criminal Trials in Scotland*. 3 vols, Edinburgh, 1833.

Power, R., 'Scotland in the Norse Sagas', in Simpson (ed.), 1990, 13–24.

Price, L., 'A Note on the Use of the Word *Baile* in Place-Names', *Celtica*, 6 (1963), 119–26.

Pryde, G. S., 'Scottish Colonization in the Province of New York', *Proceedings of the New York State Historical Association* (1935), 138–57.

Ramsay, F., *John Ramsay of Kildalton*. Aberfeldy, 1988.

———— (ed.), *The Day Book of Daniel Campbell of Shawfield 1767*. Aberdeen, 1991.

Ramsay, J., *Periodical Destitution in the Highlands and its Remedy*. A paper read at a meeting of the National Association for the Promotion of Social Science, Edinburgh, 8 October 1863 (printed as a pamphlet, consulted as ML TD 1284/11/4/1).

Ramsay, L. (ed.), *The Stent Book and Acts of the Balliary of Islay 1718–1848*. Privately printed, 1890.

RCAHMS, *Argyll Volume 5, Islay, Jura, Colonsay & Oronsay*. Edinburgh, 1984.

Reed, T. M., Currie, A. and Love, J. A., 'Birds of the Inner Hebrides', in Morton Boyd and Bowes (eds), 1983, 449–72.

Registrum Episcopatus Moraviensis. Bannatyne Club, 1837.

Registrum Monasterii de Passelet. Maitland Club, 1832.

Reeves, W., (ed.), *Life of Saint Columba*. Edinburgh, 1874.

Reeves-Smith, T. and Hammond, F. (eds), *Landscape Archaeology in Ireland*. British Archaeological Report, Oxford, 1983.

Reid, I. A., 'Shinty, Nationalism and Celtic Politics, 1870–1922', *The Sports Historian*, 18 (1998), 107–30.

Reid, N. H., (ed.), *Scotland in the Reign of Alexander III 1249–1286*. Edinburgh, 1990.

Reilly, P., *Computer Analysis of an Archaeological Landscape*. BAR British Series 190, 1988.

Rivet, A. L. F. and Smith C., *The Place-Names of Roman Britain*. London, 1979.

Rixson, D., *The West Highland Galley*. Edinburgh, 1998.

Ross, A., 'The Identity of the "Prisoner of Roxburgh": Malcolm son of Alexander or Malcolm MacHeth?', in Arbuthnot and Hollo (eds), 2007, 269–82.

Rothwell, H. (ed.), *The Chronicle of Walter of Guisborough*. Camden series 89, Royal Historical Society, London, 1957.

Royal Commission (Highlands and Islands, 1892), *Reports from Commissioners, Inspectors, and Others*, vol. 26/1. London, 1895.

Russell, C., *Three Generations of Fascinating Women*. London, 1903.

Rymer, T. (ed.), *Foedera, Conventiones, Litterae et Cuiuscunque Generis Acta Publica*. London, 1816–69.

Sanger, K., 'The Origins of Highland Piping', *Piping Times*, 41/11 (Jan. 1989), 46–52.

Scott, H. (ed.), *Fasti Ecclesiae Scoticanae*. Edinburgh, 1923.

Scottish History Society, *Miscellany*, iv (1926).

Sellar, W. D. H., 'The origins and ancestry of Somerled', *SHR*, 45 (1966), 123–42.

———, 'Hebridean Sea Kings: The Successors of Somerled, 1164–1316', in Cowan and McDonald (eds), 2000, 187–218.

Sharpe, R. (ed.), *Adomnán of Iona. Life of St Columba*. Harmondsworth, 1995.

———, 'The Thriving of Dalriada' in Taylor, (ed.), 2000, 47–61.

Shaw, F. J., *The Northern and Western Islands of Scotland: Their Economy and Society in the Seventeenth Century*. Edinburgh, 1980.

Shetelig, H., 'The Viking Graves' in Curle, Olsen and Shetelig (eds), 1954, 67–111.

Simms, K., *From Kings to Warlords*. Woodbridge, 2000.

Simpson, G. (ed.), *Scotland and Scandinavia*. Edinburgh, 1990.

Sinclair, C., *Thatched Houses. A contribution to the social history of the old Highlands*. Edinburgh, 1953.

Sinclair, Sir J. (ed.), *The Statistical Account of Scotland drawn up from the communications of the ministers of the different parishes*, vol. 11, Edinburgh, 1794 (see also Statistical Account).

Sinclair, S., 'The Journal of Donald Sinclair, Schoolmaster, Islay, 1835–71', *ROSC*, 14 (2002), 86–92.

Skene, W., *Celtic Scotland. A History of Ancient Alba*. 3 vols, Edinburgh, 1880.

Skene, W. F. (ed.), *The Historians of Scotland, vol. 4, John of Fordun's Chronicle of the Scottish Nation*. Edinburgh, 1872.

Skre, D., 'The Social Context of Settlement in Norway in the First Millennium AD', *Norwegian Archaeol. Rev.*, 34/1 (2001), 1–12.

Smith, B. (ed.), *Britain and Ireland, 900 – 1300: Insular responses to medieval European change*. Cambridge, 1999.

Smith, D. J., *Action Stations 7*, Cambridge, 1983.

Smith, G. G. (ed.), *The Book of Islay*. Privately printed, 1895.

Smith, J., *General View of the Agriculture of the County of Argyll*. Edinburgh, 1798.

Smout, T. C., 'Lead-mining in Scotland 1650–1850', in Payne (ed.), 1967, 103–35.

Smyth, A. P., *Warlords and Holy Men*. Edinburgh, 1984.

————, 'The effect of Scandinavian raiders on the English and Irish churches: a preliminary reassessment' in Smith (ed.) 1999, 17–22.

Somerville, J. E., 'Notice of an Ancient Structure Called "The Altar" in the Island of Canna', *PSAS*, 33 (1898–99), 133–40.

Stanford, E. C. C., 'On the Manufacture of Kelp', *Pharmaceutical Journal*, April 1862, 495–506.

Statistical Account, *The Statistical Account of Scotland by the Ministers of the Respective Parishes*, vol. 7, Edinburgh, 1845 (see also Sinclair, 1794).

Steer, K. A. and Bannerman, J. W. M., *Late Medieval Monumental Sculpture in the West Highlands*. Edinburgh, 1977.

Stevenson, D., *Highland Warrior. Alasdair MacColla and the Civil Wars*. Edinburgh, 2003.

Stevenson, J., *Documents Illustrative of the History of Scotland*. 2 vols, Edinburgh, 1870.

Stevenson J. H., and Wood, M, *Scottish Heraldic Seals*. 3 vols, Glasgow, 1940.

Stevenson, R. B. K., *Sylloge of Coins of the British Isles*. National Museum of Antiquities of Scotland, Edinburgh, part 1, Anglo-Saxon Coins. London, 1966.

Stewart, A. I. B., 'John Paul Jones and others', *Kintyre Magazine*, 28 (1999), 11.

Stewart, T. W., 'Lexical Imposition: Old Norse vocabulary in Scottish Gaelic', *Diachronica*, 21/2 (2004), 393–420.

Stone, J., *Illustrated Maps of Scotland from Blaeu's Atlas Novus of the 17th century*. London, 1991.

Storrie, M., 'Islay: A Hebridean Exception', *Geographical Review*, 51/1 (1961), 87–108.

————, 'Landholdings and Settlement Evolution in West Highland Scotland', *Geografiska Annaler*, 47B (1965), 138–61.

————, 'Land use and settlement history of the Southern Inner Hebrides', in Morton Boyd and Bowes (eds), 1983, 549–66.

————, *Continuity and Change. The Islay, Jura and Colonsay Agricultural Association 1838–1988*. Port Ellen, 1988.

————, *Islay Biography of an Island*. Islay, 1997.

————, 'Recovering the Historic Designed Landscape of Islay House', *Scottish Archives*, 7 (2001), 59–77.

Stuart, J., et al. (eds), *The Exchequer Rolls of Scotland*. Edinburgh, 1878–.

Sykes, B., *Adam's Curse A Future Without Men*. London, 2004.

Taylor, J. See Anonymous.

Taylor, S. (ed.), *Kings, clerics and chronicles in Scotland 500–1297*. Dublin, 2000.

Teignmouth, Lord, *Sketches of the Coasts and Islands of Scotland and of the Isle of Man*. 2 vols, London, 1836.

The Historie and Life of King James the Sext. Bannatyne Club, 1825.

Thomas, F. W. L., 'Notice of Beehive Houses in Harris and Lewis . . .', *PSAS*, 3 (1857–60), 127–44.

————, 'On The Primitive Dwellings and Hypogea of the Outer Hebrides', *PSAS*, 7 (1867–68), 153–95.

————, 'Did the Norsemen Extirpate the Inhabitants of the Hebrides in the Ninth Century', *PSAS*, 11 (1874–76), 472–507.

————, 'On Islay Place-Names', *PSAS*, 16 (1881–82), 241–76.

Thomas, S. E., 'Political rift or ambitious cleric. The election of Cormac, archdeacon of Sodor, as bishop in 1331', *Soc. Antiq. Scot. Newsletter*, 19.2 (Sept. 2007), 8.

Thompson, J., 'On the Geology of the Island of Islay', *Trans. Geol. Soc. Glasgow*, 5 (1873–76), 200–22.

Thomson, D. S., 'The MacMhuirich Bardic Family', *Trans. Gaelic Soc. Inverness*, 46 (1960–63), 276–304.

————, 'Gaelic Learned Orders and Literati in Medieval Scotland', *SS*, 12 (1968), 57–78.

————, 'The Harlaw Brosnachadh: An early fifteenth-century literary curio', in Carney and Greene (eds), 1968, 147–69.

Thomson, J. M., et al. (eds), *Registrum Magni Sigilli Regum Scotorum*. Edinburgh, 1882–1914.

Thomson, T. (ed.), *Inquistionum ad Capellam Domini Regis Retornatarum*. Edinburgh, 1811–16.

———— and Innes, C (eds), *The Acts of the Parliaments of Scotland*. Edinburgh, 1814–75.

Thomson, W. P. L., *The New History of Orkney*. Edinburgh, 2001.

Tourist's Guide The Tourist's Guide to Islay, the 'Queen of the Hebrides', with Directory of the Island . . . Glasgow, 1881.

Turnbull, J., *The Scottish Glass Industry 1610–1750*. Society of Antiquaries of Scotland, monograph no. 18, 2001.

Turner, Sir J., *Memoirs of His Own Life And Times. By Sir James Turner. MDCXXXII–MDCLXX*. Bannatyne Club, 1829.

Ureland, P. S. and Clarkson, I., *Language contact across the North Atlantic: proceedings of the working groups held at University College, Galway (Ireland), August 29–September 3, 1992 and the University of Göteborg (Sweden), August 16–21, 1993*. Tübingen, 1996.

Walker, F., 'The Islay–Jura Dyke Swarm', *Trans. Geol. Soc. Glasgow*, 24 (1961), 121–137.

Walker, F. A., *The Buildings of Scotland. Argyll And Bute*. Harmondsworth, 2000.

Walker, Revd Dr J. See McKay, 1980.

Wardlaw Manuscript. SHS, 1905.

Watson, W. J., *The History of the Celtic Place-Names of Scotland*. Edinburgh, 1926.

———— (ed.), *Scottish Verse From The Book Of The Dean Of Lismore*. Scottish Gaelic Texts Society, Edinburgh, 1937.

Watt, D. E. R., 'Bishops in the Isles before 1203: Bibliography and Biographical Lists', *IR*, 45 (1994), 99–119.

————, et al. (eds), *Walter Bower's Scotichronicon*. 9 vols, Edinburgh, 1987–97.

Welander, R., Breeze, D. J. and Clancy, T. O. (eds), *The Stone of Destiny Artefact & Icon*. Edinburgh, 2003.

Whittaker, J., *I, James Whittaker*. London, 1934.

Wiggins, J., *The Exmouth of Newcastle 1811–1847*. Bowmore (2000).

Wilkinson, S. B., *Memoirs of the Geological Survey, Scotland. The Geology of Islay, including Oronsay and portions of Colonsay and Jura*. (Explanation of Sheets 19 and 27, with the western part of Sheet 20.) Glasgow, 1907.

Williams, J., *The Natural History of the Mineral Kingdom*. Edinburgh, 1789.

Wilson, G. V. and Flett, J. S., *Memoirs of the Geological Survey, vol. 17, The Lead, Zinc, Copper and Nickel Ores of Scotland*. Edinburgh, 1921, 65–73.

Wilson, N., *Scotch and Water. Islay, Jura, Mull, Skye. An illustrated guide to the Hebridean malt whisky distilleries*. Moffat, 1985.

————, *The Island Whisky Trail. An Illustrated Guide to the Hebridean Distilleries*. Glasgow, 2003.

Withall, M., *Easdale, Belnahua, Luing & Seil: the islands that roofed the world*. Edinburgh, 2003.

Wood, D., *Attack Warning Red*. Portsmouth, 1992.

Woolf, A., *The Diocese of the Sudreyar*, in Imsen (ed.), 2003.

————, 'The Age of the Sea-Kings', in Omand (ed.), 2004, 94–109.

————, 'The origins and ancestry of Somerled: Gofraid mac Fergusa and "The Annals of the Four Masters"', *Mediaeval Scandinavia*, 15 (2005), 199–213.

————, 'Dun Nechtain, Fortriu and the Geography of the Picts', *SHR*, 85 (2006), 182–201.

————, 'A dead man at Ballyshannon', in Duffy (ed.), 2007, 77–85.

Index